BEST PLAYS OF THE SEVENTIES

Books and Plays by Stanley Richards

BOOKS:

BEST PLAYS OF THE SEVENTIES
BEST PLAYS OF THE SIXTIES
AMERICA ON STAGE: TEN GREAT PLAYS OF AMERICAN HISTORY
TWENTY ONE-ACT PLAYS
THE TONY WINNERS
GREAT MUSICALS OF THE AMERICAN THEATRE: VOLUME ONE
GREAT MUSICALS OF THE AMERICAN THEATRE: VOLUME TWO
THE MOST POPULAR PLAYS OF THE AMERICAN THEATRE
GREAT ROCK MUSICALS
BEST MYSTERY AND SUSPENSE PLAYS OF THE MODERN THEATRE
10 CLASSIC MYSTERY AND SUSPENSE PLAYS OF THE MODERN THEATRE
MODERN SHORT COMEDIES FROM BROADWAY AND LONDON
BEST SHORT PLAYS OF THE WORLD THEATRE: 1968–1973
BEST SHORT PLAYS OF THE WORLD THEATRE: 1958–1967
THE BEST SHORT PLAYS 1980
THE BEST SHORT PLAYS 1979
THE BEST SHORT PLAYS 1978
THE BEST SHORT PLAYS 1977
THE BEST SHORT PLAYS 1976
THE BEST SHORT PLAYS 1975
THE BEST SHORT PLAYS 1974
THE BEST SHORT PLAYS 1973
THE BEST SHORT PLAYS 1972
THE BEST SHORT PLAYS 1971
THE BEST SHORT PLAYS 1970
THE BEST SHORT PLAYS 1969
THE BEST SHORT PLAYS 1968
CANADA ON STAGE

PLAYS:

THROUGH A GLASS, DARKLY
AUGUST HEAT
SUN DECK
TUNNEL OF LOVE
JOURNEY TO BAHIA
O DISTANT LAND
MOOD PIECE
MR. BELL'S CREATION
THE PROUD AGE
ONCE TO EVERY BOY
HALF-HOUR, PLEASE
KNOW YOUR NEIGHBOR
GIN AND BITTERNESS
THE HILLS OF BATAAN
DISTRICT OF COLUMBIA

BEST PLAYS
OF THE
SEVENTIES

Edited with an Introductory Note
and Prefaces to the Plays by

STANLEY RICHARDS

DOUBLEDAY & COMPANY, INC., GARDEN CITY, NEW YORK
1980

Library of Congress Catalog Card Number 79–6634
ISBN: 0-385-14739-2

Copyright © 1980 by Stanley Richards
All Rights Reserved
Printed in the United States of America

for
WARREN BAYLESS

CONTENTS

AN INTRODUCTORY NOTE

In a turbulent decade that witnessed a constantly changing world, the theatre, somehow, maintained a relatively steady balance. And while, undeniably, it made some advances, there also was a bit of retrogression, particularly in the musical theatre with its plethora of revivals.

Quantity-wise, the seventies saw fewer Broadway and Off-Broadway attractions than did the previous decade, due to spiraling production costs rather than a paucity of producible new material. To mount a play during the latter part of the seventies involved a capitalization of anywhere from $400,000 upward (depending on the size of the cast and the demands of the scenic production) while musicals required $750,000 to over one million dollars to raise their first night curtains.

Nonetheless, the Broadway theatre set records in attendance and box-office receipts during the seventies. For example, the 1978–79 season attracted an attendance of 9.8 million theatregoers which yielded $136 million in ticket sales and was the sixth season in a row that saw continual increases in both totals. Although inflation, which brought higher prices for tickets, played a partial, but by no means solo, role in the rise of revenues, the attendance figures indicated a steady growth in theatregoing.

The most noticeable trend of the seventies was the reliance upon regional theatres as a source of material for Broadway and Off-Broadway playhouses. In a sense, it was a reversal of sorts. When the regional theatre movement began in force a decade or so ago, those professional companies operating outside of New York City habitually scoured the Broadway scene for material to fill their seasons. But in recent years those theatres became so acclaimed for their own productions of new plays that Broadway managements carefully scrutinized their work for dramatic properties to fill their own New York seasons. Consequently, many of the more significant new plays of the 1970s found their way to New York stages via the regional theatre route. Among these: Hugh Leonard's "*Da*," David Rabe's *Streamers*, Paul Zindel's *The Effect of Gamma Rays on Man-in-the-Moon Marigolds*, D. L. Coburn's *The Gin Game*, Michael Cristofer's *The Shadow Box*, David Mamet's *American Buffalo*, Michael Weller's *Loose Ends*, Marsha Norman's *Getting Out*, Arthur Kopit's *Wings*, and Sam Shepard's *Buried Child*. With the exception of veteran dramatist Hugh Leonard and Arthur Kopit, all of the aforementioned playwrights sprang to prominence during the decade and might never have attracted the attention of most New York impresarios were it not for their early nurturing by regional theatres.

While the new dramatists were making their mark in the New York theatre of the period, the established writers—with the exception of revivals of past works—contributed little of any significance. Tennessee Williams produced several new plays but none made much of a dent with reviewers or audiences. Similarly, Arthur Miller's single new contribution, *The Creation of the World and Other Business*, opened and closed rather precipitously and Edward Albee's *Seascape*, though winning the Pulitzer Prize, neglected to entice sizable audiences and shuttered after a comparatively brief engagement. Only Neil Simon maintained his stronghold as the theatre's most prolific and successful playwright of contemporary times with seven new comedies and a sellout musical.

Once again, as in previous decades, importations from the London stage abounded. And while all did not survive the sea change, those that did were a prevalent force including works by David Storey, Tom Stoppard, Peter Shaffer, Anthony Shaffer, Simon Gray, Harold Pinter, and Alan Ayckbourn, among others.

Serious drama also had a reawakening. For a considerable length of time, comedies and musicals prevailed in Broadway theatres but in the late seventies there was a resurgence of drama and the oft-heard complaint that a serious work could not survive in the environs of the theatre district no longer held quite true. Playgoers flocked to the likes of *The Elephant Man*, "*Da*," *Whose Life Is It Anyway?*, *The Gin Game*, and others based on substantial themes.

Although the concentration here is specifically on plays in this volume, a word or two about musicals. That ever-popular and distinctive genre of entertainment was easily dominated by composer-lyricist Stephen Sondheim who began the 1970s with the prize-winning *Company* and ended the decade with another multiple-prize winner *Sweeney Todd*. Other musicals that brightened the Broadway horizon of the seventies included *A Chorus Line, A Little Night Music, Annie, Applause, Grease* (Broadway's all-time longest-running show), *Chicago, The Wiz, Follies, Two Gentlemen of Verona, Purlie, Bubbling Brown Sugar, Pippin,* and *The Best Little Whorehouse in Texas* as well as a spate of revivals and song and dance revues.

With the exception of a well-received remounting of *The King and I,* the fabled old master of American musicals, Richard Rodgers, came a cropper each time out during the seventies. Beginning with the Danny Kaye vehicle, *Two by Two,* through his musicalized treatment of Henry VIII, *Rex,* and the embattled musicalization of *I Remember Mama,* there was hardly a Rodgers tune to sing, whistle, or remember. The equally noted lyricist-librettist Alan Jay Lerner fared little better with a stage version of *Gigi* and the lavish *1600 Pennsylvania Avenue* (with music by Leonard Bernstein) which vanished within a week.

The theatre of the seventies, then, followed its due course with the customary ratio of successes and failures, absorbing and sometimes exciting works measured against the less than inspired offerings, the surprising and the disappointing—specifics that have permeated the theatre for ages. Yet, in retrospect it was a decade, if not of complete challenge, at least of above average quality and theatrical excitement.

While compiling this volume's predecessor, *Best Plays of the Sixties,* I wrote in my introduction: "An editor charged with that distinguished, though often intimidating, descriptive 'best' on the spine of his book—and, somehow, that four-letter adjective invariably seems to loom larger and more brilliantly colored than any other word of a title—becomes instant and juicy prey for the stalkers. Even in a society that takes justifiable pride in its freedom of speech and expression, there is, quite curiously, a relatively lower degree of forbearance with, say, freedom of *choice.* Especially for editors of collections. Yet, an editor's first and foremost responsibility is to pursue his task with integrity and to express in his selections a reflection of his own tastes and standards, always, of course, hoping that the reader will be in, if not total, at least partial accord with his personal choice of material."

A decade after they first were written, those words still prevail for, once again, I have selected the plays that follow not as a lofty, dispassionate critic, but as a dedicated involved theatregoer. And I hope indeed that this collection will provide a generous sampling of the theatre of the seventies and bring to the reader, as they did to me, many hours of pleasure and dramatic gratification.

STANLEY RICHARDS
New York, New York

"DA"

Hugh Leonard

Hugh Leonard

The Irish reputation for wit, sentiment, and emotion, as well as colorfully droll characters, is magnificently upheld in Hugh Leonard's "*Da*," a highlight of the 1977–78 New York theatre season.

Paradoxically, though its roots are firmly set in Ireland, and the author is a Dubliner, the play had its world premiere in 1973 at the Olney Theatre in Maryland, thousands of miles from its setting. From there it went on, during that same year, to win top honors at the Dublin Theatre Festival and in his coverage of the event for *Plays and Players*, Gerald Colgan wrote: "Known to be a deeply autobiographical play, it tells of the return home of a successful playwright to arrange the funeral and other last affairs of his foster father, an uneducated gardener of eighty-odd years. As he winds things up, memories and ghosts fill his mind and the stage of his younger self, his mother, a friend, an employer, and above all of 'Da' and the complex bond between them for which love is both too grand and too simple a word. Brilliantly written and constructed for the theatre, it invades the emotions, gently at first, then building to a climax of revelation and pain that wrings them dry. The word 'classic' should not be used lightly, but if it means a work in which may be clearly seen truth, artistry, and the capture of something permanent in the transience that dominates our lives, then this play is a classic."

During its pre-Broadway peregrinations, "*Da*" also was seen at the Ivanhoe Theatre, Chicago, and finally at the Off-Off-Broadway Hudson Guild Theatre, where it received general acclaim and subsequently was moved to Broadway's Morosco Theatre on May 1, 1978.

As it settled in for a lengthy run, Clive Barnes imparted to readers of the New York *Post* that " '*Da*' is just the best Irish play we have had in years, and as most of the English-speaking theatre seems to have been traditionally fed by the Irish—was Shakespeare really born in Dublin?—that is pointedly high praise." And continuous high praise it did receive. "In a class with the best of Sean

O'Casey," wrote Mel Gussow in the New York *Times*, "it is steeped in Irish language, laughter and atmosphere, but it rises far above ethnicity."

A multiple-prize play, *"Da"* won the Antoinette Perry (Tony) Award, the New York Drama Critics' Circle Award, a Drama Desk and an Outer Circle Award for the year's best play. (Tonys also were awarded to Barnard Hughes for his masterly performance in the title role, to Lester Rawlins for his interpretation of the aloof employer, Mr. Drumm, and to Melvin Bernhardt for his direction of the play.)

Hugh Leonard was born in Dublin on November 9, 1926. Like the character of Charlie in the play, he was adopted at an early age. His real name is John Keyes Byrne—Keyes being the name of his adoptive parents, Byrne his mother's name (he never knew his natural father). Hughie Leonard was the name of the hero of his first play, which was rejected by the Abbey Theatre. When he submitted his second play to the Abbey, he dropped the "ie" and used the pen name of Hugh Leonard. "It was poetic justice that I take the name of the character in the play they turned down." The second play was accepted and he has used it professionally ever since. As Hugh Leonard, he now is Ireland's most successful and productive resident playwright.

Once again, like the character in *"Da,"* he worked in an office for fourteen years. "I was a temporary clerical assistant—that was the title—in the Irish Civil Service, the Department of Lands. I went in in 1945 at six dollars a week and left in 1959, with a wife and child, at twenty dollars a week." At the age of thirty-three he began to devote all his time to writing.

As for his frankly autobiographical *"Da,"* Mr. Leonard recounted during a visit to New York, "People used to say to me, it must have been a tough play to write, because it's a terrible thing in Ireland to write the word bastardy. It's a *hard* word. Well, when you don't tell 'em, when you've never told anyone . . . Once I got over that word, which comes midway through Act One, I said, oh, that's all right, and I got on with it. I never realized till I sat down to write it that I would have to be in it. Then I thought, oh my God, the only thing to do is tell the truth or it's a waste of time doing it."

The author has written some twenty plays which have been seen mainly in Ireland and London. Among these are *The Patrick Pearse*

Motel, Madigan's Lock, Some of My Best Friends Are Husbands, Mick and Mick, Thieves, Summer, and *A Suburb of Babylon.*

In addition to "*Da*," three of his earlier plays were seen in New York: *Stephen D* (an adaptation of James Joyce's *A Portrait of the Artist as a Young Man* and *Stephen Hero,* 1967), *The Poker Session* (1967), and *The Au Pair Man* (1973).

Mr. Leonard also has written extensively for television in England and worked on the screenplays for *Interlude, Great Catherine,* and *Rake's Progress.*

His newest drama, *A Life,* with Cyril Cusack as the protagonist Mr. Drumm (who also figures importantly in "*Da*") opened in the autumn of 1979 at the Abbey Theatre in Dublin.

"*Da*" was first presented in the United States at the Olney Theatre, Olney, Maryland, on August 9, 1973, and subsequently at the Ivanhoe Theatre, Chicago, and the Hudson Guild Theatre, New York City. On May 1, 1978, the Hudson Guild Theatre production, Craig Anderson, producer, was presented at the Morosco Theatre, New York City, by Lester Osterman, Marilyn Strauss, and Marc Howard, with the following cast:

CHARLIE NOW	*Brian Murray*
OLIVER	*Ralph Williams*
DA	*Barnard Hughes*
MOTHER	*Sylvia O'Brien*
YOUNG CHARLIE	*Richard Seer*
DRUMM	*Lester Rawlins*
MARY TATE	*Mia Dillon*
MRS. PRYNNE	*Lois de Banzie*

Direction by Melvin Bernhardt
Set Design by Marjorie Kellogg
Costume Design by Jennifer von Mayrhauser
Lighting Design by Arden Fingerhut

"Da" was given its European premiere at the Olympia Theatre, Dublin, as part of the Dublin Festival, on October 8, 1973. The cast was as follows:

CHARLIE NOW	*Kevin McHugh*
OLIVER	*Frank Kelly*
DA	*John McGiver*
MOTHER	*Phyl O'Doherty*
YOUNG CHARLIE	*Chris O'Neill*
DRUMM	*Edward Golden*
MARY TATE	*Dearbhla Molloy*
MRS. PRYNNE	*Pamela Mant*

Directed and Designed by Jim Waring

THE PLACE: *A kitchen and, later, places remembered.*

THE TIME: *May 1968 and, later, times remembered.*

THE SET: *There are several playing areas. The main one is the kitchen. This is the kitchen-living room plus small hallway of a corporation house. An exit at the rear to the scullery. A hint of stairs running up from the hall. There are two areas at either side of the kitchen and a series of connecting steps and ramps which climb up and over, behind the kitchen. One of the two areas is the seafront . . . it includes a park bench. Behind the seafront, on the rising platforms, is the hilltop. On the other side of the stage is a neutral area, defined by lighting. This can be a number of locales as the script requires. (In the Second Act there is an ornamental bench there; the park bench is removed.) The kitchen, however, is the womb of the play.*

ACT ONE

CHARLIE, *overcoat on, is at the kitchen table, sorting letters, family papers, old photos, etc., into two piles. He finds one paper of interest and puts on his glasses to examine it. He then goes to the range and pours boiling water from the kettle into a teapot. He then picks up the teapot as* OLIVER *comes to the door.*

He is CHARLIE's *age—early forties. His clothes are too neat for him to be prosperous; youthful bouncy step, handkerchief exploding from his breast pocket. He sees that the door is ajar. He knocks all the same.*

CHARLIE: Yes? [OLIVER *is about to come in, but stops to remove a crepe bow from the door*] Yes, who is it?

[OLIVER *steps into the hall and coughs*]

CHARLIE: [*Half to himself*] I didn't ask how you are, but who you are. [*Then, seeing him*] Oliver!

OLIVER: Instant recognition. Oh, yes, full marks.

CHARLIE: You . . . good God!

OLIVER: [*Careful speech, equal emphasis on each syllable*] Well, I'm still a native-you-know. Not a globe-trotter like some. [*Almost wagging a finger*] Oh, yes.

CHARLIE: Well, today's the day for it.

OLIVER: Par-don me?

CHARLIE: Old faces. They've turned up like bills you thought you'd never have to pay. I'm on my own . . . come in. [*He puts the teapot down on the table*]

OLIVER: Won't intrude. Thought I'd offer my . . .

CHARLIE: Sure.

OLIVER: For your trouble. [*Holding up the wreath*] I took the liberty.

CHARLIE: That's damn nice of you, Oliver. Thank you.

OLIVER: It was . . .

CHARLIE: He would have liked that.

OLIVER: It's from the door.

CHARLIE: From . . . ? [*A loud laugh*] I thought it was a . . . gift-wrapped Mass card. I mean, Masses in English, the priest facing you across the altar like a chef at a buffet luncheon . . . I thought it was one more innovation. [*Taking it purposefully*] Yes, by all means. [*He drops it into the range*]

OLIVER: Gwendolyn—the wife-you-know—saw the notice in the "Press." I would have gone to the funeral—

CHARLIE: What for!

OLIVER: But business-you-know.

CHARLIE: It's nice to see you. It must be ten . . . I don't know, fifteen years? Sit down . . . the mourners left a soldier or two still standing. [*He takes a bottle of stout out of a crate*]

OLIVER: It's seldom I take a drink.

CHARLIE: I've made tea for myself, do you mind? I never drink in this house. Every Christmas the Da would say: "Will you have a bottle of stout, son?" Couldn't. It was the stricken look I knew would come on my mother's face, as if I'd appeared in my first pair of trousers or put my hand on a girl's tit in her presence.

OLIVER: [*Dutifully*] Ho-ho-ho.

CHARLIE: So I . . . [*Blankly*] What?

OLIVER: Joll-y good.

CHARLIE: My God, Oliver, you still think saying "tit" is the height of depravity. You must find married life unbearably exciting.

OLIVER: [*Beaming*] Haven't changed, haven't changed!

CHARLIE: [*Pouring the stout*] Anyway, I kept meaning to take that Christmas drink and send her upstairs in tears with a frenzied petition to St. Ann. Next thing I knew, there I was aged thirty-nine, the year she died, a child on my lap who was capable of consuming the dregs of everyone else's tawny port to wild grandparental applause, and my wife sitting where you are, looking with disbelieving nausea at the man she had half-carried home the previous night, as he shook his greying head virtuously and said: "No, thanks, Da, I still don't." [*He hands the stout to* OLIVER] After she died, the not altogether frivolous thought occurred to me that the man who will deliberately not cause pain to his mother must be something of a sadist. I suppose I could have had a drink since then, but why spoil a perfect . . . [*Looking down at* OLIVER] You've got a bald spot.

OLIVER: Me? No . . . ha-ha, it's the wind. [*Producing a comb*] Breezy out. No, no: fine head of hair still-you-know.

[CHARLIE *smiles and pours his tea, using a pot-holder*]

OLIVER: [*As he combs*] Warm for a coat, but.

CHARLIE: Yes.

OLIVER: Month of May-you-know.

CHARLIE: [*An evasion*] I was halfway out the door when I remembered this lot. Rubbish mostly. HP agreements, rent books, insurance, broken pipe . . . [*He moves them to the bureau*]

OLIVER: Now!

CHARLIE: What?

OLIVER: [*Bowing his head for inspection*] Look, you see . . . see?

CHARLIE: Mm . . . you were right and I was wrong. Hair care is not an idle dream.

OLIVER: The old massage-you-know.

CHARLIE: Ah-hah.

OLIVER: [*Firmly*] Oh, yes. [*Stroking his hair, he picks up his glass and drinks*]

CHARLIE: Have you children? [*Drinking,* OLIVER *holds up four fingers*] Ah? [OLIVER *jabs a finger towards* CHARLIE] Um? [*Takes a sip of tea.* CHARLIE *points interrogatively towards himself and raises one finger*]

OLIVER: Ah.

CHARLIE: What else?

OLIVER: What?

CHARLIE: Is new.

OLIVER: Oh, now.

CHARLIE: Long time. So?

OLIVER: Oh, now. [*He thinks. Pause.* CHARLIE *waits, then is about to go back to his sorting*] Yes, by Jove, knew I had something to tell you. Six years ago . . .

CHARLIE: Yes?

OLIVER: I finally got the theme music from *King's Row.*

CHARLIE: Is that so?

OLIVER: Only electronically-simulated stereo-you-know. But still . . .

CHARLIE: Still . . .

OLIVER: That was a good fillum.

CHARLIE: Wasn't it.

OLIVER: I got billy-ho for going with you to that fillum. My mother wouldn't let me play with you over that fillum.

CHARLIE: Why?

OLIVER: Oh, pretend he doesn't know!

CHARLIE: Remind me.

OLIVER: You made me miss my elocution class.

CHARLIE: [*Remembering*] So I did.

OLIVER: Ah, sappy days. Do you remember that expression we had, ah, sappy days? I was glad I kept up with the old elocution-you-know. A great stand-by. Always pronounce properly and look after your appearance: that's how you get on.

CHARLIE: *Did* you get on?

OLIVER: Oh-well-you-know.

CHARLIE: How fantastic.

OLIVER: No harm being ready and waiting.

CHARLIE: None.

OLIVER: That's why I was always smart in myself.

CHARLIE: And you got all the best girls.

OLIVER: I did, though, did-n't I?

CHARLIE: Betty Brady . . .

OLIVER: Oh, now.

CHARLIE: And that one who lived in the maze of buildings behind Cross Avenue. What was it we called her?

OLIVER: The Casbah.

CHARLIE: The Casbah. And Maureen O'Reilly.

OLIVER: Maureen . . . oh, don't-be-talking. There was a girl who took pride in her appearance. With the big—well, it was-you-know—chest.

CHARLIE: Tits.

OLIVER: [*As before*] Ho-ho-ho.

CHARLIE: She once told me . . . she said: "Oliver is going to be a great man." Believed it. [OLIVER's *smile crumples; it is as if his face had collapsed from inside*] Mad about you. They all were. What's up? [OLIVER *shakes his head. He affects to peer closely at a wall picture*] All I ever seemed to get was the kind of girl who had a special dispensation from Rome to wear the thickest part of her legs below the knees. [*Looking for reaction*] Yes?

OLIVER: [*Face unseen*] Oh, now.

CHARLIE: Modelled yourself on Tyrone Power, right? I favoured Gary Cooper myself, but somehow I always came across as Akim Tamiroff. Jesus, Oliver, us in those days! We even thought Gene Autry could act.

OLIVER: [*Turning*] He could sing "Mexicali Rose," still and all.

CHARLIE: Least he could do.

OLIVER: Your drawback was you didn't take the Dale Carnegie course like I done.

CHARLIE: Too lazy.

OLIVER: Very worthwhile-you-know. Then, after you went over the Pond, as they say, I joined the Rosicrucians. That was a great comfort to me the time the mother died. It's all about the soul surviving-you-know in the Universal Consciousness. Do you think I should keep on with it?

CHARLIE: Of course if it helps.

OLIVER: Your da-you-know came to the mother's funeral. I never forgot that to him.

CHARLIE: Well, he was always fond of you.

[DA *comes in from the scullery and looks at* OLIVER]

DA: Fond of him? Fond of that one? Jesus, will you give over, my grave's too narrow to turn in. [*He goes out again.* CHARLIE, *in whose mind this has happened, winces*]

CHARLIE: In his way.

OLIVER: In the end, was it . . . 'em, if you don't mind me asking . . . ?

CHARLIE: No, it wasn't sudden. He got these silent strokes, they're called. Old age. What I mean is, it wasn't unexpected. He *went* suddenly.

OLIVER: [*Still delicately*] You weren't, em . . .

CHARLIE: I was in London: flew over yesterday, off tonight. Well, my middle-aged friend, now we're both parentless. We've gone to the head of the queue.

OLIVER: Queue for what? Oh, now. Long way to go yet, only getting started. [*He bounces to his feet*] Well!

CHARLIE: Don't go. Finish your drink.

OLIVER: The wife-you-know.

CHARLIE: Let me finish here and I'll run you home.

OLIVER: No, must be riding the trail to the old hacienda.

CHARLIE: [*A hint of urgency*] Ten minutes.

OLIVER: The little woman . . . [OLIVER *moves to the door, takes gloves from his jacket pocket*] Queer-you-know how a house looks empty after a funeral. What will happen to it now, do you think?

CHARLIE: This place? It'll be re-let, I suppose.

OLIVER: I wondered—what was it I wondered?—do you happen to know anybody in the Corporation?

CHARLIE: Me?

OLIVER: Well, I hear you got on, so they tell me. Gwendolyn and me are on the list for a house this long time. If you had a bit of pull-you-know.

CHARLIE: [*His manner cooling*] No, I haven't. Sorry.

OLIVER: Oh, now. Man who's up in the world . . .

CHARLIE: I haven't.

OLIVER: Oh. Well, ask not and you receive not.

CHARLIE: Dale Carnegie.

OLIVER: Ho-ho. Oh, now. Well, see you next time you're over. Sorry for the trouble. Sappy days, eh?

CHARLIE: Sappy days. [OLIVER *goes.* CHARLIE *closes the door*] Fucking vulture!

> [*He faces the empty room. He returns the teapot to the range with* OLIVER's *unfinished tumbler of stout. He looks briefly at* DA's *chair and then goes to the bureau and begins to sort papers. He finds a wallet and puts on his glasses to examine a photograph in it.* DA *comes in. He wears workingman's clothes: Sunday best*]

CHARLIE: [*Refusing to look at him*] Hoosh. Scat. Out.

DA: That wasn't too bad a day.

CHARLIE: Piss off. [DA *sits in his chair,* CHARLIE *looks at him*] Sit there, then! No one is minding you.

DA: I knew it would hold up for you. You were lucky with the weather when you came over at Christmas, too. [CHARLIE *ignores him and returns the papers to the table and goes on sorting them*] Mind, I wouldn't give much for tomorrow. When you can see the Mountains of Mourne, that's a sure sign it'll rain. Yis, the angels'll be having a pee.

CHARLIE: [*Whirling on him*] Now that will do!

DA: That's a good expression. Did you ever hear that expression?

CHARLIE: Did I? Thanks to you, until I was twelve years of age every time the rain came down I had a mental picture of a group of winged figures standing around a hole in the clouds relieving themselves. Go away; I'm working, I'm clearing up. [*Working, half to himself*] Oh, yes, that was him. A gardener all his life, intimately associated with rainfall: i.e., the atmospheric condensation of warm air which, when large enough to fall perceptibly to the ground, constitutes precipitation. Hot air rises, the rain falls; but as far as he was concerned that kind of elementary phenomenon was . . .

DA: Codology.

CHARLIE: Codology. No, it was easier and funnier and more theologically orientated to say that the angels were having a pee. [*He goes to the range and drops a large pile of papers in*]

DA: You ought to put that down in one of your plays.

CHARLIE: I'd die first.

[DA *rises and, without moving more than a step or two, takes a look at* CHARLIE's *teacup, then turns towards the range*]

CHARLIE: What are you doing?

DA: Sitting there without a cup of tea in your hand.

CHARLIE: I've a cupful.

DA: It's empty.

CHARLIE: It's full.

DA: [*Dismissively*] G'way out that.

CHARLIE: Now don't touch that teapot. Do you hear me? For forty-two years I've been through this, you and that bloody teapot, and I know what's going to happen. So don't touch it!

DA: Not a drop of tea in his cup . . . no wonder he's delicate.

CHARLIE: Look, will you— [*He watches dumbly, almost tearfully, as* DA *picks up the teapot and starts with it across the room. Halfway across he sets the teapot down on the floor*]

DA: [*Agonized*] Jesus, Mary and Joseph. [*He hugs his hand*]

CHARLIE: I knew it.

DA, CHARLIE: [*Together*] That's hot.

CHARLIE: Too damn headstrong. Couldn't you have waited until my ma came in and let her— [*Softly*] Jesus.

[DA *begins to stalk the teapot*]

DA: Bad cess to it for an anti-Christ of a teapot. The handle must be hollow. Whisht, now . . . say nothing. [*He takes* CHARLIE's *cup from the table and looks contemptuously into it*] Empty! [*He pours the contents—it is three-quarters full—into a scuttle, then kneels down, placing the cup in front of the teapot. He holds the handle of the pot between fingers and thumb, using the end of his necktie as a potholder, and pours the tea. Wincing*] The devil's cure to it, but it's hot. [*Rising*] Oh, be the hokey. [*He sets the cup before* CHARLIE] There you are, son.

CHARLIE: [*Controlling himself*] Thanks.

DA: [*Hovering*] That'll put the red neck on you.

CHARLIE: Right!

DA: Where's the sugar?

CHARLIE: I have it. [*Beating him to the sugar and milk*]

DA: Is there milk?

CHARLIE: Yes!

DA: If you don't want tea I'll draw you a bottle of stout.

CHARLIE: No! [*More composed*] You know I never . . . [*Correcting himself*] I don't want a bottle of stout. Now sit.

DA: Sure there's no shaggin' nourishment in tea. [*Returning to his chair, he is brought up short by the sight of the teapot*] How the hell are we going to shift it? Hoh? If herself walks in on us and sees that on the floor there'll be desolation. The gee-gees let her down today, and if the picture in the Picture House was a washout as well she'll come home ready to eat us. That's a right conundrum, hoh?

CHARLIE: [*Coldly*] Cover it with a bucket.

DA: That handle is hot for the night. [*A solution*] Don't stir. Keep your ear cocked for the squeak of the gate.

CHARLIE: Why? What . . . [DA *goes to the range, picks up a long rusting pair of tongs and starts to use them to lift the teapot*] Oh, God! [CHARLIE *rushes over, grabs the teapot and puts it back on the range.* DA *drops the tongs. He sucks his scorched hand*] Now will you get out and leave me be. You're dead. You're in Dean's Grange, in a box, six feet under . . . with her. I carried you . . . it's over, you're gone, so get out of my head. [DA *sits in the armchair, unperturbed, filling his pipe with tobacco*] Or at least stay quiet. Eighty miserable years of you is in this drawer, and as soon as I've sorted out the odds and ends, I'm slamming that front door and that's *it*. Your nephew Paddy got the TV set, I gave the radio to Maureen and Tom, and Mrs. Dunne next door got my sincere thanks for her many kindnesses and in consequence thereof has said she'll never talk to me again. The junkman can have the rest, because I've got what *I* want. An hour from now that fire will go out and there'll be no one here to light it. I'll be rid of you. I'm sweating here because I couldn't wait to put my coat on and be off. So what do you say to that?

DA: [*Amiably*] Begod, son, you're getting as grey as a badger.

CHARLIE: Old Drumm was right about you. The day he came here to give me the reference.

DA: Drumm is not the worst of them.

CHARLIE: He had *you* taped.

DA: Was he here today?

CHARLIE: He was at the Mass . . . next to the pulpit.

DA: Was that him? I wouldn't recognise him. God, he's failed greatly.

CHARLIE: You can talk.

DA: Decent poor bugger, but.

CHARLIE: Do you know what he called you? The enemy.

MOTHER: [*Off*] Charlie, will you come down when I tell you.

CHARLIE: Who's that?

MOTHER: [*Off*] Charlie! [*She comes in from the scullery. At this time she is in her late fifties;* DA *is four years older. Looking towards the ceiling*] Do you want me to come up to you?

CHARLIE: I'd forgotten what she looked like.

MOTHER: [*To* DA] Will you get off your behind and call him. He's in the lavatory with his curse-o'-God books again.

DA: [*Galvanized into action, yelling*] Do you hear your mother? Come down out of there. You pup, come when you're called. If I put my hand to you . . .

MOTHER: That will do.

DA: [*Now wound up*] Slouching around . . . skipping and jumping and acting the go-boy. Mr. Drumm is halfway up the path!

MOTHER: I said that will do. Read your paper.

DA: [*A grotesque imitation of a boy leaping about*] With your hopping and-and-and leppin' and your playing cowboys on the Green bank. Buck Jones.

CHARLIE: You were always behind the times. I hadn't played cowboys in five years.

DA: Hoot-shaggin'—Gibson, Tim McCoy and Randolph Scott.

MOTHER: You'd give a body a headache.

DA: [*Subsiding*] And-and-and-and Jeanie Autry.

MOTHER: When Mr. Drumm comes in this house you're not to say yes, aye or no to him, do you hear me?

DA: Sure *I* know Drumm. Who was it pruned his rose-trees?

MOTHER: No passing remarks. [*She picks up the teapot*]

DA: Mag, that teapot is . . .

MOTHER: Say nothing. [*She takes the teapot into the scullery*]

CHARLIE: I never knew how she did it.

DA: "Tynan," says he to me, "'clare to God, I never seen the beating of you for roses." That's as true as you're standing there, Mag. Never seen the beating of me. [*Ruddy with pleasure*] Hoh?

CHARLIE: Throw you a crumb and you'd call it a banquet.

DA: "I hear," says he to me, "you're a great man for the whist drives." Do you know, I nearly fell out of my standing. "Who told you that?" says I, looking at him. "Sure," says he, "there's not a dog or divil in the town doesn't know you!" [*He laughs.* YOUNG CHARLIE *comes downstairs. He is seventeen, shabbily dressed. He carries a book*]

DA: [*To* YOUNG CHARLIE] Charlie, I was saying, sure I know old Drumm these donkey's years.

CHARLIE: Oh, God: not that little prick. [YOUNG CHARLIE *looks at him, smarting at the insult. Their contempt is mutual*] You were, you know.

YOUNG CHARLIE: And what are you, only a big—

CHARLIE: Careful, that could lead to a compliment.

[YOUNG CHARLIE *sits at the table and opens his book*]

DA: Oh, Drumm will give you a grand reference. [MOTHER *returns with the teapot and pours water into it*] And if he didn't itself, what odds? Aren't we all grand and comfortable, owing nothing to no one, and haven't we got our health and strength and isn't that the main thing?

CHARLIE: Eat your heart out, Oscar Wilde.

MOTHER: [*To* YOUNG CHARLIE] Don't lie over the table . . . You'll get a hump-back like old Totterdel.

DA: Old Totterdel was a decent man.

CHARLIE: What's the book?

YOUNG CHARLIE: [*Surly*] Story of San Michele. [*He pronounces it "Michel" as in French*]

CHARLIE: [*Italian*] Michele, you thick.

MOTHER: The state of that shirt. I'll give you a fresh one.

YOUNG CHARLIE: It's only Tuesday.

MOTHER: Take it off.

YOUNG CHARLIE: How am I to wear one shirt all week?

MOTHER: You can go easy on it, can't you? Do as you're told. [*Going into the scullery*] More you do for them, the less thanks you get.

[YOUNG CHARLIE *removes his shirt: under it is a singlet*]

DA: You could plant seed potatoes on that shirt, son.

YOUNG CHARLIE: [*Muffled, the shirt over his head*] Ah, dry up.

DA: [*Singing to himself: the tune is "The Girl I left Behind Me"*]
"Oh, says your oul' wan to my oul' wan,
'Will you come to the Waxie Dargle?'
And says my oul' wan to your oul' wan,
'Sure I haven't a farthin'.' "
The Waxies were tailors and the Waxie Dargle was a fair they used to have beyant in Bray in old God's time. You never knew that. Hoh?

[YOUNG CHARLIE, *shivering, ignores him*]

CHARLIE: [*Glaring*] Answer him.

YOUNG CHARLIE: [*To* DA] Yeah, you told me. [*To* CHARLIE] You're a nice one to talk about being polite to him.

CHARLIE: Privilege of age, boy.

DA: [*Pinching* YOUNG CHARLIE's *arm*] Begod, son, there's not a pick on you. "I'm thin," the fella says, "and you're thin"; but says he: "Y'r man is thinner than the pair of us put together!"

[MOTHER *has returned with the shirt*]

MOTHER: This is newly-ironed. Put it on. [*She holds it for him. It has been lengthened by the addition of ill-matching pieces from another shirt to the tail and sleeves*]

YOUNG CHARLIE: What's that?

MOTHER: Put it on you.

YOUNG CHARLIE: Look at it.

MOTHER: There's not a brack on that shirt, only it's gone a bit small for you. There's many a poor person 'ud be glad of it.

YOUNG CHARLIE: Then give it to them.

MOTHER: You cur.

YOUNG CHARLIE: God, look at the tail.

MOTHER: Who's going to see it?

YOUNG CHARLIE: I'm not wearing it.

MOTHER: [*Flinging the shirt down*] Leave it there, then. Don't. [*Picking it up at once*] Put that shirt on you.

YOUNG CHARLIE: I won't.

MOTHER: [*Turning to* DA] Nick . . .

DA: [*A half-feigned, half-real rather frightened anger*] Do like the woman tells you. Can we not have a bit of peace and quiet in the house the one day of the week? Jasus Christ tonight, do you want old Drumm to walk in on top of you?

MOTHER: [*Quietly*] That will do with your Sacred Name. [*To* YOUNG CHARLIE] Lift your arms.

YOUNG CHARLIE: [*Already beaten*] I'm not wearing that— [*She slaps his face briskly and, almost in the same movement, thrusts the shirt over his head. She pulls his arms into the sleeves, jerks him to her and fastens the buttons*]

DA: [*Relieved*] That's the boy. Herself cut up one of my old shirts for that, son: didn't you, Mag?

CHARLIE: You were always there with the good news.

MOTHER: [*Coldly, wanting to hurt back*] The day you bring money in, you can start being particular. Time enough then for you to act the gentleman. You can do the big fellow in here then, as well as on the seafront. Oh, it's an old saying and a true one: the more you do for them . . .

DA: Sure that looks grand.

MOTHER: How bad he is . . . And at the end of it they'd hang you.

[YOUNG CHARLIE *puts his jacket on. He sits and picks up his book*]

CHARLIE: You always give in. Too soft to stand up to them. No guts. [MOTHER *is at the door looking out*] It could have been worse. Like the time you had the date with Ita Byrne and you asked her [MOTHER] to press your navy-blue trousers: told her it was for the altar boys' outing. She'd never pressed a pair of trousers in her life, and she put the creases down the side. And every little gurrier in the town followed you and Ita that night singing "Anchors Aweigh." Remember?

YOUNG CHARLIE: [*Now grinning*] Sappy days.

[*The gate squeaks*]

MOTHER: There he is now. [*To* YOUNG CHARLIE, *fearfully, the quarrel forgotten*] God and his holy Mother send he'll find you something. [DA *starts towards the door. She yanks him back*] Will you wait till he knocks.

DA: [*Almost an incantation*] Sure I know old Drumm.

MOTHER: And keep that mouth of yours shut. Have manners.

YOUNG CHARLIE: He's only a clerk, you know.

[*She looks at him venomously.* DRUMM *comes into view: He is in his mid-fifties thin, acerbic. He knocks.* MOTHER *and* DA *go to the door. The greetings are mimed*]

CHARLIE: He was a chief clerk. [YOUNG CHARLIE *looks towards the door, anguish on his face, fists clenched*] Five-fifty a year . . . not bad for nineteen-forty . . . what?

YOUNG CHARLIE: Four . . . November.

CHARLIE: What's up?

YOUNG CHARLIE: Nothing.

CHARLIE: Don't be proud with me, boy.

YOUNG CHARLIE: Listen to them: they always *crawl*.

CHARLIE: Blessed are the meek: they shall inherit the dirt. The shame of being ashamed of them was the worst part, wasn't it? What are you afraid of?

YOUNG CHARLIE: Tell us . . . That day.

CHARLIE: When?

YOUNG CHARLIE: Then. Now. Today. Did they say . . . say anything to him?

CHARLIE: About what?

[DRUMM *is shown in*]

MOTHER: Still, we're terrible, dragging you out of your way.

DRUMM: Is this the young man? [*Shaking hands*] How do you do?

DA: [*Belatedly*] Shake hands, son.

DRUMM: A bookworm like myself, I see.

MOTHER: [*To* DA] Move out and let the man sit down.

DA: [*Offering his chair, saluting with one finger*] Here you are, sir!

CHARLIE: [*Angry*] Don't call him sir.

MOTHER: Now you'll sit there and have a cup of tea in your hand. [*She sets about pouring the tea*]

DRUMM: [*Quite sternly*] No, I will not.

DA: [*Aggressive*] Don't mind him. Yes, he will. You will!

DRUMM: You're a foolish woman. In these times we may take hospitality for granted. A ration of a half-ounce of tea per person per week doesn't go far.

MOTHER: [*Serving him*] Now it won't poison you.

DA: And them's not your tea-leaves that are used and dried out and used again, sir. Get that down you. There's your milk and there's your sugar.

DRUMM: Look here, my dear man, will you sit. I'm not helpless.

MOTHER: Nick . . .

DA: Sure what the hell else have we only for the cup of tea? Damn all . . . amn't I right?

DRUMM: [*Ignoring him, to* YOUNG CHARLIE] Your name is . . . ?

MOTHER: Charles Patrick.

DRUMM: And you've done with school?

MOTHER: He's got a scholarship to the Presentation Brothers. There was many a one got it and took the money; but no, we said, let him have the education, because it'll stand to him when we're gone.

DA: Oh, Charlie's the boy with the brains.

DRUMM: Bright are you? Who's your favourite author?

YOUNG CHARLIE: Shakespeare.

CHARLIE: You liar.

DRUMM: And where do your talents lie?

YOUNG CHARLIE: Dunno.

DRUMM: An authority on Shakespeare shouldn't mumble. I asked, what kind of post do you want?

MOTHER: He'll take what he's offered. He's six months idle since he left school. He won't pick and choose.

DA: And if there's nothing for him, sure he can wait. There'll be any amount of jobs once the war's over.

DRUMM: Past history says otherwise. There's usually a depression.

DA: Not at all.

DRUMM: You're an expert, are you?

DA: [A *stock phrase*] What are you talking about, or do you know what you're talking about? The Germans know the Irish are their friends, and sign's on it, when the good jobs are handed out in England they'll give us the first preference.

DRUMM: Who will?

DA: The Jerries, amn't I telling you . . . when they win.

DRUMM: You support the Germans, do you?

CHARLIE: [*To* DA] Shut up. [*To* YOUNG CHARLIE] Don't go red. Smile.

[YOUNG CHARLIE *summons up an unnatural grin. He laughs. At once* DRUMM *looks at him bad-temperedly*]

DRUMM: Is something amusing you?

YOUNG CHARLIE: No.

DA: Hitler's the man that's well able for them. He'll give them lackery, the same as *we* done. Sure isn't the greatest man under the sun, himself and De Valera?

MOTHER: [*Not looking at him*] Now that will do . . .

DA: What the hell luck could the English have? Didn't they come into the town here and shoot decent people in their beds? But they won't see the day when they can crow it over Heil Hitler. He druv them back into the sea in 1940, and he'll do it again now. Sure what's Churchill anyway, bad scran to him, only a yahoo, with the cigar stuck in his fat gob and the face on him like a boiled shite. [*Pause.* DRUMM *just looks at him*]

MOTHER: There's plenty more tea in the—

DRUMM: No, I must be going.

MOTHER: [*With a false smile*] You oughtn't to mind him.

DRUMM: I don't at all. I thought the boy might walk with me, and I could ask him what it is I need to know.

MOTHER: Charlie, do you hear? Go and comb your hair and give your face a rub. [YOUNG CHARLIE *goes upstairs, glad to get away*] I know you'll do your best for him. You will.

DRUMM: It would be a poor best. There's nothing here for anyone. Have you thought of letting him go to England?

DA: England!

DRUMM: There's work there.

MOTHER: Ah, no.

DRUMM: It might be for his good.

MOTHER: No, we'd think bad of losing him.

DA: There's good jobs going here if you can keep an eye out. I'm gardening above in Jacob's these forty-six years, since I was a young lad . . . would you credit that?

DRUMM: Yes, I would.

MOTHER: What is there in England only bombs and getting into bad health? No, he'll stay where he's well looked after. Sure, Mr. Drumm, we're all he has. His own didn't want him.

DRUMM: His own?

MOTHER: [*Bitterly*] Whoever she was.

DRUMM: Do you mean the boy is adopted?

[YOUNG CHARLIE *comes downstairs at a run, anxious to be off. He hears what* DRUMM *has said and hangs back on the stairs*]

MOTHER: [*Purely as punctuation*] Ah, don't talk to me.

CHARLIE: And I listened, faint with shame, while you delivered your party-piece.

MOTHER: I took him out of Holles Street Hospital when he was ten days old, and he's never wanted for anything since. My mother that's dead and gone, the Lord have mercy on her, said to me: "Mag, he's a nurse-child. You don't know where he was got or how he was got, and you'll rue the day. He'll turn on you."

DA: [*A growl*] Not at all, woman.

MOTHER: Amn't I saying! [*To* DRUMM] You try rearing a child on thirty shillings a week then and two pounds ten now after forty years of slaving, and see where it leaves you.

CHARLIE: Stand by. Finale coming up.

MOTHER: And a child that was delicate. She tried to get rid of him.

DRUMM: Get rid?

CHARLIE: Roll of drums, *and* . . . !

MOTHER: Before he was born. Whatever kind of rotten poison she took. Dr. Enright told me; he said, "You won't rear that child, ma'am, he'll never make old bones." But I did rear him, and he's a credit to us.

CHARLIE: Band-chord. Final curtain. Speech!

MOTHER: He's more to us than our own, so he is.

CHARLIE: Thunderous applause. [*To* DRUMM] Hand her up the bouquet.

DRUMM: You're a woman out of the ordinary. The boy has cause to be grateful.

CHARLIE: Well done. House-lights.

[YOUNG CHARLIE, *his lips pressed tight together to suppress a howl, emits a high-pitched half-whimper, half-squeal, and flees into the garden*]

CHARLIE: And the scream seemed to come through my eyes.

MOTHER: Charlie?

DRUMM. [*Looking out*] I see he's leading the way. Goodbye, Mrs. Tynan: I'll do what little I can.

MOTHER: Sure I know. God never let me down yet.

DRUMM: [*He looks at* DA *and then at* MOTHER] You surprise me.

MOTHER: Nick, say goodbye.

DA: Are you off? Good luck, now. [*Giving a Nazi salute*] We shall rise again. Begod, we will.

DRUMM: You're an ignorant man. [*He nods to* MOTHER *and goes out.* DA *laughs softly and shakes his head, as if he had been complimented*]

DRUMM: [*Off*] Young man, come here.

DA: [*As* MOTHER *comes in from hall*] There's worse going than old Drumm. A decent man. "I never seen the beating of you," says he, "for roses."

[*She glares at him, too angry to speak, and takes* DRUMM'S *teacup out to the scullery*]

CHARLIE: [*To* DA] You could have stopped her. You could have tried. You never said a word.

DA: [*Calling to* MOTHER] I think I'll do me feet tonight, Mag. I have a welt on me that's a bugger.

CHARLIE: All those years you sat and looked into the fire, what went through your head? What did you think of? What thoughts? I never knew you to have a hope or a dream or say a half-wise thing.

DA: [*Rubbing his foot*] Aye, rain tomorrow.

CHARLIE: Whist drive on Wednesday, the Picture House on Sundays and the Wicklow regatta every first Monday in August. Bendigo plug-tobacco and "Up Dev" and "God bless all here when I get in meself." You worked for fifty-eight years, nine hours a day, in a garden so steep a horse couldn't climb it, and when they got rid of you with a pension of ten shillings a week you did handsprings for joy because it came from the Quality. You spent your life sitting on brambles, and wouldn't move in case someone took your seat.

DA: [*Softly*] You're a comical boy.

CHARLIE: [*Almost an appeal*] You could have stopped her.

[MOTHER *comes in*]

MOTHER: Ignorant, he said you were, and that's the word for you.

DA: [*Taken aback*] What?

MOTHER: With your "Up Hitler" in front of him and your dirty expressions. Ignorant.

DA: What are you giving out about?

MOTHER: You. You sticking your prate in where it's not wanted, so's a body wouldn't know where to look. I said to you: "Keep that mouth of yours shut," I said. But no . . it'd kill you.

DA: Sure I never said a word to the man, good, bad or indifferent.

MOTHER: You're not fit to be let loose with respectable people. I don't wonder at Charlie running out of the house.

DA: What? Who did?

MOTHER: It wouldn't be the first time you made a show of him and it won't be the last. God help the boy if he has you to depend on.

DA: [*Upset*] Ah now, Mag, go easy. No . . . sure Charlie and me is—

MOTHER: *Anyone* would be ashamed of you.

DA: No, him and me is—

MOTHER: He's done with you now. Done with you. [*She goes out*]

CHARLIE: Serves you right. You could have stopped her.

[*The lights go down on the kitchen and come up on the promenade. The sound of seagulls.* DRUMM *and* YOUNG CHARLIE *appear. They stand in front of a bench*]

DRUMM: The wind has moved to the east. Do you take a drink?

YOUNG CHARLIE: Not yet.

DRUMM: You will, please God. Do you chase girls?

YOUNG CHARLIE: Pardon?

DRUMM: Female persons. Do you indulge?

YOUNG CHARLIE: The odd time.

DRUMM: As a diversion I don't condemn it. Henry Vaughan, an otherwise unremarkable poet of the seventeenth century, summed it up happily when he wrote "How brave a prospect is a bright backside." Do you know Vaughan?

YOUNG CHARLIE: "They are all gone into the world of light."

DRUMM: So you do read poetry! Listen to me, my friend: if you and I are to have dealings you had better know that I do not tolerate liars. Don't try it on with me ever again.

YOUNG CHARLIE: I didn't . . .

DRUMM: [*Firmly*] Shakespeare is nobody's favourite author. [*He gives* YOUNG CHARLIE *a searching look*] We'll say no more about it. Yes, chase away by all means and give them a damn good squeeze if you catch them, but be slow to marry. The maximum of loneliness and the minimum of privacy. I have two daughters myself . . . no boys.

YOUNG CHARLIE: I know your daughters.

DRUMM: Oh?

YOUNG CHARLIE: To see. Not to talk to.

DRUMM: I would describe them as . . . bird-like.

YOUNG CHARLIE: [*Trying to say the right thing*] Yes, I suppose they—

DRUMM: Rhode Island Reds. You may laugh . . .

CHARLIE: I wouldn't.

DRUMM: I say you may. *I* do. No . . . no boys. [*He sits on the bench and motions for* YOUNG CHARLIE *to sit beside him*] There will be a vacancy in my office for a filing clerk. I don't recommend it to you: jobs are like lobster pots, harder to get out of than into, and you seem to me to be not cut out for clerking. But if you want to sell your soul for forty-five shillings a week I daresay my conscience won't keep me awake at nights.

YOUNG CHARLIE: Do you mean I can have it?

DRUMM: If you're fool enough. My advice—

YOUNG CHARLIE: A job. A job in an office, in out of the cold. Oh, Janey, I think I'll go mad. [*He jumps up*] Yeow! [DRUMM *taps the umbrella on the ground*] God, I think I'll split in two! I'm a millionaire. Mr. Drumm . . . any time if there's e'er an oul' favour I can do for you over this—

DRUMM: You can speak correct English.

YOUNG CHARLIE: Honest to God, Mr. Drumm, I'm so delighted, if you asked me to I'd speak Swahili. A job!

DRUMM: [*Sourly*] And this is how we throw our lives away.

YOUNG CHARLIE: [*Grins, then*] Beg your pardon?

DRUMM: You'll amount to nothing until you learn to say no. No to jobs, no to girls, no to money. Otherwise, by the time you've learned to say no to life you'll find you've swallowed half of it.

YOUNG CHARLIE: I've been looking for a job since school, Mr. Drumm. I couldn't refuse it.

DRUMM: To be sure.

YOUNG CHARLIE: I mean, I'm the only one at home . . .

DRUMM: I'm aware of that. [*Considered it settled*] So be it. There's a grey look about your face: I suggest you begin to wash yourself properly. And I'll need a copy of your birth certificate. What's your name?

YOUNG CHARLIE: [*Surprised*] Tynan.

DRUMM: I mean your real name. You overheard what your foster-mother told me, didn't you? That you're illegitimate. Don't give me that woe-begone look. It's a fact, you're going to have to live with it and you may as well make a start. Bastardy is more igno-minious in a small town than in a large one, but please God it may light a fire under you. Do your friends know? [YOUNG CHARLIE *shakes his head*] Probably they do. So don't tell them: they won't thank you for spiking their guns. What ails you? Look here, my friend: tears will get no sympathy from me. I said we'll have done with it . . . people will take me for a pederast. Your nose is run-ning: wipe it.

YOUNG CHARLIE: I haven't got a handkerchief.

DRUMM: Well, you can't have mine. Use something . . . the tail of your shirt.

[YOUNG CHARLIE *is about to comply when he remembers*]

DRUMM: Well?

YOUNG CHARLIE: I won't.

DRUMM: [*Bristling*] Won't?

YOUNG CHARLIE: [*Loftily*] It's a disgusting thing to do.

DRUMM: You think so? [*They outglare each other.* YOUNG CHARLIE *sniffs deeply. Brass band music is heard in the distance*] Well, per-haps there's hope for you yet.

YOUNG CHARLIE: There's a band on the pier.

DRUMM: [*Rising to look*] Hm? Yes, the Artane Boys, by the sound of them.

[YOUNG CHARLIE *whips out his shirt-tail, wipes his nose and re-adjusts his dress as* DRUMM *turns to face him*]

DRUMM: Your . . . mother, shall we call her? . . . is a fine woman.

YOUNG CHARLIE: Yeah. Except she tells everyone.

DRUMM: About you?

YOUNG CHARLIE: All the old ones. Then they say to her: isn't she great and how I ought to go down on my bended knees. Even the odd time I do something right, it's not enough . . . it's always the least I could do. Me da is different: if you ran into him with a motor car he'd thank you for the lift.

DRUMM: I'm fond of him.

YOUNG CHARLIE: [*Disbelieving*] Of me da?

DRUMM: I can afford that luxury: I'm not obliged to live with him. You are. That's why he's the enemy.

YOUNG CHARLIE: The what?

DRUMM: Your enemy.

YOUNG CHARLIE: [*Straight-faced, trying not to laugh*] I see.

DRUMM: Don't be polite with me, my friend, or you'll be out of that job before you're into it. Once at a whist drive I heard him say that the world would end in 1940. It was a superstition that had a fashionable currency at one time among the credulous. Well, 1940 came and went, as you may have noticed, and finding myself and the county of Dublin unscathed, I tackled him on the subject. He was unruffled. He informed me that the world hadn't ended because the German bombs had upset the weather. [YOUNG CHARLIE *laughs boisterously. He bangs his fists on his knees.* DA *enters the neutral area and rings a doorbell*] Yes, the dangerous ones are those who amuse us. [*The bell is rung again.* DA *puts his pipe in his pocket and waits*] There are millions like him: inoffensive, stupid, and not a damn bit of good. They've never said no in their lives or to their lives, and they'd cheerfully see the rest of us buried. If you have any sense, you'll learn to be frightened of him.

[*A light is flashed on* DA's *face as if a door had been opened*]

DA: [*Saluting*] That's a hash oul' day, ma'am. Certainly you know me . . . Tynan, of Begnet's Villas, sure I'm as well known as a begging ass. And do you know what I'm going to tell you? . . . that back field of yours, the meadow: if you was to clear that field of the rocks that's in it and the stumps of trees and had it dug up with a good spreading of manure on the top of it, begod, you wouldn't know yourself. There's bugger-all you couldn't grow in it.

DRUMM: From people too ignorant to feel pain, may the good God deliver us!

DA: The young lad, do you see, he's starting work. Oh, a toppin' job: running an office, sure he's made for life. And the way it is, I'd think bad of him starting off without a decent suit on his back or the couple of good shirts. Sure you couldn't let him mix with high-up people and the arse out of his trousers. Have you me?

DRUMM: I'm advising you to live in your own world, not with one foot in his.

DA: I'll come to you so on Sundays and do the field . . . sure it won't take a feather out of me. [*Embarrassed by mention of money*] Very good, yis . . . I'll leave that to yourself: sure whatever you think. [*Saluting*] Thanks very much, more power. [*He starts off, then bobs back again*] More power, says oul' Power when young Power was born, wha'? [*The door-light snaps off. As he moves away, the lights on the neutral area go down*]

DRUMM: Are we still on speaking terms?

YOUNG CHARLIE: [*Hating him*] Yes.

DRUMM: You aren't angry?

YOUNG CHARLIE: No!

DRUMM: Indeed, why should you be! Shall we stroll down and listen to the Artane Boys?

[*They walk off. Lights come up quickly on* CHARLIE *and* DA *in the kitchen as before*]

CHARLIE: And I went off with him like a trollop.

DA: Drumm is a decent skin. Came in here once to see how I was managing after herself died. Three years ago this month, yis. Gev me a packet of cigarettes. "No," says I, "I won't." "You will," says he; "take them when you're told to." So I did. Wait now till I see where I have them.

CHARLIE: We listened to the band and I even made excuses for you. Told him about your grandfather and two uncles starving to death in the Famine.

DA: Oh, aye. Them was hard times. They died in the ditches.

CHARLIE: What ditches? I made it up!

DA: Fierce times they were. Where the hell did I put them? You can smoke them in the aeroplane. [*Going to the dresser*]

CHARLIE: I don't want them.

DA: [*Searching*] Yes, you do.

CHARLIE: Don't make a— [*He takes a packet of Player's from his pocket*] It's all right . . . look, I found them.

DA: Hoh?

CHARLIE: Look.

DA: Good lad. Yis, it was in the month of— [*He breaks off*] Drumm smoked Sweet Aftons . . . that's not them.

[*He resumes the search*]

CHARLIE: Messer!

DA: It was in the month of May herself died, and it was in the month of May I went. Would you credit that? [*He climbs on a chair*]

CHARLIE: Congratulations. I should have stuck up for you and told him to keep his job. Then I could have hated you instead of myself. Because he was dead on: he described you to a— [*Seeing him*] Oh, get down. [DA *finds the cigarettes on top of the dresser. He begins to climb down*] You destroyed me, you know that? Long after I'd quit the job and seen the last of Drumm, I was dining out in London: black dickie-bow, oak paneling, picture of

Sarah Bernhardt at nine o'clock: the sort of place where you have to remember not to say thanks to the waiters. I had just propelled an erudite remark across the table and was about to shoot my cuffs, lose my head and chance another one, when I felt a sudden tug as if I was on a dog-lead. I looked, and there were you at the other end of it. Paring your corns, informing me that bejasus the weather would hold up if it didn't rain, and sprinkling sugar on my bread when ma's back was turned.

[DA *gives him the cigarettes as if he was passing on contraband*]

DA: Say nothing. Put this in your pocket.

CHARLIE: So how could I belong there if I belonged here?

DA: "Take them," says Drumm to me, "when you're told to."

CHARLIE: And it was more than a memory. She was dead then, and at that moment I knew you were sitting here on your own while the daylight went. Did you think bad of me? I wish I were a fly inside your head, like you're a wasp inside of mine. Why wouldn't you come and live with us in London when we asked you?

DA: What would I do that for?

CHARLIE: You were eighty-one.

DA: Sure I was a marvel. "Begod, Tynan," says Father Kearney to me, "we'll have to shoot you in the wind-up." What a fool I'd be to leave herself's bits and pieces here where any dog or divil could steal them. And for what? To go to England and maybe land meself in an early grave with the food they serve up to you.

CHARLIE: No, you'd rather stay here instead, like a maggot in a cabbage, and die of neglect.

DA: I fended for meself. No better man.

CHARLIE: In sight or out of it, you were a millstone. You couldn't even let me lose my virginity in peace.

DA: Lose your what?

CHARLIE: Nothing. It's a slang word, now obsolete.

[MARY TATE *walks on. She is twenty-five, a loner*]

DA: Who's that? That's a fine figure of a girl. What's she doing around here?

CHARLIE: She's not here: she's on the seafront. And she wasn't a fine girl. She was known locally as the Yellow Peril.

[YOUNG CHARLIE *and* OLIVER—*younger now—are lounging in the neutral area.* MARY *walks by. They pay her no obvious attention*]

YOUNG CHARLIE: [*Suddenly, singing*] "Underneath the lamplight . . ."

OLIVER: "By the barracks gate . . ."

YOUNG CHARLIE: "Darling, I remember . . ."

OLIVER: "The way you used to wait."

YOUNG CHARLIE, OLIVER: [*Together*]
"I heard you walking in the street,
I smelt your feet,
But could not meet,
My lily of the lamplight,
My own Lily Marlene."

[MARY'S *step falters as she hears the lyrics. She continues on to the bench, where she sits and opens a copy of* Modern Screen. *The two youths go on singing—quietly now and to themselves.* YOUNG CHARLIE *looks covertly at her once or twice*]

CHARLIE: [*To* DA] We all dreamed, privately and sweatily, about committing dark deeds with the Yellow Peril. Dark was the word, for if you were seen with her, nice girls would shun you and tell their mothers, and their mothers would tell yours: the Yellow Peril was the enemy of mothers. And the fellows would jeer at you for your beggarman's lust—you with your fine words of settling for nothing less than Veronica Lake. We always kept our sexual sights impossibly high: it preserved us from the stigma of attempt and failure on the one hand, and success and mortal sin on the other. The Yellow Peril never winked, smiled or flirted: the sure sign of an activist. We avoided her, and yet she was a comfort to us. It was like having a trusty flintlock handy in case of necessity.

[YOUNG CHARLIE *and* OLIVER *both look at* MARY]

YOUNG CHARLIE: They say she's mustard.

OLIVER: Oh, yes. Red-hot-you-know.

YOUNG CHARLIE: And she has a fine-looking pair.

OLIVER: Of legs-you-mean?

YOUNG CHARLIE: Well, yeah: them, too.

OLIVER: Oh. Ho-ho-ho. Oh, now. Joll-y good.

[MARY *looks up from her magazine as* OLIVER *raises his voice: a calm direct look, neither friendly nor hostile*]

YOUNG CHARLIE: She's looking. [*To* MARY, *bravely*] 'Evening.

OLIVER: [*Embarrassed*] Don't.

YOUNG CHARLIE: Why?

OLIVER: We'll get ourselves a bad name. Where was I? Yes . . . I was telling you about Maria Montez in *Cobra Woman*. Now there's a fine figure of a—

YOUNG CHARLIE: They say she'd let you. All you have to do is ask.

OLIVER: Maria Montez? Is that a fact?

YOUNG CHARLIE: [*Pointing*] Her.

OLIVER: Ah, yes: but who is that hard up for it?

CHARLIE: I was.

OLIVER: I mean, who wants to demean himself?

CHARLIE: I did.

YOUNG CHARLIE: God, I wouldn't touch her in a fit. I'm only—

OLIVER: And she would make a holy show of you, you-know, like she done with the man who tried to interfere with her in the Picture House.

YOUNG CHARLIE: When?

OLIVER: I think it was a Bette Davis. The man sat down next to her and as soon as the big picture came on the screen he started tampering with her in some way. And she never said a word, only got up and dragged him to the manager by his wigger-wagger.

YOUNG CHARLIE: [*Stunned*] She never.

OLIVER: True as God. He felt very small, I can tell you.

YOUNG CHARLIE: Still, if she minded she can't be all that fast.

OLIVER: Oh-I-don't-know. If she wasn't fast she'd have dragged him by something else.

[YOUNG CHARLIE *looks at* MARY *in awe*]

CHARLIE: Lust tied granny-knots in my insides. I wanted the Yellow Peril like I wanted no girl before or no woman since. What was worse, I was wearing my new suit for the first time and I had to do it now, now or never, before the newness wore off.

OLIVER: [*Who has been talking*] So will we trot up to the billiard hall?

YOUNG CHARLIE: You go.

OLIVER: Me?

YOUNG CHARLIE: I'll follow you. [*He looks almost tragically at* OLIVER. *Pause. Then* OLIVER *stares from him to* MARY]

OLIVER: Her?

YOUNG CHARLIE: [*Agonised*] Go on.

OLIVER: Ho-ho-ho-ho. Oh, now. [*Dismay*] You wouldn't.

YOUNG CHARLIE: Olly . . . fizz off.

OLIVER: But you don't want to chance your arm with her; she'd let you. [*Then*] Where will you take her?

YOUNG CHARLIE: I dunno; down the back.

OLIVER: I'll see you, then.

YOUNG CHARLIE: Yeah.

OLIVER: I suppose you know you'll destroy your good suit.

YOUNG CHARLIE: Will you go on. See you.

[OLIVER *does not move. Hostility forms on his face*]

OLIVER: I was the one you came out with-you-know. [YOUNG CHARLIE *waits for him to go*] They say it's very disappointing-you-know, very over-rated. [*Pause. Angrily*] Well, don't salute me in the town when you see me, because you won't be saluted back.

[*He goes.* YOUNG CHARLIE *goes towards the bench. He stops, suddenly panic-stricken.* CHARLIE *has by now moved out of the kitchen area*]

CHARLIE: Do you want a hand? [*Still looking at* MARY, YOUNG CHARLIE *motions to him to be quiet*] If they think you're afraid to ask them they attack you. You said yourself, all you have to do is ask.

YOUNG CHARLIE: Dry up, will you!

[MARY *looks at him*]

CHARLIE: Now . . . quick!

YOUNG CHARLIE: 'Evening.

MARY: You said that.

CHARLIE: Sit.

[YOUNG CHARLIE *sits beside her. What follows is ritual, laconic and fast*]

MARY: Didn't ask you to sit down.

YOUNG CHARLIE: Free country.

MARY: Nothing doing for you here.

YOUNG CHARLIE: Never said there was.

MARY: Ought to have gone off with that friend of yours.

YOUNG CHARLIE: Who ought?

MARY: You ought.

YOUNG CHARLIE: What for?

MARY: Nothing doing for you here.

YOUNG CHARLIE: Never said there was.

[*Pause. Phase Two in conversation*]

MARY: What's your name, anyway?

YOUNG CHARLIE: Bruce.

MARY: [*A sceptical grin*] Yeah?

YOUNG CHARLIE: It is. [*He crosses his eyes and thumbs his nose at* CHARLIE *by way of defiance*]

MARY: Bruce?

YOUNG CHARLIE: Mm.

MARY: Nice name.

YOUNG CHARLIE: [*Pointing off*] He's Oliver.

MARY: That so?

YOUNG CHARLIE: He's from the town.

MARY: Where *you* from?

YOUNG CHARLIE: Trinity College.

MARY: That right?

YOUNG CHARLIE: English Literature.

MARY: Must be hard.

YOUNG CHARLIE: Bits of it. [*She goes back to her reading. A lull. End of Phase Two*]

CHARLIE: Ask her.

YOUNG CHARLIE: She's not on.

CHARLIE: Ask.

[*Instead,* YOUNG CHARLIE *clamps his arm heavily around* MARY. *She does not look up from her magazine during the following*]

MARY: Wouldn't Edward G. Robinson put you in mind of a mon-key?

YOUNG CHARLIE: Let's see. Do you know, he does.

MARY: One of them baboons.

YOUNG CHARLIE: Yes. Yes, yes, yes, yes. [*At each "yes" he slaps her vigorously on the knee. She stares as if mesmerized at his hand as it bounces up and down and finally comes to rest on her knee in an iron grip. As she returns to her magazine he begins to massage her kneecap*]

CHARLIE: [*Staring*] You insidious devil, you.

MARY: It doesn't screw off.

YOUNG CHARLIE: What?

MARY: Me leg.

[*His other hand now slides under her armpit, intent on touching her breast. He is unaware that he is kneading and pinching her handbag, which is tucked under her arm. She watches this hand, fascinated*]

CHARLIE: I think you're getting her money all excited.

MARY: [*Having returned to her reading*] You needn't think there's anything doing for you here.

YOUNG CHARLIE: I don't.

MARY: Dunno what you take me for . . . sort of person who'd sit here and be felt with people passing. If you won't stop I'll have to go down the back. [*She looks at him directly for the first time*] If you won't stop.

YOUNG CHARLIE: [*Not stopping; hoarsely*] All right.

MARY: [*Looking off*] Wait till that old fella goes past.

YOUNG CHARLIE: Who?

MARY: [*Fondling his knee*] Not that you're getting anything.

YOUNG CHARLIE: [*Dazed with lust*] I know.

CHARLIE: My silver-tongue eloquence had claimed its helpless victim. Defloration stared me in the face. My virginhood swung by a frayed thread. Then . . . !

DA: [*Off*]
"Oh, says your oul' one to my oul' one:
'Will you come to the Waxie Dargle?'
And says my oul' one to your oul' one:
'Sure I haven't got a farthin'.' "

> [YOUNG CHARLIE'S *kneading and rubbing comes to a halt. As* DA *walks on at a good stiff pace, he tries to extract his hand from under* MARY'S *armpit but she holds it fast*]

DA: [*Passing*] More power. [*He walks a few more paces, stops, turns and stares*] Jesus, Mary and Joseph!

YOUNG CHARLIE: [*His voice cracking*] Hello.

MARY: Don't talk to him.

> [DA *looks at* MARY'S *hand on* YOUNG CHARLIE'S *knee.* YOUNG CHARLIE *removes her hand; she replaces it*]

DA: Sure the whole world is going mad.

MARY: Don't answer him.

> [DA *sits next to her*]

DA: The whist drive was cancelled, bad scran to it. Only four tables. Says I: "I'm at the loss of me tram fare down, but I won't be at the loss of it back, for I'll walk." [*He looks at* YOUNG CHARLIE'S *hand flapping helplessly*] I dunno. I dunno what to say.

MARY: He'll go away. Don't mind him.

CHARLIE: If my hand was free I'd have slashed my wrists.

DA: Oh, the young ones that's going nowadays would eat you. I dunno.

MARY: He doesn't know much.

DA: He knows too shaggin' much. [*To* YOUNG CHARLIE] If your mother was here and seen the antrumartins of you, there'd be blood spilt.

MARY: Much she'd care.

DA: Much who'd care?

MARY: Me ma.

YOUNG CHARLIE: He's talking to me.

DA: Certainly I'm talking to him, who else? That's my young lad you're trick-acting with.

MARY: [To YOUNG CHARLIE] Is he your—

DA: Oh, that's Charlie.

MARY: Who?

YOUNG CHARLIE: Bruce is me middle name.

DA: That's Charles Patrick.

YOUNG CHARLIE: Oh, thanks.

DA: [To MARY] You mind me, now. What is it they call you?

MARY: [A little cowed] Mary Tate.

YOUNG CHARLIE: Leave her alone.

DA: You hold your interference. From where?

MARY: Glasthule . . . the Dwellin's.

[DA makes a violent gesture, gets up, walks away, turns and points at her dramatically]

DA: Your mother was one of the Hannigans of Sallynoggin. Did you know that?

MARY: Yes.

DA: And your uncle Dinny and me was comrades the time of the Troubles. And you had a sister that died of consumption above in Loughlinstown.

MARY: My sister Peg.

DA: And another one in England.

MARY: Josie.

DA: Don't I know the whole seed and breed of yous! [*To* YOUNG CHARLIE] Sure this is a grand girl. [*He nudges* YOUNG CHARLIE *off the bench and sits down next to* MARY] Tell me, child, is there news of your father itself?

MARY: [*Her face clouding*] No.

DA: That's hard lines.

MARY: [*Bitterly*] We don't *want* news of him. Let him stay wherever he is—we can manage without him. He didn't give a curse about us then, and we don't give a curse about him now.

DA: There's some queer people walking the ways of the world.

MARY: Blast him!

[DA *talks to her. She listens, nods, wipes her eyes*]

CHARLIE: And before my eyes you turned the Yellow Peril into Mary Tate of Glasthule, with a father who had sailed off to look for work in Scotland five years before, and had there decided that one could live more cheaply than seven. The last thing I'd wanted that evening was a person.

[DA *rises, about to go*]

DA: [*To* YOUNG CHARLIE] You mind your manners and treat her right, do you hear me. [*To* MARY] Don't take any impudence from him. Home by eleven, Charlie.

YOUNG CHARLIE: Yes, da.

DA: 'Bye-'bye, so. Mind yourselves.

MARY: 'Bye . . . [*They watch until he is out of sight*] Your old fellow is great gas.

YOUNG CHARLIE: [*Sourly*] Oh, yeah. A whole bloody gasometer.

MARY: [*Pause, then*] Well, will we go down the back?

YOUNG CHARLIE: Uh . . . down the back . . . yeah.

MARY: He's gone, he won't see us. [*Affectionately, mocking*] Bruce!

YOUNG CHARLIE: The thing is, I promised Oliver I'd see him in the billiard hall.

MARY: Oh, yeah?

YOUNG CHARLIE: Maybe some evening next week, if you're around, we can—

MARY: Mm . . . sure.

YOUNG CHARLIE: Oliver's holding a table for us. Got to run. Well . . . see you.

MARY: Suppose you will. [*As he goes*] Y'ought to wrap yourself in cotton wool. [*Chanting*] Daddy's little baby . . . Daddy's little b— [*She stops and begins to cry, then goes off*]

CHARLIE: I stayed away from the seafront for a long time after that. [*He finds an object on the table in front of him*] Is this yours? [*He sees that he is alone. He looks at it more closely*] Tug-o-war medal. Nineteen . . . God almighty, nineteen-twelve. It was different then. It was even different when . . . when? When I was seven. You were an Einstein in those days.

[DA *comes in from the scullery. He is thirty years younger: in his prime*]

DA: [*A roar*] Hup out of that! Put up your homework, get off your backside, and we'll take the dog for a run around the Vico.

CHARLIE: [*Happily*] Yes, da.

DA: [*Summoning the dog*] Come on, Blackie . . . who's a good dog? That's the fella . . . hup, hup! [*He crouches as if holding a dog by the forepaws, and allows his face to be licked*] Give us the paw . . . give. Look at that . . . begod, wouldn't he near talk to you? Get down. Are you right, son? [*He extends his hand.* CHARLIE *takes it.* MOTHER *comes in from the scullery with a woollen scarf*]

MOTHER: No, he's not right. [*She puts the scarf around* CHARLIE's *neck, tucking it in tightly*] You have as much sense in you as a don't-know-what. Dragging him out with his chest exposed. Do you want to get him into bad health?

CHARLIE: Ah, ma . . .

MOTHER: Ah, ma! Go on. Bless yourselves going out, the pair of you.

> [CHARLIE *and* DA *go into the hall.* DA *dips his fingers into a holy-water font and flicks the water at* CHARLIE]

DA: [*Opening the front door: to the dog, stumbling*] Blast you, don't trip me up . . . hoosh owa that!

> [*They stop on the doorstep,* DA *looking at the sky. During this scene,* CHARLIE *does not attempt to imitate a child. He is an adult re-enacting a memory. Trust is evident in his attitude towards* DA]

DA: That's a fine mackerel sky. Sure isn't it the best bloody country in the world!

CHARLIE: Da, say it.

DA: Say what?

CHARLIE: What you always say. Ah, you know . . . what the country mug in the army said. Say it.

DA: [*Feigning innocence*] What did he say?

CHARLIE: Ah, do . . .

DA: Yis, well, he joins up. And he sits down to his dinner the first night, and says he . . .

CHARLIE: Yeah, yeah!

DA: Says he: "Yes, sir; no, sir; sir, if you please. Is it up the duck's arse that I shove the green peas?"

> [CHARLIE *laughs delightedly. They walk hand in hand up and around the stage, both singing "Waxie Dargle." Lights go down on the kitchen. They stop at an upper level.* DA *reaches back to help* CHARLIE *up*]

DA: Come on, now . . . big step.

CHARLIE: I can't, da.

DA: Yes, you can.

CHARLIE: I'll fall.

DA: You won't fall. Catch a hold of me hand. That's the lad . . . and there you go! Looka that, looka them mountains. There's a view, if you were rich enough you couldn't buy it. Do you know what I'm going to tell you? . . . there's them that says that view is better nor the Bay of Naples.

CHARLIE: Where's Naples, da?

DA: Ah, it's in Italy.

CHARLIE: What's Italy like, da?

DA: [*Pause, then gravely*] Sticky, son . . . sticky.

CHARLIE: Da . . .

DA: What?

CHARLIE: Will I go to Italy when I grow up?

DA: [*Comforting*] Not a fear of it . . . we wouldn't let you.

CHARLIE: [*Looking out and down*] There's a ship. Is that it, da? . . . is that our ship coming in?

DA: Where? No . . . no, son, that one's going out.

CHARLIE: Will ours come in tomorrow, da?

DA: Begod now it might.

CHARLIE: We'll be on the pig's back then, da, won't we? When we're rich.

DA: We won't be far off it.

CHARLIE: And what'll we do?

DA: Do?

CHARLIE: When we win the Sweep.

DA: [*The standard answer*] We won't do a shaggin' hand's turn.

CHARLIE: [*Awe and delight*] Gawny!

DA: [*Deadpan*] Sure the girl drew out me ticket the last time, and bad cess to her, didn't she drop it.

CHARLIE: [*Dismay*] She didn't?

DA: She did.

CHARLIE: The bloomin' bitch.

DA: The what? Where did you hear that expression?

CHARLIE: I dunno, da.

DA: Don't ever again let me hear you saying the like of that. That's a corner-boy expression.

CHARLIE: Sorry, da.

DA: Women is different from you and me: y'ought to grow up to have respect for them. No, never call a woman a name like that, son, not even if she was a right oul' whoor. [*Pause*] Do you know where we are now?

CHARLIE: Dalkey Hill, da.

DA: Not at all. In my day this was called Higgins' Hill, and oul' Higgins used to chase us off it and him up on a white horse. He never set foot in church, chapel or meeting, and sign's on it when he died no one would have him, and [*Pointing off*] that's where he's buried, under that stump of what's left of a cross after it was struck by lightnin'. Sure they say he sold his soul to the Oul' Fella himself.

CHARLIE: What oul' fella?

DA: [*Pointing down*] Your man. Isn't the mark of his hoof on the wall below on Ardbrugh Road where he tripped running down to the mailboat to go back to England?

CHARLIE: Da, let's go home.

DA: What ails you?

CHARLIE: I'm afraid of old Higgins.

DA: Are you coddlin' me?

CHARLIE: And it's getting dark. I want to go home.

DA: Sure ghosts won't mind you if you don't mind them.

CHARLIE: Da . . . [*Reaching for his hand*]

DA: Wait now till I light me pipe and then we'll go.

CHARLIE: Da, you know the thing I'm worst afraid of?

DA: What's that?

CHARLIE: Well, you know me mother? . . . Not ma: me real one.

DA: What about her?

CHARLIE: Me Aunt Bridgie says when it gets dark she comes and looks in at me through the window.

DA: Looks in at you?

CHARLIE: And she says she's tall and with a white face and a black coat, and she comes out from Dublin on the tram, and she wants me back.

DA: Is that a fact?

CHARLIE: And me Aunt Bridgie says it wasn't true what you told me when I was small, about me mother being on Lambay Island where she wasn't able to get hold of me, and living on pollack and Horny Cobblers.

DA: Not true? Did I ever tell you a word of a lie?

CHARLIE: I don't believe she's on Lambay Island.

DA: No. No, she's not there. That wasn't a lie, son: it was . . . a makey-up. Because you were too young, do you follow me . . . you wouldn't have understood.

CHARLIE: [*Apprehensive*] Understood what? Why, where is she? [DA *looks impassively out to sea*] Da, tell us.

DA: [*Seeming to change the subject*] Do you see that flashing light?

CHARLIE: That's the *Kish* lightship.

DA: Well, that's where she is.

CHARLIE: [*Stunned*] On the *Kish?*

DA: God help her.

CHARLIE: What's she doing on the *Kish?*

DA: She . . . cooks.

CHARLIE: For the lightshipmen?

DA: Yis.

CHARLIE: What does she cook?

DA: Ah, pollack, son, and Horny Cobblers.

[CHARLIE *gives him a suspicious look, then peers out to sea*]

CHARLIE: Gawny.

DA: So now you know.

CHARLIE: Da . . . what if she got off the *Kish?* What if she's at home now before us and looking through the window?

DA: Well, if she is, I'll tell you what we'll do. I'll come up behind her and I'll give her the biggest root up in the arse a woman ever got.

CHARLIE: [*Pleased*] Will you, da?

DA: I will. And bejasus it'll be nothing compared to the root I'll give your Aunt Bridgie. [*Rising, brushing his trousers-seat*] Now where the hell is that whelp of a dog?

CHARLIE: Da, I love you.

DA: [*Staring at him in puzzlement*] Certainly you do. Why wouldn't you? [*Moving away*] Blackie, come here to me! [DA'*s reply has the effect of causing* CHARLIE *to revert to his present-day self*]

CHARLIE: [*Fuming*] Why wouldn't I? I'll tell you why bloody wouldn't I. Because you were an old thick, a zombie, a mastodon. My God . . . my mother living on a lightship, trimming the wick and filleting Horn Cobblers. What a blazing, ever-fertile imagination you had—Cobblers aren't even edible!

DA: [*Whistles*] Blackie!

CHARLIE: And pollacks!

DA: You're right son, bolloxed that's what he is.

CHARLIE: The black dog was the only intelligent member of the family. He died a few years later. He was poisoned, and no one will convince me it wasn't suicide. God knows how ma ever came to marry you.

[*Lights come up in the kitchen.* MOTHER *looks on while* YOUNG CHARLIE *is writing a letter*]

CHARLIE: Oh, I know how, sort of . . . she told me. I mean why.

MOTHER: He was called Ernie Moore. He used to be on the boats . . . the B and I. The *Lady Hudson-Kinahan* it was. I was very great with him for a while. Then himself came to the house one day and said how he had the job above in Jacob's and he wanted to marry me. So that was that.

YOUNG CHARLIE: How?

MOTHER: It was fixed.

YOUNG CHARLIE: How fixed?

MOTHER: My father told him I would, so it was fixed. Things was arranged in them days.

YOUNG CHARLIE: Did you want to?

MOTHER: I had no say in it.

YOUNG CHARLIE: How well did you know him?

MOTHER: Well enough to bid the time of day to.

YOUNG CHARLIE: That was handy.

MOTHER: A body's not put into this world to pick and choose and be particular. I was seventeen, I done what I was told to.

YOUNG CHARLIE: What about Popeye the Sailor?

MOTHER: Who?

YOUNG CHARLIE: The other one.

MOTHER: Mr. Moore in your mouth. When your time comes and you have to answer to God in the next world it makes no differ who you married and who you didn't marry. That's when everything will be made up to us.

YOUNG CHARLIE: You mean they hand out free sailors?

MOTHER: What? You little jeer, you. [*She aims a blow at him which he wards off*] Well, God send that you never have to get married young for fear that if you stayed at home you might die, like many another died, of consumption for want of proper nourishment. [YOUNG CHARLIE *affects to ignore her. He resumes writing and sings "Popeye the Sailorman" under his breath in derisive counterpoint*] Waited on hand and foot, never wanting for nothing. Well, when you do get married, to whatever rip will have you, I only hope you'll be half the provider for her as himself has been for me. Is that letter done?

YOUNG CHARLIE: Yeah.

MOTHER: Read it out.

YOUNG CHARLIE: The Jacobs don't care whether I got a job or not.

MOTHER: It's manners to tell them, they ask after you. Go on.

YOUNG CHARLIE: "Dear Nelson and Jeanette . . ." [*She gives him a look. He amends*] "Dear Mr. and Mrs. Jacob: My father has told me how often you have been so good as to enquire as to whether I have yet found employment. I am grateful for your interest and am glad to say that I have now been given a clerical position. So, happily, I am no longer like Mr. Micawber, constantly expecting something to turn up. Thanking you for your—"

MOTHER: What sort of codology is that?

YOUNG CHARLIE: What?

MOTHER: You're no longer like who?

YOUNG CHARLIE: It's an expression out of a book.

MOTHER: Write it out again and do it proper.

YOUNG CHARLIE: What for?

MOTHER: Because you're told to.

YOUNG CHARLIE: Look, there's this character in a book. He's always hard up, but he's an optimist. He—

MOTHER: Do as you're bid.

YOUNG CHARLIE: There's nothing wrong with it. Maybe you don't understand it, but the Jacobs will. It's meant to be funny, they'll laugh when they read it.

MOTHER: Aye, to be sure they will. At you, for setting yourself up to be something you're not.

YOUNG CHARLIE: It's my letter. You're not writing it: I am.

MOTHER: Then write it proper.

YOUNG CHARLIE: Proper-*ly!*

MOTHER: Don't you pull *me* up. Don't act the high-up lord with *me*, not in this house. They said I'd rue the day, and the gawm I was, I didn't believe them. He'll turn on you, they said. My own mother, me good neighbours, they all—

YOUNG CHARLIE: Oh, play another record.

MOTHER: Don't you back-answer me, you cur.

YOUNG CHARLIE: Whatever it is, if you don't understand it, it's rubbish. To hell with Charles Dickens and the rest of them: Nat Gould and Ruby M. Ayres made the world.

MOTHER: Are you going to write that out again, yes or no?

YOUNG CHARLIE: No, because there's nothing the—

MOTHER: Are you not! [*She looks up at* DA, *who with* CHARLIE *is still standing in the hill area*] Nick . . .

DA: Ah, son, write it out the way she wants you to.

MOTHER: Don't beg him: tell him.

DA: [*Violently*] Will you do as you're bloody well told and not be putting the woman into a passion! Can we not have a solitary minute's peace in the house with you and your curse-o'-God Jack-acting?

MOTHER: Do that letter again.

YOUNG CHARLIE: [*In a rage*] All right, all right! I'll do it. [*He crumples up the letter, takes the notepad and writes furiously*] "Dear Mr. and Mrs. Jacob . . . I am very well. My parents hope you are well, too, as it leaves them. I have a j-o-b now. I do not know myself, I am that delighted. Thanking you and oblige . . ." [*He signs it*] Now are you happy?

MOTHER: Hand it here. I wouldn't trust you to post it. [*She takes the letter and puts it into an envelope. He cannot quite believe that she is taking it seriously*]

YOUNG CHARLIE: You're not going to send—

DA: [*Turning to* CHARLIE] Begod, son, you always made a great fist of writing a letter.

YOUNG CHARLIE: [*Barely in control*] I'm going to the billiard hall.

MOTHER: Go wherever you like.

[YOUNG CHARLIE *storms out, loudly singing "Popeye the Sail-orman." He emits a last mocking "Boop-boop!" as he vanishes. We hear the far-off barking of a dog*]

CHARLIE: It was a long time before I realized that love turned upside down is love for all that.

DA: There's the whoorin' dog gone down ahead of us in the finish. And the lights is on in the town. [*Pointing*] That's the Ulverton Road, son, where we frightened the shite out of the Black-and-Tans. And the lamp is lit in your uncle Paddy's window.

CHARLIE: If it is, he didn't light it: he's dead these donkey's years. Uncle Paddy, Kruger Doyle, Gunjer Hammond, Oats Nolan—all your cronies—and old Bonk-a-bonk with his banjo and Mammy Reilly in her madhouse of a shop, with her money, so they said, all in sovereigns, wrapped up inside her wig. All dead. Like your-self . . . and, trust you, last as usual.

DA: That's a hash old wind starting up. We'll need a couple of extra coats on the bed tonight, son.

CHARLIE: We will.

DA: Mind your step now. If you slip and cut yourself she'll ate the pair of us. Give me your hand. Let the light from the *Kish* show you where the steps are.

CHARLIE: That's it, mother: light us home. Least you can do.

CURTAIN

ACT TWO

CHARLIE *and* YOUNG CHARLIE *appear, walking towards the front door. There is a slightly exaggerated vivacity in* CHARLIE'S *manner: the result of having had a few drinks.*

CHARLIE: Ikey Meh? I remember the *name* . . .

YOUNG CHARLIE: The tram conductor. We used to yell Ikey Meh at him when the tram went past, and he'd pull the emergency stop and lep off after us—

CHARLIE: Leap off.

YOUNG CHARLIE: . . . And leave the passengers high and dry. God, he could run.

CHARLIE: Of course: yes! Ikey Meh. [*"Meh" is drawn out in imitation of a goat*] He— [*He catches sight of* DA, *who is trailing along behind them*] I told you to stop following me. Now go away.

YOUNG CHARLIE: Leave him alone.

CHARLIE: I go out for a bite to eat and a quiet jar, to get away from him, and what happens? He's in the pub ahead of me. Fizz off.

[DA *hangs back and lurks in the shadows*]

YOUNG CHARLIE: You might be civil to him. I mean, it's his day.

CHARLIE: It was. The funeral's over.

YOUNG CHARLIE: [*Coldly*] Oh, that's exquisite. You're a gem, you are.

CHARLIE: Don't get uppish with me, sonny Jim: you're as dead as he is. Come in and keep me company while I finish up.

YOUNG CHARLIE: I think I'll hump off.

CHARLIE: [Aggressively] You'll hump nowhere. You'll stay in my head until I choose to chase you out of it.

YOUNG CHARLIE: Oh, will I?

CHARLIE: There's only room in there for one of you at a time, and if I let you leave he'll come back like a yo-yo. Look at him, lurking. Get in there when you're told to.

[He has opened the front door with a key and pushed YOUNG CHARLIE in ahead of him]

YOUNG CHARLIE: Mind who you're shaggin' pushin'.

CHARLIE: Shagging. Pushing. Get in. [DA comes up to the door, moving fast] Oh, no you don't. Out, and stay out. [He shuts the door]

[DA promptly walks through the fourth wall and sits in his armchair filling his pipe]

YOUNG CHARLIE: Someone to see you.

CHARLIE: Who? [He stares angrily at DA]

DA: God, they done wonders with that public house, son. I wouldn't recognise it. All the metally bits and the red lights . . . it'd put you in mind of a whoorhouse.

YOUNG CHARLIE: When were you ever in a—

CHARLIE: Say nothing. Ignore him. [He searches through the bureau drawers]

DA: That pub used to be called Larkin's . . . you didn't know that. [CHARLIE fetches a jug from the dresser and empties it. It is filled with old keys, bits of yarn and thread, receipts, newspaper clippings, odds and ends]

YOUNG CHARLIE: If you hadn't gone out you could have been finished and away by now. But no, you couldn't wait to get maggoty drunk.

CHARLIE: Maggoty? On three small ones?

DA: I never seen you take a drink before, son. But sure what odds? Aren't you old enough?

YOUNG CHARLIE: [*Primly*] I never need artificial stimulets.

CHARLIE: Stimulants.

YOUNG CHARLIE: Booze. Look at you.

DA: [*Placidly*] The way you swally-ed them. Begod, says I to meself, that fellow would drink Lough Erin dry.

CHARLIE: Shut up. [*To* YOUNG CHARLIE] What's wrong with me?

YOUNG CHARLIE: Well, you're a bit of a disappointment.

CHARLIE: Oh, yes?

YOUNG CHARLIE: I mean, I'd hoped to do better for meself.

CHARLIE: What had you in mind?

YOUNG CHARLIE: Don't get huffy. It's not that I amn't glad to see you: at least it means I'll live till I'm forty: that's something.

CHARLIE: Thanks.

YOUNG CHARLIE: [*Looking at* CHARLIE's *wrist*] And I like the watch.

CHARLIE: Oh, good.

YOUNG CHARLIE: I suppose I could have done worse: but you can't deny you're a bit ordinary. It gives a fellow the creeps, seeing himself at your age: everything behind him and nothing to look forward to.

CHARLIE: I get the old-age pension next year: there's that.

YOUNG CHARLIE: Yesterday I was thinking: I'm only eighteen, anything can happen to me . . . anything. I mean, maybe a smashing girl will go mad for me. Now I dunno. [CHARLIE *puts on his glasses to read a receipt.* YOUNG CHARLIE *looks at him*] Ah, God.

CHARLIE: What?

YOUNG CHARLIE: Glasses. I'm blind as well.

CHARLIE: I'm sorry about that. The time I was castrated in a car crash, it affected my eyesight.

YOUNG CHARLIE: [Horrified] You weren't. [Then] You're so damn smart.

DA: Oh, them motor cars is dangerous.

YOUNG CHARLIE: Everything's a laugh, isn't it? Anyone I see who's your age . . . same thing. All lah-de-dah and make a joke of it. God, if something good happens to me, I jump up in the air, I let out a yell, I run. Your sort just sits there.

CHARLIE: Arthritis.

YOUNG CHARLIE: You're dried up. Dead.

CHARLIE: I'm a seething torrent inside.

YOUNG CHARLIE: You? You're jizzless.

CHARLIE: I'm what?

YOUNG CHARLIE: There's no jizz in you. The fun's gone out of you. What's worse, you're no good . . . wouldn't even take him with you to London when me ma died.

CHARLIE: I asked him.

YOUNG CHARLIE: Instead of forcing him.

CHARLIE: Him? Who could force him to do anything?

YOUNG CHARLIE: Did you try?

CHARLIE: Don't get righteous with me, my pasty-faced little friend. It doesn't become you. Were you any good? Who was it once gave him a packet of six razor blades for Christmas?

YOUNG CHARLIE: I was broke.

CHARLIE: Yeah, and why? Because you'd bought a pair of nylons for that typist from Cappoquin who let you grope her up against the railings of the Custom House. Six Gillette blades!

DA: Oh, there was great shaving in them blades.

YOUNG CHARLIE: You weren't even here when he died.

CHARLIE: It was sudden.

DA: [*Rising*] I think I have one of them still. Hold on.

CHARLIE, YOUNG CHARLIE: [*Together*] Sit down.

CHARLIE: It was sudden. I'm not clairvoyant.

YOUNG CHARLIE: You were glad it was sudden, though, weren't you?

CHARLIE: Why not? It's the best way. No pain . . .

YOUNG CHARLIE: No pain for you, you mean. No having to go to him and wait and watch him and say things. All the dirty bits over with when you got here.

CHARLIE: Do you think I planned it?

YOUNG CHARLIE: No, but it suited you. Didn't it?

CHARLIE: I was . . .

YOUNG CHARLIE: Relieved.

CHARLIE: [*Nodding*] Mm.

YOUNG CHARLIE: Look at me, you with your lousy watch. I haven't got a tosser, but at least I've got a few principles. Where's yours?

CHARLIE: Principles? You mean like when you took that job Drumm offered you?

YOUNG CHARLIE: That's a stop-gap.

CHARLIE: I see.

YOUNG CHARLIE: I'll be out of it in a month and doing what I want to.

CHARLIE: A month?

YOUNG CHARLIE: A month!

[DRUMM *appears in the neutral area, a letter in his hand*]

DRUMM: My friend . . . [*As* YOUNG CHARLIE *looks around*] Come in here.

YOUNG CHARLIE: Now what? [*He leaves the kitchen through the fourth wall and goes over to* DRUMM] Yes, Mr. Drumm?

DRUMM: How long have you been employed here?

YOUNG CHARLIE: Thirteen years, Mr. Drumm.

DRUMM: In those thirteen years it may not have escaped your notice that there is one filing drawer for names with the initial letter "M," and another for those which are adorned with the prefix "Mac," whether written M-a-c, M-c, or M-apostrophe. This letter pertains to one James Maguire. I found it, after a forty-minute search, in the "Mac" drawer. Spell "Maguire," would you?

CHARLIE, YOUNG CHARLIE: [*Together*] M-a-g-u-i-r-e.

DRUMM: [*Slowly, as if it were a death sentence*] M-a-g.

YOUNG CHARLIE: I must have—

DRUMM: M-a-g.

YOUNG CHARLIE: Yes.

DRUMM: You will concede that this was incorrectly filed?

YOUNG CHARLIE: Technically, yes . . .

DRUMM: [*With venom*] Don't use words you don't know the meaning of. A barely literate child could have filed this letter where it belongs. But not, apparently, a man thirty years of age, with a wife, the beginning of a family and pretensions towards intellectual superiority.

YOUNG CHARLIE: That has nothing to do with— [*He stops*]

DRUMM: [*Dangerously*] With whom? [*He nods towards the other, unseen members of the staff*] Get on with your work. [*To* YOUNG CHARLIE] With whom?

YOUNG CHARLIE: [*A retreat*] With this place.

        [DRUMM *smiles at him scornfully*]

DRUMM: File this where it—

YOUNG CHARLIE: Or with you either, Mr. Drumm.

DRUMM: Don't get insolent with me, my friend. If you don't like it here, be off with you. No one is holding you. But while you remain you will stay awake and do your work. Accurately. Do you understand? [YOUNG CHARLIE *holds out his hand for the letter*] I asked if you understood.

YOUNG CHARLIE: Yes. [*He takes the letter*]

DRUMM: We all know that you think your position here is beneath you. But you must try and put up with it and with us, Mr. Tynan. Or whatever your name is.

> [YOUNG CHARLIE *looks at him, then goes.* DRUMM *remains standing during the following*]

DA: Oh, Old Drumm is a decent man.

CHARLIE: For years, he'd taken me in hand like a Victorian father. He taught me, not by his enthusiasms—he had none—but by his dislikes.

DRUMM: Women, Mr. Tynan, should be given a damn good squeeze at the earliest opportunity, and thereafter avoided.

CHARLIE: Perhaps he wanted a son or had a fondness for strays. He made me his confidant.

DRUMM: That man Kelly is known to be a pervert. Shun him. What's more, he spits as he talks. I move away from him, and he follows me and spits on me again.

CHARLIE: One evening, I was in a hurry somewhere—to meet a girl, go to a film: I don't know. I saw him coming towards me. I didn't want to stop and talk, so I crossed over. He'd seen me avoid him. It was that simple. Except at work, he never spoke to me again.

> [*The light fades on* DRUMM. DA *gets the razor blade from the bureau*]

DA: Ah.

CHARLIE: What?

DA: I dunno is this one of the blades you gev me, son.

CHARLIE: Show. [*He sniffs at it*] A Gillette, definitely. Sheffield, I'd say . . . nineteen-forty-three. An impudent blade, sharpish after-taste . . . precocious, but not presumptuous. Damn it, I bet this *is* one of them. Anything I ever gave you, you took and wouldn't use. Wouldn't be under a compliment to me.

[DA *slips the blade into* CHARLIE's *pocket*]

DA: Say nothing . . . take them home with you.

CHARLIE: It's a wonder you cashed the cheques I sent you for to-bacco.

DA: Certainly I cashed them. Wasn't that how I got thrun out of that home you put me into last January?

CHARLIE: Home? Blast your impudence, that was a private hotel.

DA: Whatever it was.

CHARLIE: I'm telling you what it was. An hotel.

DA: [*Carelessly*] Yis.

CHARLIE: Because you'd gone dotty. Shouting out to ma, who was two years dead. Going around to my cousin Rosie for your Christmas dinner at two in the morning. Do you know how hard it was to get you into that hotel?

DA: Hotel my arse. Sure they wouldn't let me go up to the bank to cash that cheque you sent me. But begod, says I, I'll bate them yet. Do you know what I done?

CHARLIE: I heard.

DA: I got out over the shaggin' wall. And these two big impudent straps of country ones cem after me. "Come back," says they. "Leave go of me," says I; "The divil's cure to the pair of yiz." Then doesn't one of them put her mawsy red hands on me be the collar. "Be a good boy," says she to me. Well . . . [*He laughs fondly*] I drew out with me fist and I gev her a poke for herself in the stomach.

CHARLIE: They told me it was on the breast.

DA: It was in the pit of the stomach . . . I wouldn't poke a woman in the breast. Yis, I drew out with me fist . . . ! That wasn't bad for eighty-three, wha'?

CHARLIE: So they threw you out.

DA: And after that you had me put into the Union.

CHARLIE: Into the what?

DA: [*Ashamed to say it*] You know . . . the . . . the . . . the poorhouse.

CHARLIE: Oh, you malignant, lopsided old liar. It was a private room in a psychiatric hospital.

DA: I know, I know.

CHARLIE: A hospital.

DA: Yis.

CHARLIE: [*Incredulous*] Poorhouse!

DA: Sure it's greatly improved since I was a young lad. You wouldn't know a bit of it.

CHARLIE: [*Beginning to shout*] It was not the p—

DA: I amn't saying a word again' it. Sure hadn't I the best of everything, and wasn't I better off there than I was where you put me before that—in the home?

CHARLIE: [*Giving up*] Jesus!

DA: Do you know what I'm going to tell you? If the oul' heart hadn't gone on me the evenin' before last, I'd be alive today.

CHARLIE: Is that so?

DA: It is.

CHARLIE: There are no shallows to which you won't sink, are there?

DA: [*Proudly*] There aren't! [*Reminiscent*] I drew out with me fist and I give her a poke. You never seen me when I was riz, did you, son?

CHARLIE: No. [*Then*] Yes . . . once.

DA: You did not.

CHARLIE: Nineteen-fifty-one. You were sixty-seven . . . She was sixty-three then, and I still don't believe I saw it happen.

[*There is a squeak of the gate and* MOTHER *appears. She is carrying a shopping bag*]

DA: [*Looking out*] There she is at long last. It's gone half-past six; I thought she was run over. [*He opens the door.* MOTHER *comes in. She is in a good mood, humming to herself*] I say, we thought you were under the wheels of a bus. Where were you at all? The boy is home before you, with his stomach roaring for his tea.

MOTHER: [*Unruffled*] He'll get it when it's put in front of him, not before. [*She takes off her coat and hangs it up, then puts on her apron*]

DA: [*Grumbling*] We didn't know *what* happened to you. Was the picture any good itself?

MOTHER: It was an old love thing, all divorces and codology. A body couldn't make head or tail of it. Charlie, clear that rubbidge off the table and be a bit of help to me.

[CHARLIE *puts the odds and ends back in the jug.* MOTHER *begins to lay the table*]

DA: It's seldom we hear a song out of you.

MOTHER: I ought to cry to suit you.

DA: I'm only saying, any other time the picture is a washout you come home to us raging. [*Pause*] And your horse finished down the field today as well.

MOTHER: Did it? [*Nodding, not caring*] The going was too soft.

[*She goes on with her work, still humming.* CHARLIE *and* DA *exchange puzzled looks*]

DA: [*Curious, fishing*] I suppose Dun Laoghaire was packed.

MOTHER: Crowds.

DA: Nothing strange or startling, so?

MOTHER: [*Almost coyly*] Mm . . .

DA: Well, tell us or don't tell us, one or the other.

[MOTHER *turns. She cannot keep her adventure to herself*]

MOTHER: I was treated to a glass of port in the Royal Marine Hotel.

DA: You were what?

MOTHER: Someone I met in Lipton's.

CHARLIE: The grandeur of you!

DA: [*Laughing*] Was he good-looking itself?

MOTHER: It wasn't a "him" at all—don't be such a jeer. This woman comes up to me. "Excuse me," says she, "for asking. Are you not Margaret Tynan . . . Maggie Doyle, that was?" "I am," says I; "Do I know you?" "You do," says she.

DA: [*In disgust*] Ah!

MOTHER: Well, to cut a long story, who was she but Gretta Moore out of the Tivoli in Glasthule.

DA: I never heard tell of her.

MOTHER: Ah, Gretta Nolan that married Ernie Moore off of the B and I.

CHARLIE: [*Remembering*] Who?

MOTHER: He's retired these two years.

CHARLIE: [*It comes to him; singing*] "I'm . . . Popeye the sailor-man!"

MOTHER: Hold your tongue! [DA *is staring at her, numbed*] So in with the pair of us into the Royal Marine Hotel. Says she to me: "Sure we're as good as the best of them." And the style of all the old ones there, with their dyed hair and the fur coats on them. Tea, they were all having, and sweet cake. "Sure," says Gretta, "we can have *that* at home in the house." [*To* CHARLIE] So this waiter comes up in a swalla-tail coat. Oh, she was well able for him. "We want two large glasses of port wine," says she, and off he went like a hare to get them!

DA: Making a show of yourself.

CHARLIE: What show?

DA: High-up people looking at you.

MOTHER: [*Loftily*] Pity about them!

DA: The whole town'll have it tomorrow.

CHARLIE: [*To* MOTHER] Then what?

MOTHER: Three shillings for two glasses of port wine you'd be hard put to it to wet your lips with . . . and sixpence on top of that for the waiter. Oh, it was scandalous. Says I to her—

DA: Sure Ernie Moore is dead these donkey's years.

MOTHER: What?

DA: [*Dogged*] I know he's dead.

MOTHER: How do you know?

DA: I know.

MOTHER: The man's wife says different.

DA: Oh aye, ask me brother am I a liar! Oh, she must be a right good thing. And you're worse. Pouring drink into you in the Royal Marine Hotel, and the crowds of the world looking at you and . . . and . . . laughing.

CHARLIE: What crowds?

MOTHER: Don't mind him.

DA: And I say he's dead and long dead.

MOTHER: Is he? Well, I'll soon tell you next Thursday whether he's dead or no.

DA: What's next Thursday?

MOTHER: [*Almost coquettishly*] I'm invited down for me tea.

DA: Down where, for your tea?

MOTHER: To the Tivoli. [*To* CHARLIE] Gretta was telling me her eldest is beyant in Canada, and she has a grandson nearly your age, and—

DA: Well, you'll go there by yourself if you go, because I'm staying where I am.

MOTHER: You can stay wherever you like, for you weren't invited.

DA: Am I not!

MOTHER: Your own tea will be left here ready for you.

DA: Well, it needn't be, because you're not going.

MOTHER: Why amn't I?

DA: You aren't setting foot outside of here.

MOTHER: You won't stop me.

DA: Will I not!

MOTHER: [*Her fury mounting*] You were always the same and you always will be the same. The one time I'm invited to a person's house, you begrudge it to me. [*Beginning to shout*] Well, I'll go *wherever* I like and see *whoever* I like.

DA: Do, and you'll go out of this. I'm the boss in this house and I'll stay the boss in it.

CHARLIE: She's only going for a cup of tea.

DA: [*Wildly*] Oh aye . . . aye, that's what she'd like us to think. But it's to see him . . . *him*.

MOTHER: To see who?

DA: You faggot, you: don't let on you don't know. It's Ernie . . . Ernie . . . curse-o'-God Ernie! [*His fist crashes on the table*] May he die roaring for a priest . . . curse-o'-God Ernie!

[*Even* MOTHER, *who knows him, is alarmed by the violence of his rage. She stares at him. He strikes the table again*]

CHARLIE: [*Remembering*] And the floorboards barked like dogs, and the cups went mad on their hooks.

DA: You set one foot in the Tivoli, you look crossways at a whoormaster the like of him, and bejasus, I'll get jail for you, do you hear me? I won't leave a stick or a stone standing in the kip.

MOTHER: [*Recovering, still a little afraid*] Look at you . . . look at the yellow old face of you.

DA: [*Savagely, almost skipping with rage*] With your . . . your port wine, and your sweet cake, and your Royal Marine Hotel.

MOTHER: The whole town knows you for a madman . . . aye, and all belonging to you.

DA: Ernie . . . Ernie! You'll stay clear of him, Thursday and every other day.

MOTHER: Because you know I preferred him over you, and that's what you can't stand. Because I never went with you. Because you know if it wasn't for me father, God forgive him, telling me to—

[DA *makes a violent rush at her, his fist raised*]

CHARLIE: Hey . . .

[DA'S *fist comes down and stops almost touching her face, where it stays, trembling, threatening*]

MOTHER: [*Quietly*] Go on. Go on, do it. And that'll be the first time and the last. I'll leave here if I was to sleep on the footpath. [*Pause.* DA *starts past her towards the scullery. Half to herself*] You went behind my back to him because you knew I wouldn't have you.

[DA *runs to the table and raises a cup as if to dash it to pieces. Instead, he takes his pipe from the table and throws it on the ground. It breaks. He goes into the scullery.* CHARLIE *stoops to pick up the pieces of the pipe as* MOTHER *faces away from him to wipe her eyes*]

CHARLIE: [*Still stooping*] Will you go? On Thursday?

[*She faces him. Although tears are coming, there is a wry, almost mocking attempt at a smile*]

MOTHER: The jealous old bags.

[*The lights fade. Then we see a woman enter and sit on a rustic seat in the neutral area. She is* MRS. PRYNNE, *fifty, Anglo-Irish accent, dressed for the country*]

YOUNG CHARLIE: [*Off, singing: the tune is "Blaze Away"*]
"Tight as a drum,
Never been done,
Queen of all the fairies!"

[MRS. PRYNNE *opens her eyes. Through the following,* YOUNG CHARLIE *comes on carrying two quart cans*]

"Bolicky Biddy had only one diddy
To feed the baby on.
Poor little fucker had only one sucker
To grind his teeth up . . ." [*He stops on seeing* MRS. PRYNNE]

MRS. PYRNNE: Good evening. Do you know where Tynan is? The gardener.

YOUNG CHARLIE: He's in the greenhouse. Will I tell him you want him?

MRS. PRYNNE: If you would.

YOUNG CHARLIE: Sure. [*He goes across the stage*] Da! Hey . . . [DA *appears, carrying a basket of tomatoes*] You're wanted.

DA: Who wants me?

YOUNG CHARLIE: I dunno. Posh-looking old one.

DA: [*A mild panic*] It's the mistress. Hold this for me . . . will you hold it! [*He thrusts the basket at* YOUNG CHARLIE *and getting his coat from offstage struggles to put it on*]

YOUNG CHARLIE: Easy . . . she's not on fire, you know. [*Helping him*] How much do you think?

DA: How much what?

YOUNG CHARLIE: Money.

DA: [*Confidently*] I'll get me due. Poor oul' Jacob wouldn't see me stuck, Lord ha' mercy on him . . . no, nor none of us. Says he many's the time: "Yous'll all be provided for." The parlourmaid and Cook got their envelopes this morning. [*A sob in his throat*] A decent poor man.

YOUNG CHARLIE: Don't start the waterworks, will you?

DA: [*Voice breaking*] God be good to him.

YOUNG CHARLIE: Hey, is it true they bury Quakers standing up?

DA: Jasus, you don't think they do it sitting down, do you? Where's the mistress?

YOUNG CHARLIE: Yours or mine? [*As* DA *looks at him*] By the tennis court. [*He calls after him*] Da . . . how much was the cook left?

DA: A hundred.

YOUNG CHARLIE: Pounds? [*He emits a quiet "Yeoww!" of pleasure. Exits.* DA *makes his way painfully, carrying the basket of tomatoes. He salutes* MRS. PRYNNE]

MRS. PRYNNE: Oh, Tynan, isn't this garden beautiful? Mr. Prynne and I shall hate not to see it again. I'm sure you'll miss it, too. Sit down, Tynan: next to me.

[DA *salutes and sits beside her*]

We loathe selling "Enderley," but with my dear father gone and the family with homes of their own, there's no one left to live in it.

DA: I picked you the best of the tomatoes, ma'am.

MRS. PRYNNE: Aren't you the great man. We'll take them back to Mountmellick with us in the morning. And the rose-trees.

DA: [*Authoritative, tapping her knee*] Yis . . . now don't forget: a good pruning as soon as you plant them. Cut the hybrids—the Peer Gynts, the Blue Moons and the Brasilias—cut them well back to two buds from the bottom, and the floribundas to five buds.

MRS. PRYNNE: The floribundas to five buds.

DA: The harder you cut, the better the bloom: only don't cut into a stem that's more than a year old.

MRS. PRYNNE: [*Attentive*] I'll remember.

DA: [*Slapping her knee*] I'll make a rose-grower out of you yet, so I will. And feed the buggers well in July, do you hear, if you want a good second blush.

MRS. PRYNNE: I do hope they take: my father loved the Enderley roses. Did you hear we have a buyer for the house, Tynan? A schoolteacher and his wife. She owns a fashion business in the city . . . I daresay that's where their money is. Catholics, I believe.

DA: [*Contemptuous*] Huh!

MRS. PRYNNE: I'm sure they'll want a gardener.

DA: Let them. Catholics with no money, letting on they're the Quality: sure they're the worst there is. No, I wouldn't work for me own: they'd skin you. The way it is, the legs is gone stiff on me, and the missus says it's time I gev meself a rest.

MRS. PRYNNE: What age are you now, Tynan?

DA: I'm sixty-eight, and I'm here since I was fourteen.

MRS. PRYNNE: Fifty-four years?

DA: The day yourself was born, the boss called me in. Nineteen-hundred-and-three, it was. "Take this in your hand, Tynan," says he to me, "and drink it." Begod, I never seen a tumbler of whiskey the size of it. "And now," says he, "go off to hell home for the rest of the day."

MRS. PRYNNE: The world is changing, Tynan, and not for the better. People are growing hard; my father's generation is out of fashion. [DA's *eyes are moist again. She takes an envelope from her handbag.* DA *gets to his feet*] In his will he asked that Mr. Prynne and I should attend to the staff. We think you should have a pension, Tynan: you're entitled to it. We thought twenty-six pounds per annum, payable quarterly.

DA: [*Saluting automatically*] Thanks, ma'am; thanks very much.

MRS. PRYNNE: Nonsense, you've earned it. Now, the lump sum. Poor Cook is getting on and will have to find a home of her own, so we've treated her as a special case. But I'm sure you and Mrs. Tynan won't say no to twenty-five pounds, with our best wishes and compliments. [DA *takes the envelope and again salutes automatically. He looks at it dumbly*] You're a great man for the work, and whatever you may say, we know you wouldn't give it up for diamonds. And there's that boy of yours. Once he leaves school he'll be a great help to you. You did well to adopt him.

DA: The way it is, do you see, the young lad is saving up to get married . . .

MRS. PRYNNE: Married?

DA: So we'd think bad of asking him to—

MRS. PRYNNE: How old is he?

DA: Sure didn't yourself send him up to me.

MRS. PRYNNE: Was that he? But he's a young man.

DA: [*Calling*] Charlie! Come here to me. [*To* MRS. PRYNNE] Sure he's working these six years. Only every shilling he earns, do you see, has to be put by. So herself and me, we couldn't ask him to—

MRS. PRYNNE: You mustn't encourage him to be selfish. Young people can live on next to nothing. [*As* YOUNG CHARLIE *arrives*] Hello. How d'you do?

YOUNG CHARLIE: 'Evening.

DA: Shake hands now, son. [*To* MRS. PRYNNE] He cem to pick the loganberries. Sure we couldn't leave them to go rotten.

MRS. PRYNNE: You are thoughtful. I'll ask Cook to make jam and send it to us in Mountmellick. [*To* YOUNG CHARLIE] I hear you're getting married.

YOUNG CHARLIE: I hope to.

MRS. PRYNNE: Well done. But you must look after this old man. Remember how much you owe him, so be good to him, and generous. [*She looks in her handbag and finds a five-pound note*] Mr. Prynne and I would like you to have this. A wedding gift. Perhaps you'll buy something for your new home.

YOUNG CHARLIE: No . . . thank you. I—

DA: Yes, he will. Take it.

YOUNG CHARLIE: Well . . . [*Taking it*] I'm sure we could do with a Sacred Heart picture for over the bed.

DA: [*Missing the sarcasm*] That's the boy!

MRS. PRYNNE: I see you've reared an art-lover, Tynan. And now the most important thing. I know my father would want you to have a keepsake . . . one of his treasures. [*She picks up a loosely-wrapped package from the seat.* DA *and* YOUNG CHARLIE *are intrigued.* To YOUNG CHARLIE] Have you travelled?

YOUNG CHARLIE: Not much.

MRS. PRYNNE: You must. In these days of aeroplanes, young people have no excuse. When my father was your age he'd been around the world. In nineteen-hundred-and-six he was in San Francisco at the time of the earthquake. That's on the west coast of America, you know.

YOUNG CHARLIE: Yes, I saw the film.

MRS. PRYNNE: After the great fire, he was passing a gutted jewelry shop when he saw this, lying on the ground for the taking. A find in a thousand, Tynan. [*She reverently lifts the paper, unveiling a mass of tangled bits of wire mounted on a metal base*] What do you think of that? Thirty or more pairs of spectacles, fused together by the heat of the fire. [*Pause*] My father had them mounted.

DA: Sure, what else would he do with them?

MRS. PRYNNE: Extraordinary, yes?

DA: That's worth having.

MRS. PRYNNE: It is, and there you are. [*She gives it to him, then shaking hands*] Goodbye, Tynan. Take care of yourself and we'll call to see you when we're in town. [*To* YOUNG CHARLIE] See that he doesn't overdo things, won't you? Goodbye . . . our best to your intended.

> [*She goes off, taking the various cans with her.* DA *salutes her, tears in his eyes*]

YOUNG CHARLIE: It's a miracle she didn't take the bench. When she said he found it in the ruins of a jeweller's shop, I thought for sure it was the Star of India. Thirty pairs of spectacles.

DA: You hold them: me hands is dirty. Don't drop them.

YOUNG CHARLIE: Don't what?

DA: They're worth money.

YOUNG CHARLIE: [*Irate*] Ah, for— What are you bawling for?

DA: A great man, she said I was. Sure I am, too.

YOUNG CHARLIE: How much did you get?

DA: Fifty-four years in the one place. I laid that tennis court . . . aye, and rolled it, too.

YOUNG CHARLIE: I don't care if you knitted the net. How much?

DA: [*Looking up*] And I planted them trees.

YOUNG CHARLIE: [*Realising*] You've been diddled.

DA: What diddled? Sure she needn't have gev me anything. The work I done, wasn't I paid for it . . . every Friday like a clockwork. I got me week off in the summer . . .

YOUNG CHARLIE: Give me that. [*He takes the envelope and opens it*]

DA: [*Unheeding, ranting away*] And me two days at Christmas, with an extra pound note put into me fist, and the sup of whiskey poured and waiting for me in the pantry. Wasn't I—

YOUNG CHARLIE: [*Looking at the cheque*] Twenty-five?

DA: [*Snatching it back*] Don't go tricking with that.

YOUNG CHARLIE: Is that *it*?

DA: Isn't it money for doing bugger-all? And sure haven't I the offer of work from the people that's bought the house.

YOUNG CHARLIE: What work? You're giving it up.

DA: Ah, time enough to give it up when I'm going downhill. Catholics, yis. They own a dress shop. Sure if your own won't look after you, who will?

YOUNG CHARLIE: My God, she'll kill you.

DA: Who will?

YOUNG CHARLIE: She will, when you bring that home to her. [*Meaning the cheque*] Here, put this with it. [*He offers him the five-pound note*]

DA: What for?

YOUNG CHARLIE: It'll save you a couple of curses.

DA: Go 'long out of that . . . that's for yourself and Polly, to buy the holy picture with. Are you off into town to see her?

YOUNG CHARLIE: Well, I'm not going home, that's for sure. Blast her anyway, and her twenty-five quid and her Californian wire puzzle!

DA: Sure the Quakers was the only ones that was good to us the time of the Famine. Oh, the mistress is a decent skin. [*He laughs*] "Tynan," says she to me, "aren't you the greatest man that ever trod shoe-leather!" And I planted them hyacinths, too. [YOUNG CHARLIE *has gone off, taking the parcel with him.* DA *goes into the house*] Mag . . . Mag. Do you know what the mistress said to me?

[*Lights up.* CHARLIE, *his glasses on, is writing. The jug, with its contents, is back on the table*]

CHARLIE: Twenty-five pounds divided by fifty-four. I make it that your gratuity worked out at nine shillings and three pence per year of service. No wonder she didn't talk to you for a week.

DA: Who didn't?

CHARLIE: She didn't.

DA: Are you mad? In fifty-nine years there was never a cross word between us.

CHARLIE: Oh, dear God.

DA: There was not.

CHARLIE: "Ernie, Ernie, curse-o'-God Ernie!"

DA: Sure I was only letting on I was vexed with her. [*With relish*] Oh, I put a stop to her gallop, her and her . . . high tea! Son, do you remember them spectacles from San Francisco?

CHARLIE: Do I?

DA: Herself took them down to the pawn office. "How much will you give me on these?" says she. "I'll give you nothing at all on them, ma'am," says he, "for they're too valuable for me to keep under this roof." And you saying I was diddled: you thick, you!

CHARLIE: Where are they?

DA: What?

CHARLIE: The spectacles.

DA: [*Shiftily*] I musta lost them.

CHARLIE: Liar. [*Searching*] They're in this house, and if I find them I'll pulp them and bury them. You ignorant, wet, forelock-tugging old crawler. [*Mimicking him*] "Begod, ma'am, sure after fifty-four years all I needed to be set up for life was a parcel of barbed wire." And then you put in another four years, toiling for the Catholic but somewhat less than Christian Diors of Grafton Street.

DA: "Tynan," says that bitch's ghost to me, and him only a school-master, "I want more honest endeavour from you and less excuses." "Do you see this fist?" says I to him—

CHARLIE: [*Still searching*] I asked you where they were.

DA: I disrecall.

CHARLIE: You probably had them buried with you. I can hear St. Peter now—"Hey God, there's an old gobshite at the tradesmen's entrance with thirty pairs of spectacle-frames from the San Francisco earthquake. What'll I tell him?" [*God's voice, with a Jewish accent*] "Tell him we don't want any." [*He scoops up the contents of the jug and moves to dump them in the range*] Mind up: this is the last.

DA: [*Seizing on an article*] That pipe is worth keeping.

CHARLIE: It's in bits. You broke it.

DA: Sure a piece of insulating tape would—

CHARLIE: No. Move. [*He goes past* DA *and drops the lot in the range*]

DA: You could have smoked that, and you'll folly a crow for it yet. What else did you throw out? [*He opens* CHARLIE'S *dispatch case and goes through the papers*]

CHARLIE: At the funeral this morning I heard one of your old cronies muttering what a great character you were and how I'll never be the man me da was.

DA: Don't belittle yourself: yes, you will. What's this?

CHARLIE: Death certificate. Tell me, what was it like?

DA: What?

CHARLIE: Dying.

DA: [*Offhand*] Ah, I didn't care for it. [*Peering at a document*] Eighteen-hundred and—

CHARLIE: . . . Eighty-four. Birth certificate.

DA: [*Annoyed*] You kept nothing worth keeping at all. There was more to me than this rubbidge. Where's me old IRA service certificate? And the photograph of the tug-o-war team? I still have the mark under me oxter where the rope sawed into it. And the photo herself and meself had took in the Vale of Avoca.

CHARLIE: I threw them out.

DA: And yourself the day of your first Communion with me beside you.

CHARLIE: I burned them. I don't want them around.

> [DA *stares blankly at him*. CHARLIE *waits, almost daring him to be angry*]

DA: You wha'?

CHARLIE: I got rid of them. You're gone, now they're gone. So?

DA: [*Nodding*] Ah, sure what the hell good were they anyway.

CHARLIE: Eh?

DA: Bits of paper. Sure they only gather dust.

CHARLIE: I burned all that was left of you and you can't even get angry. You were a sheep when you lived: you're still a sheep. "Yes, sir; no, sir; sir, if you please—"

DA: [*Chuckling*] "Is it up the duck's arse that I shove the green peas?" Oh, that was a good poem. [*Singing*] "Is it up the—"

CHARLIE: Where's my coat? I'm going to the airport.

DA: Yis. [*Calling*] Mag . . . Mag, the lad is off.

CHARLIE: She won't answer you. Goodbye.

> [MOTHER *comes in quickly from the scullery. She pays* CHARLIE *no attention*]

MOTHER: [*Briskly*] Where is he? [*Calling upstairs*] Charlie, you'll be late. [*To* DA] Call him.

DA: [*Yelling*] You pup, will you come down before the shaggin' aeroplane is off up into the air and you're left standin'!

MOTHER: Charlie!

DA: If he misses that aeroplane they'll be no whoorin' weddin'. Then he'll be nicely destroyed. Jasus, come when you're called!

> [YOUNG CHARLIE, *carrying a suitcase, is on the stairs, followed by* OLIVER]

MOTHER: That will do. He won't miss it.

YOUNG CHARLIE: [*Coming in*] Will you quit roaring. I'm not deaf.

MOTHER: It's the last time you'll have to put up with it, so hold your tongue. Have you everything?

YOUNG CHARLIE: Yes.

MOTHER: Smarten yourself. Anyone'd think it was Oliver that was getting married.

OLIVER: Oh, now. Ho-ho. Oh, now.

YOUNG CHARLIE: I left Oliver's wedding present upstairs. Will you keep it for me?

OLIVER: It's just a bowl to float rose-petals in-you-know. Maybe your da will give you some of his roses.

DA: I only grow the shaggers. I don't learn 'em to swim.

MOTHER: You're to mind yourself in that aeroplane and bless yourself when it starts.

YOUNG CHARLIE: Yes.

DA: Oh, Charlie won't crash.

MOTHER: [Half-snapping] No one is saying to the contrary.

DA: Divil a fear of him.

MOTHER: [Aggrieved] Going off to the other side of the world to get married.

YOUNG CHARLIE: Five hundred miles . . . !

MOTHER: It's far enough. Too far.

YOUNG CHARLIE: It's where she lives.

DA: Oh, Belgium is a great country.

MOTHER: It's little you or I will ever see of it. No matter.

YOUNG CHARLIE: [Angrily] Don't start. You were both invited—

MOTHER: Oh, aye. Aye, I'm sure we were.

YOUNG CHARLIE: [To OLIVER] They damn well were. But no, it's too far, it's too foreign, his legs won't let him . . .

MOTHER: I said it's no matter.

[YOUNG CHARLIE *gives her a hostile look*]

OLIVER: When he gets time during the honeymoon, Charlie is going to drop you a line and give me all the details. [*As they look at him*] About going in an aeroplane-you-know.

[*Pause.* YOUNG CHARLIE *is chafing to be off and trying to conceal it.* CHARLIE *moves to be near him*]

MOTHER: You may as well be off, so. There's nothing to keep you.

YOUNG CHARLIE: [*Protesting*] I'll be back in a fortnight.

[*She nods, upset*]

MOTHER: Please God.

CHARLIE: Now. Goodbye, and out.

YOUNG CHARLIE: Yeah, well, mind yourselves.

MOTHER: You mind yourself. [*She reaches for him blindly. He half-resists the kiss, half-accepts it. She steps back and looks at him, eyes large. He reaches for his case as* DA *comes forward, hand extended*]

CHARLIE: Hang on . . . one to go.

DA: [*Shaking hands*] Good luck now, son. Sure you'll get there in great style. Oh, aeroplanes is all the go these days.

YOUNG CHARLIE: Yeah. 'Bye, now.

DA: [*Not letting go*] Have you your tickets?

YOUNG CHARLIE: Yes.

CHARLIE: [*To* DA] Let go.

DA: Have you your passport?

YOUNG CHARLIE: Yes.

CHARLIE: It's the Beast with Five Fingers.

DA: Have you your—

YOUNG CHARLIE: I've got to go. [*He prises his hand free and starts out*]

MOTHER: Bless yourself!

[*He dips his fingers in the holy-water font and hurries out.* MOTHER *and* DA *come to the door.* OLIVER *is caught behind them. He coughs*]

OLIVER: I'm going with him. As far as the bus-you-know.

YOUNG CHARLIE: [*Agonised, waiting for him*] For God's sake.

OLIVER: Well, 'bye-'bye now and sappy days. That's an expression him and me have-you-know. Oh, yes.

YOUNG CHARLIE: [*Half to himself*] Oliver!

OLIVER: [*Turning to wave*] Cheerio, now.

CHARLIE: [*From the house*] Well, at least wave to them.

[YOUNG CHARLIE *raises a hand without turning and climbs across to an upper level where he rests, waiting for* OLIVER]

OLIVER: That went well, I thought. I mean, they can get very sentimental-you-know. Often with my mother I can't feel anything because I'm trying to stop *her* from feeling anything. How do *you* feel? [YOUNG CHARLIE *makes a huge gesture of relief*] They're all the same-you-know. I dread the roars of my mother when I get married. She cries even if I go to a late-night dance.

YOUNG CHARLIE: Come on before we meet someone.

OLIVER: Oh-ho. Off to the altar. Can't wait.

YOUNG CHARLIE: Dry up.

OLIVER: The eager bridegroom. Oh, yes.

YOUNG CHARLIE: Well, it's the beginning, isn't it?

[*They go off*]

MOTHER: Well, that's the end of him. [*She and* DA *return to the kitchen*]

DA: Still and all, mebbe we ought to have gone, Mag, when we were asked. [*She gives him a sour look*] Sure it'd have been a . . . a . . . a change for us.

MOTHER: I never hindered him. I wasn't going to start now.

DA: What hinderment? Weren't we asked?

MOTHER: [*It is not a disparagement, but evasion*] You'd be a nice article to bring to a foreign country. [*Then*] I think I'll make his bed and have done with it. [*She goes upstairs. She is in view during part of the following*]

DA: [*Laughing, watching her*] Oh, a comical woman.

CHARLIE: She died an Irishwoman's death, drinking tea.

DA: Do you want a cup?

CHARLIE: No! Two years afterwards, I told a doctor in London about you, on your own and getting senile. I said you'd have to be made to come and live with us. He said: "Oh, yes. Then he can die among strangers in a hospital in Putney or Wandsworth, with nothing Irish around him except the nurses. But with your luck you'd probably have got Jamaicans." It's always pleasant to be told what you half-want to hear. So when I came to see you—the last time—there was no talk of your going to London. I was solicitous: asked you how you were managing, were you eating regularly . . .

[DA *is in his eighties, stooped and deaf.* CHARLIE's *attitude is paternal*]

DA: Hoh?

CHARLIE: I said are you eating regularly?

DA: Sure I'm getting fat. I go to Rosie for me tea and Mrs. Dunne next door cooks me me dinner: Are *you* eating regular.

CHARLIE: She's a widow. I'd watch her.

DA: Hoh?

CHARLIE: I say I'd watch her.

DA: I do.

CHARLIE: You reprobate. Do you need extra cash, for whist drives?

DA: I gave up going. Me hands is too stiff to sort the cards into suits. The last time I went, oul' Drumm was there. Do you remember oul' Drumm?

CHARLIE: Yes.

DA: He accused me of renagin'. "Why don't you," says he, "join the Old People's club and play there?" Says I to him back: "I would," says I, "only I'm too shaggin' old for them!" [He laughs]

CHARLIE: That was good.

DA: Sure I have the garden to do . . . fine heads of cabbage that a dog from Dublin never pissed on. I'm kept going. I say I blacked the range yesterday.

CHARLIE: You're a marvel.

DA: I am. How's all the care?

CHARLIE: They're great. Send their love.

DA: [Rising] I was meaning to ask you . . .

CHARLIE: What?

DA: [Saluting him] I do often see your young one in the town.

CHARLIE: What young one?

DA: Her . . . Maggie. Your eldest. 'Clare to God, Mr. Doyle, I never seen such shiny bright hair on a girl. [CHARLIE stares at him. (Note: this is not a flashback to DA as a young man; it is DA in his eighties, his mind wandering)] Sure she's like a young one out of the story books. The way it is, Mr. Doyle, I'm above at Jacob's these six years, since I was fourteen. I have a pound a week and the promise of one of the new dwellin's in the square. I'd think well of marrying her, so I would.

CHARLIE: Da, no, she's—

DA: You can ask anyone in the town about me. And, and, and she wouldn't want for an'thing. The job is safe, we won't go short. I'm learning roses, do you see. To grow them. Oh, yis: Polyanthas and Belles de Crecys and Cornelias and Tuscanys and Amy Robsarts and Janet's Pride and—

CHARLIE: Da, stop.

DA: And, and, Portlands and Captain John Ingrams and Heidlebergs and Munsters and Shepherdesses and Golden Jewels and Buccaneers and New Dawns and King's Ransoms and—

CHARLIE: Jesus Christ, will you stop! [*In despair*] You old get, what am I going to do with you?

DA: A rainbow of roses. I never seen a young one like her . . . so I know you'd think bad of refusing me. [*Looking at* CHARLIE] But sure you wouldn't.

CHARLIE: No.

DA: And you'll put in a good word for me? She wouldn't go again' you.

CHARLIE: I'll talk to her.

DA: [*Happy now*] I'm on the pig's back, so. On it for life. Oh, she won't be sorry. [*Looking up at the ceiling*] Mag! Mag, are you up there?

CHARLIE: Da, sh. [*He seats* DA]

DA: [*Begins to sing aimlessly*]
"I've just been down to Monto Town
To see the bould McArdle,
But he wouldn't give me half a crown
To go to the Waxie—"

CHARLIE: Stop it: it's not then any more, it's now! [*Picking up a paper*] See that? Death certificate . . . yours.

[DA *nods and straightens up, returning to the present.* CHARLIE *puts the papers back into his dispatch case and closes it*]

DA: I never carried on the like of that.

CHARLIE: How?

DA: Astray in the head. Thinking it was old God's time and you were herself's da.

CHARLIE: Oh, didn't you!

DA: And you not a bit like him. Begod, I don't wonder at you putting me into the poorhouse.

CHARLIE: [*Getting annoyed again*] You useless old man.

[*The gate squeaks*]

DA: Sure it must have gev you a laugh, anyway.

[CHARLIE *is too angry to speak. He picks up his overcoat.* DA *moves to assist him.* DRUMM *appears outside the house carrying a briefcase. He is now seventy, still erect*]

DA: Are you off, so? Well, God send you good weather, son. Tell them I was asking for them. [DRUMM *knocks at the front door*] That must be another Mass card. Do you know, I have enough of them to play whist with. [*As* CHARLIE *goes to the door*] Did you see the flowers on me coffin . . . shaggin' weeds, the half of them.

[*He sits.* CHARLIE *opens the door*]

CHARLIE: [*Surprised*] Mr. Drumm . . .

DRUMM: I'm glad I caught you. Might I have a word?

CHARLIE: Of course . . . come in.

[*They go into the kitchen*]

DA: Oh, old Drumm is not the worst of them.

DRUMM: It's been many years. Will you agree to shake hands? . . . it's a bad day for grievances. [*They do so*] There, that's done . . . I'm obliged. Mind, I won't say it's generous of you: *I* was the wounded party.

CHARLIE: It was a long time ago.

DRUMM: [*Good-humoured*] Don't play word-games with me, my friend. Time doesn't mitigate an injury; it only helps one to overlook it. [*Indicating a chair*] May I?

CHARLIE: Please.

DRUMM: [*Sitting*] Years ago I made a choice. I could have indiscriminate friendships or I could have standards. I chose standards. It's my own misfortune that so few people have come up to them.

CHARLIE: Including me.

DRUMM: You tried. You had your work cut out.

CHARLIE: I had.

DRUMM: [*Being fair*] I daresay I was difficult.

CHARLIE: Impossible.

DRUMM: [*Bridling*] And you've become impudent.

CHARLIE: [*Unruffled*] Yes.

DRUMM: A beggar on horseback.

CHARLIE: It's better than walking.

DA: There was a young fella went to confession. "Father," says he, "I rode a girl from Cork." "Yerra, boy," says the priest, "sure 'twas better than walking."

[CHARLIE's *face twitches.* DRUMM *glares at him*]

CHARLIE: I hope you're well.

DRUMM: Your hopes are unfounded.

CHARLIE: Oh?

DA: Didn't I tell you he was sick? Sure he has a face on him like a boiled—

CHARLIE: [*Hastily*] It's hard to believe. You look well.

[DRUMM *chuckles to himself as if at a private joke. He leans confidentially towards* CHARLIE]

DRUMM: I have this . . . tummy trouble. I told a certain person—I don't know why, out of mischief, it isn't like me—I told him cancer was suspected. Quite untrue. Of course he told others, and since then my popularity has soared. I said to one man: "I know you for a rogue and a blackguard." Was he offended? "You're right," he said; "come and have a drink." [*With defiant pleasure*] I did.

CHARLIE: There'll be ructions when you don't die.

DRUMM: There will.

CHARLIE: False pretences.

DRUMM: Pity about them.

CHARLIE: Still . . .

DRUMM: They shun a man because he's intelligent, but get maudlin over a few supposedly malignant body-cells. I'm as bad. Ten years ago I wouldn't have given one of them the time of day, still less have taken pleasure in their approbation.

CHARLIE: Do you?

DRUMM: People like them, like the old man—your foster-father—they thank God for a fine day and stay diplomatically silent when it rains. They deride whatever is beyond them with a laugh, a platitude and a spit. They say: "How could he be a dental surgeon?—his father was warned by the police for molesting women."

DA: Who would that be? Old Martin Conheedy used to tamper with women. Is his son a dentist now?

DRUMM: [*Answering* CHARLIE's *question*] They . . . amuse me.

DA: [*Derisive*] Who'd trust that fella to pull a tooth?

DRUMM: [*Picking up his briefcase*] When the old man was in hospital he sent word that he wanted to see me.

CHARLIE: My father?

DRUMM: Who lived here.

CHARLIE: [*Persisting*] My father.

DRUMM: [*Letting it pass*] He asked my advice. I told him that not being related by blood you would have no natural claim on his estate.

CHARLIE: What estate? He had nothing.

DRUMM: At his request I wrote out a will for him then and there. He signed it and I had it witnessed. [*He takes an envelope and hands it to* CHARLIE] It'll stand up with the best of them.

CHARLIE: But he had bugger-all.

DRUMM: There was also the matter of an heirloom which he gave into my keeping.

CHARLIE: Heirloom?

[DRUMM *dips into his briefcase and takes out a familiar-looking brown-paper parcel*]

DA: [*Jovially*] There now's a surprise for you.

CHARLIE: [*Staring at the parcel*] No . . .

DA: [*Crowing*] You won't guess what's in that!

DRUMM: He said it was valuable, so I asked my bank manager to keep it in his vault.

CHARLIE: [*Under stress*] That was in a bank vault?

DRUMM: I can see that the value was also sentimental. [*Rising*] Well, I'm glad to have discharged my trust.

CHARLIE: Thank you. [*Looking at the parcel*] His estate.

DRUMM: Oh, no. Whatever that is, it has nothing to do with what's in the will. And I'd be careful with that envelope. There's money involved!

CHARLIE: Money?

DRUMM: He mentioned the sum of a hundred and thirty-five pounds, with more to come.

CHARLIE: He never had that much in his life.

DRUMM: He thought otherwise.

CHARLIE: He was raving. I *know*. All he had was his pension and the cheques I sent him for— [*He breaks off and looks around at* DA]

DA: [*Strategically*] That dog from next door is in the garden. Hoosh . . . hoosh, you bastard.

[CHARLIE *watches him murderously as he beats a retreat into the scullery*]

DRUMM: [*Waiting for* CHARLIE *to finish*] Yes?

CHARLIE: I was wrong. I've remembered where it came from.

DRUMM: The money?

CHARLIE: Yes.

DRUMM: I imagined it was hard-earned.

CHARLIE: [*Grimly*] It was.

DRUMM: [*Sternly*] Now, my friend, no caterwauling. To whom else could he leave it? I once called him an ignorant man. I still do. And yet he may have been better off. Everything I once thought I knew for certain I have seen inverted, revised, disproved, or discredited. Shall I tell you something? In seventy years the one surviving fragment of my knowledge, the only indisputable poor particle of certainty in my entire life, is that in a public house lavatory incoming traffic has the right of way. [*Acidly*] It isn't much to take with one, is it?

CHARLIE: [*Smiling*] Well, now I know something.

DRUMM: I have always avoided him and his kind, and yet in the end we fetch up against the self-same door. I find that aggravating. [*Moving towards the door*] The old couple, had they children of their own?

CHARLIE: I was told once there were several. All still-born.

DRUMM: He didn't even create life—at least I have the edge on him there.

CHARLIE: How are the two Rhode Island Reds?

DRUMM: Moulting. [*He offers his hand*] It was pleasant to see you. I enjoyed it. Goodbye.

CHARLIE: Mr. Drumm, he never took anything from me, he

wouldn't let me help him, what I offered him he kept and wouldn't use. Why?

DRUMM: Don't you know?

CHARLIE: Do *you?*

DRUMM: The Irish national disease.

CHARLIE: Bad manners?

DRUMM: Worse, no manners. [*He holds out his hand, inspecting the sky for rain, then goes.* CHARLIE *closes the door, returns to the kitchen*]

CHARLIE: Where are you? [*Yelling*] Come . . . in . . . here!

[DA *comes in*]

DA: Do you want a cup of tea?

CHARLIE: You old shite. You wouldn't even use the money.

DA: I did.

CHARLIE: How?

DA: Wasn't it something to leave you?

CHARLIE: I'll never forgive you for this.

DA: [*Not worried*] Ah, you will.

CHARLIE: Since I was born. "Here's six-pence for the chairoplanes, a shilling for the pictures, a new suit for the job. Here's a life." When did I ever get a chance to pay it back, to get out from under, to be quit of you? You wouldn't come to us in London; you'd rather be the brave old warrior, soldiering on.

DA: And wasn't I?

CHARLIE: While I was the ingrate. The only currency you'd take, you knew I wouldn't pay. Well, I've news for you, mate. You had your chance. The debt is cancelled, welshed on. [*Tapping his head*] I'm turfing you out. Of here. See that? [*He tears the black armband from his overcoat and drops it in the range*] And this? [*He holds up the parcel containing the spectacle frames*]

DA: You wouldn't. Not at all.

CHARLIE: Wouldn't I? You think not? [*He bends and crushes the frames through the paper with increasing violence*]

DA: Ah, son . . .

CHARLIE: San Francisco earthquake!

DA: You'd want to mind your hand with them—

CHARLIE: [*Cutting his finger*] Shit!

DA: I told you you'd cut yourself.

> [CHARLIE *gives him a malevolent look and very deliberately shoves the parcel into the range. He sucks his hand*]

CHARLIE: Now wouldn't I?

DA: Is it deep? That's the kind of cut 'ud give you lock-jaw. I'd mind that.

CHARLIE: Gone . . . and you with it.

DA: Yis. [*Taking out a dirty handkerchief*] Here, tie this around it.

CHARLIE: Get away from me. Ignorant man, ignorant life!

DA: What are you talking about, or do you know what you're talking about? Sure I enjoyed meself. And in the windup I didn't die with the arse out of me trousers like the rest of them—I left money!

CHARLIE: My money.

DA: Jasus, didn't you get it back? And looka . . . if I wouldn't go to England with you before, sure I'll make it up to you. I will now.

CHARLIE: You what? Like hell you will.

DA: Sure you can't get rid of a bad thing.

CHARLIE: Can't I? You watch me. You watch! [*He picks up his case, walks out of the house and closes the front door. He locks the door and hurls the key from him. A sigh of relief. He turns to go, to find* DA *has walked out through the fourth wall]*

DA: Are we off, so? It's starting to rain. The angels must be peein' again.

CHARLIE: Don't you dare follow me. You're dead . . . get off.

DA: Sure Noah's flood was only a shower. [*Following him*] Left . . . left . . . I had a good job and I left, right, left!

CHARLIE: Hump off. Get away. Shoo. I don't want you. [*He goes to the upper level.* DA *follows, lagging behind*]

DA: Go on, go on. I'll keep up with you.

[CHARLIE *stops at the top level*]

CHARLIE: Leave me alone.

[CHARLIE *slowly walks down as* DA *follows, singing*]

DA: [*Singing*]
"Oh, says your oul' one to my oul' one:
'Will you come to the Waxie Dargle?'
And says my oul' one to your oul' one:
'Sure I haven't got a farthin'.'"

CURTAIN

THE ELEPHANT MAN

Bernard Pomerance

Bernard Pomerance

The Elephant Man would be a powerful and significant play in any decade, but coming as it did during a period when dramas (as opposed to musicals and comedies) seldom were, in theatrical parlance, a "hot ticket," it became something of a lodestar in the theatre of the late seventies. An immediate success, with long lines persisting at the box office and standees in attendance at almost every performance, it was the season's prime dramatic attraction. And deservedly, for both play and production provided theatregoers with an uncommonly mesmerizing experience.

Based on a true story, John Merrick is a hideously deformed nineteenth-century man who is rescued from life as a circus freak by a young surgeon, Frederick Treves, and under whose care and shelter reveals an acute intelligence and romantic imagination, subsequently becoming the object of compassionate attention from the elite of Victorian society. Initially, the drama was presented at the Hampstead Theatre in London in 1977 and made its American debut in January 1979, at the Theatre of St. Peter's Church, a small Off-Broadway playhouse. There it generated enough theatrical excitement to prompt its sponsors to move it across town and onto Broadway.

The critical consensus was unanimous. "A giant of a play; wonderful, moving and purely theatrical," wrote Clive Barnes in the New York *Post*. "*The Elephant Man* is lofted on poetic wings and nests in the human heart," stated T. E. Kalem of *Time* magazine, while Martin Gottfried declared in the *Saturday Review* that it contained all "the overwhelming humanity, tragedy and compassion, soaring poetry and intensity that we go to the theatre for."

Winner of the Antoinette Perry (Tony) Award and the New York Drama Critics' Circle Award for the season's best play, it also was similarly honored with a Drama Desk and Outer Circle Award matching the previous year's "*Da*" as a multiple-prize play. (Tony Awards also were presented to the director, Jack Hofsiss, and Carole Shelley for her portrayal of Mrs. Kendal.)

Bernard Pomerance was born and raised in New York City and educated at the University of Chicago. In the early 1970s he moved to London where he still lives. He was then an aspiring novelist. "It's true I didn't write plays before I came to London," he told an interviewer. "I had been working in narrative form, but I realized all my notes were coming out as dialogue. At the same time, there was the growth of what you call the fringe theatre in London. It was a good period for people to experiment with new kinds of techniques and material. The economics of the fringe were conducive to trying new things. In a very personal way, I found the rigorousness of it rewarding."

The story of John Merrick was introduced to Mr. Pomerance by his brother, following a visit to a medical museum at London Hospital where Merrick's bones are still preserved. (Later, the director of the original London production, Roland Rees, and his cast were to conduct extensive research there with the help of the medical staff.)

The Elephant Man was the first Pomerance play to reach an audience beyond the fringe devotees and also the first of his plays to be produced in New York. His previous London plays include: *High in Vietnam* and *Hot Damn* (presented at the London Polytechnic Festival, 1971, and the Almost Free Theatre, 1972); *Foco Novo* (Oval House, 1972); *Someone Else Is Still Someone* (Bush Theatre, 1974); and an adaptation of Bertolt Brecht's *A Man's a Man* (Hampstead Theatre, 1975).

INTRODUCTORY NOTE

The Elephant Man was suggested by the life of John Merrick, known as the Elephant Man. It is recounted by Sir Frederick Treves in *The Elephant Man and Other Reminiscences*, Cassell and Co. Ltd., 1923. This account is reprinted in *The Elephant Man, A Study in Human Dignity*, by Ashley Montagu, Ballantine Books, 1973, to whom much credit is due for reviving contemporary interest in the story. My own knowledge of it came via my brother Michael, who told me the story, provided me with xeroxes of Treves' memoirs until I came on my own copy, and sent me the Montagu book. In Montagu's book are included photographs of Merrick as well as of Merrick's model of St. Philip's Church. Merrick's bones are still at London Hospital.

I believe the building of the church model constitutes some kind of central metaphor, and the groping toward conditions where it can be built and the building of it are the action of the play. It does not, and should not, however, dominate the play visually, as I originally believed.

Merrick's face was so deformed he could not express any emotion at all. His speech was very difficult to understand without practice. Any attempt to reproduce his appearance and his speech naturalistically—*if* it were possible—would seem to me not only counterproductive, but, the more remarkably successful, the more distracting from the play. For how he appeared, let slide projections suffice.

If the pinheaded women are two actresses, then the play, in a pinch, can be performed with seven players, five men, two women.

No one with any history of back trouble should attempt the part of MERRICK *as contorted. Anyone playing the part of* MERRICK *should be advised to consult a physician about the problems of sustaining any unnatural or twisted position.—B.P.*

The London production of *The Elephant Man* opened at the Hampstead Theatre, co-produced by the Hampstead Theatre and the Foco Novo Company, with the following cast:

CELLIST	*Pat Arrowsmith*
FREDERICK TREVES	*David Allister*
BELGIAN POLICEMAN	
CARR GOMM	*William Hoyland*
CONDUCTOR	
ROSS	*Arthur Blake*
BISHOP WALSHAM HOW	
SNORK	
JOHN MERRICK	*David Schofield*
PINHEAD	*Judy Bridgland*
NURSE SANDWICH	
PRINCESS ALEXANDRA	
DUCHESS	
JELLY WILLOW	
PINHEAD	*Jennie Stoller*
MRS. KENDAL	
COUNTESS	
PINHEAD MANAGER	*Ken Drury*
ENGLISH POLICEMAN	
PORTER	
LORD JOHN	
WILLOW	

This production was directed by Roland Rees; set and costumes by Tanya McCallin; costumes made and supervised by Lindy Hemming; lighting by Alan O'Toole.

The Elephant Man was produced on Broadway at the Booth Theatre, on April 19, 1979, with the following cast:

FREDERICK TREVES	*Kevin Conway*
BELGIAN POLICEMAN	
CARR GOMM	*Richard Clarke*
CONDUCTOR	
ROSS	*I. M. Hobson*
BISHOP WALSHAM HOW	
SNORK	
JOHN MERRICK	*Philip Anglim*
PINHEAD MANAGER	*John Neville-Andrews*
LONDON POLICEMAN	
WILL	
EARL	
LORD JOHN	
PINHEAD	*Cordis Heard*
MISS SANDWICH	
COUNTESS	
PRINCESS ALEXANDRA	
MRS. KENDAL	*Carole Shelley*
PINHEAD	
ORDERLY	*Dennis Creaghan*
CELLIST	*David Heiss*

This production was directed by Jack Hofsiss; set by David Jenkins; costumes by Julie Weiss; lighting by Beverly Emmons; produced by Richmond Crinkley, Elizabeth I. McCann, and Nelle Nugent; Ray Larsen and Ted Snowdon, associate producers.

1884–1890. London. One scene is in Belgium.

CHARACTERS:

FREDERICK TREVES, *a surgeon and teacher*

CARR GOMM, *administrator of the London Hospital*

ROSS, *manager of the Elephant Man*

JOHN MERRICK, *the Elephant Man*

Three PINHEADS, *three women freaks whose heads are pointed*

BELGIAN POLICEMAN

LONDON POLICEMAN

MAN, *at a fairground in Brussels*

CONDUCTOR, *of Ostend–London boat train*

BISHOP WALSHAM HOW

PORTER, *at the London Hospital*

SNORK, *also a porter*

MRS. KENDAL, *an actress*

DUCHESS

COUNTESS

PRINCESS ALEXANDRA

LORD JOHN

NURSE, MISS SANDWICH

HE WILL HAVE 100 GUINEA
FEES BEFORE HE'S FORTY

The London Hospital, Whitechapel Road. Enter GOMM, *enter*
TREVES.

TREVES: Mr. Carr Gomm? Frederick Treves. Your new lecturer in
anatomy.

GOMM: Age thirty-one. Books on scrofula and applied surgical anatomy—I'm happy to see you rising, Mr. Treves. I like to see merit
credited, and your industry, accomplishment, and skill all do you
credit. Ignore the squalor of Whitechapel, the general dinginess,
neglect and poverty without, and you will find a continual medical richesse in the London Hospital. We study and treat the
widest range of diseases and disorders, and are certainly the
greatest institution of our kind in the world. The Empire provides
unparalleled opportunities for our studies, as places cruel to life
are the most revealing scientifically. Add to our reputation by
going further, and that'll satisfy. You've bought a house?

TREVES: On Wimpole Street.

GOMM: Good. Keep at it, Treves. You'll have an F.R.S. and 100
guinea fees before you're forty. You'll find it is an excellent consolation prize.

TREVES: Consolation? I don't know what you mean.

GOMM: I know you don't. You will. [*Exits*]

TREVES: A happy childhood in Dorset.
A scientist in an age of science.
In an English age, an Englishman. A teacher and a doctor at the
London. Two books published by my thirty-first year. A house. A
wife who loves me, and my God, 100 guinea fees before I'm forty.

Consolation for what?

As of the year A.D. 1884, I, Freddie Treves, have excessive blessings. Or so it seems to me.

[*Blackout*]

SCENE TWO

ART IS AS NOTHING TO NATURE

Whitechapel Road. A storefront. A large advertisement of a creature with an elephant's head. ROSS, *his manager.*

ROSS: Tuppence only, step in and see: This side of the grave, John Merrick has no hope nor expectation of relief. In every sense his situation is desperate. His physical agony is exceeded only by his mental anguish, a despised creature without consolation. Tuppence only, step in and see! To live with his physical hideousness, incapacitating deformities and unremitting pain is trial enough, but to be exposed to the cruelly lacerating expressions of horror and disgust by all who behold him—is even more difficult to bear. Tuppence only, step in and see! For in order to survive, Merrick forces himself to suffer these humiliations, I repeat, humiliations, in order to survive, thus he exposes himself to crowds who pay to gape and yawp at this freak of nature, the Elephant Man.

[*Enter* TREVES *who looks at advertisement*]

ROSS: See Mother Nature uncorseted and in malignant rage! Tuppence.

TREVES: This sign's absurd. Half-elephant, half-man is not possible. Is he foreign?

ROSS: Right, from Leicester. But nothing to fear.

TREVES: I'm at the London across the road. I would be curious to see him if there is some genuine disorder. If he is a mass of papier-mâché and paint however—

ROSS: Then pay me nothing. Enter, sir. Merrick, stand up. Ya bloody donkey, up, up.

[*They go in, then emerge.* TREVES *pays*]

TREVES: I must examine him further at the hospital. Here is my card. I'm Treves. I will have a cab pick him up and return him. My card will gain him admittance.

ROSS: Five bob he's yours for the day.

TREVES: I wish to examine him in the interests of science, you see.

ROSS: Sir, I'm Ross. I look out for him, get him his living. Found him in Leicester workhouse. His own ma put him there age of three. Couldn't bear the sight, well you can see why. We—he and I—are in business. He is our capital, see. Go to a bank. Go anywhere. Want to borrow capital, you pay interest. Scientists even. He's good value though. You won't find another like him.

TREVES: Fair enough. [*He pays*]

ROSS: Right. Out here, Merrick. Ya bloody donkey, out!

[*Lights fade out*]

SCENE THREE

WHO HAS SEEN THE LIKE
OF THIS?

TREVES *lectures.* MERRICK *contorts himself to approximate projected slides of the real Merrick.*

TREVES: The most striking feature about him was his enormous head. Its circumference was about that of a man's waist. From the brow there projected a huge bony mass like a loaf, while from the back of his head hung a bag of spongy fungous-looking skin, the surface of which was comparable to brown cauliflower. On the top of the skull were a few long lank hairs. The osseous growth on the forehead, at this stage about the size of a tangerine, almost occluded one eye. From the upper jaw there projected another mass of bone. It protruded from the mouth like a pink stump, turning the upper lip inside out, and making the mouth a wide slobbering aperture. The nose was merely a lump of flesh, only recognizable as a nose from its position. The deformities rendered the face utterly incapable of the expression of any emotion whatsoever. The back was horrible because from it hung, as far down as the middle of the thigh, huge sacklike masses of flesh covered by the same loathsome cauliflower stain. The right arm was of enormous size and shapeless. It suggested but was not elephantiasis, and was overgrown also with pendant masses of the same cauliflower-like skin. The right hand was large and clumsy—a fin or paddle rather than a hand. No distinction existed between the palm and back, the thumb was like a radish, the fingers like thick tuberous roots. As a limb it was useless. The other arm was remarkable by contrast. It was not only normal, but was moreover a delicately shaped limb covered with a fine skin and provided with a beautiful hand which any woman might have envied. From the chest hung a bag of the same repulsive flesh. It was like a dewlap suspended from the neck of a lizard. The lower limbs had the characters of the deformed arm. They were unwieldy, dropsical-looking, and grossly misshapen. There arose from the fungous skin growths a very sickening stench which was hard to tolerate. To add a further burden to his trouble, the wretched man when a boy developed hip disease which left him permanently lame, so that he could only walk with a stick. [To MERRICK] Please. [MERRICK walks] He was thus denied all means of escape from his tormentors.

VOICE: Mr. Treves, you have shown a profound and unknown disorder to us. You have said when he leaves here it is for his exhibition again. I do not think it ought to be permitted. It is a disgrace. It is a pity and a disgrace. It is an indecency in fact. It may be a danger in ways we do not know. Something ought to be done about it.

TREVES: I am a doctor. What would you have me do?

VOICE: Well. I know what to do. *I* know.

    [*Silence. A policeman enters as lights fade out*]

SCENE FOUR

THIS INDECENCY MAY NOT
CONTINUE

Music. A fair. PINHEADS *huddling together, holding a portrait of Leopold, King of the Congo. Enter* MAN.

MAN: Now, my pinheaded darlings, your attention please. Every freak in Brussels Fair is doing something to celebrate Leopold's fifth year as King of the Congo. Him. Our King. Our Empire. [*They begin reciting*] No, don't recite yet, you morons. I'll say when. And when you do, get it *right.* You don't, it's back to the asylum. Know what that means, don't you? They'll cut your heads. They'll spoon out your little brains, replace 'em in the dachshund they were nicked from. *Cut you.* Yeah. Be back with customers. Come see the Queens of the Congo! [*Exits*]

    [*Enter* MERRICK, ROSS]

MERRICK: Cosmos? Cosmos?

ROSS: Congo. Land of darkness. Hoho! [*Sees* PINS] Look at them, lad. It's freer on the continent. Loads of indecency here, no one minds. You won't get coppers sent round to roust you out like London. Reckon in Brussels here's our fortune. You have a little tête-à-tête with this lot while I see the coppers about our license to exhibit. Be right back. [*Exits*]

MERRICK: I come from England.

PINS: Allo!

MERRICK: At home they chased us. Out of London. Police. Someone complained. They beat me. You have no trouble? No?

PINS: Allo! Allo!

MERRICK: Hello. In Belgium we make money. I look forward to it. Happiness, I mean. You pay your police? How is it done?

PINS: Allo! Allo!

MERRICK: We do a show together sometime? Yes? I have saved forty-eight pounds. Two shillings. Nine pence. English money. Ross takes care of it.

PINS: Allo! Allo!

MERRICK: Little vocabulary problem, eh? Poor things. Looks like they put your noses to the grindstone and forgot to take them away.

[MAN *enters*]

MAN: They're coming. [*People enter to see the girls' act*] Now.

PINS: [*Dancing and singing*]
We are the Queens of the Congo,
The Beautiful Belgian Empire
Our niggers are bigger
Our miners are finer
Empire, Empire, Congo and power
Civilizuzu's finest hour
Admire, perspire, desire, acquire
Or we'll set you on fire!

MAN: You cretins! Sorry, they're not ready yet. Out please. [*People exit*] Get those words right, girls! Or you know what.

[MAN *exits*. PINS *weep*]

MERRICK: Don't cry. You sang nicely. Don't cry. There, there.

[*Enter* ROSS *in grip of two* POLICEMEN]

ROSS: I was promised a permit. I lined a tour up on that!

POLICEMEN: This is a brutal, indecent, and immoral display. It is a public indecency, and it is forbidden here.

ROSS: What about them with their perfect cone heads?

POLICEMEN: They are ours.

ROSS: Competition's good for business. Where's your spirit of competition?

POLICEMEN: Right here. [*Smacks* MERRICK]

ROSS: Don't do that, you'll kill him!

POLICEMEN: Be better off dead. Indecent bastard.

MERRICK: Don't cry, girls. Doesn't hurt.

PINS: Indecent, indecent, indecent, indecent!!

[POLICEMEN *escort* MERRICK *and* ROSS *out, i.e., forward. Blackout except spot on* MERRICK *and* ROSS]

MERRICK: Ostend will always mean bad memories. Won't it, Ross?

ROSS: I've decided. I'm sending you back, lad. You're a flop. No, you're a liability. You ain't the moneymaker I figured, so that's it.

MERRICK: Alone?

ROSS: Here's a few bob, have a nosh. I'm keeping the rest. For my trouble. I deserve it, I reckon. Invested enough with you. Pick up your stink if I stick around. Stink of failure. Stink of lost years. Just stink, stink, stink, stink, stink.

[*Enter* CONDUCTOR]

CONDUCTOR: This the one?

ROSS: Just see him to Liverpool Street Station safe, will you? Here's for your trouble.

MERRICK: Robbed.

CONDUCTOR: What's he say?

ROSS: Just makes sounds. Fella's an imbecile.

MERRICK: Robbed.

ROSS: Bon voyage, Johnny. His name is Johnny. He knows his name, that's all, though.

CONDUCTOR: Don't follow him, Johnny. Johnny, come on boat now. Conductor find Johnny place out of sight. Johnny! Johnny! Don't struggle, Johnny. Johnny come on.

MERRICK: Robbed! Robbed!

[*Fadeout on struggle*]

SCENE FIVE

POLICE SIDE WITH IMBECILE AGAINST THE CROWD

Darkness. Uproar, shouts.

VOICE: Liverpool Street Station!

[*Enter* MERRICK, CONDUCTOR, POLICEMAN]

POLICEMAN: We're safe in here. I barred the door.

CONDUCTOR: They wanted to rip him to pieces. I've never seen anything like it. It was like being Gordon at bleedin' Khartoum.

POLICEMAN: Got somewhere to go in London, lad? Can't stay here.

CONDUCTOR: He's an imbecile. He don't understand. Search him.

POLICEMAN: Got any money?

MERRICK: Robbed.

POLICEMAN: What's that?

CONDUCTOR: He just makes sounds. Frightened sounds is all he makes. Go through his coat.

MERRICK: Je-sus.

POLICEMAN: Don't let me go through your coat, I'll turn you over to that lot! Oh, I was joking, don't upset yourself.

MERRICK: Joke? Joke?

POLICEMAN: Sure, croak, croak, croak, croak.

MERRICK: Je-sus.

POLICEMAN: Got a card here. You Johnny Merrick? What's this old card here, Johnny? Someone give you a card?

CONDUCTOR: What's it say?

POLICEMAN: Says Mr. Frederick Treves, Lecturer in Anatomy, the London Hospital.

CONDUCTOR: I'll go see if I can find him, it's not far. [*Exits*]

POLICEMAN: What's he do, lecture you on your anatomy? People who think right don't look like that then, do they? Yeah, glung glung, glung, glung.

MERRICK: Jesus. Jesus.

POLICEMAN: Sure, Treves, Treves, Treves, Treves.

[*Blackout, then lights go up as* CONDUCTOR *leads* TREVES *in*]

TREVES: What is going on here? Look at that mob, have you no sense of decency. I am Frederick Treves. This is my card.

POLICEMAN: This poor wretch here had it. Arrived from Ostend.

TREVES: Good Lord, Merrick? John Merrick? What has happened to you?

MERRICK: Help me!

[*Fadeout*]

SCENE SIX

EVEN ON THE NIGER AND
CEYLON, NOT THIS

The London Hospital. MERRICK *in bathtub.* TREVES *outside. Enter* MISS SANDWICH.

TREVES: You are? Miss Sandwich?

SANDWICH: Sandwich. Yes.

TREVES: You have had experience in missionary hospitals in the Niger.

SANDWICH: And Ceylon.

TREVES: I may assume you've seen—

SANDWICH: The tropics. Oh, those diseases. The many and the awful scourges our Lord sends, yes, sir.

TREVES: I need the help of an experienced nurse, you see.

SANDWICH: Someone to bring him food, take care of the room. Yes, I understand. But it is somehow difficult.

TREVES: Well, I have been let down so far. He really is—that is, the regular sisters—well, it is not part of their job and they will not do it. Be ordinarily kind to Mr. Merrick. Without—well—panicking. He is quite beyond ugly. You understand that? His appearance has terrified them.

SANDWICH: The photographs show a terrible disease.

TREVES: It is a disorder, not a disease; it is in no way contagious though we don't in fact know what it is. I have found however that there is a deep superstition in those I've tried, they actually believe he somehow brought it on himself, this thing, and of course it is not that at all.

SANDWICH: I am not one who believes it is ourselves who attain grace or bring chastisement to us, sir.

TREVES: Miss Sandwich, I am hoping not.

SANDWICH: Let me put your mind to rest. Care for lepers in the East, and you have cared, Mr. Treves. In Africa, I have seen dreadful scourges quite unknown to our more civilized climes. What at home could be worse than a miserable and afflicted rotting black?

TREVES: I imagine.

SANDWICH: Appearances do not daunt me.

TREVES: It is really that that has sent me outside the confines of the London seeking help.

SANDWICH: "I look unto the hills whence cometh my help." I understand: I think I will be satisfactory.

[*Enter* PORTER *with tray*]

PORTER: His lunch. [*Exits*]

TREVES: Perhaps you would be so kind as to accompany me this time. I will introduce you.

SANDWICH: Allow me to carry the tray.

TREVES: I will this time. You are ready.

SANDWICH: I am.

TREVES: He is bathing to be rid of his odor.

[*They enter to* MERRICK]

John, this is Miss Sandwich. She—

SANDWICH: I— [*Unable to control herself*] Oh, my good God in heaven! [*Bolts room*]

TREVES: [*Puts* MERRICK's *lunch down*] I am sorry. I thought—

MERRICK: Thank you for saving the lunch this time.

TREVES: Excuse me. [*Exits to* MISS SANDWICH] You have let me down, you know. I did everything to warn you and still you let me down.

SANDWICH: You didn't say.

TREVES: But I—

SANDWICH: Didn't! You said—just words!

TREVES: But the photographs.

SANDWICH: Just pictures. No one will do this. I am sorry. [*Exits*]

TREVES: Yes. Well. This is not helping him.

[*Fadeout*]

SCENE SEVEN

THE ENGLISH PUBLIC WILL PAY
FOR HIM TO BE LIKE US

The London Hospital. MERRICK *in a bathtub reading.* TREVES, BISHOP HOW *in foreground.*

BISHOP: With what fortitude he bears his cross! It is remarkable. He has made the acquaintance of religion and knows sections of the Bible by heart. Once I'd grasped his speech, it became clear he'd certainly had religious instruction at one time.

TREVES: I believe it was in the workhouse, Dr. How.

BISHOP: They are awfully good about that sometimes. The psalms he loves, and the book of Job perplexes him, he says, for he cannot see that a just God must cause suffering, as he puts it, merely then to be merciful. Yet that Christ will save him he does not doubt, so he is not resentful.

[*Enter* GOMM]

GOMM: Christ had better; be damned if we can.

BISHOP: Ahem. In any case, Dr. Treves, he has a religious nature, further instruction would uplift him and I'd be pleased to provide it. I plan to speak of him from the pulpit this week.

GOMM: I see our visiting bather has flushed the busy Bishop How from his cruciform lair.

BISHOP: Speak with Merrick, sir. I have spoken to him of Mercy and Justice. There's a true Christian in the rough.

GOMM: This makes my news seem banal, yet yes: Frederick, the response to my letter to the *Times* about Merrick has been staggering. The English public has been so generous that Merrick may be supported for life without a penny spent from Hospital funds.

TREVES: But that is excellent.

BISHOP: God bless the English public.

GOMM: Especially for not dismembering him at Liverpool Street Station. Freddie, the London's no home for incurables, this is quite irregular, but for you I permit it—though God knows what you'll do.

BISHOP: God does know, sir, and Darwin does not.

GOMM: He'd better, sir; he deformed him.

BISHOP: I had apprehensions coming here. I find it most fortunate Merrick is in the hands of Dr. Treves, a Christian, sir.

GOMM: Freddie is a good man and a brilliant doctor, and that is fortunate indeed.

TREVES: I couldn't have raised the funds though, Doctor.

BISHOP: Don't let me keep you longer from your duties, Mr. Treves. Yet, Mr. Gomm, consider: is it science, sir, that motivates us when we transport English rule of law to India or Ireland?

When good British churchmen leave hearth and home for missionary hardship in Africa, is it science that bears them away? Sir, it is not. It is Christian duty. It is the obligation to bring our light and benefices to benighted man. That motivates us, even as it motivates Treves toward Merrick, sir, to bring salvation where none is. Gordon was a Christian, sir, and died at Khartoum for it. Not for science, sir.

GOMM: You're telling me, not for science.

BISHOP: Mr. Treves, I'll visit Merrick weekly if I may.

TREVES: You will be welcome, sir, I am certain.

BISHOP: Then good day, sirs. [*Exits*]

GOMM: Well, Jesus my boy, now we have the money, what do you plan for Merrick?

TREVES: Normality as far as is possible.

GOMM: So he will be like us? Ah. [*Smiles*]

TREVES: Is something wrong, Mr. Gomm? With us?

[*Fadeout*]

SCENE EIGHT

MERCY AND JUSTICE ELUDE
OUR MINDS AND ACTIONS

MERRICK *in bath.* TREVES, GOMM.

MERRICK: How long is as long as I like?

TREVES: You may stay for life. The funds exist.

MERRICK: Been reading this. About homes for the blind. Wouldn't mind going to one when I have to move.

TREVES: But you do not have to move; and you're not blind.

MERRICK: I would prefer it where no one stared at me.

GOMM: No one will bother you here.

TREVES: Certainly not. I've given instructions.

[PORTER *and* SNORK *peek in*]

PORTER: What'd I tell you?

SNORK: Gawd almighty. Oh. Mr. Treves. Mr. Gomm.

TREVES: You were told not to do this. I don't understand. You must not lurk about. Surely you have work.

PORTER: Yes, sir.

TREVES: Well, it is infuriating. When you are told a thing, you must listen. I won't have you gaping in on my patients. Kindly remember that.

PORTER: Isn't a patient, sir, is he?

TREVES: Do not let me find you here again.

PORTER: Didn't know you were here, sir. We'll be off now.

GOMM: No, no, Will. Mr. Treves was precisely saying no one would intrude when you intruded.

TREVES: He is warned now. Merrick does not like it.

GOMM: He was warned before. On what penalty, Will?

PORTER: That you'd sack me, sir.

GOMM: You are sacked, Will. You, his friend, you work here?

SNORK: Just started last week, sir.

GOMM: Well, I hope the point is taken now.

PORTER: Mr. Gomm—I ain't truly sacked, am I?

GOMM: Will, yes. Truly sacked. You will never be more truly sacked.

PORTER: It's not me. My wife ain't well. My sister has got to take care of our kids, and of her. Well.

GOMM: Think of them first next time.

PORTER: It ain't as if I interfered with his medicine.

GOMM: That is exactly what it is. You may go.

PORTER: Just keeping him to look at in private. That's all. Isn't it?

[SNORK *and* PORTER *exit*]

GOMM: There are priorities, Frederick. The first is discipline. Smooth is the passage to the tight ship's master. Merrick, you are safe from prying now.

TREVES: Have we nothing to say, John?

MERRICK: If all that'd stared at me'd been sacked—there'd be whole towns out of work.

TREVES: I meant, "Thank you, sir."

MERRICK: "Thank you, sir."

TREVES: We always do say please and thank you, don't we?

MERRICK: Yes, sir. Thank you.

TREVES: If we want to properly be like others.

MERRICK: Yes, sir, I want to.

TREVES: Then it is for our own good, is it not?

MERRICK: Yes, sir. Thank you, Mr. Gomm.

GOMM: Sir, you are welcome. [*Exits*]

TREVES: You are happy here, are you not, John?

MERRICK: Yes.

TREVES: The baths have rid you of the odor, have they not?

MERRICK: First chance I had to bathe regular. Lye.

TREVES: And three meals a day delivered to your room?

MERRICK: Yes, sir.

TREVES: This is your Promised Land, is it not? A roof. Food. Protection. Care. Is it not?

MERRICK: Right, Mr. Treves.

TREVES: I will bet you don't know what to call this.

MERRICK: No, sir, I don't know.

TREVES: You call it, Home.

MERRICK: Never had a home before.

TREVES: You have one now. Say it, John: Home.

MERRICK: Home.

TREVES: No, no, really say it. I have a home. This is my. Go on.

MERRICK: I have a home. This is my home. This is my home. I have a home. As long as I like?

TREVES: That is what home is.

MERRICK: That is what is home.

MERRICK: If I abide by the rules, I will be happy.

MERRICK: Yes, sir.

TREVES: Don't be shy.

MERRICK: If I abide by the rules, I will be happy.

TREVES: Very good. Why?

MERRICK: Why what?

TREVES: Will you be happy?

MERRICK: Because it is my home?

TREVES: No, no. Why do rules make you happy?

MERRICK: I don't know.

TREVES: Of course you do.

MERRICK: No, I really don't.

TREVES: Why does anything make you happy?

MERRICK: Like what? Like what?

TREVES: Don't be upset. Rules make us happy because they are for our own good.

MERRICK: Okay.

TREVES: Don't be shy, John. You can say it.

MERRICK: This is my home?

TREVES: No. About rules making us happy.

MERRICK: They make us happy because they are for our own good.

TREVES: Excellent. Now: I am submitting a follow-up paper on you to the London Pathological Society. It would help if you told me what you recall about your first years, John. To fill in gaps.

MERRICK: To fill in gaps. The workhouse where they put me. They beat you there like a drum. Boom boom: scrape the floor white. Shine the pan, boom boom. It never ends. The floor is always dirty. The pan is always tarnished. There is nothing you can do about it. You are always attacked anyway. Boom boom. Boom boom. Boom boom. Will the children go to the workhouse?

TREVES: What children?

MERRICK: The children. The man he sacked.

TREVES: Of necessity Will will find other employment. You don't want crowds staring at you, do you?

MERRICK: No.

TREVES: In your own home you do not have to have crowds staring at you. Or anyone. Do you? In your home?

MERRICK: No.

TREVES: Then Mr. Gomm was merciful. You yourself are proof. Is it not so? [Pause] Well? Is it not so?

MERRICK: If your mercy is so cruel, what do you have for justice?

TREVES: I am sorry. It is just the way things are.

MERRICK: Boom boom. Boom boom. Boom boom.

[Fadeout]

SCENE NINE

MOST IMPORTANT ARE WOMEN

MERRICK asleep, head on knees. TREVES, MRS. KENDAL foreground.

TREVES: You have seen photographs of John Merrick, Mrs. Kendal. You are acquainted with his appearance.

MRS. KENDAL: He reminds me of an audience I played Cleopatra for in Brighton once. All huge grim head and grimace and utterly unable to clap.

TREVES: Well. My aim's to lead him to as normal a life as possible. His terror of us all comes from having been held at arm's length from society. I am determined that shall end. For example, he loves to meet people and converse. I am determined he shall. For example, he had never seen the inside of any normal home before. I had him to mine, and what a reward, Mrs. Kendal; his astonishment, his joy at the most ordinary things. Most critical I feel, however, are women. I will explain. They have always shown the greatest fear and loathing of him. While he adores them of course.

MRS. KENDAL: Ah. He is intelligent.

TREVES: I am convinced they are the key to retrieving him from his exclusion. Though, I must warn you, women are not quite real to him—more creatures of his imagination.

MRS. KENDAL: Then he is already like other men, Mr. Treves.

TREVES: So I thought, an actress could help. I mean, unlike most women, you won't give in, you are trained to hide your true feelings and assume others.

MRS. KENDAL: You mean unlike most women I am famous for it, that is really all.

TREVES: Well. In any case. If you could enter the room and smile and wish him good morning. And when you leave, shake his hand, the left one is usable, and really quite beautiful, and say, "I am very pleased to have made your acquaintance, Mr. Merrick."

MRS. KENDAL: Shall we try it? Left hand out please. [*Suddenly radiant*] I am *very* pleased to have made your acquaintance, Mr. Merrick. I am very *pleased* to have made your acquaintance, Mr. Merrick. I am very pleased to have made your *acquaintance*, Mr. Merrick. I *am* very pleased to have made *your* acquaintance, Mr. Merrick. Yes. That one.

TREVES: By God, they are all splendid. Merrick will be so pleased. It will be the day he becomes a man like other men.

MRS. KENDAL: Speaking of that, Mr. Treves.

TREVES: Frederick, please.

MRS. KENDAL: Freddie, may I commit an indiscretion?

TREVES: Yes?

MRS. KENDAL: I could not but help noticing from the photographs that—well—of the unafflicted parts—ah, how shall I put it? [*Points to photograph*]

TREVES: Oh. I see! I quite. Understand. No, no, no, it is quite normal.

MRS. KENDAL: I thought as much.

TREVES: Medically speaking, uhm, you see the papillomatous extrusions which disfigure him, uhm, seem to correspond quite regularly to the osseous deformities, that is, excuse me, there is a link between the bone disorder and the skin growths, though for the life of me I have not discovered what it is or why it is, but in any case this—part—it would be therefore unlikely to be afflicted because well, that is, well, there's no bone in it. None at all. I mean.

MRS. KENDAL: Well. Learn a little every day, don't we?

TREVES: I am horribly embarrassed.

MRS. KENDAL: Are you? Then he must be lonely indeed.

[Fadeout]

SCENE TEN

WHEN THE ILLUSION ENDS HE
MUST KILL HIMSELF

MERRICK sketching. Enter TREVES, MRS. KENDAL.

TREVES: He is making sketches for a model of St. Philip's Church. He wants someday to make a model, you see. John, my boy, this is Mrs. Kendal. She would very much like to make your acquaintance.

MRS. KENDAL: Good morning, Mr. Merrick.

TREVES: I will see to a few matters. I will be back soon. [Exits]

MERRICK: I planned so many things to say. I forget them. You are so beautiful.

MRS. KENDAL: How charming, Mr. Merrick.

MERRICK: Well. Really that was what I planned to say. That I forgot what I planned to say. I couldn't think of anything else I was so excited.

MRS. KENDAL: Real charm is always planned, don't you think?

MERRICK: Well. I do not know why I look like this, Mrs. Kendal. My mother was so beautiful. She was knocked down by an elephant in a circus while she was pregnant. Something must have happened, don't you think?

MRS. KENDAL: It may well have.

MERRICK: It may well have. But sometimes I think my head is so big because it is so full of dreams. Because it is. Do you know what happens when dreams cannot get out?

MRS. KENDAL: Why, no.

MERRICK: I don't either. Something must. [*Silence*] Well. You are a famous actress.

MRS. KENDAL: I am not unknown.

MERRICK: You must display yourself for your living then. Like I did.

MRS. KENDAL: That is not myself, Mr. Merrick. That is an illusion. This is myself.

MERRICK: This is myself, too.

MRS. KENDAL: Frederick says you like to read. So: books.

MERRICK: I am reading *Romeo and Juliet* now.

MRS. KENDAL: Ah, Juliet. What a love story. I adore love stories.

MERRICK: I like love stories best, too. If I had been Romeo, guess what?

MRS. KENDAL: What?

MERRICK: I would not have held the mirror to her breath.

MRS. KENDAL: You mean the scene where Juliet appears to be dead and he holds a mirror to her breath and sees—

MERRICK: Nothing. How does it feel when he kills himself because he just sees nothing?

MRS. KENDAL: Well. My experience as Juliet has been—particularly with an actor I will not name—that while I'm lying there dead dead dead, and he is lamenting excessively, I get to thinking that if this slab of ham does not part from the hamhock of his life *toute de suite*, I am going to scream, pop off the tomb, and plunge a dagger into his scene-stealing heart. Romeos are very undependable.

MERRICK: Because he does not care for Juliet.

MRS. KENDAL: Not care?

MERRICK: Does he take her pulse? Does he get a doctor? Does he make sure? No. He kills himself. The illusion fools him because he does not care for her. He only cares about himself. If I had been Romeo, we would have got away.

MRS. KENDAL: But then there would be no play, Mr. Merrick.

MERRICK: If he did not love her, why should there be a play? Looking in a mirror and seeing nothing. That is not love. It was all an illusion. When the illusion ended he had to kill himself.

MRS. KENDAL: Why. That is extraordinary.

MERRICK: Before I spoke with people, I did not think of all these things because there was no one to bother to think them for. Now things just come out of my mouth which are true.

[TREVES *enters*]

TREVES: You are famous, John. We are in the papers. Look. They have written up my report to the Pathological Society. Look—it is a kind of apotheosis for you.

MRS. KENDAL: Frederick, I feel Mr. Merrick would benefit by even more company than you provide; in fact by being acquainted with the best, and they with him. I shall make it my task if you'll permit. As you know, I am a friend of nearly everyone, and I do pretty well as I please and what pleases me is this task, I think.

TREVES: By God, Mrs. Kendal, you are splendid.

MRS. KENDAL: Mr. Merrick, I must go now. I should like to return if I may. And so that we may without delay teach you about society, I would like to bring my good friend Dorothy Lady Neville. She would be most pleased if she could meet you. Let me tell her, yes? [MERRICK *nods yes*] Then until next time. I'm sure your church model will surprise us all. Mr. Merrick, it has been a very great pleasure to make your acquaintance.

TREVES: John. Your hand. She wishes to shake your hand.

MERRICK: Thank you for coming.

MRS. KENDAL: But it was my pleasure. Thank you. [*Exits, accompanied by* TREVES]

TREVES: What a wonderful success. Do you know he's never shook a woman's hand before?

[*As lights fade* MERRICK *sobs soundlessly, uncontrollably*]

SCENE ELEVEN

HE DOES IT WITH JUST
ONE HAND

Music. MERRICK *working on model of St. Philip's Church. Enter* DUCHESS. *At side* TREVES *ticks off a gift list.*

MERRICK: Your grace.

DUCHESS: How nicely the model is coming along, Mr. Merrick. I've come to say Happy Christmas, and that I hope you will enjoy this ring and remember your friend by it.

MERRICK: Your grace, thank you.

DUCHESS: I am very pleased to have made your acquaintance. [*Exits*]

[*Enter* COUNTESS]

COUNTESS: Please accept these silver-backed brushes and comb for Christmas, Mr. Merrick.

MERRICK: With many thanks, Countess.

COUNTESS: I am very pleased to have made your acquaintance. [*Exits*]

[*Enter* LORD JOHN]

LORD JOHN: Here's the silver-topped walking stick, Merrick. Make you a regular Piccadilly exquisite. Keep up the good work. Self-help is the best help. Example to us all.

MERRICK: Thank you, Lord John.

LORD JOHN: Very pleased to have made your acquaintance. [*Exits*]

[*Enter* TREVES *and* PRINCESS ALEXANDRA]

TREVES: Her Royal Highness Princess Alexandra.

PRINCESS: The happiest of Christmases, Mr. Merrick.

TREVES: Her Royal Highness has brought you a signed photograph of herself.

MERRICK: I am honored, your Royal Highness. It is the treasure of my possessions. I have written to His Royal Highness the Prince of Wales to thank him for the pheasants and woodcock he sent.

PRINCESS: You are a credit to Mr. Treves, Mr. Merrick. Mr. Treves, you are a credit to medicine, to England, and to Christendom. I am so very pleased to have made your acquaintance.

[PRINCESS, TREVES *exit. Enter* MRS. KENDAL]

MRS. KENDAL: Good news, John. Bertie says we may use the Royal Box whenever I like. Mrs. Keppel says it gives a unique perspective. And for Christmas, ivory-handled razors and toothbrush.

[*Enter* TREVES]

TREVES: And a cigarette case, my boy, full of cigarettes!

MERRICK: Thank you. Very much.

MRS. KENDAL: Look Freddie, look. The model of St. Philip's.

TREVES: It is remarkable, I know.

MERRICK: And I do it with just one hand, they all say.

MRS. KENDAL: You are an artist, John Merrick, an artist.

MERRICK: I did not begin to build at first. Not till I saw what St. Philip's really was. It is not stone and steel and glass; it is an imitation of grace flying up and up from the mud. So I make my imitation of an imitation. But even in that is heaven to me, Mrs. Kendal.

TREVES: That thought's got a good line, John. Plato believed this was all a world of illusion and that artists made illusions of illusions of heaven.

MERRICK: You mean we are all just copies? Of originals?

TREVES: That's it.

MERRICK: Who made the copies?

TREVES: God. The Demi-urge.

MERRICK: [*Goes back to work*] He should have used both hands, shouldn't he?

[*Music. Puts another piece on St. Philip's. Fadeout*]

SCENE   TWELVE

WHO DOES HE REMIND
YOU OF?

TREVES, MRS. KENDAL.

TREVES: Why all those toilet articles, tell me? He is much too deformed to use any of them.

THE ELEPHANT MAN   145

MRS. KENDAL: Props of course. To make himself. As I make me.

TREVES: You? You think of yourself.

MRS. KENDAL: Well. He is gentle, almost feminine. Cheerful, honest within limits, a serious artist in his way. He is almost like me.

[*Enter* BISHOP HOW]

BISHOP: He is religious and devout. He knows salvation must
radiate to us or all is lost, which it's certainly not.

[*Enter* GOMM]

GOMM: He seems practical, like me. He has seen enough of daily
evil to be thankful for small goods that come his way. He knows
what side his bread is buttered on, and counts his blessings for it.
Like me.

[*Enter* DUCHESS]

DUCHESS: I can speak with him of anything. For I know he is discreet. Like me.

[*All exit except* TREVES]

TREVES: How odd. I think him curious, compassionate, concerned
about the world, well, rather like myself, Freddie Treves, 1889 A.D.

[*Enter* MRS. KENDAL]

MRS. KENDAL: Of course he is rather odd. And hurt. And helpless
not to show the struggling. And so am I.

[*Enter* GOMM]

GOMM: He knows I use him to raise money for the London, I am
certain. He understands I would be derelict if I didn't. He is wary
of any promise, yet he fits in well. Like me.

[*Enter* BISHOP HOW]

BISHOP: I as a seminarist had many of the same doubts. Struggled
as he does. And hope they may be overcome.

[*Enter* PRINCESS ALEXANDRA]

PRINCESS: When my husband His Royal Highness Edward Prince of Wales asked Dr. Treves to be his personal surgeon, he said, "Dear Freddie, if you can put up with the Elephant bloke, you can surely put up with me."

[*All exit, except* TREVES. *Enter* LORD JOHN]

LORD JOHN: See him out of fashion, Freddie. As he sees me. Social contacts critical. Oh—by the way—ignore the bloody papers; all lies. [*Exits*]

TREVES: Merrick visibly worse than '86–87. That, as he rises higher in the consolations of society, he gets visibly more grotesque is proof definitive he is like me. Like his condition, which I make no sense of, I make no sense of mine.

[*Spot on* MERRICK *placing another piece on St. Philip's. Fadeout*]

SCENE THIRTEEN

ANXIETIES OF THE SWAMP

MERRICK, *in spot, strains to listen:* TREVES, LORD JOHN *outside.*

TREVES: But the papers are saying you broke the contracts. They are saying you've lost the money.

LORD JOHN: Freddie, if I were such a scoundrel, how would I dare face investors like yourself. Broken contracts! I never considered them actual contracts—just preliminary things, get the old deal under way. An actual contract's something between gentlemen; and this attack on me shows they are no gentlemen. Now I'm only here to say the company remains a terribly attractive proposi-

tion. Don't you think? To recapitalize—if you could spare another
—ah. [*Enter* GOMM] Mr. Gomm. How good to see you. Just
remarking how splendidly Merrick thrives here, thanks to you and
Freddie.

GOMM: Lord John. Allow me: I must take Frederick from you.
Keep him at work. It's in his contract. Wouldn't want him breaking it. Sort of thing makes the world fly apart, isn't it?

LORD JOHN: Yes. Well. Of course, mmm.

GOMM: Sorry to hear you're so pressed. Expect we'll see less of you
around the London now?

LORD JOHN: Of course, I, actually—ah! Overdue actually. Appointment in the City. Freddie. Mr. Gomm. [*Exits*]

TREVES: He plain fooled me. He was kind to Merrick.

GOMM: You have risen fast and easily, my boy. You've forgot how
to protect yourself. Break now.

TREVES: It does not seem right somehow.

GOMM: The man's a moral swamp. Is that not clear yet? Is he attractive? Deceit often is. Friendly? Swindlers can be. Another
loan? Not another cent. It may be your money, Freddie; but I will
not tolerate laboring like a navvy that the London should represent honest charitable and compassionate science, and have titled
swindlers mucking up the pitch. He has succeeded in destroying
himself so rabidly, you ought not doubt an instant it was his real
aim all along. He broke the contracts, gambled the money away,
lied, and like an infant in his mess, gurgles and wants to do it
again. Never mind details, don't want to know. Break and be glad.
Don't hesitate. Today. One-man moral swamp. Don't be sucked
in.

       [*Enter* MRS. KENDAL]

MRS. KENDAL: Have you see the papers?

TREVES: Yes.

GOMM: Yes, yes. A great pity. Freddie: today. [*Exits*]

MRS. KENDAL: Freddie?

TREVES: He has used us. I shall be all right. Come. [MRS. KENDAL, TREVES *enter to* MERRICK] John: I shall not be able to stay this visit. I must, well, unravel a few things. Nurse Ireland and Snork are—?

MERRICK: Friendly and respectful, Frederick.

TREVES: I'll look in in a few days.

MERRICK: Did I do something wrong?

MRS. KENDAL: No.

TREVES: This is a hospital. Not a marketplace. Don't forget it, ever. Sorry. Not you. Me. [*Exits*]

MRS. KENDAL: Well. Shall we weave today? Don't you think weaving might be fun? So many things are fun. Most men really can't enjoy them. Their loss, isn't it? I like little activities which engage me; there's something ancient in it, I don't know. Before all this. Would you like to try? John?

MERRICK: Frederick said I may stay here for life.

MRS. KENDAL: And so you shall.

MERRICK: If he is in trouble?

MRS. KENDAL: Frederick is your protector, John.

MERRICK: If he is in trouble? [*He picks up small photograph*]

MRS. KENDAL: Who is that? Ah, is it not your mother? She is pretty, isn't she?

MERRICK: Will Frederick keep his word with me, his contract, Mrs. Kendal? If he is in trouble.

MRS. KENDAL: What? Contract? Did you say?

MERRICK: And will you?

MRS. KENDAL: I? What? Will I?

[MERRICK *silent. Puts another piece on model. Fadeout*]

SCENE FOURTEEN

ART IS PERMITTED BUT NATURE
FORBIDDEN

Rain. MERRICK *working.* MRS. KENDAL.

MERRICK: The Prince has a mistress. [*Silence*] The Irishman had one. Everyone seems to. Or a wife. Some have both. I have concluded I need a mistress. It is bad enough not to sleep like others.

MRS. KENDAL: Sitting up, you mean. Couldn't be very restful.

MERRICK: I have to. Too heavy to lay down. My head. But to sleep alone; that is worst of all.

MRS. KENDAL: The artist expresses his love through his works. That is civilization.

MERRICK: Are you very shocked?

MRS. KENDAL: Why should I be?

MERRICK: Others would be.

MRS. KENDAL: I am not others.

MERRICK: I suppose it is hopeless.

MRS. KENDAL: Nothing is hopeless. However it is unlikely.

MERRICK: I thought you might have a few ideas.

MRS. KENDAL: I can guess who has ideas here.

MERRICK: You don't know something. I have never even seen a naked woman.

MRS. KENDAL: Surely in all the fairs you worked.

MERRICK: I mean a real woman.

MRS. KENDAL: Is one more real than another?

MERRICK: I mean like the ones in the theater. The opera.

MRS. KENDAL: Surely you can't mean they are more real.

MERRICK: In the audience. A woman not worn out early. Not deformed by awful life. A lady. Someone kept up. Respectful of herself. You don't know what fairgrounds are like, Mrs. Kendal.

MRS. KENDAL: You mean someone like Princess Alexandra?

MERRICK: Not so old.

MRS. KENDAL: Ah. Like Dorothy.

MERRICK: She does not look happy. No.

MRS. KENDAL: Lady Ellen?

MERRICK: Too thin.

MRS. KENDAL: Then who?

MERRICK: Certain women. They have a kind of ripeness. They
seem to stop at a perfect point.

MRS. KENDAL: My dear, she doesn't exist.

MERRICK: That is probably why I never saw her.

MRS. KENDAL: What would your friend Bishop How say of all this I
wonder?

MERRICK: He says I should put these things out of my mind.

MRS. KENDAL: Is that the best he can suggest?

MERRICK: I put them out of my mind. They reappeared, snap.

MRS. KENDAL: What about Frederick?

MERRICK: He would be appalled if I told him.

MRS. KENDAL: I am flattered. Too little trust has maimed my life.
But that is another story.

MERRICK: What a rain. Are we going to read this afternoon?

MRS. KENDAL: Yes. Some women are lucky to look well, that is all. It is a rather arbitrary gift; it has no really good use, though it has uses, I will say that. Anyway it does not signify very much.

MERRICK: To me it does.

MRS. KENDAL: Well. You are mistaken.

MERRICK: What are we going to read?

MRS. KENDAL: Trust is very important, you know. I trust you.

MERRICK: Thank you very much. I have a book of Thomas Hardy's here. He is a friend of Frederick's. Shall we read that?

MRS. KENDAL: Turn around a moment. Don't look.

MERRICK: Is this a game?

MRS. KENDAL: I would not call it a game. A surprise. [*She begins undressing*]

MERRICK: What kind of a surprise?

MRS. KENDAL: I saw photographs of you. Before I met you. You didn't know that, did you?

MERRICK: The ones from the first time, in '84? No, I didn't.

MRS. KENDAL: I felt it was—unjust. I don't know why. I cannot say my sense of justice is my most highly developed characteristic. You may turn around again. Well. A little funny, isn't it?

MERRICK: It is the most beautiful sight I have seen. Ever.

MRS. KENDAL: If you tell anyone, I shall not see you again, we shall not read, we shall not talk, we shall do nothing. Wait. [*Undoes her hair*] There. No illusions. Now. Well? What is there to say? "I am extremely pleased to have made your acquaintance"?

[*Enter* TREVES]

TREVES: For God's sakes. What is going on here? What is going on?

MRS. KENDAL: For a moment, Paradise, Freddie. [*She begins dressing*]

TREVES: But—have you no sense of decency? Woman, dress yourself quickly. [*Silence.* MERRICK *goes to put another piece on St.
Philip's*] Are you not ashamed? Do you know what you are? Don't
you know what is forbidden?

[*Fadeout*]

SCENE FIFTEEN

INGRATITUDE

ROSS *in* MERRICK'S *room.*

ROSS: I come actually to ask your forgiveness.

MERRICK: I found a good home, Ross. I forgave you.

ROSS: I was hoping we could work out a deal. Something new
maybe.

MERRICK: No.

ROSS: See, I was counting on it. That you were kindhearted. Like
myself. Some things don't change. Got to put your money on the
things that don't, I figure. I figure from what I read about you,
you don't change. Dukes, Ladies coming to see you. Ask myself
why? Figure it's same as always was. Makes 'em feel good about
themselves by comparison. Them things don't change. There but
for the grace of. So I figure you're selling the same service as always. To better clientele. Difference now is you ain't charging for
it.

MERRICK: You make me sound like a whore.

ROSS: You are. I am. They are. Most are. No disgrace, John. Disgrace is to be a stupid whore. Give it for free. Not capitalize on
the interest in you. Not to have a manager then is stupid.

MERRICK: You see this church. I am building it. The people who visit are friends. Not clients. I am not a dog walking on its hind legs.

ROSS: I was thinking. Charge these people. Pleasure of the Elephant Man's company. Something. Right spirit is everything. Do it in the right spirit, they'd pay happily. I'd take ten percent. I'd be okay with ten percent.

MERRICK: Bad luck's made you daft.

ROSS: I helped you, John. Discovered you. Was that daft? No. Only daftness was being at a goldmine without a shovel. Without proper connections. Like Treves has. What's daft? Ross sows, Treves harvests? It's not fair, is it, John? When you think about it. I do think about it. Because I'm old. Got something in my throat. You may have noticed. Something in my lung here, too. Something in my belly I guess, too. I'm not a heap of health, am I? But I'd do well with ten percent. I don't need more than ten percent. Ten percent'd give me a future slightly better'n a cobblestone. This lot would pay, if you charged in the right spirit. I don't ask much.

MERRICK: They're the cream, Ross. They know it. Man like you tries to make them pay, they'll walk away.

ROSS: I'm talking about doing it in the right spirit.

MERRICK: They are my friends. I'd lose everything. For you. Ross, you lived your life. You robbed me of forty-eight pounds, nine shillings, tuppence. You left me to die. Be satisfied, Ross. You've had enough. You kept me like an animal in darkness. You come back and want to rob me again. Will you not be satisfied? Now I am a man like others, you want me to return?

ROSS: Had a woman yet?

MERRICK: Is that what makes a man?

ROSS: In my time it'd do for a start.

MERRICK: Not what makes this one. Yet I am like others.

ROSS: Then I'm condemned. I got no energy to try nothing new. I may as well go to the dosshouse straight. Die there anyway. Between filthy dosshouse rags. Nothing in the belly but acid. I don't like pain, John. The future gives pain sense. Without a future— [*Pauses*] Five percent? John?

MERRICK: I'm sorry, Ross. It's just the way things are.

ROSS: By God. Then I am lost.

[*Fadeout*]

SCENE SIXTEEN

NO RELIABLE GENERAL
ANESTHETIC HAS APPEARED
YET

TREVES, *reading, makes notes.* MERRICK *works.*

MERRICK: Frederick—do you believe in heaven? Hell? What about Christ? What about God? I believe in heaven. The Bible promises in heaven the crooked shall be made straight.

TREVES: So did the rack, my boy. So do we all.

MERRICK: You don't believe?

TREVES: I will settle for a reliable general anesthetic at this point. Actually, though—I had a patient once. A woman. Operated on her for—a woman's thing. Used ether to anesthetize. Tricky stuff. Didn't come out of it. Pulse stopped, no vital signs, absolutely moribund. Just a big white dead mackerel. Five minutes later, she fretted back to existence, like a lost explorer with a great scoop of the undiscovered.

MERRICK: She saw heaven?

TREVES: Well. I quote her: it was neither heavenly nor hellish. Rather like perambulating in a London fog. People drifted by, but no one spoke. London, mind you. Hell's probably the provinces. She was shocked it wasn't more exotic. But allowed as how had she stayed, and got used to the familiar, so to speak, it did have hints of becoming a kind of bliss. She fled.

MERRICK: If you do not believe—why did you send Mrs. Kendal away?

TREVES: Don't forget. It saved you once. My interference. You know well enough—it was not proper.

MERRICK: How can you tell? If you do not believe?

TREVES: There are still standards we abide by.

MERRICK: They make us happy because they are for our own good.

TREVES: Well. Not always.

MERRICK: Oh.

TREVES: Look, if you are angry, just say so.

MERRICK: Whose standards are they?

TREVES: I am not in the mood for this chipping away at the edges, John.

MERRICK: That do not always make us happy because they are not always for our own good?

TREVES: Everyone's. Well. Mine. Everyone's.

MERRICK: That woman's, that Juliet?

TREVES: Juliet?

MERRICK: Who died, then came back.

TREVES: Oh. I see. Yes. Her standards, too.

MERRICK: So.

TREVES: So what?

MERRICK: Did you see her? Naked?

TREVES: When I was operating. Of course—

MERRICK: Oh.

TREVES: Oh what?

MERRICK: Is it okay to see them naked if you cut them up afterwards?

TREVES: Good Lord. I'm a surgeon. That is science.

MERRICK: She died. Mrs. Kendal didn't.

TREVES: Well, she came back, too.

MERRICK: And Mrs. Kendal didn't. If you mean that.

TREVES: I am trying to read about anesthetics. There is simply no comparison.

MERRICK: Oh.

TREVES: Science is a different thing. This woman came to me to be. I mean, it is not, well, love, you know.

MERRICK: Is that why you're looking for an anesthetic.

TREVES: It would be a boon to surgery.

MERRICK: Because you don't love them.

TREVES: Love's got nothing to do with surgery.

MERRICK: Do you lose many patients?

TREVES: I—some.

MERRICK: Oh.

TREVES: Oh what? What does it matter? Don't you see? If I love, if any surgeon loves her or any patient or not, what does it matter? And what conceivable difference to you?

MERRICK: Because it is your standards we abide by.

TREVES: For God's sakes. If you are angry, just say it. I won't turn you out. Say it: I am angry. Go on. I am angry. I am angry! I am angry!

MERRICK: I believe in heaven.

TREVES: And it is not okay. If they undress if you cut them up. As you put it. Make me sound like Jack the, Jack the Ripper.

MERRICK: No. You worry about anesthetics.

TREVES: Are you having me on?

MERRICK: You are merciful. I myself am proof. Is it not so? [*Pauses*] Well? Is it not so?

TREVES: Well. I. About Mrs. Kendal—perhaps I was wrong. I, these days that is, I seem to. Lose my head. Taking too much on perhaps. I do not know—what is in me these days.

MERRICK: Will she come back? Mrs. Kendal?

TREVES: I will talk to her again.

MERRICK: But—will she?

TREVES: No. I don't think so.

MERRICK: Oh.

TREVES: There are other things involved. Very. That is. Other things.

MERRICK: Well. Other things. I want to walk now. Think. Other things. [*Begins to exit. Pauses*] Why? Why won't she?

[*Silence.* MERRICK *exits*]

TREVES: Because I don't want her here when you die. [*He slumps in chair*]

[*Fadeout*]

SCENE SEVENTEEN

CRUELTY IS AS NOTHING TO
KINDNESS

TREVES *asleep in chair dreams the following:* MERRICK *and* GOMM *dressed as* ROSS *in foreground.*

MERRICK: If he is merely papier-mâché and paint, a swindler and a fake—

GOMM: No, no, a genuine Dorset dreamer in a moral swamp. Look —he has so forgot how to protect himself he's gone to sleep.

MERRICK: I must examine him. I would not keep him for long, Mr. Gomm.

GOMM: It would be an inconvenience, Mr. Merrick. He is a mainstay of our institution.

MERRICK: Exactly that brought him to my attention. I am Merrick. Here is my card. I am with the mutations cross the road.

GOMM: Frederick, stand up. You must understand. He is very very valuable. We have invested a great deal in him. He is personal surgeon to the Prince of Wales.

MERRICK: But I only wish to examine him. I had not of course dreamed of changing him.

GOMM: But he is a gentleman and a good man.

MERRICK: Therefore exemplary for study as a cruel or deviant one would not be.

GOMM: Oh, very well. Have him back for breakfast time or you feed him. Frederick, stand up. Up you bloody donkey, up!

[TREVES, *still asleep, stands up. Fadeout*]

SCENE   EIGHTEEN

WE ARE DEALING WITH
AN EPIDEMIC

TREVES *asleep.* MERRICK *at lectern.*

MERRICK: The most striking feature about him, note, is the terrifyingly normal head. This allowed him to lie down normally, and therefore to dream in the exclusive personal manner, without the weight of others' dreams accumulating to break his neck. From the brow projected a normal vision of benevolent enlightenment, what we believe to be a kind of self-mesmerized state. The mouth, deformed by satisfaction at being at the hub of the best of existent worlds, was rendered therefore utterly incapable of self-critical speech, thus of the ability to change. The heart showed signs of worry at this unchanging yet untenable state. The back was horribly stiff from being kept against a wall to face the discontent of a world ordered for his convenience. The surgeon's hands were well-developed and strong, capable of the most delicate carvings-up, for others' own good. Due also to the normal head, the right arm was of enormous power; but, so incapable of the distinction between the assertion of authority and the charitable act of giving, that it was often to be found disgustingly beating others—for their own good. The left arm was slighter and fairer, and may be seen in typical position, hand covering the genitals, which were treated as a sullen colony in constant need of restriction, governance, punishment. For their own good. To add a further burden to his trouble, the wretched man when a boy developed a disabling spiritual duality, therefore was unable to feel what others feel, nor reach harmony with them. Please. [TREVES *shrugs*] He would thus be denied all means of escape from those he had tormented.

[PINS *enter*]

FIRST PIN: Mr. Merrick. You have shown a profound and unknown disorder to us. You have said when he leaves here, it is for his prior life again. I do not think it ought to be permitted. It is a disgrace. It is a pity and a disgrace. It is an indecency in fact. It may be a danger in ways we do not know. Something ought to be done about it.

MERRICK: We hope in twenty years we will understand enough to put an end to this affliction.

FIRST PIN: Twenty years! Sir, that is unacceptable!

MERRICK: Had we caught it early, it might have been different. But his condition has already spread both East and West. The truth is, I am afraid, we are dealing with an epidemic.

[MERRICK *puts another piece on St. Philip's.* PINS *exit.* TREVES *starts awake. Fadeout*]

SCENE NINETEEN

THEY CANNOT MAKE OUT
WHAT HE IS SAYING

MERRICK, BISHOP HOW *in background.* BISHOP *gestures,* MERRICK
on knees. TREVES *foreground. Enter* GOMM.

GOMM: Still beavering away for Christ?

TREVES: Yes.

GOMM: I got your report. He doesn't know, does he?

TREVES: The Bishop?

GOMM: I meant Merrick.

TREVES: No.

GOMM: I shall be sorry when he dies.

TREVES: It will not be unexpected anyway.

GOMM: He's brought the hospital quite a lot of good repute. Quite
a lot of contributions, too, for that matter. In fact, I like him;
never regretted letting him stay on. Though I didn't imagine he'd
last this long.

TREVES: His heart won't sustain him much longer. It may even give
out when he gets off his bloody knees with that bloody man.

GOMM: What is it, Freddie? What has gone sour for you?

TREVES: It is just—it is the overarc of things, quite inescapable that
as he's achieved greater and greater normality, his condition's
edged him closer to the grave. So—a parable of growing up? To

become more normal is to die? More accepted to worsen? He—it is just a mockery of everything we live by.

COMM: Sorry, Freddie. Didn't catch that one.

TREVES: Nothing has gone sour. I do not know.

COMM: Cheer up, man. You are knighted. Your clients will be kings. Nothing succeeds, my boy, like success. [*Exits*]

[BISHOP *comes from* MERRICK's *room*]

BISHOP: I find my sessions with him utterly moving, Mr. Treves. He struggles so. I suggested he might like to be confirmed; he leaped at it like a man lost in a desert to an oasis.

TREVES: He is very excited to do what others do if he thinks it is what others do.

BISHOP: Do you cast doubt, sir, on his faith?

TREVES: No, sir, I do not. Yet he makes all of us think he is deeply like ourselves. And yet we're not like each other. I conclude that we have polished him like a mirror, and shout hallelujah when he reflects us to the inch. I have grown sorry for it.

BISHOP: I cannot make out what you're saying. Is something troubling you, Mr. Treves?

TREVES: Corsets. How about corsets? Here is a pamphlet I've written due mostly to the grotesque ailments I've seen caused by corsets. Fashion overrules me, of course. My patients do not unstrap themselves of corsets. Some cannot—you know, I have so little time in the week, I spend Sundays in the poor-wards; to keep up with work. Work being twenty-year-old women who look an abused fifty with worn-outedness; young men with appalling industrial conditions I turn out as soon as possible to return to their labors. Happily most of my patients are not poor. They are middle class. They overeat and drink so grossly, they destroy nature in themselves and all around them so fervidly, they will not last. Higher up, sir, above this middle class, I confront these same— deformities—bulged out by unlimited resources and the ruthlessness of privilege into the most scandalous dissipation yoked to the grossest ignorance and constraint. I counsel against it where I can. I am ignored of course. Then, what, sir, could be troubling me? I am an extremely successful Englishman in a successful and respected England which informs me daily by the way it lives that it wants to die. I am in despair in fact. Science, observation, practice, deduction, having led me to these conclusions, can no longer serve as consolation. I apparently see things others don't.

BISHOP: I do wish I understood you better, sir. But as for consolation, there is in Christ's Church consolation.

TREVES: I am sure we were not born for mere consolation.

BISHOP: But look at Mr. Merrick's happy example.

TREVES: Oh, yes. You'd like my garden, too. My dog, my wife, my daughter, pruned, cropped, pollarded and somewhat stupefied. Very happy examples, all of them. Well. Is it all we know how to finally do with—whatever? Nature? Is it? Rob it? No, not really, not nature I mean. Ourselves really. Myself really. Robbed, that is. You do see of course, can't figure out, really, what else to do with them. Can we? [*Laughs*]

BISHOP: It is not exactly clear, sir.

TREVES: I am an awfully good gardener. Is that clear? By God I take such good care of anything, anything you, we, are convinced —are you not convinced, him I mean, is not very dangerously human? I mean how could he be? After what we've given him? What you like, sir, is that he is so grateful for patrons, so greedy to be patronized, and no demands, no rights, no hopes; past perverted, present false, future nil. What better could you ask? He puts up with all of it. Of course I do mean taken when I say given, as in what, what, what we have given him, but. You knew that. I'll bet. Because. I. I. I. I—

BISHOP: Do you mean Charity? I cannot tell what you are saying.

TREVES: Help me. [*Weeps*]

       [BISHOP *consoles him*]

MERRICK: [*Rises, puts last piece on St. Philip's*] It is done.

       [*Fadeout*]

SCENE TWENTY

THE WEIGHT OF DREAMS

MERRICK *alone, looking at model. Enter* SNORK *with lunch.*

SNORK: Lunch, Mr. Merrick. I'll set it up. Maybe you'd like a walk after lunch. April's doing wonders for the gardens. [*A funeral procession passes slowly by*] My mate Will, his sister died yesterday. Twenty-eight she was. Imagine that. Wife was sick, his sister nursed her. Was a real bloom that girl. Now wife okay, sister just ups and dies. It's all so—what's that word? Forgot it. It means chance-y. Well. Forgot it. Chance-y'll do. Have a good lunch. [*Exits*]

> [MERRICK *eats a little, breathes on model, polishes it, goes to bed, arms on knees, head on arms, the position in which he must sleep*]

MERRICK: Chancey? [*Sleeps*]

> [*Enter* PINHEADS *singing*]

PINS: We are the Queens of the Cosmos
Beautiful darkness' empire
Darkness darkness, light's true flower,
Here is eternity's finest hour
Sleep like others you learn to admire
Be like your mother, be like your sire.

> [*They straighten* MERRICK *out to normal sleep position. His head tilts over too far. His arms fly up clawing the air. He dies. As light fades,* SNORK *enters*]

SNORK: I remember it, Mr. Merrick. The word is "arbitrary." Arbitrary. It's all so—oh. Hey! Hey! The Elephant Man is dead!

> [*Fadeout*]

SCENE TWENTY-ONE

FINAL REPORT TO THE
INVESTORS

GOMM *reading,* TREVES *listening.*

GOMM: "To the Editor of the *Times.* Sir; In November, 1886, you
were kind enough to insert in the *Times* a letter from me drawing
attention to the case of Joseph Merrick—"

TREVES: John. John Merrick.

GOMM: Well. "—known as the Elephant Man. It was one of singular and exceptional misfortune" et cetera et cetera ". . . debarred
from earning his livelihood in any other way than being exhibited
to the gaze of the curious. This having been rightly interfered
with by the police . . ." et cetera et cetera, "with great difficulty
he succeeded somehow or other in getting to the door of the London Hospital where through the kindness of one of our surgeons
he was sheltered for a time." And then . . . and then . . . and
. . . ah. "While deterred by common humanity from evicting him
again into the open street, I wrote to you and from that moment
all difficulty vanished; the sympathy of many was aroused, and although no other fitting refuge was offered, a sufficient sum was
placed at my disposal, apart from the funds of the hospital, to
maintain him for what did not promise to be a prolonged life.
As—"

TREVES: I forgot. The coroner said it was death by asphyxiation.
The weight of the head crushed the windpipe.

GOMM: Well. I go on to say about how he spent his time here,
that all attempted to alleviate his misery, that he was visited by

the highest in the land et cetera, et cetera, that in general he joined our lives as best he could, and: "In spite of all this indulgence, he was quiet and unassuming, grateful for all that was done for him, and conformed readily to the restrictions which were necessary." Will that do so far, do you think?

TREVES: Should think it would.

GOMM: Wouldn't add anything else, would you?

TREVES: Well. He was highly intelligent. He had an acute sensibility; and worst for him, a romantic imagination. No, no. Never mind. I am really not certain of any of it. [*Exits*]

GOMM: "I have given these details thinking that those who sent money to use for his support would like to know how their charity was used. Last Friday afternoon, though apparently in his usual health, he quietly passed away in his sleep. I have left in my hands a small balance of the money for his support, and this I now propose, after paying certain gratuities, to hand over to the general funds of the hospital. This course I believe will be consonant with the wishes of the contributors.

"It was the courtesy of the *Times* in inserting my letter in 1886 that procured for this afflicted man a comfortable protection during the last years of a previously wretched existence, and I desire to take this opportunity of thankfully acknowledging it.

"I am, sir, your obedient servant,

"F. C. Carr Gomm

"House Committee Room, London Hospital. 15 April 1890."

[TREVES *reenters*]

TREVES: I did think of one small thing.

GOMM: It's too late, I'm afraid. It is done. [*Smiles*]

[*Hold before fadeout*]

OTHERWISE ENGAGED

Simon Gray

Simon Gray

A stylish, urbane comedy (something of a rarity these days), *Otherwise Engaged* was another British import that added luster to the Broadway stage of the seventies. Named by the New York Drama Critics' Circle the best play of the 1976–77 season, it is a witty, satirical portrait of today's anti-hero—the unemotional, self-contented, coolly detached stoic who throws up an invisible screen between himself and the rest of the world.

Originally seen in London in 1975 (with Alan Bates as the impenetrable Simon Hench), it reaped much praise from the reviewers, who termed it "a marvelously engaging evening on the theme of emotional detachment . . . a play of unusual wit and literacy" and "incomparably Simon Gray's best work to date."

The New York critics' sector was equally impressed when the play opened at the Plymouth Theatre on February 2, 1977—this time with Tom Courtenay (making his American stage debut) in the central role. Greeted as a "brilliantly literate social comedy . . . with ironic, verbally dazzling dialogue," it also was singled out for its "sober human observations" and "perceptive undertones."

In *Otherwise Engaged* (as he did in *Butley*, produced in New York in 1972), Mr. Gray probed for the "nerve-endings that animate the world of the middle-class London intelligentsia," a particular corner of contemporary British society which the author admits is "the world I know best."

The author was born in Hayling Island, Hampshire, England, on October 21, 1936, and was educated at Westminster School and at universities in Canada and France before going to Cambridge, where he majored in English.

Professionally, he started out as a novelist and writer of short stories, one of which was sold for television. "But when I found out that the person who was to adapt my story for television would get more than I did for selling the rights, I asked if I could do the dramatization."

His next effort for television was a play about a transvestite criminal fleeing from the police. When it was turned down because of its subject matter, he reworked it for the stage and as *Wise Child* it marked his theatrical debut in 1967. A success in England with Alec Guinness in the transvestite role, it was presented in New York in 1972 with Donald Pleasence but made little dent. Nevertheless, Mr. Gray was launched as a playwright, although he had trouble "staying afloat" until *Butley* came along.

The latter, a major success, was preceded by *Dutch Uncle* (1969), an adaptation of Dostoevsky's *The Idiot* for England's National Theatre (1970), and *Spoiled* (1971).

Since 1966, he also has written extensively for television, and has published three novels: *Colmain, Simple People,* and *Little Portia.*

An energetic writer, Mr. Gray has worked on a number of plays simultaneously. "At one point," he told an interviewer, "I actually had seven plays I was moving between. The nice thing about that was, if one of them went on and went well, then there was something else to get on with. If it went badly, there was that same lifeline of another play to continue work on."

While working, his plays "change and change and change" in the course of many revisions, until quite often the result is one he never contemplated at the outset. "*Otherwise Engaged* took as many as forty drafts, I think, and wound up being about a completely opposite sort of man I had intended at the outset. It started out being about a fellow who desperately wanted to be unfaithful to his wife but who could never stop explaining and apologizing for it. The character ended up as someone who never felt that way at all—about anything."

Mr. Gray's other West End plays include: *Molly* (staged in New York at the Hudson Guild Theatre, 1978); *The Rear Column* (1978); *Close of Play,* a National Theatre presentation starring Michael Redgrave (1979); and *Stage Struck* with Alan Bates once again as his star (1979).

For the past decade, Mr. Gray also has been teaching English Literature at the University of London's Queen Mary College.

Otherwise Engaged was first presented on July 30, 1975, at the Queen's Theatre, London, by Michael Codron. The cast was as follows:

SIMON	*Alan Bates*
DAVE	*Ian Charleson*
STEPHEN	*Nigel Hawthorne*
JEFF	*Julian Glover*
DAVINA	*Jacqueline Pearce*
WOOD	*Benjamin Whitrow*
BETH	*Mary Miller*

Directed by Harold Pinter
Scenery by Eileen Diss

Otherwise Engaged was first presented in New York at the Plymouth Theatre on February 2, 1977, by James M. Nederlander, Frank Milton, and Michael Codron. The cast was as follows:

SIMON	*Tom Courtenay*
DAVE	*John Christopher Jones*
STEPHEN	*John Horton*
JEFF	*Nicolas Coster*
DAVINA	*Lynn Milgrim*
WOOD	*Michael Lombard*
BETH	*Carolyn Lagerfelt*

Directed by Harold Pinter
Scenery by Eileen Diss
Scenery Supervision and Lighting by Neil Peter Jampolis
Costumes by Jane Greenwood

ACT ONE

The living-room of the HENCHES' house in London. It is both
elegant and comfortable, but not large. Two sofas, two
armchairs, a coffee table, a telephone with an answering machine, an extremely expensive and elaborate hi-fi set, and
around the walls shelves to accommodate a great range of
books (which are evidently cherished) and an extensive
collection of records, in which Wagner and other opera sets
can be distinguished.

   Stage left is a door that leads onto a small hall, at one end
of which is the front door, and at the other a door which, in
its turn, when opened, reveals a passage that goes onto stairs
going down to the basement. More stairs lead up from the
hall to another section of the house. The house has, in fact,
recently been divided into two, so that there is a top flat.

   Stage right has a door that leads to the kitchen, and as becomes evident, there is a door that opens from the kitchen
into the garden.

   When the curtain goes up, SIMON is unwrapping a new record. He takes it out with the air of a man who is deeply looking forward to listening to it—there are several records, in
fact—the complete Parsifal. He goes to the hi-fi, puts the first
record on, listens, adjusts the level, then goes to the sofa and
settles himself in it. The opening chords of Parsifal fill the
theatre.

   The door opens, left. DAVE enters. SIMON turns, looks at
him, concealing his irritation as DAVE wanders into the
kitchen, returns, and sits restlessly in the armchair. A pause in
the music.

DAVE: What's that, then?

   [SIMON gets up and switches off the record]

SIMON: Wagner. Do you like him?

DAVE: [*Standing up*] No, well, I mean he was anti-semitic, wasn't he? Sort of early fascist, ego-manic type.

SIMON: What about his music, do you like that?

DAVE: Well, I mean, I'm not likely to like his music if I don't like his type, am I?

SIMON: [*Concealing his impatience*] Everything all right? In the flat, that is. No complaints or other urgencies?

DAVE: No, no, that's all right. Oh, you mean about the rent?

SIMON: Good God no, I wasn't thinking about the rent.

DAVE: It's all right if it waits a bit then, is it?

SIMON: Good God yes, pay us this week's when you pay us last week's—next week, or whenever.

DAVE: O.K. I'm a bit short, you know how it is. Your wife out again, then?

SIMON: Yes, she's gone to [*Thinks*] Salisbury. She left last night.

DAVE: That girl in the first year came round last night for something to eat. I dropped down to borrow a chop or something, fish fingers would have done.

SIMON: Would they really?

DAVE: But she wasn't here, your wife.

SIMON: No, she wouldn't have been, as she was either in, or on her way to, Salisbury.

DAVE: So I had to take her out for a kebab and some wine. Then I had to get her to come back.

SIMON: Ah, she stayed the night, then? Good for you!

DAVE: No, she didn't.

SIMON: Oh. You managed to get rid of her, then, instead, well done!

DAVE: She just left by herself.

SIMON: Before you had a chance to get rid of her, oh dear, why?

DAVE: Said she didn't fancy me.

SIMON: Good God, why ever not?

DAVE: I don't know. I mean, I asked her if she'd like a screw and she said no. Then I asked her why not, and she said she didn't fancy me, that was why not.

SIMON: Still, she's left the door open for a platonic relationship.

DAVE: Yeah, well, then she went off to see something on television with some friend. I haven't got a television.

SIMON: Well, I'm afraid I can't help you there, nor have we.

DAVE: Anyway she said she might be going to that Marxist bookshop down the road today.

SIMON: What time?

DAVE: About lunch time, she said.

SIMON: But good God, lunch will soon be on you, hadn't you better get going—it would be tragic to miss her.

DAVE: Yeah, well, that's it, you see. I'm a bit short, like I said. I mean we can't do anything—

[Pause]

SIMON: Can I lend you some?

DAVE: What?

SIMON: Can I lend you some money?

DAVE: Yeah, O.K.

SIMON: [Giving him a fiver] Is that enough?

DAVE: Yeah. Right. [Takes it] That's five.

SIMON: Well, I'll get back to my music while you're making your own.

STEPHEN: [*Enters, through the kitchen door*] Hello. Oh, hello.

SIMON: [*Concealing his dismay*] Oh, Stephen. This is Dave, who's taken over the upstairs flat. Dave, my brother Stephen.

STEPHEN: Oh, yes, you're at the Poly, aren't you?

DAVE: That's right.

STEPHEN: What are you studying?

DAVE: Sociology.

STEPHEN: That must be jolly interesting. What aspect?

DAVE: What?

STEPHEN: Of sociology.

DAVE: Oh, the usual stuff.

STEPHEN: Psychology, statistics, politics, philosophy, I suppose.

DAVE: We're sitting in at the moment.

STEPHEN: Really? Why?

DAVE: Oh, the usual sort of thing. Well— [*Goes towards the door and out*]

STEPHEN: What is the usual sort of thing?

SIMON: No idea.

STEPHEN: [*After a pause*] Well, I must say!

SIMON: Oh, he's not as thick as he seems.

STEPHEN: Isn't he? He certainly seems quite thick. [*Sits down*] I'm surprised a student could afford that flat, what do you charge him?

SIMON: Two pounds a week, I think.

STEPHEN: But you could get, good Heavens, even through the rent tribunal, ten times that.

SIMON: Oh, we're not out to make money from it.

STEPHEN: Well, *he* seems rather an odd choice for your charity, with so many others in real need. Beth's not here, then?

SIMON: No, she's taken some of her foreign students to Canterbury.

STEPHEN: Did she go with that teacher she was telling Teresa about?

SIMON: Chap called Ned?

STEPHEN: Yes.

SIMON: Yes.

STEPHEN: What do you think of him?

SIMON: Oh, rather a wry, sad little fellow. Bit of a failure, I'd say, from what I've seen of him.

STEPHEN: A failure? In what way?

SIMON: Oh, you know, teaching English to foreigners.

STEPHEN: So does Beth.

SIMON: True, but Beth isn't a middle-aged man with ginger hair, a pigeon-toed gait, a depressed-looking wife and four children to boot.

STEPHEN: You know, sometimes I can't help wondering how people describe me. A middle-aged public school teacher with five children to boot. A bit of a failure too, eh? Anyhow, that's how I feel today.

SIMON: Why, what's the matter?

STEPHEN: That damned interview.

SIMON: Interview?

STEPHEN: For the Assistant Headmastership. You'd forgotten, then!

SIMON: No, no, of *course* I hadn't. When is it exactly?

STEPHEN: [*Looks at him*] Yesterday.

SIMON: Good God! Was it really? Well, what happened?

STEPHEN: I didn't get it.

SIMON: Well, who did?

STEPHEN: A chap called MacGregor. And quite right too, as he's already Assistant Headmaster of a small public school in Edinburgh, very capable, written a couple of text books—in other
words he's simply the better man for the job.

SIMON: I don't see what that's got to do with it. I don't know how
your Headmaster had the face to tell you.

STEPHEN: Oh, he didn't. Nobody's had the face or the grace. Yet.

SIMON: Then how do you know he's got it.

STEPHEN: It was written all over MacGregor. I've never seen anyone so perky after an interview.

SIMON: Oh, good God, is that all? Of course he was perky. He's a
Scot, isn't he? They're always perky. Except when they're doleful.
Usually they're both at once.

STEPHEN: If you'd seen him come bouncing down the library steps.

SIMON: In my experience a bouncing candidate is a rejected candidate. No, no, Steve, my money's on your paddle feet. [He sits]

STEPHEN: Even though my interview lasted a mere half hour although his lasted fifty-seven minutes? Even though I fluffed my
mere half hour, and before a hostile board? Do you know, one of
the Governors couldn't get over the fact that I'd taken my degree
at Reading. He was unable to grasp that Reading was a university
even, he referred to it as if it were some cutprice institution where
I'd scraped up some—some diploma on the cheap. MacGregor
went to Oxford, needless to say.

SIMON: Did he? Which college?

STEPHEN: And then another Governor harped on the number of
our children—he kept saying *five* children, eh? Like that. Five
children, eh? As if I'd had—I don't know—five—five—

SIMON: Cheques returned.

STEPHEN: What?

SIMON: That's what you made it sound as if he sounded as if he were saying.

STEPHEN: Anyway, there were the two Governors manifestly hostile.

SIMON: Out of how many?

STEPHEN: Two.

SIMON: Ah, but then your Headmaster was on your side.

STEPHEN: Perhaps. [*Pause*] At least until I succeeded in putting him off.

SIMON: How?

STEPHEN: By doing something I haven't done since I was twelve years old.

SIMON: [*After a pause*] Can you be more specific?

STEPHEN: You will of course laugh, for which I shan't of course blame you, but I'm not sure that I can stand it if you do laugh at the moment. It was something very trivial, but also very embarrassing. [*Pause*] You see, the Governor who didn't feel Reading was up to snuff had a rather low, husky voice, and towards the end I bent forward, rather sharply, to catch something he said, and this movement caused me to fart.

[*They stare levelly at each other.* SIMON's *face is completely composed*]

SIMON: You haven't farted since you were twelve?

STEPHEN: In public, I meant.

SIMON: Oh. Loudly?

STEPHEN: It sounded to me like a pistol shot.

SIMON: The question, of course, is what it sounded like to Headmaster.

STEPHEN: Like a fart, I should think.

SIMON: Oh, he probably found it sympathetically human, you've no grounds for believing he'd hold anything so accidental against you, surely?

STEPHEN: I don't know, I simply don't know. [*He gets up*] But afterwards when he had us around for some of his wife's herbal coffee—

SIMON: Herbal coffee?

STEPHEN: They paid far more attention to MacGregor than they did to me. I had to struggle to keep my end up. Headmaster was distinctly aloof in his manner—and MacGregor, of course, was relaxed and I suppose a fair man would call it charming.

SIMON: What herbs does she use?

STEPHEN: What? What's that got to do with it? How would I know.

SIMON: Sorry, I was just trying to imagine the—the setting, so to speak.

STEPHEN: You know, what really hurts is that I can't complain that it's unfair. MacGregor really is better qualified, quite obviously an admirable bloke. But what I do resent, and can't help resenting, is the edge Oxford gives him—the simple fact that he went there improves his chances—but I suppose that's the way of the world, isn't it? Almost everybody goes along with it, don't they?

SIMON: Oh, I don't know—

STEPHEN: Of course you know. You subscribe to it yourself, don't you?

SIMON: Certainly not. Why should I?

STEPHEN: Because you went to Oxford yourself.

SIMON: Good God, so what?

STEPHEN: Well, how many other members of your editorial board also went there?

SIMON: Only five.

STEPHEN: Out of how many?

SIMON: Eight.

STEPHEN: And where did the other three go, Cambridge?

SIMON: Only two of them.

STEPHEN: And so only *one* of the nine went elsewhere?

SIMON: No, he didn't go anywhere. He's the Chairman's son.

STEPHEN: I think that proves my point.

SIMON: It proves merely that our editorial board is composed of Oxford and Cambridge graduates, and a half-wit. It proves absolutely nothing about your chances of beating MacDonald to the Assistant Headmastership. And it's my view that poor old Mac-Donald, whether he be Oxford MacDonald or Cambridge Mac-Donald or Reading MacDonald or plain Edinburgh MacDonald—

STEPHEN: MacGregor.

SIMON: What?

STEPHEN: His name happens to be MacGregor.

SIMON: Absolutely. Has no chance at all. Even if they do believe you have too few qualifications and too many children, even if they suspect that your single fart heralds chronic incontinence, they'll still have to appoint you. And if they've been extra courteous to MacDonald it's only to compensate him for coming all the way from Edinburgh for a London rebuff. [*Stands up*]

STEPHEN: Actually it would be better, if you don't mind, not to try and jolly me along with reasons and reassurances. I shall have to face the disappointment sooner or later, and I'd rather do it sooner—wouldn't you?

SIMON: No, I have a distinct preference for later, myself. I really do think you'll get it, you know.

STEPHEN: Yes, well thanks anyway. I'd better get back. What time's your friend coming?

SIMON: What friend?

STEPHEN: When I phoned and asked whether I could come round, you said it mightn't be worth my while as you were expecting a friend.

SIMON: Good God! Yes. Still, he's one of those people who never turns up when expected. So if I remember to expect him I should be all right.

STEPHEN: You mean you don't want him to turn up? Who is he anyway?

SIMON: Jeff Golding.

STEPHEN: Oh, *him!* Yes, well I must say that piece he wrote in one of last week's Sundays, on censorship and children—I've never read anything so posturingly half-baked.

SIMON: Oh, I doubt if he was posturing, he really is half-baked.

STEPHEN: I shall never forget—never—how he ruined the dinner party—the one time I met him—his drunkenness and his appalling behaviour. And I shall particularly never forget his announcing that people—he meant me, of course—only went into public school teaching because they were latent pederasts.

SIMON: Good God, what did you say?

STEPHEN: I told him to take it back.

SIMON: And did he?

STEPHEN: He offered to take back the latent, and congratulated me on my luck. That was his idea of badinage. By God, I don't often lose control but I made a point of cornering him in the hall when he was leaving. I got him by the lapels and warned him that I'd a good mind to beat some manners into him. If Teresa hadn't happened to come out of the lavatory just then—she'd rushed in there in tears—I might have done him some damage. I've never told you that bit before, have I?

SIMON: You haven't told me any of it before, it's very amusing. Tell me, who gave this memorable dinner party?

STEPHEN: You did.

SIMON: Did I really? I don't remember it. It must have been a long time ago.

STEPHEN: Yes, but I have a feeling your friend Jeff Golding will remember it all right.

[*The front door slams and* JEFF GOLDING *enters left*]

JEFF: Simon—ah, there you are. [*There is a pause*] Weren't you expecting me?

SIMON: I most certainly was. Oh, my brother Stephen—Jeff Golding. I believe you know each other.

STEPHEN: We do indeed.

JEFF: Really? Sorry, 'fraid I don't remember.

STEPHEN: A dinner party Simon gave—some years ago.

JEFF: [*Clearly not remembering at all*] Nice to see you again. [*To* SIMON] Could I have a Scotch please?

SIMON: Of course. [*Goes to the drinks table*] Steve?

STEPHEN: No, thank you.

JEFF: [*Collapses into a chair*] Christ! Christ! I've just had a session at the Beeb, taping a piece with Bugger Lampwith. I've got the goods on him at last.

STEPHEN: Lampwith. Isn't he a poet?

JEFF: Not even. He's an Australian. A closet Australian. Went to Oxford instead of Earl's Court. Thinks it makes him one of us. Still, I got him out of his closet with his vowels around his tonsils, once or twice. Thrice, actually. [*Laughs at the recollection*]

STEPHEN: What exactly have you got against him?

JEFF: Isn't that enough?

STEPHEN: Simply that he's an Australian?

JEFF: They're all right as dentists.

STEPHEN: But could you please explain to me why you have it in for Australians.

JEFF: Once you let them into literature they lower the property values.

STEPHEN: Really? How?

JEFF: They're too fertile, scribble, scribble, scribble like little Gibbons. They breed whole articles out of small reviews, don't mind what work they do, go from sports journalists to movie critics to novelists to poets to television pundits, and furthermore they don't mind how little they get paid as long as they fill our space. So you see if there weren't any Australians around sods like me wouldn't end up having to flog our crap to the Radio Times and even the Shiterary Supplement, let alone spend Saturday morning interviewing buggers like Bugger Lampwith.

STEPHEN: We've got half a dozen Australian boys in our school at the moment. They're not only friendly, frank and outgoing, they're also intelligent and very hard-working.

JEFF: Exactly, the little buggers. Hey! [To SIMON] Roger's been going around telling people I can't face him since my review of his turgid little turd of a novel. Have you read it?

SIMON: Which?

JEFF: My review—first things first.

SIMON: Yes, I did.

JEFF: Well?

SIMON: Some good jokes, I thought.

JEFF: Weren't there? And what did you honestly, frankly and actually think of his turd?

SIMON: I haven't read it.

JEFF: Didn't you publish it?

SIMON: Yes.

JEFF: Well, if you ask me, the blokie you got to write the blurb hadn't read it either, bloody sloppy piece of crap, who did it anyway?

SIMON: Actually I did.

JEFF: D'you know what it bloody is—I'll tell you what it bloody is —I wish I'd come out with it straight when I wrote about it—it's a piece of—*literature*, that's what it bloody is!

STEPHEN: You don't like literature?

JEFF: [*A pause*] I don't like literature, no.

STEPHEN: Why not?

JEFF: Because it's a bloody boring racket.

STEPHEN: You think literature is a *racket?*

JEFF: Are you in it, too?

STEPHEN: I happen to teach it, it so happens.

JEFF: Does it, Christ! To whom?

STEPHEN: Sixth formers. At Amplesides.

JEFF: What's Amplesides?

STEPHEN: It happens to be a public school.

JEFF: Does it? Major or minor?

STEPHEN: Let's just say that it's a good one, if you don't mind.

JEFF: I don't mind saying it even if it's not. It's a good one. Christ, can't remember when I last met a public school teacher.

STEPHEN: Probably when you last met me.

JEFF: But I don't remember that, don't forget.

STEPHEN: Would you like me to remind you? I'm the latent pederast.

JEFF: [*After a pause*] Then you're in the right job.

STEPHEN: [*To* SIMON] I think I'd better go. Before I do something I regret. [*Turns and goes out through kitchen*]

SIMON: Oh, right. [*Making an attempt to follow* STEPHEN. *Calling it out*] Love to Teresa and the kids.

[*Sound of doors slamming.* JEFF *helps himself to another Scotch*]

JEFF: Seems a real sweetie, what's he like in real life?

SIMON: Not as stupid as he seems.

JEFF: That still leaves him a lot of room to be stupid in.

SIMON: He *is* my brother.

JEFF: I'm very sorry.

SIMON: Actually, the last time he met you, he offered to fight you.

JEFF: Then he's matured since then. Where's Beth?

SIMON: Gone to Canterbury.

JEFF: With her woggies?

SIMON: Yes.

JEFF: Never seem to see her these days. You two still all right, I take it?

SIMON: Yes, thanks.

JEFF: Christ, you're lucky, don't know how you do it. She's so bloody attractive of course, as well as nice and intelligent. I suppose that helps.

SIMON: Yes, it does really.

JEFF: And she's got that funny little moral streak in her—she doesn't altogether approve of me, I get the feeling. Even after all these years. Christ, women! Listen, there's something I want to talk to you about, and I'll just lay down the guide-lines of your response. What I want from you is an attentive face and a cocked ear, the good old-fashioned friendly sympathy and concern for which you're celebrated, O bloody K?

SIMON: Well, I'll do my best.

JEFF: Remember Gwendoline?

SIMON: Gwendoline, no. Have I met her?

JEFF: Hundreds of times.

SIMON: Really, where?

JEFF: With me.

SIMON: Oh. Which one was she—to tell you the truth, Jeff, there've been so many that the only one I still have the slightest recollection of is your ex-wife.

JEFF: Are you sure?

SIMON: Absolutely.

JEFF: Well, that was Gwendoline.

SIMON: Oh, I thought her name was Gwynyth.

JEFF: Why?

SIMON: What?

JEFF: Why should you think her name was Gwynyth?

SIMON: Wasn't she Welsh?

JEFF: No, she bloody was not Welsh.

SIMON: Well, I haven't seen her for years, don't forget, not since the afternoon you threw your drink in her face and walked out on her.

JEFF: And that's all you remember?

SIMON: Well, it *did* happen in my flat, a lunch party you asked me to give so that you could meet the then Arts Editor of *The Sunday Times*, and you did leave her sobbing on my bed, into my pillow, with the stink of Scotch everywhere—

JEFF: Don't you remember anything else about my Gwendoline days, for Christ's sake? What I used to tell you about her?

SIMON: [*Thinks*] Yes. You used to tell me that she was the stupidest woman I'd ever met.

JEFF: *You'd* ever met.

SIMON: Yes.

JEFF: And was she?

SIMON: Yes.

JEFF: Well, you've met some stupider since, haven't you?

SIMON: Probably, but fortunately I can't remember them either.

JEFF: So you rather despised my poor old Gwendoline, did you?

SIMON: Absolutely. So did you.

JEFF: Then why do you think I married her?

SIMON: Because of the sex.

JEFF: Did I tell you that, too?

SIMON: No, you told her that, once or twice, in front of me.

JEFF: Christ, what a bloody swine of a fool I was. [*Pours himself another drink*] Well, now I'm suffering for it, aren't I? Listen, a few months ago I bumped into her in Oxford Street. I hadn't given her a thought in all that time, and suddenly there we were, face to face, looking at each other. For a full minute just looking. And do you know something, she cried. And I felt as if we were— Christ, you know—still married. But in the very first days of it, when we couldn't keep our hands off each other. In a matter of minutes.

SIMON: Minutes?

JEFF: Minutes. Bloody minutes. All over each other.

SIMON: In *Oxford* Street.

JEFF: I'll tell you—I put my hand out, very slowly, and stroked her cheek. The tears were running down, her mouth was trembling— and she took my hand and pressed it against her cheek. Then I took her to Nick's flat—he's still in hospital by the way.

SIMON: Really? I didn't know he'd gone in.

JEFF: They're trying aversion therapy this time, but it won't do any good. He's so bloody addictive that he'll come out hooked on the cure and still stay hooked on the gin, poor sod. Saline chasers. Anyway, I took her to Nick's, and had her, and had her, and had her. Christ! And when she left what do you think I did?

SIMON: Slept, I should think.

JEFF: I cried, that's what I did. Didn't want her to leave me, you see. I'm in love with her. I think I love her. And since then there have been times when I've thought I even liked her. Well?

SIMON: Well, Jeff, that's marvellous. Really marvellous.

JEFF: Oh, yes, bloody marvellous to discover that you want to marry your ex-wife.

SIMON: But why ever not? It just confirms that you were right the first time. Why not marry her?

JEFF: [*Taking another drink*] Because she's got a new bloody husband, that's why. In fact not so new, five years old. A bloody don in Cambridge called Manfred. Christ knows why he had to go and *marry* her!

SIMON: Perhaps he likes sex, too.

JEFF: According to Gwen he likes TV situation comedies, football matches, wrestling, comic books, horror films and sadistic thrillers, but not sex.

SIMON: What does he teach?

JEFF: Moral sciences.

SIMON: Then there's your answer. Philosophers have a long tradition of marrying stupid women, from Socrates on. They think it clever. Does she love him?

JEFF: Of course she does, she loves everyone. But she loves me most. Except for their bloody child. She bloody dotes on the bloody child.

SIMON: Oh. How old is it?

JEFF: Two—three—four—that sort of age.

SIMON: Boy or girl?

JEFF: Can't really tell. The one time I saw it, through my car window, it was trotting into its nursery school with its arm over its face, like a mobster going to the grand jury.

SIMON: Haven't you asked Gwen which it is?

JEFF: Yes, but only to show interest. Anyway, what does it matter, what matters is she won't leave Manfred because of it. She's *my* wife, not his, I had her first, and she admits as much, she'll always be mine, but all I get of her is two goes a week when I drive up to Cambridge—Tuesdays and Thursdays in the afternoon when Manfred's conducting seminars. In the rooms of some smartie-boots theologian.

SIMON: [*Pacing up and down*] Do you mean Manfred conducts his seminars in the rooms of some smartie-boots theologian or you have Gwen in the rooms of some smartie-boots theologian?

JEFF: I have Gwen there. He's a friend of Manfred's, you see.

SIMON: So Manfred's asked him to let you use his rooms?

JEFF: Oh, no, Manfred doesn't know anything about it. Or about me. No, smartie-boots seems to have some idea that it's part of his job to encourage what he calls sin. Oh, Christ, you know the type, a squalid little Anglican queen of a pimp, the little sod. Turns my stomach. [*Adds more Scotch*] Christ, you know, Simon, you want to know something about me?

SIMON: What? [*Sinks into an armchair*]

JEFF: I'm English, yes, English to my marrow's marrow. After years of buggering about as a cosmopolitan literateur, going to PEN conferences in Warsaw, hob-nobbing with Frog poets and Eyetye essayists, German novelists and Greek composers, I suddenly realise I hate the lot of them. Furthermore I detest women, love men, loathe queers. D'you know when I'm really at bloody peace with myself? When I'm caught in a traffic jam on an English road, under an English heaven—somewhere between London and Cambridge, on my way to Gwen, on my way back from her, rain sliding down the window, engine humming, dreaming—dreaming of what's past or is to come. Wrapped in the anticipation or the memory, no, the anticipation *of* the memory. [*Pause*] Oh, Christ—it's my actual bloody opinion that this sad little, bloody little country of ours is finished at last. Bloody finished at last. Yes, it truly is bloody well actually finished at last. I mean that. Had the VAT man around the other day. That's what we get now instead of the muffin man. I remember the muffin men, I'm old enough to remember the muffin men. Their bells and smells and lighting of the lamps—do you remember? Sometimes I even remember hansom cabs and crinoline, the music halls and Hobbes and Sutcliffe . . . [*Smiles*] Or the memory of the anticipation, I suppose. Stu Lampwith. Christ, the bugger! [*Pause*] Well, Christ—I suppose I'd better go and write my piece. [*He gets to his feet*] Did I tell you what that cold-hearted bitch said last night, in bed? Christ!

SIMON: Who?

JEFF: What?

SIMON: What cold-hearted bitch?

JEFF: Davina. [*Takes another Scotch*]

SIMON: Davina?

JEFF: You don't know about Davina?

SIMON: [*Wearily*] No.

JEFF: You haven't met her?

SIMON: No, no—I don't think—

JEFF: But, Christ, I've got to tell you about bitch Davina!

SIMON: Why?

JEFF: Because she is actually and completely the most utterly and totally— [*Lifts his hand. There is a ring at the doorbell*] What?

SIMON: Just a minute, Jeff. [*Goes to the door, opens it*]

DAVINA: Hello, is Jeff here, by any chance?

[JEFF *groans in recognition and sits down on the sofa*]

SIMON: Yes, yes he is. Come in.

[DAVINA *enters.* JEFF *ignores her*]

DAVINA: I'm Davina Saunders.

SIMON: I'm Simon Hench.

DAVINA: I know.

[*There is a pause*]

SIMON: Would you like a drink?

DAVINA: Small gin and bitters, please.

[SIMON *goes across to the drinks table*]

JEFF: How did you know I was here?

DAVINA: You said you would be.

JEFF: Why did I tell you?

DAVINA: Because I asked you.

JEFF: But why did I tell you? Because you see, I wanted a quiet conversation with my friend, Simon, you see.

DAVINA: You're all right then, are you?

JEFF: What?

[*A pause.* SIMON *brings* DAVINA *her drink*]

DAVINA: How did the interview go?

JEFF: All right.

DAVINA: What's he like?

JEFF: Who?

DAVINA: Bugger Lampwith.

JEFF: O.K.

DAVINA: What's O.K. about him?

JEFF: He's all right.

DAVINA: Good.

JEFF: What do you mean, good?

DAVINA: That he's all right. [*Sits down*]

JEFF: Well, what d'you want me to say, you follow me across bloody London, you turn up when I'm having a private bloody conversation with my old friend Simon, you're scarcely in the room before you ask me whether I'm drunk—

DAVINA: As a matter of sober precision, I did not ask you whether you were drunk. I asked you whether you were all right.

JEFF: Then as a matter of drunken precision, no, I'm not all right, I'm drunk.

DAVINA: That's surprising, as with you being all right and being drunk are usually precisely synonymous.

JEFF: But now you're here, aren't you, and that alters everything, doesn't it?

DAVINA: Does it?

JEFF: I thought you were going to spend the morning at the British Bloody Museum. I thought we'd agreed not to see each other for a day or two, or even a year or two—

[*There is a pause*]

SIMON: What are you doing at the BM, some research?

JEFF: That's what she's doing. On Major Bloody Barttelot. Got the idea from *my* review of that Life of Stanley—naturally.

SIMON: Really, and who is Major Bloody Barttelot?

DAVINA: Major Barttelot went with Stanley to the Congo, was left in a camp to guard the Rear Column, and ended up flogging, shooting, and even, so the story goes, eating the natives.

JEFF: Pleasant work for a woman, eh?

SIMON: Major Barttelot was a *woman?*

DAVINA: He was an English gentleman. Although he did find it pleasant work from what I've discovered, yes.

SIMON: Really? And are you planning a book?

JEFF: Of course she is, cannibalism, sadism, doing down England all at the same time, how can it miss? Why do you think she's on to it?

SIMON: I must say it sounds quite fascinating. Who's your publisher?

DAVINA: I haven't got one yet.

JEFF: Is that what summoned you away from the BM, the chance of drawing up a contract with my old friend, the publisher Simon? [Refills his glass]

DAVINA: Actually, I haven't been to the BM this morning. I've been on the telephone. And what summoned me here was first that I wanted to give you your key back. [Throws it over to him]

JEFF: [Makes no attempt to catch it] Thank you.

DAVINA: And secondly to tell you about the telephone call.

JEFF: What? Who was it?

DAVINA: Your ex-wife's husband. Manfred.

JEFF: What did he want?

DAVINA: You.

JEFF: Why?

DAVINA: He wanted you to know the contents of Gwendoline's suicide letter.

JEFF: [After a pause] What? Gwendoline—what—Gwen's dead!

SIMON: Good God!

DAVINA: No.

JEFF: But she tried—tried to commit suicide?

DAVINA: Apparently.

JEFF: What do you mean apparently, you mean she failed?

DAVINA: Oh, I'd say she succeeded. At least to the extent that Manfred was hysterical, I had a wastefully boring morning on the telephone, and you look almost sober. What more could she expect from a mere bid, after all?

JEFF: For Christ sake, what happened, what actually happened?

DAVINA: Well, Manfred's narrative was a trifle rhapsodic.

JEFF: But you said there was a letter.

DAVINA: He only read out the opening sentences—he was too embarrassed by them to go on.

JEFF: Embarrassed by what?

DAVINA: Oh, Gwendoline's epistolary style, I should think. It was rather shaming.

JEFF: Look, where is she?

DAVINA: In that hospital in Cambridge probably. And if you're thinking of going up there, you should reflect that Manfred is looking forward to beating you to a pulp. A *bloody* pulp was his phrase, and unlike yourself he seems to use the word literally, rather than for rhetorical effect or as drunken punctuation. I like people who express themselves limpidly [*To* SIMON] under stress, don't you?

JEFF: [*Throws his drink at her, splashing her blouse, etc.*] Is that limpid enough for you?

DAVINA: No, tritely theatrical, as usual. But if you're absolutely determined to go, and you might as well because what else have you to do? I advise you not to drive. Otherwise you may have to make do with one of the hospitals *en route*.

SIMON: Yes, you really shouldn't drive, Jeff . . .

[JEFF *turns, goes out, left, slamming the door. There is a pause*]

I'll get you something to wipe your shirt—

DAVINA: Don't bother, it's far too wet. But another drink please. [*Hands him her glass*]

SIMON: Of course.
[*Takes it, goes to the drinks table.*
DAVINA *takes off her shirt and throws it over a chair. She is bra-less. She goes to the large wall mirror, and dries herself with a handkerchief from her bag.*
SIMON *turns with the drink, looks at* DAVINA, *falters slightly, then brings her her drink*]

DAVINA: God, what a stupid man, don't you think?

SIMON: Well, a bit excitable at times, perhaps.

DAVINA: No, stupid really, and in an all-round way. You know, when I was at Oxford one used to take his articles quite seriously —not very seriously but quite. But now of course one sees that his facility, though it may pass in the Arts pages as intelligence and originality, was something merely cultivated in late adolescence for the examination halls. He hasn't developed, in fact his Gwendoline syndrome makes it evident that he's regressed. Furthermore his drunken bravado quickly ceases to be amusing, on top of which he's a fourth-rate fuck.

SIMON: Oh, well, perhaps he's kind to animals.

DAVINA: [*Sitting on the sofa*] To think I thought he might be of some use to me. But of course he's out of the habit, if he was ever in it, of talking to women who like to think and therefore talk concisely, for whom intelligence does actually involve judgement, and for whom judgement concludes in discrimination. Hence the appeal, I suppose, of a pair of tits from which he can dangle, with closed eyes and infantile gurglings. Especially if he has to get to them furtively, with a sense of not being allowed. Yes, stupid, don't you agree?

SIMON: Did you really go to Oxford?

DAVINA: Came down two years ago, why?

SIMON: From your style you sound more as if you went to Cambridge.

DAVINA: Anyway, he's nicely gone, you will admit, and four bad weeks have been satisfactorily concluded.

SIMON: Aren't you a little worried about him, though?

DAVINA: Why should I be?

SIMON: Well, Manfred did threaten to beat him to a bloody pulp, after all. And it may not be an idle boast. Men whose wives attempt suicide because of other men sometimes become quite animated, even if they are moral scientists.

DAVINA: Oh, I think the wretched Manfred will be more bewildered than belligerent. I composed that fiction between Great Russell Street and here. Of course I didn't know until I met his glassy gaze and received his boorish welcome whether I was actually going to work it through. It was quite thrilling, don't you think?

SIMON: You mean, Gwendoline didn't try to commit suicide?

DAVINA: Surely you don't imagine that *that* complacent old cow would attempt even an attempted suicide?

SIMON: Why did you do it?

DAVINA: Spite of course. Well, he told me he wanted to bring it all to a climax, although he wanted no such thing of course, prolonged and squalid messes that lead least of all to climaxes being his method, so my revenge has been to provide him with one that should be exactly in character—prolonged, squalid and utterly messy even by Cambridge standards, don't you think? *You're* married, aren't you? To Beth, isn't it?

SIMON: That's right.

DAVINA: I've only just realised she isn't here, is she?

SIMON: Well, I suppose that's better than just realising she was, isn't it?

DAVINA: I'd like to have met her. I've heard a great deal about you both, you mainly, of course. Are you two as imperturbably, not to say implacably *married* as he and everyone else says?

SIMON: I hope so.

DAVINA: And that you've never been unfaithful to Beth, at least as far as Jeff knows.

SIMON: Certainly never that far.

DAVINA: Don't you even fancy other women?

SIMON: [*Sits in the armchair*] My not sleeping with other women has absolutely nothing to do with not fancying them. Although I do make a particular point of not sleeping with women I don't fancy.

DAVINA: That's meant for me, is it?

SIMON: Good God, not at all.

DAVINA: You mean you do fancy me?

SIMON: I didn't mean that either.

DAVINA: But do you fancy me?

SIMON: Yes.

DAVINA: But you don't like me?

SIMON: No.

DAVINA: Ah, then do you fancy me *because* you don't like me? Some complicated set of manly mechanisms of that sort, is it?

SIMON: No, very simple ones that Jeff, for instance, would fully appreciate. I fancy you because of your breasts, you see. I'm revolted by your conversation and appalled by your behaviour. I think you're possibly the most egocentrically unpleasant woman I've ever met, but I have a yearning for your breasts. I'd like to dangle from them too, with my eyes closed and doubtless emitting infantile gurglings. Furthermore they look deceptively hospitable.

DAVINA: If they look deceptively hospitable, they're deceiving you. [*Comes over and sits on the arm of his chair*] You're very welcome to a nuzzle. [*Pause*] Go on, then. And then we'll see what *you* can do. [SIMON *sits, hesitating for a moment, then gets up, gets* DAVINA's *shirt, hands it to her*] Because of Beth?

SIMON: This is her house, as much as mine. It's *our* house, don't you see?

DAVINA: Fidelity means so much to you?

SIMON: Let's say rather more to me than a suck and a fuck with the likes of you. So, comes to that, does Jeff.

DAVINA: Yes, well I suppose that's to be expected in a friend of his. He doesn't begin to exist and nor do you.

SIMON: That's excellent. Because I haven't the slightest intention of letting you invent me.

DAVINA: And what about my Barttelot book?

SIMON: There I'm sure we shall understand each other. If it's any good, I shall be delighted to publish it. And if you've any sense, and you've got a hideous sight too much, you'll be delighted to let me. I shall give you the best advance available in London, arrange an excellent deal with an American publisher, and I shall see that it's edited to your advantage as well as ours. If it's any good.

DAVINA: That means more to me than being sucked at and fucked by the likes of you.

[*They smile.* DAVINA *turns and goes out.*
SIMON, *with the air of a man celebrating, picks up the keys and glasses, puts them away. Makes to go to the gramophone, stops, goes to the telephone answering machine*]

SIMON: [*Records*] 348-0720, Simon Hench on an answering machine. I shall be otherwise engaged for the rest of the day. If you have a message for either myself or for Beth could you please wait until after the high-pitched tone, and if that hasn't put you off, speak. Thank you.

[*Puts the button down, then goes over to the gramophone, bends over to put a record on.*
DAVE *enters,* SIMON *freezes, turns*]

DAVE: She didn't show.

SIMON: What?

DAVE: Suzy. My girl. She didn't show. You know what I'd like to do now, I'd like to get really pissed, that's what I'd like to do.

SIMON: I don't blame you, and furthermore, why don't you? You'll still catch the pubs if you hurry—

DAVE: Well, I'm a bit short, you see.

SIMON: But didn't you have a few pounds—

DAVE: Yeah, well, I spent those.

SIMON: Oh, what on?

DAVE: Usual sort of stuff.

SIMON: Well, then, let me. [*Pause*] I've got just the thing. [*Goes to the drinks table, fishes behind, takes out a bottle of Cyprus sherry*] Here. Go on, one of Beth's students gave it to her—it's yours. [*Hands it to* DAVE] A Cyprus sherry. Nice and sweet. Now you settle down in some dark corner, with a receptacle by your side, and forget yourself completely. That's what I'd want to do if I were you. [*Points him towards the door*]

> [DAVE *goes out.* SIMON *turns back to the hi-fi. Voices in the hall*]

DAVE: [*Opens the door*] Bloke here for you. [*Withdraws*]

SIMON: What? [*Turns*]

WOOD: [*Enters*] Mr. Hench?

SIMON: Yes.

WOOD: Can you spare me a few minutes? My name is Wood. Bernard Wood.

SIMON: [*As if recognising the name, then checks it*] Oh?

WOOD: It means something to you, then?

SIMON: No, just an echo. Of Birnam Wood, it must be, coming to Dunsinane. No, I'm very sorry, it doesn't. Should it?

WOOD: You don't recognise me either, I take it?

SIMON: No, I'm afraid not. Should I?

WOOD: We went to school together.

SIMON: Did we really, Wundale?

WOOD: Yes. Wundale. I was all of three years ahead of you, but I recall you. It should be the other way around, shouldn't it? But then *you* were very distinctive.

SIMON: Was I really, in what way?

WOOD: [*After a little pause*] Oh, as the sexy little boy that all the glamorous boys of my year slept with.

SIMON: [*After a pause*] But you didn't?

WOOD: No.

SIMON: Well, I do hope you haven't come to make good, because it's too late, I'm afraid. The phase is over, by some decades. [*Little pause, then with an effort at courtesy*] I'm sure I would have remembered you, though, if we had slept together.

WOOD: Well, perhaps your brother Stephen, isn't it? would remember me as we were in the same year, how is he?

SIMON: Oh, very well.

WOOD: Married, with children?

SIMON: Yes.

WOOD: And you're married?

SIMON: Yes.

WOOD: Good. Children?

SIMON: No.

WOOD: Why not?

SIMON: There's isn't enough room. What about you?

WOOD: Oh, as you might expect of someone like me. Married with children.

[*There is a pause*]

SIMON: Well . . . um—you said there was something—?

WOOD: Yes, there is. It's of a rather personal—embarrassing nature.

[*Pause*]

SIMON: [*Unenthusiastically*] Would a drink help?

WOOD: Oh, that's very kind. Some sherry would be nice, if you have it.

SIMON: Yes, I have it.

WOOD: Then some sherry, if I may.

SIMON: Yes, you may. [*Pours* WOOD *a sherry*]

WOOD: My many thanks. Your very good health. I thought you might have heard my name the day before yesterday.

SIMON: Oh, in what context?

WOOD: From my girl, Joanna. In your office, at about six in the evening.

SIMON: Joanna?

WOOD: She came to see you about getting work in publishing. She's only just left art school, but you were kind enough to give her an appointment.

SIMON: Oh, yes, yes. I do remember a girl—I'm terrible about names, a nice girl, I thought.

WOOD: Thank you. How did your meeting go? Just between us?

SIMON: Well, I thought she was really quite promising.

WOOD: But you didn't make her any promises.

SIMON: Well, no, I'm afraid I couldn't. What work of hers she showed me struck me as a—a trifle over-expressive for our needs. [*Pause*] Why, is her version of our, um, talk different, in any way?

WOOD: She hasn't said anything about it at all.

SIMON: I see. And you've come to me to find out about her potential?

WOOD: Not really, no. I've come to ask you if you know where she is.

SIMON: Have you lost her, then?

WOOD: She hasn't been home since I dropped her off at your office.

SIMON: Well, I'm very sorry, but I haven't seen her since she left my office.

WOOD: I only have one rule with her, that she come home at night. Failing that, that at least she let me know where or with whom she is spending the night. Failing that, that at least she telephone me first thing in the morning. Could I be more unreasonably reasonable? So before doing the rounds among her pals, from Ladbroke Grove to Earls Court, I thought it might be worth finding out from you if she let anything slip about her plans.

SIMON: Nothing that I can remember.

WOOD: She didn't mention any particular friend or boyfriend?

SIMON: Just the usual references to this drip and that drip in the modern manner. Look, from what one makes out of today's youth, isn't it likely that she'll come home when she feels in the mood or wants a good meal, eh?

WOOD: I suppose so.

SIMON: I can quite understand your worry—

WOOD: Can you? No, I don't think you can.

SIMON: No, perhaps not. But I really don't see how I can help you any further.

WOOD: Did you have it off with her?

SIMON: What? *What?*

WOOD: Did you have it off with her?

SIMON: Look, Wood, whatever your anxiety about your daughter, I really don't think, old chap, that you should insinuate yourself into people's homes and put a question like that to them. I mean, good God, you can't possibly expect me to dignify it with an answer, can you?

WOOD: In other words, you did.

SIMON: [*After a long pause*] In other words, I'm afraid I did. Yes. Sorry, old chap.

CURTAIN

ACT TWO

Curtain up on exactly same scene, WOOD *and* SIMON *in exactly the same postures. There is a pause.*

WOOD: Tell me, does your wife know you do this sort of thing?

SIMON: Why, are you going to tell her?

WOOD: Oh, I'm not a sneak. Beside, Joanna would never forgive me. She'd have told me herself, you know. She always does. She thinks it's good for me to know what she and her pals get up to. Do you do it often? [*Smiling*]

SIMON: Reasonably often. Or unreasonably, depending on one's point of view.

WOOD: And always with girls of my Joanna's age?

SIMON: There or thereabouts, yes.

WOOD: Because you don't love your wife?

SIMON: No, because I do. I make a point, you see, of not sleeping with friends, or the wives of friends, or acquaintances even. No one in our circle. Relationships there can be awkward enough—

WOOD: It's a sort of code, is it?

SIMON: No doubt it seems a rather squalid one, to you.

WOOD: So that's why you chose my Joanna, is it?

SIMON: I didn't really choose her, you know. She came into my office, and we looked at her work, and talked—

WOOD: Until everybody else had gone. You decided, in other words, that she was an easy lay. And wouldn't make any fuss, afterwards.

SIMON: I also realized that I couldn't possibly do her any harm.

WOOD: What about the clap? [*Pause*] I think I have a right to know.

SIMON: I keep some pills at my office.

WOOD: So your post-coital period together was passed gobbling down anti-VD pills.

SIMON: One doesn't exactly gobble them—one swallows them, as one might digestive tablets.

WOOD: What about going back to your wife, reeking of sex?

SIMON: What?

WOOD: What do you do about the stench of your adulteries?

SIMON: I confess I find this enquiry into method rather depressing. I'd willingly settle for a burst of parental outrage—

WOOD: And I'd far rather satisfy my curiosity. Won't you please tell me?

SIMON: Very well. I stop off at my squash club, play a few points with the professional, then have a shower.

WOOD: But you don't suffer from any guilt afterwards? No post-coital distress, no angst or even embarrassment?

SIMON: Not unless this counts as afterwards.

WOOD: So really, only your sexual tastes have changed, your moral organism has survived intact since the days when you were that lucky sod, the Wundale Tart?

SIMON: Look, are you here because I slept around at thirteen, with the attractive boys of your year, or because I sleep around with attractive girls of your daughter's generation, at thirty-nine. Good God, Wood, I'm beginning to find something frankly Mediterranean in this obsession with your child's sex-life and mine—after all, let's face it, in the grand scheme of things, nothing much has happened, and in the Anglo-Saxon scheme of things, your daughter's well over the age of consent. That may sound brutal, but it's also true.

WOOD: Except in one important point. She's not my daughter.

SIMON: What? What is she then?

WOOD: My [*Hesitates*] fiancée.

SIMON: Is it worth my saying sorry over again, or will my earlier apologies serve. [*Pause*] But I thought you said her name was Wood—

WOOD: Yes.

SIMON: And your name is Wood.

WOOD: Yes, I changed my name as she refuses to change hers, and won't marry me.

SIMON: In that case you're not Wood of Wundale.

WOOD: No, I'm Strapley—Strapley of Wundale. Known as Wanker Strapley. Now do you remember me?

SIMON: Strapley—Strapley, Wanker Strapley. No.

WOOD: Well, your brother certainly would. He was known as Armpits Hench. We were two of a kind, in that we were both considered drips—what was the Wundale word for drip?

SIMON: I really can't remember.

WOOD: It was "plop."

SIMON: Plop.

WOOD: Those of us who were called it are more likely to remember it than those of you who called us it. Plop. Yes, I'm a plop, Hench. Whom one can now define, after so many years ploppily lived, as a chap who goes straight from masturbation to matrimony to monogamy.

SIMON: Oh, now there I think you're underestimating yourself. After all you have a wife, didn't you say, and now Joanna—

WOOD: I haven't got my wife any more. I doubt if I've got Joanna any more. But it's only appropriate that *you* should be the last common factor in our relationship. The first time I set eyes on her she reminded me of you.

SIMON: Where was that?

WOOD: At our local amateur theatricals. Joanna was playing in *The Winslow Boy*. She came on the stage in grey flannel bags, a white shirt and starched collar. She walked with a modest boy's gait, her eyes were wide with innocent knowledge. So did you walk down the Wundale Cloisters, that first year of yours. So I watched you then as I watched her. And there on my one side, were my two poor old sons, who've never reminded me of anyone but myself. And on the other, my poor old wife, the female plop, who from that second on ceased even to remind me that we shared a ploppy past. The years we'd spent together brooding over her mastoids, my haemorrhoids, and the mortgage on our maisonette, watching over our boys' sad little defeats, their failure to get into Wundale, their scrabbling for four O levels and then two A levels, their respective roles as twelfth man and scorer—they haven't even the competitiveness for sibling rivalry, poor old boys—all seemed, it all seemed such a waste, such a waste.

SIMON: But still you did succeed, to some extent at least, in breaking free. And you did succeed, to some extent I take it, with Joanna—so not altogether a case for predestination, when you think of it.

WOOD: Free meals, lots of gifts, little loans by the usual ploppy techniques of obligation and dependence—not that she felt dependent or obliged. She took what I offered and then asked for more. A generous nature. Did she get anything from you?

SIMON: She didn't ask for anything.

WOOD: Just as you never asked for anything from those boys—Higgens, Hornby, Darcy.

SIMON: It's true that Darcy was very kind with his truck, but I hope I never took it as payment, nor did he offer it as such.

WOOD: [*Pause*] What was it like with Joanna?

SIMON: Well, it was, um, I'm sure you know—she's a very uninhibited um—

WOOD: It was, then, satisfactory?

SIMON: Well, as these things go.

WOOD: They don't for me. I'm incapacitated by devotion.

SIMON: But you live together?

WOOD: She allows me to share the flat I've leased for her. We have different rooms—I sometimes sit on the side of her bed when she's in it. More often when she's not.

SIMON: You're obviously in the grip of a passion almost Dantesque in the purity of its hopelessness. You know, I really feel quite envious—for you every moment has its significance, however tortured, I just have to get by on my small pleasures and easy accommodations, my daily contentments—

WOOD: So she actually talks of me as a drip, does she?

SIMON: The ignorance of youth. Drips have neither your capacity for ironic self-castigation, nor more importantly your gift for the futile grand gesture.

WOOD: If she comes back, do you know what she'll do? She'll tell me about the boys she's slept with, the adults she's conned, the pot she's smoked. She'll tell me what a good time she had with you on your office floor—

SIMON: Sofa, actually.

WOOD: If she comes back. And I'll sit listening and yearning and just occasionally I'll soothe myself with the thought that one day she'll be dead, or even better old and unwanted and desperate— what I resent most about you, little Hench, is the way you seem to have gone on exactly as you promised you would at Wundale. If life catches up with everybody at the end, why hasn't it with you?

SIMON: But I haven't got to the end yet, thank God. I'm sure it will eventually.

WOOD: Sweet little Hench from Wundale, who picks off my Jo in an hour at his office, munches down a few pills, and then returns, without a worry in his head, the whole experience simply showered off, to his wife, who is doubtless quite attractive enough—is she?

SIMON: I find her quite attractive enough for me. Though taste in these matters—

WOOD: I'd like to kill you, Hench. Yes—kill you!

STEPHEN: [*Enters through the kitchen*] Si— [*Sees* WOOD] Oh, sorry, I didn't realise . . . Good God, it is, isn't it? Old Strapley, from Wundale?

WOOD: The name's Wood.

STEPHEN: Oh, sorry. You look rather like a chap who used to be at school with us, or rather me, in my year, Strapley.

WOOD: Really? What sort of chap was he?

STEPHEN: Oh, actually, a bit of what we used to call a plop, wasn't he, Simon? So you're quite lucky not to be Strapley who almost certainly had a pretty rotten future before him. [*Laughs*]

WOOD: Thank you for the sherry. [*Turns quickly, goes out*]

SIMON: Not at all.

STEPHEN: I hope I haven't driven him off.

SIMON: Mmmm. Oh, no, it's not you that's driven him off.

STEPHEN: What did he want?

SIMON: He was looking for somebody I once resembled. A case of mistaken identity, that's all.

STEPHEN: Well, if he had been Strapley, he'd hardly have changed at all, except that he's a quarter of a century older. Poor old Wanker Strapley. [*Sits down. There is a pause*] Well, Si, you were quite right, of course.

SIMON: Mmmm?

STEPHEN: I got it.

SIMON: Got what?

STEPHEN: The Assistant Headmastership.

SIMON: Oh. Oh, good! [*Pause*] Goody.

STEPHEN: You can imagine how stunned I was. I was so depressed when I got home, not only because I thought I'd lost the appointment, but because of that friend of yours—

SIMON: What friend?

STEPHEN: Golding. Jeff Golding. That he didn't even remember me, let alone what I'd threatened to do to him—and I could hear the children quarrelling in the garden, the baby crying in her cot, and when I sat down in the sitting-room there was a piece in *The Times* on the phasing out of public schools and private health, lumped together, and it all seemed—well! Then Teresa called out. I couldn't face her, you know how lowering her optimism can be —but I managed to drag myself into the kitchen—she had her back to me, at the oven, cooking up some nut cutlets for the children's lunch—and she said: "Greetings, Assistant Headmaster of Amplesides." Yes, Headmaster's wife had phoned while I was here, isn't that ironic? I could hardly believe it. So. I crammed down a nut cutlet—

SIMON: What was it like?

STEPHEN: What?

SIMON: The nut cutlet.

STEPHEN: Oh, it was from one of Headmaster's wife's recipes. They're semi-vegetarian, you know.

SIMON: What did it *taste* like?

STEPHEN: Rather disgusting. But she's going to give us some more recipes if we like this one. Perhaps they'll be better.

SIMON: But you didn't like this one.

STEPHEN: [*Pause*] Aren't you pleased or even interested in my news?

SIMON: Of course I am.

STEPHEN: In spite of thinking MacDonald the better man? Well, you needn't worry about him, he's been offered a job, too. As head of sixth form English.

SIMON: But you're head of sixth form English.

STEPHEN: Not any more. Headmaster reckons that with my new responsibilities I should step down from some of my teaching. I shall be head of fifth form English.

SIMON: Ah, fewer hours then.

STEPHEN: Actually more hours, but at fifth form level.

SIMON: Ah, less celebration. That's even better. So—[*Loses thread, picks it up*] so justice has been done to two excellent candidates.

STEPHEN: I shall still be senior to MacDonald, you know.

SIMON: Isn't his name MacGregor?

STEPHEN: Yes. [*Little pause. Ironically*] Thanks, Si.

SIMON: What for?

STEPHEN: Sharing my triumph with me.

SIMON: Why don't you—have a drink.

STEPHEN: No, thank you. Headmaster's asked Teresa to ask me to look in after lunch for a celebration glass.

SIMON: Oh. Of what?

STEPHEN: Pansy wine, I expect, as that's their favourite tipple.

SIMON: [*After a pause*] Do they make it themselves?

STEPHEN: Headmaster's wife's aunt's husband does.

SIMON: Does he? [*Little pause*] What's it like?

STEPHEN: You know what it's like.

SIMON: No, I don't. What's it like?

STEPHEN: Why do you want to know what it's like?

SIMON: Because I can't imagine what it's like, I suppose.

STEPHEN: Oh, yes, you can. Oh, yes, you can.

[*Turns, goes out through the kitchen.* DAVE *enters left. He's slightly drunk. There is a pause*]

DAVE: [*Swaying slightly*] She's come. She's upstairs. She came all by herself.

SIMON: Who?

DAVE: That girl. Suzy. She dropped in for a cup of Nescafé.

SIMON: That's very good news, Dave. But should you, now you've got her, leave her to have it all by herself? She sounds a highly strung creature—

DAVE: Yeah, well, the only thing is, I'm out of Nescafé.

SIMON: Oh.

DAVE: Well, have you got any, man?

SIMON: No, I'm sorry, we don't drink it.

DAVE: Anything else?

SIMON: Nothing at all like Nescafé, I'm afraid.

DAVE: What, no coffee at all?

SIMON: Oh, yes, we've got coffee. But we use beans, a grinder, and a rather complicated filter process. Metal holders, paper cones—

DAVE: That'll do. Is it in the kitchen? [*He moves towards kitchen*]

SIMON: Actually, it's rather a precious set.

DAVE: What? [*Returning*]

SIMON: It's one of those few things I feel rather specially about.

DAVE: You mean you've got something against lending it to me?

SIMON: Not at all. The beans are in a sealed bag in an airtight tin—

DAVE: Oh, yes, you have. I can tell by your—your tone.

SIMON: My tone? Oh, come now, Dave, that's only one possible gloss of my tone. No, you take the grinder, take the filters, the jug, the paper cones and the metal holders, and the coffee beans which come from a small shop in Holborn that keeps uncertain hours and can therefore be easily replaced with a great deal of difficulty, and don't addle your head with questions about my tone, good God! [*Pause*] Go ahead. [*Wearily*] Please.

DAVE: No, thanks. No, thank you! Because you do mind all right, you bloody mind all right.

SIMON: No, I don't.

DAVE: No, you don't, no, you don't bloody mind, do you—why should you, you've got it all already, haven't you? Machines for making coffee, a table covered with booze, crates of wine in your cellar, all the nosh you want, all the books you want, all the discs, the best hi-fi on the bloody market, taxis to work every morning, taxis home in the evening, a whole bloody house just for you and your sexy little wife—oh, you don't bloody mind anything you don't, what's there for you to mind, you shit you!

SIMON: Now that's not quite fair, Dave. It's not really a whole house, you know, since we converted the top floor at considerable expense and turned it over to you at an inconsiderable rent which you don't pay anyway. But then I don't mind that either.

DAVE: 'Course you bloody don't, why should you, you bloody like to run a pet, don't you, your very own special deserving case.

SIMON: I swear to you, Dave, I've never once thought of you as my pet or as a deserving case. If we'd wanted the former to occupy our upstairs flat we'd have got a monkey, and if we'd wanted the latter we'd have selected from among the unmarried mothers or the dispossessed old age pensioners. We thought quite hard about doing that, in fact.

DAVE: Then why didn't you?

SIMON: Because unmarried mothers mean babies, and babies mean nappies, and crying. While old age pensioners mean senility and eventual death.

DAVE: So I salve your bloody conscience without being a nuisance, eh? Right?

SIMON: Wrong. You salve my conscience by being a bloody nuisance. Your manners irritate me, your smell is unusually offensive, you're extremely boring, your sex-life is both depressing and disgusting, and you're a uniquely ungrateful cadge. But you really mustn't mind, because the point is that I don't, either. You have your one great value, that you run a poor third to recent births and imminent deaths.

DAVE: I'm not staying—I'm not staying—I'm not staying in the fucking top of your fucking house another fucking minute! You— you— [Makes as if to hit SIMON]

> [SIMON remains impassive, DAVE turns, goes out left. Noise of door slamming. SIMON closes door left. As he does so STEPHEN enters right]

STEPHEN: It's sugary and tastes of onions. And it's quite revolting, just as you imagine.

SIMON: Well, I did imagine it would be revolting and probably sugary, but it never occurred to me it would taste of onions. But you can't have come back to report on its flavour already, you've only just left.

STEPHEN: I've been sitting in the car, thinking.

SIMON: What about?

STEPHEN: You, and your sneers. Oh, I don't altogether blame you, but I wish—[Sits down, looks at SIMON] you'd had the guts to say it outright.

SIMON: Say what?

STEPHEN: That it's taken me twenty-four years to advance from Second Prefect of Wundale to Assistant Headmaster of Amplesides.

SIMON: [Sitting down] But that seems very respectable progress to me. At that rate you should make it to Eton, if it still exists, by your mid-fifties. And as that's what you want, why should I have a word to say against it?

STEPHEN: Nor against the way I'm doing it? My stuffing down nut cutlets, and herbal coffee and pansy wine. And then coming back for seconds.

SIMON: But you do rather more than eat the inedible and drink the undrinkable. You're among the best Junior Colts football managers in the country.

STEPHEN: You despise my job.

SIMON: You've a family to support.

STEPHEN: So you do despise my job, and despise me for doing it. Why don't you say it. That's all I'm asking you to do.

SIMON: But I don't want to say it! I can't remember when you were last as you've been today, or what I said then to make you feel any better. I wish I could, because that's what I'd like to say now.

STEPHEN: The last time I felt like this was eleven years ago, after Teresa had broken off our engagement, and you didn't say anything to make me feel any better. What you did say was that I was well out of it.

SIMON: Well, as you've been back in it for eleven years, you'll agree that it has little relevance now.

STEPHEN: It had little relevance then either. As I was desperately in love with her.

SIMON: Good God, all I probably meant, and I don't even remember saying it, was that if she didn't want to marry you then it was better to be out of it before the wedding.

STEPHEN: Oh, no, oh, no, all you meant was that *you* were relieved to be out of it.

SIMON: Out of what?

STEPHEN: Out of having for your sister-in-law a girl you thought tedious and unattractive. And still do. And still do.

SIMON: Look, Stephen, this is really rather eccentric, even in the English fratricidal tradition. First you hold it against me that I won't join you in abusing yourself, and then you hold it against me that not only did I fail to abuse your intended wife eleven years ago, but won't join you in abusing her now that she is your wife and has borne you seven children—

STEPHEN: Six children.

SIMON: Nearly seven.

STEPHEN: Nearly six.

SIMON: Well, straight after the sixth, it'll be nearly seven. [*He gets up*]

STEPHEN: Teresa's absolutely right about you. She always has been. You're just indifferent. Absolutely indifferent!

SIMON: In what sense? As a wine is indifferent, or prepositionally, as in, say, indifferent to—

STEPHEN: Imbeciles like Teresa. Go on, say it!

SIMON: But I don't want to say it.

STEPHEN: Not to me, no. But that's what you tell your clever-clever metropolitan Jeff Goldings, isn't it? That Teresa and I are imbeciles.

SIMON: I swear to you, Stephen, I've never told a soul.

STEPHEN: Answer me one question, Simon. *One* question! What have you got against having children?

SIMON: Well, Steve, in the first place there isn't enough room. In the second place they seem to start by mucking up their parents' lives, and then go on in the third place to muck up their own. In the fourth place it doesn't seem right to bring them into a world like this in the fifth place and in the sixth place I don't like them very much in the first place. O.K.

STEPHEN: And Beth? What about her?

SIMON: [*After a little pause*] Beth and I have always known what we're doing, thank you, Stephen.

STEPHEN: You think she's happy, do you?

SIMON: Yes, I do. And let's not let you say another word about her, because I don't want to hear it. Have you got that, Steve, *I don't want to hear it.*

STEPHEN: No, I'm sure you don't. I'm sure you don't. The last thing you want to hear is how unhappy she is.

SIMON: Steve!

STEPHEN: Well, she is! So unhappy that last week she came around to Teresa and sobbed her heart out!

SIMON: Steve!

STEPHEN: She's having an affair, Simon. An affair with that Ned whom you so much despise. *That's* how unhappy your happy Beth is.

[*There is a long pause*]

SIMON: With Ned. [*Pause*] Beth's having an affair with Ned? [*Pause*] Really? With Ned? Good God! [*Sits down*]

STEPHEN: It's time you knew.

SIMON: No, it isn't.

[*There is a pause*]

STEPHEN: I had to tell you.

SIMON: Now that's a different matter.

[*There is the sound of a door opening left.* BETH *enters*]

BETH: Hello. Hello, Stephen.

STEPHEN: Hello, Beth.

SIMON: [*Goes over, gives* BETH *a kiss*] You're back nice and early, aren't you?

BETH: Yes, I got an earlier train.

SIMON: Ah, that explains it. How was it, then, old Salisbury?

BETH: Old *Canterbury,* actually. Much as it ever was, except for the parts they've turned into new Canterbury.

SIMON: But the Cathedral's still there?

BETH: Although the French students were more interested in the new Marks and Spencers.

SIMON: And Ned?

BETH: Oh, he preferred the Cathedral.

STEPHEN: I really must be getting along. Headmaster will be wondering what's happening to me.

SIMON: Oh, but first you must tell Beth your news. [*There is a slight pause*] The Assistant Headmastership, Steve.

STEPHEN: Oh. Oh, yes. I got it.

BETH: Steve—how marvellous! [*Comes over, gives him a kiss*] Congratulations—Teresa must be thrilled!

STEPHEN: Yes, she is. I've had some black moments since the interview, but she was absolutely sure—and old Si jollied me along a bit this morning. It's all a great relief, more than anything. Well, I really must dash—see you both very soon—[*Goes towards the kitchen door*] Oh, by the way, Si—I was a bit carried away just now, spoke a lot of nonsense, don't know why I said it.

SIMON: Don't you?

STEPHEN: Yes, well I suppose I meant to hurt, but I didn't mean harm, if you see.

SIMON: Well, then that's fine, because no harm's been done. I didn't take it seriously.

STEPHEN: Good. [*Hesitates, turns, goes out*]

BETH: What did he say? [*Sits and lights a cigarette*]

SIMON: Actually I could hardly make out—he was in a post-success depression, I think, suddenly realising that what he's got can therefore no longer be striven for. He'll be all right the moment he sets his sights on a full Headmastership. Or Amplesides is abolished. Triumph or disaster—you know, like a drug. What about tea or coffee?

BETH: No, I've had some, thanks.

SIMON: Where?

BETH: On the train.

SIMON: Oh, then you're probably still trying to work out which it was.

BETH: Did you enjoy your Wagner?

SIMON: I enjoyed some things about it, very much. The picture on its cover for example, its glossy and circular blackness when unsheathed, its light balance—and if the sound is any good it'll be quite perfect.

BETH: You haven't managed to play it, then?

SIMON: Very nearly, very nearly. But what with Dave and Stephen, Jeff and Davina, the odd bod and sod, you know—

BETH: Oh, you poor thing, and you'd been looking forward to it all week.

SIMON: Still, one mustn't snatch at one's pleasures, nor overplan them it seems. [He puts the record away in its box]

BETH: [Pause] How was Jeff?

SIMON: Oh, in excellent form, really. He got drunk, threw his Scotch in his girl's face, dashed off to Cambridge where he's been having it off with his ex-wife, Gwynyth. Did you know Gwynyth, or was she a little before your time?

BETH: Isn't it Gwendoline?

SIMON: Yes, yes, Gwendoline. Anyway, usual sort of Jeff saga, quite droll in its way.

BETH: And what's his girl like?

SIMON: She's got good tits and a nasty sense of humour.

BETH: And did she try to get you to bed?

SIMON: She did.

BETH: And how did you get out of it?

SIMON: Rudely, I'm afraid, as she's on to rather a good book, from the sound of it. Ah, well—

BETH: Ah, well, you can play your records now, can't you?

SIMON: Oh, no. Wouldn't dream of it.

BETH: Why not?

SIMON: Well, for one thing, you hate Wagner.

BETH: Well, I'm going to have a bath.

SIMON: A four-hour bath?

BETH: Afterwards I've got to go along to the school—sort out the fares and docket them, that sort of thing.

SIMON: Ah! Well, in that case—

[SIMON *moves to hi-fi and takes out record.* BETH *rises, hesitates, and moves towards him*]

BETH: [*Stops, looks at* SIMON] Stephen told you, didn't he?

SIMON: Mmmm? Told me what?

BETH: About me. At least I hope he has.

SIMON: Why?

BETH: So I shan't have to tell you myself.

SIMON: You don't have to.

BETH: What?

SIMON: Tell me.

BETH: What?

SIMON: Tell me anything you don't want to tell me. Stephen said nothing of significance about anything.

BETH: But you see, I may not want to tell you, but I do want you to know.

SIMON: Why?

BETH: Because there's an important problem we shall have to discuss. And I want you to understand. [*Sits on sofa*]

SIMON: In my experience, the worst thing you can do to an important problem is discuss it. You know—[*Sitting down*]—I really do think this whole business of non-communication is one of the more poignant fallacies of our zestfully over-explanatory age. Most of us understand as much as we need to without having to be told —except old Dave, of course, now I thought he had quite an effective system, a tribute really to the way in which even the lowest amongst us can put our education (or lack of it, in Dave's case) and intelligence (or lack of it, in Dave's case) to serving our needs. He's done really remarkably well out of taking the metaphors of courtesy literally, as for example when he asks for a loan that is in fact a gift, and one replies, "Of course, Dave, no trouble, pay it back when you can." *But* this system completely collapses when he's faced with a plainly literal reply, as for example when he asks to borrow our coffee set, and he's told that it'll be lent with reluctance and one would like him to be careful with it. Weird, isn't it, he can take one's courteous metaphors literally, but he can't take one's literals literally, he translates them into metaphors for insults, and plans, I'm reasonably happy to inform you, to move out at once. So I've managed one useful thing today, after all. When we come to think of his replacement, let's narrow our moral vision slightly, and settle for a pair of respectably married and out of date homosexuals who still think they've something to hide. They'll leave us entirely alone, and we can congratulate ourselves on doing them a good turn. We'll have to raise the rent to just this side of exorbitant of course, or they'll smell something fishy, but we'll pass the money straight on to charities for the aged, unmarried mothers, that sort of thing and no one need be the wiser, what do you think?

BETH: In other words, you do know.

SIMON: In other words, can't we confine ourselves to the other words.

BETH: What did Stephen tell you, please, Simon.

SIMON: Nothing. Nothing, except for the odd detail, that I haven't known for a long time. So you see it's all right. Nothing's changed for the worst, though it might if we assume we have to talk about it.

BETH: [Long pause] How long have you known for?

SIMON: Oh—[Sighs] about ten months it would be roughly. [Pause] How long has it been going on for?

BETH: For about ten months, it would be. [Pause] How did you know?

SIMON: There's no point, Beth—

BETH: Yes, there is. Yes, there is. How did you know?

SIMON: Well, frankly, your sudden habit, after years of admirable conversational economy on such day-to-day matters as what you'd done today, of becoming a trifle prolix.

BETH: You mean you knew I was having an affair because I became boring?

SIMON: No, no, over-detailed, that's all, darling. And quite naturally, as you were anxious to account for stretches of time in which you assumed I *would* be interested if I knew how you'd *actually* filled them, if you see, so you sweetly devoted considerable effort and paradoxically imaginative skill to rendering them—for my sake I know—totally uninteresting. My eyes may have been glazed but my heart was touched.

BETH: Thank you. And is that all you had to go on?

SIMON: Well, you have doubled your bath routine. Time was, you took one immediately before going out for the day. These last ten months you've taken one immediately on return, too. [Pause] And once or twice you've addressed me, when in the twilight zone, with an unfamiliar endearment.

BETH: What was it?

SIMON: Foxy. [Little pause] At least, I took it to be an endearment. Is it?

BETH: Yes. I'm sorry.

SIMON: No, no, it's quite all right.

BETH: You haven't felt it's interfered with your sex-life, then?

SIMON: On the contrary. *Quite* the contrary. In fact there seems to have been an increased intensity in your—[*Gestures*] which I suppose in itself was something of a sign.

BETH: In what way?

SIMON: Well, guilt, would it be? A desire to make up—

BETH: [*After a pause*] And did you know it was Ned, too?

SIMON: Ned *too?* Oh, did I also know it was Ned? No, that was the little detail I mentioned Stephen did provide. Ned. There I *was* surprised.

BETH: Why?

SIMON: Oh, I don't know. Perhaps because—well, no offence to Ned, whom I've *always* as you know thought of as a very engaging chap, in his way, no offence to *you* either, come to think of it, I'd just imagined when you did have an affair it would be with someone of more—more—

BETH: What?

SIMON: Consequence. *Overt* consequence.

BETH: He's of consequence to me.

SIMON: And *that's* what matters, quite.

BETH: What did you mean, when?

SIMON: Mmmm?

BETH: *When* I had an affair, you said.

SIMON: A grammatical slip, that's all. And since the hypothesis is now a fact—

BETH: But you used the emphatic form—When I *did* have an affair —which implies that you positively assumed I'd have an affair. Didn't you?

SIMON: Well, given your nature, darling, and the fact that so many people do have them these days, I can't see any reason for being *bouleversé* now that you're having one, even with Ned, can I put it that way?

BETH: Given what about my nature?

SIMON: It's marvellously responsive—warm, a warm, responsive nature. And then I realised once we'd taken the decision not to have children,—and the fact that you work every day and therefore meet chaps—and pretty exotic ones too, from lithe young Spanish counts to experienced Japanese businessmen—not forgetting old Ned himself—it was only realistic—

BETH: From boredom, you mean. You know I'm having an affair because I'm boring, and you assumed I'd have one from boredom. That's why I'm in love with Ned, is it?

SIMON: I'm absolutely prepared to think of Ned as a very, very lovable fellow. I'm sure *his* wife loves him, why shouldn't mine.

BETH: You are being astonishingly hurtful.

SIMON: I don't want to be, I don't want to be! That's why I tried to avoid this conversation, darling.

BETH: You'd like to go back, would you, to where I came in, and pretend that I'd simply caught the early train from Salisbury, and here I was, old unfaithful Beth, back home and about to take her bath, as usual?

SIMON: Yes, I'd love to. [*Little pause*] I thought it was Canterbury.

BETH: It was neither. We spent the night in a hotel in Euston, and the morning in Ned's poky little office at the school, agonizing.

SIMON: Agonizing? Good God, did you really?

BETH: About whether we should give up everything to live together properly.

SIMON: Properly?

BETH: We want, you see, to be husband and wife to each other.

SIMON: Husband *and* wife to each other? Is Ned up to such double duty? And what did you decide?

BETH: Do you care?

SIMON: Yes.

BETH: His wife isn't well. She's been under psychiatric treatment for years. And his daughter is autistic.

SIMON: Oh. I'm sorry. I can quite see why he wants to leave them.

BETH: But I could still leave you.

SIMON: Yes.

BETH: But you don't think I will. Do you?

SIMON: No.

BETH: And why not?

SIMON: Because I hope you'd rather live with me than anybody else, except Ned of course. And I know you'd rather live with almost anyone than live alone.

BETH: You think I am that pathetic?

SIMON: I don't think it's pathetic. I'd rather live with you than anyone else, including Ned. And I don't want to live alone either.

BETH: But do you want to live at all?

SIMON: What?

BETH: As you hold such a deeply contemptuous view of human life. That's Ned's diagnosis of you.

SIMON: But the description of my symptoms came from you, did it?

BETH: He says you're one of those men who only give permission to little bits of life to get through to you. He says that while we may envy you your serenity, we should be revolted by the rot from which it stems. Your sanity is of the kind that causes people to go quietly mad around you.

SIMON: What an elegant paraphrase. Tell me, did you take notes?

BETH: I didn't have to. Every word rang true.

SIMON: But if it's all true, why do you need to keep referring it back to Ned?

BETH: It's a way of keeping in touch with him. If I forgot in the middle of a sentence that he's there and mine, I might begin to scream at you and claw at you and punch at you.

SIMON: But why should you want to do that?

BETH: Because I hate you.

> [*The telephone rings.* SIMON *makes a move towards it. After the fourth ring, it stops*]

SIMON: Oh, of course. I've put on the machine. [*Pause*]

BETH: [*Quietly*] You know the most insulting thing, that you let me go on and on being unfaithful without altering your manner or your behaviour one—one—you don't care about me, or my being in love with somebody else, or my betraying you, good God! least of all that! But you do wish I hadn't actually *mentioned* it, because then we could have gone on, at least *you* could, pretending that everything was all right, no, not even pretending, as far as *you* were concerned, everything was all right, you probably still think it *is* all right—and—and—you've—you've—all those times we've made love, sometimes the very same evening as Ned and I—and yet you took me—in your usual considerate fashion, just as you take your third of a bottle of wine with dinner or your carefully measured brandy and your cigar after it, *and* enjoyed it all the more because I felt guilty, God help me *guilty* and so tried harder for your sake—and you *admit* that, no, not admit it, simply state it as if on the difference made by an extra voice or something in your bloody Wagner—don't you see, don't you see that that makes you a freak! You're—you're—Oh, damn! Damn. Damn you! [*Pause*] Oh, damn. [*There is a silence*] So you might as well listen to your Wagner.

SIMON: I must say you've quite warmed up for it. And what are *you* going to do, have your cleansing bath?

BETH: No, go to Ned for a couple of hours.

SIMON: Oh, dear, more agonizing in his poky little office. Or is that a euphemism for Ned's brand of love-play? Excuse me, but what precisely has all this been about? You complain of my reticence over the last ten months, but what good has all this exposition served, what's it been for Beth? Ned's not going to leave his wife, I don't want you to leave me, you don't even think you're going to leave me—we have a perfectly sensible arrangement, we are happy enough together you and I, insultingly so if you like but still happy. We could go on and on, with Ned, until you've gone off him, why, why did you have to muck it up between you with your infantile agonizings.

BETH: Because there's a problem.

SIMON: What problem?

BETH: I'm going to have a baby.

SIMON: [Stares at her for a long moment] What? [Another moment] Whose?

BETH: That is the problem. [Goes out]

[SIMON sits in a state of shock. DAVE enters left]

DAVE: [Stands grinning at SIMON] Well, I worked it out, you'll be unhappy to hear. Suzy put me onto you. She just laughed when I told her the stuff you'd said, she and her bloke had dealings with your type in their last place. You were trying to get me out, that's all. Well, it hasn't worked, see. I'm staying. See. And another thing, Suzy and her bloke are looking for a new place. I said they could move in upstairs with me. Got that? Got that? You won't like tangling with them either. [Stares at SIMON] Having a bit of trouble sinking in, is it? [Turns, goes out, leaving the door open]

[SIMON remains sitting, dazed. Then he goes to the drinks table, pours himself a small Scotch. Looks at it. Frowns. Adds some more. Stands uncertainly, looks at the telephone, goes over to it. Remembers something vaguely, presses the play-back machine]

WOOD: [His voice] Hello, Hench, Bernard Wood, né Strapley here. I expect by now my little visit has passed entirely out of your consciousness, it was all of an hour ago that I left, and you've no doubt had any number of amusing little things to engage your attention. Your life goes on its self-appointed way, as I sit in my empty flat, my home. I've taken off my jacket, and I've lowered my braces so that they dangle around me—a picture, you might say, of old Wood, né Strapley, quite abandoned at the last. Imagine it, the jacket off, the braces down, thinking of you as I speak into the telephone, clasped tightly in my left hand as my right brings up, not trembling too much—Hench—sweet little Hench—and point the gun at my forehead—no, through the—no, I can't do the mouth, the metal tastes too intimate—it'll have to be—picture it— picture it—and as I—as I—Hench, as I squeeze—squee . . .

[SIMON *switches off the machine, interrupting the message. He sits motionless.* JEFF *appears in the doorway left*]

SIMON: [*Sees him. Gets up slowly*] Ah, yes. Jeff. Yes. All right, are we, then? Get back to—[*Thinks*] Oxford, did you?

JEFF: I didn't get to the bloody corner.

SIMON: Oh, really. Why not?

JEFF: There was a police car, Simon, right behind me, then right beside me, then right on bloody top of me with the cops all bloody over me, breathalysing me, shaking me about, and then down at the station for the rest of it. That's why bloody not. And you tipped the buggers off, friend, Christ!

SIMON: What? [*Vaguely*] What?

JEFF: No, don't deny it, don't deny it, please Christ don't deny it. Davina told me when I phoned her. She told me—you tipped them off. Christ!

SIMON: Oh. [*Thinks*] That's what you believe, is it?

JEFF: That's what I bloody know, Simon.

SIMON: [*Calmly*] What sort of man do you think I am? [*He throws his Scotch in* JEFF's *face*] What sort of man do you think I am?

JEFF: [*Sputtering, gasping*] Christ, Christ! My eyes! My eyes! [SIMON *watches him a moment, then takes out his handkerchief, gives it to* JEFF] Christ— [*Takes the handkerchief*] Thanks. [*Little pause*] Thanks. [*Little pause*] Sorry. Sorry, Simon. [*Pause, goes and sits down*] Can I have a drink? [*Pause*] The bitch. [SIMON *hesitates, then goes and gets him a Scotch, brings it to him*] Thanks. [*There is a pause*] Don't throw me out, eh? I've got nowhere to bloody go, and I don't want to go there yet.

SIMON: I'm going to play *Parsifal*. Do you mind?

JEFF: No, lovely. Lovely.

SIMON: You sure?

JEFF: Christ, yes. You know I adore Wagner.

SIMON: No, I didn't know that.

JEFF: Christ, I introduced you. At Oxford. I bloody introduced you.

SIMON: Did you really? [*Looks at him*] Such a long time ago. Then I owe you more than I can say. Thank you, Jeff. [*Goes over to the hi-fi, puts on the record*]

[*The opening bars of* Parsifal *fill the theatre. They sit listening as the music swells.*
The light fades]

CURTAIN

WHOSE LIFE IS IT ANYWAY?
Brian Clark

Brian Clark

A provocative and enthralling play invested with—rather surprisingly, in view of its thematic material—liberal doses of humor, Brian Clark's *Whose Life Is It Anyway?* opened in New York on April 17, 1979, to virtually unanimous raves. With a galvanizing performance by Tom Conti repeating his London role as the questioning quadriplegic, it was described in the press as "a rare dramatic experience . . . a blazing light in this season." The play became an immediate Broadway hit, and brought Conti an Antoinette Perry (Tony) Award for year's best actor.

Originating as a television play, the author later prepared a stage version which he acknowledges had "laid around about seven years, and I never thought it would be done." Finally, British producer Ray Cooney picked it up and brought it to the Mermaid Theatre where it was presented in 1978. The production subsequently was transferred to the West End and played to capacity audiences for almost two years. Named the best play of 1978 by the London theatre critics, the drama has since been performed in more than a dozen foreign countries.

The questions raised in *Whose Life Is It Anyway?* are both complex and fascinating, and what lifts it above the realm of mere debate and makes it so theatrically viable is the humor and unfailing humanity with which Mr. Clark treats the situation and its characters. Ken Harrison, the patient, is mentally alert, acutely sensitive to the fact that he can never again have a meaningful, productive life. He asks only that he be given the right to decide when to die, the right to remove himself from the life-sustaining environment of the hospital. Does that power reside in a human being or an institution that holds itself responsible for him?

There have been other plays dealing with life and death before, but none in the past decade that asked so pointedly who should decide whether a patient should live or die—the doctors who treat him and whose alleged goal is to sustain his life, or the patient himself.

Essentially, the author studies human dignity, the freedom of making one's own decision. And as Clive Barnes observed in the New York *Post:* "What is important here is the dazzling irony and literacy of the writing, and the forceful arguments pro and con on the proposition."

The idea for *Whose Life Is It Anyway?* came by way of theory rather than experience. According to the author: "I simply started thinking about it one day while I was driving my car. I was thinking about euthanasia, deciding I didn't approve of it. If a man wants to die, he himself must accept that responsibility. But then I asked myself, is there anyone who can't commit suicide? I imagined a paralytic, and as soon as I thought of a situation involving a man paralyzed from the neck down, I knew I had a play."

Brian Clark was born in 1932 and was brought up in Bristol, England. As a boy, he fell in love with the theatre when his father took him to the local music hall. Later, his first job, as a clerk, left him time in the evenings for studying drama at Bristol's Old Vic School. From there he went on to the Central School of Speech and Drama in London, and eventually to the University of Nottingham. He then taught English in various schools and for four years served as Staff Tutor in Drama at the University of Hull.

Mr. Clark's big decision came in 1970, when he left teaching and turned to writing. His first attempt was the television screenplay of *Whose Life Is It Anyway?* Because of its subject matter, the author recalls: "I found it extremely difficult to sell to television and was on the point of giving up being a writer. Finally, I sold it in 1971 (it was produced the following year) and overnight I became an established television playwright." Since then he has written over twenty television plays, and the highly successful ten-part series for the BBC, *Telford's Change.*

The author's second West End play, *Can You Hear Me at the Back?* opened in London in 1979.

NOTE: A revised version of *Whose Life Is It Anyway?*—with the protagonist changed to a woman—reopened on Broadway at the Royale Theatre on February 24, 1980. The limited engagement starred the television favorite Mary Tyler Moore as the patient. This change of gender in the leading role necessitated converting the part of Doctor Scott to a male physician.

Whose Life Is It Anyway? was first presented at the Mermaid Theatre, London, in association with Ray Cooney Limited, on March 6, 1978. The cast was as follows:

KEN HARRISON	*Tom Conti*
SISTER ANDERSON	*Jennie Goossens*
KAY SADLER	*Phoebe Nicholls*
JOHN	*Trevor Thomas*
DR. SCOTT	*Jane Asher*
DR. EMERSON	*Richard Leech*
MRS. BOYLE	*Rona Anderson*
PHILIP HILL	*Richard Ireson*
DR. PAUL TRAVERS	*Edward Lyon*
PETER KERSHAW	*Alan Brown*
DR. BARR	*Peter Honri*
ANDREW EDEN	*Robert Gary*
MR. JUSTICE MILLHOUSE	*Sebastian Shaw*

Directed by Michael Lindsay-Hogg
Designed by Alan Tagg
Lighting by Andy Phillips

Whose Life Is It Anyway? was first presented in New York at the Trafalgar Theatre on April 17, 1979, by Emanuel Azenberg, James M. Nederlander and Ray Cooney, by arrangement with Mermaid Theatre Trust. The cast was as follows:

KEN HARRISON	*Tom Conti*
SISTER ANDERSON	*Beverly May*
KAY SADLER	*Pippa Pearthree*
JOHN	*Damien Leake*
DR. SCOTT	*Jean Marsh*
DR. EMERSON	*Philip Bosco*
MRS. BOYLE	*Veronica Castang*
PHILIP HILL	*Kenneth Welsh*
DR. PAUL TRAVERS	*Peter McRobbie*
PETER KERSHAW	*Russell Leib*
DR. BARR	*James Higgins*
ANDREW EDEN	*Richard De Fabees*
MR. JUSTICE MILLHOUSE	*Michael Higgins*

Directed by Michael Lindsay-Hogg
Scenery by Alan Tagg
Costumes by Pearl Somner
Lighting by Tharon Musser

The action takes place in a side ward, offices, corridors, and a road outside a general hospital in England.

ACT ONE

SISTER ANDERSON *and* NURSE KAY SADLER *enter with trolley.*

SISTER: Good morning, Mr. Harrison. A new face for you today.

KEN: That's nice.

NURSE: Hello.

KEN: Hello. I'm afraid I can't offer you my hand. You'll just have to make do with my backside like all the other nurses. [*They lower the bed*] Going down—Obstetrics, Gynaecology, Lingerie, Rubber wear. [*They roll* KEN *over and start to massage his back and heels with spirit and talc*] It's funny you know. I used to dream of situations like this.

SISTER: Being injured?

KEN: No! Lying on a bed being massaged by two beautiful women.

SISTER: [*Mock serious*] If you go on like this, Mr. Harrison, I shan't be able to send my young nurses in here.

KEN: They're perfectly safe with me, Sister.

[*The phone rings outside*]

SISTER: Can you manage for a moment, Nurse?

NURSE: Oh, yes, Sister.

SISTER: Wipe your hands and put the pillows behind Mr. Harrison; we don't want to have him on the floor.

KEN: Have me on the floor, Sister, please. Have me on the floor. [SISTER *goes out*] What's your name?

NURSE: Kay.

KEN: That's nice, but don't let Sister hear you say that.

NURSE: What?

KEN: What's your second name?

NURSE: Sadler.

KEN: Then you must answer "Nurse Sadler" with a smile that is full of warmth, but with no hint of sex.

NURSE: I'm sorry.

KEN: I'm not. I'm glad you're called Kay. I shall call you Kay when we're alone, just you and me, having my backside caressed . . .

NURSE: I'm rubbing your heels.

KEN: Well, don't spoil it. After all it doesn't matter. I can't feel anything wherever you are. Is this your first ward?

NURSE: Yes, I'm still at P.T.S.

KEN: What's that? Primary Training School?

NURSE: Yes, I finish next week.

KEN: And you can't wait to get here full time.

NURSE: I'll be glad to finish the school.

KEN: All students are the same.

NURSE: Were you a teacher?

KEN: Tut tut; second lesson. You mustn't use the past tense.

NURSE: What do you mean?

KEN: You said: "Were you a teacher?" You should have said: "Are you a teacher?" I mean, you are now part of the optimism industry. Everyone who deals with me acts as though, for the first time in the history of medical science, a ruptured spinal column will heal itself—it's just a bit of a bore waiting for it to happen.

NURSE: I'm sorry.

KEN: Don't be. Kay, you're a breath of fresh air.

[SISTER *comes back*]

SISTER: Finished, Nurse?

KEN: What do you mean? Have I finished Nurse. I haven't started her yet!

NURSE: Yes, Sister.

[*They roll him back and remake the bed*]

KEN: I must congratulate you, Sister, on your new recruit. A credit to the monstrous regiment.

SISTER: I'm glad you got on.

KEN: Well, I didn't get quite that far. Not that I didn't try, Sister. But all I could get out of her was that her name was . . . Nurse Sadler . . . and that she's looking forward to coming here.

SISTER: If she still feels like that after being five minutes with you, we'll make a nurse of her yet.

KEN: I don't know quite how to take that, Sister—lying down I suppose.

SISTER: Night Sister said you slept well.

KEN: Ah, then. I fooled her . . . After her last round, a mate of mine came in and smuggled me out . . . We went midnight skateboarding.

SISTER: Oh, yes . . . I hope it was fun . . .

KEN: It was alright . . . The only problem was that I was the skateboard.

SISTER: There, that's better. Comfortable?

KEN: Sister, it's so beautifully made, I can't feel a thing.

SISTER: Cheerio, Mr. Harrison.

[*They leave*]

NURSE: Won't he ever get better, Sister?

SISTER: No.

NURSE: What will happen to him?

SISTER: When we have him fully stabilised, he'll be transferred to a long-stay hospital.

NURSE: For the rest of his life?

SISTER: Yes.

[JOHN, *an orderly, comes along the corridor carrying shaving tackle on a tray*]

JOHN: Morning, Sister.

SISTER: Morning, John. Are you going to Mr. Harrison?

JOHN: That's right.

SISTER: He's all ready.

JOHN: Right.

[JOHN *goes into the sluice room to collect an electric razor*]

NURSE: How long has he been here?

SISTER: Four months.

NURSE: How much longer will he be here?

SISTER: Not much longer now I should think. Take the trolley into the ward, Nurse. I should start on Mr. Phillips.

[SISTER *goes into her office.* JOHN *goes into* KEN's *room. He plugs in the razor and shaves* KEN]

JOHN: Good morning, Mr. Harrison . . .

KEN: Come to trim the lawn?

JOHN: That's right.

KEN: Good . . . Must make sure that all the beds and borders are neat and tidy.

JOHN: That's my job.

KEN: Well, my gardening friend, isn't it about time you got some fertiliser to sprinkle on me and get some movement going in this plant?

JOHN: Ah, now there you have me. You see, I'm only a labourer in this here vineyard. Fertilisers and pruning and bedding out is up to the head gardener.

KEN: Still, you must be in charge of the compost heap. That's where I should be.

[SISTER *puts her head around the door*]

SISTER: John.

JOHN: Yes?

SISTER: Don't be long, will you. Dr. Scott will probably be early today; there's a consultant's round this morning.

JOHN: Right, Sister.

[SISTER *goes back to her office*]

KEN: The visitation of the Gods.

JOHN: Eh?

KEN: The Gods are walking on earth again.

JOHN: Oh, yes—they think they're a bit of alright.

KEN: What happened to the other chap—Terence he was called . . . I think?

JOHN: They come and they go . . . I think he left to get married up north somewhere.

KEN: Terence, getting married? Who to? A lorry driver?

JOHN: Catty!

KEN: No. Bloody jealous. From where I'm lying, if you can make it at all—even with your right hand—it would be heaven . . . I'm sorry . . . feeling sorry for myself this morning . . . can't even say I got out of the wrong side of the bed. Are you down to the bone yet? . . . Anyway, how long will you be staying?

JOHN: Just till we go professional, man.

KEN: Doing what?

JOHN: Music. We got a steel band—with some comedy numbers
and we're getting around a bit . . . We're auditioning for Opportunity Knocks in four months.

KEN: That's great . . . Really great . . . I like steel bands . . .
There's something fascinating about using oil drums—making
something out of scrap . . . Why not try knocking a tune out of
me?

JOHN: Why not, man!

> [He puts down his razor and, striking KEN very lightly up and
> down his body like a xylophone, sings a typical steel band
> tune, moving rhythmically to the music. KEN is delighted. DR.
> SCOTT comes in. JOHN stops]

DR. SCOTT: Don't stop . . .

JOHN: It's alright . . . I've nearly finished.

> [He makes one more pass with the razor]

KEN: I was just making myself beautiful for you, Doctor.

JOHN: There . . . Finished.

> [He goes to the door]

KEN: Work out some new tunes . . . Hey, if Doctor Scott could
drill some holes in my head, you could blow in my ear and play
me like an ocarina.

JOHN: I'll see you later.

> [He grins and goes out]

DR. SCOTT: You're bright and chirpy this morning.

KEN: [Ironically] It's marvellous, you know. The courage of the
human spirit.

DR. SCOTT: [Dryly] Nice to hear the human spirit's O.K. How's the
lungs?

> [She takes her stethoscope from her pocket. She puts the
> stethoscope to KEN's chest]

KEN: [*sings*] Boom boom.

DR. SCOTT: Be quiet. You'll deafen me.

KEN: Sorry. [*She continues to listen*] And what does it say?

DR. SCOTT: [*Gives up*] What does what say?

KEN: My heart, of course. What secrets does it tell?

DR. SCOTT: It was just telling me that it's better off than it was six months ago.

KEN: It's a brave heart. It keeps its secrets.

DR. SCOTT: And what are they?

KEN: Did you hear it going boom boom, like that? Two beats.

DR. SCOTT: Of course.

KEN: Well, I'll tell you. That's because it's broken, broken in two. But each part carries on bravely yearning for a woman in a white coat.

DR. SCOTT: And I thought it was the first and second heart sounds.

KEN: Ah! Is there a consultant's round this morning?

DR. SCOTT: That's right.

KEN: I suppose he will sweep in here like Zeus from Olympus, with his attendant nymphs and swains.

DR. SCOTT: I don't think that's fair.

KEN: Why not?

DR. SCOTT: He cares; he cares a lot.

KEN: But what about?

DR. SCOTT: His patients.

KEN: I suppose so.

DR. SCOTT: He does. When you first came in he worked his guts out to keep you going; he cares.

KEN: I was a bit flip, wasn't I . . .

DR. SCOTT: It's understandable.

KEN: But soon we shall have to ask the question why.

DR. SCOTT: Why?

KEN: Why bother. You remember the mountain laboured and brought forth not a man but a mouse. It was a big joke. On the mouse. If you're as insignificant as that, who needs a mountain for a mummy?

DR. SCOTT: I'll see you later . . . with Dr. Emerson.

KEN: And Cupbearers Limited.

DR. SCOTT: Oh, no . . . I assure you . . . We're not at all limited.

[*She goes out. She opens the door of* SISTER's *room. The* SISTER *is writing at the desk*]

Sister. It's Mr. Harrison. He seems a little agitated this morning.

SISTER: Yes, he's beginning to realise what he's up against.

DR. SCOTT: I'm changing the prescription and putting him on a small dose of Valium. I'll have a word with Dr. Emerson. Thank you, Sister.

[*She closes the door and looks up the corridor towards* KEN's *room.* NURSE SADLER *is just going in with a feeding cup*]

KEN: An acolyte, bearing a cup.

NURSE: I beg your pardon?

KEN: Nothing. I was joking. It's nothing.

NURSE: It's coffee.

KEN: You're joking now.

NURSE: I'm not.

KEN: What you have there is a coffee-flavoured milk drink.

NURSE: Don't you like it?

KEN: It's alright, but I would like some real coffee, hot and black and bitter so that I could chew it.

NURSE: I'll ask the Sister.

KEN: I shouldn't.

NURSE: Why not?

KEN: Because in an hour's time, you'll be bringing round a little white pill that is designed to insert rose-coloured filters behind my eyes. It will calm me and soothe me and make me forget for a while that you have a lovely body.

NURSE: Mr. Harrison . . . I'm . . .

KEN: [*Genuinely concerned*] I'm sorry. Really, I *am* sorry. I don't want to take it out on you—it's not your fault. You're only the vestal virgin . . . Sorry I said virgin.

NURSE: You'd better drink your coffee before it gets cold.

[*She feeds him a little, sip by sip*]

KEN: I was right; it's milky . . . What made you become a nurse?

NURSE: I'm not a nurse yet.

KEN: Oh yes, you are. [NURSE SADLER *smiles*] Nurse Sadler.

NURSE: You must have thought me a real twit.

KEN: Of course not!

NURSE: The Sister-Tutor told us we could say it.

KEN: Well, then . . .

NURSE: But I was so sure I wouldn't.

KEN: You haven't told me what made you become a nurse.

NURSE: I've always wanted to. What made you become a sculptor?

KEN: Hey there! You're learning too fast!

NURSE: What do you mean?

KEN: When you get a personal question, just ignore it—change the subject or better still, ask another question back. [NURSE SADLER *smiles*] Did Sister-Tutor tell you that, too?

NURSE: Something like it.

KEN: It's called being professional, isn't it?

NURSE: I suppose so.

KEN: I don't want any more of that, it's horrid. Patients are requested not to ask for credit for their intelligence, as refusal often offends.

NURSE: You sound angry. I hope I . . .

KEN: Not with you, Kay. Not at all. With myself I expect. Don't say it. That's futile, isn't it?

NURSE: Yes.

[SISTER *opens the door*]

SISTER: Have you finished, Nurse? Dr. Emerson is here.

NURSE: Yes, Sister. I'm just coming.

SISTER: Straighten that sheet.

[*She goes, leaving the door open*]

KEN: Hospitals are weird places. Broken necks are acceptable, but a wrinkled sheet! . . .

[NURSE SADLER *smooths the bed. She goes out as* DR. EMERSON *comes in with* SISTER *and* DR. SCOTT]

DR. EMERSON: Morning.

KEN: Good morning.

DR. EMERSON: How are you this morning?

KEN: As you see, racing around all over the place.

[DR. EMERSON *picks up the chart and notes from the bottom of the bed*]

DR. EMERSON: [*To* DR. SCOTT] You've prescribed Valium I see.

DR. SCOTT: Yes.

DR. EMERSON: His renal function looks much improved.

DR. SCOTT: Yes, the blood urea is back to normal and the cultures are sterile.

DR. EMERSON: Good . . . Good. Well, we had better go on keeping an eye on it, just in case.

DR. SCOTT: Yes, of course, sir.

DR. EMERSON: Good . . . Well, Mr. Harrison, we seem to be out of the wood now . . .

KEN: So when are you going to discharge me?

DR. EMERSON: Difficult to say.

KEN: Really? Are you ever going to discharge me?

DR. EMERSON: Well, you'll certainly be leaving *us* soon, I should think.

KEN: Discharged or transferred?

DR. EMERSON: This unit is for critical patients; when we have reached a position of stability, then you can be looked after in a much more comfortable, quiet hospital.

KEN: You mean you only grow the vetetables here—the vegetable store is somewhere else.

DR. EMERSON: I don't think I understand you.

KEN: I think you do. Spell it out for me please. What chance have I of only being partly dependent on nursing?

DR. EMERSON: It's impossible to say with certainty what the prognosis of any case is.

KEN: I'm not asking for a guarantee on oath. I am simply asking for your professional opinion. Do you believe I will ever walk again?

DR. EMERSON: No.

KEN: Or recover the use of my arms?

DR. EMERSON: No.

KEN: Thank you.

DR. EMERSON: What for?

KEN: Your honesty.

DR. EMERSON: Yes, well . . . I should try not to brood on it if I were you. It's surprising how we can come to accept things. Dr. Scott has prescribed something which will help. [To DR. SCOTT] You might also get Mrs. Boyle along . . .

DR. SCOTT: Yes, of course.

DR. EMERSON: You'll be surprised how many things you will be able to do. Good morning.

[*They go into the corridor area*]

DR. EMERSON: What dose was it you prescribed?

DR. SCOTT: Two milligrams T.I.D.

DR. EMERSON: That's very small. You might have to increase it to five milligrams.

DR. SCOTT: Yes, sir.

DR. EMERSON: We ought to aim to get him moved in a month at most. These beds are very precious.

DR. SCOTT: Yes.

DR. EMERSON: Well, thank you, Doctor. I must rush off. Damned committee meeting.

DR. SCOTT: I thought you hated those.

DR. EMERSON: I do, but there's a new heart monitoring unit I want . . . very much indeed.

DR. SCOTT: Good luck then.

DR. EMERSON: Thank you, Clare.

[*He goes.* DR. SCOTT *looks in at* SISTER's *office*]

DR. SCOTT: Did you get that Valium for Mr. Harrison, Sister?

SISTER: Yes, Doctor. I was going to give him the first at twelve o'clock.

DR. SCOTT: Give him one now, will you?

SISTER: Right.

DR. SCOTT: Thank you. [*She begins to walk away, then turns*] On second thoughts . . . give it to me. I'll take it. I want to talk with him.

SISTER: Here it is.

> [*She hands a small tray with a tablet and a feeding cup of water*]

DR. SCOTT: Thank you. [*She walks to* KEN's *room and goes in*] I've brought something to help you.

KEN: My God, they've got some highly qualified nurses here.

DR. SCOTT: Only the best in this hospital.

KEN: You're spoiling me, you know, Doctor. If this goes on I shall demand that my next enema is performed by no one less than the Matron.

DR. SCOTT: Well, it wouldn't be the first she'd done, or the thousandth either.

KEN: She worked up through the ranks, did she?

DR. SCOTT: They all do.

KEN: Yes, in training school they probably learn that at the bottom of every bed pan lies a potential Matron. Just now, for one or two glorious minutes, I felt like a human being again.

DR. SCOTT: Good.

KEN: And now you're going to spoil it.

DR. SCOTT: How?

KEN: By tranquillizing yourself.

DR. SCOTT: Me?

KEN: Oh, I shall get the tablet, but it's you that needs the tranquillizing; I don't.

DR. SCOTT: Dr. Emerson and I thought . . .

KEN: You both watched me disturbed, worried even perhaps, and you can't do anything for me—nothing that really matters. I'm paralysed and you're impotent. This disturbs you because you're a sympathetic person and as someone dedicated to an active sympathy doing something—anything even—you find it hard to accept you're impotent. The only thing you can do is to stop me thinking about it—that is—stop me disturbing you. So I get the tablet and you get the tranquillity.

DR. SCOTT: That's a tough diagnosis.

KEN: Is it so far from the truth?

DR. SCOTT: There may be an element of truth in it, but it's not the whole story.

KEN: I don't suppose it is.

DR. SCOTT: After all, there is no point in worrying unduly—you know the facts. It's no use banging your head against a wall.

KEN: If the only feeling I have is in my head and I want to feel, I might choose to bang it against a wall.

DR. SCOTT: And if you damage your head?

KEN: You mean go bonkers?

DR. SCOTT: Yes.

KEN: Then that would be the final catastrophe but I'm not bonkers—yet. My consciousness is the only thing I have and I must claim the right to use it and, as far as possible, act on conclusions I may come to.

DR. SCOTT: Of course.

KEN: Good. Then you eat that tablet if you want tranquillity, because I'm not going to.

DR. SCOTT: It is prescribed.

KEN: Oh, come off it, Doctor. I know everyone around here acts as though those little bits of paper have just been handed down from Sinai. But the writing on those tablets isn't in Hebrew . . .

DR. SCOTT: . . . Well, you aren't due for it till twelve o'clock. We'll see . . .

KEN: That's what I always say. If you don't know whether to take a tranquillizer or not—sleep on it. When you tell Dr. Emerson, impress on him I don't need it . . .

[DR. SCOTT *smiles. She leaves and goes to the* SISTER's *room*]

DR. SCOTT: Sister, I haven't given it to him . . . Leave it for a while.

SISTER: Did you alter the notes?

DR. SCOTT: No . . . Not yet.

[*She picks up a pile of notes and begins writing. Cross fade on sluice room.* NURSE SADLER *is taking kidney dishes and instruments out of the steriliser.* JOHN *creeps up behind her and seizes her round the waist.* NURSE SADLER *jumps, utters a muffled scream and drops a dish*]

NURSE: Oh, it's you . . . Don't do that . . .

JOHN: I couldn't help myself, honest my Lord. There was this vision in white and blue, then I saw red in front of my eyes. It was like looking into a Union Jack.

[NURSE SADLER *has turned round to face* JOHN, *who has his arms either side of her against the table*]

NURSE: Let go . . .

JOHN: What's a nice girl like you doing in a place like this?

NURSE: Sterilising the instruments . . .

[JOHN *gasps and holds his groin*]

JOHN: Don't say things like that! Just the thought . . .

[NURSE SADLER *is free and returns to her work*]

NURSE: I don't know what you're doing in a place like this . . . It's just a big joke to you.

JOHN: 'Course it is. You can't take a place like this seriously . . .

NURSE: Why ever not?

JOHN: It's just the ante-room of the morgue.

NURSE: That's terrible! They don't all die.

JOHN: Don't they?

NURSE: No! Old Mr. Trevellyan is going out tomorrow, for instance.

JOHN: After his third heart attack! I hope they give him a return ticket on the ambulance.

NURSE: Would you just let them die? People like Mr. Harrison?

JOHN: How much does it cost to keep him here? Hundreds of pounds a week.

NURSE: That's not the point.

JOHN: In Africa children die of measles. It would cost only a few pounds to keep them alive. There's something crazy somewhere.

NURSE: That's wrong, too—but it wouldn't help just letting Mr. Harrison die.

JOHN: No . . . [*He goes up to her again*] Nurse Sadler, when your eyes flash, you send shivers up and down my spine . . .

NURSE: John, stop it . . .

[*She is backing away*]

JOHN: Why don't we go out tonight?

NURSE: I've got some work to do for my exam.

JOHN: Let me help . . . I'm an expert on anatomy. We could go dancing, down to the Barbados Club, a few drinks and then back to my pad for an anatomy lesson.

NURSE: Let me get on . . .

[JOHN *holds* NURSE SADLER's *head and slides his hands down*]

JOHN: [*Singing*] Oh, the head bone's connected to the neck bone,

The neck bone's connected to the shoulder bone,
The shoulder bone's connected to the . . . breast bone . . .

[NURSE SADLER *escapes just in time. She backs out of the room and into* SISTER, *who is coming to see what's causing the noise*]

NURSE: Sorry, Sister.

SISTER: This hospital exists to cure accidents, not to cause them.

NURSE: No . . . Yes . . . Sister.

SISTER: Are you going to be all day with that steriliser?

NURSE: No, Sister.

[*She hurries away*]

SISTER: Haven't you any work to do, John?

JOHN: Sister, my back is bowed down with the weight of all the work resting on it.

SISTER: Then I suggest you shift some.

JOHN: Right.

[*She goes.* JOHN *shrugs and goes. Cross fade on* DR. EMERSON'S *office.* DR. EMERSON *is on the 'phone*]

DR. EMERSON: Look, Jenkins, I know the capital cost is high, but it would save on nursing costs. I've got four cardiac cases in here at the moment. With that unit I could save at least on one nurse a day. They could all be monitored in the Sister's room . . . Yes, I know . . . [DR. SCOTT *knocks on the door. She goes in*] Hello? . . . Yes, well old chap, I've got to go now. Do impress on the board how much money we'd save in the long run . . . alright . . . Thank you.

[*He puts the 'phone down*]

DR. SCOTT: Still wheeling and dealing for that monitoring unit?

DR. EMERSON: Bloody administrators. In this job a degree in accountancy would be more valuable to me than my M.D. . . . Still, what can I do for you?

DR. SCOTT: It's Harrison.

DR. EMERSON: Some sort of relapse!

DR. SCOTT: On the contrary.

DR. EMERSON: Good.

DR. SCOTT: He doesn't want to take Valium.

DR. EMERSON: Doesn't want to take it? What do you mean?

DR. SCOTT: He guessed it was some sort of tranquillizer and said he preferred to keep his consciousness clear.

DR. EMERSON: That's the trouble with all this anti-drug propaganda; it's useful of course, but it does set up a negative reaction to even necessary drugs, in sensitive people.

DR. SCOTT: I'm not sure he's not right.

DR. EMERSON: Right? When you prescribed the drug, you thought he needed it.

DR. SCOTT: Yes.

DR. EMERSON: And when I saw him, I agreed with you.

DR. SCOTT: Yes.

DR. EMERSON: It's a very small dose—two milligrams T.I.D., wasn't it?

DR. SCOTT: That's right.

DR. EMERSON: The minimum that will have any effect at all. You remember I said you might have to go up to five milligrams. A psychiatric dose, you know, is ten or fifteen milligrams.

DR. SCOTT: I know, but Mr. Harrison isn't a psychiatric case, is he?

DR. EMERSON: So how did you persuade him to take it?

DR. SCOTT: I didn't.

DR. EMERSON: Now let's get this clear. This morning when you examined him, you came to a careful and responsible decision that your patient needed a certain drug.

DR. SCOTT: Yes.

DR. EMERSON: I saw the patient and I agreed with your prescription.

DR. SCOTT: Yes.

DR. EMERSON: But in spite of two qualified opinions, you accept the decisions of someone completely unqualified to take it.

DR. SCOTT: He may be unqualified, but he is the one affected.

DR. EMERSON: Ours was an objective, his a subjective decision.

DR. SCOTT: But isn't this a case where a subjective decision may be more valid? After all, you're both working on the same subject— his body. Only he knows more about how he feels.

DR. EMERSON: But he doesn't know about the drugs and their effects.

DR. SCOTT: He can feel their effects directly.

DR. EMERSON: Makes no difference. His knowledge isn't based on experience of a hundred such cases. He can't know enough to challenge our clinical decisions.

DR. SCOTT: That's what he's doing and he's protesting about the dulling of his consciousness with Valium.

DR. EMERSON: When he came in, shocked to hell, did he protest about the dextrose-saline? Or when he was gasping for breath, he didn't use some of it to protest about the aminophylline or the huge stat dose of cortisone . . .

DR. SCOTT: Those were inevitable and emergency decisions.

DR. EMERSON: And so is this one inevitable. Just because our patient is conscious, that does not absolve us from our complete responsibility. We have to maximise whatever powers he retains.

DR. SCOTT: And how does a depressant drug improve his consciousness?

DR. EMERSON: It will help him to use his consciousness, Clare. We must help him now to turn his mind to the real problem he has. We must help him to an acceptance of his condition. Only then will his full consciousness be any use to him at all . . . You say he refused to take the tablet?

[DR. SCOTT *nods.* DR. EMERSON *picks up the 'phone and dials. The 'phone rings in the* SISTER'S *office*]

SISTER: Sister Anderson speaking.

DR. EMERSON: Emerson here. Could you prepare a syringe with five milligrams of Valium for Mr. Harrison?

SISTER: Yes, sir.

DR. EMERSON: I'll be down myself immediately to give it to him.

SISTER: Yes, sir.

[*She replaces the 'phone and immediately prepares the syringe*]

DR. SCOTT: Do you want me to come?

DR. EMERSON: No . . . It won't be necessary.

DR. SCOTT: Thank you . . .

[*She moves to the door*]

DR. EMERSON: Harrison is an intelligent, sensitive and articulate man.

DR. SCOTT: Yes.

DR. EMERSON: But don't undervalue yourself. Clare, your first decision was right.

[DR. SCOTT *nods and leaves the room. She is unhappy.* DR. EMERSON *walks to the* SISTER'S *room*]

DR. EMERSON: Have you the Valium ready, Sister?

SISTER: Yes, sir.

[*She hands him the kidney dish.* DR. EMERSON *takes it.* SISTER *makes to follow him*]

DR. EMERSON: It's alright, Sister. You've plenty of work I expect.

SISTER: There's always plenty of that.

[DR. EMERSON *goes into* KEN's *room*]

KEN: Hello, hello, they've brought up the heavy brigade.

[DR. EMERSON *pulls back the bed clothes and reaches for* KEN's *arm*]

Dr. Emerson, I am afraid I must insist that you do not stick that needle in me.

DR. EMERSON: It is important that I do.

KEN: Who for?

DR. EMERSON: You.

KEN: I'm the best judge of that.

DR. EMERSON: I think not. You don't even know what's in this syringe.

KEN: I take it that the injection is one of a series of measures to keep me alive.

DR. EMERSON: You could say that.

KEN: Then it is not important. I've decided not to stay alive.

DR. EMERSON: But you can't decide that.

KEN: Why not?

DR. EMERSON: You're very depressed.

KEN: Does that surprise you?

DR. EMERSON: Of course not; it's perfectly natural. Your body received massive injuries; it takes time to come to any acceptance of the new situation. Now I shan't be a minute . . .

KEN: Don't stick that fucking thing in me!

DR. EMERSON: There . . . It's over now.

KEN: Doctor, I didn't give you permission to stick that needle in me. Why did you do it?

DR. EMERSON: It was necessary. Now try to sleep . . . You will find that as you gain acceptance of the situation you will be able to find a new way of living.

KEN: Please let me make myself clear. I specifically refused permission to stick that needle in me and you didn't listen. You took no notice.

DR. EMERSON: You must rely on us, old chap. Of course you're depressed. I'll send someone along to have a chat with you. Now I really must go and get on with my rounds.

KEN: Doctor . . .

DR. EMERSON: I'll send someone along.

[*He places the dish on the side locker, throwing the needle in a waste bin. He goes out.* KEN *is frustrated and then his eyes close. Cross fade on* SISTER's *office.* SISTER *and* DR. SCOTT *are sitting*]

SISTER: I'm always warning my nurses not to get involved.

DR. SCOTT: Of course . . . And you never do, do you?

SISTER: [*Smiling*] . . . Never.

DR. SCOTT: You're a liar, Sister.

SISTER: Dr. Scott!

DR. SCOTT: Come on, we all do. Dr. Emerson is as involved with Ken Harrison as if he were his father.

SISTER: But you don't feel like his mother!

DR. SCOTT: . . . No comment, Sister.

[NURSE SADLER *comes into* SISTER's *office*]

NURSE: I've finished, Sister.

SISTER: Alright . . . Off you go then, Nurse.

NURSE: Yes, Sister!

SISTER: Have you been running?

NURSE: No, Sister!

SISTER: Oh . . . You just looked . . . flushed.

NURSE: . . . Oh . . . Goodnight, Sister . . . Doctor.

SISTER ⎫
        ⎬ :   Goodnight.
DR. SCOTT ⎭

> [*Cross fade to* KEN'S *room.* SISTER *and* NURSE SADLER *come in with the trolley*]

SISTER: Good morning, Mr. Harrison. How are you this morning?

KEN: Marvellous.

SISTER: Night Sister said you slept well.

KEN: I did. I had a lot of help, remember.

SISTER: Your eyes are bright this morning.

KEN: I've been thinking.

SISTER: You do too much of that.

KEN: What other activity would you suggest? . . . Football? I tell you what, Sister, just leave me alone with Nurse Sadler here. Let's see what the old Adam can do for me.

SISTER: I'm a Sister, not a Madame.

KEN: Sister—you dark horse you! All this time you've been kidding me. I've been wondering for months how on earth a woman could become a State Registered Nurse and a Sister and still think you found babies under a gooseberry bush—and you've known all along.

SISTER: Of course I've known. When I qualified as a midwife I learnt that when they pick up the babies from under the gooseberry bushes they wrap them up in women to keep them warm. I know because it was our job to unwrap them again.

KEN: The miracle of modern science! Anyway, Sister, as I said, I've been thinking, if I'm going to be around for a long time, money will help.

SISTER: It always does.

KEN: Do you remember that solicitor chap representing my insurance company a few months ago? Mr. Hill, I think he said his name was. He said he'd come back when I felt better. Do you think you could get him back as soon as possible? I'd feel more settled if we could get the compensation sorted out.

SISTER: Sounds a good idea.

KEN: You'll ring him up?

SISTER: Of course.

KEN: He left a card; it's in my drawer.

SISTER: Right. [*She goes to the locker and takes out the card*] Mr. Philip Hill, Solicitor. Right, I'll ring him.

KEN: Thanks.

SISTER: That's enough.

[*They cover him up again and straighten the bed*]

SISTER: Mrs. Boyle is waiting to see you, Mr. Harrison.

KEN: Mrs. Boyle? Who's she?

SISTER: A very nice woman.

KEN: Oh God, must I see her?

SISTER: Dr. Emerson asked her to come along.

KEN: Then I'd better see her. If I refuse, he'll probably dissolve her in water and inject her into me.

[SISTER *has to choke back a giggle*]

SISTER: Mr. Harrison! Come on, Nurse; this man will be the death of me.

KEN: [*Cheerfully*] Doubt it, Sister. I'm not even able to be the death of myself.

[SISTER *goes out with* NURSE SADLER. MRS. GILLIAN BOYLE *enters. She is thirty-five, attractive, and very professional in her manner. She is a medical social worker*]

MRS. BOYLE: Good morning.

KEN: Morning.

MRS. BOYLE: Mr. Harrison?

KEN: [*Cheerfully*] It used to be.

MRS. BOYLE: My name is Mrs. Boyle.

KEN: And you've come to cheer me up.

MRS. BOYLE: I wouldn't put it like that.

KEN: How would you put it?

MRS. BOYLE: I've come to see if I can help.

KEN: Good. You can.

MRS. BOYLE: How?

KEN: Go and convince Dr. Frankenstein that he has successfully made his monster and he can now let it go.

MRS. BOYLE: Dr. Emerson is a first-rate physician. My goodness, they have improved this room.

KEN: Have they?

MRS. BOYLE: It used to be really dismal. All dark green and cream. It's surprising what pastel colours will do, isn't it? Really cheerful.

KEN: Yes; perhaps they should try painting me. I'd hate to be the thing that ruins the decor.

MRS. BOYLE: What on earth makes you say that? You don't ruin anything.

KEN: I'm sorry. That was a bit . . . whining. Well, don't let me stop you.

MRS. BOYLE: Doing what?

KEN: What you came for I suppose. What do you do? Conjuring tricks? Funny stories? Or a belly dance? If I have any choice, I'd prefer the belly dance.

MRS. BOYLE: I'm afraid I've left my bikini at home.

KEN: Who said anything about a bikini?

MRS. BOYLE: Dr. Emerson tells me that you don't want any more treatment.

KEN: Good.

MRS. BOYLE: Why good?

KEN: I didn't think he'd heard what I'd said.

MRS. BOYLE: Why not?

KEN: He didn't take any notice.

MRS. BOYLE: Well, as you can see, he did.

KEN: He sent you?

MRS. BOYLE: Yes.

KEN: And you are my new treatment; get in.

MRS. BOYLE: Why don't you want any more treatment?

KEN: I'd rather not go on living like this.

MRS. BOYLE: Why not?

KEN: Isn't it obvious?

MRS. BOYLE: Not to me. I've seen many patients like you.

KEN: And they all want to live?

MRS. BOYLE: Usually.

KEN: Why?

MRS. BOYLE: They find a new way of life.

KEN: How?

MRS. BOYLE: You'll be surprised how many things you will be able to do with training and a little patience.

KEN: Such as?

MRS. BOYLE: We can't be sure yet. But I should think that you will be able to operate reading machines and perhaps an adapted type-writer.

KEN: Reading and writing. What about arithmetic?

MRS. BOYLE: [*Smiling*] I dare say we could fit you up with a comp-tometer if you really wanted one.

KEN: Mrs. Boyle, even educationalists have realised that the three r's do not make a full life.

MRS. BOYLE: What did you do before the accident?

KEN: I taught in an art school. I was a sculptor.

MRS. BOYLE: I see.

KEN: Difficult, isn't it? How about an electrically operated hammer and chisel? No, well. Or a cybernetic lump of clay?

MRS. BOYLE: I wouldn't laugh if I were you. It's amazing what can be done. Our scientists are wonderful.

KEN: They are. But it's not good enough you see, Mrs. Boyle. I re-ally have absolutely no desire at all to be the object of scientific virtuosity. I have thought things over very carefully. I do have plenty of time for thinking and I have decided that I do not want to go on living with so much effort for so little result.

MRS. BOYLE: Yes, well, we shall have to see about that.

KEN: What is there to see?

MRS. BOYLE: We can't just stop treatment, just like that.

KEN: Why not?

MRS. BOYLE: It's the job of the hospital to save life, not to lose it.

KEN: The hospital's done all it can, but it wasn't enough. It wasn't the hospital's fault; the original injury was too big.

MRS. BOYLE: We have to make the best of the situation.

KEN: No. "We" don't have to do anything. I have to do what is to be done and that is to cash in the chips.

MRS. BOYLE: It's not unusual, you know, for people injured as you have been to suffer with this depression for a considerable time before they begin to see that a life is possible.

KEN: How long?

MRS. BOYLE: It varies.

KEN: Don't hedge.

MRS. BOYLE: It could be a year or so.

KEN: And it could last for the rest of my life.

MRS. BOYLE: That would be most unlikely.

KEN: I'm sorry, but I cannot settle for that.

MRS. BOYLE: Try not to dwell on it. I'll see what I can do to get you started on some occupational therapy. Perhaps we could make a start on the reading machines.

KEN: Do you have many books for those machines?

MRS. BOYLE: Quite a few.

KEN: Can I make a request for the first one?

MRS. BOYLE: If you like.

KEN: "How to be a sculptor with no hands."

MRS. BOYLE: I'll be back tomorrow with the machine.

KEN: It's marvellous, you know.

MRS. BOYLE: What is?

KEN: All you people have the same technique. When I say something really awkward you just pretend I haven't said anything at all. You're all the bloody same . . . Well, there's another outburst. That should be your cue to comment on the light-shade or the colour of the walls.

MRS. BOYLE: I'm sorry if I have upset you.

KEN: Of course you have upset me. You and the doctors with your appalling so-called professionalism, which is nothing more than a series of verbal tricks to prevent you relating to your patients as human beings.

MRS. BOYLE: You must understand; we have to remain relatively detached in order to help . . .

KEN: That's alright with me. Detach yourself. Tear yourself off on the dotted line that divides the woman from the social worker and post yourself off to another patient.

MRS. BOYLE: You're very upset . . .

KEN: Christ Almighty, you're doing it again! Listen to yourself, woman. I say something offensive about you and you turn your professional cheek. If you were human, if you were treating me as human, you'd tell me to bugger off. Can't you see that this is why I've decided that life isn't worth living? I am not human and I'm even more convinced of that by your visit than I was before, so how does that grab you? The very exercise of your so-called professionalism makes me want to die.

MRS. BOYLE: I'm . . . Please . . .

KEN: Go . . . For God's sake get out . . . Go on . . . Get out . . . Get out.

[*She goes into* SISTER's *room.* SISTER *hears* KEN's *shouts*]

SISTER: What's the matter, Mrs. Boyle?

MRS. BOYLE: It's Mr. Harrison . . . He seems very upset.

KEN: [*Shouting*] . . . I am upset!

[SISTER *closes the door*]

SISTER: I should leave him for now, Mrs. Boyle. We'll send for you again when he's better.

[SISTER *hurries in to* KEN. *He is very distressed, rocking his head from side to side, desperately short of breath*]

KEN: Sis . . . ter . . .

[SISTER *reaches for the oxygen mask*]

SISTER: Now, now, Mr. Harrison, calm down.

[*She applies the mask and turns on the oxygen.* KEN *gradually becomes calmer*]

SISTER: Now why do you go getting yourself so upset? . . . There's no point . . .

KEN: [*Muffled*] But . . .

SISTER: Stop talking, Mr. Harrison. Just relax. [KEN *becomes calm.* SISTER *sees* NURSE SADLER *going past.* MRS. BOYLE *is still hovering*] Nurse.

NURSE: Sister?

SISTER: Take over here, will you?

NURSE: Yes, Sister.

[NURSE SADLER *holds the mask.* SISTER *goes to the door*]

MRS. BOYLE: Is he alright?

SISTER: Yes, perfectly.

MRS. BOYLE: I'm sorry . . .

SISTER: Don't worry. It was not you . . . We'll let you know when he's better.

MRS. BOYLE: Right . . . Thank you.

[*She goes.* SISTER *stands at the open door*]

SISTER: Just give him another ten seconds, Nurse.

NURSE: Yes, Sister.

[SISTER *takes a pace back behind the door and listens. After ten seconds,* NURSE SADLER *removes the mask*]

KEN: Oh, she's a shrewd cookie, is our Sister. [SISTER *smiles at this.* NURSE SADLER *glances backward.* KEN *catches on to the reason*] It's alright, Sister. I'm still alive, bugger it. I don't want to give her too much satisfaction.

NURSE: She's gone. [*She closes the door*]

KEN: Come on then, over here. I shan't bite you, Kay. Come and cool my fevered brow or something.

NURSE: What upset you?

KEN: Being patronised, I suppose.

NURSE: What did you mean about Sister?

KEN: She knew if she came in I'd shout at her, but if you were here I wouldn't shout.

NURSE: Why?

KEN: A good question. Because I suppose you're young and gentle and innocent and Sister knows that I am not the sort who would shout at you . . .

NURSE: You mean, you would rather patronise me.

KEN: Hey! Steady on there, Kay. If you show you're well able to take care of yourself I shall have to call you Nurse Sadler and shout at you, too, and Sister and I will have lost a valuable asset.

NURSE: What were you? . . .

[*The door opens and* SISTER *and* DR. SCOTT *come in*]

KEN: What is this? Piccadilly Circus?

SISTER: Alright, Nurse. Dr. Scott was just coming as it happened. Are you feeling better now, Mr. Harrison?

[NURSE SADLER *leaves*]

KEN: Lovely, thank you, Sister.

SISTER: I made your 'phone call to Mr. Hill. He said he'd try to get in tomorrow.

KEN: Thank you . . .

[SISTER *leaves*]

DR. SCOTT: And what was all the fuss about?

KEN: I'm sorry about that. The last thing I want is to bring down Emerson again with his pharmaceutical truncheon.

DR. SCOTT: I'm . . . sorry about that.

KEN: I don't suppose it was your fault.

DR. SCOTT: Can I give you some advice?

KEN: Please do; I may even take it.

DR. SCOTT: Take the tablets; the dose is very small—the minimum —and it won't really blunt your consciousness, not like the injection.

KEN: . . . You're on.

DR. SCOTT: Good . . . I was glad to hear about your decision to try and get your compensation settled.

KEN: How did you? . . . Oh, I suppose Sister checked with you.

DR. SCOTT: She did mention it . . .

KEN: You have lovely breasts.

DR. SCOTT: I beg your pardon?

KEN: I said you have lovely breasts.

DR. SCOTT: What an odd thing to say.

KEN: Why? You're not only a doctor, are you? You can't tell me that you regard them only as mammary glands.

DR. SCOTT: No.

KEN: You're quite safe.

DR. SCOTT: Of course.

KEN: I'm not about to jump out of bed and rape you or anything.

DR. SCOTT: I know.

KEN: Did it embarrass you?

DR. SCOTT: Surprised me.

KEN: And embarrassed you.

DR. SCOTT: I suppose so.

KEN: But why exactly? You are an attractive woman. I admit that it's unusual for a man to compliment a woman on her breasts when only one of them is in bed, only one of the people that is, not one of the breasts, but that wasn't the reason, was it?

DR. SCOTT: I don't think it helps you to talk like this.

KEN: Because I can't do anything about it, you mean.

DR. SCOTT: I didn't mean that exactly.

KEN: I watch you walking in the room, bending over me, tucking in your sweater. It's surprising how relaxed a woman can become when she is not in the presence of a man.

DR. SCOTT: I'm sorry if I provoked you . . . I can assure you . . .

KEN: You haven't "provoked" me, as you put it, but you are a woman and even though I've only a piece of knotted string between my legs, I still have a man's mind. One change that I have noticed is that I now engage in sexual banter with young nurses, searching for the double entendre in the most innocent remark. Like a sexually desperate middle-aged man. Then they leave the room and I go cold with embarrassment. It's fascinating, isn't it? Laughable. I still have tremendous sexual desire. Do you find that disgusting?

DR. SCOTT: No.

KEN: Pathetic?

DR. SCOTT: Sad.

KEN: I am serious you know . . . about deciding to die.

DR. SCOTT: You will get over that feeling.

KEN: How do you know?

DR. SCOTT: From experience.

KEN: That doesn't alter the validity of my decision now.

DR. SCOTT: But if we acted on your decision now, there wouldn't be an opportunity for you to accept it.

KEN: I grant you, I may become lethargic and quiescent. Happy when a nurse comes to put in a new catheter, or give me an enema, or to turn me over. These could become the high spots of my day. I might even learn to do wonderful things, like turn the pages of a book with some miracle of modern science, or to type letters with flicking my eyelids. And you would look at me and say: "Wasn't it worth waiting?" and I would say: "Yes" and be proud of my achievements. Really proud. I grant you all that, but it doesn't alter the validity of my present position.

DR. SCOTT: But if you became happy?

KEN: But I don't want to become happy by becoming the computer section of a complex machine. And morally, you must accept my decision.

DR. SCOTT: Not according to my morals.

KEN: And why are yours better than mine? They're better because you're more powerful. I am in your power. To hell with a morality that is based on the proposition that might is right.

DR. SCOTT: I must go now. I was halfway through Mr. Patel.

[*She walks to the door*]

KEN: I thought you were just passing. Oh, Doctor . . . one more thing . . .

DR. SCOTT: Yes?

KEN: You still have lovely breasts.

[*She smiles and goes out into the* SISTER's *office. She is very upset.* SISTER *passes and looks at her*]

SISTER: Are you alright? Would you like a cup of tea?

DR. SCOTT: Yes, Sister, I would.

SISTER: . . . Nurse! Would you bring a cup of tea please.

[NURSE SADLER *looks from the kitchen*]

NURSE: Yes, Sister.

[*They walk into the* SISTER's *room and sit down*]

DR. SCOTT: I've never met anyone like Ken Harrison before.

SISTER: No.

DR. SCOTT: He's so . . . bright . . . intelligent . . . He says he wants to die.

SISTER: Many patients say that.

DR. SCOTT: I know that, Sister, but he means it. It's just a calm rational decision.

SISTER: I thought this morning, when he was talking about the compensation, he was beginning to plan for the future.

DR. SCOTT: Not really, you know. That was just to keep us happy. He probably thinks that if he pretends to be planning for the future we'll stop tranquillizing him or something like that.

[A knock on the door]

SISTER: Come in.

NURSE: Here's the tea, Sister.

SISTER: Thank you, Nurse. For Doctor.

[NURSE SADLER gives the cup to DR. SCOTT and goes out]

DR. SCOTT: It's marvellous, you know. We bring him back to life using everything we've got. We give him back his consciousness, then he says: "But how do I use it?" So what do we do? We put him back to sleep.

[Cross fade on KEN's room. JOHN goes in to empty the rubbish. He taps KEN lightly as if to repeat the steel band game but KEN is asleep]

JOHN: Ping-Pong . . . You poor bastard.

[He leaves]

CURTAIN

ACT TWO

SISTER: A visitor for you, Mr. Harrison.

HILL: Good afternoon, Mr. Harrison.

KEN: Good afternoon.

HILL: You're looking very much better.

[SISTER *has placed a chair by the bed*]

KEN: It's the nursing, you know.

SISTER: I'm glad you realise it, Mr. Harrison.

KEN: Oh I do, Sister, I do.

SISTER: I'll leave you gentlemen now.

HILL: Thank you, Sister. [*She goes out*] You really do look better.

KEN: Yes. I'm as well now as I shall ever be . . .

HILL: [*Unzipping his briefcase*] I've brought all the papers . . . Things are moving along very satisfactorily now and . . .

KEN: I don't want to talk about the accident.

HILL: I understand it must be very distressing . . .

KEN: No, no. It's not that. I didn't get you along about the compensation.

HILL: Oh . . . Sister said on the 'phone . . .

KEN: Yes, I know. Could you come away from the door? Look, do you work for yourself? I mean, you don't work for an insurance company or something, do you? . . .

HILL: No. I'm in practice as a solicitor, but I . . .

KEN: Then there's no reason why you couldn't represent me generally . . . apart from this compensation thing . . .

HILL: Certainly, if there's anything I can do . . .

KEN: There is.

HILL: Yes?

KEN: . . . Get me out of here.

HILL: . . . I don't understand, Mr. Harrison.

KEN: It's quite simple. I can't exist outside the hospital, so they've got to keep me here if they want to keep me alive and they seem intent on doing that. I've decided that I don't want to stay in hospital any longer.

HILL: But surely they wouldn't keep you here longer than necessary?

KEN: I'm almost completely paralysed and I always will be. I shall never be discharged by the hospital. I have coolly and calmly thought it out and I have decided that I would rather not go on. I therefore want to be discharged to die.

HILL: And you want me to represent you?

KEN: Yes. Tough.

HILL: . . . And what is the hospital's attitude?

KEN: They don't know about it yet. Even tougher.

HILL: This is an enormous step . . .

KEN: Mr. Hill, with all respect, I know that our hospitals are wonderful. I know that many people have succeeded in making good lives with appalling handicaps. I'm happy for them and respect and admire them. But each man must make his own decision. And mine is to die quietly and with as much dignity as I can muster and I need your help.

HILL: Do you realise what you're asking me to do?

KEN: I realise. I'm not asking that you make any decision about my life and death, merely that you represent me and my views to the hospital.

HILL: . . . Yes, well, the first thing is to see the Doctor. What is his name?

KEN: Dr. Emerson.

HILL: I'll try and see him now and come back to you.

KEN: Then you'll represent me? . . .

HILL: Mr. Harrison, I'll let you know my decision after I've seen Dr. Emerson.

KEN: Alright, but you'll come back to tell me yourself, even if he convinces you he's right?

HILL: Yes, I'll come back.

[*Cross fade on the sluice room.* NURSE SADLER *and* JOHN *are talking*]

JOHN: So why not? . . .

NURSE: It's just that I'm so busy . . .

JOHN: All work and no play . . . makes for a boring day.

NURSE: Anyway, I hardly know you.

JOHN: Right . . . That's why I want to take you out . . . to find out what goes on behind those blue eyes . . .

NURSE: At present, there's just lists of bones and organs, all getting themselves jumbled up.

JOHN: Because you're working too hard . . .

NURSE: Ask me next week . . .

JOHN: O.K. It's a deal . . .

NURSE: Right!

JOHN: And I'll ask you this afternoon as well.

[*Cross fade on* DR. EMERSON'S *room*]

DR. EMERSON: Mr. Hill? Sister just rang through.

HILL: Dr. Emerson?

[*They shake hands*]

DR. EMERSON: You've been seeing Mr. Harrison?

HILL: Yes.

DR. EMERSON: Tragic case . . . I hope you'll be able to get enough money for him to ease his mind.

HILL: Dr. Emerson. It's not about that I wanted to see you. I thought I was coming about that, but Mr. Harrison wishes to retain me to represent him on quite another matter.

DR. EMERSON: Oh?

HILL: Yes, he wants to be discharged.

DR. EMERSON: That's impossible.

HILL: Why?

DR. EMERSON: To put it bluntly, he would die if we did that.

HILL: He knows that. It's what he wants.

DR. EMERSON: And you are asking me to kill my patient?

HILL: I am representing Mr. Harrison's wishes to you and asking for your reaction.

DR. EMERSON: Well, you've had it. It's impossible. Now if that's really all you came about . . .

HILL: Dr. Emerson, you can, of course, dismiss me like that if you choose to, but I would hardly think it serves anyone's interests, least of all Mr. Harrison's.

DR. EMERSON: I am trying to save Mr. Harrison's life. There is no need to remind me of my duty to my patient, Mr. Hill.

HILL: Or mine to my client, Dr. Emerson.

DR. EMERSON: . . . Are you telling me that you have accepted the job of coming to me to urge a course of action that will lose your client his life?

HILL: I hadn't accepted it . . . no . . . I told Mr. Harrison I would talk to you first. Now I have and I begin to see why he thought it necessary to be represented.

DR. EMERSON: Alright . . . Let's start again. Now tell me what you want to know.

HILL: Mr. Harrison wishes to be discharged from hospital. Will you please make the necessary arrangements?

DR. EMERSON: No.

HILL: May I ask why not?

DR. EMERSON: Because Mr. Harrison is incapable of living outside the hospital and it is my duty as a doctor to preserve life.

HILL: I take it that Mr. Harrison is a voluntary patient here.

DR. EMERSON: Of course.

HILL: Then I fail to see the legal basis for your refusal.

DR. EMERSON: Can't you understand that Mr. Harrison is suffering from depression? He is incapable of making a rational decision about his life and death.

HILL: Are you maintaining that Mr. Harrison is mentally unbalanced?

DR. EMERSON: Yes.

HILL: Would you have any objection to my bringing in a psychiatrist for a second opinion?

DR. EMERSON: Of course not, but why not ask the consultant psychiatrist here? I'm sure he will be able to convince you.

HILL: Has he examined Mr. Harrison?

DR. EMERSON: No, but that can be quickly arranged.

HILL: That's very kind of you, Dr. Emerson, but I'm sure you'll understand if I ask for my own—whose opinion you are not sure of *before* he examines the patient.

DR. EMERSON: Good afternoon, Mr. Hill.

HILL: Good afternoon.

[MR. HILL *takes up his briefcase and leaves*]

DR. EMERSON: [*Picks up the 'phone*] Could you find out where Dr. Travers is please? I want to see him urgently, and put me through to the hospital secretary please. Well, put me through when he's free.

[*Cross fade on* KEN'S *room. The door opens and* MR. HILL *comes in*]

KEN: Well, how was it on Olympus?

HILL: Cloudy.

KEN: No joy then?

HILL: Dr. Emerson does not wish to discharge you.

KEN: Surprise, surprise. So what do we do now?

HILL: Mr. Harrison, I will be perfectly plain. Dr. Emerson claims that you are not in a sufficiently healthy mental state to make a rational decision, especially one of this seriousness and finality. Now my position is, I am not competent to decide whether or not he is right.

KEN: So how will you decide?

HILL: I should like to have you examined by an independent psychiatrist and I will accept his view of the case and advise you accordingly.

KEN: Fair enough. Will Dr. Emerson agree?

HILL: He has already. I ought to warn you that Dr. Emerson is likely to take steps to have you admitted here as a person needing treatment under the Mental Health Act of 1959. This means that he can keep you here and give you what treatment he thinks fit.

KEN: Can he do that?

HILL: He probably can.

KEN: Haven't I any say in this?

HILL: Oh, yes. He will need another signature and that doctor will have to be convinced that you ought compulsorily to be detained. Even if he agrees, we can appeal.

KEN: Let's get on with it then.

HILL: One thing at a time. First, you remember, our own psychiatrist.

KEN: Wheel him in . . .

HILL: I'll be in touch soon, then.

KEN: Oh, before you go. Yesterday I refused to take a tranquillizer and Dr. Emerson came and gave me an injection. It made me pretty dopey. If I was like that when the psychiatrist came, he'd lock me up for life!

HILL: I'll mention it to him. Goodbye for now, then.

KEN: Goodbye.

> [*Cross fade on* DR. EMERSON's *office.* DR. EMERSON *is writing.* DR. TRAVERS *knocks on his door and looks in*]

DR. EMERSON: [*On the 'phone*] Can you find me Dr. Scott please?

> [*He puts the 'phone down*]

DR. TRAVERS: You wanted to see me?

DR. EMERSON: Ah, yes. If you can spare a moment.

DR. TRAVERS: What's the problem?

DR. EMERSON: Nasty one really. I have a road accident case, paralysed from the neck down. He's naturally very depressed and wants to discharge himself. But with a neurogenic bladder and all the rest of it, he couldn't last a week out of here. I need time to get him used to the idea.

DR. TRAVERS: How long ago was the accident?

DR. EMERSON: Six months.

DR. TRAVERS: A long time.

DR. EMERSON: Yes, well there were other injuries but we've just about got him physically stabilised. The trouble is that he's got himself a solicitor and if I am to keep him here, I'll have to admit him compulsorily under the Mental Health Act. I wondered if you'd see him.

DR. TRAVERS: I'll see him of course, but my signature won't help you.

DR. EMERSON: Why not? You're the psychiatrist, aren't you?

DR. TRAVERS: Yes, but under the Act, you need two signatures and only one can come from a practitioner of the hospital where the patient is to be kept.

DR. EMERSON: Bloody hell!

DR. TRAVERS: Not to worry. I take it you regard this as an emergency.

DR. EMERSON: Of course I do.

DR. TRAVERS: Well, sign the application and then you've got three days to get another signature.

DR. EMERSON: There'll be no problem about that surely?

DR. TRAVERS: Depends upon whether he's clinically depressed or not.

DR. EMERSON: You haven't understood. He's suicidal. He's determined to kill himself.

DR. TRAVERS: I could name you several psychiatrists who wouldn't take that as evidence of insanity.

DR. EMERSON: Well, I could name several psychiatrists who *are* evidence of insanity. I've had a lot of experience in this kind of case. I'm sure, absolutely sure, I can win him around, given time—a few months . . .

DR. TRAVERS: I understand, Michael.

DR. EMERSON: . . . So you'll look at him, will you? . . . And get another chap in? . . .

DR. TRAVERS: Yes, I'll do that.

DR. EMERSON: [*Twinkling*] And . . . do me a favour, will you? Try and find an old codger like me, who believes in something better than suicide.

DR. TRAVERS: [*Grinning*] There's a chap at Ellertree . . . a very staunch Catholic, I believe. Would that suit you?

DR. EMERSON: Be Jasus—sounds just the man!

DR. TRAVERS: I'll see his notes and drop in on him . . .

DR. EMERSON: Thank you very much, Paul . . . I'm very grateful— and Harrison will be too.

[DR. SCOTT *comes in the room*]

DR. SCOTT: Oh, sorry.

DR. TRAVERS: It's alright . . . I'm just off . . . I'll see him then, Michael, this afternoon.

[DR. TRAVERS *leaves.* DR. SCOTT *looks at* DR. EMERSON *questioningly*]

DR. SCOTT: You wanted me?

DR. EMERSON: Ah, yes. Harrison's decided to discharge himself.

DR. SCOTT: Oh, no, but I'm not surprised.

DR. EMERSON: So, Travers is seeing him now.

DR. SCOTT: Dr. Travers won't make him change his mind.

DR. EMERSON: I am committing him under Section 26.

DR. SCOTT: Oh, will Dr. Travers sign it?

DR. EMERSON: Evidently if I do, he can't, but he knows a chap over in Ellertree who probably will.

DR. SCOTT: I see.

DR. EMERSON: I have no choice, do you see, Clare? He's got himself a solicitor. It's the only way I can keep him here.

DR. SCOTT: Are you sure you should?

DR. EMERSON: Of course. No question.

DR. SCOTT: It's his life.

DR. EMERSON: But my responsibility.

DR. SCOTT: Only if he's incapable of making his own decision.

DR. EMERSON: But he isn't capable. I refuse to believe that a man with a mind as quick as his, a man with enormous mental resources, would calmly choose suicide.

DR. SCOTT: But he has done just that.

DR. EMERSON: And, therefore, I say he is unbalanced.

DR. SCOTT: But surely a wish to die is not *necessarily* a symptom of insanity? A man might want to die for perfectly sane reasons.

DR. EMERSON: No, Clare, a doctor cannot accept the choice for death; he's committed to life. When a patient is brought into my unit, he's in a bad way. I don't stand about thinking whether or not it's worth saving his life, I haven't the time for doubts. I get in there, do whatever I can to save life. I'm a doctor, not a judge.

DR. SCOTT: I hope you will forgive me, sir, for saying this, but I think that is just how you are behaving—as a judge.

DR. EMERSON: You must, of course, say what you think—but I am the responsible person here.

DR. SCOTT: I know that, sir.

[*She makes to go*]

DR. EMERSON: I'm sure it's not necessary for me to say this but I'd rather there was no question of misunderstanding later . . . Mr. Harrison is now physically stable. There is no reason why he should die; if he should die suddenly, I would think it necessary to order a post-mortem and to act on whatever was found.

DR. SCOTT: . . . Mr. Harrison is your patient, sir.

DR. EMERSON: [*Smiling*] Of course, of course. You make that sound a fate worse than death.

DR. SCOTT: Perhaps for him it is.

[*She goes out. Cross fade on* KEN'S *room.* DR. TRAVERS *comes in.*]

DR. TRAVERS: Mr. Harrison?

KEN: That's right.

DR. TRAVERS: Dr. Travers.

KEN: Are you a psychiatrist?

DR. TRAVERS: Yes.

KEN: For or against me . . . Or does that sound like paranoia?

DR. TRAVERS: You'd hardly expect me to make an instant diagnosis.

KEN: Did Dr. Emerson send you?

DR. TRAVERS: I work here, in the hospital.

KEN: Ah.

DR. TRAVERS: Would you describe yourself as suffering from paranoia?

KEN: No.

DR. TRAVERS: What would you say paranoia was?

KEN: Difficult. It depends on the person. A man whose feelings of security are tied to his own sense of what is right and can brook no denial. If he were, say, a sculptor, then we would describe his mental condition as paranoia. If, on the other hand, he was a doctor, we would describe it as professionalism.

DR. TRAVERS: [*Laughing*] You don't like doctors!

KEN: Do you like patients?

DR. TRAVERS: Some.

KEN: I like some doctors.

DR. TRAVERS: What's wrong with doctors, then?

KEN: Speaking generally, I suppose that as a profession you've not learnt that the level of awareness of the population has risen dramatically; that black magic is no longer much use and that people *can* and *want* to understand what's wrong with them and many of them can make decisions about their own lives.

DR. TRAVERS: What they need is information.

KEN: Of course, but as a rule, doctors dole out information like a kosher butcher gives out pork sausages.

DR. TRAVERS: That's fair. But you'd agree that patients need medical knowledge to make good decisions?

KEN: I would. Look at me, for example. I'm a sculptor, an airy-fairy artist, with no real hard knowledge and no capability to understand anything about my body. You're a doctor but I think I would hold my own with a competition in anatomy with *you*.

DR. TRAVERS: It's a long time since I did any anatomy.

KEN: Of course. Whereas I was teaching it every day up to six months ago. It wouldn't be fair.

DR. TRAVERS: Your knowledge of anatomy may be excellent, but what's your neurology like, or your dermatology, endocrinology, urology and so on.

KEN: Lousy, and in so far as these bear on my case, I should be grateful for information so that I can make a proper decision. But it is my decision. If you came to my studio to buy something, and look at all my work, and you say: "I want that bronze" and I say to you: "Look, you don't know anything about sculpture. The proportion of that is all wrong, the texture is boring and it should have been made in wood anyway. You are having the marble!" You'd think I was nuts. If you were sensible you'd ask for my professional opinion but if you were a mature adult, you'd reserve the right to choose for yourself.

DR. TRAVERS: But we're not talking about a piece of sculpture to decorate a room, but about your life.

KEN: That's right Doctor. *My* life.

DR. TRAVERS: But your obvious intelligence weakens your case. I'm not saying that you would find life easy but you do have resources that an unintelligent person doesn't have.

KEN: That sounds like Catch-22. If you're clever and sane enough to put up an invincible case for suicide, it demonstrates you ought not to die. [DR. TRAVERS *moves the stool near the bed*] That's a disturbing tidiness compulsion you've got there.

DR. TRAVERS: I was an only child; enough of me. Have you any relationships outside the hospital? . . . You're not married, I see.

KEN: No, thank God.

DR. TRAVERS: A girl friend?

KEN: A fiancée actually. I asked her not to visit me any more. About a fortnight ago.

DR. TRAVERS: She must have been upset.

KEN: Better that than a lifetime's sacrifice.

DR. TRAVERS: She wanted to . . . stay with you, then?

KEN: Oh, yes . . . Had it all worked out . . . But she's a young healthy woman. She wants babies—real ones. Not ones that never *will* learn to walk.

DR. TRAVERS: But if that's what she really wants.

KEN: Oh, come on, Doctor. If that's what she really wants, there's plenty of other cripples who want help. I told her to go to release her, I hope, from the guilt she would feel if she did what she really wanted to.

DR. TRAVERS: That's very generous.

KEN: Balls! Really, Doctor, I did it for *me*. It would destroy *my* self-respect if I allowed myself to become the object with which people can safely exploit their masochist tendencies.

DR. TRAVERS: That's putting it very strongly.

KEN: Yes. Too strong. But you are beginning to sound like the chaplain. He was in here the other day. He seemed to think I should be quite happy to be God's chosen vessel into which people could pour their compassion . . . That it was alright being a cripple because it made other folk feel good when they helped me.

DR. TRAVERS: What about your parents?

KEN: Working class folk—they live in Scotland. I thought it would break my mother—I always thought of my father as a very tough egg. But it was the other way round. My father can only think with his hands. He used to stand around here—completely at a loss. My mother would sit there—just understanding. She knows what suffering's about. They were here a week ago—I got rid of my father for a while and told my mother what I was going to do. She looked at me for a minute. There were tears in her eyes. She said: "Aye, lad, it's thy life . . . don't worry about your dad—I'll get him over it." . . . She stood up and I said: "What about you?" "What about me?" she said, "Do you think life's so precious to me, I'm frightened of dying?" . . . I'd like to think I was my mother's son.

DR. TRAVERS: . . . Yes, well, we shall have to see . . .

KEN: What about? You mean you haven't made up your mind?

DR. TRAVERS: . . . I shall have to do some tests . . .

KEN: What tests, for Christ's sake? I can tell you now, my time over a hundred metres is lousy.

DR. TRAVERS: You seem very angry.

KEN: Of course I'm angry . . . No, no . . . I'm . . . Yes. I am angry. [Breathing] But I am trying to hold it in because you'll just write me off as in a manic phase of a manic depressive cycle.

DR. TRAVERS: You are very free with psychiatric jargon.

KEN: Oh, well then, you'll be able to say I'm an obsessive hypochondriac. [Breathing]

DR. TRAVERS: I certainly wouldn't do that, Mr. Harrison.

KEN: Can't you see what a trap I am in? Can anyone prove that they are sane? Could you?

DR. TRAVERS: . . . I'll come and see you again.

KEN: No, don't come and see me again, because every time you come I'll get more and more angry, and more and more upset and depressed. And eventually you will destroy my mind.

DR. TRAVERS: I'm sorry if I upset you, Mr. Harrison.

[DR. TRAVERS *replaces the stool and exits. He crosses to the* SISTER's *office. Enter* DR. SCOTT *and* MR. HILL]

DR. SCOTT: I hate the idea. It's against all my training and instincts . . .

HILL: Mine, too. But in this case, we're not dealing with euthanasia, are we?

DR. SCOTT: Something very close.

HILL: No. Something very far away. Suicide.

DR. SCOTT: Thank you for a lovely meal.

HILL: Not at all, I am glad you accepted. Tell me, what would you think, or rather feel, if there was a miracle and Ken Harrison was granted the use of his arms for just one minute and he used them to grab a bottle of sleeping tablets and swallowed the lot?

DR. SCOTT: . . . It's irrational but . . . I'd be very . . . relieved.

HILL: It wouldn't go against your instincts? . . . You wouldn't feel it was a wasted life and fight with stomach pumps and all that?

DR. SCOTT: No . . . not if it was my decision.

HILL: You might even be sure there *was* a bottle of tablets handy and you not there.

DR. SCOTT: You make it harder and harder . . . but yes, I might do that . . .

HILL: Yes. Perhaps we ought to make suicide respectable again. Whenever anyone kills himself there's a whole legal rigmarole to go through—investigations, inquests and so on—and it all seems designed to find someone or something to *blame*. Can you ever recall a coroner saying something like: "We've heard all the evidence of how John Smith was facing literally insuperable odds and he made a courageous decision. I record a verdict of a noble death?"

DR. SCOTT: No . . . It's been a . . . very pleasant evening.

HILL: Thank you. For me, too.

DR. SCOTT: I don't know if I've helped you though.

HILL: You have. I've made up my mind.

DR. SCOTT: You'll help him?

HILL: Yes . . I hope you're not sorry.

DR. SCOTT: I'm pleased . . .

HILL: I'm sure it is morally wrong for anyone to try to hand the responsibility for their death to anyone else. And it's wrong to accept that responsibility, but Ken isn't trying to do that.

DR. SCOTT: I'm glad you've made up your mind . . . Goodnight.

[*They stop*]

HILL: I hope I see you again.

DR. SCOTT: I'm on the 'phone . . . Goodnight.

HILL: Goodnight.

[*They exit,* NURSE SADLER *goes into* KEN's *room with a meal*]

KEN: You still on duty?

NURSE: We're very short-staffed . . . [*She prepares to feed* KEN *with a spoon*] It looks good tonight . . . Minced beef.

KEN: Excellent . . . and what wine shall we order, then? How about a '48 claret. Yes, I think so . . . Send for the wine waiter.

NURSE: You are a fool Mr. Harrison.

KEN: Is there any reason why I shouldn't have wine?

NURSE: I don't know. I'll ask Sister if you like . . .

KEN: After all, the hospital seems determined to depress my consciousness. But they'd probably think it's immoral if I enjoy it. [NURSE SADLER *gives him a spoonful of mince*] It's a bit salty.

NURSE: Do you want some water?

KEN: That would be good. Very nice . . . Not too full of body, Château Ogston Reservoir, I think, with just a cheeky little hint of Jeyes fluid from the steriliser.

NURSE: We use Milton.

KEN: Oh, dear . . . you'd better add to my notes. The final catastrophe. Mr. Harrison's palate is failing; rush up the emergency taste resuscitation unit. [*In a phoney American accent*] "Nurse, give me orange . . . No response . . . Quick the lemon . . . God! Not a flicker . . . We're on the tightrope . . . Nurse pass the ultimate . . . Quick, there's no time to lose . . . Pass the hospital mince." That would bring people back from the dead. Don't tell Emerson that or he'll try it. I don't want any more of that.

[NURSE SADLER *exits.* DR. SCOTT *comes in*]

KEN: Sister.

DR. SCOTT: No, it's me. Still awake?

KEN: Yes.

DR. SCOTT: It's late.

KEN: What time is it?

DR. SCOTT: Half past eleven.

KEN: The Night Sister said I could have the light for half an hour. I couldn't sleep. I wanted to think.

DR. SCOTT: Yes.

KEN: You look lovely.

DR. SCOTT: Thank you.

KEN: Have you been out?

DR. SCOTT: For a meal.

KEN: Nice. Good company?

DR. SCOTT: You're fishing.

KEN: That's right.

DR. SCOTT: Yes, it was good company.

KEN: A colleague?

DR. SCOTT: No. Actually it was Philip Hill, your solicitor.

KEN: Well, well, well . . . The randy old devil. He didn't take long to get cracking, did he?

DR. SCOTT: It was just a dinner.

KEN: I know I engaged him to act for me. I didn't realise he would see his duties so comprehensively.

DR. SCOTT: It was just a dinner!

KEN: Well, I hope my surrogate self behaved myself.

DR. SCOTT: You were a perfect gentleman.

KEN: Mm . . . then perhaps I'd better engage another surrogate.

DR. SCOTT: Do you mind really?

KEN: . . . No. Unless you convinced him that Emerson was right.

DR SCOTT: . . . I didn't try.

KEN: Thank you.

DR. SCOTT: I think you are enjoying all this.

KEN: I suppose I am in a way. For the first time in six months I feel like a human being again.

DR. SCOTT: Yes. [A *pause*] Isn't that the whole point, Ken, that . . .

KEN: You called me Ken.

DR. SCOTT: Do you mind?

KEN: Oh! No, I liked it. I'll just chalk it up as another credit for today.

DR. SCOTT: I was saying, isn't that just the point; isn't that what this fight has shown you? That you are a human being again. You're not fighting for death. I don't think you want to win.

KEN: That was what I had to think about.

DR. SCOTT: And have you . . . changed your mind?

KEN: . . . No. I know I'm enjoying the fight and I had to be sure that I wanted to win, really get what I'm fighting for, and not just doing it to convince myself I'm still alive.

DR. SCOTT: And are you sure?

KEN: Yes, quite sure; for me life is over. I want it recognised because I can't do the things that I want to do. That means I can't say the things I want to say. Is that a better end? You understand, don't you?

[NURSE SADLER *comes in with a feeding cup*]

NURSE: I didn't know you were here, Doctor?

DR. SCOTT: Yes, I'm just going.

KEN: See what I mean, Doctor. Here is my substitute mum, with her porcelain pap. This isn't for me.

DR. SCOTT: No . . .

KEN: So tomorrow, on with the fight!

DR. SCOTT: Goodnight . . . and good luck.

[*Fade*]

KERSHAW: So our psychiatrist is prepared to state that Harrison is sane.

HILL: Yes, he was sure. I'll have his written report tomorrow. He said he could understand the hospital fighting to save their patient from himself, but no matter how much he sympathised with them and how much he wished he could get Harrison to change his mind, nevertheless, he was sane and knew exactly what he was doing and why he was doing it.

KERSHAW: And you say that the hospital are holding him here under Section 26.

HILL: Yes, they rang me this morning. They got another chap in from Ellertree to sign it as well as Emerson.

KERSHAW: Hm . . . Tricky. There's no precedent for this, you know. Fascinating.

HILL: Yes.

KERSHAW: And you're sure in your mind he knows what he's doing?

HILL: Yes.

KERSHAW: . . . Well . . . Let's see him, shall we?

HILL: Here's the Sister's office.

KERSHAW: Is she your standard gorgon?

HILL: Only on the outside. But under that iron surface beats a heart of stainless steel.

[*They go into* SISTER'S *office*]

HILL: Good morning, Sister.

SISTER: Morning, Mr. Hill.

HILL: This is a colleague, Mr. Kershaw.

SISTER: Good morning.

KERSHAW: Good morning.

HILL: Is it alright to see Mr. Harrison? . . .

SISTER: Have you asked Dr. Emerson?

HILL: Oh, yes . . . before we came . . .

SISTER: I see . . .

HILL: You can check with him . . .

SISTER: . . . I don't think that's necessary . . . However, I'm afraid I shall have to ask you if I can stay with Mr. Harrison whilst you interview him.

HILL: Why?

SISTER: We are very worried about Mr. Harrison's mental condition, as you know. Twice recently he has . . . got excited . . . and his breathing function has not been able to cope with the extra demands. Dr. Emerson has ordered that at any time Mr. Harrison is subjected to stress, someone must be there as a precaution.

HILL: . . . I see. [*He glances at* MR. KERSHAW, *who shrugs*] Very well.

SISTER: This way, gentlemen.

[*They go into* KEN's *room*]

HILL: Good morning, Mr. Harrison.

KEN: Morning.

HILL: I've brought along Mr. Kershaw. He is the barrister who is advising us.

KERSHAW: Good morning, Mr. Harrison.

HILL: Your doctor has insisted that Sister remains with us—to see you don't get too excited.

KEN: Oh! Sister, you know very well that your very presence always excites me tremendously. It must be the white apron and black stockings. A perfect mixture of mother and mistress. [SISTER *grins a little sheepishly and takes a seat at the head of the bed.* KEN *strains his head to look at her.* SISTER *turns back the covers*] Sister, what are you doing! Oh. Just for a minute there, Sister . . .

[SISTER *takes his pulse*]

HILL: . . . Well . . .

SISTER: Just a moment, Mr. Hill . . . [*She finishes taking the pulse*] Very well.

KEN: So, Mr. Kershaw, what is your advice?

[MR. KERSHAW *pauses.* MR. HILL *makes to speak but* MR. KERSHAW *stops him with a barely perceptible shake of the head. A longer pause*]

KERSHAW: . . . If you succeed in your aim you will be dead within a week.

KEN: I know.

KERSHAW: . . . I am informed that without a catheter the toxic substance will build up in your bloodstream and you will be slowly poisoned by your own blood.

KEN: [*Smiles*] . . . You should have brought along a tape-recorder. That speech would be much more dramatic with sound effects!

KERSHAW: [*relaxing and smiling*] I had to be sure you know what you are doing.

KEN: I know.

KERSHAW: And you have no doubt whatsoever; no slightest reservations? . . .

KEN: None at all.

KERSHAW: Let's look at the possibilities. You are now being held under the Mental Health Act Section 26, which means they can keep you here and give you any treatment they believe you need. Under the law we can appeal to a tribunal.

KEN: How long will that take?

KERSHAW: . . . Up to a year.

KEN: A year! A year! Oh God, can't it be quicker than that?

KERSHAW: It might be quicker, but it could be a year.

KEN: Jesus Christ! I really would be crazy in a year.

KERSHAW: That's the procedure.

KEN: I couldn't stay like this for another year, I couldn't.

HILL: We could always try habeas corpus.

KERSHAW: That would depend if we could find someone.

KEN: Habeas corpus? What's that? I thought it was something to do with criminals.

KERSHAW: Well, it usually is, Mr. Harrison. Briefly, it's against the law to deprive anyone of their liberty without proper cause. If anyone is so deprived, they or a friend can apply for a writ of habeas corpus, which is the Latin for "you may have the body."

KEN: Particularly apt in my case.

KERSHAW: . . . The people who are doing the detaining have to produce the . . . person, before the judge and if they can't give a good enough reason for keeping him, the judge will order that he be released.

KEN: It sounds as if it will take as long as that tribunal you were talking about.

KERSHAW: No. Habeas corpus is one of the very few legal processes that move very fast. We can approach any judge at any time even when the courts aren't sitting and he will see that it's heard straight away—in a day or so usually.

HILL: If you could find a judge to hear it.

KEN: Why shouldn't a judge hear it.

KERSHAW: Habeas corpus itself is fairly rare. This would be rarer.

KEN: Will I have to go to court?

KERSHAW: I doubt it. The hearing can be in court or in private, in the Judge's Chambers, as we say. The best thing to do in this case is for Mr. Hill and I to find a judge, issue the writ, then I'll get together with the hospital's barrister and we'll approach the judge together and suggest we hold the subsequent hearing here.

KEN: In this room?

KERSHAW: I expect the judge will agree. If he ordered you to be produced in court and anything happened to you, it would be a classical case of prejudging the issue.

KEN: I wouldn't mind.

KERSHAW: But the judge would feel rather foolish. I should think it would be in a few days.

KEN: Thank you. It'll be an unusual case for you—making a plea for the defendant's death.

KERSHAW: I'll be honest with you. It's a case I could bear to lose.

KEN: If you do—it's a life sentence for me.

KERSHAW: Well, we shall see. Good morning, Mr. Harrison.

[*They go out with the* SISTER. *They pause at the* SISTER'S *office*]

HILL: Thank you very much, Sister . . . I'm very sorry about all this. I do realise it must be upsetting for you.

SISTER: Not at all, Mr. Hill. As I have a stainless steel heart, it's easy to keep it sterilised of emotion. Good morning.

[*She goes into her room.* HILL *and* KERSHAW *go out. Cross fade on* KEN's *room.* JOHN *and* NURSE SADLER *are setting chairs for the hearing.* JOHN *begins to sing "Dry Bones"*]

NURSE: John!

JOHN: What's the matter?

[NURSE SADLER *is confused*]

NURSE: Nothing, of course . . . silly . . .

[KEN *picks up the vibes between the two*]

KEN: Hello, hello . . . What have we here? Don't tell me that Cupid has donned his antiseptic gown and is flying the corridors of the hospital, shooting his hypodermic syringes into maidens' hearts . . .

NURSE: No!

KEN: John?

JOHN: Honestly, your honour, I'm not guilty. I was just walking down the corridor when I was struck dumb by the beauty of this nurse.

NURSE: Don't be an idiot, John . . . We need an extra chair . . . Can you go and find one please?

JOHN: Your wishes, oh queen, are my command.

[*He bows and goes out*]

NURSE: He is a fool.

KEN: He isn't. He's been bloody good to me. Have you been out with him? . . . It's none of my business, of course.

NURSE: We went to a club of his last night . . . He plays in a band, you know.

KEN: Yes, I know.

NURSE: They're really good. They should go a long way . . . Still, I shouldn't be going on like this.

KEN: Why not? . . . Because I'm paralysed? Because I can't go dancing?

NURSE: Well . . .

KEN: The other day I was low and said to John, who was shaving me, I was useless, what could I do? I served no purpose and all the rest of the whining miseries. John set about finding things I could do. He said, first, because I could move my head from side to side [KEN *does so*] I could be a tennis umpire; then as my head was going, I could knock a pendulum from side to side and keep a clock going. Then he said I could be a child-minder and because kids were always doing what they shouldn't I could be perpetually shaking my head. He went on and on getting more and more fantastic—like radar scanners. I laughed so much that the Sister had to rush in and give me oxygen.

NURSE: He is funny.

KEN: He's more than that. He's free!

NURSE: Free?

KEN: Free of guilt. Most everybody here feels guilt about me— including you. That's why you didn't want to tell me what a fantastic time you had dancing. So everybody makes me feel worse because I make them feel guilty. But not John. He's sorry for me but he knows bloody well it isn't his fault. He's a tonic.

[JOHN *comes back carrying* SISTER's *armchair*]

NURSE: John! Did Sister say you could have that chair?

JOHN: She wasn't there . . .

NURSE: She'll kill you; no one ever sits in her chair.

JOHN: Why? Is it contaminated or something? I just thought that if the poor old Judge had to sit here listening to that miserable bugger moaning on about wanting to die, the least we could do was to make him comfortable.

KEN: [*Laughing to* NURSE SADLER] See?

[JOHN *sits in the chair and assumes a grave face*]

JOHN: Now, this is a very serious case. The two charges are proved . . . Firstly, this hospital has been found guilty of using drugs to make people happy. That's terrible. Next and most surprising of all, this hospital, in spite of all their efforts to the contrary, are keeping people alive! We can't have that.

   [*Footsteps outside*]

NURSE: Sister's coming!

   [JOHN *jumps up and stands between the chair and the door.* SISTER *comes in and as she approaches the bed with her back to the chair,* JOHN *slips out of the room*]

KEN: Well now, we have some very important visitors today, Sister.

SISTER: Indeed we have.

KEN: Will you be here?

SISTER: No.

KEN: I feel a bit like a traitor.

SISTER: . . . We all do what we've got to.

KEN: That's right, but not all of us do it as well as you, Sister . . .

SISTER: [*Quickly*] . . . Thank you.

   [*She moves quickly to go.* DR. SCOTT *comes in*]

DR. SCOTT: Good morning, Sister.

SISTER: [*Brightly*] Good morning.

   [*She goes quickly without noticing the chair.* DR. SCOTT *watches her go.*]

KEN: I've upset her I'm afraid.

DR. SCOTT: You shouldn't do that. She is a marvellous Sister. You ought to see some of the others.

KEN: That's what I told her.

DR. SCOTT: Oh, I see. Well, I should think that's just about the one way past her defences. How are you this morning?

KEN: Fine.

DR. SCOTT: And you're going ahead with it?

KEN: Of course.

DR. SCOTT: Of course.

KEN: I haven't had any tablets, yesterday or today.

DR. SCOTT: No.

KEN: Thank you.

DR. SCOTT: Thank the Judge. He ordered it.

KEN: Ah!

[DR. EMERSON *comes in*]

DR. EMERSON: Good morning, Mr. Harrison.

KEN: Morning, Doctor.

DR. EMERSON: There's still time.

KEN: No, I want to go on with it . . . unless you'll discharge me.

DR. EMERSON: I'm afraid I can't do that. The Judge and lawyers are conferring. I thought I'd just pop along and see if you were alright. We've made arrangements for the witnesses to wait in the Sister's office. I am one, so I should be grateful if you would remain here, with Mr. Harrison.

DR. SCOTT: Of course.

DR. EMERSON: Well, I don't want to meet the Judge before I have to. I wish you the best of luck, Mr. Harrison, so that we'll be able to carry on treating you.

KEN: [*Smiling*] Thank you for your good wishes.

[DR. EMERSON *nods and goes out*]

DR. SCOTT: If I didn't know *you* I'd say *he* was the most obstinate man I've ever met.

[*As* DR. EMERSON *makes for his office,* MR. HILL *comes down the corridor*]

HILL: Good morning.

DR. EMERSON: Morning.

[MR. HILL *stops and calls after* DR. EMERSON]

HILL: Oh, Dr. Emerson . . .

DR. EMERSON: Yes?

HILL: I don't know . . . I just want to say how sorry I am that you have been forced into such a . . . distasteful situation.

DR. EMERSON: It's not over yet, Mr. Hill. I have every confidence that the law is not such an ass that it will force me to watch a patient of mine die unnecessarily.

HILL: We are just as confident that the law is not such an ass that it will allow anyone arbitrary power.

DR. EMERSON: My power isn't arbitrary; I've earned it with knowledge and skill and it's also subject to the laws of nature.

HILL: And to the laws of the state.

DR. EMERSON: If the state is so foolish as to believe it is competent to judge a purely professional issue.

HILL: It's always doing that. Half the civil cases in the calendar arise because someone is challenging a professional's opinion.

DR. EMERSON: I don't know about other professions but I do know this one, medicine, is being seriously threatened because of the intervention of law. Patients are becoming so litigious that doctors will soon be afraid to offer any opinion or take any action at all.

HILL: Then they will be sued for negligence.

DR. EMERSON: We can't win.

HILL: Everybody wins. You wouldn't like to find yourself powerless in the hands of, say, a lawyer or a . . . bureaucrat. I wouldn't like to find myself powerless in the hands of a doctor.

DR. EMERSON: You make me sound as if I were some sort of Dracula . . .

HILL: No! . . . I for one certainly don't doubt your good faith but in spite of that I wouldn't like to place *anyone* above the law.

DR. EMERSON: I don't want to be above the law; I just want to be under laws that take full account of professional opinion.

HILL: I'm sure it will do that, Dr. Emerson. The question is, whose professional opinion?

DR. EMERSON: We shall see.

[MR. ANDREW EDEN, *the hospital's barrister, and* MR. HILL *and* MR. KERSHAW *come into* KEN's *room*]

HILL: Morning, Mr. Harrison. This is Mr. Eden who will be representing the hospital.

KEN: Hello.

[*They settle themselves into the chairs. The* SISTER *enters with the* JUDGE]

SISTER: Mr. Justice Millhouse.

JUDGE: Mr. Kenneth Harrison?

KEN: Yes, my Lord.

JUDGE: This is an informal hearing which I want to keep as brief as possible. You are, I take it, Dr. Scott?

DR. SCOTT: Yes, my Lord.

JUDGE: I should be grateful, Doctor, if you would interrupt the proceedings at any time you think it necessary.

DR. SCOTT: Yes, my Lord.

JUDGE: I have decided in consultation with Mr. Kershaw and Mr. Hill that we shall proceed thus. I will hear a statement from Dr. Michael Emerson as to why he believes Mr. Harrison is legally detained, and then a statement from Dr. Richard Barr, who will support the application. We have decided not to subject Mr. Harrison to examination and cross-examination.

KEN: But I . . .

JUDGE: [*Sharply*] Just a moment, Mr. Harrison. If, as appears likely, there remains genuine doubt as to the main issue, I shall question Mr. Harrison myself. Dr. Scott, I wonder if you would ask Dr. Emerson to come in.

DR. SCOTT: Yes, my Lord. [*She goes out*] Would you come in now, sir.

[SISTER *and* DR. EMERSON *come into* KEN's *room*]

JUDGE: Dr. Emerson, I would like you to take the oath.

[*The* JUDGE *hands* DR. EMERSON *a card with the oath written on it*]

DR. EMERSON: I swear the evidence that I give shall be the truth, the whole truth and nothing but the truth.

JUDGE: Stand over there please.

[*The* JUDGE *nods to* MR. EDEN]

EDEN: You are Dr. Michael Emerson?

DR. EMERSON: I am.

EDEN: And what is your position here?

DR. EMERSON: I am a consultant physician and in charge of the intensive care unit.

EDEN: Dr. Emerson, would you please give a brief account of your treatment of this patient.

DR. EMERSON: [*Referring to notes*] Mr. Harrison was admitted here on the afternoon of October 9th, as an emergency following a road accident. He was suffering from a fractured left tibia and right tibia and fibia, a fractured pelvis, four fractured ribs, one of which had punctured the lung, and a dislocated fourth vertebra, which had ruptured the spinal cord. He was extensively bruised and had minor lacerations. He was deeply unconscious and remained so for thirty hours. As a result of treatment all the broken bones and ruptured tissue have healed with the exception of a severed spinal cord and this, together with a mental trauma, is now all that remains of the initial injury.

EDEN: Precisely, Doctor. Let us deal with those last two points. The spinal cord. Will there be any further improvement in that?

DR. EMERSON: In the present state of medical knowledge, I would think not.

EDEN: And the mental trauma you spoke of?

DR. EMERSON: It's impossible to injure the body to the extent that Mr. Harrison did and not affect the mind. It is common in these cases that depression and the tendency to make wrong decisions goes on for months, even years.

EDEN: And in your view Mr. Harrison is suffering from such a depression?

DR. EMERSON: Yes.

EDEN: Thank you, Doctor.

JUDGE: Mr. Kershaw?

KERSHAW: Doctor. Is there any objective way you could demonstrate this trauma? Are there, for example, the results of any tests, or any measurements you can take to show it to us?

DR. EMERSON: No.

KERSHAW: Then how do you distinguish between a medical syndrome and a sane, even justified, depression?

DR. EMERSON: By using my thirty years' experience as a physician, dealing with both types.

KERSHAW: No more questions, my Lord.

JUDGE: Mr. Eden, do you wish to re-examine?

EDEN: No, my Lord.

JUDGE: Thank you, Doctor. Would you ask Dr. Barr if he would step in please?

[DR. EMERSON *goes out*]

DR. EMERSON: It's you now, Barr.

[SISTER *brings* DR. BARR *into* KEN's *room*]

SISTER: Dr. Barr.

JUDGE: Dr. Barr, will you take the oath please. [*He does so*] Mr. Kershaw.

KERSHAW: You are Dr. Richard Barr?

DR. BARR: I am.

KERSHAW: And what position do you hold?

DR. BARR: I am a consultant psychiatrist at Norwood Park Hospital.

KERSHAW: That is primarily a mental hospital, is it not?

DR. BARR: It is.

KERSHAW: Then you must see a large number of patients suffering from depressive illness.

DR. BARR: I do, yes.

KERSHAW: You have examined Mr. Harrison?

DR. BARR: I have, yes.

KERSHAW: Would you say that he was suffering from such an illness?

DR. BARR: No, I would not.

KERSHAW: Are you quite sure, Doctor?

DR. BARR: Yes, I am.

KERSHAW: The court has heard evidence that Mr. Harrison is depressed. Would you dispute that?

DR. BARR: No, but depression is not necessarily an illness. I would say that Mr. Harrison's depression is reactive rather than endogenous. That is to say, he is reacting in a perfectly rational way to a very bad situation.

KERSHAW: Thank you, Dr. Barr.

JUDGE: Mr. Eden?

EDEN: Dr. Barr. Are there any objective results that you could produce to prove Mr. Harrison is capable?

DR. BARR: There are clinical symptoms of endogenous depression, of course, disturbed sleep patterns, loss of appetite, lassitude, but, even if they were present, they would be masked by the physical condition.

EDEN: So how can you be sure this *is* in fact just a reactive depression?

DR. BARR: Just by experience, that's all, and by discovering when I talk to him that he has a remarkably incisive mind and is perfectly capable of understanding his position and of deciding what to do about it.

EDEN: One last thing, Doctor; do you think Mr. Harrison has made the right decision?

KERSHAW: [*Quickly*] Is that really relevant, my Lord? After all . . .

JUDGE: Not really . . .

DR. BARR: I should like to answer it though.

JUDGE: Very well.

DR. BARR: No, I thought he made the wrong decision. [*To* KEN] Sorry.

EDEN: No more questions, my Lord.

JUDGE: Do you wish to re-examine, Mr. Kershaw?

KERSHAW: No thank you, my Lord.

JUDGE: That will be all, Dr. Barr.

[DR. BARR *goes out. The* JUDGE *stands*]

JUDGE: Do you feel like answering some questions?

KEN: Of course.

JUDGE: Thank you.

KEN: You are too kind.

JUDGE: Not at all.

KEN: I mean it. I'd prefer it if you were a hanging judge.

JUDGE: There aren't any any more.

KEN: Society is now much more sensitive and humane?

JUDGE: You could put it that way.

KEN: I'll settle for that.

JUDGE: I would like you to take the oath. Dr. Scott, his right hand please. [KEN *takes the oath*] The consultant physician here has given evidence that you are not capable of making a rational decision.

KEN: He's wrong.

JUDGE: When then do you think he came to that opinion?

KEN: He's a good doctor and won't let a patient die if he can help it.

JUDGE: He found that you were suffering from acute depression.

KEN: Is that surprising? I am almost totally paralysed. I'd be insane if I *weren't* depressed.

JUDGE: But there is a difference between being unhappy and being depressed in the medical sense.

KEN: I would have thought that my psychiatrist answered that point.

JUDGE: But, surely, wishing to die must be strong evidence that the depression has moved beyond a mere unhappiness into a medical realm?

KEN: I don't wish to die.

JUDGE: Then what is this case all about?

KEN: Nor do I wish to live at any price. Of course I want to live but as far as I am concerned, I'm dead already. I merely require the doctors to recognise the fact. I cannot accept this condition constitutes life in any real sense at all.

JUDGE: Certainly, you're alive legally.

KEN: I think I could challenge even that.

JUDGE: How?

KEN: Any reasonable definition of life must include the idea of its being self-supporting. I seem to remember something in the papers—when all the heart transplant controversy was on—about it being alright to take someone's heart if they require constant attention from respirators and so on to keep them alive.

JUDGE: There also has to be absolutely no brain activity at all. Yours is certainly working.

KEN: It is and sanely.

JUDGE: That is the question to be decided.

KEN: My Lord, I am not asking anyone to kill me. I am only asking to be discharged from this hospital.

JUDGE: It comes to the same thing.

KEN: Then that proves my point; not just the fact that I will spend the rest of my life in hospital, but that whilst I am here, everything is geared just to keeping my brain active, with no real possibility of it ever being able to direct anything. As far as I can see, that is an act of deliberate cruelty.

JUDGE: Surely, it would be more cruel if society let people die, when it could, with some effort, keep them alive.

KEN: No, not *more* cruel, *just* as cruel.

JUDGE: Then why should the hospital let you die—if it is just as cruel?

KEN: The cruelty doesn't reside in saving someone or allowing them to die. It resides in the fact that the choice is removed from the man concerned.

JUDGE: But a man who is very desperately depressed is not capable of making a reasonable choice.

KEN: As you said, my Lord, that is the question to be decided.

JUDGE: Alright. You tell me why it is a reasonable choice that you decided to die.

KEN: It is a question of dignity. Look at me here. I can do nothing, not even the basic primitive functions. I cannot even urinate, I have a permanent catheter attached to me. Every few days my bowels are washed out. Every few hours two nurses have to turn me over or I would rot away from bedsores. Only my brain functions unimpaired but even that is futile because I can't act on any conclusions it comes to. This hearing proves that. Will you please listen?

JUDGE: I am listening.

KEN: I choose to acknowledge the fact that I am in fact dead and I find the hospital's persistent effort to maintain this shadow of life an indignity and it's inhumane.

JUDGE: But wouldn't you agree that many people with appalling physical handicaps have overcome them and lived essentially creative, dignified lives?

KEN: Yes, I would, but the dignity starts with their choice. If I choose to live, it would be appalling if society killed me. If I choose to die, it is equally appalling if society keeps me alive.

JUDGE: I cannot accept that it is undignified for society to devote resources to keeping someone alive. Surely it enhances that society.

KEN: It is not undignified if the man wants to stay alive, but I must restate that the dignity starts with his choice. Without it, it is degrading because technology has taken over from human will. My Lord, if I cannot be a man, I do not wish to be a medical achievement. I'm fine . . . I am fine.

JUDGE: It's alright. I have no more questions.

[The JUDGE stands up and walks to the window. He thinks a moment]

JUDGE: This is a most unusual case. Before I make a judgement I want to state that I believe all the parties have acted in good faith. I propose to consider this for a moment. The law on this is fairly clear. A deliberate decision to embark on a course of action that will lead inevitably to death is not *ipso facto* evidence of insanity. If it were, society would have to reward many men with a dishonourable burial rather than a posthumous medal for gallantry. On the other hand, we do have to bear in mind that Mr. Harrison has suffered massive physical injuries and it is possible that his mind is affected. Any judge in his career will have met men who are without doubt insane in the meaning of the Act and yet appear in the witness box to be rational. We must, in this case, be most careful not to allow Mr. Harrison's obvious wit and intelligence to blind us to the fact that he could be suffering from a depressive illness . . . and so we have to face the disturbing fact of the divided evidence . . . and bear in mind that, however much we may sympathise with Mr. Harrison in his cogently argued case to be allowed to die, the law instructs us to ignore it if it is the product of a disturbed or clinically depressed mind . . . However, I am satisfied that Mr. Harrison is a brave and cool man who is in complete control of his mental faculties and I shall therefore make an order for him to be set free. [*A pause. The* JUDGE *walks over to* KEN] Well, you got your hanging judge!

KEN: I think not, my Lord. Thank you.

[*The* JUDGE *nods and smiles*]

JUDGE: Goodbye. [*He turns and goes. He meets* DR. EMERSON *in the* SISTER's *room. Whilst he talks to him everyone else, except* DR. SCOTT, *comes out*] Ah, Dr. Emerson.

DR. EMERSON: My Lord?

JUDGE: I'm afraid you'll have to release your patient.

DR. EMERSON: I see.

JUDGE: I'm sorry. I understand how you must feel.

DR. EMERSON: Thank you.

JUDGE: If ever I have to have a road accident, I hope it's in this town and I finish up here.

DR. EMERSON: Thank you again.

JUDGE: Goodbye.

[*He walks down the corridor.* DR. EMERSON *stands a moment, then slowly goes back to the room.* KEN *is looking out of the window.* DR. SCOTT *is sitting by the bed*]

DR. EMERSON: Where will you go?

KEN: I'll get a room somewhere.

DR. EMERSON: There's no need.

KEN: Don't let's . . .

DR. EMERSON: We'll stop treatment, remove the drips. Stop feeding you if you like. You'll be unconscious in three days, dead in six at most.

KEN: There'll be no last minute resuscitation?

DR. EMERSON: Only with your express permission.

KEN: That's very kind; why are you doing it?

DR. EMERSON: Simple! You might change your mind.

[KEN *smiles and shakes his head*]

KEN: Thanks. I won't change my mind, but I'd like to stay.

[DR. EMERSON *nods and goes.* DR. SCOTT *stands and moves to the door. She turns and moves to* KEN *as if to kiss him*]

KEN: Oh, don't, but thank you.

[DR. SCOTT *smiles weakly and goes out. The lights are held for a long moment and then snap out*]

CURTAIN

ONCE A CATHOLIC
Mary O'Malley

Mary O'Malley

A big, thumping hit in London, Mary O'Malley's *Once a Catholic* opened in New York on October 10, 1979, and closed within the week. What happened? Was the play's irreverence too much for our local reviewers? (Audiences, unfortunately, had little time to judge for themselves because of the precipitous posting of the closing notice.) Were there too many damaging alterations to the original script or was it the inconclusive ending that abruptly brought the curtain down for domestic playgoers? Or was it the overdrawn performances (that often verged on caricature rather than comedy) or the miscasting of certain key roles that ballasted the play?

Whatever the reasons for its rather swift demise on this side of the Atlantic, this editor still concurs with British critic Sheridan Morley who wrote in *Punch* that *Once a Catholic* is "a marvelous, irreverent, affectionate and warmly comic play about the confusions and contradictions of being a Catholic schoolgirl."

The play originally was presented at the Royal Court Theatre on August 10, 1977, then moved to Wyndham's Theatre in the West End, where, at this writing, it is well into its third year.

Once a Catholic earned Miss O'Malley a number of significant honors including an award for playwriting from Thames Television, awards from the London *Evening Standard* and *Plays and Players* for the most promising new playwright of 1977, and the first Susan Smith Blackburn Prize, given annually to a woman for an outstanding contribution to the English-speaking theatre.

The version published within these pages is the original London script.

Once a Catholic takes place in and around a convent school where Irish nuns teach by rote, relate everything to dogma, and regard questions about sex as evidence of a filthy mind. While there might be some who are offended by the play (there have been scant complaints in London or in Belfast where it recently opened to a warm reception) the author admits, "I think what I have written is not offensive on the page. When a play goes into production, it can be misinterpreted. I didn't set out to offend anybody, particularly my parents, who are very good Catholics."

Actually, much of what is depicted in *Once a Catholic* no longer exists: the play is set a decade before the radical reforms of the Second Vatican Council. On the other hand, the play reflects current concerns—lack of communication between teachers and pupils, and prejudice. "Everything I write is about religious bigotry, about narrow-minded religion," says Miss O'Malley, who has written about a dozen plays both for television and the theatre.

Mary O'Malley was born in Harrow, England, and like the students in her play attended a convent school for girls in suburban London in the mid-1950s and recalls feeling fearful but rebellious because the nuns deemed so much in life to be a sin. "We were told not to do so many things, we went out and did a few," she remembers.

"*Once a Catholic* is not an autobiographical play. It's an epitaph to the fifties, to the Irish living in England as I remember them in my youth and to Catholicism as taught before the Second Vatican Council. I went to a convent in Harlesden, yes, and some of the scenes in the play are based on incidents remembered, but the characters were created out of bits of various people glued together with imagination."

Miss O'Malley's interest in the theatre began at an early age when she and her two brothers ("Impossible scholars, the three of us, though natural mimics and musicians") wrote and acted in a steady stream of plays in the back garden of their home.

"I decided to be a writer at the age of fifteen but had no idea how to go about it. There didn't seem to be a course for dramatists. But I read a lot of plays and enrolled for evening classes at an Institute in St. John's Wood where we improvised plays and I met up with a young man who had a similar sense of humor, Paul Thompson." It was Thompson who later encouraged her to write a short play for the Soho Poly. Dealing with a "bloke" living in style on Social Security and charities, it "went down well with reviewers and audiences." From there she went on to write a second play, *A 'Nevolent Society*, about three Jewish brothers in Stoke Newington. She turned to an Irish family in her third work, *If Ever a Man Suffered*, presented at both the Soho Poly and Hampstead Theatre. After that "it was encouragement all the way from people in the theatre, especially from more established writers."

She soon joined the Royal Court Theatre as resident writer and was promptly commissioned to write a play for its main stage. The result was *Once a Catholic*, her first full-length play and first commercial success.

The author, who is the mother of two teenage sons, was recently represented again on the London stage by *Look Out, Here Comes Trouble*, presented in 1978 by the Royal Shakespeare Company's Warehouse Theatre.

Once a Catholic was first produced at the Royal Court Theatre, London, on August 10, 1977, by the English Stage Company. The cast was as follows:

MOTHER PETER	*Pat Heywood*
MOTHER BASIL	*Jeanne Watts*
MOTHER THOMAS AQUINAS	*Doreen Keogh*
MR. EMANUELLI	*John Boswall*
FATHER MULLARKEY	*John Rogan*
MARY MOONEY	*Jane Carr*
MARY MCGINTY	*June Page*
MARY GALLAGHER	*Anna Keaveney*
MARY O'GRADY	*Kim Clifford*
MARY HENNESSY	*Lilian Rostkowska*
MARY MURPHY	*Sally Watkins*
MARY FLANAGAN	*Rowena Roberts*
DEREK	*Daniel Gerroll*
CUTHBERT	*Mike Grady*

Directed by Mike Ockrent
Designed by Poppy Mitchell
Lighting by Jack Raby

Once a Catholic was first presented in New York at the Helen Hayes Theatre on October 10, 1979, by Doris Cole Abrahams and Eddie Kulukundis in association with Leon Becker. The cast was as follows:

MOTHER PETER	*Rachel Roberts*
MOTHER BASIL	*Peggy Cass*
MOTHER THOMAS AQUINAS	*Pat Falkenhain*
MR. EMANUELLI	*Joseph Leon*
FATHER MULLARKEY	*Roy Poole*
MARY MOONEY	*Mia Dillon*
MARY MCGINTY	*Terry Calloway*
MARY GALLAGHER	*Virginia Hut*
MARY HENNESSY	*Bonnie Hellman*
MARY FLANAGAN	*Joyce Cohen*
MARY O'GRADY	*Christine Mitchell*
MARY MURPHY	*Loretta Scott*
DEREK	*Bill Buell*
CUTHBERT	*Charley Lang*

Directed by Mike Ockrent
Scenery by William Ritman
Costumes by Patricia Adshead
Lighting by Marc B. Weiss

MOTHER THOMAS AQUINAS: *A tall, thin, fairly young and very refined Irish nun with spectacles. Headmistress of the Convent of Our Lady of Fatima.*

MOTHER PETER: *A tall, fat, middle-aged Irish teaching nun.*

MOTHER BASIL: *A short, fat, elderly Irish teaching nun.*

MARY MOONEY: *A 5th-former. She is plain and scruffy and has ginger hair, freckles and a very good soprano singing voice.*

MARY MCGINTY: *A well-developed, blonde and pretty 5th-former.*

MARY GALLAGHER: *A sensible, attractive, dark-haired 5th-former.*

FATHER MULLARKEY: *An Irish Priest.*

MR. EMANUELLI: *A very old Music Master, non-specifically foreign. He has white hair down to his shoulders, a bandage on one leg, two walking sticks and a baritone voice.*

DEREK: *A tall, thin Teddy boy in his late teens.*

CUTHBERT: *A Catholic 6th-former with a fairly bad case of acne.*

Pupils of Form 5A:

MARY O'GRADY   MARY MURPHY

MARY HENNESSY   MARY FLANAGAN

The play is set in the Convent of Our Lady of Fatima—a Grammar School for Girls, and in and around the streets of Willesden and Harlesden, London N.W.10, from September, 1956 to July, 1957.

ACT ONE

The Chapel. FATHER MULLARKEY *is officiating at Morning Mass assisted by* CUTHBERT *dressed as an altar boy.* MR. EMANUELLI *is on the organ and the congregation consists of* MOTHER THOMAS AQUINAS, MOTHER PETER, MOTHER BASIL, MARY MOONEY, MARY MCGINTY, MARY GALLAGHER *and the* MEMBERS OF FORM 5A.

CONGREGATION: [*Singing*] "Qui cum Patre et Filio simul adoratur et conglorificatur: qui locutus est per Prophetas. Et unam, sanctam, catholicam et apostolicam Ecclesiam. Confiteor unum baptisma in remissionem peccatorum. Et exspecto resurrectionem mortuorum. Et vitam venturi saeculi. Amen."

[FATHER MULLARKEY *kisses the altar and turns to the congregation*]

FATHER MULLARKEY: "Dominus vobiscum."

CONGREGATION: "Et cum spiritu tuo."

FATHER MULLARKEY: [*Turning back to the altar*] "Oremus."

SCENE TWO

The Classroom. The girls of Form 5A are at their desks. MOTHER PETER *walks on carrying some books and a brown paper parcel.*

GIRLS: Good morning, Mother Peter.

MOTHER PETER: Good morning, 5A. [*She makes the Sign of the Cross*]

MOTHER PETER *and* GIRLS: In the name of the Father and of the Son and of the Holy Ghost, Amen. Oh Jesus through the most pure heart of Mary I offer thee all the prayers, works and sufferings of this day for all the intentions of thy divine heart. [*She makes the Sign of the Cross again*] In the name of the Father and of the Son and of the Holy Ghost, Amen.

[MOTHER PETER *sits down and opens the register*]

MOTHER PETER: [*Reading the names rapidly*]
Mary Brennan
Mary Clancy
Mary Delaney
Mary Fahy
Mary Flanagan
Mary Gallagher
Mary Hennessy
Mary Hogan
Mary Kelly
Mary Keogh
Mary Looney
Mary Mooney
Mary McGettigan
Mary McGinty
Mary McGuinness
Mary McHugh
Mary McLoughlin
Mary McManahon
Mary Murphy
Mary Nolan
Mary O'Connor
Mary O'Driscoll
Mary O'Gorman
Mary O'Grady
Mary O'Malley
Mary O'Rourke
Mary O'Shea

Mary O'Toole
Mary Walsh
Mary Whelan
Maria Zajaczkowski

[MOTHER PETER *gets up from her desk*]

MOTHER PETER: Now. Who's going to tell me what day it is today?
Mary Mooney?

MARY MOONEY: It's Tuesday, Mother Peter.

MOTHER PETER: Oh, sit down, you little simpleton and think before
you speak. Will somebody with a bit of sense please tell me what
day it is today? [*Long pause*] Well? Doesn't the eighth of September ring a bell? A very important bell indeed? [*Pause*] Evidently it
does not. Oh, aren't you the fine pack of heathens! It's Our
Blessed Lady's birthday, that's what day it is. I hope you're all
ashamed of yourselves. Just imagine how insulted Our Lady must
be feeling. Go into the chapel every one of you at dinner time and
beg for her forgiveness. Is this an example of the standard I can
expect from form 5A this year? I hope you realise that this is the
most crucial year of your academic life. In January you'll be sitting
the mock O level exams. And in June the O levels proper. And I
don't intend to have any failures in my form. Any girl showing
signs of imbecility will be sent straight down to 5B. And see will
that get you to Oxford or Cambridge. Of course, nobody ever
passed any exam of their own accord. Only prayer will get results.
The best thing each one of you can do is to pick out a particular
saint and pray to him or her to get you through. Your Confirma-
tion saint, perhaps, or any saint you fancy. But not St. Peter the
Apostle, if you wouldn't mind. He's my saint, so he is, and don't
any of you go annoying him now. We've a great understanding,
myself and Peter. He's never let me down in all the years I've
been beseeching him for favours. Oh, he's a wonderful man and a
glorious martyr. I'm mad about him. There are plenty of other
saints who'll be happy to intercede for you. Indeed, you've a
choice of five thousand and more. From St. Aaron the Hermit to
St. Zoticus the Roman Martyr. And, you know, there are lots of
other St. Peters apart from the real St. Peter. A hundred and
thirty-three of them altogether. St. Peter of Nicodemia, St. Peter
Gonzalez, St. Peter the Venerable, St. Peter Pappacarbone. And a

big batch of Chinese and Japanese St. Peters. So take your pick of
them. Now you must be prepared for a heavy burden of homework all this year. At least three hours every evening. Plus revi-
sion. And double that amount at the weekend. If any girl has
ideas about delivering papers or serving behind the counter of a
Woolworth on a Saturday she can put such ideas right out of her
head. Under no circumstances will Mother Thomas Aquinas give
permission for a girl from Our Lady of Fatima to take on a job of
work. And anyway, your parents have a duty to provide you with
sufficient pocket money. They also have a duty to supply you with
the correct school uniform, which must be obtained from Messrs.
Houlihan and Hegarty and only Messrs. Houlihan and Hegarty.
There's no greater insult to this school than to see a girl dressed
up in a shoddy imitation of the uniform. Mary Mooney, step up
here to me and face the class. [MARY MOONEY *comes forward and
stands next to* MOTHER PETER's *desk. She is wearing a large, shapeless hand-knitted cardigan and a thick pair of striped, knitted
knee-length socks*] Will you look at this girl's cardigan! Who knitted you that monstrosity, Mary Mooney?

MARY MOONEY: My mother, Mother Peter.

MOTHER PETER: Did she now? Have you no school cardigan to
wear?

MARY MOONEY: No, Mother Peter.

MOTHER PETER: Will you please inform your mother that she must
order you two school cardigans from Houlihan and Hegarty immediately. And don't dare come into school wearing that thing again.

MARY MOONEY: No, Mother. Sorry, Mother.

[MARY MOONEY *goes off*]

MOTHER PETER: Come back here a minute. [MARY MOONEY *comes
back*] Mary Mooney, have you joined a football team?

MARY MOONEY: No, Mother.

MOTHER PETER: Well, what are those horrible socks doing on your
feet? Is this another example of your mother's handiwork?

MARY MOONEY: Yes, Mother.

MOTHER PETER: God help the girl. Isn't her mother a martyr for the knitting. Go back to your place now and don't ever let me see you wearing socks like that again.

MARY MOONEY: No, Mother. Sorry, Mother.

[MARY MOONEY *goes off.* MOTHER PETER *opens the brown paper parcel and holds up a thick pair of long-legged bloomers*]

MOTHER PETER: Now you all know what this is, don't you? It's the Our Lady of Fatima knicker and it's the only type of knicker we want to see worn at this school. An increasing number of girls have been leaving off this knicker and coming to school in . . . in scanty bits of things that wouldn't cover the head of a leprechaun and showing them off under their PE shorts. Hands up any girl who has on a knicker like this. Is that all? Hands up every girl who has a knicker like this at home. And why haven't you got them on you, that's what I'd like to know. Oh, aren't you the brazen little madams. You know well there's a man out in the garden. A man who has to walk up and down with his wheelbarrow right past the tennis courts. Mary Gallagher, come right up here to me and give out two knickers to every girl who hasn't any. I'll collect the cash first thing tomorrow morning. [MARY GALLAGHER *gives out the knickers*] Well now, let us turn our attention to Our Lady on the occasion of her birthday. No woman on this earth was ever worthy of the holy name of Mary. The Mother of God is elevated high above all other human creatures. Because of the special privileges given to her by God. Mary Murphy, will you name one of Our Lady's special privileges.

MARY MURPHY: The Immaculate Conception, Mother Peter.

MOTHER PETER: Yes, indeed. Every ordinary baby comes into the world with a stain upon its soul. The big, black stain of original sin. But Our Lady came into the world with a soul of sparkling white. Because the Mother of Jesus had to be immaculate. Immaculate through and through. Mary Mooney, who were Our Lady's parents?

MARY MOONEY: I'm sorry, Mother Peter. I can't remember.

MOTHER PETER: You can't remember the names of Our Lady's parents? Why can't you?

MARY MOONEY: I don't know, Mother Peter.

MOTHER PETER: Mary Gallagher, will you enlighten this irreligious girl.

MARY GALLAGHER: Our Lady's mother was St. Anne, Mother Peter. And Our Lady's father was St. Joachim.

MOTHER PETER: Quite correct. It's a very great pity we don't know more about the lives of St. Anne and St. Joachim. Indeed we know nothing at all about either one of them. But they must have been two of the holiest saints that ever walked the earth. Mary Mooney, tell your mother you'll be late home from school tomorrow evening. You'll be staying behind to write out the names of Our Lady's parents one hundred times. And I want to see the lines written out in a legible hand. The same applies to all work handed in to me. I hope you each have your very own fountain pen. If you haven't then you must go out and get one. And I'll tell you what you must do when you get the pen home. Take a clean sheet of paper and write on it the holy names of Jesus, Mary and Joseph. Then throw the sheet of paper into the fire. That way the pen will never let you down. Mary O'Grady, will you tell me another of Our Lady's special privileges?

MARY O'GRADY: The Assumption, Mother Peter.

MOTHER PETER: Correct. At the completion of her life on earth Our Lady did not die. Our Lady was assumed into Heaven. Taken straight up, body and soul, to reign as Queen in everlasting glory. The Mother of God could not be subjected to such an indignity as death. Death and corruption in the coffin are part of the penalty of original sin, and the rest of us will have to wait until the end of the world when we'll all rise again on the Last Day of Judgement to be finally reunited with our bodies. What is it, Mary Flanagan?

MARY FLANAGAN: Please, Mother Peter. If somebody loses a leg on earth will he get it back on the Day of Judgement?

MOTHER PETER: Indeed he will. And he'll get a higher place in

Heaven into the bargain. Provided he's been a good man on earth. Mary McGinty?

MARY MCGINTY: Please, Mother, will the souls in Hell get their bodies back at the end of the world?

MOTHER PETER: Oho, they most certainly will. They'll be brought up for the Day of Judgement with the rest of us. And when their wickedness has been revealed to the whole of mankind they'll go back down to Hell taking their bodies with them into the everlasting fire. And remember, no sin ever goes unrecorded. Every little lapse will be brought to judgement. And not just your actual deeds. But every iniquitous thought that was ever carried inside your head will be revealed. And the sinner will stand alone and be shamed in front of family, friends, neighbours, teachers, and every member of the human race. [Pause] Well now, 5A, we've a hard year's work ahead of us. But there are nevertheless a number of treats in store. Mother Basil has one of her fillum shows planned, the sixth form will be giving us another operetta in the summer, and this year you'll all have a chance to be in the chorus. But the most exciting event of all will be in the Easter holidays. When we'll be taking a party of girls away on a pilgrimage. A very special pilgrimage to Fatima. What do you think of that now? Isn't it wonderful news? We'll be sending the full information out to your parents later on, and I'm sure they'll all be happy to make a financial sacrifice in order to give you the benefit of this splendid opportunity. And now we'd better have some nominations for the election of a captain of the form.

SCENE THREE

The Canteen. MARY MCGINTY *and* MARY GALLAGHER *are sitting at a table.* MOTHER BASIL *is pacing up and down.* MARY GALLAGHER *is laboriously eating a plate of rice pudding. She has an empty dinner plate in front of her.* MARY MCGINTY *is still struggling through her dinner.*

MOTHER BASIL: Mary McGinty, will you stop playing about with that stew and eat it up properly.

MARY MCGINTY: I can't swallow the meat, Mother Basil.

MOTHER BASIL: Oh, isn't it a pity for you? Why don't you try opening your mouth and see if that will help you at all.

MARY MCGINTY: There's great big lumps of gristle in this meat, Mother Basil.

MOTHER BASIL: There's no gristle in that meat, is there, Mary Gallagher? You don't realise how lucky you are. Think of all the poor black fellows dropping down dead in the heart of Africa for want of a bit of stewing steak. Look at Mary Gallagher. She's finished all hers and is eating her pudding up nicely.

MARY GALLAGHER: Please may I leave this last little bit, Mother Basil?

MOTHER BASIL: You may not! Eat every single bit and offer it up for all the souls in Purgatory. Come on now. Think of each grain of rice as a poor soul in agony. And remember, an hour in Purgatory is as long as a century on earth. As you swallow every mouthful just imagine all the souls you're getting a bit of remission for. Oh, come on and eat it up! Will you eat it! [*She stamps her foot*] Oh, damn the two of yeez with your fussing and finicking. D'you think I have all day to be standing here? Well, I haven't. I've a lot of things to do. A lot of very important things. D'you hear me?

MARY GALLAGHER: I've finished it, Mother.

MOTHER BASIL: All right. Go on and get out of it. [MARY GALLAGHER *goes off*] Come on now, Mary McGinty. Eat it up or I . . . I . . . I . . . I . . . I'm not going to stand for any more of this old nonsense.

MARY MCGINTY: Please Mother, I think I'm going to be sick.

MOTHER BASIL: Ah! Puke away then. Go on and be as sick as you like. But you'll stay behind and clear it all up after you.

MARY MCGINTY: I just can't eat it, Mother. I can't. I honestly can't.

MOTHER BASIL: You can't? You mean you won't. Well, you will! Give me that knife and fork!

MARY MCGINTY: I'm eating it, Mother. I'm eating it.

MOTHER BASIL.:   That's the idea. Keep it up now. I'll tell you what we'll do. Let's see if you can polish it all off in the time it takes me to say a Hail Holy Queen. Are you ready now? In the name of the Father and of the Son and of the Holy Ghost Amen. Hail Holy Queen Mother of Mercy, Hail Our Life, Our Sweetness and Our Hope. To thee do we cry, poor banished children of Eve. To thee do we send up our sighs, mourning and weeping in this vale of tears. Turn then, most gracious advocate, thine eyes of mercy towards us and after this our exile, show unto us the blessed fruit of thy womb, Jesus. [*She beats her breast three times*] O clement! O loving! O sweet Virgin Mary! Pray for us O holy Mother of God . . .

MARY MCGINTY: [*Nearly choking*] That we may be made worthy of the promises of Christ.

MOTHER BASIL.:   Good girl.

[MARY MCGINTY *retches*]

SCENE FOUR

The Music Room. MR. EMANUELLI *comes hobbling in with two walking sticks. He sits down at the piano.*

GIRLS: Good afternoon, Mr. Emanuelli.

MR. EMANUELLI: What good afternoon? My leg is giving me gip. I am crucified with pain and you tell me good afternoon. It's a rotten afternoon. [*He points with one stick*] Look at me! Don't look to the left or the right, look straight up here at me, please! Now. [*He sings*]
"When Jesus Christ was four years old
The angels brought him toys of gold
Which no man ever bought or sold."
[*He stops singing and points with his stick*] You! The girl with the frizzly hair. Sing for me! Come on, come on. Stand up and sing it if you please. "When Jesus Christ . . ." [*He gets ready to conduct with his walking stick*]

MARY FLANAGAN: [*Extremely off key*]
"When Jesus Christ was four years old
The angels brought him toys of . . ."

MR. EMANUELLI: No, no! No, no, no, no, no, no, no, no, no. That is not singing. That is ruddy awful caterwauling. Can you hold in your hand a broom? Well? Can you?

MARY FLANAGAN: Yes, sir.

MR. EMANUELLI: Good. Then you will sweep the stage for my production of *The Mikado* next July. Look at me! [*He sings*]
"And yet with these he would not play
He made him small fow-ow-owl out of clay
And blessed them till they floo-oo-oo-oo-oo-oo-oo away.
O Laudate domine."
[*He points with his stick*] You! The girl with the glasses. What do you call. National Health. Sing it!

MARY HENNESSY: [*Croaking in a very low octave*]
"And yet with these he would not play
He made him small fow-ow-owl . . ."

MR. EMANUELLI: Enough! Enough! Where am I? I can't be in the Convent of Our Lady of Fatima. I must be in the zoological gardens. At Regents Park. This voice is bad. Bad, bad, bad. I will not have such a honking in my Gilbert and Sullivan chorus. I want a chorus of Japanese schoolgirls, nobles, guards and coolies for *The Mikado*. And I need a Nanki-Poo. There is a shortage of prima donnas in the sixth form. So let us see who we can find in here. I will not have second-raters in my productions. You have seen my *Iolanthe*, my *H.M.S. Pinafore*, my *Pirates*. You know what a professional standard I demand. I was once a professional myself, you know. You have heard all about my reputation, eh? "Psst, psst, psst, psst, psst. He was a famous opera singer before the 1914–18 war." You have heard that, eh? You! [*He points with his stick*] The little tiny girl. Have you heard such a rumour about me?

MARY O'GRADY: Yes, sir.

MR. EMANUELLI: It's a fact. I was famous all over the world. But

what happened to me, eh? You think you know what happened?
Something to do with my leg? Eh? "Psst, psst, psst. I wonder
what is wrong with Mr. Emanuelli's leg. Is it gangrene? Is it gout?
Is it a war wound? Whatever it is, it certainly stinks out the music
room." Can anyone smell this leg? Well? Speak out! Yes or no?

GIRLS: No, sir.

MR. EMANUELLI: You are all a load of liars because I can ruddy
well smell it myself. Look at me! [*He sings*]
"Jesus Christ thou child so wise
Bless my hands and fill my eyes."
[*He points with his stick*] You! The girl with the ginger hair, lurk-
ing low. Sing it!

MARY MOONEY:

"Jesus Christ thou child so wise
Bless my hands and fill my eyes."

MR. EMANUELLI: Again! [*He sings*]
"And bring my soul to Par-ar-adise
To Par-ar-adise."

MARY MOONEY:

"And bring my soul to Par-ar-adise
To Par-ar-adise."

MR. EMANUELLI: Yes. Yes, yes, yes, yes. This one is good. Quite
good. But I don't believe it. Such a plain young missy. Come here.
Come on, come on. Come right up here and let me look at you.
[MARY MOONEY *comes forward*] Yes. You will be Nanki-Poo. He is
a young man. And you are a boyish-looking girl. Come to see me
later. Now go away. [MARY MOONEY *goes off*] We will all sing
"Jesus Christ" together. [*He gets up*] My ear is coming close to
every mouth. So warble away and don't let me hear any cacoph-
ony. One, two, three, four.

GIRLS: [*Singing*]
"When Jesus Christ was four years old
The angels brought him toys of gold
Which no man ever bought or sold . . ."

SCENE FIVE

A Street in Harlesden. MARY MCGINTY, MARY GALLAGHER *and* MARY MOONEY *are walking along carrying heavy satchels and eating Mars Bars.* MARY MCGINTY *has her hat in her hand.*

MARY GALLAGHER: Put your hat back on, McGinty.

MARY MCGINTY: No. I refuse to walk the streets with a pisspot on my head. It's bad enough having to wear these socks and a stupid-looking gymslip.

MARY GALLAGHER: What if a prefect sees you? You'll only get reported.

MARY MCGINTY: It wouldn't worry me if I got expelled. I wonder what you have to do to get expelled from that old dump.

MARY GALLAGHER: You could tell them you'd become a member of the pudding club.

MARY MCGINTY: Yeah. Or you could make a big long willy out of plasticine and stick it on the crucifix in the chapel.

MARY MOONEY: You mustn't say things like that.

MARY MCGINTY: Why not? D'you reckon a thunderbolt is gonna come hurtling down from Heaven?

MARY MOONEY: It doesn't happen straight away. It happens when you're least expecting it. You'd better make an Act of Contrition.

MARY MCGINTY: [*Looking up*] Sorry, Jesus.

MARY MOONEY: My Dad knows this man who used to be a monk. But he couldn't keep his vows so he asked if he could be released. On the day he left he came skipping down the path with his collar in his hand. And when he opened the monastery gate he saw an Alsatian sitting outside. So he hung his collar round the Alsatian's neck and went on his way laughing all along the road. After that he started going into pubs every night and boasting to all the people about what he'd gone and done with his collar. Then one day he went and got married. And while he was on his honeymoon he started to get a really bad pain in his back. He was in such a terrible agony he could only walk about with a stoop. And after a while he was completely bent up double. Then he started to lose his voice. He went to loads of different doctors but none of them could do anything to help him. And now he can only get about on all fours. And when he opens his mouth to say anything he barks just like a dog.

MARY GALLAGHER: Is that true?

MARY MOONEY: Yes. He lives in Shepherds Bush.

MARY MCGINTY: Why can't you keep your stupid old stories to yourself. You're as bad as Mother Peter, you are.

MARY MOONEY: No, I am not. Huh. I bet if you were knocked down by a trolley bus this evening you'd be yelling your head off for a priest.

MARY MCGINTY: Oh, no, I wouldn't.

MARY GALLAGHER: Well I certainly would.

MARY MCGINTY: Oh, shit! I was only having a joke about trying to get expelled. I don't even have to get expelled, come to think of it. I'm old enough to go out to work.

MARY GALLAGHER: You wouldn't get much of a job without any qualifications.

[DEREK, *the Teddy boy, comes swaggering along the street behind them*]

MARY MCGINTY: Huh. I couldn't care less about exams.

MARY GALLAGHER: Well, that's the main difference between you and me, McGinty, because I do happen to care.

MARY MOONEY: Yes, and so do I.

MARY MCGINTY: Huh. There's millions of jobs I could do. [*She sees* DEREK] Oh, blimey!

DEREK: Afternoon, girls. I must say you're looking very smart.

MARY MCGINTY: Leave off. What you doing round here, anyway?

DEREK: Just having a bit of a promenade. You don't mind, do you?
Or is this a private road?

MARY MCGINTY: Aren't you supposed to be at work?

DEREK: Had to take the day off, didn't I. Touch of the old neuralgia.

MARY MCGINTY: Don't give me that.

DEREK: Are you calling me a liar, darling?

MARY MCGINTY: No . . .

DEREK: Well, just make sure you don't, 'cos nobody accuses me of
telling lies. All right? [*He looks over at the other two girls*] How
you doing, girls? [*To* MARY MCGINTY] Ain't you gonna introduce
me to your two lovely mates?

MARY MCGINTY: Yeah, well, that's Mary Gallagher. And that's
Mary Mooney. His name's Derek.

[DEREK *winks and clicks his tongue at them, then he turns
back to* MARY MCGINTY]

DEREK: You gonna be down the White Hart tonight, by any
chance?

MARY MCGINTY: I might be.

DEREK: Oh, well, I'll see you inside, then, shall I?

MARY MCGINTY: You've got to be joking. You don't think I'm
gonna go wandering in there and have everybody staring at me all
on me tod.

DEREK: All right, all right. I'll see you outside then. Half past
seven. And you be there, darling. Right?

[*He clicks his tongue and winks at the other two, then he
goes swaggering off*]

MARY GALLAGHER: Is that your bloke?

MARY MCGINTY: Sort of.

MARY GALLAGHER: How long have you been going out with him?

MARY MCGINTY: About two and a half weeks. D'you think he's nice looking?

MARY GALLAGHER: Well . . . he's not exactly my sort of bloke.

MARY MCGINTY: No, well, of course we all know your type, don't we. Smarmy little Catholic schoolboys, with short back and sides. And acne.

MARY GALLAGHER: Cuthbert has not got acne.

MARY MCGINTY: He did have the day I saw him. He had a beautiful crop of blackheads on his boatrace. And he had a load of pimples, all about ready to pop. Ugh!

MARY GALLAGHER: Well, at least he's not bowlegged like that long streak of paralysed piss that's just gone by. I wonder where he left his horse.

MARY MCGINTY: Oh, shut your face.

MARY MOONEY: I'd like to know how you're going to get your homework done if you're going to be gadding about all night.

MARY MCGINTY: I was thinking of copying your History on the trolley bus tomorrow morning. And having a lend of Gallagher's Latin after lunch.

MARY GALLAGHER: You've got some nerve.

MARY MCGINTY: I'll do the same for you some time.

MARY GALLAGHER: Oh, yes, and pigs might fly.

MARY MCGINTY: [To MARY MOONEY] You'd better be waiting for me tomorrow morning at Willesden Green.

MARY MOONEY: All right.

MARY GALLAGHER: And don't forget your knicker money, will you.

MARY MOONEY: I didn't have to have any knickers off Mother Peter.

MARY MCGINTY: Oh, no, you wouldn't, of course. You always wear passion killers, don't you.

MARY MOONEY: You'll be wearing them yourself from tomorrow.

[MARY MCGINTY *takes a pair of bloomers out of her satchel and puts them over her head*]

MARY MCGINTY: How's that? She didn't actually say you had to put them on your bum.

[*They go off*]

SCENE SIX

The Biology Lab. MOTHER BASIL, *wearing a bloodstained apron, is dissecting a female rabbit.*

MOTHER BASIL: Now this is the abdomen, which contains the remainder of the alimentary canal together with the organs of excretion and reproduction. The female ova are produced in the two ovaries which you can see here lying behind the kidneys. Close to each ovary there's a Fallopian tube. Each Fallopian tube widens out into an oviduct leading to a uterus, which in turn opens out together with the second uterus, here, into a much larger tube, the vagina. [*The Angelus bell tolls loudly several times.* MOTHER BASIL *wipes her hands and makes the Sign of the Cross. The "Hail Mary" part of the following prayer is recited very rapidly indeed*] In the name of the Father and of the Son and of the Holy Ghost Amen. The Angel of the Lord declared unto Mary.

GIRLS: And she conceived of the Holy Ghost.

MOTHER BASIL: Hail Mary full of grace the Lord is with thee. Blessed art thou amongst women and blessed is the fruit of thy womb Jesus.

GIRLS: Holy Mary Mother of God pray for us sinners now and at the hour of our death Amen.

MOTHER BASIL: Behold the handmaid of the Lord.

GIRLS: Be it done unto me according to thy word.

MOTHER BASIL: Hail Mary full of grace the Lord is with thee. Blessed art thou amongst women and blessed is the fruit of thy womb Jesus.

GIRLS: Holy Mary Mother of God pray for us sinners now and at the hour of our death Amen.

MOTHER BASIL: And the word was made flesh.

GIRLS: And dwelt amongst us.

MOTHER BASIL: Hail Mary full of grace the Lord is with thee. Blessed art thou amongst women and blessed is the fruit of thy womb Jesus.

GIRLS: Holy Mary Mother of God pray for us sinners now and at the hour of our death Amen.

MOTHER BASIL: Pray for us O Holy Mother of God.

GIRLS: That we may be made worthy of the promises of Christ.

MOTHER BASIL: Pour forth we beseech thee O Lord thy grace into our hearts that we to whom the Incarnation of Christ thy Son was made known by the message of an Angel, may by his Passion and Cross be brought to the glory of his resurrection through the same Christ Our Lord Amen. [*Sign of the Cross*] In the name of the Father and of the Son and of the Holy Ghost Amen. Now, this organ here, the vagina, at its anal end leads to a much smaller tube, the urethra, which opens to the exterior. As the breeding season approaches the ova will pass down the Fallopian tube through the oviduct and into the uterus. For the purposes of reproduction an enormous number of sperm from the male will be introduced into the vagina. The sperm will swim along the uterus and through the oviduct into the Fallopian tube. Yes, Mary Mooney?

MARY MOONEY: Please, Mother Basil, could you tell us how the sperm from the male gets introduced into the vagina?

MOTHER BASIL: What?

MARY MOONEY: Could you tell us how . . .

MOTHER BASIL: I heard what you said, you little madam. Get out of here this minute and stand outside till the lesson is over. [MARY MOONEY *gets up and goes off*] God bless us and save us! I'm going to send that girl upstairs to see Mother Thomas Aquinas. Now. When an ovum has been fertilised it'll be implanted in the uterus where the protective membranes and the placenta will be formed. The dirty little devil! Trying to make a laughing stock out of me! The placenta is the organ by which the embryo is attached to the uterus of the mother. Oh, the cheek of it! Mother Thomas Aquinas will deal with her. This uterus here, by the way, is known as a duplex uterus. I never heard the like of it before! The little trollop! All rabbits and rodents have this type of uterus. There is also the simplex uterus which is found in the higher primates including man, or rather woman, but we don't want to be going into that. A detention is no good to that one. What she wants is a good, hard kick up the behind.

SCENE SEVEN

Mother Thomas Aquinas' Office. MARY MOONEY *is standing in front of* MOTHER THOMAS AQUINAS' *desk.*

MOTHER THOMAS AQUINAS: How dare you ask Mother Basil such a precocious question? How dare you?

MARY MOONEY: I'm sorry, Mother Thomas Aquinas, but I didn't know I was asking anything wrong.

MOTHER THOMAS AQUINAS: You didn't know? Are you sure you didn't know?

MARY MOONEY: No, Mother. I mean yes, Mother.

MOTHER THOMAS AQUINAS: In that case you must be an extremely ignorant girl. Is that what you are, Mary Mooney? Ignorant?

MARY MOONEY: I don't know, Mother Thomas Aquinas.

MOTHER THOMAS AQUINAS: Don't you? Hasn't your mother ever had a little chat with you?

MARY MOONEY: Yes, Mother. But she doesn't ever chat about rabbits.

MOTHER THOMAS AQUINAS: Never mind the rabbits. Hasn't she ever warned you about boys?

MARY MOONEY: No, Mother Thomas Aquinas.

MOTHER THOMAS AQUINAS: The woman is evidently guilty of neglecting her duties. Such ignorance is inexcusable in a girl of fifteen. I must write to your mother this afternoon and tell her to start instructing you immediately on certain matters. Go along now. And try to be a bit more mature.

MARY MOONEY: Yes, Mother Thomas. Thank you, Mother Thomas. Sorry, Mother Thomas.

SCENE EIGHT

The Classroom. MARY MCGINTY, MARY MOONEY *and* MARY GALLAGHER *are at their desks.*

MARY MCGINTY: Fancy her not knowing the facts of life.

MARY MOONEY: So what?

MARY MCGINTY: You know a man's willy?

MARY MOONEY: Yes.

MARY MCGINTY: D'you know what it's for?

MARY MOONEY: Yes. For being excused.

[MARY MCGINTY *and* MARY GALLAGHER *exchange looks*]

MARY GALLAGHER: Yes, well, he does do that with it, of course. But he can do something else with it as well.

MARY MCGINTY: Not at the same time, though.

MARY GALLAGHER: No. Did you know he had two balls as well?

MARY MOONEY: Two what?

MARY MCGINTY: Bollocks.

MARY GALLAGHER: And the same to you.

MARY MCGINTY: You know when you get married you have to go to bed with your husband.

MARY MOONEY: No. My Mum and Dad don't.

MARY GALLAGHER: Don't they?

MARY MOONEY: No. My Dad always goes to bed at nine o'clock. Me and my Mum go at ten. After she's finished her packing.

MARY GALLAGHER: Her what?

MARY MOONEY: Well, she gets out all our best dresses and packs them in a suitcase with her real fox fur and her jewellery. Then she gets out her canteen of cutlery and her best bone china tea set and she puts them in with a tin of corned beef and a crucifix.

MARY MCGINTY: What for?

MARY MOONEY: In case we have an air raid in the night.

MARY GALLAGHER: I heard the war ended eleven years ago.

MARY MOONEY: Yes, but we have to be ready for the next one. The devil works in threes, don't forget. And this country's got a lot more coming to it for the things it did to Ireland.

MARY GALLAGHER: What things?

MARY MOONEY: Things that'd make your hair stand up on end if only you knew.

MARY GALLAGHER: Such as what?

MARY MOONEY: I don't know. I wasn't there. My Mum was, though.

MARY MCGINTY: D'you share a bedroom with your Mum?

MARY MOONEY: Yes. And my Dad.

MARY MCGINTY: Bloody hell!

MARY MOONEY: Well, we've only got one bedroom. Me and my Mum have the double bed. And he's got one of his own.

MARY GALLAGHER: Does she ever get in his bed?

MARY MOONEY: No!

MARY MCGINTY: She must have done once.

MARY GALLAGHER: You have to get in bed with your husband to have a baby.

MARY MCGINTY: And they both have to take their pyjamas off.

MARY MOONEY: Oh, no! How could they. I'd never do anything so rude.

MARY GALLAGHER: You'll have to if you ever get married. Our Lady was the only one who never had to do it.

MARY MOONEY: Wasn't she lucky.

MARY MCGINTY: It wasn't so lucky for poor old Joseph, though. I reckon he must have used it to stir his tea.

MARY MOONEY: Used what?

MARY MCGINTY: His cock.

MARY GALLAGHER: Prick.

MARY MCGINTY: Dick.

MARY GALLAGHER: Tool.

MARY MCGINTY: Sssh!

[MOTHER PETER *comes in, gets something out of her desk and goes off*]

MARY GALLAGHER: When you're expecting a baby you stop having the curse. That's how they can tell.

MARY MOONEY: Are you sure?

MARY GALLAGHER: Yes, of course.

MARY MCGINTY: You don't always have to have a baby, though. Not if the man uses a French letter.

MARY GALLAGHER: You often see a used one lying about in the park.

MARY MCGINTY: Yeah. Don't ever sit on the seat in a public toilet.

MARY GALLAGHER: No. Just hover over it. In case you get VD.

MARY MCGINTY: Your body breaks out in big sores. And after a while it starts to rot away.

MARY GALLAGHER: I know someone who's had VD. She stands outside Dollis Hill station selling papers. All her nose has been eaten away. She's just got a hole in the middle of her face.

MARY MCGINTY: Cor, I wouldn't buy a paper off her.

MARY MOONEY: My Mum must be having a baby. I know for a fact she's stopped having the curse. I thought it was a bit funny.

MARY GALLAGHER: She must have got in his bed while you were fast asleep.

MARY MOONEY: There isn't enough room for the two of them.

MARY MCGINTY: They don't need all that much room. The man lies on top of the woman.

[MOTHER BASIL *comes in*]

MOTHER BASIL: Get up this minute and go and take some healthy exercise. Sitting nattering like a bunch of old fishwives. [*The girls get up*] I'd like to know what all that whispering was about. That's what I'd like to know.

SCENE NINE

The Classroom. MOTHER PETER *is at her desk. Two extra chairs have been placed nearby.*

MOTHER PETER: Now sit up straight and clear the tops of your desks. Give your answers loud and clear and God help any girl who lets me down.

[FATHER MULLARKEY *makes an entrance with* MOTHER THOMAS AQUINAS]

GIRLS: Good morning, Father Mullarkey. Good morning, Mother Thomas Aquinas.

FATHER MULLARKEY: Good morning, Mother Peter. Good morning, girls. [MOTHER PETER *goes to sit on one of the side chairs with* MOTHER THOMAS AQUINAS] Have they been working hard, Mother Peter?

MOTHER PETER: Indeed they have, Father. [*From his pocket* FATHER MULLARKEY *takes a little red booklet:* A Catechism of Christian Doctrine. *Throughout the following scene he flicks through this booklet*] And do they know their Catechism?

MOTHER PETER: There's no excuse for any girl who doesn't.

FATHER MULLARKEY: Which girl is the Captain of the form, Mother Peter?

MOTHER PETER: Mary Hennessy is the Captain, Father.

FATHER MULLARKEY: Well now, Mary Hennessy. Stand up and tell me who is the head of the Catholic Church.

MARY HENNESSY: The Pope.

FATHER MULLARKEY: Is that a fact? Are you sure this girl is fit to be the Captain, Mother Peter? Are the duties of leadership so exacting that she hasn't time to study her religion? Sit down, Captain Hennessy, and let the blondy girl over there tell us the answer to the question. Who is the Head of the Catholic Church?

MARY FLANAGAN: The Head of the Catholic Church is Jesus Christ Our Lord.

FATHER MULLARKEY: And has the Church a visible head on earth?

MARY FLANAGAN: The Church has a visible head on earth. The Bishop of Rome, who is the Vicar of Christ.

FATHER MULLARKEY: What is the Bishop of Rome called?

MARY FLANAGAN: The Bishop of Rome is called the Pope, which word signifies Father.

FATHER MULLARKEY: Make a note of that, Mary Hennessy. And now stand up and tell me is the Pope infallible?

MARY HENNESSY: The Pope is infallible.

FATHER MULLARKEY: Correct. That girl there. Which are the four sins crying to Heaven for vengeance?

MARY MOONEY: The four sins crying to Heaven for vengeance are Wilful Murder, The Sin of Sodom, Oppression of the Poor and Defrauding Labourers of Their Wages.

FATHER MULLARKEY: Is it a great evil to fall into mortal sin?

MARY MOONEY: It is the greatest of all evils to fall into mortal sin.

FATHER MULLARKEY: Why is it called mortal sin?

MARY MOONEY: It is called mortal sin because it kills the soul and deserves Hell.

FATHER MULLARKEY: Now you there with the horse's tail. Is it a mortal sin to neglect to hear Mass on Sundays and Holy Days of Obligation?

MARY MURPHY: It is a mortal sin to neglect to hear Mass on Sundays and Holy Days of Obligation.

FATHER MULLARKEY: Make no mistake about it, there's no greater sin on all this earth than the deliberate missing of Mass. [He bangs on the desk] A person who lies in bed and refuses to get up for Mass is committing a far more serious sin than a man who lashes out and murders his wife in a fit of fury. God would surely be merciful to the man who lost control. But you can't expect God to condone a premeditated decision to stay away from Holy Mass. The blondy girl again. Where is God?

MARY FLANAGAN: God is everywhere.

FATHER MULLARKEY: Had God any beginning?

MARY FLANAGAN: God had no beginning. He always was, He is and He always will be.

FATHER MULLARKEY: Has God any body?

MARY FLANAGAN: God has no body. He is a spirit.

FATHER MULLARKEY: Is there only one God?

MARY FLANAGAN: There is only one God.

FATHER MULLARKEY: Are there three persons in God?

MARY FLANAGAN: There are three persons in God: God the Father, God the Son and God the Holy Ghost.

FATHER MULLARKEY: Are these three persons three Gods?

MARY FLANAGAN: These three persons are not three Gods. The Father, the Son and the Holy Ghost are all one and the same God.

FATHER MULLARKEY: Does God know and see all things?

MARY FLANAGAN: God knows and sees all things, even our most secret thoughts.

FATHER MULLARKEY: How are you to know what God has revealed?

MARY FLANAGAN: I am to know what God has revealed by the testimony, teaching and authority of the Catholic Church.

FATHER MULLARKEY: Now then, Captain Hennessy! What is the Sixth Commandment?

MARY HENNESSY: The Sixth Commandment is: "Thou shalt not commit adultery."

FATHER MULLARKEY: What does the Sixth Commandment forbid?

MARY HENNESSY: The Sixth Commandment forbids all sins of impurity with another's wife or husband.

FATHER MULLARKEY: Does the Sixth Commandment forbid whatever is contrary to holy purity?

MARY HENNESSY: The Sixth Commandment forbids whatever is contrary to holy purity, in looks, words or actions.

FATHER MULLARKEY: Good. Now I want to say a little word to you about the vital importance of purity. You're all getting to be big girls now. Indeed some of you are bigger than others. Isn't it a great joy to be young and healthy with all your life before you. Sooner or later you might want to share your life with a member of the opposite sex. The best way to find a boyfriend is to join a Catholic Society where you'll have scope for all sorts of social activities. Now when you've met your good Catholic boy and you're getting to know each other he might suggest a bit of a kiss and a cuddle. Well, let him wait. And if he doesn't want to wait let him go. Any cuddling and kissing is bound to arouse bad feelings and desires for the intimate union allowed only in Matrimony. [*He bangs on the desk*] The intimate union of the sexes is a sacred act. A duty to be done in a state of grace by a man and his wife and nobody else. So until the day you kneel at the altar with a bridal veil on your head you must never be left alone in a room with a boyfriend. Or in a field for that matter. Let the two of you go out and about with other young couples to dances and to parties and the like. But a particular word of warning about the latter. There's no doubt at all that alcoholic drinks make a party go with a swing. The danger is that after a couple of drinks a boy and a girl are more inclined to take liberties with each other. To indulge in such liberties is sinful. The girl has the special responsibility in the matter because a boy's passions are more readily aroused, God help him. Show your affection by all means. But keep to holding hands with an occasional kiss on the cheek. A Catholic boy, in his heart of hearts, will be impressed by such insistence on perfect chastity. Ask Our Blessed Lady to keep you free from the temptations of the flesh. And make no mistake about it, a passionate kiss on the lips between a boy and a girl is a serious mortal sin. [*He bangs on the desk*] When you've the wedding ring on your finger you can fire away to your heart's content. Now has any girl any question she'd like to ask? Yes? That girl there.

MARY MOONEY: Please, Father, could you tell me what is the Sin of Sodom?

FATHER MULLARKEY: The what? Whatever put that into your head?

MARY MOONEY: It's one of the four sins crying to Heaven for vengeance, Father.

FATHER MULLARKEY: Oh, yes. So it is. That's right. Well, it's a very bad sin indeed. But it's nothing you need bother your head about. Sit down now. Are there any more questions? No? That'll be all then. Thank you, Mother Peter. Mother Thomas Aquinas. [*He blesses the class*] In nomine Patris et Filii et Spiritus Sancti. Amen.

GIRLS: Good morning, Father. Thank you, Father.

SCENE TEN

Mother Thomas Aquinas' Office. MARY MOONEY *is standing in front of* MOTHER THOMAS AQUINAS' *desk.*

MOTHER THOMAS AQUINAS: What a foul, despicable creature you are. I'm thoroughly disgusted with you. Was it your own idea to ask that question, or did somebody put you up to it?

MARY MOONEY: No, Mother Thomas.

MOTHER THOMAS AQUINAS: No, what? It wasn't your own idea?

MARY MOONEY: Yes, Mother Thomas. But . . .

MOTHER THOMAS AQUINAS: It was your own idea. To embarrass the poor priest in front of the entire class. May I ask why?

MARY MOONEY: I don't know, Mother Thomas.

MOTHER THOMAS AQUINAS: I'm sorry, but I don't believe you. I suggest you know full well why you chose such a question. To make yourself the centre of attraction and procure a cheap laugh at Father Mullarkey's expense. The last time you were in this office you tried to hoodwink me into believing you to be an innocent girl, immature for your years. You might like to know that I wasn't entirely convinced. And I'm now quite certain that you're not in the least bit innocent. You're an exceedingly sophisticated girl, full of knowing far beyond your years. As to the punishment, I hardly think a detention would serve any useful purpose. Instead, I am going to send you into the chapel after lunch today and every day for nine consecutive days to recite a Novena to Our Lady of Perpetual Succour. On the Saturday and Sunday you will visit your parish church. Take this. [*She takes a small booklet from her desk drawer*] And recite the prayer on page five. "O Mother of Perpetual Succour behold me a miserable sinner at thy feet," and so on. Followed by nine Hail Marys. The intention of this Novena is to ask Our Lady to alleviate your apparent obsession with carnal

knowledge and to restore your mind and heart to childlike innocence.

MARY MOONEY: Thank you, Mother Thomas.

MOTHER THOMAS AQUINAS: Now get out!

SCENE ELEVEN

A Street Corner. MARY MCGINTY, *wearing a slightly tarty
fifties outfit, is leaning up against a wall with* DEREK *who has
one arm around her. He puts his other arm around her and
tries to kiss her. She turns her face away.*

DEREK: Here, what's up with you?

MARY MCGINTY: Nothing.

[DEREK *tries to kiss her again. She turns her face away again*]

DEREK: What you playing at?

MARY MCGINTY: Nothing. It's dead late, Derek. I'd better be getting indoors.

DEREK: What about my goodnight?

MARY MCGINTY: Yeah. Well, goodnight then. [*She pulls away from
him and gives him a peck on the cheek*]

DEREK: Oh, yeah? You trying to drop me a hint, by any chance?
Trying to tell me something without saying nothing? Look here,
darling, if I've done something wrong I've got a right to know
what it is.

MARY MCGINTY: It's nothing to do with you yourself personally.

DEREK: No? Well, what is it to do with then? Eh? Come on. I
wanna know.

MARY MCGINTY: If you must know, it's to do with mortal sins.

DEREK: How's that?

MARY MCGINTY: Mortal sins. They're sins what you go to Hell for if you die with one on your soul. You know, like murder. Or eating meat on a Friday.

DEREK: Oh, yeah?

MARY MCGINTY: Look, the priest came to school today to give us this big long lecture. And one of the things he said was that snogging is a mortal sin.

DEREK: Pull the other leg.

MARY MCGINTY: That's what he told us. Honestly.

DEREK: Never. You must have got it wrong. How can you go to Hell for having a snog? I mean, it's only your bloomin' cakehole after all. Wrapping it around somebody else's. Where's the harm in that for Christ's sake? You sure he wasn't talking about something a bit more on the sexy side? I mean, I know for a fact that Catholics are not allowed to . . . er . . . you know . . . until they're married. Everyone's aware of that. And myself I don't reckon it's altogether a bad idea. At least as far as girls are concerned. Myself, I wouldn't er . . . whatsname with a girl if I respected her. And I wouldn't respect a girl if she let me . . . er . . . you know. Have a bit.

MARY MCGINTY: He definitely meant snogging, Derek. I swear to you. A passionate kiss on the lips between a boy and a girl is a serious mortal sin. That's what he said. And he must know if he's the priest. D'you realise I've gone and committed hundreds of mortal sins, thanks to you?

DEREK: Oh, that's right. Put the blame on me. Ain't it marvellous, eh? I never even heard of a mortal bleedin' sin until five fucking minutes ago. Er . . . sorry about using that word in front of you.

MARY MCGINTY: That's all right.

DEREK: Well, I mean, it's no sin for me, is it, darling?

MARY MCGINTY: No, and it's not bloomin' fair. Protestants don't have sins, the lucky sods. I wonder where they go when they die, though.

DEREK: They stop in the cemetery like everybody else.

MARY MCGINTY: What are you supposed to be? Church of England?

DEREK: Yeah, well, that's what I stick down if I have to fill up a form for something or other. C of E. It don't mean nothing, do it, except you're an ordinary English person. It's hard luck for you, ain't it, having an Irish Mum and Dad. You know, you don't strike me as being one bit Irish yourself. I mean, you could easy pass yourself off as a normal person. Funny how you can spot a mick a mile off. No offence to your old man or nothing. I mean, I've got nothing against them 'part from the fact that they drink too much and they're always picking fights among themselves. It makes me die laughing the way their hair stands all up on end. Half of them have got that diabolical ginger hair, ain't they. And all of them have got them big red faces. And them bleedin' great flapping trousers you see them wearing down the Kilburn High Road. You could fit half a dozen navvies into one leg alone. I never can understand a word they're saying. Bejasus and all that boloney. Myself I reckon they all take religion a bit too serious. I mean, you can understand it more with the Italians, having the Pope stuck in the Vatican there, keeping his eye on them. But the Irish are bleedin' miles away. Why should they have to take orders from the Pope? If I was you I'd be a bit suspicious of that Heaven you're so keen to get up to. It's gonna be packed out with some of the worst types of foreigners. The Irish'll be the only ones up there speaking English. The rest of them'll be Italians, Spaniards, Portuguese . . .

MARY MCGINTY: Mexicans.

DEREK: Yeah. Bolivians. Peruvians. All that mob. I can't see you fitting in somehow. No. If I was you I'd start taking it all with a pinch of salt. You don't really believe in it, do you?

MARY MCGINTY: I don't know. One minute I do, the next minute I don't.

DEREK: I know you have to make out you believe it in front of all them nuns and priests and your Mum and Dad. You don't wanna cause them no trouble. Fair enough. You can play along with it for a few more more years. Then you can go your own sweet way.

MARY MCGINTY: I can't, you know. Once a Catholic always a Catholic. That's the rule.

DEREK: Yeah? Tough. Oh, well. Might see you around some time.

MARY MCGINTY: Couldn't we just be mates?

DEREK: What? I've got more mates than I know what to do with. I can't have you dragging round with us up the billiard hall and down the football field. Leave off.

MARY MCGINTY: It's not that I don't wanna go out with you any more, Derek. It's just . . .

   [DEREK *puts his arms around her*]

DEREK: Come here. You can always go up to Confession on Saturday and get your soul dry cleaned. [*He kisses her. His hands go wandering and she moves them*] Where is your soul anyway?

MARY MCGINTY: It's inside your heart.

DEREK: Don't talk rubbish.

MARY MCGINTY: I always imagine it in the heart. It could be inside your head, I suppose.

DEREK: It's not in your heart or your head. It's not in your bum neither. It don't exist.

MARY MCGINTY: There's definitely something mysterious about Confession though. It's not very nice having to tell your sins. But when you come out you feel all good and holy and all sort of excited in your head. A bit like when you've had a couple of gin and limes.

DEREK: Oooh. Touch of the old voodoo if you ask me.

MARY MCGINTY: It only lasts for about ten minutes. Then you come down to earth again and realise that just about everything you do or say or even think is a sin according to them and you just can't help committing the buggers if you're a normal human being.

DEREK: Oh, well. You're just gonna have to choose between me and Jesus. [*He kisses her*]

MARY MCGINTY: Oh, Christ! Another fucking mortal sin.

DEREK: Oy! I don't wanna hear you using that sort of language.

SCENE TWELVE

CUTHBERT's *House.* MARY GALLAGHER *and* CUTHBERT, *both in school uniform, are sitting on chairs.* CUTHBERT *is holding a school copy of* Macbeth.

MARY GALLAGHER: [*Gabbling without expression*]
"Duncan is in his grave;
After life's fitful fever he sleeps well;
Treason has done his worst: nor steel, nor
poison,
Malice domestic, foreign levy, nothing
Can touch him further."

CUTHBERT: [*In a high voice*] "Come on;
Gentle my lord, sleek o'er your rugged looks;
Be bright and jovial 'mong your guests
tonight."

MARY GALLAGHER: "So shall I, love; and so, I pray, be
you:
Let your remembrance apply to Banquo;
Present him eminence, both with eye and
tongue:
Unsafe the while, that we
Must lave our honours in these flattering
streams,
And make our faces vizards to our hearts,
Disguising what they are."

CUTHBERT: [*In a high voice*] "You must leave this."

MARY GALLAGHER: "O, full of scorpions is my mind, dear wife!

Thou know'st that Banquo, and his Fleance, lives."

CUTHBERT: [*In a high voice*] "But in them nature's copy's not eterne."

MARY GALLAGHER: "There's comfort yet" . . . er . . . er . . .

CUTHBERT: "They are assailable."

MARY GALLAGHER: "They are assailable." [*She looks blank*]

CUTHBERT: "Then be thou jocund."

MARY GALLAGHER: Oh, yes. "Then be thou jocund:
ere the bat hath flown,
His cloistered flight; ere to black Hecate's
summons." Er . . . the . . . er . . . the
something beetle with his . . . er . . .
Tut! Oh, shit! I don't know it.

CUTHBERT: Yes, you do. More or less.

MARY GALLAGHER: It's got to be word perfect for Mother Peter. Just in case she picks on me. She's such a crafty old cow. She makes us all learn it but she'll only pounce on one of us to test it. Whoever she happens to pick on will have to get up and act it. In front of the whole form. With her. She always gives herself the part of Lady Macbeth. God, it's so embarrassing. Especially when she starts putting on an English accent and doing all the fancy gestures. Every time she opens her mouth a spray of spit comes flying across the classroom. We've all got to go on an outing with her next Wednesday. To see *Macbeth*. She's taking us up to the Old Vic.

CUTHBERT: Big deal.

MARY GALLAGHER: Yeah. Have you ever been there?

CUTHBERT: God, who hasn't been to the Old Vic.

MARY GALLAGHER: Lots of people haven't. My Mum and Dad for a start. Neither of them have ever set foot inside a theatre.

CUTHBERT: Peasants! [*He takes out a packet of Senior Service cigarettes, sticks one in a holder and lights it up*]

MARY GALLAGHER: They only ever go to the pictures if a film comes round the Coliseum with a Catholic in the starring role.

CUTHBERT: Typical.

MARY GALLAGHER: They think an awful lot of Spencer Tracy. And Bing Crosby. He can do no wrong. And they both reckon the sun shines right out of Grace Kelly's arse.

CUTHBERT: How about Mario Lanza?

MARY GALLAGHER: Is he a Catholic?

CUTHBERT: He's entitled to be with a name like that.

MARY GALLAGHER: My Dad refuses to see a film if he thinks the star in it has ever been divorced. And he gets in a flaming temper if he catches sight of a picture of Lana Turner in the paper. Just because she's been married a few times. He rips the picture out of the paper and screws it up and stamps on it. [*In an Irish accent*] "One husband wouldn't satisfy you, ah? Ye two-legged animal! Aaah!"

CUTHBERT: I could quite fancy a session with Lana Turner.

MARY GALLAGHER: She's a bit old for you, isn't she?

CUTHBERT: Not half. I've got a definite weakness for the older woman.

MARY GALLAGHER: Oh, have you?

CUTHBERT: Yes. I have actually. [*He takes a half bottle of whisky out of his blazer pocket and has a swig*]

MARY GALLAGHER: Can I have a drop of that?

[CUTHBERT *hands her the bottle and she takes a long swig*]

CUTHBERT: Go easy with it. Bloody hell! That cost me eighteen and fourpence, you know.

MARY GALLAGHER: You're just stingy, you are.

CUTHBERT: No I'm not. But I only get ten bob a week off my Dad.

MARY GALLAGHER: Yeah. And the rest.

CUTHBERT: Come over here a minute.

MARY GALLAGHER: No.

CUTHBERT: Don't then.

MARY GALLAGHER: Guess who came to school today.

CUTHBERT: Cardinal Godfrey.

MARY GALLAGHER: No. Father Mullarkey actually. He was shouting his mouth off about purity.

CUTHBERT: Oh, was he? Huh. I only have to hear the word purity and immediately I conjure up a picture of a fanny. And it's never any ordinary fanny. It's always a withered, shrivelled up old thing like the one the Virgin Mary's supposed to have had that they're forever saluting.

MARY GALLAGHER: I think I'd better be going.

CUTHBERT: [*Offering her the whisky*] Would you like another sip? There's no such sin as impurity, you know.

MARY GALLAGHER: There is.

CUTHBERT: No, there is not. A couple of thousand years ago it was taken for granted that people had uncontrollable urges. Monks used to take loose women up to their monasteries and nobody thought anything about it.

MARY GALLAGHER: Well, why haven't we been taught that?

CUTHBERT: They don't want you to know, do they? Or they might not know themselves. There's an awful lot of ignorance about. I once asked my Mum if she knew how many illegitimate children Pope Alexander the Sixth had.

MARY GALLAGHER: What?

CUTHBERT: Christ, you're as bad as her. She gave me a clip round the ear. [*In an Irish accent*] "You dirty little swine! Get out of here this minute and go and swill your mouth with soap." She's under the impression that all the Popes were paragons of purity. Well, they bloody well weren't. They got up to all sorts of spicy things.

MARY GALLAGHER: They didn't! Did they really?

CUTHBERT: Alexander the Sixth, he was a filthy old fucker. His real name was Rodrigo Borgia. He used to knock about with various tarts. One of them owned a string of brothels. Some old bag called Vanozza. He probably picked up the syphilis off her. He was riddled with it. I found out how many bastards he had. Four. He used to have it off with his daughter. His son had the syphilis as well. I'm not making it up, you know. It's all on record in the Vatican. They've got a load of dirty documents in there all about the Popes and their concubines and bastard kids. I'm definitely going to take a trip to Rome as soon as I get the chance and have a read of them for myself.

MARY GALLAGHER: What makes you think they'd let you into the Vatican to read about stuff like that?

CUTHBERT: It happens to be open to the public. Of course they don't just let anyone in. They give out special permits. They have to, otherwise there'd be queues down there day and night.

MARY GALLAGHER: D'you think Pope Pius has girl friends?

CUTHBERT: No. They don't do it any more. They haven't been doing it for quite a few centuries. I think it was Gregory the Seventh who put a stop to it. The cunt. Well, the way I see it is if it wasn't a sin once then it's not a sin now. You wouldn't catch me discussing my sexual habits in Confession.

MARY GALLAGHER: I don't know why you bother to go.

CUTHBERT: I'm quite prepared to confess any genuine misdeeds. Any sins against the religion itself. I mean, I really believe in some of the mysteries and the majority of the doctrines. It's definitely the one true faith. And the Mass is the greatest ceremony on earth. "Ecce Agnus Dei. Ecce qui tollit peccata mundi." I've seriously thought about becoming a priest. It's a bloody great life.

Especially if you can get into a better class of parish where they all put ten bob notes in the collection plate. I wonder if I've got a vocation. Of course, I'd have to make sure there was a bit of discreet crumpet in the background. Or I might go off my head.

MARY GALLAGHER: Cuthbert, would you know if the Sin of Sodom is supposed to be something impure according to them?

CUTHBERT: Oh, yes, well that definitely is impure. Not only according to them. According to everyone. It's illegal.

MARY GALLAGHER: What exactly is it, though?

CUTHBERT: Haven't you got the slightest idea?

MARY GALLAGHER: No. That's why I'm asking you.

CUTHBERT: Well, it's two blokes in one bed having it off together up their bums.

MARY GALLAGHER: Really?

CUTHBERT: Yes. I could show you some pictures if you like.

MARY GALLAGHER: Could you?

CUTHBERT: Yes. There's some going round the school at the moment. I'll let you have a look when it's my turn to borrow them. There's quite a few homosexuals at St. Vincent's. I keep well out of their way. You've probably got some lessies at your school. Lesbian. That's what you call a woman homosexual. It's easy to spot a lesbian, you know. They all have very short hair and big gruff voices. They go to bed with each other and get up to all sorts of tricks with cucumbers and carrots and bananas. And candles. Most people think all nuns are rollicking lesbians. They probably are but I like to think of them keeping their vows of chastity if it kills them. There's something quite erotic about a completely celibate woman. Their natural lust gets all dammed up inside them and comes exploding out in all sorts of unexpected directions. That's why your Lady of Fatima nuns are so bad-tempered.

MARY GALLAGHER: You can say that again. They'd love to hit us if they were allowed to. But instead they find all sorts of spiteful ways to punish us. Saying sarcastic things and showing us up in front of other people. I'd sooner have corporal punishment any day.

CUTHBERT: You wouldn't say that if you'd ever had the cane off Canon O'Flynn. He's a bastard. The biggest bastard ever to come across the Irish Sea. You have to go up to his office to get it. He's always waiting for you, pacing up and down with the shillelagh in his hand and the saliva dribbling down his chin. [*In an Irish accent*] "Are you sorry for what you've done, boy? Are you? Well, you will be in a minute. Oho, you will." Then he gets up on his chair like this. [CUTHBERT *stands on his chair and holds the copy of* Macbeth *above his head*] "Put out your posterior." [MARY GALLAGHER *bends over.* CUTHBERT *jumps off the chair with a roar and hits her on the bottom with the book. She yells.* CUTHBERT *puts his arm around her*] Oh, sorry. [*He pulls her onto his lap and puts his arms around her and kisses her*]

MARY GALLAGHER: If I don't tell this in Confession are you sure it'll be all right to go to Holy Communion afterwards?

CUTHBERT: Of course. I've been doing that for years. Nothing's happened so it must be all right.

SCENE THIRTEEN

A Lavatory. MARY GALLAGHER *and* MARY MCGINTY *are sitting on the seat with a Bible between them.* MARY MOONEY *is standing up.*

MARY MOONEY: "And if a woman have an issue, and her issue in her flesh be blood, she shall be put apart seven days: and whosoever toucheth her shall be unclean until the even."

MARY MCGINTY: Cor! Fancy putting that in the Bible.

MARY MOONEY: There's some better bits in Chapter Eighteen. I've underlined them in pencil. Don't let me forget to rub it out, though. My Mum would do her nut if she ever found it.

[*They turn the page*]

MARY GALLAGHER: "Thou shalt not uncover the nakedness of a

woman and her daughter, neither shalt thou take her son's daughter or her daughter's daughter, to uncover her nakedness." Christ, those Jews must have been sex mad.

MARY MCGINTY: Look at this. "Thou shalt not lie with mankind, as with womankind: it is abomination."

MARY GALLAGHER: That's the Sin of Sodom.

MARY MCGINT`
MARY MOONE\ } it?

MARY GALLAGHER: Yes. Listen to this. "Neither shalt thou lie with any beast to defile thyself therewith."

MARY MCGINTY: A beast! Cor, blimey O'Riley.

MARY GALLAGHER: "Neither shall any woman stand before a beast to lie down thereto: it is confusion."

MARY MCGINTY: I should say it is. Bloody hell! What sort of animals did they do it with?

MARY GALLAGHER: Whatever happened to be trotting about at the time.

MARY MCGINTY: Camels.

MARY GALLAGHER: I suppose so. Horses. Pigs. Anything.

MARY MOONEY: What would it be like now if Jesus hadn't come down to put a stop to all that?

MARY MCGINTY: I'd probably be going down the White Hart tonight with a monkey.

MARY GALLAGHER: You are, anyway.

MARY MCGINTY: Oh, shut up!

[MOTHER PETER and MOTHER BASIL enter and go to the lavatory door]

MARY MOONEY: Have a look at Chapter Twenty.

[They turn the page]

MARY MCGINTY: "And if a man shall take his sister, his father's daughter, or his mother's daughter, and see her nakedness, and she see his nakedness . . ."

[MOTHER PETER *raps on the door*]

MOTHER PETER: Who's in this toilet?

[*The girls jump up and look alarmed.* MARY GALLAGHER *puts the Bible down and shushes them silently*]

MARY GALLAGHER: [*Calling out*] Me, Mother.

MOTHER PETER: Who's me?

MARY GALLAGHER: Mary Gallagher, Mother.

MOTHER PETER: Come out of there this minute, Mary Gallagher.

[MARY GALLAGHER *pulls the chain, opens the door, comes out and closes the door behind her.* MOTHER BASIL *pushes open the door and sees the other two*]

MOTHER BASIL: Oho! We knew well there were three of you in here. Come on out of it! [*She drags them out*]

MOTHER PETER: How dare you go into the toilet together. Big girls of your age. Were you doing anything immodest in there? Were you? Tell the truth now and shame the devil.

GIRLS: [*In unison*] No, Mother.

MOTHER BASIL: I think they were smoking. Hand over the cigarettes.

MARY GALLAGHER: We haven't been smoking, Mother.

MOTHER PETER: Well, what have you been doing in there all this time?

MARY MOONEY: We were reading the Bible, Mother.

MOTHER BASIL: You lying little toad.

MOTHER PETER: You impudent little madam, you.

[MOTHER BASIL *goes into the toilet*]

MOTHER BASIL: There's a Bible inside of this toilet, Mother Peter, believe it or not.

MOTHER PETER: Why would anyone go into the toilet to read the Bible?

[MOTHER BASIL *comes out and hands the Bible to* MOTHER PETER]

MOTHER PETER: Whose Bible is this?

[*Pause*]

MOTHER BASIL: Is it a Catholic Bible, Mother Peter?

MOTHER PETER: Indeed it is. But I've a very strong suspicion there's more to it than meets the eye. I'm going to hand it in to Mother Thomas Aquinas and ask her to give it a thorough inspection. If the owner of this Bible wants it back let her go up to Mother Thomas Aquinas' office and explain herself.

MOTHER BASIL: What are we going to do with them, Mother Peter?

MOTHER PETER: I'll deal with them later, Mother Basil. I can't imagine what kind of bad things have been going on inside that toilet. But I'll find out. I'll find out, so I will.

SCENE FOURTEEN

The Classroom. MOTHER PETER *is at her desk.*

MOTHER PETER: There will be no lessons this afternoon. And no lessons again on the afternoon of the twenty-first. On that day we'll be having our little Christmas celebration, so bring in your cakes and snacks and your bottles of lemonade. And bring your party dresses with you to change in to. You may have the use of the gramophone, so bring along some records to dance to. Bring your hit parade records by all means. But do not attempt to bring any Elvis Presley records into this school.

VOICES OFF: Oh, no!

MOTHER PETER: Never mind your protesting. That man is a positive menace to decent young girls. I might as well tell you now that Mother Thomas Aquinas is sending out a letter to all parents to warn them about the corruption caused to innocent young minds by such a lewd and bestial artiste. Your parents have every right to go through your records, to take out the Elvis Presleys and put them into the dustbin where he belongs. There are plenty of good wholesome singers to enjoy. Joseph Locke now. He's one of the finest singers in the land. And I've heard great reports about Donald Peers. So forget about that old devil of a Presley. Now, this afternoon we're going to have a fillum show. Mother Basil is going to show us *The Barretts of Wimpole Street*. When the bell goes after lunch I want you to go straight into the Assembly Hall and take your seats for the fillum. With the exception of Mary Gallagher, Mary McGinty and Mary Mooney. These three girls will come back here to the classroom where they'll find a passage of Latin waiting to be translated into English on their desks. Mother Thomas Aquinas has asked me to make it clear that any girls seen going into the toilet together will be banned from taking their O levels.

SCENE FIFTEEN

The Classroom. MARY MCGINTY *and* MARY GALLAGHER *are singing and jiving.*

MARY MCGINTY: Shall we show old Mooney how to jive?

[*She gets hold of* MARY MOONEY's *hand and tries to turn her round but she doesn't catch on*]

MARY GALLAGHER: Oh, Mooney. You've got absolutely no sense of rhythm.

MARY MOONEY: Yes, I have. When I used to go Irish dancing I was one of the best in the class.

MARY MCGINTY: Irish dancing! Sod that for a lark.

MARY GALLAGHER: Show us what you learnt.

MARY MOONEY: No fear. You'd only laugh.

MARY MCGINTY: We won't, will we.

MARY GALLAGHER: No. Come on. Just show us a couple of steps.

MARY MOONEY: No.

MARY MCGINTY: Oh, go on. Be a sport.

MARY MOONEY: Oh, all right.

> [MARY MOONEY *starts to do an Irish dance, with her arms glued to her sides and her legs leaping high in the air. The other two hum, "diddly di, diddly di," and clap their hands.* MOTHER BASIL *comes creeping in.* MARY MCGINTY *and* MARY GALLAGHER *make frantic signals to* MARY MOONEY *but she is too engrossed in her dance*]

MOTHER BASIL: I see you're making a show of yourself again, Mary Mooney. Huh. I've seen better dancing done by a headless chicken. [*To* MARY GALLAGHER *and* MARY MCGINTY] Get your things and go off home, you two. [*They go off*] Show me the work you were given, Mary Mooney. [MARY MOONEY *gives her paper to* MOTHER BASIL] I can't understand a word of this at all.

MARY MOONEY: It's Latin, Mother Basil.

MOTHER BASIL: Oh, aren't you the sharp one, Mary Mooney. You're so sharp you'd cut the cost of living. I'll give you Latin, you little bitch! It isn't the Latin I'm looking at at all. It's your own translation into English. Or is it Chinese or Arabic, or what? I never saw such a bad bit of writing in my life. Sit down and copy it all out again.

> [*She flings the paper back at* MARY MOONEY]

SCENE SIXTEEN

The Classroom. MOTHER PETER *is at her desk.*

MOTHER PETER: In 1917, in the thick of the first world war, a festering abscess broke out upon the face of the earth. Communism. The devil's own doctrine. When the wicked Red scoundrels took control of Russia in the 1917 Revolution this was only the start of a Communist crusade to be spread throughout the whole wide world. But in the very same year, thanks be to God, Our Blessed Lady revealed herself to three little children in Fatima. God had seen fit to intervene in the affairs of the world by sending his own Blessed Mother down to earth to start a counter-revolution. [MARY MOONEY *comes in and stands next to* MOTHER PETER's *desk*] Fatima is a village in the very centre of Portugal, about seventy miles from Lisbon. The scenery in those parts is stark and severe. I've heard tell it would put you in mind of Connemara but without the green. Mary Mooney, what time of day is this to come creeping into school?

MARY MOONEY: I'm sorry, Mother Peter, but the trolley bus came off the rails.

MOTHER PETER: Did it indeed? And why couldn't you hop off it and on to another like any normal person?

MARY MOONEY: We weren't anywhere near a bus stop, Mother Peter.

MOTHER PETER: Never mind your feeble excuses. You've missed your morning prayers. Go into the chapel now and say a few for the souls in Purgatory.

MARY MOONEY: Yes, Mother Peter.

MOTHER PETER: Now, have you got your deposit for Fatima?

MARY MOONEY: No, Mother Peter. I . . .

MOTHER PETER: You haven't. Well, isn't that just typical, Mary Mooney. You knew that money had to be in by today at the very latest. Isn't it just like you to be upsetting the whole schedule and making extra work for myself and Mother Thomas Aquinas. Oh, Mary Mooney, I've a good mind to exclude you from the pilgrimage altogether.

MARY MOONEY: I won't be going anyway, Mother Peter.

MOTHER PETER: Oh? And why won't you?

MARY MOONEY: My father says he can't afford it, Mother.

MOTHER PETER: Nonsense. We're getting greatly reduced rates both for the journey and the accommodation. Didn't you make that clear to your father? Of course, we know it's not a compulsory pilgrimage. Nobody is being dragged out to Fatima by the scruff of the neck. It just happens that all the other girls in this form will be going of their own free will. No doubt they'll tell you all about it when they get back. Now go to the Chapel. [MARY MOONEY *goes off*] On the thirteenth of each month from May to October, Our Lady appeared to Lucia dos Santos and her two little cousins Jacinta and Francisco while they were tending their sheep. There was a blinding flash and Our Lady appeared hovering over an evergreen tree. She wore a snowy white dress and veil, the dress embroidered with stars of gold, a golden cord around her neck. She had on little gold earrings and held rosary beads of sparkling white in one hand. In the other hand she held her own Immaculate Heart, bleeding and wreathed with thorns. "I want you to do something special for me," she told Lucia. "I want you to ask the Pope to consecrate my Immaculate Heart to Russia. If this is done I promise that Russia will be converted. But if Russia is not converted she will spread her dreadful Communism throughout the world arousing wars and persecutions against the Church." Our Lady promised the children that she would work a miracle and indeed she did. On the thirteenth of October seventy thousand people came to wait for the promised miracle. It was pouring with rain and the crowd made a roof of umbrellas. At noon the rain stopped and the Queen of Heaven appeared to the children. "I am the Lady of the Rosary," she said to Lucia. "Let them say the rosary every day. Let them offend Our Lord no more. The war is going to end but if men do not repent then another and far more disastrous war will come." And then she disappeared. "Oh, look at the sun!" cried Lucia. The sun was trembling and dancing and turning like a wheel of fireworks, changing colour as it turned round and round. Then suddenly it seemed to fall towards the earth casting the colours of the rainbow onto the people and the land. The people fell into a panic thinking the world was coming to an end. But Lucia, Jacinta and Francisco were gazing in rapture up at the sky as they saw Our Lady standing to the right of the sun. She was now dressed in the blue and white robes of Our Lady of the Rosary. To the left of the sun St.

Joseph emerged from the clouds. He held the child Jesus in his arms. Then Our Lord himself appeared in the red robes of the Divine Redeemer and made the Sign of the Cross three times over the world. Beside him stood Our Lady now clad in the purple robes of Our Lady of Sorrows. And then finally Our Lady appeared again in the simple brown robes of Our Lady of Carmel. The sun stopped dancing and the crowd breathed a sigh of relief. The world hadn't come to an end but the miracle promised by Our Lady had come to pass. Two years later Our Lady came to take the boy Francisco up to Heaven. And Jacinta went up to join him the following year. Lucia entered a convent and is still alive and well, guarding an important secret entrusted to her by Our Lady. This secret will be told to all the world as soon as Lucia receives permission from Heaven. But until then we must all be kept in suspense. If any of your families or friends are in need of a miracle get them to write out their petitions and we'll deliver them to Our Lady's shrine. And while we're there we'll say a prayer for Mary Mooney's unfortunate father. That his arms may grow long enough to reach into his pockets. And, by the way, even though we are going to Fatima during the Easter holiday, Mother Thomas Aquinas has given orders that school uniform will be worn for the duration of the pilgrimage.

VOICES OFF: Oh, no!

MOTHER PETER: Oh, yes. Oh, yes indeed.

SCENE SEVENTEEN

The Street. MARY MOONEY, *dowdily dressed, is walking along carrying a couple of library books.* DEREK *comes swaggering along in the opposite direction. They pass each other.*

MARY MOONEY: Hello, Derek.

DEREK: Eh? [*He stops and turns around*] Er . . . do I know you, darling?

MARY MOONEY: Not really. But I was with Mary McGinty that day you met her along the street near our school.

DEREK: Oh, yeah?

MARY MOONEY: You probably won't remember me but I'm Mary Mooney. There was another Mary with us as well that day. Mary Gallagher.

DEREK: Oh, really?

MARY MOONEY: Yes. You asked Mary McGinty if she'd meet you outside the White Hart that night. D'you remember?

DEREK: Er . . . vaguely. Bit of a long time ago, wasn't it?

MARY MOONEY: The beginning of last term. But I've got a good memory for faces.

DEREK: Oh, have you?

MARY MOONEY: Yes.

DEREK: Well, you'll have to excuse me not recognising you, darling. I mean, in them uniforms you all look like peas in a bleedin' pod. Seeing you all dressed up the way you are today, I wouldn't lump you in with none of them Lady of Fatima girls, now would I? Here, why ain't you in Fatima?

MARY MOONEY: I didn't want to go.

DEREK: Very wise, darling. Very wise. They're having a diabolical time, you know. I had a postcard Tuesday. She's got corns coming up on her kneecaps from having to say so many prayers. They have to be in bed by nine o'clock every night. And they have to go marching about all over the place in a crocodile. [He laughs] I bet you're glad you stopped in Willesden, ain't you? [He laughs] I hear they carted a midget along with 'em.

MARY MOONEY: Oh, you mean Mary Finnegan in 5B. She's only as big as this. [She holds her hand up about three feet in the air]

DEREK: Gonna be coming back as big as this, is she? [He holds his hand up about six feet in the air]

MARY MOONEY: They're hoping she'll grow a bit bigger.

DEREK: She won't, you know. She'll be coming back as little as what she went. You wait and see.

MARY MOONEY: They won't be back for nearly another week.

DEREK: Yeah, I know. Poor sods. Here, turn your face to the side a minute. D'you know who you remind me of?

MARY MOONEY: Who?

DEREK: Rhonda Fleming.

MARY MOONEY: I don't.

DEREK: Yes, you do. I seen her in a film last Saturday. Yeah, you're definitely her double, you are.

MARY MOONEY: Am I?

DEREK: I'm telling you. Er . . . d'you fancy coming for a bag of chips?

MARY MOONEY: I've just had my dinner.

DEREK: Oh. Well, how about a cup of tea then?

MARY MOONEY: I don't drink tea.

DEREK: Well, what do you drink?

MARY MOONEY: Milk. Or water, or . . .

DEREK: What, holy water?

MARY MOONEY: Oooh, no.

DEREK: Don't look so serious, darling. They can probably do you a glass of whatever you happen to fancy round the caff.

MARY MOONEY: Well, actually, I was just on my way to the library.

DEREK: Yeah? [*He takes one of the books from under her arm*] What's this? *The Keys of the Kingdom*, eh? Do a lot of reading do you, darling?

MARY MOONEY: There's not much else to do during the holidays.

DEREK: What's this one all about then?

MARY MOONEY: It's about a Catholic priest. Father Chisholm. He's a missionary and he goes out to China and . . .

DEREK: Sounds highly intriguing, I must say. Of course, I don't go in for reading much myself. No. I'd sooner watch the old TV.

MARY MOONEY: So would I if we had one. But we haven't.

DEREK: Ain't you? Oh well, you'll have to come round my house some time and have a watch of mine. Come round this afternoon if you like.

MARY MOONEY: Oh, I don't know.

DEREK: You're more than welcome, darling. I'm not doing nothing special this afternoon. I would have gone in to work but I had such a diabolical neuralgia this morning I couldn't lift me head off the pillow. You gonna come then?

MARY MOONEY: D'you really want me to?

DEREK: I wouldn't ask you, would I?

MARY MOONEY: All right then. I suppose I can always go to the library another day.

DEREK: Course you can. Come on then, Rhonda. Let's go and get the bus.

SCENE EIGHTEEN

DEREK'S *House*. MARY MOONEY *is sitting on the settee watching "Bill and Ben the Flowerpot Men," which is just ending.* DEREK *comes in carrying a glass of orange liquid and a very large biscuit tin.*

DEREK: Here we are, mate. Glass of Tizer gone flat. That's all she had in the cupboard.

MARY MOONEY: Oh, thanks.

[DEREK *switches off the television*]

DEREK: Cor, bleedin' chronic, ain't it. I don't know why they can't put nothing decent on of a daytime. Still, we've got *The Cisco Kid* coming on a bit later, if you fancy watching that.

MARY MOONEY: I don't know what it's all about. I've only ever seen *Carroll Levis's Discoveries.*

DEREK: That's always good for a giggle if nothing else.

MARY MOONEY: Where's your Mum, Derek?

DEREK: Down the biscuit factory, ain't she. She does afternoons down there. [*He offers her the tin*] Want one?

MARY MOONEY: Oh, thanks.

[DEREK *takes off his Edwardian jacket*]

DEREK: You can't move in this house for biscuits. She brings 'em home by the bleedin' sackful. I don't know how she gets 'em past the gate. The old man goes round flogging 'em to all the neighbours. [*He sits down very close to* MARY MOONEY *and puts his arm around the back of the settee*] You . . . er . . . you going out with a regular bloke at all?

MARY MOONEY: No.

DEREK: You must have been out with a feller or two in your time.

MARY MOONEY: Oh, yes.

DEREK: Yeah, you would have done of course, a fair-looking bird like yourself. I expect you've had quite a few blokes after you, eh?

[MARY MOONEY *goes all coy*]

DEREK: [*Putting his hands up to his eyes*] Cor, that sunshine ain't half playing havoc with me neuralgia. I'm gonna have to draw them curtains. [*He gets up*]

[*Blackout*]

MARY MOONEY: I can't see a thing.

DEREK: No, well, I'm supposed to lie down in a darkened room whenever I get one of me attacks.

MARY MOONEY: Have you taken any aspirin?

DEREK: No. They don't do no good. Where are you? Oh, there you are. [*Pause*] What's the matter, darling?

MARY MOONEY: I thought you were supposed to be Mary McGinty's boyfriend.

DEREK: She's in Fatima, ain't she?

MARY MOONEY: She will be coming back though.

DEREK: Look, darling, I don't wanna talk about her when I'm with you. [*Pause.* DEREK *tuts. Whispering*] Cor, that's a choice little pair of bristol cities you got there.

MARY MOONEY: Oh, no! No! No!

[*Pause. Sounds of protest from* MARY MOONEY]

DEREK: Ssh! It's all right. We don't have to go the whole way. Not if you don't want to. Even if we did, which I'm not saying we would, but just supposing we did, which we wouldn't of course, but if we did, you wouldn't have to worry 'cos I have got something on me, know what I mean? Give us your hand. See what you're doing to me, darling. Cor, yeah! Now that's better than taking an aspirin. Cor!

CURTAIN

ACT TWO

SCENE ONE

Outside DEREK's *Front Door.*

DEREK: Er . . . D'you reckon you can find your own way to the bus stop, darling?

MARY MOONEY: I don't know.

DEREK: Well, what you do is, you turn left outside the gate, then you go right at the bottom of the road. Then it's the first on the right, second on the left, second on the right. Go round by the garage and through the little alleyway. That brings you out to the butcher's. Then you go left. No. I tell a lie. You go right. Walk down as far as the Coliseum, cross over the road and there's your bus stop. Right?

MARY MOONEY: I think so.

DEREK: You wouldn't mind hurrying up, would you, only I want to get the place straightened up before me Mum gets in. [MARY MOONEY *puts her coat on*] Yeah. Well, I might see you around some time. There's just one thing. Er . . . you wouldn't go saying nothing to Mary McGinty, would you?

MARY MOONEY: No.

DEREK: No, well, just make sure you don't, otherwise there could be a bit of bother and we don't want none of that. I have been known to get nasty before now, know what I mean? If you ever do bump into me any time when I'm with her, just act a little bit casual like. All right? [MARY MOONEY *nods*] Right? You ready?

MARY MOONEY: I haven't got any money to get home with.

DEREK: Oh, yeah. Here you are. Here's a tanner. All right? Don't forget your library books. Ta ta, mate.

[*He pats her on the bottom. She goes*]

SCENE TWO

The Presbytery. FATHER MULLARKEY *is sitting at his dinner table. He is eating a plate of sausage and mash. A plate of pudding is in front of him.* MARY MOONEY *comes in.*

FATHER MULLARKEY: Come in and sit down, Mary Mooney. [*She sits down at the table*] Miss Gavigan tells me you want to see me on a very urgent matter. Is that right?

MARY MOONEY: Yes, Father.

FATHER MULLARKEY: D'you want a sausage? [*He holds out one on a fork*]

MARY MOONEY: No, thank you, Father.

FATHER MULLARKEY: Ah, go on and have one. She's given me too many, the way she always does. [*He puts the sausage on a side plate and pushes it towards her*] Miss Gavigan is only used to feeding great big hulks of men. She's eleven brothers back at home, not one of them under eighteen stone. Help yourself to the Lot's wife.

MARY MOONEY: The what, Father?

FATHER MULLARKEY: The salt. And put a good dollop of ketchup on it. What did you want to see me about?

MARY MOONEY: I must go to Confession, Father. Urgently.

FATHER MULLARKEY: Well, you can't go to Confession tonight. The church is all locked up and I have to get down to the off-licence.

MARY MOONEY: But I've committed a mortal sin, Father.

FATHER MULLARKEY: Ah, well, make an Act of Contrition and come up to Confession on Saturday. Could you manage a half of this old steamed pudding at all?

MARY MOONEY: No, thank you, Father.

FATHER MULLARKEY: Ah, come on and help me out. I keep telling that woman, don't be giving me any more of them steamed puddings. But she doesn't take a blind bit of notice. [*He gives her half the pudding. Then he burps*] Beg your pardon. [*He lights up a cigarette*]

MARY MOONEY: Father, I've committed a very serious mortal sin.

FATHER MULLARKEY: Ah well, it'll surely keep till Saturday.

MARY MOONEY: I might die before then.

FATHER MULLARKEY: Not at all. A big strapping girl like yourself in the best of health.

MARY MOONEY: But I might have an accident, Father. And if I did and I died I'd be sent straight down to Hell. [*She bursts into tears*]

FATHER MULLARKEY: Oh, come on now. You can't have done anything that bad, surely.

MARY MOONEY: Oh, I have, Father. I have.

FATHER MULLARKEY: Well, if it's that serious you'd better make a quick Confession now. Come over here and kneel down.

MARY MOONEY: In here, Father?

FATHER MULLARKEY: It's as good a place as any. I'll turn me back on you.

[*She kneels down by the side of his chair. He turns away from her*]

MARY MOONEY: Bless me, Father, for I have sinned. It is five days since my last Confession.

FATHER MULLARKEY: Never mind about the venial sins. Save them up for the next time. Just concentrate on the big mortal sin.

MARY MOONEY: I . . . er . . . I . . . er . . . [*Pause*] I . . . er . . .
I . . . er . . .

FATHER MULLARKEY: Was it a sin against holy purity?

MARY MOONEY: Yes, Father.

FATHER MULLARKEY: I thought as much. With another person?

MARY MOONEY: Yes, Father.

FATHER MULLARKEY: A male or a female?

MARY MOONEY: A male, Father.

FATHER MULLARKEY: A boyfriend?

MARY MOONEY: Somebody else's boyfriend.

FATHER MULLARKEY: Indeed. What did you do with him? Did you
have sexual intercourse?

MARY MOONEY: No, Father. I don't think so.

FATHER MULLARKEY: You must surely know if you did or you
didn't. Unless . . . Were you drunk at all?

MARY MOONEY: No, Father. But it was dark.

FATHER MULLARKEY: Did he force you to do anything?

MARY MOONEY: No, Father. But I didn't know what he was going
to do until he was actually doing it.

FATHER MULLARKEY: He handled you, did he?

MARY MOONEY: Yes, Father.

FATHER MULLARKEY: How many times?

MARY MOONEY: I wasn't counting, Father.

FATHER MULLARKEY: More than once?

MARY MOONEY: Yes, Father.

FATHER MULLARKEY: And you think that's all he did?

MARY MOONEY: Yes, Father. But . . . but I did something impure
as well.

FATHER MULLARKEY: What?

MARY MOONEY: I don't know exactly, Father. But I think he said it was a Twentieth Century-Fox.

FATHER MULLARKEY: What the devil?

MARY MOONEY: Oh, no it wasn't. It was a J. Arthur Rank.

FATHER MULLARKEY: Glory be to God! I hope you're not going to be seeing this scoundrel ever again.

MARY MOONEY: No, Father.

FATHER MULLARKEY: You know you shouldn't be left alone in a room with any man.

MARY MOONEY: Yes, Father.

FATHER MULLARKEY: You must put the whole episode right out of your mind. If it ever comes into your mind uninvited you mustn't entertain it at all.

MARY MOONEY: No, Father.

FATHER MULLARKEY: Unless, of course, you think of it with disgust instead of delight. Do you?

MARY MOONEY: Yes, Father.

FATHER MULLARKEY: That's the idea. For your penance say five Our Fathers and five Hail Marys. Now make a good Act of Contrition. Oh, my God . . .

MARY MOONEY: Oh, my God because thou art so good I am very sorry that I have sinned against thee and by thy grace I will not sin again.

FATHER MULLARKEY: Ego te absolvo a peccatis tuis, in nomine Patris et Filii et Spiritus Sancti. Amen. [He gets up and puts on a pair of bicycle clips] I must be going out now. You can stay behind and say the penance. I'll tell Miss Gavigan not to disturb you. Are you coming to the social on Saturday week?

MARY MOONEY: Yes, Father. I'll be coming with my mother and father.

FATHER MULLARKEY: Give my best regards to the two of them. [*He puts his hand into his pocket and brings out a booklet*] I wonder, would you take a book of raffle tickets and see how many you can sell. We've a first prize of ten pounds. And the second is a bottle of whisky.

MARY MOONEY: Yes, Father.

FATHER MULLARKEY: Good girl. I'll leave you to it then. Goodnight.

MARY MOONEY: Goodnight, Father.

[*He goes off*]

SCENE THREE

The Classroom. MOTHER PETER *is at her desk.*

MOTHER PETER: Now on Friday we're going to have a retreat. The entire day will be devoted to prayer and contemplation. Father Mullarkey will give us a little talk followed by a collection for black babies in Africa. So bring in your sixpences and shillings. If the weather stays fine, please God, we plan to spend the afternoon out in the garden. You may walk up and down and say the rosary, perhaps. Or sit down and read a good book. And I don't mean any old novel. I mean the biography of a saint or some other devotional work. [MOTHER BASIL *comes in*] Yes, Mother?

MOTHER BASIL: Carry on, please, Mother. I'll wait until you've finished.

MOTHER PETER: Absolute silence must be the rule for the whole day. And please do not resort to any preposterous sign language except in a case of absolute necessity. You will find the day will pass very quickly and the spiritual rewards will be very great indeed. Now, Mother Basil, can I help you at all?

MOTHER BASIL: I'm afraid I have a rather unpleasant duty to perform, Mother Peter. [*She reaches into her pocket and brings out a box of Tampax, which she holds up*] This box of . . . of . . .

things was found lying about on the floor of the downstairs cloak-room. I've been into 5B and 5C but no girl there has come for-ward to claim them. Indeed, they have given me their word of honour that they know nothing about them at all. And I'm in-clined to believe them which means, I'm sorry to say, Mother Peter, that they must belong to a girl in 5A.

MOTHER PETER: I can't believe any girl in my form would dream of using such an immodest method of . . .

MOTHER BASIL: No self-respecting girl would abuse her body with such a contraption and that's a fact.

MOTHER PETER: Will the owner of this container please step for-ward and claim it. [*Long pause*] I see. If this is to be the case then you will come to see me individually for questioning after the les-son. I'll find out whose they are. I'll find out, so I will. And who-ever it is, let her shame be her only punishment.

SCENE FOUR

The Classroom. FATHER MULLARKEY *is standing behind a table.* MOTHER THOMAS AQUINAS *is sitting to one side of him.*

FATHER MULLARKEY: When Adam bit into the apple and defied his creator he put a plague upon mankind forever after. The plague of original sin. All babies emerge from the womb infected with Adam's original sin. And there's only one way to remove this sin. By the Sacrament of Baptism. What happens to babies who die without receiving Baptism? They are prevented from entering Heaven. They must therefore go down into Hell. Not into the wretched furnace, no. But into that part of Hell known as Limbo. And what is it like in Limbo? Is it anything like Purgatory? Not a bit of it. In Purgatory the souls are punished by being heated to a degree of real discomfort. But this is only a temporary punish-ment. Sooner or later all the souls in Purgatory will have earned themselves a place up in Heaven. But the souls in Limbo must stay where they are for all eternity. It's a bleak old prison of a place so it is. The majority of babies in Limbo are black, yellow and brown, and if it wasn't for the wonderful work carried on by the missionaries throughout the pagan world there'd be many more babies piled up in Limbo. I'm going to send round the mission box [*He picks it up and rattles it*] and I hope it'll be filled to the brim. Now wouldn't it be a marvellous idea if you started your very own mission box at home. Think of a little black baby and give him a name. Every week put in a percentage of your pocket money and say to yourself this is for Patrick or Joseph or Eamon so that he can be baptised and grow up to be a good Catholic. I want you to remember that Baptism is the one Sacrament that doesn't have to be administered by a priest. Anyone may baptise in a case of necessity when a priest cannot be had. If you should ever find yourself in the house of a non-Catholic friend where there's a baby who hasn't been baptised you'd do well to sprinkle water on that baby's head and say, "I baptise thee in the name of the Father and of the Son and of the Holy Ghost. Amen." And when you meet that child above in Heaven you can be sure he'll come up and shake you by the hand. Is it only babies that are sent to Limbo? Mostly it is. Babies and little children under the age of seven. After the age of seven a child has reached the age of reason and must decide for himself whether he wants to be good or bad. If he's wicked he'll end up in Hell like all other wicked persons. And it's the sins of the flesh that put people into Hell, make no mistake about it. The sins of the flesh. [*He bangs on the table*] Now you may wonder about the sort of Baptism administered to our poor misguided brethren, who, though following the teachings of Christ do so within the confines of a false religion. Is the quality of their Baptism as good as our own? Indeed it is, bearing in mind that anyone can administer Baptism. We must never consider non-Catholics to be in any way inferior to ourselves. God knows it is through no fault of their own that they were born into heretical households. We must continue to pray hard for Christian unity. Pray that the heresy be removed from their hearts and that they may be guided back under the infallible umbrella of Rome. There is no other church but the Catholic Church. The Catholic Church is the one true religion. [*He bangs on the table*] The one and only Ark of Salvation for the whole of Mankind. [*He bangs on the table again*]

GIRLS: Good morning, Father Mullarkey. Good morning, Mother Thomas Aquinas.

SCENE FIVE

The Garden. The girls are in summer uniform. MARY
GALLAGHER, MOTHER PETER *and* MARY MOONEY *are walking up
and down in silence with rosary beads in their hands.* MOTHER
PETER's *lips are moving. She makes the Sign of the Cross and
goes off.* MARY GALLAGHER *does a "V" sign after her.*

MARY GALLAGHER: Oh, Jesus, I'm bored out of my mind. [MARY
MOONEY *puts her finger to her lips*] Don't tell me you're not
bored. [MARY MOONEY *shrugs her shoulders*] I'm sure they're trying to drive us mad. It's a well known fact that too much silence
can drive a person insane. It's all right for them. They're already
round the bend. Especially Mother Peter. If she hadn't put herself
into a convent somebody would have locked her up in a loony
bin.

MARY MOONEY: Sssh!

MARY GALLAGHER: It's all right. There's nobody about. Although
they've probably put a load of microphones into the bushes. And
they're sure to have stationed Reverend Mother down in the basement on a periscope. Why the hell can't they have their idiotic re-
treats in the holidays. D'you want a Smartie? [*She takes a tube
out of her pocket.* MARY MOONEY *shakes her head*] Oh, have one,
will you, for Christ's sake. We're not supposed to be fasting, you
know. Hold out your hand. [*She pours some Smarties into* MARY
MOONEY's *reluctant hand*] Are you keeping quiet just to annoy
me, by any chance? [MARY MOONEY *shakes her head*] I suppose
you're scared of getting caught.

MARY MOONEY: No, I'm not.

MARY GALLAGHER: You are.

MARY MOONEY: I'm not.

MARY GALLAGHER: Well, what are you being so holy for? Come to
think of it, though, you always have been a bit that way inclined.

MARY MOONEY: I have not. I'm no more holy than you are.

MARY GALLAGHER: Not much. I doubt if you've ever committed a genuine mortal sin in all your life.

MARY MOONEY: Oh, yes, I have. I've definitely committed one.

MARY GALLAGHER: Oooh, one. That's a lot, isn't it.

MARY MOONEY: Why, how many have you committed?

MARY GALLAGHER: Millions.

MARY MOONEY: Have you really?

MARY GALLAGHER: Yes. You know that box of Tampax?

MARY MOONEY: Yes.

MARY GALLAGHER: They were mine.

MARY MOONEY: They weren't!

MARY GALLAGHER: They were, you know.

MARY MOONEY: Why didn't you go up and claim them?

MARY GALLAGHER: You must be joking. She didn't suspect me for a minute.

MARY MOONEY: Who got the blame in the end?

MARY GALLAGHER: Maria Zajaczkowski.

MARY MOONEY: That wasn't very fair.

MARY GALLAGHER: She's not bothered. They could just as easily have been hers. She went red when Mother Peter cross-examined her. Did you know she's going out with a really old man?

MARY MOONEY: No.

MARY GALLAGHER: Yes. He must be at least twenty-five. Nearly everybody in our form has got a bloke. It's time you got yourself one, isn't it?

MARY MOONEY: You think I've never been out with a bloke, don't you?

MARY GALLAGHER: Well, you haven't, have you?

MARY MOONEY: Oh, yes, I have, if you want to know.

MARY GALLAGHER: Oh, yes? Since when?

MARY MOONEY: Since just after Easter, actually.

MARY GALLAGHER: How come you've kept so quiet about it, then?

MARY MOONEY: If I told you something really confidential would you promise to keep it a secret?

MARY GALLAGHER: Yes, of course.

MARY MOONEY: Would you swear to God never to tell a soul?

MARY GALLAGHER: Yes. You can trust me.

MARY MOONEY: Cross your heart and hope to die.

MARY GALLAGHER: All right.

MARY MOONEY: You know when you were in Fatima?

MARY GALLAGHER: Yes.

MARY MOONEY: Well, I met a bloke in the street and he asked me to go to his house with him, so I did.

MARY GALLAGHER: What, you let a bloke pick you up just like that? And you didn't even know who he was?

MARY MOONEY: No. I mean yes. I did know who he was. That's just the trouble. You know who he is too.

MARY GALLAGHER: Who?

MARY MOONEY: Promise you won't tell anyone in all the world. Especially not Mary McGinty.

MARY GALLAGHER: Why not her?

MARY MOONEY: Well, see, this bloke . . . It was her boyfriend Derek.

MARY GALLAGHER: Cor! No!

MARY MOONEY: Yes.

MARY GALLAGHER: Are you sure you're not making it up? I can't imagine you and him together.

MARY MOONEY: Well, we were.

MARY GALLAGHER: Christ! She'd go berserk if she ever knew.

MARY MOONEY: You won't tell her, will you? Please.

MARY GALLAGHER: I wouldn't dare. Did he ask to see you again?

MARY MOONEY: I wouldn't want to see him again, not as long as I live. He's horrible.

MARY GALLAGHER: Is he? How come Mary McGinty's so mad about him then?

MARY MOONEY: He was nice at first. But then he turned nasty. Well, not exactly nasty but rude. Do all blokes try to do rude things to girls?

MARY GALLAGHER: The majority of them, yes, if they get the chance.

MARY MOONEY: Has Cuthbert ever tried to be impure?

MARY GALLAGHER: He never thinks about anything else.

MARY MOONEY: But he's a Catholic.

MARY GALLAGHER: Yes. Terrible, isn't it.

MARY MOONEY: You've been going out with Cuthbert for a long time, haven't you?

MARY GALLAGHER: What about it?

MARY MOONEY: Is that why you've committed so many mortal sins? Because he makes you?

MARY GALLAGHER: He doesn't make me. What a thing to say. It's the devil who makes you commit sins.

MARY MOONEY: That Derek must be possessed by the devil.

MARY GALLAGHER: Why? What did he do? Oh, dear, you haven't lost your priceless virginity, have you?

MARY MOONEY: No. No . . . but . . .

MARY GALLAGHER: What?

MARY MOONEY: I couldn't possibly tell you.

MARY GALLAGHER: I've probably heard it all before.

MARY MOONEY: I couldn't possibly say what he did. But I've got it written down in my diary. [*She takes a book out of her pocket*] I have to keep it with me all the time in case anyone should ever find it. My Mum'd swing for me if she saw it. You can have a look at it if you like.

MARY GALLAGHER: [*Reading the diary*] Cor, fancy letting a bloke do that to you the first time you ever go out with him.

MARY MOONEY: I didn't want him to. But he was a lot stronger than me. He's not like a boy, that Derek. He's a proper big man, you know.

MARY GALLAGHER: They will usually stop if you tell them to.

MARY MOONEY: I did. But he said we all know "no" means "yes." That doesn't make any sense though, does it?

MARY GALLAGHER: It means you liked what he was doing but you didn't want to admit it.

MARY MOONEY: I did not like it.

MARY GALLAGHER: Didn't you? You must be abnormal then.

MARY MOONEY: I'm not.

MARY GALLAGHER: You must be. Everybody else likes it.

MARY MOONEY: Well, it wasn't all that bad, I suppose.

MARY GALLAGHER: You want to find a bloke of your own. It's not the done thing to go round borrowing other people's.

MARY MOONEY: Oh, shut your rotten face! And give me back my diary.

[*She snatches the diary and goes marching off.* MARY MCGINTY *is sitting on a bench with a book.* MARY GALLAGHER *goes up and sits next to her*]

MARY MCGINTY: How much longer have we got?

MARY GALLAGHER: Another couple of hours.

MARY MCGINTY: Oh, Christ! I can't stand it. Have you finished your book?

MARY GALLAGHER: No. I haven't read a word of it. I've been talking to Mary Mooney.

MARY MCGINTY: I bet she was keeping her mouth well shut.

MARY GALLAGHER: Not exactly, no. Actually, there's more to that girl than you might think.

MARY MCGINTY: How d'you mean?

MARY GALLAGHER: She's a bit of a dark horse if you did but know. I've found out she's got a dead sly streak in her.

MARY MCGINTY: Really?

MARY GALLAGHER: I know it for a fact. I can't very well tell you what I've found out about her, though. I would tell you only it's something to do with you and you wouldn't like it if you knew.

MARY MCGINTY: You might as well tell me. Go on.

MARY GALLAGHER: You'll only be furious, I warn you. It's something that happened while we were away in Fatima.

MARY MCGINTY: What? Come on?

MARY GALLAGHER: Well . . . she met a bloke in the street and went back to his house with him.

MARY MCGINTY: What's that got to do with me?

MARY GALLAGHER: It was your Derek. The bloke.

MARY MCGINTY: My Derek?

MARY GALLAGHER: Yes.

MARY MCGINTY: He wouldn't look at Mary Mooney.

MARY GALLAGHER: He might not look at her. But he definitely went and touched her.

MARY MCGINTY: Eh? Is that what she told you?

MARY GALLAGHER: She's got it all written down in her diary. All the sordid details.

MARY MCGINTY: What, you mean you've read it?

MARY GALLAGHER: Yes.

MARY MCGINTY: [*Jumping up*] I'll bleedin' kill her! Little slag. And him. Filthy dirty sod!

> [*She goes marching off.* MOTHER BASIL *and* MARY MOONEY *enter followed by* MARY MCGINTY. MARY MCGINTY *goes over to* MARY MOONEY]

MARY MCGINTY: I wanna talk to you.

MARY MOONEY: What about?

MARY MCGINTY: You know bleedin' well what about.

MARY MOONEY: I suppose you've been gossiping with your friend Mary Gallagher.

MARY MCGINTY: Haven't I just.

MARY MOONEY: She promised me she wouldn't tell you.

MARY MCGINTY: You should know better than to open your big fat mouth, shouldn't you, you little scrubber. Making out you're so frigging holy. Why can't you get a bloke of your own?

MARY MOONEY: Look, I'm sorry. I didn't mean . . . Oh, I wish I'd never.

MARY MCGINTY: You gonna let me have a look at that dirty little diary of yours?

MARY MOONEY: No.

MARY MCGINTY: Why not? You let Mary Gallagher see it. You can just let me see it and all. It's my bleedin' bloke you've been scribbling about. Where is it?

[*She tries to take the diary out of* MARY MOONEY's *pocket.* MARY MOONEY *struggles but* MARY MCGINTY *gets hold of it*]

MARY MOONEY: Give it back. You mustn't read it. Please give it back to me. Please!

[MOTHER BASIL *comes marching along.* MARY MCGINTY *drops the diary and goes off.* MOTHER BASIL *comes up to* MARY MOONEY *and shakes her fist at her. They both bend down to pick up the diary and their heads collide.* MOTHER BASIL *gives* MARY MOONEY *a punch. She falls down.* MOTHER BASIL *starts kicking her.* MOTHER BASIL *goes marching off in a temper with the diary but turns round and comes back again to deliver one final kick*]

SCENE SIX

DEREK's *House.* MARY MCGINTY *is sitting on the settee.* DEREK *is pacing up and down, chain-smoking.*

DEREK: Look, I've told you a hundred times, she didn't mean nothing. And I didn't do nothing neither. Nothing much anyway. I mean, be fair. She come up and spoke to me in the street. I never knew her from Old Mother Hubbard, did I? You know how it is when I get me attacks of neuralgia. Me eyesight gets affected, don't it? I couldn't make out what she looked like in the street. She could have been a really beautiful bird for all I knew. When I got her inside the house and see what she really looked like I had to draw the curtains double quick. I should have known that was asking for trouble, though, 'cos once you're in the dark with somebody it might just as well be anybody, you know how it is. Oh, no, you don't, of course. Well, I'm only human, know what I mean? Not like you. No. You're about as warm as a Lyons choc ice you are, darling. It's about bleedin' time you faced up to the fact that I've been impairing me capabilities for the sake of respecting you. It's a wonder I ain't done myself some sort of a permanent mischief. Not that I get any credit for it, oh, no. It's all been a bleedin' waste of time. It's quite obvious you don't wanna go out with me no more.

MARY MCGINTY: I didn't say that.

DEREK: You don't have to say it. I'm going by the way you're acting towards me.

MARY MCGINTY: Did she sit on this?

DEREK: I don't remember.

MARY MCGINTY: Yes, you do. Which side did she sit on?

DEREK: The other side.

MARY MCGINTY: You sure?

DEREK: What difference does it make? Me Mum's been over it with the Hoover tons of times since then. She's got one of them attachments that gets right into all the corners.

MARY MCGINTY: I'm just wondering how many other birds you've been out with behind my back while you're supposed to have been going out with me.

DEREK: None.

MARY MCGINTY: I don't believe you. Anyway, I've heard otherwise.

DEREK: Who from?

MARY MCGINTY: Somebody who's seen you about.

DEREK: Well . . . they was only a couple of little tarts. I mean, I don't go looking for it, darling. But if it happens to come my way . . . I can't very well help myself, can I? And who in this world would blame me the way you behave towards me. You know my old Nan was half Italian, don't you?

MARY MCGINTY: Never mind your Nan. How many girls did you say you'd been out with?

DEREK: I told you. A couple.

MARY MCGINTY: How many's a couple?

DEREK: I don't know. Five or six.

MARY MCGINTY: What were their names?

DEREK: Gloria. Joyce. I don't know. I wasn't bothered about their names. Here, what's all this interrogation in aid of? I don't ask you no questions, do I? For all I know you could have been running about with all sorts of greasy foreigners out in Fatima.

MARY MCGINTY: Oh, yeah? Some chance of that with the nuns breathing down our necks day and night.

DEREK: That's what you tell me.

MARY MCGINTY: I did not go out with anyone in Fatima or anywhere else. But I bleedin' well would in the future.

DEREK: Would you?

MARY MCGINTY: You bet your life I would.

DEREK: Oh, well. Please yourself.

MARY MCGINTY: Don't worry. I will.

[Pause]

DEREK: Er . . . you wouldn't . . . er . . . No. It's just a thought. No. I mean . . . You can laugh if you like but how about . . . no. How about . . . er . . . d'you . . . er . . . d'you . . . d'you . . . er . . . d'you fancy getting engaged?

MARY MCGINTY: What?

DEREK: You heard.

MARY MCGINTY: Are you in love with me?

DEREK: Eh? [He takes out his comb and combs his hair]

MARY MCGINTY: Yes or no.

DEREK: [Doing a terrible impersonation of Elvis Presley singing and gyrating]
"Well bless my soul what's wrong with me
I'm shaking like a bear up in a honey tree

My friends say I'm acting just as wild as a bug
I'm in love, Ooh, I'm all shook up.
Uh huh huh, uh huh, yeah, yeah, yeah."

MARY MCGINTY: You don't have to take the piss.

DEREK: I wasn't in actual fact. I meant what I was singing.

MARY MCGINTY: Oh. Are you offering to buy me a ring by any chance?

DEREK: Yeah. Don't expect nothing too flash, though. I ain't no millionaire.

MARY MCGINTY: Does that mean you'd actually want to get married some time?

DEREK: I probably would in a couple of years.

MARY MCGINTY: Before or after you do your National Service?

DEREK: There won't be none of that, darling. No. Not with this neuralgia.

MARY MCGINTY: I hope you get away with it.

DEREK: I will.

MARY MCGINTY: Why d'you want to marry me, Derek?

DEREK: Be a bit of a laugh, wouldn't it?

MARY MCGINTY: Oh, thanks very much.

DEREK: Well . . . I just happen to think you're one of the best-looking birds I've seen knocking about Willesden for a long time. And I wouldn't mind kipping down in the same bed as you every night. If it was all right with you.

MARY MCGINTY: I wouldn't mind getting engaged to you.

DEREK: Oh. I didn't think you'd want to somehow.

MARY MCGINTY: Don't you want me to, then?

DEREK: Course I do, darling. I wouldn't have asked you, would I?

MARY MCGINTY: Well, I've said I would.

DEREK: Yeah, well that's all right then, ain't it.

[*Long pause*]

MARY MCGINTY: How would you feel about changing your religion, though?

DEREK: Do what? Leave off, mate!

MARY MCGINTY: But if you really want to marry me, Derek, you'll have to marry me in a Catholic church.

DEREK: Oh, no! No chance. No. That's definitely out, darling. I was thinking more along the lines of a register office myself.

MARY MCGINTY: If I got married in a register office I'd be living in sin in the eyes of the Catholic Church.

DEREK: All right, so change over to the Church of England.

MARY MCGINTY: Look, Derek, I've told you before. It's once a Catholic always a Catholic and that's all there is to it. We're not even allowed to set foot inside the door of a Protestant church without getting permission off of a Bishop.

DEREK: No, but you expect people to come crawling into your churches whenever it suits you, oh, yes.

MARY MCGINTY: That's only because the Catholic Church is the real Christian church. In fact it's the only proper religion in the world. The others are all phoney.

DEREK: Is that right? Who said so, eh? Who laid that one down?

MARY MCGINTY: Jesus.

DEREK: He's got some cheek, ain't he. The only religion, eh? That's a downright diabolical insult to all the people in this country who go toddling off to the Church of England of a Sunday morning. And that includes my Aunt Ada and my Uncle Ernie. And my cousin Freda. Yeah, and the Queen. They're all in the wrong, are they? And the Irish are in the right? Yeah? Rhubarb. Fucking rhubarb, darling! And I don't intend to apologise for saying that word in front of you. And what about all the other people in the world, eh? The Hindus and the Mohammedans and the Four by

Twos. They don't count for nothing with Jesus, do they? Oh, no. Jesus only cares about the Irish. Anybody else is just a load of bleedin' riff-raff. He come all the way down to Earth, did he, all the way to Nazareth for the benefit of the bleedin' Irish. Yeah. Very likely. Why didn't he go straight to Dublin, eh? Why not? He could have had a great time changing all the water into Guinness and dancing about to ceilidh bands.

MARY MCGINTY: Oh, shut up, Derek! I can't help the way I was brought up. I've got to think of my Mum and Dad. How would they feel if I went and got married out of the church?

DEREK: And what about my Mum and Dad? Of course I realise they're only a pair of little old Protestants. It don't matter about them having to get stunk out with incense and having to listen to a load of hocus fucking pocus. No. Don't worry about them.

MARY MCGINTY: Oh, sod you, Derek.

DEREK: Sod you and all, mate.

[MARY MCGINTY *gets up and grabs her coat*]

MARY MCGINTY: I'm going home.

DEREK: Go on then.

MARY MCGINTY: I hope they put you in the bleedin' army and shave off all your hair.

DEREK: Thanks. [MARY MCGINTY *moves off but* DEREK *goes after her and gets hold of her*] Come here, you silly cow. Look, why can't we just leave it at getting engaged and save all the rest of the rubbish for later on.

MARY MCGINTY: No. It's something that has to be settled now.

DEREK: Well, I ain't changing into no Catholic, darling. I just ain't got it in me.

MARY MCGINTY: You don't have to change. But I have to get married in a Catholic church.

[DEREK *puts his arms around her*]

DEREK: What if I said I might. They wouldn't expect nothing of me, would they?

MARY MCGINTY: You'd have to sign a document to promise you'd bring all your children up as Catholics.

DEREK: All me what? Here, hang about. You're being a little bit previous, ain't you. It just so happens I ain't all that struck on little nippers with nappies full of squashed up turds.

MARY MCGINTY: But we'd have to have children if we got married.

DEREK: Yeah. One maybe. Or possibly two. But I draw the line at fucking football teams. Er . . . sorry about using that word. But I've seen enough of them Irish women down in Kilburn. Two in the pram. Three more hanging on to the handle. And half a dozen more waiting outside the boozer for the Daddy to come rolling out. No. You have your Catholic wedding, mate, and I'll have me packet of three. All right?

SCENE SEVEN

> CUTHBERT'S *House.* CUTHBERT *is lying on the settee. He is wearing a silk dressing gown, school socks and carpet slippers.* MARY GALLAGHER *is sitting on the floor with a bottle of whisky by the side of her. They each have a glass of whisky and their speech is slightly slurred.* CUTHBERT *is smoking a Senior Service cigarette in a holder.*

CUTHBERT: [*Holding out his glass*] Pass the bottle up, would you. It's time I had a refill.

MARY GALLAGHER: You'll be lucky. It's nearly all gone.

[*She shows him the empty bottle*]

CUTHBERT: We haven't drunk all that, have we? Fucking hell! I was hoping to top it up with water and put it back in the cupboard.

MARY GALLAGHER: You wouldn't have got away with that.

CUTHBERT: I've done it before enough times. He drinks so much himself he doesn't know what he's drinking half the time. And he'll be completely out of his mind by the time he comes rolling back from the County Mayo.

MARY GALLAGHER: And your Mum'll still be crying.

CUTHBERT: Yeah. Christ knows what for. She's been waiting for the old faggot to snuff it for the past twenty years.

MARY GALLAGHER: Did you know your Granny very well?

CUTHBERT: I only met her a couple of times when I was a little kid. I remember she had a beard. And bunions. Two of the biggest bunions you ever saw in your life, trying to force their way out of the side of each boot. Apparently she never used to wear any drawers. Whenever she wanted to go for a piddle she'd just walk out to the cowshed, stand with her legs apart and let it flow. I can well believe it. They never had any toilets when I was taken over there as a kid. You had to sit on a smelly old bucket and wipe your arse with a handful of shamrock. Or whatever it is that grows over there. I'm bleedin' glad I didn't have to go this time. Although I hear they have got toilets now.

MARY GALLAGHER: My Mum and Dad would never have trusted me on my own for a whole week.

CUTHBERT: They didn't have much choice. I couldn't very well leave my exams.

MARY GALLAGHER: One of them would have stayed behind in our house. They're a hell of a lot more suspicious than yours.

CUTHBERT: That's because you're a girl.

MARY GALLAGHER: Yeah. You're probably right. I only hope they don't go checking up to see if I'm at Mary McGinty's tonight.

CUTHBERT: Oh, sod 'em. Could you do me a big favour? See if there's anything else to drink in the cupboard.

[MARY GALLAGHER *gets up and goes to the cupboard and brings out a load of bottles*]

MARY GALLAGHER: There's no more whisky.

CUTHBERT: I know, worse luck.

MARY GALLAGHER: There's one bottle of Guinness. And apart from that it's mostly just dregs.

CUTHBERT: You might as well get it all out and we'll finish it up.

MARY GALLAGHER: Are you sure you won't get into trouble?

CUTHBERT: I'll think about that when the time comes. We'll have half the Guinness each and we can top it up with the various dregs. [MARY GALLAGHER *pours out the drinks*] I'll have to go and buy another bottle of whisky though. She's left me forty-five bob for food and stuff. A bottle of whisky is what? Thirty-six bob. Christ, I won't have much left over, will I?

MARY GALLAGHER: You could always come round to our house for dinner one night.

CUTHBERT: I wouldn't mind. But your Mum doesn't like me very much, does she?

MARY GALLAGHER: It's not you she doesn't like as much as your language.

CUTHBERT: Eh?

MARY GALLAGHER: She says it's a bit too ripe for a boy of your age.

CUTHBERT: What does she mean, ripe?

MARY GALLAGHER: She said she heard you swearing in our front room.

CUTHBERT: She shouldn't be fucking listening, should she?

MARY GALLAGHER: You might know they'd listen when you're in there with me. And they look through the keyhole. It's only to be expected.

CUTHBERT: Wait till she hears I'm going to be a priest.

MARY GALLAGHER: You're not going to be any priest.

CUTHBERT: Oh, yes, I am. I went into Canon O'Flynn the other day and told him I'd got a vocation.

MARY GALLAGHER: What did he say to that?

CUTHBERT: He said he wasn't at all surprised. He'd guessed it all along.

MARY GALLAGHER: I bet you didn't tell him your views on celibacy.

CUTHBERT: There's no reason why I should. He hasn't told me his.

MARY GALLAGHER: They're bound to be slightly more conventional than yours. How could you possibly be a priest?

CUTHBERT: I can. And I will. There's nothing else I want to do. [*He sings*] "Credo in unum Deum, Patrem omnipotentem, factorem caeli et terrae, visibilium omnium, et invisibilium. Et in unum Dominum . . ."

MARY GALLAGHER: Oh, shut up, will you. I hear enough of that every Sunday.

CUTHBERT: Well, I don't. I never get tired of the Mass.

MARY GALLAGHER: Mother Peter says they'll be saying it in English before another decade is out.

CUTHBERT: What? They'd better not or I'll be kicking up the most appalling stink. It'd be no better than the Church of England. I'd have to do a defection to the Russian Orthodox. Or the Greek. No, they couldn't possibly change it. It's only a rumour.

MARY GALLAGHER: It might not be such a bad idea. At least ordinary people would be able to understand it.

CUTHBERT: Huh. They can understand the Stations of the Cross and look how boring they are.

MARY GALLAGHER: You'd have to say them if you become a priest.

CUTHBERT: Only during Lent. I could always speed them up a bit or miss a couple out. Nobody'd notice. I can't expect to enjoy every duty I'd have to perform.

MARY GALLAGHER: How do you feel about hearing Confessions?

CUTHBERT: I'd never ask anyone: "How many times?" [*He yawns*] I think it's time for bed.

MARY GALLAGHER: It's not. It's only half past eight.

CUTHBERT: You'd better go out by the back door in the morning. Just to be on the safe side. In case one of the neighbours happens to see you.

MARY GALLAGHER: I'll go straight round to Mary McGinty's and go to Mass with her.

CUTHBERT: Are you any good at washing?

MARY GALLAGHER: What d'you mean?

CUTHBERT: Well, you know my bed's only a little one. It's the same one I've had since I was six. We could go in my Mum and Dad's only I'd have to put some clean sheets on afterwards. There's one or two shirts I'd like washing as well. And some socks.

MARY GALLAGHER: Oh. All right.

CUTHBERT: Shall we go?

MARY GALLAGHER: Not yet. You will still respect me tomorrow, won't you, Cuthbert?

CUTHBERT: Yes, of course.

MARY GALLAGHER: D'you promise?

CUTHBERT: Yes. Come on. I've got to be serving on the altar at seven o'clock Mass tomorrow morning.

SCENE EIGHT

A Side Room. MR. EMANUELLI *is sitting on a chair.* MARY MOONEY *is standing in front of him, singing. He is conducting her with one of his walking sticks. She is wearing Nanki-Poo's Japanese costume with a false bald head and a pigtail.*

MARY MOONEY: [*Singing*]
"And if you call for a song of the sea
We'll heave the capstan round
With a yeo-heave ho, for the wind is free

Her anchor's a-trip and her helm's a-lee
Hurrah for the homeward bound."

MR. EMANUELLI: [*Singing*]
"Yeo-ho, heave ho.
Hurrah for the homeward bound."

MARY MOONEY:
"To lay aloft in a howling breeze
May tickle a landsman's taste
But the happiest hour a sailor sees
Is when he's down at an inland town
With his Nancy on his knees, yeo-ho
And his arm around her waist."

MR. EMANUELLI:
"Then man the capstan off we go
As the fiddler swings us round
With a yeo-heave ho and a rum below
Hurrah for the homeward bound
With a yeo-heave ho
And a rum below
Yeo-ho, heave ho,
Yeo-ho, heave ho, heave ho, heave ho,
      yeo-ho."
[*He hums*] La, la, la, la . . .

MARY MOONEY:
"A wandering minstrel I
A thing of shreds and patches
Of ballads, songs and snatches
And dreamy lullaby
And dreamy lul-la, lul-la-by
Lul-la-by."

MR. EMANUELLI: It will have to do. The vibrato is all up the creek
but it's the best we can manage for the moment. But please,
please do not let me see you slinking onto the stage and apologis-
ing to the audience for your presence.

MARY MOONEY: No, sir.

MR. EMANUELLI: You must learn to stand up for yourself or you'll

find yourself trampled right into the ruddy ground. It will be better for you when you go away from this dump of a sanctimonious
institution. You will go and study music. Learn to control your
respiration, sing in Italian and enlighten your ear. I will help you.
Do you have a gramophone at home?

MARY MOONEY: Oh, yes, sir.

MR. EMANUELLI: What do you listen to on it?

MARY MOONEY: Irish records mostly, sir.

MR. EMANUELLI: Huh. What ruddy use is that to you? Eh? No.
You will come in the holidays to my house and you will hear
Mozart and Puccini. Come the first Wednesday afternoon at
three o'clock. Do you know how to get to Hendon Central?

MARY MOONEY: Yes, sir. But . . .

MR. EMANUELLI: [Getting out pen and paper] Here is my address.
Bang hard on the window and I will throw you out the key. It
will be good to have a visitor. Nobody comes to see me any more.
I can't say I blame them. I wouldn't come to see me myself. Why
such a face? Eh? Do you think I am putting you into a catapult
and firing you off into a career you don't want really?

MARY MOONEY: No, sir.

MR. EMANUELLI: Well, I cannot guess what is in your mind. Does
this leg of mine offend you?

MARY MOONEY: No, sir.

MR. EMANUELLI: I don't see why it shouldn't when it certainly
offends me.

MARY MOONEY: I've got used to it, sir.

MR. EMANUELLI: Well, I tell you something. I can't ever get used
to it. What kind of God is he up there to send me such an affliction when I haven't done nothing to him?

MARY MOONEY: He often sends suffering to good people, sir. It's
really a privilege in disguise.

MR. EMANUELLI: What kind of talk is that, eh? It's not the talk of

a young girl. It's the talk of a blasted nun. I loathe and detest
nuns. I despise every one of them in this building. They should be
tied up with string, laid out in a line and raped by the local
police. Take no notice. I am being cantankerous. Some days I feel
so cantankerous I could take a machine gun into the streets and
shoot down the whole population of Hendon Central. I don't
know why. I would never have come to this convent if I could
have found a little work somewhere else.

MARY MOONEY: I'll pray for your leg to get better, sir.

MR. EMANUELLI: Thank you very much but don't bother. I've tried
it myself. Candle after candle burning uselessly in front of a
statue of St. Francis of Assisi. A million Hail Marys wafting up
into the empty atmosphere. Even a journey to Lourdes, wouldn't
you know. Never in all my life did I experience such humiliation.
Seeing myself lumped in among so many wretched unfortunates. I
came hobbling home and decided it was time for Maximilian
Emanuelli to disappear from the face of the earth. I was going to
go by way of the gas oven. With one hundred codeine tablets inside my belly. Every day I had a dress rehearsal. There never could
be an actual performance. Of course there couldn't. How could
there be? No matter how unbearable his precious life on earth if a
Catholic dares to put an end to it himself there'll be a far worse
existence waiting on the other side. Huh. I don't believe a word of
it and yet I know it's true. I will be shouting for the priest to
come running with the Sacrament of Extreme Unction as soon
as I see the Angel of Death approaching. I must be saved from
the fires of Hell even though I know I would find in Hell all the
people with whom I have anything in common. Especially Rudolph, who always said he would happily burn in Hell, the swine.
For eighteen years he and I were together, all the time laughing,
mostly at other people. It's a good thing he went on before me.
He never would have stood for this leg. You are too young and
green to comprehend such things but I hope in your life one day
there will be a Rudolph. But you won't find him in Willesden or
Harlesden or Neasden or Acton or Dollis Hill. You must travel all
over the world and meet lots of fascinating people. And you must
learn to be fascinating yourself. You are not a good-looking girl
but you can cheat. With the help of something colourful out of a

bottle you can soon enrich the miserliness of nature. [*He sings*] "Paint the pretty face, dye the coral lip. Emphasise the grace of her ladyship." [*He gets up*] Now I have to go and inspect the orchestra. You will show me a good performance, yes?

MARY MOONEY: Yes, sir.

MR. EMANUELLI: [*Taking a medal and chain out of his pocket*] I have something nice for you. Here. It was once given to me and now I give it to you with my very best wishes.

MARY MOONEY: Thank you, sir. What is it?

MR. EMANUELLI: The eye of Horus. [*He puts it round her neck*] Horus was an Egyptian god who roamed the earth a long long time ago. He was highly esteemed by the pagans. Let him bring you a little bit of luck.

[MR. EMANUELLI *pats* MARY MOONEY *on the shoulder and goes off.* MARY MOONEY *wrenches the chain from her neck and hurls it across the room*]

SCENE NINE

Mother Thomas Aquinas' Office. MOTHER THOMAS AQUINAS *is at her desk.* MARY GALLAGHER *is sitting in front of her.*

MOTHER THOMAS AQUINAS: Well, congratulations, Mary Gallagher.

MARY GALLAGHER: Thank you, Mother Thomas.

MOTHER THOMAS AQUINAS: You've done extremely well and we're all very pleased with you indeed. You'll go into the academic sixth form next year and we'll work towards getting you a place at university. Have you any idea at all about what you might like to take up as a career?

MARY GALLAGHER: I've thought about working in a laboratory, Mother. And I've thought about teaching Physics and Chemistry.

MOTHER THOMAS AQUINAS: You could do a lot worse than teach, my dear. Do you know, I really miss the teaching myself, after so many years of it. I never imagined I'd be sitting behind a desk all day with so much responsibility on my shoulders. But God knows best of course. It isn't for me to question his methods. Ah, well. You'll find things very different in the academic sixth. Would you like to be a prefect?

MARY GALLAGHER: I'm not sure, Mother.

MOTHER THOMAS AQUINAS: Well, I'd like you to become a prefect and help me keep the younger girls on their toes. There's just one thing that worries me slightly about you, my dear, and that's your rather strange choice of companions. When you do go up to the sixth form you will be mixing with a different set of girls. You can look forward to a most satisfactory and perhaps even a brilliant future with the help of God. All the best to you now and have a very enjoyable holiday.

MARY GALLAGHER: Yes, Mother Thomas. Thank you, Mother Thomas.

[MARY GALLAGHER *gets up and goes off.* MARY MCGINTY *comes in and stands in front of* MOTHER THOMAS AQUINAS]

MOTHER THOMAS AQUINAS: Well now, Mary McGinty, I'm sorry to have to say, your examination results were very disappointing indeed. Do you get nervous during exams at all?

MARY MCGINTY: Yes, Mother. A bit.

MOTHER THOMAS AQUINAS: Your work has always been up to standard if not particularly original. It's a shame to see you ending up with such a poor record. Have you any thoughts on a career at all?

MARY MCGINTY: No, Mother.

MOTHER THOMAS AQUINAS: Well, I'd like you to go into the Secretarial sixth form in September.

MARY MCGINTY: Er . . . No, thank you, Mother. I'd rather not.

MOTHER THOMAS AQUINAS: I beg your pardon?

MARY MCGINTY: I'd rather leave school now, Mother Thomas.

MOTHER THOMAS AQUINAS: You can't possibly leave school now.

You must get yourself qualified for some kind of job and maybe even acquire an A level into the bargain.

MARY MCGINTY: I don't want to be a secretary, thank you, Mother.

MOTHER THOMAS AQUINAS: And what do you think you're going to be out in the world with no training of any kind and only the one solitary O level to your name?

MARY MCGINTY: I might go and work in a shop.

MOTHER THOMAS AQUINAS: You didn't come to Our Lady of Fatima for five years to learn how to stand behind the counter of a shop, my dear girl.

MARY MCGINTY: Well, I wouldn't mind being a hairdresser.

MOTHER THOMAS AQUINAS: Jesus, Mary and Joseph, did you ever hear the like! A hairdresser.

MARY MCGINTY: Well, the thing is, Mother. I'll probably be getting married quite soon.

MOTHER THOMAS AQUINAS: Indeed. Is this just wishful thinking? Or do you actually have a fiancé?

MARY MCGINTY: Yes, Mother.

MOTHER THOMAS AQUINAS: You have? At your age?

MARY MCGINTY: Yes, Mother.

MOTHER THOMAS AQUINAS: I take it he's a Catholic boy.

MARY MCGINTY: Er . . . not exactly, Mother. He might be changing his religion soon though.

MOTHER THOMAS AQUINAS: I see. Well, we can never have enough converts, that's for sure. But you can't possibly think of marriage for a long time yet. You'll have to go out and earn some sort of living. And you never know when you might need to help your husband support the children. What does the young man do for a living?

MARY MCGINTY: He's a Co-op milkman, Mother.

MOTHER THOMAS AQUINAS: Indeed.

MARY MCGINTY: But what he really wants to be is a train driver.

MOTHER THOMAS AQUINAS: Oh, take your head out of the clouds
and come back down to earth, you silly girl. I'm certainly not
going to accept your decision to leave school and go drifting into
some dead-end job and wasting your life. And I'm sure your parents will be on my side. Be a good girl now and come back here in
September and into the Secretarial sixth form, even if it's only for
the one year.

MARY MCGINTY: No, Mother. I don't want to.

MOTHER THOMAS AQUINAS: Never mind what you want or what you
don't want. You'll do what I tell you to do.

MARY MCGINTY: No, I won't. I don't have to. I'm leaving at the
end of this term.

MOTHER THOMAS AQUINAS: Oh, I think you'd better leave now, this
minute, if that's how you're going to behave. Go on. Get out.
Take your things home and don't bother coming back for the rest
of the term. You think you know what's best for you, you don't
want to be helped, well off you go then. And I hope you end up
in the gutter.

MARY MCGINTY: [*Jumping up and going to the door*] Yeah—and
the same to you. You fucking old cunt!

> [MARY MCGINTY *runs away.* MOTHER THOMAS AQUINAS *makes
> the Sign of the Cross and says a silent prayer.* MARY MOONEY
> *comes in*]

MOTHER THOMAS AQUINAS: Don't stand there gawping at me like
an idiot! Well, I see you've done all right for yourself exam-wise.
Not that there's any reason why you shouldn't have. You've brain
enough inside your head. The question is, where do you go from
here? Mr. Emanuelli has told me you're keen to start studying
singing full-time as soon as possible. He seems to think you have
the vocal equipment for nothing less than the grand opera and
I'm sure he knows about such things having been in the business
himself. All I can say is you seem like a different girl altogether up
on the stage, so maybe it'll be the makings of you. Now if you
were any other girl with all these O level passes I'd have no hesita-

tion at all in sending you straight into the academic sixth form in September. But taking into account your past behaviour and keeping in mind that you're aiming for a musical career, I see no point at all in your remaining at this school. The best course of action for you, I should think, would be to go out and get yourself some little job which would leave you time enough for lessons with Mr. Emanuelli. Unless of course your parents have any objections. Have you discussed your musical aspirations with them at any length?

MARY MOONEY: No, Mother Thomas.

MOTHER THOMAS AQUINAS: And for heaven's sake why not?

MARY MOONEY: I don't want to be a singer, Mother Thomas.

MOTHER THOMAS AQUINAS: But I spoke to Mr. Emanuelli only yesterday and he was quite adamant . . .

MARY MOONEY: I haven't told him yet, Mother Thomas.

MOTHER THOMAS AQUINAS: You let that poor man spend hours of his time instructing you and going to no end of trouble on your behalf and now you want to turn round and tell him he needn't have bothered. Oh, Mary Mooney, isn't that just like your impudence.

MARY MOONEY: I don't get on with him very well, Mother Thomas.

MOTHER THOMAS AQUINAS: Well, that's a fine thing to say when he has nothing but praise for you.

MARY MOONEY: I don't want to be left alone with him in his house, Mother Thomas. He's asked me to go there in the holidays.

MOTHER THOMAS AQUINAS: Indeed. It wouldn't be the first time you were alone with a man in his house, would it? [She opens a drawer and brings out MARY MOONEY's diary] At least not according to this diary of yours which you may have back but you needn't go looking for the two pages of obscenities because they've been ripped out and thrown into the boiler where they belong. You're on the right road to Hell, Mary Mooney.

MARY MOONEY: But I am still a virgin, Mother Thomas.

MOTHER THOMAS AQUINAS: Oh, be quiet! [*She takes a Bible out of her desk*] You may also take back the Bible that you did not come forward to claim. I went through it very carefully indeed and besides finding several dubious passages underlined in pencil I also came across a Mass card for the soul of a certain Dominic Aloysius Mooney. You can be sure your sins will always find you out.

MARY MOONEY: Please, Mother Thomas, I . . . I . . .

MOTHER THOMAS AQUINAS: Well, what is it? We haven't much time. Benediction will be starting in a minute.

MARY MOONEY: Please, Mother, I'd like to be a nun.

MOTHER THOMAS AQUINAS: Oh, would you now.

MARY MOONEY: Please, Mother, I've always wanted to be a nun. Ever since I was six years old.

MOTHER THOMAS AQUINAS: There was never a Catholic girl born that didn't want to be a nun at some stage of her developing years. But you're not a little girl now. You're a big girl with a great deal of experience. Go away now and be thankful you can sing for your supper.

MARY MOONEY: But, Mother, I have to be a nun. I want to be as perfect as I possibly can and be sure of getting a high place in Heaven.

MOTHER THOMAS AQUINAS: You haven't the necessary qualities, Mary Mooney. No. You're much more the type to go into show business.

MARY MOONEY: But, Mother, I want to give my voice back to Our Lord.

MOTHER THOMAS AQUINAS: What, fling it back in His face?

MARY MOONEY: No, Mother. Offer it up to Him by singing only for Him. Please, Mother, could you help me, please? I don't know who else I can go to.

MOTHER THOMAS AQUINAS: I can't believe a creature like you could possibly have a vocation. And I can't imagine what order would accept you. Certainly this one would not. Although, there again . . . I don't know. I suppose we can't all be Maria Goretti. Don't you feel ashamed of yourself when you think of that wonderful virgin martyr?

MARY MOONEY: Yes, Mother Thomas.

MOTHER THOMAS AQUINAS: Saint Maria Goretti was only eleven years old when her purity was put to the test. In 1902. She too was left alone in a house with a man. A great lout of a fellow who tempted her again and again but she would not give in to him. And when he found he could persuade her by no other means he threatened her with a shoemaker's awl. But still she would not commit a sin. She would not. So he got mad and took up the weapon and stabbed her with it no less than fourteen times. Mary Mooney, if you really think you have a vocation pray to Saint Maria Goretti for a positive sign. Now what about Mr. Emanuelli? You'll have to tell him what you've just told me.

MARY MOONEY: Oh, I couldn't, Mother. I couldn't face him.

MOTHER THOMAS AQUINAS: Oh, but you'll have to. And I must have a word with your mother. Why does she never come near the school?

MARY MOONEY: She's always tired after work, Mother Thomas.

MOTHER THOMAS AQUINAS: What does your father do?

MARY MOONEY: Nothing, Mother. He's been retired for years.

MOTHER THOMAS AQUINAS: Is he a sick man?

MARY MOONEY: No, Mother. He's just old.

MOTHER THOMAS AQUINAS: Is he a great deal older than your mother?

MARY MOONEY: No, Mother. She's old too. She was nearly fifty when I was born. And now she's going to have another baby.

MOTHER THOMAS AQUINAS: Don't be so ridiculous. She can't be having a baby at that age.

MARY MOONEY: But she is, Mother. I know she is.

MOTHER THOMAS AQUINAS: If she is then she should be going into the *Guinness Book of Records*. Will you tell her to come and see me before the end of term?

MARY MOONEY: Yes, Mother Thomas.

MOTHER THOMAS AQUINAS: Go into the chapel. Kneel down in front of the crucifix and offer yourself body and soul to Our Blessed Lord who died for you.

MARY MOONEY: Yes, Mother Thomas.

MOTHER THOMAS AQUINAS: And this is your very last chance, Mary Mooney, I hope you realise. Your very last chance. Go along now.

MARY MOONEY: Yes, Mother Thomas. Thank you, Mother Thomas. Thank you very much indeed.

SCENE TEN

The Classroom. MOTHER PETER *is at her desk.*

MOTHER PETER: When you come back in September you may wear nylon stockings and a smart grey skirt instead of a gymslip. But don't let me see any sign of lipstick or bits of old jewellery. Apart from a holy medal or a crucifix. Those of you going out into the world must remember that the devil will be beckoning to you from every corner. But you can just tell him to go to Hell because you're not going to be fooled by him and his wily ways. You're going to show him a shining example of Christian purity. You may often be puzzled when you see decent young men hovering around young women who wear scanty clothes and say provocative things. But you can be sure that such women are really the object of those men's secret contempt. Oh, yes indeed. Remember that God made your body for Himself. He lives in it and He may well want to use it for His own work later on when you marry, as a tabernacle for brand-new life. All parts of the body are sacred but none more so than the parts connected with the mystery of motherhood. They should be treated with the greatest respect and guarded with absolute modesty. Scrupulous hygiene is, of course, vitally important and you need not imagine you are sinning when you sit in the bath and see yourself or touch yourself with the flannel. Just say a little prayer, think of Our Lady and remember that she had a body just like yours. Oh, yes, and beware of indecent articles of news in what may otherwise appear to be innocent publications on sale in any shop. The *News of the World* is the one that springs most readily to mind. If you ever see the *News of the World* lying about on a bus or a train or in any public place don't hesitate to tear it up. And the very same applies to the *Daily Worker*. The rotten old rag of the Communists. Rip it into pieces. It's no easy task to live a good life in the adult world. We must take up our cross every day just like Our Blessed Lord and carry it with us wherever we go. And when God sends us any sickness or trouble we must accept it willingly and say, "Thy will be done. I take this for my sins." And the best of luck to you. [*She makes the Sign of the Cross*]

MOTHER   ⎞   In the name of the Father and of the Son and of the
PETER: ⎬   Holy Ghost. Amen.
GIRLS: ⎠   Jesus, Mary and Joseph I give you my heart and my soul.
Jesus, Mary and Joseph assist me in my last agony.
Jesus, Mary and Joseph may I die in peace and in your blessed company. [*Sign of the Cross*]
In the name of the Father and of the Son and of the Holy Ghost. Amen.

SCENE ELEVEN

The Back of the Chapel. A very large crucifix is hanging on the wall with candlesticks and a candle box by the side of it. MARY MOONEY *comes in, genuflects in the direction of the altar and kneels down in front of the crucifix and prays.*

VOICES OFF: [*Singing*]
"Tantum ergo Sacramentum
Veneremur cernui:
Et antiquum documentum

Novo cedat ritui:
Praestet fides supplementum
Sensuum defectui.
Genitori, Genitoque
Laus et jubilatio.
Salus, honor, virtus quoque
Sit et benedictio;
Procedenti ab ubtroque
Compar sit laudatio.
Amen."

[MARY MOONEY *stands up, takes a candle, kisses it, blesses herself with it, lights it and puts it into a candlestick. Then she genuflects and goes off in the opposite direction to which she came in, walking backwards with her hands joined*]

PRIEST: [*Voice off, chanting*] "Panem de caelo praestitisti eis. Alleluia."

VOICES OFF: [*Chanting*] "Omne delectamentum in se habentem."

[*Enter* MARY MCGINTY. *She genuflects in the direction of the altar, goes up to the crucifix and sticks something on it: a very long penis made of plasticine. She runs off*]

PRIEST: [*Voice off, speaking*] "Oremus. Deus, qui nobis sub Sacramento mirabili passionis tuae memoriam reliquisti, tribue, quaesumus, ita nos corporis et sanguinis tui sacra mysteria venerari ut redemptionis tuae fructum in nobis jugiter sentiamus, Qui vivis et regnat cum Deo Patri in unitate Spiritus Sancti per omnia saecula saeculorum. Amen."

[*During the above prayer* MOTHER THOMAS AQUINAS *comes in. She genuflects, glances over at the crucifix, sees the plasticine penis and dashes over to remove it. Then she goes off in the opposite direction. She comes back holding* MARY MOONEY *by the scruff of the neck. They genuflect together in the direction of the altar then go off*]

CURTAIN

THE SUNSHINE BOYS

Neil Simon

Neil Simon

Without any conceivable doubt, Neil Simon was the most prolific American dramatist of the 1970s. Within a period of ten years, he contributed to the New York theatre eight new works, all but two of these being extraordinarily successful.

One of his most felicitous, as well as touching, comedies of the period was *The Sunshine Boys*, a dramatic study of two partners in a retired vaudeville team who despise each other yet beneath the surface tensions of their relationship reveal deeper feelings of affection.

Opening on December 20, 1972, the play was viewed by most of the press as a turning point for the author: here was a play endowed with Simon's exceptional comedic expertise but also one that had more pathos, depth, and scope than most of his previous comedies. Clive Barnes promulgated this fact in the New York *Times* when he wrote that Neil Simon has finally emerged as "a serious writer." While there is much amusement and laughter in *The Sunshine Boys*, there also is a good deal of human nature exposed as the play unfolds.

As Otis L. Guernsey, Jr., wrote in the theatre yearbook, *The Best Plays of 1972–1973*: "The best American play of the year, other opinions to the contrary notwithstanding, was Neil Simon's *The Sunshine Boys*, a study of human beings on the threshold of senility so amazingly sensitive, with a touch so light and yet so accurate, you hardly realized how good a play it was until you'd had time to reflect on it. Simon may have written funnier plays, but never one that demonstrated such total mastery of his art."

The play ran for 538 performances and was later made into a film with Walter Matthau and George Burns, the latter winning an Academy Award for his performance as Willie Clark.

For almost two decades, Neil Simon has reigned supreme as America's foremost writer of contemporary comedies. While his plays may be regarded by some as lighthearted entertainments, there is behind the laughter an underlying element of human truths and a revelatory dissection of characters, particularly in *The Sunshine Boys* and, most recently, in the author's partially autobiographical *Chapter Two*.

Mr. Simon's gilt-edged chain of successes began in 1961 with his initial Broadway play, *Come Blow Your Horn*, which ran for 677 performances. This was followed by the book for the musical *Little Me* (music by Cy Coleman, lyrics by Carolyn Leigh, 1962), *Barefoot in the Park* (1963), *The Odd Couple* (1965), the musical *Sweet Charity* (music by Cy Coleman, lyrics by Dorothy Fields, 1966), *The Star-Spangled Girl* (1966), *Plaza Suite* (1968), the musical *Promises, Promises* (music by Burt Bacharach, lyrics by Hal David, 1968), and *Last of the Red Hot Lovers* (1969).

In the seventies, Mr. Simon was represented on the Broadway stage by *The Gingerbread Lady* (1970), *The Prisoner of Second Avenue* (1971), *The Sunshine Boys* (1972), *The Good Doctor*, adapted from short stories of Chekhov (1973), *God's Favorite* (1974), *California Suite* (1976), *Chapter Two* (1977), and the musical *They're Playing Our Song* (music by Marvin Hamlisch, lyrics by Carole Bayer Sager, 1979). His initial play of the new decade, *I Ought to Be in Pictures*, opened in New York on April 3, 1980.

The author was born in the Bronx, New York, on July 4, 1927. He attended New York University and the University of Denver. His first theatrical affiliation came as a sketch writer (in collaboration with his brother Danny) for resort revues at Camp Tamiment, Pennsylvania. From there he moved on to television, supplying comedy material for many leading personalities of the medium including Sid Caesar and Imogene Coca in *Your Show of Shows*. An accomplished hand at comedy, he also contributed sketches to two Broadway revues, *Catch a Star* (1955) and *New Faces of 1956*.

In 1965 the dramatist won an Antoinette Perry (Tony) Award as the year's best author for *The Odd Couple*, and in 1968 he was the recipient of the Sam S. Shubert Award in recognition of his outstanding contribution to the American theatre. A similar honor was bestowed upon him in 1975 by the presentation of a Special Tony Award for his overall work in the theatre.

In recent years, Mr. Simon has divided his working hours by writing for the screen as well as the stage. In addition to preparing the movie versions of his own plays, he has written the screenplays for, among others, *The Out-of-Towners*, *The Heartbreak Kid*, *Murder by Death*, *The Cheap Detective*, and *The Goodbye Girl*.

The Sunshine Boys was first presented on December 20, 1972, by Emanuel Azenberg and Eugene V. Wolsk at the Broadhurst Theatre, New York. The cast was as follows:

WILLIE CLARK	*Jack Albertson*
BEN SILVERMAN	*Lewis J. Stadlen*
AL LEWIS	*Sam Levene*
PATIENT	*Joe Young*
EDDIE	*John Batiste*
NURSE	*Lee Meredith*
REGISTERED NURSE	*Minnie Gentry*

Directed by Alan Arkin
Scenery by Kert Lundell
Costumes by Albert Wolsky
Lighting by Tharon Musser

The action takes place in New York City.

ACT ONE

SCENE 1: *A small apartment in an old hotel on upper Broadway, in the mid-Eighties. It is an early afternoon in midwinter.*

SCENE 2: *The following Monday, late morning.*

ACT TWO

SCENE 1: *A Manhattan television studio.*

SCENE 2: *The same as Act One. It is two weeks later, late afternoon.*

ACT ONE

SCENE ONE

The scene is a two-room apartment in an old hotel on upper Broadway, in the mid-Eighties. It's rather a depressing place. There is a bed, a bureau, a small dining table with two chairs, an old leather chair that faces a TV set on a cheap, metal stand. There is a small kitchen to one side—partitioned off from the living room by a curtain—a small bathroom on the other. A window looks out over Broadway. It is early afternoon, midwinter.

At rise, the TV is on, and the banal dialogue of a soap opera drones on. In the leather chair sits WILLIE CLARK, *in slippers, pajamas and an old bathrobe.* WILLIE *is in his seventies. He watches the program but is constantly dozing off, then catching himself and watching for a few more minutes at a time. The set drones on and* WILLIE *dozes off. The tea kettle on the stove in the kitchen comes to a boil and whistles.* WILLIE's *head perks up at the sound; he reaches over and picks up the telephone.*

WILLIE: [*Into the phone*] Hello? . . . Who's this?

[*The whistle continues from the kettle, and* WILLIE *looks over in that direction. He hangs up the phone and does not seem embarrassed or even aware of his own absentmindedness. He simply crosses into the kitchen and turns off the flame under the kettle*]

VOICE FROM TV: We'll be back with *Storm Warning* after this brief message from Lipton Tea.

WILLIE: Don't worry, I'm not going anywhere.

[*He puts a tea ball into a mug and pours the boiling water in. Then he goes over to the dining table in the living room,* takes a spoon, dips into a jar of honey, and pours it into his tea. He glances over at the TV set, which has just played the Lipton Tea commercial]

VOICE FROM TV: And now for Part Three of today's Storm Warning . . .

WILLIE: What happened to Part Two? I missed Part Two? [He drinks his tea as Part Three continues and the banal dialogue drones on. WILLIE listens as he shuffles toward his chair. The TV set, which is away from the wall, has an electric plug running from it, along the ground and into the wall. WILLIE, who never seems to look where he's going, comes up against the cord with his foot, inadvertently pulling the cord out of its socket in the wall. The TV set immediately dies. WILLIE sits, then looks at the set. Obviously, no picture. He gets up and fiddles with the dials. How could his best friend desert him at a time like this? He hits the set on the top with his hand] What's the matter with you? [He hits the set again and twists the knobs futilely, never thinking for a moment it might be something as simple as the plug. He slaps the picture tube] Come on, for Pete's sakes, what are you doing there? [He stares at it in disbelief. He kicks the stand on which it rests. Then he crosses to the phone, and picks it up] Hello? . . . Sandy? . . . Let me have Sandy . . . Sandy? . . . My television's dead . . . My television . . . Is this Sandy? . . . My television died . . . No, not Willie. Mr. Clark to you, please . . . Never mind the jokes, wise guy, it's not funny . . . Send up somebody to fix my dead television . . . I didn't touch nothing . . . Nothing, I'm telling you . . . It's a crappy set . . . You live in a crappy hotel, you get a crappy television . . . The what? . . . The plug? . . . What plug? . . . Wait a minute. [He lays the phone down, crosses to behind the set, bends down, picks up the plug and looks at it. He goes back to the telephone. Into the phone] Hello? . . . It's not the plug. It's something else. I'll fix it myself. [He hangs up, goes over to the wall plug and plugs it in. The set goes back on] He tells me the plug . . . When he calls me Mr. Clark then I'll tell him it was the plug. [He sits and picks up his cup of tea] The hell with all of 'em. [There is a knock on the door. WILLIE looks at the wall on the opposite side of the room] Bang all you want, I'm not turning it off. I'm lucky it works.

[*There is a pause; then a knock on the front door again, this time accompanied by a male voice*]

BEN'S VOICE: Uncle Willie? It's me. Ben.

[WILLIE *turns and looks at the front door, not acknowledging that he was mistaken about the knocking on the other wall*]

WILLIE: Who's that?

BEN'S VOICE: Ben.

WILLIE: Ben? Is that you?

BEN'S VOICE: Yes, Uncle Willie, it's Ben. Open the door.

WILLIE: Wait a minute. [*He rises, crosses to the door, tripping over the TV cord again, disconnecting the set. He starts to unlatch the door, but has trouble manipulating it. His fingers are not too manipulative*] Wait a minute . . . [*He is having great difficulty with it*] . . . Wait a minute.

BEN'S VOICE: Is anything wrong?

WILLIE: [*Still trying*] Wait a minute. [*He tries forcing it*]

BEN'S VOICE: What's the matter?

WILLIE: I'm locked in. The lock is broken, I'm locked in. Go down and tell the boy. Sandy. Tell Sandy that Mr. Clark is locked in.

BEN'S VOICE: What is it, the latch?

WILLIE: It's the latch. It's broken, I'm locked in. Go tell the boy Sandy, they'll get somebody.

BEN'S VOICE: That happened last week. Don't try to force it. Just slide it out. [WILLIE *stares at the latch*] Uncle Willie, do you hear me? Don't force it. Slide it out.

WILLIE: [*Fiddling with the latch*] Wait a minute. [*Carefully, he slides it open*] It's open. Never mind, I did it myself.

[*He opens the door.* BEN SILVERMAN, *a well dressed man in his early thirties, enters. He is wearing a topcoat and carrying a shopping bag from Bloomingdale's, filled to the brim with assorted foodstuffs and a copy of the weekly* Variety]

BEN: You probably have to oil it.

WILLIE: I don't have to oil nothing. The hell with 'em.

[BEN *hangs up his coat in the closet*]

BEN: [*Crosses to the table with the shopping bag*] You feeling all right?

WILLIE: What is this, Wednesday?

BEN: [*Puzzled*] Certainly. Don't I always come on Wednesdays?

WILLIE: But this is Wednesday today?

BEN: [*Puts his bag down*] Yes, of course. Haven't you been out?

WILLIE: When?

BEN: Today. Yesterday. This week. You haven't been out all week?

WILLIE: Sunday. I was out Sunday. I went to the park Sunday.

[BEN *hands* WILLIE *the* Variety. WILLIE *tucks it under his arm and starts to look through the shopping bag*]

BEN: What are you looking for?

WILLIE: [*Going through the bag*] My Variety.

BEN: I just gave it to you. It's under your arm.

WILLIE: [*Looks under his arm*] Why do you put it there? He puts it under my arm.

BEN: [*Starts taking items out of the bag*] Have you been eating properly? No corned beef sandwiches, I hope.

WILLIE: [*Opens to the back section*] Is this today's?

BEN: Certainly it's today's. Variety comes out on Wednesday, doesn't it? And today is Wednesday.

WILLIE: I'm just asking, don't get so excited. [BEN *shakes his head in consternation*] . . . Because I already read last Wednesday's.

BEN: [*Takes more items out*] I got you six different kinds of soups. All low-sodium, salt-free. All very good for you . . . Are you listening?

WILLIE: [*His head in the paper*] I'm listening. You got six lousy-tasting soups . . . Did you see this?

BEN: What?

WILLIE: What I'm looking at. Did you see this?

BEN: How do I know what you're looking at?

WILLIE: Two new musicals went into rehearsals today and I didn't even get an audition. Why didn't I get an audition?

BEN: Because there were no parts for you. One of them is a young rock musical and the other show is all black.

WILLIE: What's the matter, I can't do black? I did black in 1928. And when I did black, you understood the words, not like today.

BEN: I'm sorry, you're not the kind of black they're looking for. [*He shivers*] Geez, it's cold in here. You know it's freezing in here? Don't they ever send up any heat?

WILLIE: [*Has turned a page*] How do you like that? Sol Burton died.

BEN: Who?

WILLIE: Sol Burton. The songwriter. Eighty-nine years old, went like that, from nothing.

BEN: Why didn't you put on a sweater?

WILLIE: I knew him very well . . . A terrible person. Mean, mean. He should rest in peace, but he was a mean person. His best friends didn't like him.

BEN: [*Goes to the bureau for a sweater*] Why is it so cold in here?

WILLIE: You know what kind of songs he wrote? . . . The worst. The worst songs ever written were written by Sol Burton. [*He sings*] "Lady, Lady, be my baby . . ." Did you ever hear anything so rotten? Baby he rhymes with lady . . . No wonder he's dead.

[*He turns the page*]

BEN: This radiator is ice-cold. Look, Uncle Willie, I'm not going to let you live here any more. You've got to let me find you another place . . . I've been asking you for seven years now. You're going to get sick.

WILLIE: [*Still looking at* Variety] Tom Jones is gonna get a hundred thousand dollars a week in Las Vegas. When Lewis and I were headlining at the Palace, the *Palace* didn't cost a hundred thousand dollars.

BEN: That was forty years ago. And forty years ago this hotel was twenty years old. They should tear it down. They take advantage of all you people in here because they know you don't want to move.

[WILLIE *crosses to the table and looks into the shopping bag*]

WILLIE: No cigars?

BEN: [*Making notes on his memo pad*] You're not supposed to have cigars.

WILLIE: Where's the cigars?

BEN: You know the doctor told you you're not supposed to smoke cigars any more. I didn't bring any.

WILLIE: Gimme the cigars.

BEN: What cigars? I just said I don't have them. Will you forget the cigars?

WILLIE: Where are they, in the bag?

BEN: On the bottom. I just brought three. It's the last time I'm doing it.

WILLIE: [*Takes out a bag with three cigars*] How's your family? The children all right?

[*He removes one cigar*]

BEN: Suddenly you're interested in my family? It's not going to work, Uncle Willie. I'm not bringing you any more cigars.

WILLIE: I just want to know how the children are.

BEN: The children are fine. They're wonderful, thank you.

WILLIE: Good. Next time bring the big cigars.

[*He puts two cigars in the breast pocket of his bathrobe and the other one in his mouth. He crosses into the kitchen looking for a light*]

BEN: You don't even know their names. What are the names of my children?

WILLIE: Millie and Sidney.

BEN: Amanda and Michael.

WILLIE: What's the matter, you didn't like Millie and Sidney?

BEN: I was *never* going to name them Millie and Sidney. You forgot, so you made something up. You forget everything. I'll bet you didn't drink the milk from last week. I'll bet it's still in the refrigerator. [*Crosses quickly, and opens the refrigerator and looks in*] There's the milk from last week.

WILLIE: [*Comes out of the kitchen, still looking for a light*] Do they know who I am?

BEN: [*Looking through the refrigerator*] Who?

WILLIE: Amanda and Sidney.

BEN: Amanda and Michael. That you were a big star in vaudeville? They're three years old, Uncle Willie, you think they remember vaudeville? *I* never saw vaudeville . . . This refrigerator won't last another two days.

WILLIE: Did you tell them six times on *The Ed Sullivan Show?*

[*He sits, tries a cigarette lighter. It's broken*]

BEN: They never heard of Ed Sullivan. Uncle Willie, they're three years old. They don't follow show business. [*Comes back into the living room and sees* WILLIE *with the cigar in his mouth*] What are you doing? You're not going to smoke that now. You promised me you'd only smoke one after dinner.

WILLIE: Am I smoking it? Do you see smoke coming from the cigar?

BEN: But you've got it in your mouth.

WILLIE: I'm rehearsing . . . After dinner I'll do the show.

BEN: [*Crossing back into the kitchen*] I'm in the most aggravating business in the whole world and I never get aggravated until I come here.

[*He opens the cupboards and looks in*]

WILLIE: [*Looking around*] So don't come. I got Social Security.

BEN: You think that's funny? I don't think that's funny, Uncle Willie.

BEN: [*Thumbing through* Variety] If you had a sense of humor, you'd think it was funny.

BEN: [*Angrily, through gritted teeth*] I have a *terrific* sense of humor.

WILLIE: Like your father—he laughed once in 1932.

BEN: I can't talk to you.

WILLIE: Why, they're funny today? Tell me who you think is funny today, and I'll show you where he's not funny.

BEN: Let's not get into that, huh? I've got to get back to the office. Just promise me you'll have a decent lunch today.

WILLIE: If I were to tell a joke and got a laugh from you, I'd throw it out.

BEN: How can I laugh when I see you like this, Uncle Willie? You sit in your pajamas all day in a freezing apartment watching soap operas on a thirty-five-dollar television set that doesn't have a horizontal hold. The picture just keeps rolling from top to bottom— pretty soon your eyes are gonna roll around your head . . . You never eat anything. You never go out because you don't know how to work the lock on the door. Remember when you locked yourself in the bathroom overnight? It's a lucky thing you keep bread in there, you would have starved . . . And you wonder why I worry.

WILLIE: Calvin Coolidge, that's your kind of humor.

BEN: Look, Uncle Willie, promise me you'll eat decently.

WILLIE: I'll eat decently. I'll wear a blue suit, a white shirt and black shoes.

BEN: And if you're waiting for a laugh, you're not going to get one from me.

WILLIE: Who could live that long? Get me a job instead of a laugh.

BEN: [Sighs, exasperatedly] You know I've been trying, Uncle Willie. It's not easy. There's not much in town. Most of the work is commercials and . . . well, you know, we've had a little trouble in that area.

WILLIE: The potato chips? The potato chips wasn't my fault.

BEN: Forget the potato chips.

WILLIE: What about the Schick Injector? Didn't I audition funny on the Schick Injector?

BEN: You were very funny but your hand was shaking. And you can't show a man shaving with a shaky hand.

WILLIE: Why couldn't you get me on the Alka-Seltzer? That's my kind of comedy. I got a terrific face for an upset stomach.

BEN: I've submitted you twenty times.

WILLIE: What's the matter with twenty-one?

BEN: Because the word is out in the business that you can't remember the lines, and they're simply not interested.

WILLIE: [That hurt] I couldn't remember the lines? I COULDN'T REMEMBER THE LINES? I don't remember that.

BEN: For the Frito-Lays potato chips. I sent you over to the studio, you couldn't even remember the address.

WILLIE: Don't tell me I didn't remember the lines. The lines I remembered beautifully. The name of the potato chip I couldn't remember . . . What was it?

BEN: Frito-Lays.

WILLIE: Say it again.

BEN: Frito-Lays.

WILLIE: I still can't remember it—because it's not funny. If it's funny, I remember it. Alka-Seltzer is funny. You say "Alka-Seltzer," you get a laugh. The other word is not funny. What is it?

BEN: Frito-Lays.

WILLIE: Maybe in *Mexico* that's funny, not here. Fifty-seven years I'm in this business, you learn a few things. You know what makes an audience laugh. Do you know which words are funny and which words are *not* funny?

BEN: You told me a hundred times, Uncle Willie. Words with a "K" in it are funny.

WILLIE: Words with a "K" in it are funny. You didn't know that, did you? If it doesn't have a "K," it's not funny. I'll tell you which words always get a laugh.

[*He is about to count on his fingers*]

BEN: Chicken.

WILLIE: Chicken is funny.

BEN: Pickle.

WILLIE: Pickle is funny.

BEN: Cupcake.

WILLIE: Cupcake is funny . . . Tomato is *not* funny. Roast beef is *not* funny.

BEN: But cookie is funny.

WILLIE: But cookie is funny.

BEN: Uncle Willie, you've explained that to me ever since I was a little boy.

WILLIE: Cucumber is funny.

BEN: [*Falling in again*] Car keys.

WILLIE: Car keys is funny.

BEN: Cleveland.

WILLIE: Cleveland is funny . . . Maryland is *not* funny.

BEN: Listen, I have to get back to the office, Uncle Willie, but there's something I'd like to talk to you about first. I got a call yesterday from C.B.S.

WILLIE: Casey Stengel, that's a funny name; Robert Taylor is not funny.

BEN: [*Sighs exasperatedly*] Why don't you listen to me?

WILLIE: I heard. You got a call from N.B.C.

BEN: C.B.S.

WILLIE: Whatever.

BEN: C.B.S. is doing a big special next month. An hour and a half variety show. They're going to have some of the biggest names in the history of show business. They're trying to get Flip Wilson to host the show.

WILLIE: Him I like. He gives me a laugh. With the dress and the little giggle and the red wig. That's a funny boy . . . What's the boy's name again?

BEN: Flip Wilson. And it doesn't have a K.

WILLIE: But he's *black,* with a "K." You see what I mean?

BEN: [*Looks to heaven for help. It doesn't come*] I do, I do. The theme of this variety show—

WILLIE: What's the theme of the show?

BEN: *The theme of the show* is the history of comedy dating from the early Greek times, through the days of vaudeville, right up to today's stars.

WILLIE: Why couldn't you get me on this show?

BEN: I *got* you on the show.

WILLIE: Alone?

BEN: With Lewis.

WILLIE: [*Turns away*] You ain't got me on the show.

BEN: Let me finish.

WILLIE: You're finished. It's no.

BEN: Can't you wait until I'm through before you say "no"? Can't we discuss it for a minute?

WILLIE: I'm busy.

BEN: Doing what?

WILLIE: Saying "no."

BEN: You can have the courtesy of hearing me out. They begged me at C.B.S. *Begged* me.

WILLIE: Talk faster, because you're coming up to another "no."

BEN: They said to me the history of comedy in the United States would not be complete unless they included one of the greatest teams ever to come out of vaudeville, Lewis and Clark, The Sunshine Boys. The vice-president of C.B.S. said this to me on the phone.

WILLIE: The vice-president said this?

BEN: Yes. He is the greatest Lewis and Clark fan in this country. He knows by heart every one of your old routines.

WILLIE: Then let *him* go on with that bastard!

BEN: It's one shot. You would just have to do it one night, one of the old sketches. They'll pay ten thousand dollars for the team. That's top money for these shows, I promise you. Five thousand dollars apiece. And that's more money than you've earned in two years.

WILLIE: I don't need money. I live alone. I got two nice suits, I don't have a pussycat, I'm very happy.

BEN: You're *not* happy. You're miserable.

WILLIE: *I'm happy!* I just *look* miserable!

BEN: You're dying to go to work again. You call me six times a day in the office. I can't see over my desk for all your messages.

WILLIE: Call me back sometime, you won't get so many messages.

BEN: I call you every day of the week. I'm up here every Wednesday, rain or shine, winter or summer, flu or diptheria.

WILLIE: What are you, a mailman? You're a nephew. I don't ask you to come. You're my brother's son, you've been very nice to me. I appreciate it, but I've never asked you for anything . . . except for a job. You're a good boy but a stinking agent.

BEN: I'M NOT A GOOD AGENT? Damn it, don't say that to me, Uncle Willie, I'm a *goddamn good agent!*

WILLIE: What are you screaming for? What is it, such a wonderful thing to be a good agent?

BEN: [*Holds his chest*] I'm getting chest pains. You give me chest pains, Uncle Willie.

WILLIE: It's *my* fault you get excited?

BEN: Yes, it's *your* fault! I only get chest pains on Wednesdays.

WILLIE: So come on Tuesdays.

BEN: [*Starts for the door*] I'm going. I don't even want to discuss this with you any more. You're impossible to talk to. FORGET THE VARIETY SHOW!

[*He starts for the door*]

WILLIE: I forgot it.

BEN: [*Stops*] I'm not coming back any more. I'm not bringing you your *Variety* or your cigars or your low-sodium soups—do you understand, Uncle Willie? I'm not bringing you anything any more.

WILLIE: Good. Take care of yourself. Say hello to Millie and Phyllis.

BEN: I'm not asking you to be partners again. If you two don't get along, all right. But this is just for one night. One last show. Once you get an exposure like that, Alka-Seltzer will come begging to *me* to sign you up. Jesus, how is it going to look if I go back to the office and tell them I couldn't make a deal with my own uncle?

WILLIE: My personal opinion? Lousy!

BEN: [*Falls into a chair, exhausted*] Do you really hate Al Lewis that much?

WILLIE: [*Looks away*] I don't discuss Al Lewis any more.

BEN: [*Gets up*] We *have* to discuss him, because C.B.S. is waiting for an answer today, and if we turn them down, I want to have a pretty good reason why. You haven't seen him in—what? ten years now.

WILLIE: [*Takes a long time before answering*] Eleven years!

BEN: [*Amazed*] You mean to tell me you haven't spoken to him in eleven years?

WILLIE: I haven't *seen* him in eleven years. I haven't *spoken* to him in twelve years.

BEN: You mean you saw him for a whole year that you didn't speak to him?

WILLIE: It wasn't easy. I had to sneak around backstage a lot.

BEN: But you spoke to him onstage.

WILLIE: Not to *him*. If he played a gypsy, I spoke to the gypsy. If he played a lunatic, I spoke to the lunatic. But that bastard I didn't speak to.

BEN: I can't believe that.

WILLIE: You don't believe it? I can show you witnesses who *saw* me never speaking to him.

BEN: It's been eleven years, Uncle Willie. Hasn't time changed anything for you?

WILLIE: Yes. I hate him eleven years more.

BEN: Why?

WILLIE: Why? . . . You never met him?

BEN: Sure I met him. I was fifteen years old. I met him once at that benefit at Madison Square Garden and once backstage at some television show. He seemed nice enough to me.

WILLIE: That's only twice. You had to meet him three times to hate him.

BEN: Uncle Willie, could I make a suggestion?

WILLIE: He used to give me the finger.

BEN: The what?

WILLIE: The finger! The finger! He would poke me in the chest with the finger. [*He crosses to* BEN *and demonstrates on him by poking a finger in* BEN's *chest every time he makes a point*] He would say, "Listen, Doctor." [*Pokes finger*] "I'm *telling* you, Doctor." [*Pokes finger*] "You know what I *mean*, Doctor." [*Pokes finger.* BEN *rubs his chest in pain*] Hurts, doesn't it? How'd you like it for forty-three years? I got a black and blue hole in my chest. My wife to her dying day thought it was a tattoo. I haven't worked with him in eleven years, it's just beginning to fade away . . . The man had the sharpest finger in show business.

BEN: If you work with him again, I promise you I'll buy you a thick padded undershirt.

WILLIE: You think I never did that? One night I put a steel plate under my shirt. He gave me the finger, he had it in a splint for a month.

BEN: Something else must have happened you're not telling me about. You don't work with a person for forty-three years without some bond of affection remaining.

WILLIE: You wanna hear other things? He used to spit in my face. Onstage *the man would spit in my face!*

BEN: Not on purpose.

WILLIE: [*Turns away*] He tells me "not on purpose" . . . If there was some way I could have saved the spit, I would show it to you.

BEN: You mean he would just stand there and spit in your face?

WILLIE: What do you think, he's stupid? He worked it into the

act. He would stand with his nose on top of my nose and purposely only say words that began with a "T." [*As he demonstrates,
he spits*] "Tootsie Roll." [*Spit*] "Tinker Toy." [*Spit*] "Typing on
the typewriter." [*Spits.* BEN *wipes his face*] Some nights I thought
I would drown! I don't know where he got it all from . . . I think
he would drink all day and save it up for the night.

BEN: I'll put it in the contract. If he spits at you, he won't get
paid.

WILLIE: If he can get another chance to spit at me, he wouldn't
want to get paid.

BEN: Then will you answer me one question? If it was all that bad,
why did you stick together for forty-three years?

WILLIE: [*Turns; looks at him*] Because he was terrific. There'll
never be another one like him . . . Nobody could time a joke the
way he could time a joke. Nobody could say a line the way he said
it. I knew what he was thinking, he knew what I was thinking.
One person, that's what we were . . . No, no. Al Lewis was the
best. The *best!* You understand?

BEN: I understand.

WILLIE: As an actor, no one could touch him. As a human being,
no one *wanted* to touch him.

BEN: [*Sighs*] So what do I tell C.B.S.? No deal because Al Lewis
spits?

WILLIE: You know when the last time was we worked together?

BEN: Eleven years ago on *The Ed Sullivan Show.*

WILLIE: Eleven years ago on *The Ed Sullivan Show.* July twenty-
seventh. He wouldn't put us on in the winter when people were
watching, but never mind. We did The Doctor and the Tax Examination. You never saw that, did you?

BEN: No, but I heard it's wonderful.

WILLIE: What about a "classic"? A *classic!* A *dead* person watching
that sketch would laugh. We did it maybe eight thousand times,
it never missed . . . *That* night it missed. Something was wrong

with him, he was rushing, his timing was off, his mind was someplace else. I thought he was sick. Still, we got terrific applause. Five times Ed Sullivan said, "How about that?" We got back into the dressing room, he took off his make-up, put on his clothes, and said to me, "Willie, if it's all the same to you, I'm retiring." I said, "What do you mean, retiring? It's not even nine o'clock. Let's have something to eat." He said, "I'm not retiring for the night. I'm retiring for what's left of my life." And he puts on his hat, walks out of the theater, becomes a stockbroker and I'm left with an act where I ask questions and there's no one there to answer. Never saw the man again to this day. Oh, he called me, I wouldn't answer. He wrote me, I tore it up. He sent me telegrams, they're probably still under the door.

BEN: Well, Uncle Willie, with all due respect, you really weren't getting that much work any more. Maybe he was getting tired of doing the same thing for forty-three years. I mean a man has a right to retire when he wants, doesn't he?

WILLIE: Not him. Don't forget, when he retired himself, he retired me too. And goddamn it, I wasn't ready yet. Now suddenly maybe he needs five thousand dollars, and he wants to come crawling back, the hell with him. I'm a single now . . .

BEN: I spoke to Al Lewis on the phone last night. He doesn't even care about the money. He just wants to do the show for old times' sake. For his grandchildren who never saw him.

WILLIE: Sure. He probably retired broke from the stock market. I guarantee you *those* high-class people never got a spit in the face once.

BEN: Did you know his wife died two years ago? He's living with his daughter now, somewhere in New Jersey. He doesn't do anything any more. He's got very bad arthritis, he's got asthma, he's got poor blood circulation—

WILLIE: I'll send him a pump. He'll outlive *you*, believe me.

BEN: He wants very much to do this show, Willie.

WILLIE: With arthritis? Forget it. Instead of a finger, he'll poke me with a cane.

BEN: C.B.S. wants you to do the doctor sketch. Lewis told me he could get on a stage tonight and do that sketch letter perfect. He doesn't even have to rehearse it.

WILLIE: I don't even want to discuss it . . . And in the second place, I would definitely not do it without a rehearsal.

BEN: All right, then will you agree to this? Just rehearse with him one day. If it doesn't work out, we'll call it off.

WILLIE: I don't trust him. I think he's been planning this for eleven years. We rehearse all week and then he walks out on me just before the show.

BEN: Let me call him on the phone. [*Going over to the phone*] Let me set up a rehearsal time for Monday.

WILLIE: WAIT A MINUTE! I got to think about this.

BEN: We don't have that much time. C.B.S. is waiting to hear.

WILLIE: What's their rush? What are they, going out of business?

BEN: [*Picks up the phone*] I'm dialing. I'm dialing him, Uncle Willie, okay?

WILLIE: Sixty-forty—I get six thousand, he gets four thousand . . . What the hell can he buy in New Jersey anyway?

BEN: [*Holding the phone*] I can't do that, Uncle Willie . . . God, I hope this works out.

WILLIE: Tell him I'm against it. I want him to know. I'll do it with an "against it."

BEN: It's ringing.

WILLIE: And he's got to come here. I'm not going there, you understand?

BEN: He's got to be home. I told him I would call about one.

WILLIE: Sure. You know what he's doing? He practicing spitting.

BEN: [*Into the phone*] Hello? . . . Mr. Lewis? . . . Ben Silverman . . . Yes, fine, thanks . . . I'm here with him now.

WILLIE: Willie Clark. The one he left on *The Ed Sullivan Show.* Ask him if he remembers.

BEN: It's okay, Mr. Lewis . . . Uncle Willie said yes.

WILLIE: With an "against it." Don't forget the "against it."

BEN: No, he's very anxious to do it.

WILLIE: [*Jumping up in anger*] WHO'S ANXIOUS? I'M AGAINST IT! TELL HIM, you lousy nephew.

BEN: Can you come here for rehearsal on Monday? . . . Oh, that'll be swell . . . In the morning. [*To* WILLIE] About eleven o'clock? How long is the drive. About two hours?

WILLIE: Make it nine o'clock.

BEN: Be reasonable, Willie. [*Into the phone*] Eleven o'clock is fine, Mr. Lewis . . . Can you give me your address, please, so I can send you the contracts? [*He takes a pen out of his pocket and writes in his notebook*] One-one-nine, South Pleasant Drive . . .

WILLIE: Tell him if he starts with the spitting or poking, I'm taking him to court. I'll have a man on the show watching. Tell him.

BEN: West Davenport, New Jersey . . . Oh-nine-seven-seven-oh-four . . .

WILLIE: I don't want any—[*Spitting*]—"Toy telephones tapping on tin turtles." Tell him. Tell him.

CURTAIN

SCENE TWO

It is the following Monday, a few minutes before eleven in the morning.

The stage is empty. Suddenly the bathroom door opens and WILLIE *emerges. He is still wearing his slippers and the same pajamas, but instead of his bathrobe, he has made a concession to the occasion. He is wearing a double-breasted blue*

*suit-jacket, buttoned, and he is putting a handkerchief in his
pocket. He looks in the mirror, and brushes back his hair. He
shuffles over to the windows and looks out.*
    There is a knock on the door. WILLIE *turns and stares at it.
He doesn't move. There is another knock, and then we hear*
BEN's *voice.*

BEN's VOICE: Uncle Willie. It's Ben.

WILLIE: Ben? Is that you?

BEN's VOICE: Yes. Open up.

[WILLIE *starts toward the door, then stops*]

WILLIE: You're alone or he's with you?

BEN's VOICE: I'm alone.

WILLIE: [*Nods*] Wait a minute. [*The latch is locked again, and
again he has trouble getting it open*] Wait a minute.

BEN's VOICE: Slide it, don't push it.

WILLIE: Wait a minute. I'll push it.

BEN's VOICE: *DON'T PUSH IT! SLIDE IT!*

WILLIE: Wait a minute. [*He gets the lock open and opens the
door.* BEN *walks in*] You're supposed to slide it.

BEN: I rushed like crazy. I didn't want him getting here before me.
Did he call or anything?

WILLIE: Where's the *Variety?*

BEN: [*Taking off his coat*] It's Monday, not Wednesday. Didn't
you know it was Monday?

WILLIE: I remembered, but I forgot.

BEN: What are you wearing? What is that? You look half-dressed.

WILLIE: Why, for him I should get *all* dressed?

BEN: Are you all right? Are you nervous or anything?

WILLIE: Why should *I* be nervous? *He* should be nervous. I don't
get nervous.

BEN: Good.

WILLIE: Listen, I changed my mind. I'm not doing it.

BEN: *What?*

WILLIE: Don't get so upset. Everything is the same as before, except I'm not doing it.

BEN: When did you decide this?

WILLIE: I decided it when you asked me.

BEN: No, you didn't. You told me you *would* do it.

WILLIE: Well, it was a bad decision. This time I made a good one.

BEN: Well, I'm sorry, you have to do it. I've already told C.B.S. that you would be rehearsing this week and, more important, that man is on his way over here now and I'm not going to tell him that you called it off.

WILLIE: We'll leave him a note outside the door.

BEN: We're not leaving any notes. That's why I came here this morning, I was afraid you would try something like this. I'm going to stay until I think you're both acting like civilized human beings, and then when you're ready to rehearse, I'm going to leave you alone. Is that understood?

WILLIE: I'm sick. I woke up sick today.

BEN: No, you're not.

WILLIE: What are you, a doctor? You're an agent. I'm telling you I'm sick.

BEN: What's wrong?

WILLIE: I think I got hepatitis.

BEN: You don't even know what hepatitis is.

WILLIE: If you got it, what's the difference?

BEN: There's nothing wrong with you except a good case of the nerves. You're not backing out, Willie. I don't care what kind of excuse you make, you're going to go through with this. You promised me you would give it at least one day.

WILLIE: I'll pick another day.

BEN: TODAY! You're going to meet with him and rehearse with him TODAY. Now *stop* and just behave yourself.

WILLIE: What do you mean, "behave yourself"? Who do you think you're talking to, Susan and Jackie?

BEN: *Amanda* and Jackie!—Michael. I wish I were. I can reason with them. And now I'm getting chest pains on Monday.

WILLIE: Anyway, he's late. He's purposely coming late to aggravate me.

BEN: [*Looking out the window*] He's not late. It's two minutes after eleven.

WILLIE: So what is he, early? He's *late!*

BEN: You're *looking* to start trouble, I can tell.

WILLIE: I was up and dressed at eight o'clock, don't tell me.

BEN: Why didn't you shave?

WILLIE: Get me the Schick commercial, I'll shave [*He looks in the mirror*] I really think I got hepatitis. Look how green I look.

BEN: You don't get green from hepatitis. You get yellow.

WILLIE: Maybe I got a very bad case.

BEN: [*Looks at his watch*] Now you got me nervous. I wonder if I should call him? Maybe he's sick.

WILLIE: [*Glares at him*] You believe *he's* sick, but me you won't believe . . . Why don't you become *his* nephew?

[*Suddenly there is a knock on the door.* WILLIE *freezes and stares at it*]

BEN: That's him. You want me to get it—

WILLIE: Get what? I didn't hear anything.

BEN: [*Starts toward the door*] All right, now take it easy. Please just behave yourself and give this a chance. Promise me you'll give it a chance.

WILLIE: [*Starts for the kitchen*] I'll give it every possible chance in the world . . . But it's not gonna work.

BEN: Where are you going?

WILLIE: To make tea. I feel like some hot tea.

[*He crosses into the kitchen and closes the curtain. Starts to fill up the kettle with water*]

BEN: [*Panicky*] NOW? NOW? [BEN *looks at him exasperated; a knock on the door again and* BEN *crosses to it and opens it.* AL LEWIS *stands there. He is also about seventy years old and is dressed in his best blue suit, hat, scarf, and carries a walking stick. He was probably quite a gay blade in his day, but time has slowed him down somewhat. Our first impression is that he is soft-spoken and pleasant—and a little nervous*] Mr. Lewis, how do you do? I'm Ben Silverman.

[BEN, *nervous, extends his hand*]

AL: How are you? Hello. It's nice to see you. [*His eyes dart around looking for* WILLIE. *He doesn't see him yet*] How do you do? . . . Hello . . . Hello . . . How are you?

BEN: We met before, a long time ago. My father took me backstage, I forget the theater. It must have been fifteen, twenty years ago.

AL: I remember . . . Certainly . . . It was backstage . . . Maybe fifteen, twenty years ago . . . I forget the theater.

BEN: That's right.

AL: Sure, I remember.

[*He has walked into the room and shoots a glance toward the kitchen.* WILLIE *doesn't look up from his tea-making*]

BEN: Please sit down. Uncle Willie's making some tea.

AL: Thank you very much.

[*He sits on the edge of the table*]

BEN: [*Trying hard to make conversation*] Er . . . Did you have any trouble getting in from Jersey?

AL: My daughter drove me in. She has a car.

BEN: Oh. That's nice.

AL: A 1972 Chrysler . . . black . . .

BEN: Yes, the Chrysler's a wonderful car.

AL: The big one . . . the Imperial.

BEN: I know. I drove it.

AL: My daughter's car?

BEN: No, the big Chrysler Imperial. I rented one in California.

AL: [*Nods*] No, she owns.

BEN: I understand . . . Do you come into New York often?

AL: Today's the first time in two years.

BEN: Really? Well, how did you find it?

AL: My daughter drove.

BEN: No, I mean, do you find the city different in the two years since you've been here?

AL: It's not my New York.

BEN: No, I suppose it's not. [*He shoots a glance toward the kitchen.* WILLIE *still hasn't looked in*] Hey, listen, I'm really very excited about all this. Well, for that matter, everyone in the industry is.

AL: [*Nods, noncommittally*] Well, we'll see.

[*He looks around the room, scrutinizing it*]

BEN: [*He calls out toward the kitchen*] Uncle Willie, how we doing? [*No answer. Embarrassed, to* AL] I guess it's not boiling yet . . . Oh, listen, I'd like to arrange to have a car pick you up and take you home after you're through rehearsing.

AL: My daughter's going to pick me up.

BEN: Oh, I see. What time did you say? Four? Five?

AL: She's going to call me every hour.

BEN: Right . . .

[*Suddenly* WILLIE *sticks his head out of the kitchen, but looks at* BEN *and not at* AL]

WILLIE: One tea or two teas?

BEN: Oh, here he is. Well, Uncle Willie, I guess it's been a long time since you two—

WILLIE: One tea or two teas?

BEN: Oh. Er, nothing for me, thanks. I'm just about leaving. Mr. Lewis? Some tea?

AL: [*Doesn't look toward* WILLIE] Tea would be nice, thank you.

BEN: [*To* WILLIE] Just the one, Uncle Willie.

WILLIE: You're sure? I got two tea balls. I could dunk again.

BEN: [*Looks at his watch*] No, I've got to get back to the office. Honestly.

WILLIE: [*Nods*] Mm-hmm. One tea.

[*On his way back in, he darts a look at* LEWIS, *then goes back into the kitchen. He pulls the curtain shut*]

BEN: [*To* LEWIS] Well, er . . . Do you have any questions you want to ask about the show? About the studio or rehearsals or the air date? Is there anything on your mind that I could help you with?

AL: Like what?

BEN: Like, er the studio? Or the rehearsals? Or air date? Things like that?

AL: You got the props?

BEN: Which props are those?

AL: The props. For the doctor sketch. You gotta have props.

BEN: Oh, props. Certainly. What do you need? I'll tell them.

[*Takes out a pad; writes*]

AL: You need a desk. A telephone. A pointer. A blackboard. A piece of white chalk, a piece of red chalk. A skeleton, not too tall, a stethoscope, a thermometer, an "ahh" stick—

BEN: What's an "ahh" stick?

AL: To put in your mouth to say "ahh."

BEN: Oh, right, an "ahh" stick.

AL: A look stick, a bottle of pills—

BEN: A look stick? What's a look stick?

AL: A stick to look in the ears. With cotton on the end.

BEN: Right. A look stick.

AL: A bottle of pills. Big ones, like for a horse.

BEN: [*Makes a circle with his two fingers*] About this big?

AL: That's for a pony. [*Makes a circle using the fingers of both hands*] For a horse is like this. Some bandages, cotton, and eye chart—

BEN: Wait a minute, you're going too fast.

AL: [*Slowly*] A-desk . . . *a*-telephone . . . *a*-pointer . . .

BEN: No, I got all that—after the cotton and eye chart.

AL: A man's suit. Size forty. Like the one I'm wearing.

BEN: Also in blue?

AL: What do I need two blue suits— Get me a brown.

BEN: A brown suit. Is that all?

AL: That's all.

WILLIE: [*From the kitchen, without looking in*] A piece of liver.

AL: That's all, plus a piece of liver.

BEN: What kind of liver?

AL: Regular calves' liver. From the butcher.

BEN: Like how much? A pound?

AL: A little laugh is a pound. A big laugh is two pounds. Three pounds with a lot of blood'll bring the house down.

BEN: Is that it?

AL: That's it. And a blonde.

BEN: You mean a woman—

AL: You know a blond nurse that's a man? . . . Big! As big as you can find. With a big chest—a forty-five, a fifty—and a nice bottom.

BEN: You mean a sexy girl with a full, round, rear end?

AL: [Spreads hands apart] About like this. [Makes a smaller behind with his hands] This is too small. [Makes a bigger one] And this is too big. [Goes back to the original one] Like this is perfect.

BEN: I know what you mean.

AL: If you can bring me pictures, I'll pick out one.

BEN: There's a million girls like that around.

AL: The one we had was the best. I would call her, but she's maybe fifty-five, sixty.

BEN: No, no. I'll get a girl. Anything else?

AL: Not for me.

BEN: Uncle Willie?

WILLIE: [From the kitchen] I wasn't listening.

BEN: Well, if either of you thinks of anything, just call me. [Looks at his watch again] Eleven-fifteen—I've got to go. [He gets up] Uncle Willie, I'm going. [He crosses to LEWIS and extends his hand] Mr. Lewis, I can't express to you enough how happy I am, and speaking for the millions of young people in this country who never had the opportunity of seeing Lewis and Clark work, I just want to say "thank you." To both of you. [Calls out] To both of you, Uncle Willie.

AL: [Nods] I hope they won't be disappointed.

BEN: Oh, they won't.

AL: I know they won't. I'm just saying it.

BEN: [*Crosses to the kitchen*] Goodbye, Uncle Willie. I'm going.

WILLIE: I'll show you the elevator.

BEN: I *know* where it is. I'll call you tonight. I just want to say that this is a very happy moment for me. To see you both together again, reunited . . . The two kings of comedy. [*Big smile*] I'm sure it must be *very exciting* for the both of you, isn't it? [*No answer. They both just stare at him*] Well, it looks like we're off to a great start. I'll call you later . . . Goodbye.

> [*He leaves and closes the door. They are alone.* WILLIE *carries the two teas to the dining table, where the sugar bowl is. He pours himself a teaspoonful of sugar*]

WILLIE: [*Without looking in* AL's *direction*] Sugar?

AL: [*Doesn't turn*] If you got.

WILLIE: [*Nods*] I got sugar. [*He bangs the sugar bowl down in front of* AL, *crosses with his own tea to his leather chair and sits. And then the two drink tea . . . silently and interminably. They blow, they sip, they blow, they sip and they sit. Finally:*] You like a cracker?

AL: [*Sips*] What kind of cracker?

WILLIE: Graham, chocolate, coconut, whatever you want.

AL: Maybe just a plain cracker.

WILLIE: I don't have plain crackers. I got graham, chocolate and coconut.

AL: All right, a graham cracker.

WILLIE: [*Without turning, points into the kitchen*] They're in the kitchen, in the closet.

> [AL *looks over at him, a little surprised at his uncordiality. He nods in acknowledgment*]

AL: Maybe later.

[*They both sip their tea*]

WILLIE: [*Long pause*] I was sorry to hear about Lillian.

AL: Thank you.

WILLIE: She was a nice woman. I always liked Lillian.

AL: Thank you.

WILLIE: And how about you?

AL: Thank God, knock wood—[*Raps knuckles on his cane*]—perfect.

WILLIE: I heard different. I heard your blood didn't circulate.

AL: Not true. My blood circulates . . . I'm not saying *everywhere*, but it circulates.

WILLIE: Is that why you use the cane?

AL: It's not a cane. It's a walking stick . . . Maybe once in a great while it's a cane.

WILLIE: I've been lucky, thank God. I'm in the pink.

AL: I was looking. For a minute I thought you were having a flush.

WILLIE: [*Sips his tea*] You know Sol Burton died?

AL: Go on . . . Who's Sol Burton?

WILLIE: You don't remember Sol Burton?

AL: [*Thinks*] Oh, yes. The manager from the Belasco.

WILLIE: That was Sol Bernstein.

AL: Not Sol Bernstein. Sol *Burton* was the manager from the Belasco.

WILLIE: Sol *Bernstein* was the manager from the Belasco, and it wasn't the Belasco, it was the Morosco.

AL: Sid *Weinstein* was the manager from the Morosco. Sol *Burton* was the manager from the Belasco. Sol *Bernstein* I don't know *who* the hell was.

WILLIE: How can you remember anything if your blood doesn't circulate?

AL: It circulates in my *head*. It doesn't circulate in my *feet*.

[*He stomps his foot on the floor a few times*]

WILLIE: Is anything coming down?

AL: Wait a minute. Wasn't Sid Weinstein the songwriter?

WILLIE: No, for chrissakes! That's SOL BURTON!

AL: Who wrote "Lady, lady, be my baby"?

WILLIE: That's what I'm telling you! Sol Burton, the lousy songwriter.

AL: Oh, *that* Sol Burton . . . He died?

WILLIE: Last week.

AL: Where?

WILLIE: [*Points*] In V*ariety*.

AL: Sure, now I remember . . . And how is Sol Bernstein?

WILLIE: I didn't read anything.

AL: Good. I always liked Sol Bernstein. [*They quietly sip their tea. AL looks around the room*] So-o-o . . . this is where you live now?

WILLIE: Didn't I always live here?

AL: [*Looks again*] Not in here. You lived in the big suite.

WILLIE: This *is* the big suite . . . Now it's five small suites.

[AL *nods, understanding*]

AL: [*Looks around*] That's what they do today. Anything to squeeze a dollar. What do they charge now for a small suite?

WILLIE: The same as they used to charge for the big suite.

[AL *nods, understanding*]

AL: I have a very nice room with my daughter in New Jersey. I have my own bathroom. They don't bother me, I don't bother them.

WILLIE: What is it, in the country?

AL: Certainly it's in the country. Where do you think New Jersey is, in the city?

WILLIE: [Shrugs] New Jersey is what I see from the bench on Riverside Drive. What have they got, a private house?

AL: Certainly it's a private house. It's some big place. Three quarters of an acre. They got their own trees, their own bushes, a nice little swimming pool for the kids they blow up in the summertime, a big swing in the back, a little dog house, a rock garden—

WILLIE: A what?

AL: A rock garden.

WILLIE: What do you mean, a rock garden? You mean for rocks?

AL: You never saw a rock garden?

WILLIE: And I'm not that anxious.

AL: It's beautiful. A Chinaman made it. Someday you'll take a bus and you'll come out and I'll show you.

WILLIE: I should drive all the way out to New Jersey on a bus to see a rock garden?

AL: You don't even know what I'm talking about. You have to live in the country to appreciate it. I never thought it was possible I could be so happy in the country.

WILLIE: You don't mind it's so quiet?

AL: [Looks at him] They got noise in New Jersey. But it's a quiet noise. Birds . . . drizzling . . . Not like here with the buses and trucks and screaming and yelling.

WILLIE: Well, it's different for you. You like the country better because you're retired. You can sit on a porch, look at a tree, watch a bush growing. You're still not active like me. You got a different temperament, you're a slow person.

AL: I'm a slow person?

WILLIE: You're here fifteen minutes, you still got a whole cup of tea. I'm finished already.

AL: That's right. You're finished, and I'm still enjoying it. That was always the difference with us.

WILLIE: You're wrong. I can get up and make a *second* cup of tea and enjoy it twice as much as you. I like a busy life. That's why I love the city. I gotta be near a phone. I never know when a picture's gonna come up, a musical, a commercial . . .

AL: When did you do a picture?

WILLIE: They're negotiating.

AL: When did you do a musical?

WILLIE: They're talking.

AL: When did you do a commercial?

WILLIE: All the time. I did one last week.

AL: For what?

WILLIE: For, er, for the . . . what's it, the potato chips.

AL: What potato chips?

WILLIE: The big one. The crispy potato chips . . . er . . . you know.

AL: What do I know? I don't eat potato chips.

WILLIE: Well, what's the difference what the name is?

AL: They hire you to sell potato chips and you can't remember the name?

WILLIE: Did you remember Sol Burton?

AL: [*Shrugs*] I'm not selling Sol Burton.

WILLIE: Listen, I don't want to argue with you.

AL: I didn't come from New Jersey to argue.

[*They sit quietly for a few seconds.* AL *sips his tea;* WILLIE *looks at his empty cup*]

WILLIE: [*Finally*] So-o-o . . . What do you think? . . . You want to do the doctor sketch?

AL: [*Thinks*] Well, listen, it's very good money. It's only a few days' work, I can be back in New Jersey. If you feel you'd like to do it, then my feeling is I'm agreeable.

WILLIE: And my feeling they told you.

AL: What?

WILLIE: They didn't tell you? My feeling is I'm against it.

AL: You're against it?

WILLIE: Right. But I'll do it if you want to.

AL: I don't want to do it if you're against it. If you're against it, don't do it.

WILLIE: What do you care if I'm against it as long as we're doing it? I just want you to know *why* I'm doing it.

AL: Don't do me any favors.

WILLIE: Who's doing you a favor? I'm doing my nephew a favor. It'll be good for him in the business if we do it.

AL: You're sure?

WILLIE: Certainly I'm sure. It's a big break for a kid like that to get big stars like us.

AL: That's different. In that case, I'm against it too but I'll do it.

WILLIE: [*Nods*] As long as we understand each other.

AL: And I want to be sure you know I'm not doing it for the money. The money goes to my grandchildren.

WILLIE: The whole thing?

AL: The whole thing. But not now. Only if I die. If I don't die, it'll be for my old age.

WILLIE: The same with me.

AL: You don't have grandchildren.

WILLIE: My *nephew's* children. Sidney and Marvin.

AL: [*Nods*] Very good.

WILLIE: Okay . . . So-o-o, you wanna rehearse?

AL: You're not against rehearsing?

WILLIE: Why should I be against rehearsing? I'm only against doing the show. Rehearsing is important.

AL: All right, let's rehearse. Why don't we move the furniture, and we'll make the set.

> [*They both get up and start to move the furniture around. First each one takes a single chair and moves it into a certain position. Then they both take a table and jointly move it away. Then they each take the chair the other one had moved before, and move it into a different place. Every time one moves something somewhere, the other moves it into a different spot. Finally* WILLIE *becomes aware that they are getting nowhere*]

WILLIE: Wait a minute, wait a minute. What the hell are we doing here?

AL: I'm fixing up the set, I don't know what you're doing.

WILLIE: You're fixing up the set?

AL: That's right.

WILLIE: You're fixing up the set for the doctor sketch?

> [AL *looks at him for a long time without saying a word. It suddenly becomes clear to him*]

AL: Oh, the *doctor* sketch?

> [*He then starts to pick up a chair and move it into another position.* WILLIE *does the same with another chair. They both move the table . . . and then they repeat what they did before. Every time one moves a chair, the other one moves the*

same chair to a different position. WILLIE *stops and looks again*]

WILLIE: Wait a minute! Wait a minute! We're doing the same goddamn thing. Are you fixing up for the doctor sketch or are you redecorating my apartment?

AL: I'm fixing up for the doctor sketch. If you'd leave what I'm doing alone, we'd be finished.

WILLIE: We'd be finished, but we'd be wrong.

AL: Not for the doctor sketch. I know what I'm doing. I did this sketch for forty-three years.

WILLIE: And where was I all that time, taking a smoke? Who did you think did it with you for forty-three years? That was *me*, mister.

AL: Don't call me mister, you know my name. I never liked it when you called me mister.

WILLIE: It's not a dirty word.

AL: It is when you say it.

WILLIE: Forgive me, *sir*.

AL: Let's please, for Pete's sakes, fix up for the doctor sketch.

WILLIE: You think *you* know how to do it? You fix it up.

AL: It'll be my pleasure. [WILLIE *stands aside and watches with arms folded as* AL *proceeds to move table and chairs and stools until he arranges them exactly the way he wants them. Then he stands back and folds his arms the same way*] There! *That's* the doctor sketch!

WILLIE: [*Smiles arrogantly*] For how much money?

AL: I don't want to bet you.

WILLIE: You're afraid to lose?

AL: I'm afraid to *win*. You don't even have enough to buy a box of plain crackers.

WILLIE: —Don't be so afraid you're gonna win—because you're gonna lose! That's not the doctor sketch. That's the gypsy chiropractor sketch.

AL: You're positive?

WILLIE: I'm *more* than positive. I'm *sure*.

AL: All right. Show me the doctor sketch.

WILLIE: [*Looks at him confidently, then goes to a chair, picks it up and moves it to the left about four inches, if that much. Then he folds his arms over his chest*] There, *that's* the doctor sketch!

AL: [*Looks at him*] You know what you are, Willie? You're a lapalooza.

WILLIE: [*Nods*] If I'm a lapalooza, you're a mister.

AL: Let's please rehearse the sketch.

WILLIE: All right, go outside. I'm in the office.

AL: You gonna do the part with the nurse first?

WILLIE: You see a nurse here? How can I rehearse with a nurse that's not here?

AL: I'm just asking a question. I'm not allowed to ask questions?

WILLIE: Ask whatever you want. But try to make them intelligent questions.

AL: I beg your pardon. I usually ask the kind of question to the kind of person I'm talking to . . . You get my drift?

WILLIE: I get it, mister.

AL: All right. Let's skip over the nurse. We'll start from where I come in.

WILLIE: All right, from where you come in. First go out.

AL: [*Takes a few steps toward the door, stops and turns*] All right, I'm outside. [*Pantomimes with his fist, knocking on a door*] Knock, knock, knock! I was looking for the doctor.

WILLIE: Wait a minute. You're not outside.

AL: Certainly I'm outside.

WILLIE: If you were outside, you couldn't see me, could you?

AL: No.

WILLIE: Can you see me?

AL: Yes.

WILLIE: So you're not outside. Go *all* the way outside. What the hell kind of a rehearsal is this?

AL: It's a rehearsing rehearsal. Can't you make believe I'm all the way out in the hall?

WILLIE: I could also make believe you were still in New Jersey, but you're not. You're here. Let's have a professional rehearsal, for chrissakes! We ain't got a nurse, but we got a door. Let's use what we got.

AL: [*Sighs deeply*] Listen, we're not gonna stop for every little thing, are we? I don't know how many years I got left, I don't wanna spend it rehearsing.

WILLIE We're not gonna stop for the little things. We're gonna stop for the big things . . . The door is a big thing.

AL: All right, I'll go through the door, I'll come in, and then we'll run through the sketch once or twice, and that'll be it for today. All right?

WILLIE: Right . . . Unless another big thing comes up.

AL: [*Glares at him*] All right, I'm going out. I'll be right back in. [*He crosses to the door, opens it, stops and turns*] If I'm outside and my daughter calls, tell her to pick me up in an hour.

[*He goes out and closes the door behind him*]

WILLIE: [*Mumbles, half to himself*] She can pick you up *now* for all I care. [*He puts his hands behind his back, clasps them, and paces back and forth. He calls out*] All right! Knock, knock, knock!

AL:　[*From outside*] Knock, knock, knock!

WILLIE:　[*Screams*] *Don't say it*, for God's sakes, *do it!* [*To himself*] He probably went *crazy* in the country.

AL:　[*From outside*] You ready?

WILLIE:　[*Yells*] I'm ready. Knock, knock, knock! [AL *knocks three times on the door*] Come in. [*We see and hear the doorknob jiggle, but it doesn't open. This is repeated*] All right, come in already.

AL:　[*From outside*] It doesn't open—it's stuck.

WILLIE:　[*Wearily*] All right, wait a minute. [*He shuffles over to the door and puts his hand on the knob and pulls. It doesn't open*] Wait a minute.

　　　[*He tries again, to no avail*]

AL:　[*From outside*] What's the matter?

WILLIE:　Wait a minute.

　　　[*He pulls harder, to no avail*]

AL:　Is it locked?

WILLIE:　It's not locked. Wait a minute. [*He tries again; it doesn't open*] It's locked. You better get somebody. Call the boy downstairs. Sandy. Tell him it's locked.

AL:　[*From outside*] Let me try it again.

WILLIE:　What are you wasting time? Call the boy. Tell him it's locked.

　　　[AL *tries it again, turning it in the other direction, and the door opens. They stand there face-to-face*]

AL:　I fixed it.

WILLIE:　[*Glares at him*] You didn't fix it. You just don't know how to open a door.

AL:　Did my daughter call?

WILLIE:　You know, I think you went crazy in the country.

AL: You want to stand here and insult me, or do you want to rehearse the sketch?

WILLIE: I would like to do *both,* but we ain't got the time . . . Let's forget the door. Stand in here and say "Knock, knock, knock."

AL: [AL *comes in and closes the door. Sarcastically*] I hope I can get *out* again.

WILLIE: I hope so, too. [*He places his hands behind his back and paces*] All right. "Knock, knock, knock."

AL: [*Pantomimes with his fist*] Knock, knock, knock.

WILLIE: [*Singsong*] Enter!

AL: [*Stops and looks at him*] What do you mean "Enter"? [*He does it in the same singsong way*] What happened to "Come in"?

WILLIE: It's the same thing, isn't it? "Enter" or "Come in." What's the difference, as long as you're in?

AL: The difference is we've done this sketch twelve thousand times, and you've always said "Come in," and suddenly today it's "Enter." Why today, after all these years, do you suddenly change it to "Enter"?

WILLIE: [*Shrugs*] I'm trying to freshen up the act.

AL: Who asked you to freshen up the act? They asked for the doctor sketch, didn't they? The doctor sketch starts with "Come in," not "Enter." You wanna freshen up something, put some flowers in here.

WILLIE: It's a new generation today. This is not 1934, you know.

AL: No kidding? I didn't get today's paper.

WILLIE: What's bad about "Enter" instead of "Come in"?

AL: Because it's different. You know why we've been doing it the same way for forty-three years? Because it's good.

WILLIE: And you know why we don't do it any more? Because we've been doing it the same way for forty-three years.

AL: So, if we're not doing it any more, why are we changing it?

WILLIE: Can I make a comment, nothing personal? I think you've been sitting on a New Jersey porch too long.

AL: What does that mean?

WILLIE: That means I think you've been sitting on a New Jersey porch too long. From my window, I see everything that goes on in the world. I see old people, I see young people, nice people, bad people, I see holdups, drug addicts, ambulances, car crashes, jumpers from buildings—I see everything. You see a lawn mower and a milkman.

AL: [*Looks at him for a long moment*] And that's why you want to say "Enter" instead of "Come in"?

WILLIE: Are you listening to me?

AL: [*Looks around*] Why, there's someone else in the room?

WILLIE: You don't know the first thing that's going on today?

AL: All right, what's going on today?

WILLIE: Did you ever hear the expression "That's where it is"? Well, this is where it is, and that's where I am.

AL: I see . . . Did you ever hear the expression "You don't know what the hell you're talking about"? It comes right in front of the *other* expression "You *never* knew what the hell you were talking about."

WILLIE: *I* wasn't the one who retired. You know why you retired? Because you were tired. You were getting old-fashioned. I was still new-fashioned, and I'll *always* be.

AL: I see. That's why you're in such demand. That's why you're such a "hot" property today. That's why you do movies you don't do, that's why you're in musicals you're not in, and that's why you make commercials you don't make—because you can't even remember them to *make* them.

WILLIE: You know what I *do* remember? I remember what a pain in the ass you are to work with, that's what I remember.

AL: That's right. And when you worked with this pain in the ass, you lived in a *five*-room suite. Now you live in a *one*-room suite . . . And you're still wearing the same goddamn pajamas you wore in the five-room suite.

WILLIE: I don't have to take this crap from you.

AL: You're lucky you're getting it. No one else wants to give it to you.

WILLIE: I don't want to argue with you. After you say "Knock, knock, knock," I'm saying "Enter," and if you don't like it you don't have to come in.

AL: You can't say nothing without my permission. I own fifty percent of this act.

WILLIE: Then say *your* fifty percent. I'm saying "Enter" in my fifty percent.

AL: If you say "Enter" after "Knock, knock, knock" . . . I'm coming in all right. But not alone. I'm bringing a lawyer with me.

WILLIE: Where? From New Jersey? You're lucky if a *cow* comes with you.

AL: Against *you* in court, I could *win* with a cow.

[*He enunciates each point by poking* WILLIE *in the chest*]

WILLIE: [*Slaps his hand away*] The *finger?* You're starting with the finger again?

[*He runs into the kitchen and comes out brandishing* a *knife*]

AL: I'll tell you the truth now. I didn't retire. I *escaped.*

WILLIE: [*Wielding the knife*] The next time you give me the finger, say goodbye to the finger.

AL: [*Hiding behind a chair*] Listen, I got a terrific idea. Instead of working together again, let's never work together again. You're crazy.

WILLIE: I'm crazy, heh? I'M CRAZY!

AL: Keep saying it until you believe it.

WILLIE: I may be crazy, but you're *senile!* You know what that is?

AL: I'm not giving you any straight lines.

WILLIE: Crazy is when you got a couple of parts that go wrong. Senile is when you went the hell out of business. That's you, mister. [*The phone rings.* AL *moves toward the phone*] Get away from that phone. [*He drives the knife into the table.* AL *backs away in shock.* WILLIE *picks up the phone*] Hello?

AL: Is that my daughter?

WILLIE: Hello . . . How are you?

AL: Is that my daughter? Is that her?

WILLIE: [*To* AL] Will you shut up? Will you be quiet? Can't you see I'm talking? Don't you see me on the phone with a person? For God's sakes, behave like a human being for five seconds, will you? WILL YOU BEHAVE FOR FIVE SECONDS LIKE A HUMAN BEING? [*Into the phone*] Hello? . . . Yes . . . Just a minute. [*To* AL] It's your daughter.

[*He sits, opens up* Variety]

AL: [*Takes the phone, turns his back to* WILLIE, *speaks low*] Hello . . . Hello, sweetheart . . . No . . . No . . . I can't talk now . . . I said I can't talk now . . . Because he's a crazy bedbug, that's why.

WILLIE: [*Jumps up*] Mister is no good but bedbug is all right?? [*Yells into the phone*] Your father is sick! Come and get your sick father!

AL: [*Turns to him*] Don't you see me on the phone with a person? Will you please be quiet, for God's sakes! [*Back into the phone*] Listen, I want you to pick me up now . . . I don't want to discuss it. Pick me up now. In front of the hotel. Don't park too close, it's filthy here . . . I *know* what I promised. Don't argue with me. I'm putting on my coat. I'll wait in the street—I'll probably get mugged . . . All right, just a minute. [*He hands the phone to* WILLIE] She'd like to talk to you for a second.

WILLIE: Who is it?

AL: [*Glares at him*] Mrs. Eleanor Roosevelt . . . What do you mean, who is it? Didn't you just say it's my daughter?

WILLIE: I know it's your daughter. I forgot her name.

AL: Doris.

WILLIE: What does she want?

AL: [*Yells*] Am I Doris? She'll tell you.

WILLIE: [*Takes the phone*] Hello? . . . Hello, dear, this is Willie Clark . . . Unpleasantness? There was no unpleasantness . . . There was stupidity maybe but no unpleasantness . . .

AL: Tell her I'm getting into my coat. [*He is putting his coat on*] Tell her I got one sleeve on.

WILLIE: [*Into the phone*] I was hoping it would work out too . . . I bent over backwards and forwards. He didn't even bend sideways . . .

AL: I got the other sleeve on . . . Tell her I'm up to my hat and then I'm out the door.

WILLIE: It's a question of one word, darling. "Enter"! . . . "Enter" —that's all it comes down to.

AL: [*Puts his hat on*] The hat is on. I'm bundled up, tell her.

WILLIE: [*Into the phone*] Yes . . . Yes, I will . . . I'll tell him myself. I promise . . . Goodbye, Dorothy. [*He hangs up*] I told her we'll give it one more chance.

AL: Not if you say "Enter." "Come in," I'll stay. "Enter," I go.

WILLIE: Ask me "Knock, knock, knock."

AL: Don't fool around with me. I got enough pains in my neck. Are you going to say "Come in"?

WILLIE: Ask me "Knock, knock, knock."

AL: I know you, you bastard!

WILLIE: ASK ME "KNOCK, KNOCK, KNOCK"!

AL: KNOCK, KNOCK, KNOCK!

WILLIE: [*Grinding it in*] EN-TERRR!

AL: BEDBUG! CRAZY BEDBUG!

[*He starts to run out*]

WILLIE: [*Big smile*] ENNN-TERRRRR!

[*The curtain starts down*]

AL: [*Heading for the door*] LUNATIC BASTARD!

WILLIE: ENNN-TERRRR!

CURTAIN

ACT TWO

SCENE ONE

The scene is a doctor's office or, rather, an obvious stage "flat" representation of a doctor's office. It has an old desk and chair, a telephone, a cabinet filled with medicine bottles, a human skeleton hanging on a stand, a blackboard with chalk and pointer, an eye chart on the wall.

Overhead television lights surround the top of the set. Two boom microphones extend from either end of the set over the office.

At rise, the set is not fully lit. A thin, frail man in a hat and business suit sits in the chair next to the doctor's desk, patiently waiting.

VOICE OF TV DIRECTOR: [*Over the loudspeaker*] Eddie! *EDDIE!*

[EDDIE, *a young assistant TV director with headset and speaker, trailing wires and carrying a clipboard, steps out on the set. He speaks through his mike*]

EDDIE: Yeah, Phil?

VOICE OF TV DIRECTOR: Any chance of doing this today?

EDDIE: [*Shrugs*] We're all set here, Phil. We're just waiting on the actors.

VOICE OF TV DIRECTOR: What the hell is happening?

EDDIE: I don't know. There's a problem with the makeup. Mr. Clark wants a Number Seven amber or something.

VOICE OF TV DIRECTOR: Well, get it for him.

EDDIE: Where? They stopped making it thirty-four years ago.

VOICE OF TV DIRECTOR: Christ!

EDDIE: And Mr. Lewis says the "ahh" sticks are too short.

VOICE OF TV DIRECTOR: The what?

EDDIE: The "ahh" sticks. Don't ask me. I'm still trying to figure out what a "look" stick is.

VOICE OF TV DIRECTOR: What the hell are we making, *Nicholas and Alexandra?* Tell them it's just a dress rehearsal. We'll worry about the props later. Let's get moving, Eddie. Christ Almighty!

   [WILLIE's *nephew* BEN *appears onstage. He talks up into the overhead mike*]

BEN: Mr. Schaefer . . . Mr. Schaefer, I'm awfully sorry about the delay. Mr. Lewis and Mr. Clark have had a few technical problems backstage.

VOICE OF TV DIRECTOR: Yeah, well, we've had it all week . . . I'm afraid we're running out of time here. I've got twelve goddamned other numbers to get through today!

BEN: I'll get them right out. There's no problem.

VOICE OF TV DIRECTOR: Tell them I want to run straight through, no stopping. They can clean up whatever they want afterwards.

BEN: Absolutely.

VOICE OF TV DIRECTOR: I haven't seen past "Knock, knock, knock"– "Come in" since Tuesday.

BEN: [*Looks offstage*] Right. There they are. [*Into the mike*] We're ready, Mr. Schaefer. I'll tell them we're going to go straight through, no stopping. Thank you very much.

   [BEN *exits very quickly*]

VOICE OF TV DIRECTOR: All right, Eddie, bring in the curtains.

EDDIE: What?

VOICE OF TV DIRECTOR: Bring in the curtains. Let's run it from the top with the voice over.

EDDIE: [*Calls up*] Let's have the curtains.

[*The curtains come in*]

VOICE OF TV DIRECTOR: Voice over!

ANNOUNCER: The golden age of comedy reached its zenith during a fabulous and glorious era known as Vaudeville—Fanny Brice, W. C. Fields, Eddie Cantor, Ed Wynn, Will Rogers and a host of other greats fill its Hall of Fame. There are two other names that belong on this list, but they can never be listed separately. They are more than a team. They are two comic shining lights that beam as one. For, Lewis without Clark is like laughter without joy. We are privileged to present tonight, in their first public performance in over eleven years, for half a century known as "The Sunshine Boys"—Mr. Al Lewis and Mr. Willie Clark, in their beloved scene, "The Doctor Will See You Now."

> [*The curtain rises, and the set is fully lit. The frail man in the hat is sitting on the chair as* WILLIE, *the doctor, dressed in a floor-length white doctor's jacket, a mirror attached to his head and a stethoscope around his neck is looking into the* PATIENT'S *mouth, holding his tongue down with an "ahh" stick*]

WILLIE: Open wider and say "Ahh."

PATIENT: Ahh.

WILLIE: Wider.

PATIENT: *Ahhh!*

WILLIE: [*Moves with his back to the audience*] A little wider.

PATIENT: Ahhh!

WILLIE: [*Steps away*] Your throat is all right, but you're gonna have some trouble with your stomach.

PATIENT: How come?

WILLIE: You just swallowed the stick.

> [*The* PATIENT *feels his stomach*]

PATIENT: Is that bad?

WILLIE: It's terrible. I only got two left.

PATIENT: What about getting the stick out?

WILLIE: What am I, a tree surgeon? . . . All right, for another ten dollars, I'll take it out.

PATIENT: That's robbery.

WILLIE: Then forget it. Keep the stick.

PATIENT: No, no. I'll pay. Take the stick out.

WILLIE: Come back tomorrow. On Thursdays I do woodwork. [*The* PATIENT *gets up and crosses to the door, then exits.* WILLIE *calls out*] Oh, Nurse! Nursey!

[*The* NURSE *enters. She is a tall, voluptuous and overstacked blonde in a tight dress*]

NURSE: Did you want me, Doctor?

WILLIE: [*He looks at her, knowingly*] Why do you think I hired you? . . . What's your name again?

NURSE: Miss MacKintosh. You know, like the apples.

WILLIE: [*Nods*] The name I forgot, the apples I remembered . . . Look in my appointment book, see who's next.

NURSE: It's a Mr. Kornheiser.

WILLIE: Maybe you're wrong. Look in the book. It's better that way.

[*She crosses to the desk and bends way over as she looks through the appointment book. Her firm, round rear end faces us and* WILLIE. WILLIE *shakes his head from side to side in wonderful contemplation*]

NURSE: [*Still down*] No, I was right.

WILLIE: So was I.

NURSE: [*Straightens up and turns around*] It's Mr. Kornheiser.

WILLIE: Are you sure? Spell it.

NURSE: [*Turns, bends and gives us the same wonderful view again*] K-o-r-n-h-e-i-s-e-r!

[*She turns and straightens up*]

WILLIE: [*Nods*] What's the first name?

NURSE: [*Turns, bends*] Walter.

WILLIE: Stay down for the middle name.

NURSE: [*Remains down*] Benjamin.

WILLIE: Don't move and give me the whole thing.

NURSE: [*Still rear end up, reading*] Walter Benjamin Kornheiser.

[*She turns and straightens up*]

WILLIE: Oh, boy. From now on I only want to see patients with long names.

NURSE: Is there anything else you want?

WILLIE: Yeah. Call a carpenter and have him make my desk lower.

[*The* NURSE *walks sexily right up to* WILLIE *and stands with her chest practically on his, breathing and heaving*]

NURSE: [*Pouting*] Yes, Doctor.

WILLIE: [*Wipes his brow*] Whew, it's hot in here. Did you turn the steam on?

NURSE: [*Sexily*] No, Doctor.

WILLIE: In that case, take a five-dollar raise. Send in the next patient before I'm the next patient.

NURSE: Yes, Doctor. [*She coughs*] Excuse me, I think I have a chest cold.

WILLIE: Looks more like an epidemic to me.

NURSE: Yes, Doctor. [*She wriggles her way to the door*] Is there anything else you can think of?

WILLIE: I can *think* of it, but I'm not so sure I can *do* it.

NURSE: Well, if I *can* help you, Doctor, that's what the nurse is for.

[*She exits and closes the door with an enticing look*]

WILLIE: I'm glad I didn't go to law school. [*Then we hear three knocks on the door. "Knock, knock, knock"*] Aha. That must be my next patient. [*Calls out*] Come in! [*The door starts to open*]— and *enter!*

[AL *steps in and glares angrily at* WILLIE. *He is in a business suit, wears a wig, and carries a cheap attaché case*]

AL: I'm looking for the doctor.

WILLIE: Are you sick?

AL: Are *you* the doctor?

WILLIE: Yes.

AL: I'm not *that* sick.

WILLIE: What's your name, please?

AL: Kornheiser. Walter Benjamin Kornheiser. You want me to spell it?

WILLIE: Never mind. I got a better speller than you . . . [*Takes a tongue depressor from his pocket*] Sit down and open your mouth, please.

AL: There's nothing wrong with my mouth.

WILLIE: Then just sit down.

AL: There's nothing wrong with that either.

WILLIE: Then what are you doing here?

AL: I came to examine you.

WILLIE: I think you got everything backwards.

AL: It's possible. I dressed in a hurry this morning.

WILLIE: You mean you came here for me to examine *you*.

AL: No, I came here for me to examine *you*. I'm a tax collector.

WILLIE: [*Nods*] That's nice. I'm a stamp collector. What do you do for a living?

AL: I find out how much money people make.

WILLIE: Oh, a busybody. Make an appointment with the nurse.

AL: I did. I'm seeing her Friday night . . .

WILLIE: [*Jumps up and down angrily*] Don't fool around with my nurse! DON'T FOOL AROUND WITH MY NURSE! She's a nice girl. She's a *Virginian!*

AL: A what?

WILLIE: A *Virginian*. That's where she's from.

AL: Well, she ain't going *back*, I can tell you that. [*He sits, opens the attaché case*] I got some questions to ask you.

WILLIE: I'm too busy to answer questions. I'm a doctor. If you wanna see me, you gotta be a patient.

AL: But I'm not sick.

WILLIE: Don't worry. We'll find something.

AL: All right, you examine me and I'll examine you . . . [*Takes out a tax form as* WILLIE *wields the tongue depressor*] The first question is, How much money did you make last year?

WILLIE: Last year I made—

[*He moves his lips mouthing a sum, but it's not audible*]

AL: I didn't hear that.

WILLIE: Oh. Hard of hearing. I knew we'd find something. Did you ever have any childhood diseases?

AL: Not lately.

WILLIE: Father living or deceased?

AL: Both.

WILLIE: What do you mean, both?

AL: First he was living, now he's deceased.

WILLIE: What did your father die from?

AL: My mother . . . Now it's my turn. Are you married?

WILLIE: I'm looking.

AL: Looking to get married?

WILLIE: No, looking to get out.

[He looks in AL's ear with a flashlight]

AL: What are you doing?

WILLIE: I'm examining your lower intestines.

AL: So why do you look in the ear?

WILLIE: If I got a choice of two places to look, I'll take this one.

AL: [Consulting his form] Never mind. Do you own a car?

WILLIE: Certainly I own a car. Why?

AL: If you use it for medical purposes, you can deduct it from your taxes. What kind of car do you own?

WILLIE: An ambulance.

AL: Do you own a house?

WILLIE: Can I deduct it?

AL: Only if you use it for medical purposes. Where do you live?

WILLIE: In Mount Sinai Hospital . . . Open your shirt, I want to listen to your heartbeat.

AL: [Unbuttons two buttons on his shirt] Will this take long?

WILLIE: Not if I hear something. [He puts his ear to AL's chest and listens] Uh-huh. I hear something . . . You're all right.

AL: Aren't you going to listen with the stethoscope?

WILLIE: Oh, sure. I didn't know you wanted a thorough examination. [*Puts the stethoscope to his ears and listens to* AL's *chest*] Oh, boy. Ohhh, boyyyy! You know what you got?

AL: What?

WILLIE: A filthy undershirt.

AL: Never mind that. Am I in good health?

WILLIE: Not unless you change your undershirt.

AL: What is this, a doctor's office or a laundry? I bet you never went to medical school.

WILLIE: [*Jumping up and down again*] What are you talkin'? . . . WHAT ARE YOU TALKIN'? . . . I went to Columbia Medical School.

AL: Did you pass?

WILLIE: Certainly.

AL: Well, you should have gone *in!*

WILLIE: Never mind . . . I'm gonna examine your eyes now.

AL: They're perfect. I got twenty-twenty eyes.

WILLIE: That's too much. All you need is one and one. Look at that chart on the wall. Now put your left hand over your left eye and your right hand over your right eye. [AL *does so*] Now tell me what you see.

AL: I don't see nothing.

WILLIE: Don't panic, I can cure you . . . Take your hands away. [AL *does*] Can you see now?

AL: Certainly I can see now.

WILLIE: You know, I fixed over two thousand people like that.

AL: It's a miracle.

WILLIE: Thank you.

AL: A miracle you're not in jail . . . What do you charge for a visit?

WILLIE: A dollar.

AL: A dollar? That's very cheap for an examination.

WILLIE: It's not an examination. It's just a visit. "Hello and Goodbye" . . . "Hello and How Are You?" is ten dollars.

AL: If you ask me, you're a quack.

WILLIE: If I was a duck I would ask you . . . Now roll up your sleeve, I wanna take some blood.

AL: I can't do it.

WILLIE: Why not?

AL: If I see blood, I get sick.

WILLIE: Do what I do. Don't look.

AL: I'm sorry. I'm not giving blood. I'm anemic.

WILLIE: What's anemic?

AL: You're a doctor and you don't know what anemic means?

WILLIE: That's because I'm a specialist.

AL: What do you specialize in?

WILLIE: Everything but anemic.

AL: Listen, can I continue my examination?

WILLIE: You continue yours, and I'll continue mine. All right, cross your legs. [He hits AL's knee with a small hammer] Does it hurt if I hit you with the hammer?

AL: Yes.

WILLIE: Good. From now on, try not to get hit with a hammer. [He throws the hammer over his shoulder. He takes a specimen bottle from the cabinet and returns] You see this bottle?

AL: Yes.

WILLIE: You know what you're supposed to do with this bottle?

AL: I think so.

WILLIE: You *think* so or you *know* so? If you're not sure, let me know. The girl doesn't come in to clean today.

AL: What do you want me to do?

WILLIE: I want you to go in this bottle.

AL: I haven't got time. I have to go over your books.

WILLIE: *The hell you will!*

AL: If I don't go over your books, the *government* will come in here and go over your books.

WILLIE: Don't they have a place in Washington?

AL: Certainly, but they have to go where the books are.

WILLIE: The whole government?

AL: No, just the Treasury Department.

WILLIE: That's a relief.

AL: I'm glad you're relieved.

WILLIE: I wish *you* were before you came in here.

[*The door opens and the big-chested* NURSE *steps in*]

NURSE: Oh, Doctor. Doctor Klockenmeyer.

WILLIE: Yes.

NURSE: Mrs. Kolodny is on the phone. She wants you to rush right over and deliver her baby.

WILLIE: I'm busy now. Tell her I'll mail it to her in the morning.

NURSE: Yes, Doctor.

[*She exits and closes the door*]

AL: Where did you find a couple of nurses like that?

WILLIE: She was standing on Forty-third and Forty-fourth Street . . . Let me see your tongue, please.

AL: I don't want to.

[WILLIE *squeezes* AL's *throat, and his tongue comes out*]

WILLIE: Open the mouth . . . How long have you had that white coat on your tongue?

AL: Since January. In the spring I put on a gray sports jacket.

WILLIE: Now hold your tongue with your fingers and say "shish kabob."

AL: [*Holds his tongue with his fingers*] Thickabob.

WILLIE: Again.

AL: Thickabob.

WILLIE: I have bad news for you.

AL: What is it?

WILLIE: If you do that in a restaurant, you'll never get shish kabob.

AL: [*Stands with his face close to* WILLIE's] Never mind that. What about your taxes?

[*On the "T," he spits a little*]

WILLIE: [*Wipes his face*] The what?

AL: The taxes. It's time to pay your taxes to the Treasury.

[*All the "T's" are quite fluid.* WILLIE *wipes his face and glares angrily at* AL]

WILLIE: I'm warning you, don't start in with me.

AL: What are you talking about?

WILLIE: You know what I'm talking about. [*Illustrates*] "It's time to pay the taxes." You're speaking with spitting again.

AL: I said the right line, didn't I? If it comes out juicy, I can't help that.

WILLIE: [*Quite angry*] It doesn't come out juicy unless you squeeze the "T's." I'm warning you, don't squeeze them on me.

[VOICE OF TV DIRECTOR *is heard over the loudspeaker*]

VOICE OF TV DIRECTOR: Okay, let's hold it a second. Mr. Clark, I'm having trouble with the dialogue. I don't find those last few lines in the script.

WILLIE: [*Shouts up*] It's not in the script, it's in *his mouth.*

AL: [*Talking up into the mike*] I said the right line. Look in the script, you'll find it there.

WILLIE: [*Shouting*] You'll find the words, you won't find the spit. The spit's his own idea. He's doing it on *purpose!*

AL: I don't spit on purpose. I spit on accident. I've *always* spitted on accident. It's not possible to say that line without spitting a little.

WILLIE: [*Addressng all his remarks to the unseen director*] I can say it. [*He says the line with great delicacy, especially on the "T's"*] "It's time to pay your taxes to the Treasury." [*Back to his normal inflection*] There wasn't a spit in my entire mouth. Why doesn't he say it like *that?*

AL: What am I, an Englishman? I'm talking the same as I've talked for forty-three years.

VOICE OF TV DIRECTOR: Gentlemen, can we argue this point after the dress rehearsal and go on with the sketch?

WILLIE: I'm not going to stand here and get a shower in the face. If you want me to go on, either take out the line or get me an umbrella.

VOICE OF TV DIRECTOR: Can we *please* go on? With all due respect, gentlemen, we have twelve other scenes to rehearse and we cannot spend all day on personal squabbles . . .

WILLIE: I'll go on, but I'm moving to a safer spot.

VOICE OF TV DIRECTOR: Don't worry about the moves, we'll pick you up on camera. Now, let's skip over this spot and pick it up on "I hope you don't have what Mr. Melnick had." [WILLIE *moves away from* AL] All right, Mr. Clark, whenever you're ready.

WILLIE: [*Waits a minute, then goes back into the doctor character*] I hope you don't have what Mr. Melnick had.

AL: What did Mr. Melnick have?

WILLIE: [*Points to standing skeleton*] Ask him yourself, he's standing right there.

AL: That's Mr. Melnick?

WILLIE: It could be Mrs. Melnick. Without high heels, I can't tell.

AL: If he's dead, why do you leave him standing in the office?

WILLIE: He's still got one more appointment with me.

AL: [*Crosses to him*] You know what you are? You're a charlatan! [*As* AL *says that line, he punctuates each word by poking* WILLIE *in the chest with his finger. It does not go unnoticed by* WILLIE] Do you know what a charlatan is? [*More pokes*]

WILLIE: It's a city in North Carolina. And if you're gonna poke me again like that, you're gonna end up in Poughkeepsie.

VOICE OF TV DIRECTOR: [*Over the loudspeaker*] Hold it, hold it. Where does it say, "You're going to end up in Poughkeepsie"?

WILLIE: [*Furious*] Where does it say he can poke me in the chest? He's doing it on purpose. He *always* did it on purpose, just to get my goat.

AL: [*Looking up to the mike*] I didn't poke him, I tapped him. A light little tap, it wouldn't hurt a baby.

WILLIE: Maybe a baby elephant. I *knew* I was going to get poked. First comes the spitting, then comes the poking. I know his routine already.

AL: [*To the mike*] Excuse me. I'm sorry we're holding up the rehearsal, but we have a serious problem on our hands. The man I'm working with is a lunatic.

WILLIE: [*Almost in a rage*] I'm a lunatic, heh? He breaks my chest and spits in my face and calls *me* a lunatic! I'm gonna tell you something now I never told you in my entire life. I hate your guts.

AL: You told it to me on Monday.

WILLIE: Then I'm telling it to you again.

VOICE OF TV DIRECTOR: Listen, gentlemen, I really don't see any point in going on with this rehearsal.

AL: I don't see any point in going on with this *show*. This man is persecuting me. For eleven years he's been waiting to get back at me, only I'm not gonna give him the chance.

[*The assistant director,* EDDIE, *walks out in an attempt to make peace*]

WILLIE: [*Half-hysterical*] I knew it! I knew it! He planned it! He's been setting me up for eleven years just to walk out on me again.

EDDIE: [*Trying to be gentle*] All right, Mr. Clark, let's settle down. Why don't we all go into the dressing room and talk this out?

AL: I didn't want to do it in the first place.

WILLIE: [*Apoplectic*] Liar! Liar! His daughter *begged* me on the phone. She *begged* me!

[BEN *rushes out to restrain* WILLIE]

BEN: Uncle Willie, please, that's enough. Come back to the dressing room.

EDDIE: Gentlemen, we need the stage. Can we please do this over on the side?

AL: [*To the assistant director*] The man is hysterical, you can see for yourself. He's been doing this to me all week long.

[*He starts taking off the wig and suit jacket*]

WILLIE: Begged me. She begged me. His own daughter begged me.

BEN: Uncle Willie, stop, please!

AL: [*To the others*] I'm sorry we caused everyone so much trouble.

I should have stayed in New Jersey in the first place. [*On his way out. To the assistant director*] He pulled a knife on me last week. In his own apartment he pulled a knife on me. A crazy man.

[*He is gone*]

WILLIE: I don't need you. I *never* needed you. You were nothing when I found you, and that's what you are today.

BEN: Come on, Willie. [*Out front*] I'm sorry about this, Mr. Schaefer.

WILLIE: He thinks I can't get work without him. Maybe *his* career is over, but not mine. Maybe he's finished, but not me. You hear? not me! NOT M—

[*He clutches his chest*]

BEN: [*Turns and sees him stagger*] Grab him, quick! [EDDIE *rushes to* WILLIE, *but it's too late*—WILLIE *falls to the floor.* BEN *rushes to his side*] All right, take it easy, Uncle Willie, just lie there. [*To* EDDIE] Get a doctor, please hurry.

[*A "bit" actor and the* NURSE *rush onstage behind* BEN]

WILLIE: [*Breathing hard*] I don't need a doctor. Don't get a doctor, I don't trust them.

BEN: Don't talk, Willie, you're all right. [*To the* NURSE] Somebody get a blanket, please.

WILLIE: [*Breathing fast*] Don't tell him. Don't tell him I fell down. I don't want to give him the satisfaction.

BEN: Of course, I won't tell him, Willie. There's nothing to tell. You're going to be all right.

WILLIE: Frito-Lays . . . That's the name of the potato chip . . . You see? I remembered . . . I remembered the name! Frito-Lays.

[BEN *is holding* WILLIE's *hand as the lights dim. The* CURTAIN *falls on the scene. In the dark, we hear the voice of the* ANNOUNCER]

ANNOUNCER: The golden age of comedy reached its zenith during a fabulous and glorious era known as Vaudeville—Fanny Brice,

W. C. Fields, Eddie Cantor, Ed Wynn, Will Rogers and a host of other greats fill its Hall of Fame. There are two other names that belong on this list, but they can never be listed separately. They are more than a team. They are two comic shining lights that beam as one. For, Lewis without Clark is like laughter without joy. When these two greats retired, a comic style disappeared from the American scene that will never see its likes again . . . Here, then, in a sketch taped nearly eleven years ago on *The Ed Sullivan Show*, are Lewis and Clark in their classic scene, "The Doctor Will See You Now."

[*We hear* WILLIE's *voice and that of the first* PATIENT]

WILLIE: Open wider and say "Ahh."

PATIENT: Ahh.

WILLIE: Wider.

PATIENT: Ahh.

WILLIE: A little wider.

PATIENT: Ahhh!

WILLIE: Your throat is all right, but you're gonna have some trouble with your stomach.

PATIENT: How come?

WILLIE: You just swallowed the stick.

SCENE TWO

The curtain rises. The scene is WILLIE's *hotel room, two weeks later. It is late afternoon.* WILLIE *is in his favorite pajamas in bed, propped up on the pillows, his head hanging down, asleep.*

The television is droning away—another daytime serial. A black REGISTERED NURSE *in uniform, a sweater draped over her shoulders, and her glasses on a chain around her neck, is sitting in a chair watching the television. She is eating from a big box of chocolates. Two very large vases of flowers are on the bureau.* WILLIE's *head bobs a few times; then he opens his eyes.*

WILLIE: What time is it?

NURSE: [*Turns off the TV and glances at her watch*] Ten to one.

WILLIE: Ten to one? . . . Who are you?

NURSE: Don't give me that. You know who I am.

WILLIE: You're the same nurse from yesterday?

NURSE: I'm the same nurse from every day for two weeks now. Don't play your games with me.

WILLIE: I can't even chew a piece of bread, who's gonna play games? . . . Why'd you turn off the television?

NURSE: It's either watching that or watching you sleep—either one ain't too interesting.

WILLIE: I'm sorry. I'll try to sleep more entertaining . . . What's today, Tuesday?

NURSE: Wednesday.

[*She bites into a piece of chocolate*]

WILLIE: How could this be Wednesday? I went to sleep on Monday.

NURSE: Haven't we already seen Mike Douglas twice this week?

WILLIE: Once.

NURSE: Twice.

WILLIE: [*Reluctantly*] All right, twice . . . I don't even remember. I was all right yesterday?

NURSE: We are doing very well.

WILLIE: We are? When did *you* get sick?

NURSE: [*Deadly serious, no smile*] That's funny. That is really funny, Mr. Clark. Soon as I get home tonight I'm gonna bust out laughing.

WILLIE: You keep eating my candy like that, you're gonna bust out a lot sooner.

NURSE: Well, *you* can't eat it and there's no sense throwing it out. I'm just storing up energy for the winter.

WILLIE: Maybe you'll find time in between the nougat and the peppermint to take my pulse.

NURSE: I took it. It's a little better today.

WILLIE: When did you take my pulse?

NURSE: When you were sleeping.

WILLIE: *Everybody's* pulse is good when they're sleeping. You take a pulse when a person is up. Thirty dollars a day, she takes a sleeping pulse. I'll tell you the truth, I don't think you know what you're doing . . . and I'm not a prejudiced person.

NURSE: Well, *I* am: I don't like sick people who tell registered nurses how to do their job. You want your tea now?

WILLIE: I don't want to interrupt your candy.

NURSE: And don't get fresh with me. You can get fresh with your nephew, but you can't get fresh with me. Maybe *he* has to take it, but I'm not a blood relative.

WILLIE: That's for sure.

NURSE: That's even funnier than the other one. My *whole* evening's gonna be taken up tonight with nothing but laughing.

WILLIE: I don't even eat candy. Finish the whole box. When you're through, I hope you eat the flowers too.

NURSE: You know why I don't get angry at anything you say to me?

WILLIE: I give up. Why?

NURSE: Because I have a good sense of humor. I am *known* for my good sense of humor. That's why I can take anything you say to me.

WILLIE: If you nurse as good as your sense of humor, I won't make it to Thursday . . . Who called?

NURSE: No one.

WILLIE: I thought I heard the phone.

NURSE: [*Gets up*] No one called. [*She crosses and puffs up his pillow*] Did you have a nice nap?

WILLIE: It was a nap, nothing special . . . Don't puff up the pillows, please. [*He swats her hands away*] It takes me a day and a night to get them the way I like them, and then you puff them up.

NURSE: Oh, woke up a little grouchy, didn't we?

WILLIE: Stop making yourself a partner all the time. I woke up grouchy. Don't make the bed, please. I'm still sleeping in it. Don't make a bed with a person in it.

NURSE: Can't stand to have people do things for you, can you? If you just want someone to sit here and watch you, you're better off getting a dog, Mr. Clark. I'll suggest that to your nephew.

WILLIE: Am I complaining? I'm only asking for two things. Don't take my pulse when I'm sleeping and don't make my bed when I'm in it. Do it the other way around and then we're in business.

NURSE: It doesn't bother me to do nothing as long as I'm getting paid for it.

[*She sits*]

WILLIE: [*A pause*] I'm hungry.

NURSE: You want your junket?

WILLIE: Forget it. I'm not hungry. [*She reads*] Tell me something, how old is a woman like you?

NURSE: That is none of your business.

WILLIE: I'm not asking for business.

NURSE: I am fifty-four years young.

WILLIE: Is that so? . . . You're married?

NURSE: My husband passed away four years ago.

WILLIE: Oh . . . You were the nurse?

NURSE: No, I was not the nurse . . . You could use some sleep and I could use some quiet.

[*She gets up*]

WILLIE: You know something? For a fifty-four-year-old registered widow, you're an attractive woman.

[*He tries to pat her. She swings at him*]

NURSE: And don't try that with me!

WILLIE: Who's trying anything?

NURSE: You are. You're getting fresh in a way I don't like.

WILLIE: What are you worried about? I can't even put on my slippers by myself.

NURSE: I'm not worried about your slippers. And don't play on my sympathy. I don't have any, and I ain't expecting any coming in, in the near future.

WILLIE: Listen, how about a nice alcohol rub?

NURSE: I just gave you one.

WILLIE: No, I'll give *you* one.

NURSE: I know you just say things like that to agitate me. You like to agitate people, don't you? Well, I am not an agitatable person.

WILLIE: You're right. I think I'd be better off with the dog.

NURSE: How did your poor wife stand a man like you?

WILLIE: Who told you about my poor wife?

NURSE: Your poor nephew . . . Did you ever think of getting married again?

[*She takes his pulse*]

WILLIE: What is this, a proposal?

NURSE: [*Laughs*] Not from me . . . I am *not* thinking of getting married again . . . Besides, you're just not my type.

WILLIE: Why? It's a question of religion?

NURSE: It's a question of age. You'd wear me out in no time.

WILLIE: You think I can't support you? I've got Medicare.

NURSE: You never stop, do you?

WILLIE: When I stop, I won't be here.

NURSE: Well, that's where you're gonna be unless you learn to slow up a little.

WILLIE: Slow up? I moved two inches in three weeks, she tells me slow up.

NURSE: I mean, if you're considering getting well again, you have to stop worrying about telephone calls and messages, and especially about when you're going back to work.

WILLIE: I'm an actor—I have to act. It's my profession.

NURSE: Your profession right now is being a sick person. And if you're gonna act anywhere, it's gonna be from a sick bed.

WILLIE: Maybe I can get a job on Marcus Welby.

NURSE: You can turn everything I say into a vaudeville routine if you want, but I'm gonna give you a piece of advice, Mr. Clark . . .

WILLIE: What?

NURSE: The world is full of sick people. And there just ain't enough doctors or nurses to go around to take care of all these sick people. And all the doctors and all the nurses can do just so much, Mr. Clark. But God, in His Infinite Wisdom, has said He will help those who help themselves.

WILLIE: [Looks at her] So? What's the advice?

NURSE: *Stop bugging me!*

WILLIE: All right, I'll stop bugging you . . . I don't even know what the hell it means.

NURSE: That's better. Now you're my type again.

[*The doorbell rings. The* NURSE *crosses to the door*]

WILLIE: Here comes today's candy.

[*She opens the door.* BEN *enters with packages*]

BEN: Hello. How is he?

NURSE: Fine. I think we're gonna get married.

BEN: Hey, Uncle Willie, you look terrific.

WILLIE: You got my *Variety*?

BEN: [*Goes over to him, and hands him* Variety] I also got about two hundred get-well telegrams from just about every star in show business—Lucille Ball, Milton Berle, Bob Hope, the mayor. It'll take you nine months just to answer them.

WILLIE: What about a commercial? Did you hear from Alka-Seltzer?

BEN: We have plenty of time to talk about that . . . Miss O'Neill, did you have your lunch yet?

NURSE: Not yet.

WILLIE: She just finished two pounds of appetizers.

BEN: Why don't you go out, take an hour or so? I'll be here for a while.

NURSE: Thank you. I could use some fresh air. [*Gets her coat. To* WILLIE] Now, when I'm gone, I don't want you getting all agitated again, you hear?

WILLIE: I hear, I hear. Stop bugging me.

NURSE: And don't get up to go to the bathroom. Use the you-know-what.

WILLIE: [*Without looking up from his* Variety] And if not, I'll do it you-know-where.

[*The* NURSE *exits*]

BEN: [*Pulling up a chair next to the bed*] Never mind, she's a very good nurse.

WILLIE: [*Looks in the paper*] Oh, boy, Bernie Eisenstein died.

BEN: Who?

WILLIE: Bernie Eisenstein. Remember the dance team "Ramona and Rodriguez"? Bernie Eisenstein was Rodriguez . . . He would have been seventy-eight in August.

BEN: [*Sighs*] Uncle Willie, could you put down V*ariety* for a second?

WILLIE: [*Still reading*] Did you bring a cigar?

BEN: Uncle Willie, you realize you've had a heart attack, don't you? . . . You've been getting away with it for years—the cigars, the corned beef sandwiches, the tension, the temper tantrums. You can't do it any more, Willie. Your heart's just not going to take it.

WILLIE: This is the good news you rushed up with? For this we could have skipped a Wednesday.

BEN: [*A pause*] I talked to the doctor this morning . . . and I'm going to have to be very frank and honest with you, Willie . . . You've got to retire. I mean give it up. Show business is out.

WILLIE: Until when?

BEN: Until *ever!* Your blood pressure is abnormally high, your heart is weak—if you tried to work again you would kill yourself.

WILLIE: All right, let me think it over.

BEN: *Think what over?* There's nothing to think over. You can't work any more, there's no decision to be made. Can't you understand that?

WILLIE: You decide for Ben Silverman, I'll decide for Willie Clark.

BEN: No, *I'll* decide for Willie Clark. I am your closest and *only* living relative, and I am responsible for your welfare . . . You can't live here any more, Willie. Not alone . . . And I can't afford to keep this nurse on permanently. Right now she's making more than I am. Anyway she already gave me her notice. She's leaving Monday. She's going to Buffalo to work for a very wealthy family.

WILLIE: Maybe she'll take me. I always did well in Buffalo.

BEN: Come on, Willie, face the facts. We have to do something, and we have to do it quickly.

WILLIE: I can't think about it today. I'm tired, I'm going to take a nap.

[*He closes his eyes and drops his head to the side on the pillow*]

BEN: You want to hear my suggestion?

WILLIE: I'm napping. Don't you see my eyes closed?

BEN: I'd like you to move in with me and Helen and the kids. We have the small spare room in the back, I think you would be very comfortable . . . Uncle Willie, did you hear what I said?

WILLIE: What's the second suggestion?

BEN: What's the matter with the first?

WILLIE: It's not as good as the second.

BEN: I haven't made any yet.

WILLIE: It's still better than the first. Forget it.

BEN: Why?

WILLIE: I don't like your kids. They're noisy. The little one hit me in the head with a baseball bat.

BEN: And I've also seen you talk to them for hours on end about vaudeville and had the time of your life. Right?

WILLIE: If I stopped talking, they would hit me with the bat. No offense, but I'm not living with your children. If you get rid of them, then we'll talk . . .

BEN: I know the reason you won't come. Because Al Lewis lives with his family, and you're just trying to prove some stupid point about being independent.

WILLIE: What's the second suggestion?

BEN: [*A long sigh*] All right . . . Now, don't jump when I say this, because it's not as bad as it sounds.

WILLIE: Say it.

BEN: There's the Actors' Home in New Brunswick—

WILLIE: It's as bad as it sounds.

BEN: You're wrong. I drove out there last Sunday and they showed me around the whole place. I couldn't believe how beautiful it was.

WILLIE: You went out there? You didn't have the decency to wait until I turned down living with you first?

BEN: I just went out to investigate, that's all. No commitments.

WILLIE: The Old Actors' Home: the first booking you got me in ten years.

BEN: It's on a lake, it's got twenty-five acres of beautiful grounds, it's an old converted mansion with a big porch . . .

WILLIE: I knew it. You got me on a porch in New Jersey. He put you up to this, didn't he?

BEN: You don't have to sit on the porch. There's a million activities there. They put on shows every Friday and Saturday night. I mean, it's all old actors—what could be better for you?

WILLIE: Why New Jersey? I hate New Jersey . . . I'm sorry they ever finished the George Washington Bridge.

BEN: I couldn't get over how many old actors were there that I knew and remembered. I thought they were all dead.

WILLIE: Some recommendation. A house in the swamps with forgotten people.

BEN: They're not forgotten. They're well taken care of . . . Uncle Willie, I promise you, if you spend one day there that you're not happy, you can come back and move in with me.

WILLIE: That's my choice—New Jersey or the baseball bat.

BEN: All right, I feel a lot better about everything.

WILLIE: And what about you?

BEN: What do you mean what about me?

WILLIE: [A *pause; looks away*] I won't see you no more?

BEN: Certainly you'll see me. As often as I can . . . Did you think I wouldn't come to visit you, Uncle Willie?

WILLIE: Well, you know . . . People don't go out to New Jersey unless they have to.

BEN: Uncle Willie, I'll be there every week. *With* the *Variety*. I'll even bring Helen and the kids.

WILLIE: *Don't bring the kids!* Why do you think I'm going to the home for?

BEN: You know, this is the first moment since I've known you, that you've treated me like a nephew and not an agent. It's like a whole new relationship.

WILLIE: I hope this one works out better than the other one.

BEN: I've been waiting for this for fifteen years. You just wouldn't ever let me get close, Uncle Willie.

WILLIE: If you kiss me, I call off the whole thing.

BEN: No kiss, I promise . . . Now there's just one other thing I'd like you to do for me.

WILLIE: With my luck it's a benefit.

BEN: In a way it is a benefit. But not for any organization. It's for another human being.

WILLIE: What are you talking about?

BEN: Al Lewis wants to come and see you.

WILLIE: If you wanted to kill me, why didn't you bring the cigars?

BEN: He's been heartsick ever since this happened.

WILLIE: What do you think I've been? What is this, the mumps?

BEN: You know what I mean . . . He calls me twice a day to see how you are. He's worried to death.

WILLIE: Tonight tell him I'm worse.

BEN: He's not well himself, Willie. He's got diabetes, hardening of the arteries, his eyes are getting very bad . . .

WILLIE: He sees good enough to spit in my face.

BEN: He's lost seven pounds since you were in the hospital. Who do you think's been sending all the candy and flowers every day? He keeps signing other people's names because he knows otherwise you'd throw them out.

WILLIE: They're *his* flowers? Throw 'em out!

BEN: Uncle Willie, I've never asked you to do a personal favor for me as long as I've known you. But this is important—for me, and for you, for Al Lewis. He won't even stay. He just wants to come up and say hello . . .

WILLIE: Hello, heh?

BEN: That's all.

WILLIE: And if he pokes me in the chest with the finger, I'm a dead man. That's murder, you know.

BEN: Come on, Willie. Give us all a break.

WILLIE: Well, if he wants to come up, I won't stop him. But I can't promise a "hello." I may be taking a nap.

BEN: [*Starts toward the phone*] I knew I could count on you, Willie. He's going to be very happy.

   [*He picks up the phone*]

WILLIE: You don't have to call him from here. Why should I pay sixty cents for him to come say hello?

BEN: [*He dials "O"*] It's not going to cost you sixty cents. [*To the operator*] Hello. Would you tell the boy at the desk to send Mr. Lewis up to Mr. Clark's room, please? Thank you.

   [*He hangs up*]

WILLIE: [*As near to shouting as he can get*] You mean he's here now in the hotel?

BEN: He's been with me all morning. I knew it would be all right.

WILLIE: First you commit me to the Old Man's Home, bring that bastard here and *then* you ask me?

BEN: [*All smiles*] I'm sorry. I apologize. Never speak to me again . . . But just promise you'll be decent to Al Lewis.

WILLIE: I'll be wonderful to him. In my will, I'll leave him *you!*

[*He starts to get out of bed*]

BEN: What are you doing? You're not supposed to be out of bed.

WILLIE: You think I'm going to give him the satisfaction of seeing me laying in bed like a sick person? I'm gonna sit in my chair and I'm gonna look healthier than he does.

[*He tries weakly to get on his slippers*]

BEN: The doctor said you're not to get out of bed for *anything.*

WILLIE: Lewis coming to apologize to Clark is not anything. To me, this is worth another heart attack. Get my coat from the closet.

BEN: [*Starting for the closet*] All right, but just walk slowly, will you, please?

[*He opens the closet*]

WILLIE: And then I want you to move my chair all the way back. I want that son-of-a-bitch to have a long walk.

BEN: [*Takes out a bathrobe from the closet*] Here, put this on.

WILLIE: Not the bathrobe, the jacket. The blue sports jacket. This is gonna be a *formal* apology.

BEN: [*Puts back the bathrobe and takes out the blue sports jacket*] He's not coming to apologize. He's just coming to say hello.

WILLIE: If he doesn't apologize, I'll drop dead in the chair for spite. And you can tell him that.

[BEN *helps him into the blue sports jacket over the pajamas*]

BEN: Now I'm sorry I started in with this.

WILLIE: That's funny. Because now I'm starting to feel good. [*Buttons the jacket*] Push the chair back. All the way.

[BEN *picks up the chair and carries it to the far side of the room*]

BEN: I thought I was bringing you two together.

WILLIE: [*He shuffles over to the chair.* BEN *helps him to sit*] Put a pillow underneath. Make it two pillows. When I sit, I wanna look down on him.

[BEN *puts a pillow under* WILLIE]

BEN: This is the last time. I'm never going to butt into your lives again.

WILLIE: The only thing that could have made today better is if it was raining. I would love to see him apologize dripping wet. [*And then come three knocks on the door: "Knock, knock, knock"*] Aha! This is it! . . . *This* was worth getting sick for! Come on, knock again. [*Points his finger in the air, his crowning moment.* AL *knocks again*] En-terrr!

[BEN *crosses to the door and opens it.* AL LEWIS *timidly steps in, with his hat in his hand.* WILLIE *immediately drops his head to his side, closes his eyes and snores, feigning a nap*]

AL: [*Whispers*] Oh, he's sleeping. I could come back later.

BEN: [*Also whispers*] No, that's all right. He must be dozing. Come on in. [AL *steps in and* BEN *closes the door*] Can I take your hat?

AL: No, I'd like to hold on to something, if you don't mind.

[BEN *crosses over to* WILLIE, *who is still dozing. He bends over and speaks softly in* WILLIE's *ear*]

BEN: Uncle Willie. There's someone here to see you.

WILLIE: [*Opens his eyes, stirs*] Heh? What?

BEN: Look who's here to see you, Uncle Willie.

WILLIE: [*Squints*] I don't have my glasses. Who's that?

AL: It's me, Willie. Al . . . Al Lewis.

WILLIE: [*Squints harder*] Al Lewis? You're so far away . . . Walk all the way over here. [AL *sheepishly makes the trek across the room with hat in hand. He squints again*] Oh, *that* Al Lewis.

AL: I don't want to disturb you, Willie. I know you're resting.

WILLIE: That's all right. I was just reading my telegrams from Lucille Ball and Bob Hope.

AL: Oh, that's nice . . . [*Turns, looks at the vase*] Oh, look at the beautiful flowers.

WILLIE: I'm throwing them out. I don't like the smell. People send them to me every day with boxes of cheap candy. They mean well.

AL: [*Nods*] They certainly do . . . Well, I just came up to see how you're doing. I don't want to take up your time. I just wanted to say hello . . . So "hello"—and goodbye.

[*He starts to put on his hat to go*]

WILLIE: Wait a minute. You got a few minutes before my next nap. Sit down and talk for a while.

AL: You're sure it's okay?

WILLIE: I'm sure you got a lot more to say than just "hello" . . . Would you like some tea?

AL: I would love some.

WILLIE: Go in the kitchen and make it.

BEN: I've got a better idea. I'll go down and have the kitchen send up a tray. If I call room service it'll take forever.

[*He starts for the door*]

WILLIE: [*To* BEN] You're going? You don't want to hear what Al has to say?

BEN: I don't think it's necessary. I'll be back in ten minutes. [*At the door*] It's good to see you, Mr. Lewis . . . It's good to see the *both* of you.

[*He nods, then exits, closing the door. There is an awkward silence between the two men for a moment*]

AL: [*Finally*] He's a nice boy.

WILLIE: He's the best . . . Not too bright, but a good boy.

AL: [*Nods*] You've got everything you need here?

WILLIE: What could I need here?

AL: Some books? Some magazines?

WILLIE: No, I got plenty to do. I got all my fan mail to answer.

AL: You get fan mail?

WILLIE: Don't you?

AL: I don't even get jury duty.

WILLIE: Sure, plenty of people still remember . . . [*He coughs*] Excuse me.

AL: You're sure it's all right for you to talk like this?

WILLIE: I'm not talking. I'm just answering. *You're* talking. [*There is a long pause*] Why? Is there something special you wanted to talk about?

AL: Like what?

WILLIE: What do I know like what? How should I know what's on your mind? Do I know why you can't sleep at night?

AL: Who said I don't sleep at night! I sleep beautifully.

WILLIE: Funny, to me you look tired. A little troubled. Like a person who had something on his conscience, what do I know?

AL: I have nothing on my conscience.

WILLIE: [*A pause*] Are you sure you looked good?

AL: I have *nothing* on my conscience. The only thing I feel badly about is that you got sick.

WILLIE: Thank you. *I accept your apology!*

AL: What apology? Who apologized? I just said I'm sorry you got sick.

WILLIE: Who do you think *made* me sick?

AL: Who? *You* did, that's who! Not me. You yelled and screamed and carried on like a lunatic until you made yourself sick . . . and for that I'm sorry.

WILLIE: All right, as long as you're sorry for something.

AL: I'm also sorry that people are starving in India, but I'm not going to apologize. I didn't do it.

WILLIE: I didn't accuse you of India. I'm just saying you're responsible for making me sick, and since you've come up here to apologize, I am gentleman enough to accept it.

AL: Don't be such a gentleman, because there's nothing to accept.

WILLIE: You're the one who came up here with your hat in your hand not me.

AL: It's a twenty-five-dollar hat, what was I gonna do, fold it up in my pocket?

WILLIE: If you didn't come to apologize, why did you send me the candy and flowers?

AL: I sent you candy and flowers?

WILLIE: Yes. Because it was on your conscience and *that's* why you couldn't sleep at night and *that's* why you came up here with your hat in your hand to apologize, only *this* time I'm not a gentleman any more and I *don't accept the apology!* How do you like that?

[AL *stares at* WILLIE]

AL: I knew there was gonna be trouble when you said "Enter" instead of "Come in."

WILLIE: There's no trouble. The trouble is over. I got what I want and now I'm happy.

AL: What did you get? You got "no apology" from me, which you didn't accept.

WILLIE: I don't want to discuss it any more, I just had a heart attack.

[AL *stares at* WILLIE *silently*]

AL: [*Calmly*] You know something, Willie. I don't think we get along too good.

WILLIE: Well, listen, everybody has their ups and downs.

AL: In forty-three years, we had maybe one "up" . . . To tell the truth, I can't take the "downs" any more.

WILLIE: To be honest with you, for the first time I feel a little tired myself. In a way this heart attack was good for me. I needed the rest.

AL: So what are you going to do now?

WILLIE: Well, my nephew made me two very good offers today.

AL: Is that right?

WILLIE: I think I'm gonna take the second one.

AL: Are you in any condition to work again?

WILLIE: Well, it wouldn't be too strenuous . . . Mostly take it easy, maybe do a show on Saturday night, something like that.

AL: Is that so? Where, in New York?

WILLIE: No, no. Out of town . . .

AL: Isn't that wonderful.

WILLIE: Well, you know me, I gotta keep busy . . . What's with you?

AL: Oh, I'm very happy. My daughter's having another baby. They're gonna need my room, and I don't want to be a burden on them. . . . So we talked it over, and I decided I'm gonna move to the Actors' Home in New Brunswick.

WILLIE: [*He sinks back onto his pillow, his head falls over to one side, and he sighs deeply*] Ohh, God! I got the finger again.

AL: What's the matter? You all right? Why are you holding your chest? You got pains?

WILLIE: Not yet. But I'm expecting.

AL: [*Nervously*] Can I get you anything? Should I call the doctor?

WILLIE: It wouldn't help.

AL: It wouldn't hurt.

[*The realization that they slipped accidentally into an old vaudeville joke causes* WILLIE *to smile*]

WILLIE: "It wouldn't hurt" . . . How many times have we done that joke?

AL: It always worked . . . Even from you I just got a laugh.

WILLIE: You're a funny man, Al . . . You're a pain in the ass, but you're a funny man.

AL: You know what your trouble was, Willie? You always took the jokes too seriously. They were just jokes. We did comedy on the stage for forty-three years, I don't think you enjoyed it once.

WILLIE: If I was there to enjoy it, I would buy a ticket.

AL: Well, maybe now you can start enjoying it . . . If you're not too busy, maybe you'll come over one day to the Actors' Home and visit me.

WILLIE: You can count on it.

AL: I feel a lot better now that I've talked to you . . . Maybe you'd like to rest now, take a nap.

WILLIE: I think so . . . Keep talking to me, I'll fall asleep.

AL: [*Looks around*] What's new in *Variety?*

WILLIE: Bernie Eisenstein died.

AL: Go on. Bernie Eisenstein? The house doctor at the Palace?

WILLIE: That was Sam Hesseltine. Bernie Eisenstein was "Ramona and Rodriguez."

AL: Jackie Aaronson was Ramona and Rodriguez. Bernie Eisenstein was the house doctor at the Palace. Sam Hesseltine was Sophie Tucker's agent.

WILLIE: Don't argue with me, I'm sick.

AL: I know. But why should I get sick too? [*The curtain starts to fall.* WILLIE *moans*] Bernie Eisenstein was the house doctor when we played for the first time with Sophie Tucker, and that's when we met Sam Hesseltine . . . Jackie Aaronson wasn't Rodriguez yet . . . He was "DeMarco and Lopez" . . . Lopez died, and DeMarco went into real estate, so Jackie became Rodriguez . . .

CURTAIN

CURTAIN CALL

AL: Don't you remember Big John McCafferey? The Irishman? He owned the Biltmore Theater in Pittsburgh? And the Adams Theater in Syracuse? Always wore a two-pound diamond ring on his finger? He was the one who used to take out Mary Donatto, the cute little Italian girl from the *Follies*. Well, she used to go with Abe Berkowitz who was then the booker for the Orpheum circuit and Big John hated his guts because of the time when Harry Richman . . .

STREAMERS
David Rabe

David Rabe

With *Streamers*, David Rabe brought to a conclusion his Vietnam trilogy which began with *The Basic Training of Pavlo Hummel* and continued with *Sticks and Bones*—a powerful assemblage of works that dramatically ignited the stage of the seventies.

Although *Streamers* is set in a 1965 Virginia army barracks, and designated as part of the Vietnam trilogy, it isn't, in essence, a play about war. Rather, it is an attempt to delineate the American way of violence: the inhabitants of the barracks room where the action transpires have not seen combat yet, their individual stresses are of a personal nature, and the barracks, in effect, represents a social microcosm.

Initially presented at the Long Wharf Theatre in New Haven, Connecticut, the play opened at the Mitzi E. Newhouse Theatre, Lincoln Center, New York City, on April 21, 1976.

Clive Barnes reported in the New York *Times:* "In some ways, *Streamers* is the best play of the trilogy. It has a dramatic power and, more significant, a dramatic idea that is absolutely a knockout. What is violence? What is the concatenation of violence—what is the domino effect? No, not in Southeast Asia, but in the ordinary, deadly practices of everyday life? What are the promptings of seemingly illogical murder—the moment when mind and hands become derailed and irrational? *Streamers* is a shocking, provocative play that emerges with something of a touch of the poet."

Named the year's best American play by the New York Drama Critics' Circle, *Streamers* ran for 478 performances, making it the longest-running serious drama ever performed at Lincoln Center.

David Rabe's emergence into the front ranks of young American playwrights began in 1971 when the New York Shakespeare Festival (Joseph Papp, producer) presented the first play of his Vietnam trilogy, *The Basic Training of Pavlo Hummel*. It brought him a Drama Desk Award for "most promising playwright," an "Obie" for Off-Broadway excellence, as well as the Elizabeth Hull-Kate Warriner

Award voted by the Dramatists Guild Council as the season's best play on a controversial subject.

While *Pavlo Hummel* was still attracting capacity audiences, *Sticks and Bones* opened on November 7, 1971, at another theatre in the Off-Broadway Shakespeare Festival complex. Lauded by most of the press, the production later transferred to Broadway and, at season's end, received the Antoinette Perry (Tony) Award for best play.

David Rabe was born on March 10, 1940, in Dubuque, Iowa. He was educated at Loras Academy and Loras College, both in Dubuque, and served in the U. S. Army for two years, the final eleven months in Vietnam.

Mr. Rabe studied writing at Villanova University where he wrote the first drafts of *The Basic Training of Pavlo Hummel* and *Sticks and Bones*.

In his introduction to the first publication of both plays, the author admitted: "When I returned from Vietnam, I was home for six months before I thought seriously of writing (finally there was nothing else to do with the things I was thinking). But oddly enough, it was a novel rather than a play that I wanted to work on. I had written both plays and novels earlier in my life and my writing came from something in me not dedicated to any one form. And upon return, theatre seemed lightweight, all fluff and metaphor, spangle, posture, and glitter crammed into a form as rigid as any machine geared to reproduce the shape of itself endlessly. In the way that all machines are unnatural in a natural universe, theatrical form seemed artificial beyond what was necessary.

"But then I chanced upon a grant of money, a Rockefeller grant in playwriting, enough to live on for a year and a half. I remember thinking, 'I'll dash off some plays real quick, then focus in on the novel.'

"But when I sat down to write, regardless of the form, I found it impossible to avoid the things most crowding my mind, and because these memories and ideas were of such extreme value to me, I could deal with them with nothing less than my best effort.

"What I am trying to say is simply that if things had turned out differently, I don't know if I would have written what I have in the way I have, but the grant was a playwriting grant."

After Villanova, Mr. Rabe joined the staff of the New Haven

Register, where he won an Associated Press Award for feature writing. Other honors that have been bestowed upon the writer are a New York Drama Critics' Circle Citation and an Outer Circle Award, both for *Sticks and Bones,* a Drama Desk Award for *Streamers,* and an award from the National Institute of Arts and Letters.

Streamers was produced at the Long Wharf Theatre, New Haven, Connecticut, on January 30, 1976, under the direction of Mike Nichols, with the following cast:

MARTIN	*Michael-Raymond O'Keefe*
RICHIE	*Peter Evans*
CARLYLE	*Joe Fields*
BILLY	*John Heard*
ROGER	*Herbert Jefferson, Jr.*
COKES	*Dolph Sweet*
ROONEY	*Kenneth McMillan*
M.P. LIEUTENANT	*Stephen Mendillo*
PFC HINSON (M.P.)	*Ron Siebert*
PFC CLARK (M.P.)	*Michael Kell*

Produced by Arvin Brown
Setting by Tony Walton
Costumes by Bill Walker
Lighting by Ronald Wallace

Streamers was produced in New York by Joseph Papp on April 21, 1976, at the Mitzi E. Newhouse Theatre, Lincoln Center, New York City, under the direction of Mike Nichols, with the following cast:

MARTIN	*Michael Kell*
RICHIE	*Peter Evans*
CARLYLE	*Dorian Harewood*
BILLY	*Paul Rudd*
ROGER	*Terry Alexander*
COKES	*Dolph Sweet*
ROONEY	*Kenneth McMillan*
M.P. LIEUTENANT	*Arlen Dean Snyder*
PFC HINSON (M.P.)	*Les Roberts*
PFC CLARK (M.P.)	*Mark Metcalf*
FOURTH M.P.	*Miklos Horvath*

Associate Producer: Bernard Gersten
Setting by Tony Walton
Costumes by Bill Walker
Lighting by Ronald Wallace

TIME: *1965.*

PLACE: *An Army Barracks in Virginia.*

ACT ONE

The set is a large cadre room thrusting angularly toward the audience. The floor is wooden and brown. Brightly waxed in places, it is worn and dull in other sections. The back wall is brown and angled. There are two lights at the center of the ceiling. They hang covered by green metal shades. Against the back wall and to the stage right side are three wall lockers, side by side. Stage center in the back wall is the door, the only entrance to the room. It opens onto a hallway that runs off to the latrines, showers, other cadre rooms and larger barracks rooms. There are three bunks. BILLY's bunk is parallel to ROGER's bunk. They are upstage and on either side of the room, and face downstage. RICHIE's bunk is downstage and at a right angle to BILLY's bunk. At the foot of each bunk is a green wooden footlocker. There is a floor outlet near ROGER's bunk. He uses it for his radio. A reading lamp is clamped on to the metal piping at the head of RICHIE's bunk. A wooden chair stands beside the wall lockers. Two mops hang in the stage left corner near a trash can.

It is dusk as the lights rise on the room. RICHIE is seated and bowed forward wearily on his bunk. He wears his long-sleeved khaki summer dress uniform. Upstage behind him is MARTIN, a thin, dark young man, pacing, worried. A white towel stained red with blood is wrapped around his wrist. He paces several steps and falters, stops. He stands there.

RICHIE: Honest to God, Martin, I don't know what to say anymore. I don't know what to tell you.

MARTIN: [*Beginning to pace again*] I mean it. I just can't stand it. Look at me.

RICHIE: I know.

MARTIN: I hate it.

RICHIE: We've got to make up a story. They'll ask you a hundred questions.

MARTIN: Do you know how I hate it?

RICHIE: Everybody does. Don't you think I hate it too?

MARTIN: I enlisted, though. I enlisted and I hate it.

RICHIE: I enlisted too.

MARTIN: I vomit every morning. I get the dry heaves. In the middle of every night.

[*He flops down on the corner of* BILLY's *bed and sits there, slumped forward, shaking his head*]

RICHIE: You can stop that. You can.

MARTIN: No.

RICHIE: You're just scared. It's just fear.

MARTIN: They're all so mean; they're all so awful. I've got two years to go. Just thinking about it is going to make me sick. I thought it would be different from the way it is.

RICHIE: But you could have died, for God's sake.

[RICHIE *has turned now; he is facing* MARTIN]

MARTIN: I just wanted out.

RICHIE: I might not have found you, though. I might not have come up here.

MARTIN: I don't care. I'd be out.

[*The door opens and a black man in filthy fatigues—they are grease-stained and dark with sweat—stands there. He is* CARLYLE, *looking about.* RICHIE, *seeing him, rises and moves toward him*]

RICHIE: No. Roger isn't here right now.

CARLYLE: Who isn't?

RICHIE: He isn't here.

CARLYLE: They tole me a black boy livin' in here. I don't see him.

[*He looks suspiciously about the room*]

RICHIE: That's what I'm saying. He isn't here. He'll be back later. You can come back later. His name is Roger.

MARTIN: I slit my wrist. [*Thrusting out the bloody, towel-wrapped wrist toward* CARLYLE]

RICHIE: Martin! Jesus!

MARTIN: I did.

RICHIE: He's kidding. He's kidding.

CARLYLE: What was his name? Martin? [CARLYLE *is confused and the confusion has made him angry. He moves toward* MARTIN] You Martin?

MARTIN: Yes.

[*As* BILLY, *a white in his mid-twenties, blond and trim, appears in the door, whistling, carrying a slice of pie on a paper napkin. Sensing something, he falters, looks at* CARLYLE, *then* RICHIE]

BILLY: Hey, what's goin' on?

CARLYLE: [*Turning, leaving*] Nothin', man. Not a thing.

[BILLY *looks questioningly at* RICHIE. *Then, after placing the piece of pie on the chair beside the door, he crosses to his footlocker*]

RICHIE: He came in looking for Roger, but he didn't even know his name.

BILLY: [*Sitting on his footlocker, he starts taking off his shoes*] How come you weren't at dinner, Rich? I brought you a piece of pie. Hey, Martin.

[MARTIN *thrusts out his towel-wrapped wrist*]

MARTIN: I cut my wrist, Billy.

RICHIE: Oh, for God's sake, Martin!

[*He whirls away*]

BILLY: Huh?

MARTIN: I did.

RICHIE: You are disgusting, Martin.

MARTIN: No. It's the truth. I did. I am not disgusting.

RICHIE: Well, maybe it isn't disgusting, but it certainly is disappointing.

BILLY: What are you guys talking about?

[*Sitting there, he really doesn't know what is going on*]

MARTIN: I cut my wrists, I slashed them, and Richie is pretending I didn't.

RICHIE: I am not. And you only cut one wrist and you didn't slash it.

MARTIN: I can't stand the army anymore, Billy.

[*He is moving now to petition* BILLY, *and* RICHIE *steps between them*]

RICHIE: Billy, listen to me. This is between Martin and me.

MARTIN: It's between me and the army, Richie.

RICHIE: [*Taking* MARTIN *by the shoulders as* BILLY *is now trying to get near* MARTIN] Let's just go outside and talk, Martin. You don't know what you're saying.

BILLY: Can I see? I mean, did he really do it?

RICHIE: No!

MARTIN: I did.

BILLY: That's awful. Jesus! Maybe you should go to the infirmary.

RICHIE: I washed it with peroxide. It's not deep. Just let us be. Please. He just needs to straighten out his thinking a little, that's all.

BILLY: Well, maybe I could help him?

MARTIN: Maybe he could.

RICHIE: [*Suddenly pushing at* MARTIN. RICHIE *is angry and exasperated. He wants* MARTIN *out of the room*] Get out of here, Martin! Billy, you do some push-ups or something.

[*Having been pushed toward the door,* MARTIN *wanders out*]

BILLY: No.

RICHIE: I know what Martin needs.

[RICHIE *whirls and rushes into the hall after* MARTIN, *leaving* BILLY *scrambling to get his shoes on*]

BILLY: You're no doctor, are you? I just want to make sure he doesn't have to go to the infirmary, then I'll leave you alone. [*One shoe on, he grabs up the second and runs out the door into the hall after them*] Martin! Martin, wait up!

[*Silence. The door has been left open. Fifteen or twenty seconds pass. Then someone is heard coming down the hall. He is singing "Get a Job" and trying to do the voices and harmonies of a vocal group.* ROGER, *a tall, well-built black in long-sleeved khakis, comes in the door. He has a laundry bag over his shoulder, a pair of clean civilian trousers and a shirt on a hanger in his other hand. After dropping the bag on his bed, he goes to his wall locker, where he carefully hangs up the civilian clothes. Returning to the bed, he picks up the laundry and then, as if struck, he throws the bag down on the bed, tears off his tie and sits down angrily on the bed. For a moment, with his head in his hands, he sits there. Then, resolutely, he rises, takes up the position of attention, and simply topples forward, his hands leaping out to break his fall at the last instant and put him into the push-up position. Counting in a hissing, whispering voice, he does ten push-ups before giving up and flopping onto his belly. He simply doesn't have the will to do any more. Lying there, he counts rapidly on*]

ROGER: Fourteen, fifteen. Twenty. Twenty-five.

[BILLY, *shuffling dejectedly back in, sees* ROGER *lying there.* ROGER *springs to his feet, heads toward his footlocker, out of which he takes an ashtray and a pack of cigarettes*]

You come in this area, you come in here marchin', boy: standin' tall.

[BILLY, *having gone to his wall locker, is tossing a* Playboy *magazine onto his bunk. He will also remove a towel, a Dopp kit and a can of foot powder*]

BILLY: I was marchin'.

ROGER: You call that marchin'?

BILLY: I was as tall as I am; I was marchin'—what do you want?

ROGER: Outa here, man; outa this goddamn typin'-terrors outfit and into some kinda real army. Or else out and free.

BILLY: So go; who's stoppin' you; get out. Go on.

ROGER: Ain't you a bitch.

BILLY: You and me are more regular army than the goddamn sergeants around this place, you know that?

ROGER: I was you, Billy boy, I wouldn't be talkin' so sacrilegious so loud, or they be doin' you like they did the ole sarge.

BILLY: He'll get off.

ROGER: Sheee-it, he'll get off. [*Sitting down on the side of his bed and facing* BILLY, ROGER *lights up a cigarette.* BILLY *has arranged the towel, Dopp kit and foot powder on his own bed*] Don't you think L.B.J. want to have some sergeants in that Vietnam, man? In Disneyland, baby? Lord have mercy on the ole sarge. He goin' over there to be Mickey Mouse.

BILLY: Do him a lot of good. Make a man outa him.

ROGER: That's right, that's right. He said the same damn thing about himself and you too, I do believe. You know what's the ole boy's MOS? His Military Occupation Specialty? Demolitions, baby. Expert is his name.

BILLY: [*Taking off his shoes and beginning to work on a sore toe,* BILLY *hardly looks up*] You're kiddin' me.

ROGER: Do I jive?

BILLY: You mean that poor ole bastard who cannot light his own cigar for shakin' is supposed to go over there blowin' up bridges and shit? Do they wanna win this war or not, man?

ROGER: Ole sarge was over in Europe in the big one, Billy. Did all kinds a bad things.

BILLY: [*Swinging his feet up onto the bed,* BILLY *sits, cutting the cuticles on his toes, powdering his feet*] Was he drinkin' since he got the word?

ROGER: Was he breathin', Billy? Was he breathin'?

BILLY: Well, at least he ain't cuttin' his fuckin' wrists. [*Silence.* ROGER *looks at* BILLY, *who keeps on working*] Man, that's the real damn army over there, ain't it? That ain't shinin' your belt buckle and standin' tall. And we might end up in it, man. [*Silence.* ROGER, *rising, begins to sort his laundry*] Roger . . . you ever ask yourself if you'd rather fight in a war where it was freezin' cold or one where there was awful snakes? You ever ask that question?

ROGER: Can't say I ever did.

BILLY: We used to ask it all the time. All the time. I mean, us kids sittin' out on the back porch tellin' ghost stories at night. 'Cause it was Korea time and the newspapers were fulla pictures of soldiers in snow with white frozen beards; they got these rags tied around their feet. And snakes. We hated snakes. Hated 'em. I mean, it's bad enough to be in the jungle duckin' bullets, but then you crawl right into a goddamn snake. That's awful. That's awful.

ROGER: It don't sound none too good.

BILLY: I got my draft notice, goddamn Vietnam didn't even exist. I mean, it existed, but not as in a war we might be in. I started crawlin' around the floor a this house where I was stayin' 'cause I'd dropped outa school, and I was goin' "Bang, bang," pretendin'. Jesus!

ROGER: [*Continuing with his laundry, he tries to joke*] My first goddamn formation in basic, Billy, this NCO's up there jammin'
away about how some a us are goin' to be dyin' in the war. I'm
sayin', "What war? What that crazy man talkin' about?"

BILLY: Us too. I couldn't believe it. I couldn't believe it. And now
we got three people goin' from here.

ROGER: Five.

> [*They look at each other, and then turn away, each returning
> to his task*]

BILLY: It don't seem possible. I mean, people shootin' at you.
Shootin' at you to kill you. [*Slight pause*] It's somethin'.

ROGER: What did you decide you preferred?

BILLY: Huh?

ROGER: Did you decide you would prefer the snakes or would you
prefer the snow? 'Cause it look like it is goin' to be the snakes.

BILLY: I think I had pretty much made my mind up on the snow.

ROGER: Well, you just let 'em know that, Billy. Maybe they get
one goin' special just for you up in Alaska. You can go to the
Klondike. Fightin' some snowmen.

> [RICHIE *bounds into the room and shuts the door as if to keep
> out something dreadful. He looks at* ROGER *and* BILLY *and
> crosses to his wall locker, pulling off his tie as he moves. Toss-
> ing the tie into the locker, he begins unbuttoning the cuffs of
> his shirt*]

RICHIE: Hi, hi, hi, everybody. Billy, hello.

BILLY: Hey.

ROGER: What's happenin', Rich?

> [*Moving to the chair beside the door,* RICHIE *picks up the pie*
> BILLY *left there. He will place the pie atop the locker, and
> then, sitting, he will remove his shoes and socks*]

RICHIE: I simply did this rather wonderful thing for a friend of mine, helped him see himself in a clearer, more hopeful light—little room in his life for hope? And I feel very good. Didn't Billy tell you?

ROGER: About what?

RICHIE: About Martin.

ROGER: No.

BILLY: [*Looking up and speaking pointedly*] No.

[RICHIE *looks at* BILLY *and then at* ROGER. RICHIE *is truly confused*]

RICHIE: No? No?

BILLY: What do I wanna gossip about Martin for?

RICHIE: [*He really can't figure out what is going on with* BILLY. *Shoes and socks in hand, he heads for his wall locker*] Who was planning to gossip? I mean, it did happen. We could talk about it. I mean, I wasn't hearing his goddamn confession. Oh, my sister told me Catholics were boring.

BILLY: Good thing I ain't one anymore.

RICHIE: [*Taking off his shirt, he moves toward* ROGER] It really wasn't anything, Roger, except Martin made this rather desperate, pathetic gesture for attention that seems to have brought to the surface Billy's more humane and protective side. [*Reaching out, he tousles* BILLY's *hair*]

BILLY: Man, I am gonna have to obliterate you.

RICHIE: [*Tossing his shirt into his locker*] I don't know what you're so embarrassed about.

BILLY: I just think Martin's got enough trouble without me yappin' to everybody.

[RICHIE *has moved nearer* BILLY, *his manner playful and teasing*]

RICHIE: "Obliterate"? "Obliterate," did you say? Oh, Billy, you better say "shit," "ain't" and "motherfucker" real quick now or we'll all know just how far beyond the fourth grade you went.

ROGER: [*Having moved to his locker, into which he is placing his folded clothes*] You hear about the ole sarge, Richard?

BILLY: [*Grinning*] You ain't . . . shit . . . motherfucker.

ROGER: [*Laughing*] All right.

RICHIE: [*Moving center and beginning to remove his trousers*] Billy, no, no. Wit is my domain. You're in charge of sweat and running around the block.

ROGER: You hear about the ole sarge?

RICHIE: What about the ole sarge? Oh, who cares? Let's go to a movie. Billy, wanna? Let's go. C'mon. [*Trousers off, he hurries to his locker*]

BILLY: Sure. What's playin'?

RICHIE: I don't know. Can't remember. Something good, though.

[*With a* Playboy *magazine he has taken from his locker,* ROGER *is settling down on his bunk, his back toward both* BILLY *and* RICHIE]

BILLY: You wanna go, Rog?

RICHIE: [*In mock irritation*] Don't ask Roger! How are we going to kiss and hug and stuff if he's there?

BILLY: That ain't funny, man.

[*He is stretched out on his bunk, and* RICHIE *comes bounding over to flop down and lie beside him*]

RICHIE: And what time will you pick me up?

BILLY: [*He pushes at* RICHIE, *knocking him off the bed and onto the floor*] Well, you just fall down and wait, all right?

RICHIE: Can I help it if I love you?

[*Leaping to his feet, he will head to his locker, remove his shorts, put on a robe*]

ROGER: You gonna take a shower, Richard?

RICHIE: Cleanliness is nakedness, Roger.

ROGER: Is that right? I didn't know that. Not too many people know that. You may be the only person in the world who know that.

RICHIE: And godliness is in there somewhere, of course.

[*Putting a towel around his neck, he is gathering toiletries to carry to the shower*]

ROGER: You got your own way a lookin' at things, man. You cute.

RICHIE: That's right.

ROGER: You g'wan, have a good time in that shower.

RICHIE: Oh, I will.

BILLY: [*Without looking up from his feet, which he is powdering*] And don't drop your soap.

RICHIE: I will if I want to. [*Already out the door, he slams it shut with a flourish*]

BILLY: Can you imagine bein' in combat with Richie—people blastin' away at you—he'd probably want to hold your hand.

ROGER: Ain't he somethin'?

BILLY: Who's zat?

ROGER: He's all right.

BILLY: [*Rising, he heads toward his wall locker, where he will put the powder and Dopp kit*] Sure he is, except he's livin' under water.

[*Looking at* BILLY, ROGER *senses something unnerving; it makes* ROGER *rise, and return his magazine to his footlocker*]

ROGER: I think we oughta do this area, man. I think we oughta do our area. Mop and buff this floor.

BILLY: You really don't think he means that shit he talks, do you?

ROGER: Huh? Awwww, man . . . Billy, no.

BILLY: I'd put money on it, Roger, and I ain't got much money.

[BILLY *is trying to face* ROGER *with this, but* ROGER, *seated on his bed, has turned away. He is unbuttoning his shirt*]

ROGER: Man, no, no. I'm tellin' you, lad, you listen to the ole Rog. You seen that picture a that little dolly he's got in his locker? He ain't swish, man, believe me—he's cool.

BILLY: It's just that ever since we been in this room, he's been different somehow. Somethin'.

ROGER: No, he ain't.

[BILLY *turns to his bed, where he carefully starts folding the towel. Then he looks at* ROGER]

BILLY: You ever talk to any a these guys—queers, I mean? You ever sit down, just rap with one of 'em?

ROGER: Hell, no; what I wanna do that for? Shit, no.

BILLY: [*Crossing to the trash can in the corner, where he will shake the towel empty*] I mean, some of 'em are okay guys, just way up this bad alley, and you say to 'em, "I'm straight, be cool," they go their own way. But then there's these other ones, these bitches, man, and they're so crazy they think anybody can be had. Because they been had themselves. So you tell 'em you're straight and they just nod and smile. You ain't real to 'em. They can't see nothin' but themselves and these goddamn games they're always playin'. [*Having returned to his bunk, he is putting on his shoes*] I mean, you can be decent about anything, Roger, you see what I'm sayin'? We're all just people, man, and some of us are hardly that. That's all I'm sayin'. [*There is a slight pause as he sits there thinking. Then he gets to his feet*] I'll go get some buckets and stuff so we can clean up, okay? This area's a mess. This area ain't standin' tall.

ROGER: That's good talk, lad; this area a midget you put it next to an area standin' tall.

BILLY: Got to be good fuckin' troopers.

ROGER: That's right, that's right. I know the meanin' of the words.

BILLY: I mean, I just think we all got to be honest with each other —you understand me?

ROGER: No, I don't understand you; one stupid fuckin' nigger like me—how's that gonna be?

BILLY: That's right; mock me, man. That's what I need. I'll go get the wax.

[*Out he goes, talking to himself and leaving the door open. For a moment* ROGER *sits, thinking, and then he looks at* RICHIE's *locker and gets to his feet and walks to the locker which he opens and looks at the pinup hanging on the inside of the door. He takes a step backward, looking*]

ROGER: Sheee-it!

[*Through the open door comes* CARLYLE. ROGER *doesn't see him. And* CARLYLE *stands there looking at* ROGER *and the picture in the locker*]

CARLYLE: Boy . . . whose locker you lookin' into?

ROGER: [*He is startled, but recovers*] Hey, baby, what's happenin'?

CARLYLE: That ain't your locker, is what I'm askin', nigger. I mean, you ain't got no white goddamn woman hangin' on your wall.

ROGER: Oh, no—no, no.

CARLYLE: You don't wanna be lyin' to me, 'cause I got to turn you in you lyin' and you do got the body a some white goddamn woman hangin' there for you to peek at nobody around but you— you can be thinkin' about that sweet wet pussy an' maybe it hot an' maybe it cool.

ROGER: I could be thinkin' all that, except I know the penalty for lyin'.

CARLYLE: Thank God for that.

[*Extending his hand, palm up*]

ROGER: That's right. This here the locker of a faggot.

[*And* ROGER *slaps* CARLYLE's *hand, palm to palm*]

CARLYLE: Course it is; I see that; any damn body know that.
[ROGER *crosses toward his bunk and* CARLYLE *swaggers about, pull-ing a pint of whiskey from his hip pocket*] You want a shot? Have
you a little taste, my man.

ROGER: Naw.

CARLYLE: C'mon. C'mon. I think you a Tom you don't drink outa
my bottle.

[*He thrusts the bottle toward* ROGER *and wipes a sweat-and-grease-stained sleeve across his mouth*]

ROGER: [*Taking the bottle*] Shit!

CARLYLE: That right. How do I know? I just got in. New boy in
town. Somewhere over there; I dunno. They dump me in amongst
a whole bunch a pale, boring motherfuckers. [CARLYLE *is exploring
the room. Finding* BILLY's *Playboy, he edges onto* BILLY's *bed and
leafs nervously through the pages*] I just come in from P Company, man, and I been all over this place, don't see too damn
many of us. This outfit look like it a little short on soul. I been
walkin' all around, I tell you, and the number is small. Like one
hand you can tabulate the lot of 'em. We got few brothers I been
able to see, is what I'm sayin'. You and me and two cats down in
the small bay. That's all I found. [*As* ROGER *is about to hand the
bottle back,* CARLYLE, *almost angrily, waves him off*] No, no, you
take another; take you a real taste.

ROGER: It ain't so bad here. We do all right.

CARLYLE: [*He moves, shutting the door. Suspiciously, he approaches* ROGER] How about the white guys? They give you any
sweat? What's the situation? No jive. I like to know what is goin'
on within the situation before that situation get a chance to be
closin' in on me.

ROGER: [*Putting the bottle on the footlocker, he sits down*] Man,
I'm tellin' you, it ain't bad. They're just pale, most of 'em, you
know. They can't help it; how they gonna help it? Some of 'em
got little bit a soul, couple real good boys around this way. Get
'em little bit of Coppertone, they be straight, man.

CARLYLE: How about the NCOs? We got any brother NCO watchin' out for us or they all white, like I goddamn well KNOW all the officers are? Fuckin' officers always white, man; fuckin' snow cones and bars everywhere you look.

[CARLYLE *cannot stay still. He moves to his right, his left; he sits, he stands*]

ROGER: First sergeant's a black man.

CARLYLE: All right; good news. Hey, hey, you wanna go over the club with me, or maybe downtown? I got wheels. Let's be free. [*Now he rushes at* ROGER] Let's be free.

ROGER: Naw . . .

CARLYLE: Ohhh, baby . . . !

[*He is wildly pulling at* ROGER *to get him to the door*]

ROGER: Some other time. I gotta get the area straight. Me and the guy sleeps in here too are gonna shape the place up a little.

[ROGER *has pulled free, and* CARLYLE *cannot understand. It hurts him, depresses him*]

CARLYLE: You got a sweet deal here an' you wanna keep it, that right? [*He paces about the room, opens a footlocker, looks inside*] How you rate you get a room like this for yourself—you and a couple guys?

ROGER: Spec 4. The three of us in here Spec 4.

CARLYLE: You get a room then, huh? [*And suddenly, without warning or transition, he is angry*] Oh, man, I hate this goddamn army. I hate this bastard army. I mean, I just got outa basic—off leave—you know? Back on the block for two weeks—and now here. They don't pull any a that petty shit, now, do they—that goddamn petty basic training bullshit? They do and I'm gonna be bustin' some head—my hand is gonna be upside all kinds a heads, 'cause I ain't gonna be able to endure it, man, not that kinda crap —understand? [*And again, he is rushing at* ROGER] Hey, hey, oh, c'mon, let's get my wheels and make it, man, do me the favor.

ROGER: How'm I gonna? I got my obligations.

[*And* CARLYLE *spins away in anger*]

CARLYLE: Jesus, baby, can't you remember the outside? How long it been since you been on leave? It is so sweet out there, nigger; you got it all forgot. I had such a sweet, sweet time. They doin' dances, baby, make you wanna cry. I hate this damn army. [*The anger overwhelms him*] All these mother-actin' jacks givin' you jive about what you gotta do and what you can't do. I had a bad scene in basic—up the hill and down the hill; it ain't somethin' I enjoyed even a little. So they do me wrong here, Jim, they gonna be sorry. Some-damn-body! And this whole Vietnam THING—I do not dig it. [*He falls on his knees before* ROGER. *It is a gesture that begins as a joke, a mockery. And then a real fear pulses through him to nearly fill the pose he has taken*] Lord, Lord, don't let 'em touch me. Christ, what will I do, they DO! Whooooooooooooo! And they pullin' guys outa here, too, ain't they? Pullin' 'em like weeds, man; throwin' 'em into the fire. It's shit, man!

ROGER: They got this ole sarge sleeps down the hall—just today they got him.

CARLYLE: Which ole sarge?

ROGER: He sleeps just down the hall. Little guy.

CARLYLE: Wino, right?

ROGER: Booze hound.

CARLYLE: Yeh; I seen him. They got him, huh?

ROGER: He's goin'; gotta be packin' his bags. And three other guys two days ago. And two guys last week.

CARLYLE: [*Leaping up from* BILLY's *bed*] Ohhh, them bastards! And everybody just takes it. It ain't our war, brother. I'm tellin' you. That's what gets me, nigger. It ain't our war nohow because it ain't our country, and that's what burns my ass—that and everybody just sittin' and takin' it. They gonna be bustin' balls, man—kickin' and stompin'. Everybody here maybe one week from shippin' out to get blown clean away and, man, whata they doin'? They doin' what they told. That what they doin'. Like you? Shit! You gonna straighten up your goddamn area! Well, that ain't for

me; I'm gettin' hat, and makin' it out where it's sweet and the
people's livin'. I can't cut this jive here, man. I'm tellin' you. I
can't cut it! [*He has moved toward* ROGER, *and behind him now*
RICHIE *enters, running, his hair wet, traces of shaving cream on his
face. Toweling his hair, he falters, seeing* CARLYLE. *Then he
crosses to his locker.* CARLYLE *grins at* ROGER, *looks at* RICHIE, *steps
toward him and gives a little bow*] My name is Carlyle; what is
yours?

RICHIE: Richie.

CARLYLE: [*He turns toward* ROGER *to share his joke*] Hello. Where
is Martin? That cute little Martin. [*And* RICHIE *has taken off his
robe as* CARLYLE *turns back*] You cute too, Richie.

RICHIE: Martin doesn't live here.

[*Hurriedly putting on underpants to cover his nakedness*]

CARLYLE: [*Watching* RICHIE, *he slowly turns toward* ROGER] You
ain't gonna make it with me, man?

ROGER: Naw . . . like I tole you. I'll catch you later.

CARLYLE: That's sad, man; make me cry in my heart.

ROGER: You g'wan get your head smokin'. Stop on back.

CARLYLE: Okay, okay. Got to be one man one more time. [*On the
move for the door, his hand extended palm up behind him, de-
manding the appropriate response*] Baby! Gimme! Gimme!

[*Lunging,* ROGER *slaps the hand*]

ROGER: G'wan home! G'wan home.

CARLYLE: You gonna hear from me. [*And he is gone out the door
and down the hallway*]

ROGER: I can . . . and do . . . believe . . . that.

[RICHIE, *putting on his T-shirt, watches* ROGER, *who stubs out
his cigarette, then crosses to the trash can to empty the ashtray*]

RICHIE: Who was that?

ROGER: Man's new, Rich. Dunno his name more than that "Carlyle" he said. He's new—just outa basic.

RICHIE: [*Powdering his thighs and under his arms*] Oh, my God . . .

[*As* BILLY *enters, pushing a mop bucket with a wringer attached and carrying a container of wax*]

ROGER: Me and Billy's gonna straighten up the area. You wanna help?

RICHIE: Sure, sure; help, help.

BILLY: [*Talking to* ROGER, *but turning to look at* RICHIE, *who is still putting powder under his arms*] I hadda steal the wax from Third Platoon.

ROGER: Good man.

BILLY: [*Moving to* RICHIE, *joking, yet really irritated in some strange way*] What? Whata you doin', singin'? Look at that, Rog. He's got enough jazz there for an entire beauty parlor. [*Grabbing the can from* RICHIE's *hand*] What is this? Baby powder! *Baby powder!*

RICHIE: I get rashes.

BILLY: Okay, okay, you get rashes, so what? They got powder for rashes that isn't baby powder.

RICHIE: It doesn't work as good; I've tried it. Have you tried it?

[*Grabbing* BILLY's *waist,* RICHIE *pulls him close.* BILLY *knocks* RICHIE's *hands away*]

BILLY: Man, I wish you could get yourself straight. I'll mop too, Roger—okay? Then I'll put down the wax and you can spread it?

[*He has walked away from* RICHIE]

RICHIE: What about buffing?

ROGER: In the morning. [*He is already busy mopping up near the door*]

RICHIE: What do you want me to do?

BILLY: [*Grabbing up a mop, he heads downstage to work*] Get inside your locker and shut the door and don't holler for help. Nobody'll know you're there; you'll stay there.

RICHIE: But I'm so pretty.

BILLY: NOW! [*Pointing to* ROGER. *He wants to get this clear*] Tell that man you mean what you're sayin', Richie.

RICHIE: Mean what?

BILLY: That you really think you're pretty.

RICHIE: Of course I do; I am. Don't you think I am? Don't *you* think I am, Roger?

ROGER: I tole you—you fulla shit and you cute, man. Carlyle just tole you you cute too.

RICHIE: Don't you think it's true, Billy?

BILLY: It's like I tole you, Rog.

RICHIE: What did you tell him?

BILLY: That you go down; that you go up and down like a yo-yo and you go blowin' all the trees like the wind.

> [RICHIE *is stunned. He looks at* ROGER, *and then he turns and stares into his own locker. The others keep mopping.* RICHIE *takes out a towel, and putting it around his neck, he walks to where* BILLY *is working. He stands there, hurt, looking at* BILLY]

RICHIE: What the hell made you tell him I been down, Billy?

BILLY: [*Still mopping*] It's in your eyes; I seen it.

RICHIE: What?

BILLY: You.

RICHIE: What is it, Billy, you think you're trying to say? You and all your wit and intelligence—your *humanity*.

BILLY: I said it, Rich; I said what I was tryin' to say.

RITCHIE: *Did* you?

BILLY: I think I did.

RICHIE: *Do* you?

BILLY: Loud and clear, baby. [*Still mopping*]

ROGER: They got to put me in with the weirdos. Why is that, huh? How come the army *hate* me, do this shit to me—*know* what to do. [*Whimsical and then suddenly loud, angered, violent*] Now you guys put socks in your mouths, right now—get shut up—or I am gonna beat you to death with each other! Roger got work to do. To be doin' it!

RICHIE: [*Turning to his bed, he kneels upon it*] Roger, I think you're so innocent sometimes. Honestly, it's not such a terrible thing. Is it, Billy?

BILLY: How would I know? [*He slams his mop into the bucket*] Oh, go fuck yourself!

RICHIE: Well, I can give it a try, if that's what you want. Can I think of you as I do?

BILLY: [*Throwing down his mop*] GODDAMMIT! That's it! IT! [*He exits, rushing into the hall and slamming the door behind him.* ROGER *looks at* RICHIE. *Neither quite knows what is going on. Suddenly the door bursts open and* BILLY *storms straight over to* RICHIE, *who still kneels on the bed*] Now I am gonna level with you. Are you gonna listen? You gonna hear what I say, Rich, and not what you think I'm sayin'? [RICHIE *turns away as if to rise, his manner flippant, disdainful*] No! Don't get cute; don't turn away cute. I wanna say somethin' straight out to you and I want you to hear it!

RICHIE: I'm all ears, goddammit! For what, however, I do not know, except some boring evasion.

BILLY: At least wait the hell till you hear me!

RICHIE: [*In irritation*] Okay, okay! What?

BILLY: Now this is level, Rich; this is straight talk. [*He is quiet, intense. This is difficult for him. He seeks the exactly appropriate words of explanation*] No b.s. No tricks. What you do on the

side, that's your business and I don't care about it. But if you
don't cut the cute shit with me, I'm gonna turn you off. Completely. You ain't gonna get a good mornin' outa me, you understand, because it's gettin' bad around here. I mean, I know how
you think—how you keep lookin' out and seein' yourself, and
that's what I'm tryin' to tell you because that's all that's happenin', Rich. That's all there is to it when you look out at me and
think there's some kind of approval or whatever you see in my
eyes—you're just seein' yourself. And I'm talkin' the simple quiet
truth to you, Rich. I swear I am.

[BILLY *looks away from* RICHIE *now and tries to go back to
the mopping. It is embarrassing for them all.* ROGER *has
watched, has tried to keep working.* RICHIE *has flopped back
on his bunk. There is a silence*]

RICHIE: How . . . do . . . you want me to be? I don't know how
else to be.

BILLY: Ohhh, man, that ain't any part of it.

[*The mop is clenched in his hands*]

RICHIE: Well, I don't come from the same kind of world as you do.

BILLY: Damn, Richie, you think Roger and I come off the same
street?

ROGER: Shit . . .

RICHIE: All right. Okay. But I've just done what I wanted all of my
life. If I wanted to do something, I just did it. Honestly. I've
never had to work or anything like that and I've always had nice
clothing and money for cab fare. Money for whatever I wanted.
Always. I'm not like you are.

ROGER: You ain't sayin' you really done that stuff, though, Rich.

RICHIE: What?

ROGER: That fag stuff.

RICHIE: [*He continues looking at* ROGER *and then he looks away*]
Yes.

ROGER: Do you even know what you're sayin', Richie? Do you even know what it means to be a fag?

RICHIE: Roger, of course I know what it is. I just told you I've done it. I thought you black people were supposed to understand all about suffering and human strangeness. I thought you had depth and vision from all your suffering. Has someone been misleading me? I just told you I did it. I know all about it. Everything. All the various positions.

ROGER: Yeh, so maybe you think you've tried it, but that don't make you it. I mean, we used to . . . in the old neighborhood, man, we had a couple dudes swung that way. But they was weird, man. There was this one little fella, he was a screamin' goddamn faggot . . . uh . . . [*He considers* RICHIE, *wondering if perhaps he has offended him*] Ohhh, ohhh, you ain't no screamin' goddamn faggot, Richie, no matter what you say. And the baddest man on the block was my boy Jerry Lemon. So one day Jerry's got the faggot in one a them ole deserted stairways and he's bouncin' him off the walls. I'm just a little fella, see, and I'm watchin' the baddest man on the block do his thing. So he come bouncin' back into me instead of Jerry, and just when he hit, he gave his ass this little twitch, man, like he thought he was gonna turn me on. I'd never a thought that was possible, man, for a man to be twitchin' his ass on me, just like he thought he was a broad. Scared me to death. I took off runnin'. Oh, oh, that ole neighborhood put me into all kinds a crap. I did some sufferin', just like Richie says. Like this once, I'm swingin' on up the street after school, and outa this phone booth comes this man with a goddamned knife stickin' outa his gut. So he sees me and starts tryin' to pull his mother-fuckin' coat out over the handle, like he's worried about how he looks, man. "I didn't know this was gonna happen," he says. And then he falls over. He was just all of a sudden dead, man; just all of a sudden dead. You ever seen anything like that, Billy? Any crap like that?

[BILLY, *sitting on* ROGER's *bunk, is staring at* ROGER]

BILLY: You really seen that?

ROGER: Richie's a big-city boy.

RICHIE: Oh, no; never anything like that.

ROGER: "Momma, help me," I am screamin'. "Jesus, Momma, help me." Little fella, he don't know how to act, he sees somethin' like that.

[*For a moment they are still, each thinking*]

BILLY: How long you think we got?

ROGER: What do you mean?

[ROGER *is hanging up the mops;* BILLY *is now kneeling on* ROGER's *bunk*]

BILLY: Till they pack us up, man, ship us out.

ROGER: To the war, you mean? To Disneyland? Man, I dunno; that up to them IBM's. Them machines is figurin' that. Maybe tomorrow, maybe next week, maybe never.

[*The war—the threat of it—is the one thing they share*]

RICHIE: I was reading they're planning to build it all up to more than five hundred thousand men over there. Americans. And they're going to keep it that way until they win.

BILLY: Be a great place to come back from, man, you know? I keep thinkin' about that. To have gone there, to have been there, to have seen it and lived.

ROGER: [*Settling onto* BILLY's *bunk, he lights a cigarette*] Well, what we got right here is a fool, gonna probably be one a them five hundred thousand, too. Do you know I cry at the goddamn anthem yet sometimes? The flag is flyin' at a ball game, the ole Roger gets all wet in the eye. After all the shit been done to his black ass. But I don't know what I think about this war. I do not know.

BILLY: I'm tellin' you, Rog—I've been doin' a lot a readin' and I think it's right we go. I mean, it's just like when North Korea invaded South Korea or when Hitler invaded Poland and all those other countries. He just kept testin' everybody and when nobody said no to him, he got so committed he couldn't back out even if he wanted. And that's what this Ho Chi Minh is doin'. And all these other Communists. If we let 'em know somebody is gonna stand up against 'em, they'll back off, just like Hitler would have.

ROGER: There is folks, you know, who are sayin' L.B.J. is the Hitler, and not ole Ho Chi Minh at all.

RICHIE: [*Talking as if this is the best news he's heard in years*] Well, I don't know anything at all about all that, but I am certain I don't want to go—whatever is going on. I mean, those Vietcong don't just shoot you and blow you up, you know. My God, they've got these other awful things they do: putting elephant shit on these stakes in the ground and then you step on 'em and you got elephant shit in a wound in your foot. The infection is horrendous. And then there's these caves they hide in and when you go in after 'em, they've got these snakes that they've tied by their tails to the ceiling. So it's dark and the snake is furious from having been hung by its tail and you crawl right into them—your face. My God!

BILLY: They do not.

[BILLY *knows he has been caught; they all know it*]

RICHIE: I read it, Billy. They do.

BILLY: [*Completely facetious, yet the fear is real*] That's bullshit, Richie.

ROGER: That's right, Richie. They maybe do that stuff with the elephant shit, but nobody's gonna tie a snake by its tail, let ole Billy walk into it.

BILLY: That's disgusting, man.

ROGER: Guess you better get ready for the Klondike, my man.

BILLY: That is probably the most disgusting thing I ever heard of. I DO NOT WANT TO GO! NOT TO NOWHERE WHERE THAT KINDA SHIT IS GOIN' ON! L.B.J. is Hitler; suddenly I see it all very clearly.

ROGER: Billy got him a hatred for snakes.

RICHIE: I hate them too. They're hideous.

BILLY: [*And now, as a kind of apology to* RICHIE, BILLY *continues his self-ridicule far into the extreme*] I mean, that is one of the most awful things I ever heard of any person doing. I mean, any person who would hang a snake by its tail in the dark of a cave in the hope that some other person might crawl into it and get bitten to death, that first person is somebody who oughta be shot. And I hope the five hundred thousand other guys that get sent over there kill 'em all—all them gooks—get 'em all driven back into Germany, where they belong. And in the meantime, I'll be holding the northern border against the snowmen.

ROGER: [*Rising from* BILLY's *bed*] And in the meantime before that, we better be gettin' at the ole area here. Got to be strike troopers.

BILLY: Right.

RICHIE: Can I help?

ROGER: Sure. Be good. [*And* ROGER *crosses to his footlocker and takes out a radio*] Think maybe I put on a little music, though it's gettin' late. We got time. Billy, you think?

BILLY: [*Getting nervously to his feet*] Sure.

ROGER: Sure. All right. We can be doin' it to the music.

[*He plugs the radio into the floor outlet as* BILLY *bolts for the door*]

BILLY: I gotta go pee.

ROGER: You watch out for the snakes.

BILLY: It's the snowmen, man; the snowmen.

[BILLY *is gone and "Ruby," sung by Ray Charles, comes from the radio. For a moment, as the music plays,* ROGER *watches* RICHIE *wander about the room, pouring little splashes of wax onto the floor. Then* RICHIE *moves to his bed and lies down, and* ROGER, *shaking his head, starts leisurely to spread the wax, with* RICHIE *watching*]

RICHIE: How come you and Billy take all this so seriously—you know.

ROGER: What?

RICHIE: This army nonsense. You're always shining your brass and keeping your footlocker neat and your locker so neat. There's no point to any of it.

ROGER: [*Still working the wax*] We here, ain't we, Richie? We in the army.

RICHIE: There's no point to any of it. And doing those push-ups, the two of you.

ROGER: We just see a lot a things the same way is all. Army ought to be a serious business, even if sometimes it ain't.

RICHIE: You're lucky, you know, the two of you. Having each other for friends the way you do. I never had that kind of friend ever. Not even when I was little.

ROGER: [*After a pause during which* ROGER, *working, sort of peeks at* RICHIE *every now and then*] You ain't really inta that stuff, are you, Richie?

[*It is a question that is a statement*]

RICHIE: [*Coyly he looks at* ROGER] What stuff is that, Roger?

ROGER: That fag stuff, man. You know. You ain't really into it, are you? You maybe messed in it a little is all—am I right?

RICHIE: I'm very weak, Roger. And by that I simply mean that if I have an impulse to do something, I don't know how to deny myself. If I feel like doing something, I just do it. I . . . will . . . admit to sometimes wishin' I . . . was a little more like you . . . and Billy, even, but not to any severe extent.

ROGER: But that's such a bad scene, Rich. You don't want that. Nobody wants that. Nobody wants to be a punk. Not nobody. You wanna know what I think it is? You just got in with the wrong bunch. Am I right? You just got in with a bad bunch. That can happen. And that's what I think happened to you. I bet you never had a chance to really run with the boys before. I mean, regular normal guys like Billy and me. How'd you come in the army, huh, Richie? You get drafted?

RICHIE: No.

ROGER: That's my point, see.

[*He has stopped working. He stands, leaning on the mop, looking at* RICHIE]

RICHIE: About four years ago, I went to this party. I was very young, and I went to this party with a friend who was older and . . . this "fag stuff," as you call it, was going on . . . so I did it.

ROGER: And then you come in the army to get away from it, right? Huh?

RICHIE: I don't know.

ROGER: Sure.

RICHIE: I don't know, Roger.

ROGER: Sure; sure. And now you're gettin' a chance to run with the boys for a little, you'll get yourself straightened around. I know it for a fact; I know that thing.

[*From off there is the sudden loud bellowing sound of* SERGEANT ROONEY]

ROONEY: THERE AIN'T BEEN NO SOLDIERS IN THIS CAMP BUT ME. I BEEN THE ONLY ONE—I BEEN THE ONLY ME!

[*And* BILLY *comes dashing into the room*]

BILLY: Oh, boy!

ROGER: Guess who?

ROONEY: FOR SO LONG I BEEN THE ONLY GODDAMN ONE!

BILLY: [*Leaping onto his bed and covering his face with a* Playboy *magazine as* RICHIE *is trying to get the wax put away so he can get into his own bunk*] Hut who hee whor—he's got some yo-yo with him, Rog!

ROGER: Huh?

[*As* COKES *and* ROONEY *enter. Both are in fatigues and drunk and big-bellied. They are in their fifties, their hair whitish and cut short. Both men carry whiskey bottles, beer bottles.* COKES *is a little neater than* ROONEY, *his fatigue jacket tucked in and not so rumpled, and he wears canvas-sided jungle boots.* ROONEY, *very disheveled, chomps on the stub of a big cigar. They swagger in, looking for fun, and stand there side by side*]

ROONEY: What kinda platoon I got here? You buncha shit sacks. Everybody look sharp. [*The three boys lie there, unmoving*] Off and on!

COKES: *Off and on!*

[*He seems barely conscious, wavering as he stands*]

ROGER: What's happenin', Sergeant?

ROONEY: [*Shoving his bottle of whiskey at* ROGER, *who is sitting up*] Shut up, Moore! You want a belt? [*Splashing whiskey on* ROGER's *chest*]

ROGER: How can I say no?

COKES: My name is Cokes!

BILLY: [*Rising to sit on the side of his bed*] How about me too?

COKES: You wait your turn.

ROONEY: [*He looks at the three of them as if they are fools. Indicates* COKES *with a gesture*] Don't you see what I got here?

BILLY: Who do I follow for my turn?

ROONEY: [*Suddenly, crazily petulant*] Don't you see what I got here? Everybody on their feet and at attention! [BILLY *and* ROGER *climb from their bunks and stand at attention. They don't know what* ROONEY *is mad at*] I mean it! [RICHIE *bounds to the position of attention*] This here is my friend, who in addition just come back from the war! The goddamn war! He been to it and he come back. [ROONEY *is patting* COKES *gently, proudly*] The man's a fuckin' hero! [ROONEY *hugs* COKES, *almost kissing him on the cheek*] He's always been a fuckin' hero!

[COKES, *embarrassed in his stupor, kind of wobbles a little from side to side*]

COKES: No-o-o-o-o-o . . .

[*And* ROONEY *grabs him, starts pushing him toward* BILLY's *footlocker*]

ROONEY: Show 'em your boots, Cokes. Show 'em your jungle boots. [*With a long, clumsy step,* COKES *climbs onto the footlocker,* ROONEY *supporting him from behind and then bending to lift one of* COKES's *booted feet and display it for the boys*] Lookee that boot. That ain't no everyday goddamn army boot. That is a goddamn jungle boot! That green canvas is a jungle boot 'cause a the heat, and them little holes in the bottom are so the water can run out when you been walkin' in a lotta water like in a jungle swamp. [*He is extremely proud of all this; he looks at them*] The army ain't no goddamn fool. You see a man wearin' boots like that, you might as well see he's got a chestful a medals, 'cause he been to the war. He don't have no boots like that unless he been to the war! Which is where I'm goin' and all you slaphappy motherfuckers too. Got to go kill some gooks. [*He is nodding at them, smiling*] That's right.

COKES: [*Bursting loudly from his stupor*] Gonna piss on 'em. Old booze. 'At's what I did. Piss in the rivers. Goddamn GI's secret weapon is old booze and he's pissin' it in all their runnin' water. Makes 'em yellow. Ahhhha ha, ha, ha!

   [*He laughs and laughs, and* ROONEY *laughs too, hugging* COKES]

ROONEY: Me and Cokesy been in so much shit together we oughta be brown. [*And then he catches himself, looks at* ROGER] Don't take no offense at that, Moore. We been swimmin' in it. One Hundred and First Airborne, together. One-oh-one. Screamin' goddamn Eagles! [*Looking at each other, face to face, eyes glinting, they make sudden loud screaming-eagle sounds*] This ain't the army; you punks ain't in the army. You ain't ever seen the army. The army is Airborne! Airborne!

COKES: [*Beginning to stomp his feet*] Airborne, Airborne! ALL THE WAY!

   [*As* RICHIE, *amused and hoping for a drink too, reaches out toward* ROONEY]

RICHIE: Sergeant, Sergeant, I can have a little drink too.

[ROONEY *looks at him and clutches the bottle*]

ROONEY: Are you kiddin' me? You gotta be kiddin' me. [*He looks to* ROGER] He's kiddin' me, ain't he, Moore? [*And then to* BILLY *and then to* COKES] Ain't he, Cokesy?

[COKES *steps forward and down with a thump, taking charge for his bewildered friend*]

COKES: Don't you know you are tryin' to take the booze from the hand a the future goddamn Congressional Honor winner . . . Medal . . . ? [*And he looks lovingly at* ROONEY. *He beams*] Ole Rooney, Ole Rooney. [*He hugs* ROONEY's *head*] He almost done it already.

[*And* ROONEY, *overwhelmed, starts screaming "Agggggg-hhhhhhhhhh," a screaming-eagle sound, and making clawing eagle gestures at the air. He jumps up and down, stomping his feet.* COKES *instantly joins in, stomping and jumping and yelling*]

ROONEY: Let's show these shit sacks how men are men jumpin' outa planes. Agggggghhhhhhhhhh. [*Stomping and yelling, they move in a circle,* ROONEY *followed by* COKES] A plane fulla yellin' stompin' men!

COKES: All yellin' stompin' men! [*They yell and stomp, making eagle sounds, and then* ROONEY *leaps up on* BILLY's *bed and runs the length of it until he is on the footlocker,* COKES *still on the floor, stomping.* ROONEY *makes a gesture of hooking his rip cord to the line inside the plane. They yell louder and louder and* ROONEY *leaps high into the air, yelling,* "GERONIMO-O-O-O!" *as* COKES *leaps onto the locker and then high into the air, bellowing,* "GERONIMO-O-O-O!" *They stand side by side, their arms held up in the air as if grasping the shroud lines of open chutes. They seem to float there in silence*] What a feelin' . . .

ROONEY: Beautiful feelin' . . .

[*For a moment more they float there, adrift in the room, the sky, their memory.* COKES *smiles at* ROONEY]

COKES: Remember that one guy, O'Flannigan . . . ?

ROONEY: [*Nodding, smiling, remembering*] O'Flannigan . . .

COKES: He was this one guy . . . O'Flannigan . . . [*He moves now toward the boys,* BILLY, ROGER *and* RICHIE, *who have gathered on* ROGER's *bed and footlocker.* ROONEY *follows several steps, then drifts backward onto* BILLY's *bed, where he sits and then lies back, listening to* COKES] We was testing chutes where you could just pull a lever by your ribs here when you hit the ground—see—and the chute would come off you, because it was just after a whole bunch a guys had been dragged to death in an unexpected and terrible wind at Fort Bragg. So they wanted you to be able to release the chute when you hit if there was a bad wind when you hit. So O'Flannigan was this kinda joker who had the goddamn sense a humor of a clown and nerves, I tell you, of steel, and he says he's gonna release the lever midair, then reach up, grab the lines and float on down, hanging. [*His hand paws at the air, seeking a rope that isn't there*] So I seen him pull the lever at five hundred feet and he reaches up to two fistfuls a air, the chute's twenty feet above him, and he went into the ground like a knife.

> [*The bottle, held high over his head, falls through the air to the bed, all watching it*]

BILLY: Geezus.

ROONEY: [*Nodding gently*] Didn't get to sing the song, I bet.

COKES: [*Standing, staring at the fallen bottle*] No way.

RICHIE: What song?

ROONEY: [*He rises up, mysteriously angry*] Shit sack! Shit sack!

RICHIE: What song, Sergeant Rooney?

ROONEY: "Beautiful Streamer," shit sack.

> [COKES, *gone into another reverie, is staring skyward*]

COKES: I saw this one guy—never forget it. Never.

BILLY: That's Richie, Sergeant Rooney. He's a beautiful screamer.

RICHIE: He said "streamer," not "screamer," asshole.

[COKES *is still in his reverie*]

COKES: This guy with his chute goin' straight up above him in a streamer, like a tulip, only white, you know. All twisted and never gonna open. Like a big icicle sticking straight up above him. He went right by me. We met eyes, sort of. He was lookin' real puzzled. He looks right at me. Then he looks up in the air at the chute, then down at the ground.

ROONEY: Did *he* sing it?

COKES: He didn't sing it. He started going like this. [COKES *reaches desperately upward with both hands and begins to claw at the sky while his legs pump up and down*] Like he was gonna climb right up the air.

RICHIE: Ohhhhh, Geezus!

BILLY: God!

[ROONEY *has collapsed backward on* BILLY's *bed and he lies there and then he rises*]

ROONEY: Cokes got the Silver Star for rollin' a barrel a oil down a hill in Korea into forty-seven chinky Chinese gooks who were climbin' up the hill and when he shot into it with his machine gun, it blew them all to grape jelly.

[COKES, *rocking a little on his feet, begins to hum and then sing "Beautiful Streamer," to the tune of Stephen Foster's "Beautiful Dreamer"*]

COKES: "Beautiful streamer, open for me . . . The sky is above me . . ." [*And then the singing stops*] But the one I remember is this little guy in his spider hole, which is a hole in the ground with a lid over it. [*And he is using* RICHIE's *footlocker before him as the spider hole. He has fixed on it, is moving toward it*] And he shot me in the ass as I was runnin' by, but the bullet hit me so hard— [*His body kind of jerks and he runs several steps*]—it knocked me into this ditch where he couldn't see me. I got behind him. [*Now at the head of* RICHIE's *bed, he begins to creep along the side of the bed as if sneaking up on the footlocker*] Crawlin'. And I dropped a grenade into his hole. [*He jams a whiskey bottle into the footlocker, then slams down the lid*] Then sat on the lid, him bouncin' and yellin' under me. Bouncin' and yellin' under the lid. I could hear him. Feel him. I just sat there.

[*Silence.* ROONEY *waits, thinking, then leans forward*]

ROONEY: He was probably singin' it.

COKES: [*Sitting there*] I think so.

ROONEY: You think we should let 'em hear it?

BILLY: We're good boys. We're good ole boys.

COKES: [*Jerking himself to his feet, he staggers sideways to join* ROONEY *on* BILLY'S *bed*] I don't care who hears it, I just wanna be singin' it.

[ROONEY *rises; he goes to the boys on* ROGER'S *bed and speaks to them carefully, as if lecturing people on something of great importance*]

ROONEY: You listen up; you just be listenin' up, 'cause if you hear it right you can maybe stop bein' shit sacks. This is what a man sings, he's goin' down through the air, his chute don't open.

[*Flopping back down on the bunk beside* COKES, ROONEY *looks at* COKES *and then at the boys. The two older men put their arms around each other and they begin to sing*]

ROONEY AND COKES: [*Singing*]
Beautiful streamer,
Open for me,
The sky is above me,
But no canopy.

BILLY: [*Murmuring*] I don't believe it.

ROONEY AND COKES:
Counted ten thousand,
Pulled on the cord.
My chute didn't open,
I shouted, "Dear Lord."

Beautiful streamer,
This looks like the end,
The earth is below me,
My body won't end.

Just like a mother
Watching o'er me,
Beautiful streamer,
Ohhhhh, open for me.

ROGER: Un-fuckin'-believable.

ROONEY: [*Beaming with pride*] Ain't that a beauty.

[*And then* COKES *topples forward onto his face and flops limply to his side. The three boys leap to their feet.* ROONEY *lunges toward* COKES]

RICHIE: Sergeant!

ROONEY: Cokie! Cokie!

BILLY: Jesus!

ROGER: Hey!

COKES: Huh? Huh?

[COKES *sits up.* ROONEY *is kneeling beside him*]

ROONEY: Jesus, Cokie!

COKES: I been doin' that; I been doin' that. It don't mean nothin'.

ROONEY: No, no.

COKES: [*Pushing at* ROONEY, *who is trying to help him get back to the bed.* ROONEY *agrees with everything* COKES *is now saying and the noises he makes are little animal noises*] I told 'em when they wanted to send me back I ain't got no leukemia; they wanna check it. They think I got it. I don't think I got it. Rooney? Whata you think?

ROONEY: No.

COKES: My mother had it. She had it. Just 'cause she did and I been fallin' down.

ROONEY: It don't mean nothin'.

COKES: [*He lunges back and up onto the bed*] I tole 'em I fall down 'cause I'm drunk. I'm drunk all the time.

ROONEY: You'll be goin' back over there with me, is what I know, Cokie. [*He is patting* COKES, *nodding, dusting him off*] That's what I know.

[*As* BILLY *comes up to them, almost seeming to want to be a part of the intimacy they are sharing*]

BILLY: That was somethin', Sergeant Cokes. Jesus!

[ROONEY *whirls on him, ferocious, pushing him*]

ROONEY: Get the fuck away, Wilson! Whata you know? Get the fuck away. You don't know shit. Get away! You don't know shit. [*And he turns to* COKES, *who is standing up from the bed*] Me and Cokes are goin' to the war zone like we oughta. Gonna blow it to shit. [*He is grabbing at* COKES, *who is laughing. They are both laughing.* ROONEY *whirls on the boys*] Ohhh, I'm gonna be so happy to be away from you assholes; you pussies. Not one regular army people among you possible. I swear it to my mother who is holy. You just be watchin' the papers for doin' darin' brave deeds. 'Cause we're old hands at it. Makin' shit disappear. Goddamn whooosh!

COKES: Whooosh!

ROONEY: Demnalitions. Me and . . . [*And then he knows he hasn't said it right*] Me and Cokie . . . Demnal . . . Demnali . . .

RICHIE: [*Still sitting on* ROGER's *bed*] You can do it, Sergeant.

BILLY: Get it.

[*He stands by the lockers and* ROONEY *glares at him*]

ROGER: 'Cause you're cool with dynamite, is what you're tryin' to say.

ROONEY: [*Charging at* ROGER, *bellowing*] Shut the fuck up, that's what you can do; and go to goddamn sleep! You buncha shit . . . sacks. Buncha mothers—know-it-all motherin' shit sacks—that's what you are.

COKES: [*Shoulders back, he is taking charge*] Just goin' to sleep is what you can do, 'cause Rooney and me fought it through two wars already and we can make it through this one more and leukemia that comes or doesn't come—who gives a shit? Not guys like us. We're goin' just pretty as pie. And it's lights-out time, ain't it, Rooney?

ROONEY: Past it, goddammit. So the lights are goin' out. [*There is fear in the room, and the three boys rush to their wall lockers, where they start to strip to their underwear, preparing for bed.* ROONEY *paces the room, watching them, glaring*] Somebody's gotta teach you soldierin'. You hear me? Or you wanna go outside and march around awhile, huh? We can do that if you wanna. Huh? You tell me? Marchin' or sleepin'? What's it gonna be?

RICHIE: [*Rushing to get into bed*] Flick out the ole lights, Sergeant; that's what we say.

BILLY: [*Climbing into bed*] Put out the ole lights.

ROGER: [*In bed and pulling up the covers*] Do it.

COKES: Shut up! [*He rocks forward and back, trying to stand at attention. He is saying good night*] And that's an order. Just shut up. I got grenades down the hall. I got a pistol. I know where to get nitro. You don't shut up, I'll blow . . . you . . . to . . . fuck. [*Making a military left face, he stalks to the wall switch and turns the lights out.* ROONEY *is watching proudly, as* COKES *faces the boys again. He looks at them*] That's right.

[*In the dark, there is only a spill of light from the hall coming in the open door.* COKES *and* ROONEY *put their arms around each other and go out the door, leaving it partly open.* RICHIE, ROGER *and* BILLY *lie in their bunks, staring. They do not move. They lie there. The sergeants seem to have vanished soundlessly once they went out the door. Light touches each of the boys as they lie there*]

ROGER: [*He does not move*] Lord have mercy, if that ain't a pair. If that ain't one pair a beauties.

BILLY: Oh, yeh.

[*He does not move*]

ROGER: Too much, man—too, too much.

RICHIE: They made me sad; but I loved them, sort of. Better than movies.

ROGER: Too much. Too, too much.

[*Silence*]

BILLY: What time is it?

ROGER: Sleep time, men. Sleep time.

[*Silence*]

BILLY: Right.

ROGER: They were somethin'. Too much.

BILLY: Too much.

RICHIE: Night.

ROGER: Night. [*Silence*] Night, Billy.

BILLY: Night.

[RICHIE *stirs in his bed.* ROGER *turns onto his side.* BILLY *is motionless*]

BILLY: I . . . had a buddy, Rog—and this is the whole thing, this is the whole point—a kid I grew up with, played ball with in high school, and he was a tough little cat, a real bad man sometimes. Used to have gangster pictures up in his room. Anyway, we got into this deal where we'd drive on down to the big city, man, you know, hit the bad spots, let some queer pick us up . . . sort of . . . long enough to buy us some good stuff. It was kinda the thing to do for a while, and we all did it, the whole gang of us. So we'd let these cats pick us up, most of 'em old guys, and they were huntin' and happy as hell to have us, and we'd get a lot of free booze, maybe a meal, and we'd turn 'em on. Then pretty soon they'd ask us did we want to go over to their place. Sure, we'd say, and order one more drink, and then when we hit the street, we'd tell 'em to kiss off. We'd call 'em fag and queer and jazz like that and tell 'em to kiss off. And Frankie, the kid I'm tellin' you about, he had a mean streak in him and if they gave us a bad time at all, he'd put 'em down. That's the way he was. So that kinda jazz went on and on for sort of a long time and it was a good deal if we were low on cash or needed a laugh and it went on for a while. And then Frankie—one day he come up to me—and he says he was goin' home with the guy he was with. He said, what the hell, what did it matter? And he's sayin'—Frankie's sayin'—why don't I tag along? What the hell, he's sayin', what does it matter who does it to you, some broad or some old guy, you close your eyes, a mouth's a mouth, it don't matter—that's what he's sayin'. I tried to talk him out of it, but he wasn't hearin' anything I was sayin'. So the next day, see, he calls me up to tell me about it. Okay, okay, he says, it was a cool scene, he says; they played poker, a buck minimum, and he made a fortune. Frankie was eatin' it up, man. It was a pretty way to live, he says. So he stayed at it, and he had this nice little girl he was goin' with at the time. You know the way a real bad cat can sometimes do that—have a good little girl who's crazy about him and he is for her, too, and he's a different cat when he's with her?

ROGER: Uh-huh.

[*The hall light slants across* BILLY's *face*]

BILLY: Well, that was him and Linda, and then one day he dropped her, he cut her loose. He was hooked, man. He was into it, with no way he knew out—you understand what I'm sayin'? He had got his ass hooked. He had never thought he would and then one day he woke up and he was on it. He just hadn't been told, that's the way I figure it; somebody didn't tell him somethin' he shoulda been told and he come to me wailin' one day, man, all broke up and wailin', my boy Frankie, my main man, and he was a fag. He was a faggot, black Roger, and I'm not lyin'. I am not lyin' to you.

ROGER: Damn.

BILLY: So that's the whole thing, man; that's the whole thing.

[*Silence. They lie there*]

ROGER: Holy . . . Christ! Richie . . . you hear him? You hear what he said?

RICHIE: He's a storyteller.

ROGER: What you mean?

RICHIE: I mean, he's a storyteller, all right; he tells stories, all right.

ROGER: What are we into now? You wanna end up like that friend a his, or you don't believe what he said? Which are you sayin'? [*The door bursts open. The sounds of machine guns and cannon are being made by someone, and* CARLYLE, *drunk and playing, comes crawling in.* ROGER, RICHIE *and* BILLY *all pop up, startled, to look at him*] Hey, hey, what's happenin'?

BILLY: Who's happenin'?

ROGER: You attackin' or you retreatin', man?

CARLYLE: [*Looking up; big grin*] Hey, baby . . . ?

[*Continues shooting, crawling. The three boys look at each other*]

ROGER: What's happenin' man? Whatcha doin'?

CARLYLE: I dunno, soul; I dunno. Practicin' my duties, my new abilities. [*Half sitting, he flops onto his side, starts to crawl*] The low crawl, man; like I was taught in basic, that's what I'm doin'. You gotta know your shit, man, else you get your ass blown so far away you don't ever see it again. Oh, sure, you guys don't care. I know it. You got it made. You got it made. I don't got it made. You got a little home here, got friends, people to talk to. I got nothin'. You got jobs they probably ain't ever gonna ship you out, you got so important jobs. I got no job. They don't even wanna give me a job. I know it. They are gonna kill me. They are gonna send me over there to get me killed, goddammit! WHAT'S A MAT-TER WITH ALL YOU PEOPLE?

[*The anger explodes out of the grieving and* ROGER *rushes to kneel beside* CARLYLE. *He speaks gently, firmly*]

ROGER: Hey, man, get cool, get some cool; purchase some cool, man.

CARLYLE: Awwwww . . . [*Clumsily, he turns away*]

ROGER: Just hang in there.

CARLYLE: I don't wanna be no DEAD man. I don't wanna be the one they all thinkin' is so stupid he's the only one'll go, they tell him; they don't even have to give him a job. I got thoughts, man, in my head; alla time, burnin', burnin' thoughts a understandin'.

ROGER: Don't you think we know that, man? It ain't the way you're sayin' it.

CARLYLE: It is.

ROGER: No. I mean, we all probably gonna go. We all probably gonna have to go.

CARLYLE: No-o-o-o-o.

ROGER: I mean it.

CARLYLE: [*Suddenly he nearly topples over*] I am very drunk. [*And he looks up at* ROGER] You think so?

ROGER: I'm sayin' so. And I am sayin', "No sweat." No point.

[CARLYLE *angrily pushes at* ROGER, *knocking him backward*]

CARLYLE: Awwwww, dammit, dammit, mother . . . shit . . . it . . . ohhhhhhh. [*Sliding to the floor, the rage and anguish softening into only breathing*] I mean it. I mean it. [*Silence. He lies there*]

ROGER: What . . . a you doin' . . . ?

CARLYLE: Huh?

ROGER: I don't know what you're up to on our freshly mopped floor.

CARLYLE: Gonna go sleep—okay? No sweat . . . [*Suddenly very polite, he is looking up*] Can I, soul? Izzit all right?

ROGER: Sure, man, sure, if you wanna, but why don't you go where you got a bed? Don't you like beds?

CARLYLE: Dunno where's zat. My bed. I can' fin' it. I can' fin' my own bed. I looked all over, but I can' fin' it anywhere. GONE! [*Slip-*

ping back down now, he squirms to make a nest. He hugs his bottle]

ROGER: [*Moving to his bunk, where he grabs a blanket*] Okay, okay, man. But get on top a this, man. [*He is spreading the blanket on the floor, trying to help* CARLYLE *get on it*] Make it softer. C'mon, c'mon . . . get on this.

[BILLY *has risen with his own blanket, and is moving now to hand it to* ROGER]

BILLY: Cat's hurtin', Rog.

ROGER: Ohhhhh, yeh.

CARLYLE: Ohhhhh . . . it was so sweet at home . . . it was so sweet, baby; so-o-o good. They doin' dances make you wanna cry . . . [*Hugging the blankets now, he drifts in a kind of dream*]

ROGER: I know, man.

CARLYLE: So sweet . . . !

[BILLY *is moving back to his own bed, where, quietly, he sits*]

ROGER: I know, man.

CARLYLE: So sweet . . . !

ROGER: Yeh.

CARLYLE: How come I gotta be here?

[*On his way to the door to close it,* ROGER *falters, looks at* CARLYLE *then moves on toward the door*]

ROGER: I dunno, Jim.

[BILLY *is sitting and watching, as* ROGER *goes on to the door, gently closes it and returns to his bed*]

BILLY: I know why he's gotta be here, Roger. You wanna know? Why don't you ask me?

ROGER: Okay. How come he gotta be here?

BILLY: [*Smiling*] Freedom's frontier, man. That's why.

ROGER: [*Settled on the edge of his bed and about to lie back*] Oh
. . . yeh . . . [*As a distant bugle begins to play taps and* RICHIE,
carrying a blanket, is approaching CARLYLE. ROGER *settles back;*
BILLY *is staring at* RICHIE; CARLYLE *does not stir; the bugle plays*]
Bet that ole sarge don't live a year, Billy. Fuckin' blow his own ass
sky high.

> [RICHIE *has covered* CARLYLE. *He pats* CARLYLE's *arm, and
> then straightens in order to return to his bed*]

BILLY: Richie . . . ! [BILLY's *hissing voice freezes* RICHIE. *He
stands, and then he starts again to move, and* BILLY's *voice comes
again and* RICHIE *cannot move*] Richie . . . how come you gotta
keep doin' that stuff? [ROGER . . . *looks at* BILLY, *staring at* RICHIE,
who stands still as a stone over the sleeping CARLYLE] How come?

ROGER: He dunno, man. Do you? You dunno, do you, Rich?

RICHIE: No.

CARLYLE: [*From deep in his sleep and grieving*] It . . . was . . . so
. . . pretty . . . !

RICHIE: No.

> [*The lights are fading with the last soft notes of taps*]

ACT TWO

SCENE ONE

Lights come up on the cadre room. It is late afternoon and
BILLY *is lying on his stomach, his head at the foot of the bed,*
his chin resting on his hands. He wears gym shorts and sweat
socks; his T-shirt lies on the bed and his sneakers are on the
floor. ROGER *is at his footlocker, taking out a pair of sweat*
socks. His sneakers and his basketball are on his bed. He is
wearing his khakis.

A silence passes, and then ROGER *closes his footlocker and sits*
on his bed, where he starts lacing his sneakers, holding them
on his lap.

BILLY: Rog . . . you think I'm a busybody? In any way? [*Silence.*
ROGER *laces his sneakers*] Roger?

ROGER: Huh? Uh-uh.

BILLY: Some people do. I mean, back home. [*He rolls slightly to*
look at ROGER] Or that I didn't know how to behave. Sort of.

ROGER: It's time we maybe get changed, don't you think?

[ROGER *rises and goes to his locker. He takes off his trousers,*
shoes and socks]

BILLY: Yeh. I guess. I don't feel like it, though. I don't feel good,
don't know why.

ROGER: Be good for you, man; be good for you.

[*Pulling on his gym shorts,* ROGER *returns to his bed, carrying*
his shoes and socks]

BILLY: Yeh. [BILLY *sits up on the edge of his bed.* ROGER, *sitting, is*
bowed over, putting on his socks] I mean, a lot of people thought

like I didn't know how to behave in a simple way. You know? That I overcomplicated everything. I didn't think so. Don't think so. I just thought I was seein' complications that were there but nobody else saw. [*He is struggling now to put on his T-shirt. He seems weary, almost weak*] I mean, Wisconsin's a funny place. All those clear-eyed people sayin' "Hello" and lookin' you straight in the eye. Everybody's good, you think, and happy and honest. And then there's all of a sudden a neighbor who goes mad as a hatter. I had a neighbor who came out of his house one morning with axes in both hands. He started then attackin' the cars that were driving up and down in front of his house. An' we all knew why he did it, sorta. [*He pauses; he thinks*] It made me wanna be a priest. I wanted to be a priest then. I was sixteen. Priests could help people. Could take away what hurt 'em. I wanted that, I thought. Somethin', huh?

ROGER: [*He has the basketball in his hands*] Yeh. But everybody's got feelin's like that sometimes.

BILLY: I don't know.

ROGER: You know, you oughta work on a little jump shot, my man. Get you some kinda fall-away jumper to go with that beauty of a hook. Make you tough out there.

BILLY: Can't fuckin' do it. Not my game. I mean, like that bar we go to. You think I could get a job there bartendin', maybe? I could learn the ropes. [*He is watching* ROGER, *who has risen to walk to his locker*] You think I could get a job there off-duty hours?

ROGER: [*Pulling his locker open to display the pinup on the inside of the door*] You don't want no job. It's that little black-haired waitress you wantin' to know.

BILLY: No, man. Not really.

ROGER: It's okay. She tough, man.

[*He begins to remove his uniform shirt. He will put on an O.D. T-shirt to go to the gym*]

BILLY: I mean, not the way you're sayin' it, is all. Sure, there's somethin' about her. I don't know what. I ain't even spoke to her yet. But somethin'. I mean, what's she doin' there? When she's dancin', it's like she knows somethin'. She's degradin' herself, I sometimes feel. You think she is?

ROGER: Man, you don't even know the girl. She's workin'.

BILLY: I'd like to talk to her. Tell her stuff. Find out about her. Sometimes I'm thinkin' about her and it and I got a job there, I get to know her and she and I get to be real tight, man—close, you know. Maybe we screw, maybe we don't. It's nice . . . whatever.

ROGER: Sure. She a real fine-lookin' chippy, Billy. Got nice cakes. Nice little titties.

BILLY: I think she's smart, too. [ROGER *starts laughing so hard he almost falls into his locker*] Oh, all I do is talk. "Yabba-yabba." I mean, my mom and dad are really terrific people. How'd they ever end up with somebody so weird as me?

  [ROGER *moves to him, jostles him*]

ROGER: I'm tellin' you, the gym and a little ball is what you need. Little exercise. Little bumpin' into people. The soul is tellin' you.

  [BILLY *rises and goes to his locker, where he starts putting on his sweat clothes*]

BILLY: I mean, Roger, you remember how we met in P Company? Both of us brand-new. You started talkin' to me. You just started talkin' to me and you didn't stop.

ROGER: [*Hardly looking up*] Yeh.

BILLY: Did you see somethin' in me made you pick me?

ROGER: I was talkin' to everybody, man. For that whole day. Two whole days. You was just the first one to talk back friendly. Though you didn't say much, as I recall.

BILLY: The first white person, you mean.

  [*Wearing his sweat pants,* BILLY *is now at his bed, putting on his sneakers*]

ROGER: Yeh. I was tryin' to come outa myself a little. Do like the fuckin' head shrinker been tellin' me to stop them fuckin' headaches I was havin', you know. Now let us do fifteen or twenty push-ups and get over to that gymnasium, like I been sayin'. Then we can take our civvies with us—we can shower and change at the gym.

[ROGER *crosses to* BILLY, *who flops down on his belly on the bed*]

BILLY: I don't know . . . I don't know what it is I'm feelin'. Sick like.

[ROGER *forces* BILLY *up onto his feet and shoves him playfully downstage, where they both fall forward into the push-up position, side by side*]

ROGER: Do 'em, trooper. Do 'em. Get it.

[ROGER *starts.* BILLY *joins in. After five,* ROGER *realizes that* BILLY *has his knees on the floor. They start again. This time,* BILLY *counts in double time. They start again. At about "seven,"* RICHIE *enters. Neither* BILLY *nor* ROGER *sees him. They keep going*]

ROGER AND BILLY: . . . seven, eight, nine, ten . . .

RICHIE: No, no; no, no; no, no, no. That's not it; that's not it.

[*They keep going, yelling the numbers louder and louder*]

ROGER AND BILLY: . . . eleven, twelve, thirteen . . .

[RICHIE *crosses to his locker and gets his bottle of cologne, and then returning to the center of the room to stare at them, he stands there dabbing cologne on his face*]

ROGER AND BILLY: . . . fourteen, fifteen.

RICHIE: You'll never get it like that. You're so far apart and you're both humping at the same time. And all that counting. It's so unromantic.

ROGER: [*Rising and moving to his bed to pick up the basketball*] We was exercisin', Richard. You heard a that?

RICHIE: Call it what you will, Roger. [*With a flick of his wrist,* ROGER *tosses the basketball to* BILLY] Everybody has their own cute little pet names for it.

BILLY: Hey! [*And he tosses the ball at* RICHIE, *hitting him in the chest, sending the cologne bottle flying.* RICHIE *yelps, as* BILLY *retrieves the ball and, grabbing up his sweat jacket from the bed, heads for the door.* ROGER, *at his own locker, has taken out his suit bag of civilian clothes*] You missed.

RICHIE: Billy, Billy, Billy, please, please, the ruffian approach will not work with me. It impresses me not even one tiny little bit. All you've done is spill my cologne.

[*He bends to pick up the cologne from the floor*]

BILLY: That was my aim.

ROGER: See you.

[BILLY *is passing* RICHIE. *Suddenly* RICHIE *sprays* BILLY *with cologne, some of it getting on* ROGER, *as* ROGER *and* BILLY, *groaning and cursing at* RICHIE, *rush out the door*]

RICHIE: Try the more delicate approach next time, Bill. [*Having crossed to the door, he stands a moment, leaning against the frame. Then he bounces to* BILLY's *bed, sings "He's just my Bill," and squirts cologne on the pillow. At his locker, he deposits the cologne, takes off his shirt, shoes and socks. Removing a hardcover copy of Pauline Kael's* I Lost It at the Movies *from the top shelf of the locker, he bounds to the center of the room and tosses the book the rest of the way to the bed. Quite pleased with himself, he fidgets, pats his stomach, then lowers himself into the push-up position, goes to his knees and stands up*] Am I out of my fucking mind? Those two are crazy. I'm not crazy.

[RICHIE *pivots and strides to his locker. With an ashtray, a pack of matches and a pack of cigarettes, he hurries to his bed and makes himself comfortable to read, his head propped up on a pillow. Settling himself, he opens the book, finds his place, thinks a little, starts to read. For a moment he lies there. And then* CARLYLE *steps into the room. He comes through the doorway looking to his left and right. He comes*] *several steps into the room and looks at* RICHIE. RICHIE *sees him. They look at each other*]

CARLYLE: Ain't nobody here, man?

RICHIE: Hello, Carlyle. How are you today?

CARLYLE: Ain't nobody here?

[*He is nervous and angrily disappointed*]

RICHIE: Ẁho do you want?

CARLYLE: Where's the black boy?

RICHIE: Roger? My God, why do you keep calling him that? Don't you know his name yet? Roger. Roger.

[*He thickens his voice at this, imitating someone very stupid.* CARLYLE *stares at him*]

CARLYLE: Yeh. Where is he?

RICHIE: I am not his keeper, you know. I am not his private secretary, you know.

CARLYLE: I do not know. I do not know. That is why I am asking. I come to see him. You are here. I ask you. I don't know. I mean, Carlyle made a fool outa himself comin' in here the other night, talkin' on and on like how he did. Lay on the floor. He remember. You remember? It all one hype, man; that all one hype. You know what I mean. That ain't the real Carlyle was in here. This one here and now the real Carlyle. Who the real Richie?

RICHIE: Well . . . the real Richie . . . has gone home. To Manhattan. I, however, am about to read this book.

[*Which he again starts to try to do*]

CARLYLE: Oh. Shit! Jus' you the only one here, then, huh?

RICHIE: So it would seem. [*He looks at the air and then under the bed as if to find someone*] So it would seem. Did you hear about Martin?

CARLYLE: What happened to Martin? I ain't seen him.

RICHIE: They are shipping him home. Someone told about what he did to himself. I don't know who.

CARLYLE: Wasn't me. Not me. I keep that secret.

RICHIE: I'm sure you did. [*Rising, walking toward* CARLYLE *and the door, cigarette pack in hand*] You want a cigarette? Or don't you smoke? Or do you have to go right away? [*Closing the door*] There's a chill sometimes coming down the hall, I don't know from where. [*Crossing back to his bed and climbing in*] And I think I've got the start of a little cold. Did you want the cigarette?

[CARLYLE *is staring at him. Then he examines the door and looks again at* RICHIE. *He stares at* RICHIE, *thinking, and then he walks toward him*]

CARLYLE: You know what I bet? I been lookin' at you real close. It just a way I got about me. And I bet if I was to hang my boy out in front of you, my big boy, man, you'd start wantin' to touch him. Be beggin' and talkin' sweet to ole Carlyle. Am I right or wrong? [*He leans over* RICHIE] What do you say?

RICHIE: Pardon?

CARLYLE: You heard me. Ohhh. I am so restless, I don't even understand it. My big black boy is what I was talkin' about. My thing, man; my rope, Jim. HEY, RICHIE! [*And he lunges, then moves his fingers through* RICHIE's *hair*] How long you been a punk? Can you hear me? Am I clear? Do I talk funny? [*He is leaning close*] Can you smell the gin on my mouth?

RICHIE: I mean, if you really came looking for Roger, he and Billy are gone to the gymnasium. They were—

CARLYLE: No. [*He slides down on the bed, his arms placed over* RICHIE's *legs*] I got no athletic abilities. I got none. No moves. I don't know. HEY, RICHIE! [*Leaning close again*] I just got this question I asked. I got no answer.

RICHIE: I don't know . . . what . . . you mean.

CARLYLE: I heard me. I understood me. "How long you been a punk?" is the question I asked. Have you got a reply?

RICHIE: [*Confused, irritated, but fascinated*] Not to that question.

CARLYLE: Who do if you don't? I don't. How'm I gonna? [*Suddenly there is whistling in the hall, as if someone might enter, footsteps approaching, and* RICHIE *leaps to his feet and scurries away toward the door, tucking in his undershirt as he goes*] Man, don't you wanna talk to me? Don't you wanna talk to ole Carlyle?

RICHIE: Not at the moment.

CARLYLE: [*He is rising, starting after* RICHIE, *who stands nervously near* ROGER's *bed*] I want to talk to you, man; why don't you want to talk to me? We can be friends. Talkin' back and forth, sharin' thoughts and bein' happy.

RICHIE: I don't think that's what you want.

CARLYLE: [*He is very near to* RICHIE] What do I want?

RICHIE: I mean, to talk to me.

[RICHIE, *as if repulsed, crosses away. But it is hard to tell if the move is genuine or coy*]

CARLYLE: What am I doin'? I am talkin'. DON'T YOU TELL ME I AIN'T TALKIN' WHEN I AM TALKIN'! COURSE I AM. Bendin' over backwards. [*And pressing his hands against himself in his anger, he has touched the grease on his shirt, the filth of his clothing, and this ignites the anger*] Do you know they still got me in that goddamn P Company? That goddamn transient company! It like they think I ain't got no notion what a home is. No nose for no home—like I ain't never had no home. I had a home. I LIKE THEY THINK THERE AIN'T NO PLACE FOR ME IN THIS MOTHER ARMY BUT K.P. ALL SUDSY AND WRINKLED AND SWEATIN'. EVERY DAY SINCE I GOT TO THIS SHIT HOUSE, MISTER! HOW MANY TIMES YOU BEEN ON K.P.? WHEN'S THE LAST TIME YOU PULLED K.P.?

[*He has roared down to where* RICHIE *had moved, the rage possessing him*]

RICHIE: I'm E.D.

CARLYLE: You E.D.? You E.D.? You Edie, are you? I didn't ask you what you friends call you, asked you when's the last time you had K.P.

RICHIE: [*Edging toward his bed. He will go there, get and light a cigarette*] E.D. is "Exempt from Duty."

CARLYLE: [*Moving after* RICHIE] You ain't got no duties? What shit you talkin' about? Everybody in this fuckin' army got duties. That what the fuckin' army all about. You ain't got no duties, who got 'em?

RICHIE: Because of my job, Carlyle. I have a very special job. And my friends don't call me Edie. [*Big smile*] They call me Irene.

CARLYLE: That mean what you sayin' is you kiss ass for somebody, don't it? Good for you. [*Seemingly relaxed and gentle, he settles down on* RICHIE's *bed. He seems playful and charming*] You know the other night I was sleepin' there. You know.

RICHIE: Yes.

CARLYLE: [*Gleefully, enormously pleased*] You remember that? How come you remember that? You sweet.

RICHIE: We don't have people sleeping on our floor that often, Carlyle.

CARLYLE: But the way you crawl over in the night, gimme a big kiss on my joint. That nice.

RICHIE: [*Shocked, he blinks*] What?

CARLYLE: Or did I dream that?

RICHIE: [*Laughing in spite of himself*] My God, you're outrageous!

CARLYLE: Maybe you dreamed it.

RICHIE: What . . . ? No. I don't know.

CARLYLE: Maybe you did it, then; you didn't dream it.

RICHIE: How come you talk so much?

CARLYLE: I don't talk, man, who's gonna talk? YOU? [*He is laughing and amused, but there is an anger near the surface now, an ugliness*] That bore me to death. I don't like nobody's voice but my own. I am so pretty. Don't like nobody else face. [*And then viciously, he spits out at* RICHIE] You goddamn face ugly fuckin' queer punk!

[*And* RICHIE *jumps in confusion*]

RICHIE: What's the matter with you?

CARLYLE: You goddamn ugly punk face. YOU UGLY!

RICHIE: Nice mouth.

CARLYLE: That's right. That's right. And you got a weird mouth. Like to suck joints. [*As* RICHIE *storms to his locker, throwing the book inside. He pivots, grabbing a towel, marching toward the door*] Hey, you gonna jus' walk out on me? Where you goin'? You c'mon back. Hear?

RICHIE: That's my bed, for chrissake! [*He lunges into the hall*]

CARLYLE: You'd best. [*Lying there, he makes himself comfortable. He takes a pint bottle from his back pocket*] You come back, Richie, I tell you a good joke. Make you laugh, make you cry. [*He takes a big drink*] That's right. Ole Frank and Jesse, they got the stagecoach stopped, all the peoples lined up—Frank say, "All right, peoples, we gonna rape all the men and rob all the women." Jesse say, "Frank, no, no—that ain't it—we gonna—" And this one little man yell real loud, "You shut up, Jesse; Frank knows what he's doin'." [*Loudly, he laughs and laughs.* BILLY *enters. Startled at the sight of* CARLYLE *there in* RICHIE's *bed,* BILLY *falters, as* CARLYLE *gestures toward him*] Hey, man . . . ! Hey, you know, they send me over to that Vietnam, I be cool, 'cause I been dodgin' bullets and shit since I been old enough to get on pussy make it happy to know me. I can get on, I can do my job. [BILLY *looks weary and depressed. Languidly he crosses to his bed. He still wears his sweat clothes.* CARLYLE *studies him, then stares at the ceiling*] Yeh. I was just layin' here thinkin' that and you come in and out it come, words to say my feelin'. That my problem. That the black man's problem altogether. You ever considered that? Too much feelin'. He too close to everything. He is, man; too close to his blood, to his body. It ain't that he don't have no good mind, but he BELIEVE in his body. Is . . . that Richie the only punk in this room, or is there more?

BILLY: What?

CARLYLE: The punk; is he the only punk?

[Carefully he takes one of RICHIE's *cigarettes and lights it]*

BILLY: He's all right.

CARLYLE: I ain't askin' about the quality of his talent, but is he the only one, is my question?

BILLY: *[He does not want to deal with this. He sits there]* You get your orders yet?

CARLYLE: Orders for what?

BILLY: To tell you where you work.

CARLYLE: I'm P Company, man. I work in P Company. I do K.P. That all. Don't deserve no more. Do you know I been in this army three months and ten days and everbody still doin' the same shit and sayin' the same shit and wearin' the same green shitty clothes? I ain't been happy one day, and that a lotta god-damn misery back to back in this ole boy. Is that Richie a good punk? Huh? Is he? He takes care of you and Roger—that how come you in this room, the three of you?

BILLY: What?

CARLYLE: *[Emphatically]* You and Roger are hittin' on Richie, right?

BILLY: He's not queer, if that's what you're sayin'. A little effeminate, but that's all, no more; if that's what you're sayin'.

CARLYLE: I'd like to get some of him myself if he a good punk, is what I'm sayin'. That's what I'm sayin'! You don't got no under-standin' how a man can maybe be a little diplomatic about what he's sayin' sorta sideways, do you? Jesus!

BILLY: He don't do that stuff.

CARLYLE: *[Lying there]* What stuff?

BILLY: Listen, man. I don't feel too good, you don't mind.

CARLYLE: What stuff?

BILLY: What you're thinkin'.

CARLYLE: What . . . am I thinkin'?

BILLY: You . . . know.

CARLYLE: Yes, I do. It in my head, that how come I know. But how do you know? I can see your heart, Billy boy, but you cannot see mine. I am unknown. You . . . are known.

BILLY: [*As if he is about to vomit, and fighting it*] You just . . . talk fast and keep movin', don't you? Don't ever stay still.

CARLYLE: Words to say my feelin', Billy boy. [RICHIE *steps into the room. He sees* BILLY *and* CARLYLE, *and freezes*] There he is. There he be.

[RICHIE *moves to his locker to put away the towel*]

RICHIE: He's one of them who hasn't come down far out of the trees yet, Billy; believe me.

CARLYLE: You got rudeness in your voice, Richie—you got meanness I can hear about ole Carlyle. You tellin' me I oughta leave—is that what you think you're doin'? You don't want me here?

RICHIE: You come to see Roger, who isn't here, right? Man like you must have important matters to take care of all over the quad; I can't imagine a man like you not having extremely important things to do all over the world, as a matter of fact, Carlyle.

CARLYLE: [*He rises. He begins to smooth the sheets and straighten the pillow. He will put the pint bottle in his back pocket and cross near to* RICHIE] Ohhhh, listen—don't mind all the shit I say. I just talk bad, is all I do; I don't do bad. I got to have friends just like anybody else. I'm just bored and restless, that all; takin' it out on you two. I mean, I know Richie here ain't really no punk, not really. I was just talkin', just jivin' and entertainin' my own self. Don't take me serious, not ever. I get on out and see you all later. [*He moves for the door,* RICHIE *right behind him, almost ushering him*] You be cool, hear? Man don't do the jivin', he the one gettin' jived. That what my little brother Henry tell me and tell me.

[*Moving leisurely, he backs out the door and is gone.* RICHIE *shuts the door. There is a silence as* RICHIE *stands by the door.* BILLY *looks at him and then looks away*]

BILLY: I am gonna have to move myself outa here, Roger decides to adopt that sonofabitch.

RICHIE: He's an animal.

BILLY: Yeh, and on top a that, he's a rotten person.

RICHIE: [*He laughs nervously, crossing nearer to* BILLY] I think you're probably right. [*Still laughing a little, he pats* BILLY's *shoulder and* BILLY *freezes at the touch. Awkwardly* RICHIE *removes his hand and crosses to his bed. When he has lain down,* BILLY *bends to take off his sneakers, then lies back on his pillow staring, thinking, and there is a silence.* RICHIE *does not move. He lies there, struggling to prepare himself for something*] Hey . . . Billy? [*Very slight pause*] Billy?

BILLY: Yeh.

RICHIE: You know that story you told the other night?

BILLY: Yeh . . . ?

RICHIE: You know . . .

BILLY: What . . . about it?

RICHIE: Well, was it . . . about you? [*Pause*] I mean, was it . . . ABOUT you? Were you Frankie? [*This is difficult for him*] Are . . . you Frankie? Billy?

[BILLY *is slowly sitting up*]

BILLY: You sonofabitch . . . !

RICHIE: Or was it really about somebody you knew . . . ?

BILLY: [*Sitting, outraged and glaring*] You didn't hear me at all!

RICHIE: I'm just asking a simple question, Billy, that's all I'm doing.

BILLY: You are really sick. You know that? Your brain is really, truly rancid! Do you know there's a theory now it's genetic? That it's all a matter of genes and shit like that?

RICHIE: Everything is not so ungodly cryptic, Billy.

BILLY: You. You, man, and the rot it's makin' outa your feeble fuckin' brain!

[ROGER, *dressed in civilian clothes, bursts in and* BILLY *leaps to his feet*]

ROGER: Hey, hey, anyone got a couple bucks he can loan me?

BILLY: Rog, where you been?

ROGER: [*Throwing the basketball and his sweat clothes into his locker*] I need five. C'mon.

BILLY: Where you been? That asshole friend a yours was here.

ROGER: I know, I know. Can you gimme five?

RICHIE: [*He jumps to the floor and heads for his locker*] You want five. I got it. You want ten or more, even?

[BILLY, *watching* RICHIE *turns, and nervously paces down right, where he moves about, worried*]

BILLY: I mean, we gotta talk about him, man; we gotta talk about him.

ROGER: [*As* RICHIE *is handing him two fives*] 'Cause we goin' to town together. I jus' run into him out on the quad, man, and he was feelin' real bad 'bout the way he acted, how you guys done him, he was fallin' down apologizin' all over the place.

BILLY: [*As* RICHIE *marches back to his bed and sits down*] I mean, he's got a lotta weird ideas about us; I'm tellin' you.

ROGER: He's just a little fucked up in his head is all, but he ain't trouble.

[*He takes a pair of sunglasses from the locker and puts them on*]

BILLY: Who needs him? I mean, we don't need him.

ROGER: You gettin' too nervous, man. Nobody said anything about anybody needin' anybody. I been on the street all my life; he brings back home. I played me a little ball, Billy; took me a shower. I'm feelin' good!

[*He has moved down to* BILLY]

BILLY: I'm tellin' you there's something wrong with him, though.

ROGER: [*Face to face with* BILLY, ROGER *is a little irritated*] Every black man in the world ain't like me, man; you get used to that idea. You get to know him, and you gonna like him. I'm tellin' you. You get to be laughin' just like me to hear him talk his shit. But you gotta relax.

RICHIE: I agree with Billy, Roger.

ROGER: Well, you guys got it all worked out and that's good, but I am goin' to town with him. Man's got wheels. Got a good head. You got any sense, you'll come with us.

BILLY: What are you talkin' about—come with you? I just tole you he's crazy.

ROGER: And I tole you you're wrong.

RICHIE: We weren't invited.

ROGER: I'm invitin' you.

RICHIE: No, I don't wanna.

ROGER: [*He moves to* RICHIE; *it seems he really wants* RICHIE *to go*] You sure, Richie? C'mon.

RICHIE: No.

ROGER: Billy? He got wheels, we goin' in drinkin', see if gettin' our heads real bad don't just make us feel real good. You know what I mean. I got him right; you got him wrong.

BILLY: But what if I'm right?

ROGER: Billy, Billy, the man is waitin' on me. You know you wanna. Jesus! Bad cat like that gotta know the way. He been to D.C. before. Got cousins here. Got wheels for the weekend. You always talkin' how you don't do nothin'—you just talk it. Let's do it tonight—stop talkin'. Be cruisin' up and down the strip, leanin' out the window, bad as we wanna be. True cool is a car. We can flip a cigarette out the window—we can watch it bounce. Get us some chippies. You know we can. And if we don't, he knows a cathouse, it fulla cats.

BILLY: You serious?

RICHIE: You mean you're going to a whorehouse? That's disgusting.

BILLY: Listen who's talkin'. What do you want me to do? Stay here with you?

RICHIE: We could go to a movie or something.

ROGER: I am done with this talkin'. You goin', you stayin'?

[*He crosses to his locker, pulls into view a wide-brimmed black and shiny hat, and puts it on, cocking it at a sharp angle*]

BILLY: I don't know.

ROGER: [*Stepping for the door*] I am goin'.

BILLY: [*Turning,* BILLY *sees the hat*] I'm going. Okay! I'm going! Going, going, going! [*And he runs to his locker*]

RICHIE: Oh, Billy, you'll be scared to death in a cathouse and you know it.

BILLY: BULLSHIT!

[*He is removing his sweat pants and putting on a pair of gray corduroy trousers*]

ROGER: Billy got him a lion-tamer 'tween his legs!

[*The door bangs open and* CARLYLE *is there, still clad in his filthy fatigues, but wearing a going-to-town black knit cap on his head and carrying a bottle*]

CARLYLE: Man, what's goin' on? I been waitin' like throughout my fuckin' life.

ROGER: Billy's goin' too. He's gotta change.

CARLYLE: He goin' too! Hey! Beautiful! That beautiful!

[*His grin is large, his laugh is loud*]

ROGER: Didn't I tell you, Billy?

CARLYLE: That beautiful, man; we all goin' to be friends!

RICHIE: [*Sitting on his bed*] What about me, Carlyle?

[CARLYLE *looks at* RICHIE, *and then at* ROGER *and then he and* ROGER *begin to laugh.* CARLYLE *pokes* ROGER *and they laugh as they are leaving.* BILLY, *grabbing up his sneakers to follow, stops at the door, looking only briefly at* RICHIE. *Then* BILLY *goes and shuts the door. The lights are fading to black*]

SCENE TWO

In the dark, taps begins to play. And then slowly the lights rise, but the room remains dim. Only the lamp attached to RICHIE's *bed burns and there is the glow and spill of the hallway coming through the transom.* BILLY, CARLYLE, ROGER *and* RICHIE *are sprawled about the room.* BILLY, *lying on his stomach, has his head at the foot of his bed, a half-empty bottle of beer dangling in his hand. He wears a blue oxford-cloth shirt and his sneakers lie beside his bed.* ROGER, *collapsed in his own bed, lies upon his back, his head also at the foot, a* Playboy *magazine covering his face and a half-empty bottle of beer in his hands, folded on his belly. Having removed his civilian shirt, he wears a white T-shirt.* CARLYLE *is lying on his belly on* RICHIE's *bed, his head at the foot, and he is facing out.* RICHIE *is sitting on the floor, resting against* ROGER's *footlocker. He is wrapped in a blanket. Beside him is an unopened bottle of beer and a bottle opener.*

They are all dreamy in the dimness as taps plays sadly on and then fades into silence. No one moves.

RICHIE: I don't know where it was, but it wasn't here. And we were all in it—it felt like—but we all had different faces. After you guys left, I only dozed for a few minutes, so it couldn't have been long. Roger laughed a lot and Billy was taller. I don't remember all the details exactly, and even though we were the ones in it, I know it was about my father. He was a big man. I was six. He was a very big man when I was six and he went away, but I remember him. He started drinking and staying home making model airplanes and boats and paintings by the numbers. We had money from Mom's family, so he was just home all the time. And then one day I was coming home from kindergarten, and as I was starting up the front walk he came out the door and he had these suitcases in his hands. He was leaving, see, sneaking out, and I'd caught him. We looked at each other and I just knew and I started crying. He yelled at me, "Don't you cry; don't you start crying." I tried to grab him and he pushed me down in the grass. And then he was gone. G-O-N-E.

BILLY: And that was it? That was it?

RICHIE: I remember hiding my eyes. I lay in the grass and hid my eyes and waited.

BILLY: He never came back?

RICHIE: No.

CARLYLE: Ain't that some shit. Now, I'm a jive-time street nigger. I knew where my daddy was all the while. He workin' in this butcher shop two blocks up the street. Ole Mom used to point him out. "There he go. That him—that your daddy." We'd see him on the street, "There he go."

ROGER: Man couldn't see his way to livin' with you—that what you're sayin'?

CARLYLE: Never saw the day.

ROGER: And still couldn't get his ass outa the neighborhood?

[RICHIE *begins trying to open his bottle of beer*]

CARLYLE: Ain't that a bitch. Poor ole bastard just duck his head— Mom pointin' at him—he git this real goddamn hang-dog look like he don't know who we talkin' about and he walk a little faster. Why the hell he never move away I don't know, unless he was crazy. But I don't think so. He come up to me once—I was playin'. "Boy," he says, "I ain't your daddy. I ain't. Your momma's crazy." "Don't you be callin' my momma crazy, Daddy," I tole him. Poor ole thing didn't know what to do.

RICHIE: [*Giving up; he can't get the beer open*] Somebody open this for me? I can't get this open.

[BILLY *seems about to move to help, but* CARLYLE *is quicker, rising a little on the bunk and reaching*]

CARLYLE: Ole Carlyle get it.

[RICHIE *slides along the floor until he can place the bottle in* CARLYLE's *outstretched hand*]

RICHIE: Then there was this once—there was this TV documentary about these bums in San Francisco, this TV guy interviewing all these bums, and just for maybe ten seconds while he was talkin' . . . [*Smiling,* CARLYLE *hands* RICHIE *the opened bottle*] . . . to this one bum, there was this other one in the background jumpin' around like he thought he was dancin' and wavin' his hat, and even though there wasn't anything about him like my father and I didn't really ever see his face at all, I just kept thinkin': That's him. My dad. He thinks he's dancin'.

[*They lie in silence and suddenly, softly,* BILLY *giggles, and then he giggles a little more and louder*]

BILLY: Jesus!

RICHIE: What?

BILLY: That's ridiculous, Richie; sayin' that, thinkin' that. If it didn't look like him, it wasn't him, but you gotta be makin' up a story.

CARLYLE: [*Shifting now for a more comfortable position, he moves his head to the pillow at the top of the bed*] Richie first saw me, he didn't like me much nohow, but he thought it over now, he changed his way a thinkin'. I can see that clear. We gonna be one big happy family.

RICHIE: Carlyle likes me, Billy; he thinks I'm pretty.

CARLYLE: [*Sitting up a little to make his point clear*] No, I don't think you pretty. A broad is pretty. Punks ain't pretty. Punk—if he good-lookin'—is cute. You cute.

RICHIE: He's gonna steal me right away, little Billy. You're so slow, Bill. I prefer a man who's decisive.

[*He is lying down now on the floor at the foot of his bed*]

BILLY: You just keep at it, you're gonna have us all believin' you are just what you say you are.

RICHIE: Which is more than we can say for you.

[*Now* ROGER *rises on his elbow to light a cigarette*]

BILLY: Jive, jive.

RICHIE: You're arrogant, Billy. So arrogant.

BILLY: What are you—on the rag?

RICHIE: Wouldn't it just bang your little balls if I were!

ROGER: [*To* RICHIE] Hey, man. What's with you?

RICHIE: Stupidity offends me; lies and ignorance offend me.

BILLY: You know where we was? The three of us? All three of us, earlier on? To the wrong side of the tracks, Richard. One good black upside-down whorehouse where you get what you buy, no jive along with it—so if it's a lay you want and need, you go! Or don't they have faggot whorehouses?

ROGER: IF YOU GUYS DON'T CUT THIS SHIT OUT I'M GONNA BUST SOME-BODY'S HEAD!

[*Angrily he flops back on his bed. There is a silence as they all lie there*]

RICHIE: "Where we *was*," he says. Listen to him. "Where we *was*." And he's got more school, Carlyle, than you have fingers and . . . [*He has lifted his foot onto the bed; it touches, presses,* CARLYLE'S *foot*] . . . toes. It's this pseudo-earthy quality he feigns—but inside he's all cashmere.

BILLY: That's a lie. [*Giggling, he is staring at the floor*] I'm polyester, worsted and mohair.

RICHIE: You have a lot of school, Billy; don't say you don't.

BILLY: You said "fingers and toes"; you didn't say "a lot."

CARLYLE: I think people get dumber the more they put their butts into some schoolhouse door.

BILLY: It depends on what the hell you're talkin' about.

[*Now he looks at* CARLYLE, *and sees the feet touching*]

CARLYLE: I seen cats back on the block, they knew what was shakin'—then they got into all this school jive and, man, every year they went, they come back they didn't know nothin'.

[BILLY *is staring at* RICHIE's *foot pressed and rubbing* CARLYLE's *foot.* RICHIE *sees* BILLY *looking.* BILLY *cannot believe what he is seeing. It fills him with fear. The silence goes on and on*]

RICHIE: Billy, why don't you and Roger go for a walk?

BILLY: What?

[*He bolts to his knees. He is frozen on his knees on the bed*]

RICHIE: Roger asked you to go downtown, you went, you had fun.

ROGER: [*Having turned, he knows almost instantly what is going on*] I asked you, too.

RICHIE: You asked me; you *begged* Billy. I said no. Billy said no. You took my ten dollars. You begged Billy. I'm asking you a favor now—go for a walk. Let Carlyle and me have some time.

[*Silence*]

CARLYLE: [*He sits up, uneasy and wary*] That how you work it?

ROGER: Work what?

CARLYLE: Whosever turn it be.

BILLY: No, no, that ain't the way we work it, because we don't work it.

CARLYLE: See? See? There it is—that goddamn education showin' through. All them years in school. Man, didn't we have a good

time tonight? You rode in my car. I showed you a good cathouse,
all that sweet black pussy. Ain't we friends? Richie likes me. How
come you don't like me?

BILLY: 'Cause if you really are doin' what I think you're doin',
you're a fuckin' animal!

[CARLYLE *leaps to his feet, hand snaking to his pocket to draw
a weapon*]

ROGER: Billy, no.

BILLY: NO, WHAT?!

ROGER: Relax, man; no need. [*He turns to* CARLYLE; *patiently,
wearily, he speaks*] Man, I tole you it ain't goin' on here.
We both tole you it ain't goin' on here.

CARLYLE: Don't you jive me, nigger. You goin' for a walk like I'm
askin', or not? I wanna get this clear.

ROGER: Man, we live here.

RICHIE: It's my house too, Roger; I live here too.

[RICHIE *bounds to his feet, flinging the blanket that has been
covering him so it flies and lands on the floor near* ROGER's
footlocker]

ROGER: Don't I know that? Did I say somethin' to make you think
I didn't know that?

[*Standing,* RICHIE *is removing his trousers and throwing them
down on his footlocker*]

RICHIE: Carlyle is my guest.

[*Sitting down on the side of his bed and facing out, he puts
his arms around* CARLYLE's *thigh.* ROGER *jumps to his feet and
grabs the blanket from the foot of his bed. Shaking it open,
he drops onto the bed, his head at the foot of the bed and
facing off as he covers himself*]

ROGER: Fine. He your friend. This your home. So that mean he can
stay. It don't mean I gotta leave. I'll catch you all in the mornin'.

BILLY: Roger, what the hell are you doin'?

ROGER: What you better do, Billy. It's gettin' late. I'm goin' to sleep.

BILLY: What?

ROGER: Go to fucking bed, Billy. Get up in the rack, turn your back and look at the wall.

BILLY: You gotta be kiddin'.

ROGER: DO IT!

BILLY: Man . . . !

ROGER: Yeah . . . !

BILLY: You mean just. . .

ROGER: It been goin' on a long damn time, man. You ain't gonna put no stop to it.

CARLYLE: You . . . ain't . . . serious.

RICHIE: [*Both he and* CARLYLE *are staring at* ROGER *and then* BILLY, *who is staring at* ROGER] Well, I don't believe it. Of all the childish . . . infantile . . .

CARLYLE: Hey! [*Silence*] HEY! Even I got to say this is a little weird, but if this the way you do it . . . [*And he turns toward* RICHIE *below him*] . . . it the way I do it. I don't know.

RICHIE: With them right there? Are you kidding? My God, Carlyle, that'd be obscene.

[*Pulling slightly away from* CARLYLE]

CARLYLE: Ohhh, man . . . they backs turned.

RICHIE: No.

CARLYLE: What I'm gonna do? [*Silence. He looks at them, all three of them*] Don't you got no feelin' for how a man feel? J don't understand you two boys. Unless'n you a pair of motherfuckers. That what you are, you a pair of motherfuckers? You slits, man. DON'T YOU HEAR ME!? I DON'T UNDERSTAND THIS SITUATION. I

THOUGHT WE MADE A DEAL! [RICHIE *rises, starts to pull on his trou-sers.* CARLYLE *grabs him*] YOU GET ON YOUR KNEES, YOU PUNK, I MEAN NOW, AND YOU GONNA BE ON MY JOINT FAST OR YOU GONNA BE ONE BUSTED PUNK. AM I UNDERSTOOD?

[*He hurls* RICHIE *down to the floor*]

BILLY: I ain't gonna have this going on here; Roger, I can't.

ROGER: I been turnin' my back on one thing or another all my life.

RICHIE: Jealous, Billy?

BILLY: [*Getting to his feet*] Just go out that door, the two of you. Go. Go on out in the bushes or out in some field. See if I follow you. See if I care. I'll be right here and I'll be sleepin', but it ain't gonna be done in my house. I don't have much in this goddamn army, but *here* is mine.

[*He stands beside his bed*]

CARLYLE: I WANT MY FUCKIN' NUT! HOW COME YOU SO UPTIGHT? HE WANTS ME! THIS BOY HERE WANTS ME! WHO YOU TO STOP IT?

ROGER: [*Spinning to face* CARLYLE *and* RICHIE] *That's right*, Billy. Richie one a those people want to get fucked by niggers, man. It what he know was gonna happen all his life—can be his dream come true. Ain't that right, Richie! [*Jumping to his feet*, RICHIE *starts putting on his trousers*] Want to make it real in the world, how a nigger is an animal. Give 'em an inch, gonna take a mile. Ain't you some kinda fool, Richie? Hear me, Carlyle.

CARLYLE: Man, don't make me no nevermind what he think he's provin' an' shit, long as I get my nut. I KNOW I ain't no animal, don't have to prove it.

RICHIE: [*Pulling at* CARLYLE's *arm, wanting to move him toward the door*] Let's go. Let's go outside. The hell with it!

[*But* CARLYLE *tears himself free; he squats furiously down on the bunk, his hands seizing it, his back to all of them*]

CARLYLE: Bullshit! Bullshit! I ain't goin' no-fuckin'-where—this jive ass ain't runnin' me. Is this you house or not?

[*He doesn't know what is going on; he can hardly look at any of them*]

ROGER: [*Bounding out of bed, hurling his pillow across the room*] I'm goin' to the fuckin' john, Billy. Hang it up, man; let 'em be.

BILLY: No.

ROGER: I'm smarter than you—do like I'm sayin'.

BILLY: It ain't right.

ROGER: Who gives a big rat's ass!

CARLYLE: Right on, bro! That boy know; he do. [*He circles the bed toward them*] Hear him. Look into his eyes.

BILLY: This fuckin' army takin' everything else away from me, they ain't takin' more than they got. I see what I see—I don't run, don't hide.

ROGER: [*Turning away from* BILLY, *he stomps out the door, slamming it*] You fuckin' well better learn!

CARLYLE: That right. Time for more schoolin'. Lesson number one. [*Stealthily he steps and snaps out the only light, the lamp clamped to* RICHIE'S *bed*] You don't see what you see so well in the dark. It dark in the night. Black man got a black body—he disappear.

[*The darkness is so total they are all no more than shadows*]

RICHIE: Not to the hands; not to the fingers.

[*Moving from across the room toward* CARLYLE]

CARLYLE: You do like you talk, boy, you gonna make me happy.

[*As* BILLY, *nervously clutching his sneaker, is moving backward*]

BILLY: Who says the lights go out? Nobody goddamn asked me if the lights go out.

[BILLY, *lunging to the wall switch, throws it. The overhead lights flash on, flooding the room with light.* CARLYLE *is seated on the edge of* RICHIE's *bed,* RICHIE *kneeling before him*]

CARLYLE: I DO, MOTHERFUCKER, I SAY! [*And the switchblade seems to leap from his pocket to his hand*] I SAY! CAN'T YOU LET PEOPLE BE? [BILLY *hurls his sneaker at the floor at* CARLYLE's *feet. Instantly* CARLYLE *is across the room, blocking* BILLY's *escape out the door*] Goddamn you, boy! I'm gonna cut your ass, just to show you how it feel—and cuttin' can happen. This knife true.

RICHIE: Carlyle, now c'mon.

CARLYLE: Shut up, pussy!

RICHIE: Don't hurt him, for chrissake!

CARLYLE: Goddamn man throw a shoe at me, he don't walk around clean in the world thinkin' he can throw another. He get some shit come back at him. [BILLY *doesn't know which way to go, and then* CARLYLE, *jabbing the knife at the air before* BILLY's *chest, has* BILLY *running backward, his eyes fixed on the moving blade. He stumbles, having run into* RICHIE's *bed. He sprawls backward and* CARLYLE *is over him*] No, no; no, no. Put you hand out there. Put it out. [*Slight pause;* BILLY *is terrified*] DO THE THING I'M TELLIN'! [BILLY *lets his hand rise in the air and* CARLYLE *grabs it, holds it*] That's it. That's good. See? See?

[*The knife flashes across* BILLY's *palm; the blood flows,* BILLY *winces, recoils, but* CARLYLE's *hand still clenches and holds*]

BILLY: Motherfucker!

[*Again the knife darts, cutting, and* BILLY *yelps.* RICHIE, *on his knees beside them, turns away*]

RICHIE: Oh, my God, what are you—

CARLYLE: [*In his own sudden distress,* CARLYLE *flings the hand away*] That you blood. The blood inside you, you don't ever see it there. Take a look how easy it come out—and enough of it come out, you in the middle of the worst goddamn trouble you ever gonna see. And know I'm the man can deal that kinda trouble, easy as I smile. And I smile . . . easy. Yeah. [BILLY *is curled in upon himself, holding the hand to his stomach as* RICHIE *now reaches tentatively and shyly out as if to console* BILLY, *who repulses the gesture.* CARLYLE *is angry and strangely depressed. Forlornly he slumps onto* BILLY'S *footlocker as* BILLY *staggers up to his wall locker and takes out a towel*] Bastard ruin my mood, Richie. He ruin my mood. Fightin' and lovin' real different in the feelin's I got. I see blood come outa somebody like that, it don't make me feel good—hurt me—hurt on somebody I thought was my friend. But I ain't supposed to see. One dumb nigger. No mind, he thinks, no heart, no feelings a gentleness. You see how that ain't true, Richie. Goddamn man threw a shoe at me. A lotta people woulda cut his heart out. I gotta make him know he throw shit, he get shit. But I don't hurt him bad, you see what I mean?

[BILLY'S *back is to them, as he stands hunched at his locker, and suddenly his voice, hissing, erupts*]

BILLY: Jesus . . . H. . . . Christ . . . ! Do you know what I'm doin'? Do you know what I'm standin' here doin'? [*He whirls now; he holds a straight razor in his hand. A bloody towel is wrapped around the hurt hand.* CARLYLE *tenses, rises, seeing the razor*] I'm a twenty-four-year-old goddamn college graduate—intellectual goddamn scholar type—and I got a razor in my hand. I'm thinkin' about comin' up behind one black human being and I'm thinkin' nigger this and nigger that—I wanna cut his throat. THAT IS RIDICULOUS. I NEVER FACED ANYBODY IN MY LIFE WITH ANYTHING TO KILL THEM. YOU UNDERSTAND ME? I DON'T HAVE A GODDAMN THING ON THE LINE HERE! [*The door opens and* ROGER *rushes in, having heard the yelling.* BILLY *flings the razor into his locker*] Look at me, Roger, look at me. I got a cut palm—I don't know what happened. Jesus Christ, I got sweat all over me when I think a what I was near to doin'. I swear it. I mean, do I think I need a reputation as a killer, a bad man with a knife? [*He is wild with the energy of feeling free and with the anger at what these others almost made him do.* CARLYLE *slumps down on the footlocker; he sits there*] Bullshit! I need shit! I got sweat all over me. I got the mile record in my hometown. I did four forty-two in high school and that's the goddamn record in Windsor County. I don't need approval from either one of the pair of you. [*And he rushes at* RICHIE] You wanna be a goddamn swish—a goddamn faggot-queer—GO! Suckin' cocks and takin' it in the ass, the thing of which you dream—GO! AND YOU—[*Whirling on* CARLYLE] You wanna be a bad-assed animal, man, get it on—go—but I wash my hands. I am not human as you are. I put you down, I put you down—[*He almost hurls himself at* RICHIE]—you gay little piece a shit cake—shit cake. And you—[*Hurt, confused,* RICHIE *turns away, nearly pressing his face into the bed beside which he kneels, as* BILLY *has spun back to tower over the pulsing, weary* CARLYLE] —you are your own goddamn fault, SAMBO! SAMBO! [*And the knife flashes up in* CARLYLE's *hand into* BILLY's *stomach, and* BILLY *yelps*] Ahhhhhhhh.

> [*And pushes at the hand.* RICHIE *is still turned away*]

RICHIE: Well, fuck you, Billy!

BILLY: [*He backs off the knife*] Get away, get away!

RICHIE: [*As* ROGER, *who could not see because* BILLY's *back is to him, is approaching* CARLYLE *and* BILLY *goes walking up toward the lockers as if he knows where he is going, as if he is going to go out the door and to a movie, his hands holding his belly*] You're so-o messed up.

ROGER: [*To* CARLYLE] Man, what's the matter with you?

CARLYLE: Don't nobody talk that weird shit to me, you understand?

ROGER: You jive, man. That's all you do—jive!

> [BILLY *striding swiftly, walks flat into the wall lockers; he bounces, turns. They are all looking at him*]

RICHIE: Billy! Oh, Billy!

> [ROGER *looks at* RICHIE]

BILLY: Ahhhhhhh. Ahhhhhhh.

> [ROGER *looks at* CARLYLE *as if he is about to scream, and beyond him,* BILLY *turns from the lockers, starts to walk again, now staggering and moving toward them*]

RICHIE: I think . . . he stabbed him. I think Carlyle stabbed Billy. Roger!

[ROGER *whirls to go to* BILLY, *who is staggering downstage and angled away, hands clenched over his belly*]

BILLY: Shut up! It's just a cut, it's just a cut. He cut my hand, he cut gut. [*He collapses onto his knees just beyond* ROGER's *footlocker*] It took the wind out of me, scared me, that's all.

[*Fiercely he tries to hide the wound and remain calm*]

ROGER: Man, are you all right?

[*He moves to* BILLY, *who turns to hide the wound. Till now no one is sure what happened.* RICHIE *only "thinks"* BILLY *has been stabbed.* BILLY *is pretending he isn't hurt. As* BILLY *turns from* ROGER, *he turns toward* RICHIE *and* RICHIE *sees the blood.* RICHIE *yelps and they all begin talking and yelling simultaneously*]

CARLYLE: You know what I was learnin', he was learnin' to talk all that weird shit, cuttin', baby, cuttin', the ways and means a shit, man, razors!

ROGER: You all right? Or what? He slit you?

BILLY: Just took the wind outa me, scared me.

RICHIE: Carlyle, you stabbed him; you stabbed him!

CARLYLE: Ohhhh, pussy, pussy, pussy, Carlyle know what he do.

ROGER: [*Trying to lift* BILLY] Get up, okay? Get up on the bed.

BILLY: [*Irritated, pulling free*] I am on the bed.

ROGER: What?

RICHIE: No, Billy, no, you're not.

BILLY: Shut up!

RICHIE: You're on the floor.

BILLY: I'm on the bed. I'm on the bed. [*Emphatically. And then he looks at the floor*] What?

ROGER: Let me see what he did. [BILLY's *hands are clenched on the wound*] Billy, let me see where he got you.

BILLY: [*Recoiling*] NO-O-O-O-O-O, you nigger!

ROGER: [*He leaps at* CARLYLE] What did you do?

CARLYLE: [*Hunching his shoulders, ducking his head*] Shut up!

ROGER: What did you do, nigger—you slit him or stick him? [*And then he tries to get back to* BILLY] Billy, let me see.

BILLY: [*Doubling over till his head hits the floor*] NO-O-O-O-O-O! Shit, shit, shit!

RICHIE: [*Suddenly sobbing and yelling*] Oh, my God, my God, ohhhh, ohhhh, ohhhh!

[*Bouncing on his knees on the bed*]

CARLYLE: FUCK IT, FUCK IT, I STUCK HIM, I TURNED IT. This mother army break my heart. I can't be out there where it pretty, don't wanna live! Wash me clean, shit face!

RICHIE: Ohhhh, ohhhhh, ohhhhhhhhhhh. Carlyle stabbed Billy, oh, ohhhh, I never saw such a thing in my life. Ohhhhhh. [*As* ROGER *is trying gently, fearfully, to straighten* BILLY *up*] Don't die, Billy; don't die.

ROGER: Shut up and go find somebody to help. Richie, go!

RICHIE: [*Scrambling off the bed*] Who? I'll go, I'll go.

ROGER: I don't know. JESUS CHRIST! DO IT!

RICHIE: Okay. Okay. Billy, don't die. Don't die.

[*Backing for the door, he turns and runs*]

ROGER: The sarge, or C.Q.

BILLY: [*Suddenly doubling over, vomiting blood.* RICHIE *is gone*] Ohhhhhhhhhh. Blood. Blood.

ROGER: Be still, be still.

BILLY: [*Pulling at a blanket on the floor beside him*] I want to stand up. I'm—vomiting—[*Making no move to stand, only to cover himself*]—blood. What does that mean?

ROGER: [*Slowing standing*] I don't know.

BILLY: Yes, yes, I want to stand up. Give me blanket, blanket.

[*He rolls back and forth, fighting to get the blanket over him*]

ROGER: RIICCHHHIIIEEEE! [*As* BILLY *is furiously grappling with the blanket*] No, no. [*He looks at* CARLYLE, *who is slumped over, muttering to himself.* ROGER *runs for the door*] Wait on, be tight, be cool.

BILLY: Cover me. Cover me. [*At last he gets the blanket over his face. The dark makes him grow still. He lies there beneath his blanket. Silence. No one moves. And then* CARLYLE *senses the quiet; he turns, looks. Slowly, wearily, he rises and walks to where* BILLY *lies. He stands over him, the knife hanging loosely from his left hand as he reaches with his right to gently take the blanket and lift it slowly from* BILLY's *face. They look at each other.* BILLY *reaches up and pats* CARLYLE's *hand holding the blanket*] I don't want to talk to you right now, Carlyle. All right? Where's Roger? Do you know where he is? [*Slight pause*] Don't stab me anymore, Carlyle, okay? I was dead wrong doin' what I did. I know that now. Carlyle, promise me you won't stab me anymore. I couldn't take it. Okay? I'm cold . . . my blood . . . is . . .

[*From off comes a voice*]

ROONEY: Cokesy? Cokesy wokesy? [*And* ROONEY *staggers into the doorway, very drunk, a beer bottle in his hand*] Ollie-ollie oxen-freeee. [*He looks at them.* CARLYLE *quickly, secretly, slips the knife into his pocket*] How you all doin'? Everybody drunk, huh? I los' my friend. [*He is staggering sideways toward* BILLY's *bunk, where he finally drops down, sitting*] Who are you, soldier? [CARLYLE *has straightened, his head ducked down as he is edging for the door*] Who are you, soldier?

[*And* RICHIE, *running, comes roaring into the room. He looks at* ROONEY *and cannot understand what is going on.* CARLYLE

is standing. ROONEY *is just sitting there. What is going on?*
RICHIE *moves along the lockers, trying to get behind* ROONEY,
his eyes never off CARLYLE]

RICHIE: Ohhhhhh, Sergeant Rooney, I've been looking for you
everywhere—where have you been? Carlyle stabbed Billy, he
stabbed him.

ROONEY: [*Sitting there*] What?

RICHIE: Carlyle stabbed Billy.

ROONEY: Who's Carlyle?   .

RICHIE: He's Carlyle. [*As* CARLYLE *seems about to advance, the
knife again showing in his hand*] Carlyle, don't hurt anybody
more!

ROONEY: [*On his feet, he is staggering toward the door*] You got a
knife there? What's with the knife? What's goin' on here?
[CARLYLE *steps as if to bolt for the door, but* ROONEY *is in the way,
having inserted himself between* CARLYLE *and* RICHIE, *who has
backed into the doorway*] Wait! Now wait!

RICHIE: [*As* CARLYLE *raises the knife*] Carlyle, don't!

        [RICHIE *runs from the room*]

ROONEY: You watch your step, you understand. You see what I got
here? [*He lifts the beer bottle, waves it threateningly*] You watch
your step, motherfucker. Relax. I mean, we can straighten all this
out. We—[CARLYLE *lunges at* ROONEY, *who tenses*] I'm just askin'
what's goin' on, that's all I'm doin'. No need to get all—[*And*
CARLYLE *swipes at the air again;* ROONEY *recoils*] Motherfucker!
Motherfucker! [*He seems to be tensing, his body gathering itself
for some mighty effort. And he throws his head back and
gives the eagle yell*] Eeeeeeeeeeaaaaaaaaaaaaaaaahhhhhhh!
Eeeeaaaaaaaaaaaaaahhhhhhhhhhhhh! [CARLYLE *jumps; he looks
left and right*] Goddammit, I'll cut you good! [*He lunges to break
the bottle on the edge of the wall lockers. The bottle shatters and
he yelps, dropping everything*] Ohhhhhhhh! Ohhhhhhhhhhhhhhh!
[CARLYLE *bolts, running from the room*] I hurt myself, I cut myself. I hurt my hand. [*Holding the wounded hand, he scurries to*
BILLY's *bed, where he sits on the edge, trying to wipe the blood*

away so he can see the wound] I cut—[*Hearing a noise, he whirls, looks;* CARLYLE *is plummeting in the door and toward him.* ROONEY *stands*] I hurt my hand, goddammit! [*The knife goes into* ROONEY's *belly. He flails at* CARLYLE] I HURT MY HAND! WHAT ARE YOU DOING? WHAT ARE YOU DOING? WAIT! WAIT! [*He turns away, falling to his knees, and the knife goes into him again and again*] No fair. No fair!

[ROGER, *running, skids into the room, headed for* BILLY, *and then he sees* CARLYLE *on* ROONEY, *the leaping knife.* ROGER *lunges, grabbing* CARLYLE, *pulling him to get him off* ROONEY. CARLYLE *leaps free of* ROGER, *sending* ROGER *flying backward. And then* CARLYLE *begins to circle* ROGER's *bed. He is whimpering, wiping at the blood on his shirt as if to wipe it away.* ROGER *backs away as* CARLYLE *keeps waving the knife at him.* ROONEY *is crawling along the floor under* BILLY's *bed and then he stops crawling, lies there*]

CARLYLE: You don't tell nobody on me you saw me do this, I let you go, okay? Ohhhhhhhhh. [*Rubbing, rubbing at the shirt*] Ohhhhhh, how'm I gonna get back to the world now, I got all this mess to—

ROGER: What happened? That you—I don't understand that you did this! That you did—

CARLYLE: YOU SHUT UP! Don't be talkin' all that weird shit to me—don't you go talkin' all that weird shit!

ROGER: Noooooooooooooo!

CARLYLE: I'm Carlyle, man. You know me. You know me.

[*He turns, he flees out the door.* ROGER, *alone, looks about the room.* BILLY *is there.* ROGER *moves toward* BILLY, *who is shifting, undulating on his back*]

BILLY: Carlyle, no; oh, Christ, don't stab me anymore. I'll die. I will—I'll die. Don't make me die. I'll get my dog after you. I'LL GET MY DOG AFTER YOU!

[ROGER *is saying, "Oh, Billy, man, Billy." He is trying to hold* BILLY. *Now he lifts* BILLY *into his arms*]

ROGER: Oh, Billy; oh, man. GODDAMMIT, BILLY!

[*As a* MILITARY POLICE LIEUTENANT *comes running in the door, his .45 automatic drawn, and he levels it at* ROGER]

LIEUTENANT: Freeze, soldier! Not a quick move out of you. Just real slow, straighten your ass up.

[ROGER *has gone rigid; the* LIEUTENANT *is advancing on him. Tentatively* ROGER *turns, looks*]

ROGER: Huh? No.

LIEUTENANT: Get your ass against the lockers.

ROGER: Sir, no. I—

LIEUTENANT: [*Hurling* ROGER *away toward the wall lockers*] MOVE! [*As another M.P.,* PFC HINSON, *comes in, followed by* RICHIE, *flushed and breathless*] Hinson, cover this bastard.

HINSON: [*Drawing his .45 automatic, moving on* ROGER] Yes, sir.

[*The* LIEUTENANT *frisks* ROGER, *who is spread-eagled at the lockers*]

RICHIE: What? Oh, sir, no, no. Roger, what's going on?

LIEUTENANT: I'll straighten this shit out.

ROGER: Tell 'em to get the gun off me, Richie.

LIEUTENANT: SHUT UP!

RICHIE: But, sir, sir, he didn't do it. Not him.

LIEUTENANT: [*Fiercely he shoves* RICHIE *out of the way*] I told you, all of you, to shut up. [*He moves to* ROONEY'S *body*] Jesus, God, this Sfc is cut to shit. He's cut to shit. [*He hurries to* BILLY'S *body*] This man is cut to shit.

[*As* CARLYLE *appears in the doorway, his hands cuffed behind him, a third M.P.,* PFC CLARK, *shoving him forward.* CARLYLE *seems shocked and cunning, his mind whirring*]

CLARK: Sir, I got this guy on the street, runnin' like a streak a shit.

[*He hurls the struggling* CARLYLE *forward and* CARLYLE *stumbles toward the head of* RICHIE's *bed as* RICHIE, *seeing him coming, hurries away along* BILLY's *bed and toward the wall lockers*]

RICHIE: He did it! Him, him!

CARLYLE: What is going on here? I don't know what is going on here!

CLARK: [*Club at the ready, he stations himself beside* CARLYLE] He's got blood all over him, sir. All over him.

LIEUTENANT: What about the knife?

CLARK: No, sir. He must have thrown it away.

[*As a fourth M.P. has entered to stand in the doorway, and* HINSON, *leaving* ROGER, *bends to examine* ROONEY. *He will also kneel and look for life in* BILLY]

LIEUTENANT: You throw it away, soldier?

CARLYLE: Oh, you thinkin' about how my sister got happened, too. Oh, you ain't so smart as you think you are! No way!

ROGER: Jesus God almighty.

LIEUTENANT: What happened here? I want to know what happened here.

HINSON: [*Rising from* BILLY's *body*] They're both dead, sir. Both of them.

LIEUTENANT: [*Confidential, almost whispering*] I know they're both dead. That's what I'm talkin' about.

CARLYLE: Chicken blood, sir. Chicken blood and chicken hearts is what all over me. I was goin' on my way, these people jump out the bushes be pourin' it all over me. Chicken blood and chicken hearts. [*Thrusting his hands out at* CLARK] You goin' take these cuffs off me, boy?

LIEUTENANT: Sit him down, Clark. Sit him down and shut him up.

CARLYLE: This my house, sir. This my goddamn house.

[CLARK *grabs him, begins to move him*]

LIEUTENANT: I said to shut him up.

CLARK: Move it; move!

> [*Struggling to get* CARLYLE *over to* ROGER'S *footlocker as* HINSON *and the other M.P. exit*]

CARLYLE: I want these cuffs taken off my hands.

CLARK: You better do like you been told. You better sit and shut up!

CARLYLE: I'm gonna be thinkin' over here. I'm gonna be thinkin' it all over. I got plannin' to do. I'm gonna be thinkin' in my quietness; don't you be makin' no mistake.

> [*He slumps over, muttering to himself.* HINSON *and the other M.P. return, carrying a stretcher. They cross to* BILLY, *chatting with each other about how to go about the lift. They will lift him; they will carry him out*]

LIEUTENANT: [*To* RICHIE] You're Wilson?

RICHIE: No, sir. [*Indicating* BILLY] That's Wilson. I'm Douglas.

LIEUTENANT: [*To* ROGER] And you're Moore. And you sleep here.

ROGER: Yes, sir.

RICHIE: Yes, sir. And Billy slept here and Sergeant Rooney was our platoon sergeant and Carlyle was a transient, sir. He was a transient from P Company.

LIEUTENANT: [*Scrutinizing* ROGER] And you had nothing to do with this? [*To* RICHIE] He had nothing to do with this?

ROGER: No, sir, I didn't.

RICHIE: No, sir, he didn't. I didn't either. Carlyle went crazy and he got into a fight and it was awful. I didn't even know what it was about exactly.

LIEUTENANT: How'd the Sfc get involved?

RICHIE: Well, he came in, sir.

ROGER: I had to run off to call you, sir. I wasn't here.

RICHIE: Sergeant Rooney just came in—I don't know why—he

heard all the yelling, I guess—and Carlyle went after him. Billy was already stabbed.

CARLYLE: [*Rising, his manner that of a man who is taking charge*] All right now, you gotta be gettin' the fuck outa here. All of you. I have decided enough of the shit has been goin' on around here and I am tellin' you to be gettin' these motherfuckin' cuffs off me and you be gettin' me a bus ticket home. I am quittin' this jive-time army.

LIEUTENANT: You are doin' what?

CARLYLE: No, I ain't gonna be quiet. No way. I am quittin' this goddamn—

LIEUTENANT: You shut the hell up, soldier. I am ordering you.

CARLYLE: I don't understand you people! Don't you people understand when a man be talkin' English at you to say his mind? I have quit the army!

[*As* HINSON *returns*]

LIEUTENANT: Get him outa here!

RICHIE: What's the matter with him?

LIEUTENANT: Hinson! Clark!

[*They move, grabbing* CARLYLE, *and they drag him, struggling, toward the door*]

CARLYLE: Oh, no. Oh, no. You ain't gonna be doin' me no more. I been tellin' you. To get away from me. I am stayin' here. This my place, not your place. You take these cuffs off me like I been tellin' you! My poor little sister Lin Sue understood what was goin' on here! She tole me! She knew! [*He is howling in the hall-way now*] You better be gettin' these cuffs off me!

[*Silence.* ROGER, RICHIE *and the* LIEUTENANT *are all staring at the door. The* LIEUTENANT *turns, crosses to the foot of* ROGER's *bed*]

LIEUTENANT: All right now. I will be getting to the bottom of this. You know I will be getting to the bottom of this.

[*He is taking two forms from his clipboard*]

RICHIE: Yes, sir.

> [HINSON *and the fourth M.P. return with another stretcher.*
> *They walk to* ROONEY, *talking to one another about how to*
> *lift him. They drag him from under the bed. They will roll*
> *him onto the stretcher, lift him and walk out.* ROGER *moves,*
> *watching them, down along the edge of* BILLY's *bed*]

LIEUTENANT: Fill out these forms. I want your serial number, rank, your MOS, the NCOIC of your work. Any leave coming up will be canceled. Tomorrow at 0800 you will report to my office at the provost marshal's headquarters. You know where that is?

ROGER: [*As the two M.P.'s are leaving with the stretcher and* ROONEY's *body*] Yes, sir.

RICHIE: Yes, sir.

LIEUTENANT: [*Crossing to* ROGER, *he hands him two cards*] Be prepared to do some talking. Two perfectly trained and primed strong pieces of U.S. Army property got cut to shit up here. We are going to find out how and why. Is that clear?

RICHIE: Yes, sir.

ROGER: Yes, sir.

> [*The* LIEUTENANT *looks at each of them. He surveys the*
> *room. He marches out*]

RICHIE: Oh, my God! Oh. Oh.

> [*He runs to his bed and collapses, sitting hunched down at*
> *the foot. He holds himself and rocks as if very cold.* ROGER,
> *quietly, is weeping. He stands and then walks to his bed. He*
> *puts down the two cards. He moves purposefully up to the*
> *mops hanging on the wall in the corner. He takes one down.*
> *He moves with the mop and the bucket to* BILLY's *bed, where*
> ROONEY's *blood stains the floor. He mops.* RICHIE, *in horror, is*
> *watching*]

RICHIE: What . . . are you doing?

ROGER: This area a mess, man.

[*Dragging the bucket, carrying the mop, he moves to the spot where* BILLY *had lain. He begins to mop*]

RICHIE: That's Billy's blood, Roger. His blood.

ROGER: Is it?

RICHIE: I feel awful.

ROGER: [*He keeps mopping*] How come you made me waste all that time talkin' shit to you, Richie? All my time talkin' shit, and all the time you was a faggot, man; you really was. You shoulda jus' tole ole Roger. He don't care. All you gotta do is tell me.

RICHIE: I've been telling you. I did.

ROGER: Jive, man, jive!

RICHIE: No!

ROGER: You did bullshit all over us! ALL OVER US!

RICHIE: I just wanted to hold his hand, Billy's hand, to talk to him, go to the movies hand in hand like he would with a girl or I would with someone back home.

ROGER: But he didn't wanna; *he* didn't wanna.

[*Finished now,* ROGER *drags the mop and bucket back toward the corner.* RICHIE *is sobbing; he is at the edge of hysteria*]

RICHIE: He did.

ROGER: No, man.

RICHIE: He did. He did. It's not my fault.

[ROGER *slams the bucket into the corner and rams the mop into the bucket. Furious, he marches down to* RICHIE. *Behind him* SERGEANT COKES, *grinning and lifting a wine bottle, appears in the doorway*]

COKES: Hey! [RICHIE, *in despair, rolls onto his belly.* COKES *is very, very happy*] Hey! What a day, gen'l'men. How you all doin'?

ROGER: [*Crossing up near the head of his own bed*] Hello, Sergeant Cokes.

COKES: [*Affectionate and casual, he moves near to* ROGER] How you all doin'? Where's ole Rooney? I lost him.

ROGER: What?

COKES: We had a hell of a day, ole Rooney and me, lemme tell you. We been playin' hide-and-go-seek, and I was hidin', and now I think maybe he started hidin' without tellin' me he was gonna and I can't find him and I thought maybe he was hidin' up here.

RICHIE: Sergeant, he—

ROGER: No. No, we ain't seen him.

COKES: I gotta find him. He knows how to react in a tough situation. He didn't come up here looking for me?

[ROGER *moves around to the far side of his bed, turning his back to* COKES. *Sitting,* ROGER *takes out a cigarette, but he does not light it*]

ROGER: We was goin' to sleep, Sarge. Got to get up early. You know the way this mother army is.

COKES: [*Nodding, drifting backward, he sits down on* BILLY's *bed*] You don't mind I sit here a little. Wait on him. Got a little wine. You can have some. [*Tilting his head way back, he takes a big drink and then, looking straight ahead, corks the bottle with a whack of his hand*] We got back into the area—we had been downtown—he wanted to play hide-and-go-seek. I tole him okay, I was ready for that. He hid his eyes. So I run and hid in the bushes and then under this Jeep. 'Cause I thought it was better. I hid and I hid and I hid. He never did come. So finally, I got tired—I figured I'd give up, come lookin' for him. I was way over by the movie theater. I don't know how I got there. Anyway, I got back here and I figured maybe he come up here lookin' for me, figurin' I was hidin' up with you guys. You ain't seen him, huh?

ROGER: No, we ain't seen him. I tole you that, Sarge.

COKES: Oh.

RICHIE: Roger!

ROGER: He's drunk, Richie! He's blasted drunk. Got a brain turned to mush!

COKES: [*In deep agreement*] That ain't no lie.

ROGER: Let it be for the night, Richie. Let him be for the night.

COKES: I still know what's goin' on, though. Never no worry about that. I always know what's goin' on. I always know. Don't matter what I drink or how much I drink. I always still know what's goin' on. But . . . I'll be goin' maybe and look for Rooney. [*But rising, he wanders down center*] But . . . I mean, we could be doin' that forever. Him and me. Me under the Jeep. He wants to find me, he goes to the Jeep. I'm over here. He comes here. I'm gone. You know, maybe I'll just wait a little while more I'm here. He'll find me then if he comes here. You guys want another drink? [*Turning, he goes to* BILLY's *footlocker, where he sits and takes another enormous guzzle of wine*] Jesus, what a goddamn day we had. Me and Rooney started drivin' and we was comin' to this intersection and out comes this goddamn Chevy. I try to get around her, but no dice. BINGO! I hit her in the left rear. She was furious. I didn't care. I gave her my name and number. My car had a headlight out, the fender bashed in. Rooney wouldn't stop laughin'. I didn't know what to do. So we went to D.C. to this private club I know. Had ten or more snorts and decided to get back here after playin' some snooker. That was fun. On the way, we picked up this kid from the engineering unit, hitchhiking. I'm starting to feel real clear-headed now. So I'm comin' around this corner and all of a sudden there's this car stopped dead in front of me. He's not blinkin' to turn or anything. I slam on the brakes, but it's like puddin' the way I slide into him. There's a big noise and we yell. Rooney starts laughin' like crazy and the kid jumps outa the back and says he's gonna take a fuckin' bus. The guy from the other car is swearin' at me. My car's still workin' fine, so I move it off to the side and tell him to do the same, while we wait for the cops. He says he wants his car right where it is and he had the right of way 'cause he was makin' a legal turn. So we're waitin' for the cops. Some cars go by. The guy's car is this big fuckin' Buick. Around the corner comes this little red Triumph. The driver's this blond kid got this blond girl next to him. You can see what's

gonna happen. There's this fuckin' car sittin' there, nobody in it.
So the Triumph goes crashin' into the back of the Buick with
nobody in it. BIFF-BANG-BOOM. And everything stops. We're staring. It's all still. And then that fuckin' Buick kinda shudders and
starts to move. With nobody in it. It starts to roll from the im-
pact. And it rolls just far enough to get where the road starts a
downgrade. It's driftin' to the right. It's driftin' to the shoulder
and over it and onto this hill, where it's pickin' up speed 'cause
the hill is steep and then it disappears over the side, and into the
dark, just rollin' real quiet. Rooney falls over, he's laughin' so
hard. I don't know what to do. In a minute the cops come and in
another minute some guy comes runnin' up over the hill to tell us
some other guy had got run over by this car with nobody in it.
We didn't know what to think. This was fuckin' unbelievable to
us. But we found out later from the cops that this wasn't true and
some guy had got hit over the head with a bottle in a bar and
when he staggered out the door it was just at the instant that this
fuckin' Buick with nobody in it went by. Seein' this, the guy stops
cold and turns around and just goes back into the bar. Rooney is
screamin' at me how we been in four goddamn accidents and
fights and how we have got out clean. So then we got everything
all straightened out and we come back here to play hide-and-seek
'cause that's what ole Rooney wanted. [He is taking another
drink, but finding the bottle empty] Only now I can't find him.
[Near RICHIE's footlocker stands a beer bottle and COKES begins to
move toward it. Slowly he bends and grasps the bottle; he
straightens, looking at it. He drinks. And settles down on RICHIE's
footlocker] I'll just sit a little. [RICHIE, lying on his belly, shudders. The sobs burst out of him. He is shaking. COKES, blinking,
turns to study RICHIE] What's up? Hey, what're you cryin' about,
soldier? Hey? [RICHIE cannot help himself] What's he cryin'
about?

ROGER: [Disgustedly, he sits there] He's cryin' 'cause he's a queer.

COKES: Oh. You a queer, boy?

RICHIE: Yes, Sergeant.

COKES: Oh. [Pause] How long you been a queer?

ROGER: All his fuckin' life.

RICHIE: I don't know.

COKES: [*Turning to scold* ROGER] Don't be yellin' mean at him.
Boy, I tell you it's a real strange thing the way havin' leukemia
gives you a lotta funny thoughts about things. Two months ago—
or maybe even yesterday—I'da called a boy who was a queer a
lotta awful names. But now I just wanna be figurin' things out. I
mean, you ain't kiddin' me out about old Rooney, are you, boys,
'cause of how I'm a sergeant and you're enlisted men, so you got
some idea a vengeance on me? You ain't doin' that, are you, boys?

ROGER: No.

RICHIE: Ohhhh. Jesus! Ohhhh. I don't know what's hurtin' in me.

COKES: No, no, boy. You listen to me. You gonna be okay. There's
a lotta worse things in this world than bein' a queer. I seen a lot
of 'em, too. I mean, you could have leukemia. That's worse. That
can kill you. I mean, it's okay. You listen to the ole sarge. I mean,
maybe I was a queer, I wouldn't have leukemia. Who's to say?
Lived a whole different life. Who's to say? I keep thinkin' there
was maybe somethin' I coulda done different. Maybe not drunk so
much. Or if I'd killed more gooks, or more Krauts or more dinks.
I was kind-hearted sometimes. Or if I'd had a wife and I had
some kids. Never had any. But my mother did and she died of it
anyway. Gives you a whole funny different way a lookin' at things,
I'll tell you. Ohhhhh, Rooney, Rooney. [*Slight pause*] Or if I'd let
that little gook outa that spider hole he was in, I was sittin' on
it. I'd let him out now, he was in there. [*He rattles the footlocker lid under him*] Oh, how'm I ever gonna forget it? That
funny little guy. I'm runnin' along, he pops up outa that hole. I'm
never gonna forget him—how'm I ever gonna forget him? I see
him and dive, goddamn bullet hits me in the side, I'm midair, everything's turnin' around. I go over the edge of this ditch and
I'm crawlin' real fast. I lost my rifle. Can't find it. Then I come
up behind him. He's half out of the hole. I bang him on top of
his head, stuff him back into the hole with a grenade for company. Then I'm sittin' on the lid and it's made outa steel. I can
feel him in there, though, bangin' and yellin' under me, and his

yelling I can hear is begging for me to let him out. It was like a goddamn Charlie Chaplin movie, everybody fallin' down and clumsy, and him in there yellin' and bangin' away, and I'm just sittin' there lookin' around. And he was Charlie Chaplin. I don't know who I was. And then he blew up. [*Pause*] Maybe I'll just get a little shut-eye right sittin' here while I'm waitin' for ole Rooney. We figure it out. All of it. You don't mind I just doze a little here, you boys?

ROGER: No.

RICHIE: No.

[ROGER *rises and walks to the door. He switches off the light and gently closes the door. The transom glows.* COKES *sits in a flower of light.* ROGER *crosses back to his bunk and settles in, sitting*]

COKES: Night, boys.

RICHIE: Night, Sergeant.

[COKES *sits there fingers entwined, trying to sleep*]

COKES: I mean, he was like Charlie Chaplin. And then he blew up.

ROGER: [*Suddenly feeling very sad for this old man*] Sergeant . . . maybe you was Charlie Chaplin too.

COKES: No. No. [*Pause*] No. I don't know who I was. Night.

ROGER: You think he was singin' it?

COKES: What?

ROGER: You think he was singin' it?

COKES: Oh, yeah. Oh, yeah; he was singin' it.

[*Slight pause.* COKES, *sitting on the footlocker, begins to sing a makeshift language imitating Korean, to the tune of "Beautiful Streamer." He begins with an angry, mocking energy that slowly becomes a dream, a lullaby, a farewell, a lament*]

Yo no som lo no
Ung toe lo knee

Ra so me la lo
La see see oh doe.
Doe no tee ta ta
Too low see see
Ra mae me lo lo
Ah boo boo boo eee.
Boo boo eee booo eeee
La so lee lem
Lem lo lee da ung
Uhhh so ba booooo ohhhh.
Boo booo eee ung ba
Eee eee la looo
Lem lo lala la
Eeee oohhh ohhh ohhh ohhhhh.

[*In the silence, he makes the soft, whispering sound of a child imitating an explosion, and his entwined fingers come apart. The dark figures of* RICHIE *and* ROGER *are near. The lingering light fades*]

SLEUTH

Anthony Shaffer

Anthony Shaffer

Sleuth, another play that originated on the London stage, was a reigning success of the early seventies and the most adroit thriller of the decade.

Until its West End opening on February 12, 1970, Anthony Shaffer was best known to his fellow Londoners as a television writer, an occasional novelist, and perhaps most of all as the twin brother of one of Britain's leading dramatists, Peter Shaffer. By the end of that same evening, however, Anthony Shaffer had vanquished his secondary status, for there was unequivocal evidence that an outstanding new dramatist had emerged from the wings. Here indeed was a playwright of major resources whose ingenious plotting was complemented by an impressive hand at creating singular characters and honing dialogue to its wittiest, most chillingly effective, "where laughter and the scent of horror are intriguingly harnessed together."

Felix Barker of the London *Evening News* hailed *Sleuth* as "the most ingenious detective play we have seen for years." While Harold Hobson proclaimed in *The Sunday Times*: "*Sleuth* is an outstanding example of the thriller considered as a fine art . . . It treats the conventional detective story with a Peacockian Gothic mockery, with a baroque juxtaposition of exotic phrases, an amused frenzy of alliteration, a cool mastery of impermissible insult: and simultaneously it is both exciting and endlessly surprising. *Sleuth* is a play to see, to be astonished by, and to brood over."

Described by *Variety* as "a smart, gripping and civilized murder yarn which also is a slick parody of the popular type of detective whodunit novel of the thirties," *Sleuth* ran for 2,359 performances in London; on Broadway, 1,222.

The play had its equally lauded New York premiere on November 12, 1970, with the original stars, Anthony Quayle and Keith Baxter, repeating their London roles. According to the press, the three other listed cast members either performed their tasks "admirably" or had "missed their cues." Since their stage existence is handled by the author in a very special way and is an integral component of the play's unique design, the editor must herewith abstain from further comment.

The Shaffer twins were born in Liverpool, England, on May 15, 1926. Their first nine years were spent, as Peter has described it, in "a nice, middle-class neighborhood," and then their father, who was in real estate, moved the family of five (a third son, Brian, was born in 1929) to London in 1935. At the outbreak of World War II, to ensure the children's safety and to accommodate the sudden decentralization of the father's real estate business, there followed a whole series of moves, terminated by the enrollment of Anthony and Peter at St. Paul's, a highly regarded public school "with a fine academic reputation, comparable to Eton but with none of that English public school snobbery." Their studies were interrupted in 1944 when, instead of being drafted into the armed forces, the brothers were conscripted for service as coal miners. After a grueling tour of duty in the mines of Kent and Yorkshire, they were released and Anthony, as well as Peter, entered Trinity College, Cambridge.

Anthony came down from Cambridge (where he was editor of the university magazine, *Granta*) in 1950. He then became a barrister, but the lure of writing persisted. After several years of poring over legal briefs and documents, he decided to enter journalism and started writing commercials and documentaries and, for a while, had his own advertising agency.

It was during this period that Anthony Shaffer also began to write plays, principally for television, and collaborated with Peter on a mystery novel, *How Doth the Little Crocodile?* which was published in England under the pseudonym "Peter Anthony." Later, when the novel was issued in the United States, it appeared under their individual names, and was followed by a second collaborative suspense effort: *Withered Murder.*

Although genuine recognition and acclaim as a playwright came more than a decade later to Anthony than it did to Peter, he has since been the recipient of numerous awards and honors. *Sleuth* received an Antoinette Perry (Tony) Award for the year's best play, while the London theatre critics voted him the year's "most promising playwright."

An established screen writer as well, Mr. Shaffer's most recent endeavors for that medium include the film adaptation of Agatha

Christie's *Death on the Nile*, and *Absolution* which won the 1979 Oxford Film Festival's Best Film and Best Screenplay awards.

The author's newest comedy melodrama, *The Case of the Oily Levantine*, opened at Her Majesty's Theatre, London, in September 1979.

Sleuth was first produced by Michael White at the St. Martin's Theatre, London, on February 12, 1970. The cast was as follows:

ANDREW WYKE   *Anthony Quayle*
MILO TINDLE   *Keith Baxter*
INSPECTOR DOPPLER   *Stanley Rushton*
DETECTIVE SERGEANT TARRANT *Robin Mayfield*
POLICE CONSTABLE HIGGS *Liam McNulty*

Directed by Clifford Williams
Designed by Carl Toms
Lighting by Francis Reid

Sleuth had its New York premiere on November 12, 1970, at the Music Box Theatre, under the auspices of Helen Bonfils, Morton Gottlieb, and Michael White. The cast was as follows:

ANDREW WYKE	*Anthony Quayle*
MILO TINDLE	*Keith Baxter*
INSPECTOR DOPPLER	*Philip Farrar*
DETECTIVE SERGEANT TARRANT	*Harold K. Newman*
POLICE CONSTABLE HIGGS	*Roger Purnell*

Directed by Clifford Williams
Designed by Carl Toms
Lighting by William Ritman

ACT ONE

A summer evening.

ACT TWO

Two days later.

ACT ONE

The living room of ANDREW WYKE'S *Norman Manor House in Wiltshire, England. It is stone flagged, and a tall window runs the height of the back wall. It is divided laterally by a minstrels gallery which, in turn, is approached by a winding staircase. A wardrobe, stage left, and a grandfather clock, and bureau stage right stand on the gallery. Upstage right is the hallway leading to the unseen front door. Upstage left a corridor leads into another part of the house. Standing in this corridor is a large basket hamper. Games of all kinds adorn the room, ranging in complexity from chess, draughts and checkers, to early dice and card games and even earlier blocking games like Senat and Nine Men Morris. Sitting by the window, under the gallery, is a life-sized figure of a Laughing Sailor.*

A summer evening.

ANDREW WYKE *is sitting at his desk, typing. He is a strongly built, tall, fleshy man of fifty-seven, gone slightly to seed. His fair hair carries on it the suspicion that chemical aid has been invoked to keep the grey at bay. His face, sourly amused and shadowed with evaded self-knowledge, is beginning to reflect the absence of constant, arduous employment. He wears a smoking jacket and black tie.*

The clock strikes eight o'clock. ANDREW *turns to look at clock, finishes typing, takes the page from the typewriter and begins to read.*

ANDREW: "Since you appear to know so much, Lord Merridew, sir," said the Inspector humbly, "I wonder if you could explain just how the murderer managed to leave the body of his victim in the middle of the tennis court, and effect his escape without leaving any tracks behind him in the red dust. Frankly, sir, we in the Police Force are just plain baffled. There seems no way he could have done it, short of black magic." St. John Lord Merridew, the great detective, rose majestically, his huge Father Christmas face glowing with mischievous delight. Slowly he brushed the crumbs of seedy cake from the folds of his pendulous waistcoat. "The police may be baffled, Inspector," he boomed, "but Merridew is not. It's all a question of a little research and a little ratiocination. Thirty years ago, the murderer, Doctor Grayson, was a distinguished member of the Ballets Russes, dancing under the name of Oleg Graysinski. The years may have altered his appearance, but his old skill had not deserted him. He carried the body out to the center of the tennis court, walking on his points along the white tape which divides the service boxes. From there he threw it five feet into the court, towards the base line, where it was found, and then, with a neatly executed fouetté, faced about and returned the way he had come, thus leaving no traces. There, Inspector, that is Merridew's solution." [He picks up his drink] Splendid! Absolutely splendid! Merridew loses none of his cunning, I'm glad to say. He's as neat *and* as gaudy as ever he was.

[The doorbell rings. ANDREW finishes his drink slowly, then exits to hallway]

ANDREW: [Offstage in hall] Oh, hullo. Good evening. Milo Tindle, is it?

MILO: [Offstage in hall] Yes. Mr. Wyke?

ANDREW: Yes. Do come in, won't you?

MILO: Thank you.

[The front door is heard to close. ANDREW walks back into the room, followed by MILO TINDLE. He is about thirty-five, slim, dark-haired and of medium height. He has a sharp, sallow face alive with a faintly Mediterranean wariness. Everything about him is neat, from his exactly parted hair to the squared-off white handkerchief in the breast pocket of his blue mohair suit]

ANDREW: Let me take your coat. [He hangs coat on coat rack] Did you find the entrance to the lane all right?

MILO: Yes. [He walks about surveying room]

ANDREW: Well done. Most people go straight past it. It's very nice of you to come.

MILO: Not at all. I found your note when I got down from London this afternoon.

ANDREW: Oh, good. I pushed it through your letter box.

MILO: Er . . . What's this? [*He indicates the figure of the Laughing Sailor*]

ANDREW: Oh, that's Jolly Jack Tar the Jovial Sailor. He and I have a very good relationship. I make the jokes and he laughs at them. [*He moves the sailor's head manually*] You see, ha-ha-ha! Now let me get you a drink. [*He crosses to drinks table*] What will you have? Scotch, gin, vodka?

MILO: Scotch.

ANDREW: How do you like it? Soda, water, ice?

MILO: Just ice. And what's this?

[MILO *has crossed to a table on which there is a large game*]

ANDREW: Oh, that's a game.

MILO: A child's game. [*He picks up one of the pieces*]

ANDREW: It's anything but childish, I can assure you. I've been studying it for months, and I'm still only a novice. It's called Senat, played by the ancient Egyptians. It's an early blocking game, not unlike our own Nine Men Morris. Would you mind putting that back where you found it? It's taken me a long time to get it there. How are you settling in at Laundry Cottage?

MILO: Very well.

ANDREW: Using it for weekends, that sort of thing?

MILO: Yes, that's the sort of thing.

ANDREW: It's a charming little place. Well, cheers.

MILO: Cheers.

ANDREW: Now do come and sit down. Forgive me if I just tidy up a bit. I've just reached the denouement of my new book, "The Body on the Tennis Court." Tell me, would you agree that the detective story is the normal recreation of noble minds?

MILO: Who said that?

ANDREW: Oh, I'm quoting Philip Guedalla. A biographer of the thirties. The golden age when every cabinet minister had a thriller by his bedside, and all the detectives were titled. Before your time, I expect.

MILO: Perhaps it would have been truer to say that noble minds were the normal recreation of detective story writers.

ANDREW: Yes. Good point. You know, even in these days I still set my own work among the gentry. And a great number of people enjoy it, in spite of the Welfare State.

MILO: I'm surprised they haven't done any of your stuff on television.

ANDREW: Oh, God forbid.

MILO: Well, they're always doing crime stories.

ANDREW: What—you mean those ghastly things where the police race around in cars and call all the suspects chummy?

MILO: Yes. That's the kind of thing.

ANDREW: Oh, no. That's not my line of country at all. That is detective fact, not detective fiction.

MILO: And of course as such is of much less interest to noble minds.

ANDREW: Yes, yes, you've put it in a nutshell, my dear Milo, if I may so address you?

MILO: Of course.

ANDREW: Thank you, we need to be friendly. Now do sit down and let me get you another drink. I'm one up on you already. [MILO *starts to sit in chair below staircase.* ANDREW *moves to drinks table*] I understand you want to marry my wife. [*A pause.* MILO *is disconcerted by the directness of the question*] You'll forgive me raising the matter, but as Marguerite is away for a few days, she's up in the North you know, visiting some relatives . . .

MILO: Is she?

ANDREW: Yes, so I thought it an appropriate time for a little chat.

MILO: Yes.

ANDREW: Well, is it true?

MILO: Well . . . Well, yes, with your permission of course.

ANDREW: Oh, yes, of course. [*He crosses to* MILO *with his drink*] Zere, put zat behind your necktie.

MILO: Cheers.

ANDREW: Prost. [*He stands in front of fireplace*] Yes, I'm glad to see you're not like so many young men these days, seem to think they can do anything they like without asking anyone's permission.

MILO: Certainly not.

ANDREW: Good. I'm pleased to hear it. I know you won't object then if I ask you a few questions about your parents and so on.

MILO: My mother was born in Hereford, a farmer's daughter. My father is an Italian who came to this country in the thirties.

ANDREW: Jewish?

MILO: Half, on his mother's side, that for the Fascists was the important side. The male, they felt, didn't transmit the disease so virulently.

ANDREW: [*Tut-tutting*] Dreadful business, dreadful.

MILO: Of course I'm not at all religious myself. I'm an agnostic.

ANDREW: [*Crosses to center of room*] My dear boy, you don't have to explain to me. We're all liberals here. I have no prejudice against Jews, or even half-Jews. Why some of my best friends are half-Jews . . . Mind you, I hope you have no objections to any children that you and my wife may have being brought up Church of England?

MILO: None whatsoever if that's what Marguerite wants.

ANDREW: You haven't discussed it yet?

MILO: Not yet, it doesn't seem to have cropped up.

ANDREW: Well, I suppose in some ways that's rather a relief. But if you take my advice, you'll opt for the Established Church. It's so much simpler. A couple of hours on Christmas Eve and Good Friday and you've seen the whole thing off nicely. And if you throw in Remembrance Sunday, they give you the Good Christian medal with oak leaf cluster.

MILO: It's the same with a lot of Jews. My father used to say, "Most people only talk to their really old friends two or three times a year. Why should God be angry if He gets the same treatment?"

ANDREW: [Insincerely] Very amusing. Your father? Was his name Tindle? It doesn't sound very Italian.

MILO: His name was Tindolini. But if you had a name like that in England in those days, you had to make "a-da-nice cream." He was a watchmaker and so he changed it.

ANDREW: Was he a successful man?

MILO: No. His business failed. He went back to Italy. I send him money from time to time and go and visit him and get a little sun or skiing, depending, of course, on the season.

ANDREW: Ah!

MILO: It's not that I'm disloyal to Britain, you understand. It's just that the Scottish Highlands and Brighton don't offer the same attractions.

ANDREW: And you? What do you do?

MILO: I'm in the travel business. I have my own agency in Dulwich.

ANDREW: Tindle's Travels, eh? I see, and where do you live?

MILO: I live above the office.

ANDREW: In Dulwich?

MILO: Yes, I rent the whole house. It's really most convenient, and . . . and it's most attractive, too. It's Georgian.

ANDREW: H'm, I'm sure it's perfectly delightful, but I doubt whether an eighteenth-century architectural gem in Dulwich whispers quite the same magic to Marguerite as it does to you.

MILO: She adores old houses. She can't wait to live there.

ANDREW: I understood she was already living there—at least for a couple of nights a week. I'm not mistaken, am I? [MILO *shrugs in embarrassment*] And surely your motive in renting the cottage down here was to increase the incidence of this hebdomadal coupling?

MILO: I came to be near the woman I love. It is a great pain for us to be apart. You wouldn't understand.

ANDREW: Possibly. But I understand Marguerite well enough to know that she does not adore old houses. She's lived here quite a time, and between them the rising damp and the deathwatch beetle have put the boot into her good and proper. She's only got to see a mullioned window and it brings her out in lumps.

MILO: [*Hotly*] Perhaps it wasn't the house so much as the person she had to share it with.

ANDREW: Now, now. I thought you were well brought up. Surely you know it's very rude to make personal remarks.

MILO: I'm sorry. You were disparaging my lover.

ANDREW: On the contrary, I was reminiscing about my wife.

MILO: It comes to the same thing.

ANDREW: Things mostly do, you know. I'll wager that within a year, it's *you* who will be doing the disparaging, and *I* who will be doing the rhapsodizing, having quite forgotten how intolerably tiresome, vain, spendthrift, self-indulgent and generally bloody crafty she really is.

MILO: If you don't love Marguerite, you don't have to abuse her.

ANDREW: Never speak ill of the deadly, eh?

MILO: Now look here . . .

ANDREW: If I choose to say that my wife converses like a child of six, cooks like a Brightlingsea landlady, and makes love like a coelacanth, I shall.

MILO: That's just about enough . . .

ANDREW: And I certainly don't need her lover's permission to do so either. In fact, the only thing I need to know from you is, can you afford to take her off my hands?

MILO: Afford to . . .

ANDREW: Afford to support her in the style to which she wasn't accustomed before she met me, but now is.

MILO: [*Gestures around the room*] She won't need all this when we're married. It'll be a different life—a life of love and simplicity. Now go ahead—sneer at that. It's almost a national sport in this country—sneering at love.

ANDREW: I don't have to sneer at it. I simply don't believe you. For Marguerite, love is the fawning of a willing lap dog, and simplicity a square-cut ten-carat diamond from Van Cleef and Arpels.

> [MILO *rises to his feet, and moves to drinks table to put down glass*]

MILO: I don't know what I'm doing here. With a little effort I'm sure you could find a much more appreciative audience!

ANDREW: Oh, now, Milo. You disappoint me. Rising to your feet like that and *bridling.*

MILO: [*Abashed*] I wasn't bridling. I was *protesting.*

ANDREW: It looked like a good old-fashioned Hedy Lamarr bridle to me.

MILO: [*Turning to* ANDREW] Who?

ANDREW: Oh, very good! Very good! Why don't you just sit down and we'll talk about something that matters desperately to both of us.

MILO: Marguerite?

ANDREW: Money! Have you got any?

MILO: Well, I'm not a millionaire, but I've got the lease on the house and some capital equipment, and the turnover in the business this year has been growing every month. By this time next year, I . . .

ANDREW: This year, next year, sometime never. What you're saying in fact is that at present you're skint.

MILO: I'll survive.

ANDREW: I'm sure you will, but survival is not the point. Presumably when you're married to Marguerite you'll want a fast car, a little place in the sun, and a couple of mistresses.

MILO: Why "presumably"? Just because you need those things.

ANDREW: Certainly I do. And so does every right-thinking, insecure, deceitful man. The point is how to get them. [*He moves to drinks table*]

MILO: I'm sure you do all right. [*He crosses to fireplace*]

ANDREW: Me? Oh, *no*. Just this fading mansion, the slowest Bentley in Wiltshire, and only one mistress, I'm afraid.

MILO: Téä? The Finnish lady who runs the sauna bath at Swindon.

ANDREW: Oh, so you know about her, do you?

MILO: Marguerite and I have no secrets from each other.

ANDREW: Not even mine, it seems. [*Mock mystical*] Téä is a Karelian Goddess. Her mother was Ilma, supreme divinity of the air; her father was Jumala, the great Creator. Her golden hair smells of pine, and her cobalt eyes are the secret forest pools of Finlandia.

MILO: I hear she's a scrubbed blonde with all the sex appeal of chilled Lysol.

ANDREW: [*With dignity*] There are those who believe that cleanliness is next to sexiness. And if I were you, I wouldn't pay much attention to what Marguerite says. You can take it from me that Téa's an engaging little trollop, and she suits me mightily. Mind you, she takes a bit of keeping up with; it's a good thing I'm pretty much of an Olympic sexual athlete.

MILO: I suppose these days you're concentrating on the sprints rather than the long distance stuff.

ANDREW: Not so, dear boy. [*He sits*] I'm in the pink of condition. I could copulate for England at any distance.

MILO: Well, they do say in Olympic circles, that the point is to take part, rather than to win, so I suppose there's hope for us all. Are you going to marry her?

ANDREW: Marry a goddess? I wouldn't presume. I might get turned into a birch tree for my audacity. Oh, no, I simply want to live with her.

MILO: So what's stopping you?

ANDREW: Basically the firm of Prurient and Pry Ltd., whom you and Marguerite have seen fit to employ. Don't look so innocent. Those nicotine-stained private detectives who've been camping outside Téa's flat for the last week.

MILO: [*Crossing to center of room*] So you spotted them?

ANDREW: A Bantu with glaucoma couldn't have missed them. No one can read the *Evening News* for four hours in a Messerschmitt bubble car, and expect to remain undetected.

MILO: Sorry about that. It was Marguerite's idea.

ANDREW: Who else's? Who paid?

MILO: I did.

ANDREW: I wonder you could afford it.

MILO: It was an insurance policy against you changing your mind about divorcing Marguerite.

ANDREW: My dear boy, let us have no misunderstanding. I've nothing against you marrying Marguerite. There's nothing I want more than to see you two tucked up together. But it's got to be a fixture. I want to be rid of her for life, not just a two-week Tindle Tour, economy class. No, you listen to me. You don't know her like I do. You think you do, but you don't. The real truth of the matter is that if you fail her, by which I mean canceling the account at Harrods, or shortchanging her on winter in Jamaica, she'll be back to me in a jiffy, mewing for support—and guilty wife or no, she may be entitled to get it.

MILO: Don't be so bloody pathetic. Winter in Jamaica? I'm not going to take her for winter in Jamaica. You're worrying unnecessarily. Once Marguerite is married to me she'll never think of returning to you. Never. And don't worry about me being able to look after her either.

ANDREW: I see. You mean that as soon as you and she are married, Marguerite will joyously substitute plain water in the bath for her customary asses milk?

MILO: So she's used to luxury. Whose fault is that?

ANDREW: It's not a fault if you can afford it. But can you? Knowing you to be hard up has she shown any sign of mending her ways in these last idyllic three months? Come on now, let's get down to the good guts of the matter. When did she last turn down Bolinger for the blandishments of Babycham? Or reject crêpes suzette in favor of roly-poly? No, no, I'm not joking, how much has this brief liaison cost you so far? Five hundred pounds? Eight hundred, a thousand? And that father of yours in Italy, when did you last send him any money? You see why I'm concerned. I tell you. She'll ruin you. To coin a phrase, in two years you'll be a used gourd. And what's more, a used gourd with a sizable overdraft.

MILO: We've often talked about money. I've told her we spend too much.

ANDREW: And she takes no notice?

MILO: [Low] None.

ANDREW: A silvery laugh? A coquettish turn of the head?

MILO: Something like that.

ANDREW: Exactly. Well, it's to solve this little problem that I have invited you here tonight. This, as they say, is where the plot thickens.

MILO: Ah!

ANDREW: I'll get you another drink. [*He crosses to drinks table. In "Listen with Mother" style:*] Are you sitting comfortably? Then I'll begin. Once upon a time there was an Englishman called Andrew Wyke who, in common with most of his countrymen, was virtually castrated by taxation. To avoid total emasculation, his accountants advised him, just before the last devaluation, to put a considerable part of his money, some 135,000 pounds, into jewelry. His wife, of course, was delighted.

MILO: You made her a present of it?

ANDREW: Absolutely not. It's still mine, as well she knows. But we felt she might as well wear it, as bank it. After all, it's fully insured.

MILO: I see what you mean by the plot thickening. It usually does when insurance is mentioned.

ANDREW: I'm glad you follow me so readily. I want you to steal that jewelry.

MILO: [*Astounded*] What?

ANDREW: Tonight, for choice. Marguerite is out of the house. It's an admirable opportunity.

MILO: You must be joking.

ANDREW: You would know it if I were.

MILO: [*Playing for time*] But . . . But what about the servants?

ANDREW: I've sent Mr. and Mrs. Hawkins to the seaside for a forty-eight-hour paddle. They won't be back till Sunday night. So, the house is empty.

MILO: I see.

ANDREW: What do you say?

MILO: It sounds criminal.

ANDREW: Of course it's criminal. All good money-making schemes in England have *got* to be these days. The jewelry, when it's not in the bank, lives in the safe under the stairs. It's there now. All you have to do is steal them, and sell them abroad and live happily ever after with Marguerite. All I have to do is to claim the insurance money and live happily ever after with Têa. [*Pause*] Well, in my case perhaps, not ever after, but at least until I get fed up with a cuisine based on the elk.

MILO: Is that what you asked me over to hear? A scummy little plot to defraud the insurance company?

ANDREW: I'm sorry you find the plot scummy. I thought it was nicely clear and simple.

MILO: Nicely obvious and clearly unworkable. Supposing I do as you say and take the jewels. If I sell them under my own name, I'll be picked up just as soon as you report their loss. If I sell them to a fence, always supposing I could find one, I'd get a fraction of their value.

ANDREW: Not with the fences I know.

MILO: [*Derisory*] What fences would you know?

ANDREW: I know some of the finest fences in Europe. Prudent yet prodigal. I met them some years ago while researching *The Deadly Affair of the Druce Diamond.*

MILO: Never read it.

ANDREW: Pity, it was an absolute fizzer—sold a hundred thousand copies. Anyway, on your behalf I have already contacted a certain gentleman in Amsterdam. He will treat you very well; you won't get full value of the jewels but you will get two thirds, say ninety thousand pounds, and you'll get it in cash.

MILO: Why should this man be so generous?

ANDREW: Because he will have what fences never have—title to the jewels. I will see to it that in addition to the jewels, you also steal the receipts I got for them. All you have to do is hand them over together. Now what does my insurance company discover when it swings into action, antennae pulsing with suspicion? It discovers that someone impersonating Andrew Wyke sold the jewels for ninety thousand pounds cash. They've still got to pay me. Hard cheese. Think it over. Take your time. There's no hurry.

[*A pause.* MILO *considers the proposition.* ANDREW *walks away from* MILO, *humming lightly to himself. He stops by a roll-a-penny wall game and plays it to a successful conclusion.* MILO *paces up and down, indecisive. He suddenly turns and faces* ANDREW]

MILO: Look, I know this sounds stupid, but . . . but well, have you had any experience—I mean, have you ever actually committed a crime before?

ANDREW: Only in the mind's eye, so to speak. For the purpose of my books. St. John Lord Merridew would have a pretty lean time of it if I didn't give him any crime to solve.

MILO: Who?

ANDREW: My detective, St. John Lord Merridew. Known to millions all over the civilized world. "An ambulatory tun of port with the face of Father Christmas." That's how I describe him. "A classical scholar with a taste for good pipes and bad puns, but with a nose for smelling out evil, superior to anything in the force."

MILO: Oh, yes, the police are always stupid in your kind of story, aren't they? They never solve anything. Only an amateur sleuth ever knows what's happening. But that is detective fiction. This is fact.

ANDREW: I am aware of the difference, Milo. I also know that insurance investigators are sharp as razors, and that's why, as Queen Victoria said to Lord Melbourne on the occasion of her coronation, everything's got to be done kosher and according to cocker.

MILO: I'm just saying there's a difference between writing and real life, that's all. And there's another thing. How do I know this thing isn't one big frame-up?

ANDREW: Frame-up?

MILO: Yes. That you really hate my association with your wife, and would give five years of Olympian sexual athleticism to see me in jail. Once I'm clear of the house, an anonymous phone call to the police . . .

ANDREW: And be stuck with Marguerite for another bickering eternity? Bodystockings on the breakfast tray, false eyelashes in the washbasin, the bottles, the lotions, the unguents, the oils, the tribal record player and that ceaseless vapid yak. Oh, yes, I could shop you to the police, nothing easier, but whatever for? Still, it's for you to evaluate, old boy.

MILO: Well, I . . . I, er . . .

ANDREW: If you don't trust me . . .

MILO: Oh, I trust you, but . . .

ANDREW: It's a very simple proposition. You have an expensive woman and no money. It seems to me if you want to keep Marguerite, there is only one thing you can do—you must steal those jewels.

MILO: Why don't *you* steal them and simply hand them over to me?

ANDREW: I should have thought that was obvious. The burglary has to look real. The house has actually to be broken into.

MILO: Well, why don't *you* break into it?

ANDREW: [*Brooklyn accent*] Hey, Milo baby, will you do me a favor. Leave this to me, huh? You know what I mean? Crime is my specialty. I've got such a great plan and I've got it all worked out to the last detail. You're the star, I'm just the producer.

MILO: Ninety thousand pounds?

ANDREW: Ninety thousand pounds tax free. In cash. It would take a lot of Tindle Tours to make that kind of money.

MILO: All right, I'll do it. Where shall I break in [*He rushes for the stairs*]

ANDREW: Hold your horses. Now the first thing you've got to do is disguise yourself.

MILO: What on earth for?

ANDREW: Supposing someone saw you climbing in?

MILO: Who? You're not overlooked.

ANDREW: Who knows? A dallying couple. A passing sheep rapist. And, dear boy, remember the clues we're to leave for the police and the insurance company. We don't want your footsteps in the flower beds, or your coat button snagged on the window sill. Oh, no, you *must* be disguised.

MILO: All right, what do you suggest?

ANDREW: [*He crosses to corridor and brings back a large hamper*] As Marguerite has assuredly told you, in younger days we were always dressing up in this house. What with amateur dramatics and masquerades and costume balls, there was virtually no end to the concealment of identity.

MILO: She's never mentioned it.

ANDREW: No . . . ? [*A touch wistful*] Well, it was all some years ago. [*Briskly*] Anyway, let's see what we've got. [*He opens basket and holds up the pieces of the burglar suit, one by one*] Item. A face mask, a flat cap, a striped jersey and bag marked Loot.

MILO: I thought the idea was that I was *not* to be taken as a burglar.

ANDREW: Fashions have changed, you know.

MILO: Not quickly enough. It's asking for trouble.

[ANDREW *puts the costume back and brings out a Ku Klux Klan outfit*]

ANDREW: Ku Klux Klan invade country home. Fiery cross, flames on Salisbury plain. Police baffled.

MILO: Isn't it a trifle conspicuous for Wiltshire?

ANDREW: Yes, you may be right! [*He holds up a monk's costume*] Here is one of my favorites. How about Brother Lightfingers?

MILO: Oh, for God's sake . . . [*He shakes his head decisively*]

ANDREW: Oh, come on. Let's make this a Gothic folly. [*Edgar Lustgarten voice*] Perhaps we shall never know the identity of the cowled figure seen haunting the grounds of the Manor House on the night of the terrible murder. Even today, some locals claim to hear the agonized screams of the victim echoing around the chimney pots.

MILO: Murder? Anguished screams of the victim? What are you talking about? It's a simple robbery we're staging here, that's all.

[*An uneasy pause*]

ANDREW: [*Normal voice*] Quite right, Milo. I was carried away for a moment. I'm not sure I wasn't going to add a crucified countess entombed in her bedroom, guarded by a man-eating sparrow hawk.

MILO: Look here, Andrew, you probably think this is one huge joke. But it's my freedom you're playing with.

ANDREW: I'm merely trying to bring a little romance into modern crime, and incidentally into your life.

MILO: Marguerite will bring all the romance into my life I need, thank you all the same.

ANDREW: Marguerite romantic? Marguerite couldn't have got Johann Strauss to waltz!

MILO: Look, Andrew, these are great costumes, but haven't you just got an old pair of wellies, a raincoat and a sock that I call pull over my head?

ANDREW: Old pair of wellies and a sock? How dreary! That's the whole trouble with crime today. No imagination. I mean, you tell me, does your heart beat any faster when you hear that a truck load of cigarettes has been knocked off in the Walworth Road?

MILO: Not particularly.

ANDREW: Well, of course not. Or that a ninety-three-year-old night watchman has had his silly interfering old skull split open with a lead pipe?

MILO: Of course not.

ANDREW: Well, then, what's the matter with you? Where's your spunk? Let's give our crime the true sparkle of the thirties, a little amateur aristocratic quirkiness. Think of all that wonderful material. There's the ice dagger, the poison that leaves no trace, the Regie cigarette stubbed in the ash tray, charred violet notepaper in the grate, Duesenberg tire marks in the driveway, the gramophone record simulating conversation, the clutching hand from behind the arras, sinister Orientals, twin brothers from Australia—"Hi there, cobber, hi there, blue"—where were you on the night of the thirteenth? I swear I didn't do it, Inspector, I'm innocent I tell you, innocent . . .

MILO: God, you've gone off like a firecracker!

ANDREW: And why not? We're on the brink of a great crime. Don't you feel the need to give your old arch-enemy, Inspector Plodder of the Yard, a run for his money? And you're the *star*, you're the *who-what-dun-it!*

MILO: Well, what about this? [*He holds up courtier's costume*]

ANDREW: Ah! Monsieur Beaucaire. He's very good. Lots of beauty spots and wig powder to let fall all over the place. Or what about this? Little Bo Peep?

   [ANDREW *sings "Little Bo Peep" and dances about holding up the costume*]

MILO: No.

ANDREW: Why not?

MILO: I haven't got the figure for it.

ANDREW: Are you quite sure? An indifferent figure shouldn't materially affect the execution of this crime.

MILO: Quite sure.

ANDREW: Well, you are choosy, aren't you? There's not a great deal left. [*He pulls out a clown's costume. Large pantaloons, waiter's dicky, tail coat*] We'll have to settle for "Joey."

MILO: Wow!

ANDREW: Can't you see it all, the tinsel, the glitter, the lights, the liberty horses, the roar of the crowd, and, Milo, all the kiddies love you.

MILO: [*Happily*] All right! It seems the costume most appropriate to this scheme.

ANDREW: Well, give me your coat. I'll hang it up for you. We don't want the police to find any fibers of this beautiful suit. [MILO *takes off his jacket and gives it to* ANDREW] Oh, and the shirt and trousers too.

MILO: What?

ANDREW: Oh, yes, you know how clever they are in those laboratories of theirs. That's it. Don't be shy. Into your smalls. Oh, I know a well-brought-up boy when I see one. Folds his pants at night.

> [MILO *gives him his carefully folded trousers.* ANDREW *runs up the stairs, and with a sudden violent gesture, roughly throws the suit into the wardrobe, while* MILO *takes off his shirt and tie and shoes*]

MILO: Shirt and shoes. [MILO *holds up his shirt, shoes and tie*]

ANDREW: Very good, sir. The Quick Clean Valet Service always at your disposal, sir. [*He pushes them into the wardrobe, then watches* MILO *changing with great satisfaction. Softly*] Give a clown your finger and he'll take your hand.

MILO: What was that?

ANDREW: Just an old English proverb I was thinking of.

> [MILO *sings to himself* "On with the Motley" *and ends it with* "Ninety thousand pounds tax free, in cash" *as he dresses*]

MILO: Ecco, Milo!

ANDREW: Bravissimo! Now all you need are the boots.

> [MILO *pulls a huge pair of boots from the basket*]

MILO: Hey, I could go skiing on these when I go to Italy.

ANDREW:

"The clown is such a happy chap,
His nose is painted red,
His trousers baggy as can be,
A topper on his head.
He jumps around the circus ring.
And juggles for his bread,
Then comes the day he tries a trick,
And drops down . . ."
Come on, do us a trick.

MILO: What sort of trick?

ANDREW: Oh, I don't know. Trip up—fall on your arse.

MILO: Certainly not, I don't think that's a very good idea.

ANDREW: Well, what about a bit of juggling then.

[ANDREW *takes two oranges from the drinks table and throws them to* MILO. *He then produces an umbrella from the basket and throws it to* MILO *who opens it and runs about the room and finally trips up on his boots*]

MILO: Christ!

ANDREW: Sorry, dear boy. But you know the rule of the circus. If at first you don't succeed . . .

MILO: Give up. Can we get on with this charade, please!

ANDREW: Of course. Yours to command. [*He opens swag bag*] Here are the tools of your trade. One glass cutter to break in with; a piece of putty for holding on to the cut piece of glass so it doesn't clatter onto the floor and awake the ravenous Doberman pinscher you suspect lurks inside; and a stethoscope.

MILO: A stethoscope?

ANDREW: Safe breakers, for the use of. The theory is you tried to pick the lock by listening to the tumblers, failed, and then employed gelignite.

MILO: [*Alarmed*] Gelignite?

ANDREW: Yes. Leave that to me. Now how about some bizarre touch—say a signed photograph of Grock left impaled on a splinter of glass.

MILO: A signed photograph of Grock. [*Angry*] Why don't you take a full page ad in *The Times* and tell them what we're doing.

ANDREW: I was only trying to lighten Inspector Plodder's day for him . . . If you don't like the idea . . .

MILO: [*Earnestly*] There's no such animal as Inspector Plodder outside of books. It'll be Inspector Early Bird, or Superintendent No Stone Unturned. You can bet your bottom dollar on that and I can't walk in this costume. These boots are ridiculous. [*He stumbles and starts to take them off*]

ANDREW: Keep them on. Can't you see it all. Wiltshire paralyzed. The West Country in a ferment. Where will Big Boot strike next?

MILO: But . . .

ANDREW: [*Reasonably*] All these boots will tell the police is that a true professional realized the flower beds would carry footprints, and decided to disguise his own perhaps a trifle eccentrically. Now are you ready? Got everything? Glass cutter? Putty?

ANDREW: ⎫
         ⎬ The mask!
MILO: ⎭

[ANDREW *takes top hat and mask from basket.* MILO *puts them on*]

ANDREW: Good. Now go through that door, round the house and across the lawn. To your right you will discover a shed. In it is a ladder. Bring the ladder back and stand it against the house so you can break in at the gallery.

MILO: Will you come out and hold it steady?

ANDREW: Certainly not. I don't want *my* footprints in the flower beds.

MILO: I'm not very good at heights.

ANDREW: Improvise. Place one foot above the other. It's called climbing.

MILO: O.K.

ANDREW: Good luck.

[MILO *bows and goes through the hall door.* ANDREW *takes a length of flex and black box with gelignite, black tape and detonator from desk drawer. After a few minutes* MILO *appears at window*]

ANDREW: For Christ's sake, can't you keep those bloody boots off my Busy Lizzies. [MILO *disappears and presently reappears with the ladder which he places against the window and starts to climb.* ANDREW *sits with his back to the window and reacts to the noises he hears. As he attaches the detonator to the flex he speaks in an old woman's voice*] Puss, Puss, Puss, do you hear a noise, Puss! Was that a step on the stairs. No, it was just the wind. You know, Puss, I sometimes think there's a curse on this house. But you shouldn't pay any attention to me. I'm just a silly old woman who is afraid of her own shadow. [*Noise of glass cutter scoring window*] What was that, Puss? Someone's prowling in the grounds. We're all going to be murdered in our beds. No, no, the front door's locked, and the window's too high, no one can get into our snug little home.

[MILO *drops pane of glass*]

ANDREW: [*Exasperated*] What *are* you doing now?

MILO: I dropped the glass. [ANDREW *groans theatrically. After a further struggle,* MILO *succeeds in climbing in through the window, onto the gallery*] Whew! What do I do with the putty? [*He indicates the putty*]

ANDREW: Stick it on the wall.

MILO: I can lose this at any rate. [*He puts mask on bureau*] Now for the safe!

ANDREW: No. Not straight away. You're not meant to know where they are. Search around. Go into the bedroom. Disturb a few things. Throw some clothes on the floor—Marguerite's for choice . . . That's it.

[MILO *goes into the bedroom and returns with a pile of women's clothes which he puts neatly on the floor*]

ANDREW: [*Rushes up to gallery*] Don't pack 'em. Ravage 'em. Don't you know how burglars leave a place? [*He takes a flying kick at the pile of his wife's clothes—sending them flying all over the room*] Now try the wardrobe. Rumple the contents a little. Actually that's enough. Those shirts were made for me by Baget and Grub, chemise makers to monarchs.

MILO: [*Throws the shirts out with relish*] Got to be thorough. It would be suspicious if the burglar played favorites.

[ANDREW's *socks and underwear follow, cascading out all over the gallery*]

ANDREW: Oh, it's a martyrdom. [*Shouting*] Will you stop that, Milo, and rifle that bureau immediately.

[*Reluctantly* MILO *crosses to the bureau and tries a drawer*]

MILO: It's locked.

ANDREW: Of course it's bloody locked! Use your jimmy on it.

MILO: I haven't got a jimmy. You didn't give me one.

ANDREW: [*Exasperated*] Well, we'd better go and find one, hadn't we? [*They tramp downstairs*] Honestly, Milo, you are the soppiest night interloper I've ever met. I can't think what Marguerite sees in you.

MILO: The sympathy and kindness of a kindred spirit, actually.

ANDREW: It's like a Bengali tiger lying down with a bush baby.

MILO: I know we're a damn sight happier than you are with your ice maiden.

ANDREW: You probably take it more seriously, that's all.

MILO: You have to be serious if you want to be in love.

ANDREW: You have to be serious about crime if you want to afford to be in love. Now get cracking on that bureau.

[MILO *climbs the stairs. He starts work on the bureau with the jimmy. After a pause the drawer yields and he opens it*]

MILO: There is a set of false teeth. They look like a man's.

ANDREW: [*Furious*] Put them back at once.

MILO: Sorry. Your spares?

ANDREW: [*Pause*] Come down at once. [MILO *comes down the stairs and crosses to* ANDREW *who has plugged the flex into a light switch*] Keep your feet off the flex. Right, stand by for count down five—four—three—two—one. Contact!

[*Noise of explosion and puff of smoke from safe*]

MILO: There she blows. Ah! It's hot.

ANDREW: You've got gloves on! Get in there! [MILO *rummages in the safe and finds a large jewel box. He examines it carefully, occasionally shaking it gently*] What the hell are you shaking it for? It's a jewel box, not a maraca.

MILO: I thought it might have some secret catch on it. It's locked, you see.

ANDREW: Well, smash it open. Jesus! You've all the killer instinct of a twenty-year-old Sealyham.

[MILO *attacks the box with his jimmy*]

MILO: It's such a pretty box—it seems such a waste. [*The box opens to reveal its precious contents.* MILO *stands entranced, letting the jewels flash and sparkle through his fingers*] Dear God!

ANDREW: Ah! Moses looks upon the promised land.

MILO: [*Sits at base of stairs*] They're very beautiful. Look at this ruby necklace!

ANDREW: That we got on our honeymoon.

MILO: It's fantastic.

ANDREW: I never cared for it myself. I always thought it made Marguerite look like a blood sacrifice.

MILO: I'd like my father to be here now. Poor blighter, he had no idea what it was all about . . . sitting there every night, hunched up over those watches like a little old gnome, squinting his eyesight away, and for what—to give me an education at a second-rate prep school. I suppose he thought he had to do it—that he owed it to me and the brave new Anglo-Saxon world he'd adopted. Poor old bugger.

ANDREW: Here, put them in your pocket for a start. I'll get you the receipts in a moment. Now! This is the fun bit. It's the moment when the householder, his attention attracted by the noise of the explosion, surprises his burglar. In the ensuing struggle, the house is sacked.

MILO: Why is it necessary for you to surprise me at all?

ANDREW: Because if I've seen you at close quarters, I can always describe you to the police . . .

[MILO *reacts as if hit*]

MILO: Now look here . . .

ANDREW: . . . wrongly. [INSPECTOR's *voice*] Did you manage to get a good look at the intruder's face, sir? [*Normal voice*] Yes, Inspector, I did. It may just have been a trick of the light, but his face didn't look wholly human. If you can imagine a kind of prognathic stoat, fringed about with lilac-colored hair, and seemingly covered with a sort of boot polish . . .

MILO: [*Patiently*] I understand. How much sacking do you want done?

ANDREW: A decent bit, I think, a few chairs on their backs, some china ornaments put to the sword. You know—convincing but not Carthaginian. [MILO *carefully turns a chair over and leans a small table against the sofa. He takes a china ornament and stands it upright on the floor.* ANDREW *watches impatiently*] Surely you don't call that convincing? ANDREW *throws over another table, spills the contents of a drawer, and turns books out of his bookcase*] That's better. Let the encyclopedias fly like autumn leaves. [MILO *throws papers in the air*] We'll let my assistant sort that lot out. You know, I never liked salt glaze. [*He drops a china ornament to the floor where it breaks*] I can't think why Marguerite is devoted to it. [*The two men survey the room*] It still doesn't look right. Come on. Let's see what accident does to artifice.

[ANDREW *seizes* MILO *and wrestles him round the room, over-turning things as they go.* MILO, *apart from being the shorter, is much hampered by his big boots and floppy clown's cloth-ing, so that* ANDREW *is able to pummel him severely*]

MILO: You're bigger than I am. It's not fair.

ANDREW: Nonsense. You're the underdog, aren't you? You've got the support of the crowd.

MILO: A good big 'un will always lick a good little 'un.

ANDREW: The bigger they are the harder they fall.

[MILO *receives a particularly hard blow*]

MILO: Here, steady on, old man!

ANDREW: They never come back. [*He pushes* MILO *over the fender into the fireplace*]

MILO: Christ! That hurt!

[ANDREW *helps him up*]

ANDREW: Come on, back into the ring. Don't despair. This fight is fixed. It's about now that I take a dive. This is where you lay me out cold.

MILO: What? For real?

ANDREW: Naturally. When the police come I must be able to show them a real bump. [MILO *smiles weakly*] I thought you'd like this bit.

MILO: [*Tentatively moving towards a lamp*] What shall I use?

ANDREW: Not my opaline, if you don't mind.

MILO: [*Picks up the brass poker*] This is it. The poker, the original blunt instrument. [*He beats logs viciously*]

ANDREW: [*Eyes the poker apprehensively*] Steady on, Milo. Don't get carried away.

MILO: Well, I'm doing my best.

ANDREW: We are not talking about a murder weapon. We are discussing an object from which I receive, in the classic formula, a glancing blow which renders me temporarily unconscious.

MILO: Such as?

ANDREW: Well, I don't know exactly. Why don't you use your imagination? Ask yourself what those fathers of the scientific detective story—R. Austin Freeman or Arthur B. Reeve—would have come up with.

MILO: Huh?

ANDREW: You know—"The Red Thumb Mark," 1907. "The Silent Bullet," 1912. [MILO *still looks blank*] Oh, do try . . . I know, perhaps we could think of a device which will raise a lump but not damage the cranium.

MILO: [*Trapped into joining in*] How about a bee sting projected into the scalp with a blowpipe?

ANDREW: Do you have such sting, pipe or bee?

MILO: Well . . . no.

ANDREW: No. Still seven out of ten for trying. I know, you can always tie me up and gag me and leave me to be found by the cleaning woman. [*Charlady's voice*] Lawks, Mr. Wyke, what are doing all trussed up like a turkey cock? [*He mimes being tied up and gagged and trying to get the Charlady to untie him*] Mmmmmmmmmmmmmm . . . Mmmmmmmmmmmm . . . Mmmmmmmmmmm . . . [*Charlady's voice*] Trying out something for one of them creepy books of yours, are you, sir? Well, don't mind me. I won't disturb you. I'll just get on with the dusting.

MILO: [*Patiently*] If I don't knock you out, how do I manage to tie you up?

ANDREW: [*Normal voice*] That's a very good question. I know. You could hold a gun on me.

MILO: We professional burglars don't like firearms much.

ANDREW: But, as you're a rank amateur, you can conquer your scruples. [*He produces a gun from the desk drawer*] Here. How about this? Don't you think its wicked-looking blue barrel is just the thing?

MILO: Is it loaded?

ANDREW: Naturally. What use would it be otherwise? Perhaps it should go off in the struggle.

MILO: Why?

ANDREW: It would add credence to my story of your holding a gun on me. Hearing a noise and fearing burglars, I took my revolver and went to investigate. You attacked me. In the struggle it went off, blowing to smithereens several priceless heirlooms. Being an old fraidy-cat householder, I allowed brutish you to take possession of it. You then held it on me while you tied me up. Right?

MILO: I suppose so.

ANDREW: Uninventive but believable. Now then, what to sacrifice? What do you say to the demolition of that gaudy Swansea puzzle jug? The gloriously witty idea is that when you tip it up the liquid pours out of a hole in the back, and not through the spout.

MILO: A bit obvious, really.

ANDREW: Exactly! Obvious and ugly. Let us expose its short-comings. [*He draws a bead on it, then lowers the gun*] On the other hand, the crème brûlée coloring lends it an attractive solidity I should miss. Now how about that giant Staffordshire mug with the inscription on it? What does it say?

MILO: [*Moves a little toward it and reads aloud*] "In the real cabinet of friendship everyone helped his neighbor and said to his brother, be of good cheer."

ANDREW: Proletarian pomposity! [*He suddenly raises his gun and fires, shattering the jug.* MILO *turns in surprise, as he realizes the*

bullet must have passed reasonably close to his head] You might
have said good shot.

MILO: Good shot.

ANDREW: [*Insouciant*] It's nothing. [*He looks around him. His eye
falls on a china figurine poised on the banister rail above him. He
takes aim*] Down with all imperialistic, deviationist, reactionary
Dresden shepherdesses! [*He shoots and the Dresden shepherdess
flies into pieces*]

MILO: Bravo!

ANDREW: What fun this is! Did you ever know Charlie Begby?

MILO: I don't think so.

ANDREW: Terribly funny fellow. I once saw him bag three brace of
duck with one shot. The only trouble was they were china ducks
on his auntie's drawing room wall. I said, "Oh, Charlie, you can't
do that, it's the closed season." [*He presses button on desk and
the sailor laughs*] I told you he always laughs at my jokes. [MILO
laughs. ANDREW's *mood changes abruptly*] It's not really all that
funny. There's an open season on some creatures all the year
round. [*He turns the gun on* MILO] Seducers and wife stealers for
example.

MILO: [*Nervous*] Only in Italian opera, surely.

ANDREW: [*Hard*] You should know. It's your country of origin, is it
not?

MILO: No. I was actually born here in England.

ANDREW: Were you now! Dear old cradle-of-the-parliamentary-
system-who-screws-my-wife-merits-a-large-pink-gin-England?

MILO: Sense-of-humor-fair-trial-England, I mean.

ANDREW: That's the way a foreigner talks. In private he thinks,
filthy wet country, ugly red cold men who don't know how to treat
women.

MILO: What's brought all this on? What are you doing with that
gun?

ANDREW: Pretty obviously pointing it at you.

MILO: For God's sake, why?

ANDREW: [*Slowly, Italian accent*] Because I'm going to kill you.

MILO: You're going to . . . [*Laughs nervously*] Oh, Jesus! I suppose this is some sort of game.

ANDREW: Yes. We've been playing it all evening. It's called "You're going to die and no one will suspect murder."

[*A pause.* MILO *considers his position*]

MILO: You mean all this steal-my-wife's-jewels stuff was just a . . .

ANDREW: Of course! I invited you here to set up the circumstances of your own death. The break-in, the disguise, the jewels in your pocket, the householder aroused, the gun going off in the struggle and then the final fatal shot. I might even get a commendation from the police, for "having a go."

MILO: For God's sake, Andrew, knock it off!

ANDREW: Can you find a flaw in it?

MILO: [*Beginning to feel desperate*] Marguerite! They'll trace the connection between me and Marguerite. They'll know that's why you did it.

ANDREW: I am quite entitled to tackle a man wearing a mask, plundering my house in the middle of the night. How was *I* expected to know who you were? Oh no, the law will have every sympathy with me. Property has always been more highly regarded than people in England. Even Marguerite will assume you were just an adventurer who only loved her for her jewels—a petty sneak thief who found larceny less burdensome than marriage. You really are a dead duck, aren't you? Not a moral or romantic attitude left.

MILO: I believe you *are* serious.

ANDREW: I'm not afraid of killing you, if that's what you mean.

MILO: You've got to be. Mortally afraid for your soul.

ANDREW: I didn't think the Jews believed in hell.

MILO: We believe in not playing games with life.

ANDREW: Ha! Wit in the face of adversity. You've learnt *something* from the English. All right, here's another thing. A sporting chance. Why don't you make a run for it?

MILO: And give you the chance to shoot me down in cold blood?

ANDREW: Hot blood, you mean. I'm going to shoot you down in cold blood anyway.

[MILO *tries to run but falls over his boots*]

MILO: Look, stop pointing that gun at me . . . I hate guns . . . please . . . this is sick.

ANDREW: You should be flattered by the honor I'm doing you—to take your life light-heartedly—to make your death the centerpiece of an arranged bit of fun. To put it another way, your demise will recreate a noble mind.

MILO: This is where I came in.

ANDREW: And where you go out, I'm afraid. The only question to be decided is where the police shall find you. Sprawled over the desk like countless colonels in countless studies? Or propped up in the log basket like a rag doll? Which do you think? Early Agatha Christie or middle S. S. Van Dine?

MILO: For Christ's sake, Andrew, this is not a detective story, this is real life. You are talking of doing a real murder. Of killing a real man—don't you understand?

ANDREW: Perhaps I shouldn't do it with a gun at all. Perhaps I should shove the ham knife into you, and leave you face down in the middle of the room—[*Melodramatic voice*]—your blood staining the flagstones a deep carmine.

MILO: [*Shudders*] Oh God!

ANDREW: Or best of all, how about a real 1930's murder weapon— the mashie niblick. I've got one in my golf bag. [*He fetches the golf club from the hall.* MILO *dives for the telephone but is too late*] You would be discovered in the fireplace, I think, in a fair old mess. [*Dramatic voice*] The body lay on its back, its limbs grotesquely splayed like a broken puppet. The whole head had been pulped as if by some superhuman force. "My God," breathed the Inspector, blanching. "Thompson, you'd better get a tarpaulin . . . Excuse me, sir, but was all this violence strictly necessary?" "I'm sorry, Inspector. It was when I saw him handling my wife's nightdresses. I must have completely lost control of myself." [ANDREW *throws down the golf club*] No. I think the scene the police find is simply this. After the fight you flee up the stairs, back to your ladder. I catch you on the landing and in the renewed struggle I shoot you. Nothing succeeds like simplicity, don't you agree, Milo? Now then, some of my own fingerprints on my own revolver. [*He takes his glove off and holds the gun in his naked hand*] On your feet, up! [ANDREW *forces* MILO *to mount the stairs by shoving the gun in his back.* MILO *gives a sudden spasmodic shudder*] Did you know that Charles I put on two shirts the morning of his execution? "If I tremble with cold," he said, "my enemies will say it was from fear; I will not expose myself to such reproaches." You must also attempt dignity as you mount the steps to the scaffold.

[MILO *demurs and sinks to his knees near the top step*]

MILO: [*Terrified and pleading*] But why, Andrew? Why?

ANDREW: Don't snivel. You can't think it'll gain you mercy.

MILO: I must know why!

ANDREW: I'm amazed you have to ask. But since you do, it's perfectly simple. I hate you. I hate your smarmy, good-looking Latin face and your easy manner. I'll bet you're easy in a ski lodge, and easy on a yacht, and easy on a beach. I'll bet you a pound to a penny, that you wear a gold charm round your neck, and that your chest is hairy and in summer matted with sun oil. I hate you because you are a mock humble, jeweled, shot cufflinked sponger, a world is my oyster-er, a seducer of silly women, and a king among marshmallow snakes. I hate you because you are a culling spick. A wop—a not one-of-me. Come, little man, did you really believe I would give up my wife and jewels to you? That I would make myself *that* ridiculous.

MILO: Why not? You're not in love with her.

ANDREW: She's mine whether I love her or not. I found her, I've kept her. I am familiar with her. And once, she was in love with me.

MILO: And now she's in love with me, and the dog in the manger won't let go. [*He tries to attack him*] The mad dog in the manger who should be put down for everyone's sake!

ANDREW: [*Deadly*] And you are a young man, dressed as a clown about to be murdered. Put the mask on, Milo. [*A pause*]

MILO: No, please.

[ANDREW *reaches up and lifts the clown mask off the banister where* MILO *had previously hung it*]

ANDREW: Put it on! [MILO *takes the mask and fumbles it onto his face*] Excellent. Farewell, Punchinello!

[ANDREW *lifts the pistol to* MILO's *head.* MILO *is shaking with fear*]

MILO: [*High falsetto*] Please . . .

[ANDREW *slowly pulls the trigger.* MILO *falls backwards down the stairs and lies still.* ANDREW *walks past him, pausing to peer closely to see whether there is any sign of life. He lifts the lolling head and lets it thump back, carelessly, onto the stairs. Satisfied that he has done his work well, he straightens up, and smiles to himself*]

ANDREW: Game and set, I believe.

SLOW CURTAIN

ACT TWO

Two days later.

The curtain rises to the sound of the slow movement of Beethoven's Seventh Symphony which is playing on a record player. ANDREW *enters from kitchen with a tray containing a large pot of caviare, toast, wedge of lemon, a bottle of champagne and glass. He puts tray on desk and stands conducting the music. The movement comes to an end.* ANDREW *crosses to record player and turns over the record. He returns to desk and starts to eat. The telephone rings.*

ANDREW: Hullo . . . Yes, Hawkins, where are you? What? Well you should have checked the times of the trains . . . I've had to get my own supper for the third time running . . . Yes, yes, I daresay, but you know how helpless I am without you and Mrs. H. Man cannot live by baked beans alone, you know . . . All right . . . All right, tomorrow morning. But first thing, mind you.

[ANDREW *continues eating for some minutes. The front doorbell rings. After a slight pause,* ANDREW *goes to answer it*]

DOPPLER: [*Offstage, in hall*] Good evening, sir.

ANDREW: [*Offstage*] Evening.

DOPPLER: Mr. Wyke.

ANDREW: Yes?

DOPPLER: My name is Inspector Doppler, sir. Detective Inspector Doppler. Of the Wiltshire County Constabulary. I'm sorry to be calling so late. May I have a few words with you on a very important matter?

[ANDREW *enters, followed by* INSPECTOR DOPPLER, *a heavily built, tallish man of about fifty. His hair is balding, and he*

wears cheap, round spectacles on his fleshy nose, above a grey-
ing moustache. His clothes—dark rumpled suit, under a half-
open light-colored mackintosh—occasion no surprise, nor
does his pork pie hat]

ANDREW: The Wiltshire County Constabulary you say? [*Turning off music*] Come in. Always pleased to see the police.

DOPPLER: Can't say the same about everyone, sir. Most people seem to have what you might call an allergy to us.

ANDREW: Would you join me in a brandy, Inspector? Or are you going to tell me you don't drink on duty?

DOPPLER: Oh, no, sir. I always drink on duty. I can't afford to in my own time. [*He sits down*]

ANDREW: [*Handing the* INSPECTOR *a brandy*] Well, what can I do for you, Inspector?

DOPPLER: I'm investigating a disappearance, sir.

ANDREW: Disappearance?

DOPPLER: Yes, sir. Of a Mr. Milo Tindle. Do you know him, sir?

ANDREW: Yes, that's the chap who's taken Laundry Cottage.

DOPPLER: He walked out of his cottage on Friday night and hasn't been seen since.

ANDREW: Great Scott!

DOPPLER: Do you know this gentleman well, sir?

ANDREW: Vaguely. He came to the house once or twice. How can I help you?

DOPPLER: When did you last see Mr. Tindle, sir?

ANDREW: Oh, months ago. I can't exactly remember. As I told you, he wasn't a close friend; rather more an acquaintance.

DOPPLER: Really, sir? That doesn't quite accord with our informa-tion. In fact, he told Jack Benn, the licensee of the White Lion, he was coming to see you, two nights ago.

ANDREW: Barmen are notorious opponents of exactitude, Inspector.

Vinous gossip is their stock in trade. In particular, I've always found that Jack Benn's observations need constant correction.

DOPPLER: Really, sir? I was wondering if you could correct something else for me.

ANDREW: What's that?

DOPPLER: The impression gained by a man who happened to be passing your house two nights ago, that a fierce struggle was taking place in here.

ANDREW: Does it look like it?

DOPPLER: And that shots were fired?

ANDREW: [*Uncertainly*] Shots?

DOPPLER: Three, our man thinks.

ANDREW: A car backfiring?

DOPPLER: No, sir. These were shots. From a gun. Our man is positive.

ANDREW: May I ask why you took two days to call round and ask me about all this?

DOPPLER: Well, sir, things take longer to check out than you think. We like to be certain of our facts before troubling a gentleman like yourself.

ANDREW: Facts? What facts?

DOPPLER: After our informant reported the incident, we did a spot of checking in the village, and as I say, Mr. Benn was very helpful.

ANDREW: There's an upright citizen, then.

DOPPLER: Quite so, sir.

ANDREW: If there were more like him . . .

DOPPLER: He told us that Mr. Tindle popped into the pub Friday evening for a quick one, and said he was just on his way up to you. Well, what with him being a newcomer to these parts and all, we thought we'd better have a word with him, and see if he could throw any light on the subject. But as I previously indicated, he seems to have disappeared, sir.

ANDREW: But what's that got to do with me?

DOPPLER: He wasn't at his cottage all of Saturday, nor all today. We must have called half a dozen times.

ANDREW: By, Jove, Merridew would have been proud of you. Now, Inspector, if that's all you have to say . . .

DOPPLER: When we stepped inside Mr. Tindle's cottage to make sure he'd come to no harm, we found this note, sir. [*Reading*] "Urgent we talk. Come Friday night eight o'clock. Wyke." May I ask whether this is your handwriting, sir?

> [DOPPLER *shows him the note.* ANDREW *tries to retain it, but* DOPPLER *takes it back*]

ANDREW: [*Trapped*] Yes. It's mine all right.

DOPPLER: So Mr. Tindle *was* here?

ANDREW: Yes. The Potman spoke sooth.

DOPPLER: Perhaps you wouldn't mind answering my original question now, sir.

ANDREW: Which one?

DOPPLER: Was there a struggle here two nights ago?

ANDREW: In a manner of speaking, yes. It was a game we were playing.

DOPPLER: A game? What kind of game?

ANDREW: It's rather difficult to explain. It's called Burglary.

DOPPLER: Please don't joke, sir.

ANDREW: Isn't it about time you told me I don't know the seriousness of my own position?

DOPPLER: A man comes here, there is a fight. Shots are heard. He disappears. What would you make of that if you were me?

ANDREW: An open and shut case. But things are not always what they seem, Inspector. In "The Case of the Drowned Dummy" my man, Merridew, once proved by a phonetic misspelling the forgery of a document allegedly written by a deaf mute.

DOPPLER: I'm waiting for an explanation, sir.

ANDREW: Tindle arrived at eight and left about an hour and a half later. I haven't seen him since.

DOPPLER: And nor has anyone else, sir.

ANDREW: This is absurd. Are you suggesting that I killed Tindle?

DOPPLER: Killed Tindle, sir. I never mentioned kill.

ANDREW: Oh really! You can't pull that old one on me. [*Mimicking* INSPECTOR'S *voice*] Garrotted, sir? Might I ask how you knew that her ladyship was garrotted? [*Normal voice*] Surely *you* told me so, Inspector. [INSPECTOR'S *voice*] No, sir. I never mentioned it.

DOPPLER: I'm sorry you find us so comic, sir. On the whole what we do is necessary.

ANDREW: "You're just doing your job," that's the overworked phrase, isn't it?

DOPPLER: Possibly, sir. Your wife and Mr. Tindle have been associating closely for some time.

ANDREW: Oh, so you know about that, do you? I suppose you can't keep anything quiet in a small village.

DOPPLER: Perfectly true, sir.

ANDREW: You aren't suggesting a crime passionale, I hope, Inspector—not over Marguerite. It would be like knifing somebody for a tablespoonful of Cooperative white blancmange.

DOPPLER: I'm very partial to blancmange, sir. I find it a great standby.

ANDREW: [*Oratorically*] "All of you had either means, motive or opportunity," said Inspector Doppler as he thoughtfully digested another spoonful of his favorite pud. "But only *one* of you had all three."

DOPPLER: Exactly so, sir! That person is you.

ANDREW: Forgive me, Inspector. I suppose I'd better tell you what happened.

DOPPLER: Yes.

ANDREW: Want a bribe to believe it?

DOPPLER: I'll have another drink.

ANDREW: As you seem to know, Tindle was having an affair with my wife. Now, I'm one of that rare breed of men who genuinely don't mind losing gracefully to a gent who's playing by the same rules. But to be worsted by a flash crypto-Italian lover, who mistakes my boredom for impotence and my provocative energy for narcissism is too much. It's like starting every game—thirty down, and the umpire against you.

DOPPLER: You mean you couldn't bring yourself to accept the situation, sir. Is that what you're saying?

ANDREW: I think what infuriated me most was the things he said about me—things that Marguerite repeated to me. I mean, no man likes to listen to the other man's witticisms when he's trying to choke down his late night Ovaltine.

DOPPLER: What sort of things, sir?

ANDREW: Oh, you know, smarmy, deceitful things which any lover can make about any husband. It's just too easy for them with a captive audience groggy on rediscovered youth and penis envy. [Pause] It's not really playing the game.

DOPPLER: You seem to regard marriage as a game, sir.

ANDREW: Not marriage, Inspector. Sex. Sex is the game with marriage the penalty. Round the board we jog towards each futile anniversary. Pass go. Collect two hundred rows, two hundred silences, two hundred scars in the deep places. It's just as well that I don't lack for amorous adventure. Finlandia provides.

DOPPLER: Are you trying to tell me that because of your indifference to your wife, you had no motive for killing Mr. Tindle?

ANDREW: I'm simply saying that in common with most men I want to have my cookie and ignore it. That's rather witty!

DOPPLER: Well, sir. I must say you're very frank.

ANDREW: Disarmingly so, I hope.

DOPPLER: Please go on.

ANDREW: As I say. I thought I'd teach Mr. Tindle a lesson for his presumption. In a curious way, some of his remarks, which Marguerite repeated to me, led me to believe that he was worth taking a little trouble with—even perhaps worth getting to know. Well, the shortest way to a man's heart is humiliation. You soon find out what he's made of.

DOPPLER: So you invited him here and humiliated him?

ANDREW: I did indeed. I took a leaf out of the book of certain eighteenth-century secret societies. They knew to a nicety how to determine whether someone was worthy to be included among their number and also how to humiliate him in the process. I refer of course to the initiation ceremony.

DOPPLER: Would it be something like bullying a new boy at school?

ANDREW: Not unlike, but the victim had the choice of refusal. When Count Cagliostro, the noted magician, sought admission to one such society, he was asked whether he was prepared to die for it, if need be. He said he was. He was then sentenced to death, blindfolded and a pistol containing powder but no shot placed against his temple and discharged.

DOPPLER: And you did this to Mr. Tindle?

ANDREW: More or less. I invited Milo here and suggested to him that as my wife had expensive tastes and he was virtually a pauper, the only course open for him was to steal some valuable jewels which I had in the safe.

DOPPLER: And he agreed to this?

ANDREW: With alacrity. I persuaded him to get out of his clothes and to dress as Grock, in which ludicrous disguise he broke into the house and blew open the safe. He then pocketed the jewels, struggled convincingly round this room and was about to make off, when I turned nasty and revealed the purpose of the evening. This, of course, was that I had maneuvered him into a position where by pretending to mistake him for a burglar, I could, as the outraged householder, legitimately shoot him as he raced away up the stairs. By the time the police arrived I would be standing in my night attire, innocent, bewildered and aggrieved. And as you well know, Inspector, there's no liar in Britain, however unconvincing, more likely to be believed than an owner-occupier standing with his hair ruffled in front of his own fireplace, wearing striped Viyella pajamas under a camel Jaeger dressing gown.

DOPPLER: What was Mr. Tindle's reaction to all this?

ANDREW: It was electrifying! He swallowed my story hook, line and sinker. He fell on his knees, and pleaded for his life, but I was implacable. I put the gun against his head and shot him with a *blank* cartridge. He fainted dead away. It was most gratifying.

DOPPLER: Gratifying or not, sir, Mr. Tindle must have been put in fear for his life. Such action invites a grave charge of assault.

ANDREW: Well, I suppose that's marginally better than the murder charge you were contemplating a few minutes ago.

DOPPLER: I still am contemplating it, sir.

ANDREW: Oh, come now, Inspector. I've told you what happened. After a few minutes, Mr. Tindle recovered his senses, realized shrewdly that he wasn't dead after all and went off home.

DOPPLER: [*Shaking his head in disbelief*] Just like that?

ANDREW: Well, he needed a glass or two of cognac to get the parts working. I mean, wouldn't you?

DOPPLER: I doubt whether I would have survived completely undamaged, sir. The whole thing sounds like the most irresponsible trick.

ANDREW: Irresponsible? It was quite the contrary. I was upholding the sanctity of marriage. That's more than most people are prepared to do these days. By this action I was clearly stating "Marriage isn't dead. It's alive and well and living in Wiltshire."

DOPPLER: Tell me, did Mr. Tindle say anything when he left?

ANDREW: No. He seemed speechless. [*Laughs*] He just lurched off.

DOPPLER: I'm sorry you appear to find all this so funny, Mr. Wyke. We may not take quite the same attitude.

ANDREW: Look, why don't you see this from my point of view. In a sense, Milo *was* a burglar. He was stealing my wife.

DOPPLER: So you tortured him?

ANDREW: [*Exploding*] Don't you see? It was a *game!*

DOPPLER: A game?

ANDREW: A bloody game, yes!

DOPPLER: It sounds rather sad, sir—like a child not growing up.

ANDREW: What's so sad about a child playing, eh!

DOPPLER: Nothing, sir—if you're a child.

ANDREW: Let me tell you, Inspector. I have played games of such complexity that Jung and Einstein would have been honored to have been asked to participate in them. Games of construction and games of destruction. Games of hazard, and games of callidity. Games of deductive logic, inductive logic, semantics, color association, mathematics, hypnosis and prestidigitation. I have achieved leaps of the mind and leaps of the psyche unknown in ordinary human relationships. And I've had a great deal of not wholly innocent fun.

DOPPLER: And now, sir, you have achieved murder.

ANDREW: No!

DOPPLER: I believe so, sir.

ANDREW: No!

DOPPLER: Would you mind if I looked around?

ANDREW: Go ahead. Crawl about the floor on hands and knees. Get your envelope out and imprison hairs. Gather ye blunt instruments while ye may.

[DOPPLER *rises and starts to examine the room*]

ANDREW: [*Slowly*] I ask myself, if I wanted to conceal Milo . . . [DOPPLER *shakes the sailor on his passage round the room*] . . . where would I put him? In the cellar? . . . Too traditional! In the water tank? . . . Too poisonous! In the linen chest? . . . Too aromatic! In the furnace? . . . Too residual! In the herbaceous border? . . . Too ossiferous! In the . . .

DOPPLER: Excuse me, sir, but these holes in the wall here and here. They look like bullet holes.

ANDREW: [*Slowly*] Quite right, Inspector. So they are.

DOPPLER: I understood you to say, sir, that you used a blank.

ANDREW: Two live bullets to set up the trick. One blank to complete it. I had to persuade Tindle I was in earnest. After all, there's really no point in playing a game unless you play it to the hilt.

DOPPLER: I see, sir. One blank. I'd like you to show me where Mr. Tindle was when you killed him.

ANDREW: Pretended to kill him, you mean.

DOPPLER: Quite so, sir. Show me, please, exactly where he was when the bullet hit him.

ANDREW: You do realize, of course, there wasn't a real bullet.

DOPPLER: [*Skeptically*] Very well, sir. Show me where he was when the blank cartridge was fired.

[ANDREW *mounts the stairs, followed by the* INSPECTOR]

ANDREW: He was standing, kneeling, crouching about here. He fainted and fell down the stairs. Bang!

[DOPPLER *passes* ANDREW]

DOPPLER: I see. About here you say, sir?

ANDREW: Towards me. Come on. Come on. Stop.

DOPPLER: Were you close to Mr. Tindle when you fired the gun?

ANDREW: Very. I was standing over him, in fact, with the gun pressed against his head. The actual feel of the gun coupled with the noise of the explosion was what did the trick. [DOPPLER *scrutinizes the staircase*] Could I interest you in a magnifying glass?

[DOPPLER *bends down to examine the staircase, then the banisters. Suddenly he rubs a finger on them, and straightens up, wiping them on his handkerchief*]

DOPPLER: Joke blood, sir?

ANDREW: [*Nervous*] I'm not quite sure I follow, Inspector.

DOPPLER: This here on the banisters. It's dried blood.

ANDREW: Blood? Where?

DOPPLER: Here in the angle of the banister—

[*Warily* ANDREW *crosses to the stairs. He examines the banisters and slowly straightens up. His expression is confused and fearful*]

DOPPLER: Don't touch it, sir! Oh, look sir, here's some more. Someone's been rubbing at the carpet. Do you see, sir? There, deep in the pile, that's blood, sir. Oh! It's still damp. Could you explain how it got there, sir?

ANDREW: I have no idea, Milo . . . er he was a little burnt . . . You must believe me!

DOPPLER: Why should I, sir?

ANDREW: But it's impossible, it was only a game.

DOPPLER: A game, sir? With real bullets and real blood?

ANDREW: [*Gabbling*] There's the hole cut in the pane of glass with the diamond cutter . . . and there are the marks of the ladder on the sill outside . . . and if you look down, you'll see the imprint of the other end of the ladder and of size twenty-eight shoes, or whatever they were, still there in the flower bed and this is the bureau that he broke open . . .

[DOPPLER *descends the stairs*]

DOPPLER: [*Hard*] Thank you, sir, but I don't require a conducted tour. Over the years my eyes have been adequately trained to see things for themselves.

ANDREW: I'm sure they have, Inspector. I only meant to point out facts which would help substantiate my story. And that's the safe we blew open . . .

DOPPLER: Where are the jewels now, sir?

ANDREW: I put them in the bank yesterday.

DOPPLER: On a Saturday?

ANDREW: Yes, Inspector, on a Saturday. I went to Salisbury and I put them in the night safe. I felt they'd be better off there. I mean, anyone could break in and steal them.

DOPPLER: How provident, sir.

ANDREW: And look down the corridor, you'll see the dressing-up basket . . .

[DOPPLER *turns away and looks out of the window, over the garden*]

DOPPLER: You didn't point out that mound of earth in the garden, did you, sir?

[ANDREW *joins* DOPPLER *at the window*]

ANDREW: Mound of earth? What mound of earth?

DOPPLER: Over there—by the far wall. In the shadow of that yew tree. Would you say it had been freshly dug, sir?

ANDREW: [*Shouting*] How the hell should I know! It's probably something the gardener's doing. A new flower bed I think he said.

DOPPLER: A flower bed under a yew tree, sir?

ANDREW: [*Shouting*] I've already told you I don't know! Why don't you ask him yourself? He's probably out there somewhere; maundering around on his moleskinned knees, aching for an opportunity to slander his employer.

DOPPLER: Funny, sir. I've always found gardeners make excellent witnesses. Slow, methodical, positive.

ANDREW: Inspector, I've had just about enough of this farce. Go and dig the damned thing up, if you want to.

DOPPLER: Oh, we shall, sir. Don't worry.

ANDREW: [*Persuasive*] Look, do you really think that I'd bury Tindle in the garden, and leave all that newly turned earth for everyone to find?

DOPPLER: If you weren't expecting us, sir, yes. In a couple of weeks, with some bulbs or a little grass seed, it would be difficult to tell it had ever been disturbed. We in the police know just how fond murderers are of their back gardens, sir.

ANDREW: [*Attempts a laugh*] You're nearer a killer's heart in a garden than anywhere else on earth, eh?

DOPPLER: Except a bedroom, sir. I think you'll find that's still the favorite. [*He starts rummaging in the wardrobe*] Tch! Tch! Tch! What a way to keep clothes! All screwed up at the back of your wardrobe. Why should you do that, I wonder? [*He holds up* MILO's *shirt*] That's an interesting monogram. I.W. No, I've got it the wrong way up—M.T.

ANDREW: Let me see that.

DOPPLER: [*Reading*] Made by Owen and Smith of Percy Street. Sixteen—eight—sixty-nine for Mr. Milo Tindle. Tell me something, sir. [ANDREW *seizes the shirt and stares at it in horror, unable to speak.* DOPPLER *holds up* MILO's *jacket and carefully reads the name in the inside pocket*] When Mr. Tindle lurched off as you put it, did he lurch naked?

ANDREW: [*In great distress*] Believe me, Inspector. I have no idea how those clothes got there.

DOPPLER: Didn't you tell me that Mr. Tindle stripped off here the other night to disguise himself as a clown?

ANDREW: Yes, that's right.

DOPPLER: Another part of the humiliation process, I suppose?

ANDREW: But he changed back before he left. I mean, you can't really see him walking through the village dressed as a clown, can you?

DOPPLER: No, sir, I can't. Which makes the appearance of his clothes here all the more significant.

ANDREW: It's all so difficult . . .

DOPPLER: On the contrary, sir, I think it's all very simple. I think you started this as a game, exactly as you say you did, in order to play a diabolical trick on Mr. Tindle, but that it went wrong. Your third shot was not a blank as you had supposed, but was in fact a live bullet which killed Mr. Tindle stone dead, spattering his blood on the banisters in the process. When you realized what you'd done, you panicked and simply buried him in the garden. It was silly of you not to wash the blood properly off the banisters and burn his clothes, though.

ANDREW: I swear Tindle left here alive.

DOPPLER: I don't believe it.

ANDREW: I didn't murder him.

DOPPLER: I accept that. As I said, I think it happened by accident. We'll be quite content with a charge of manslaughter.

ANDREW: [Shouting] I did not kill him! He left here alive.

DOPPLER: If you will pardon a flippancy, sir, you had better tell that to the judge.

ANDREW: Look. There's one way of settling this. If you think Tindle is in the garden, go and dig him up.

DOPPLER: We don't need to find him, sir. Recent decisions have relieved the prosecution of producing the corpus delicti. If Mr.

Tindle is not under the newly turned earth, it will merely go to indicate that in your panic you first thought of putting him there, then changed your mind and buried him somewhere else.

ANDREW: Where?

DOPPLER: Does it matter? Spook Spinney! Flasher's Heath! It's all the same to us. He'll turn up sooner or later—discovered by some adulterous salesman or rutting boy scout. And if he doesn't, it scarcely matters, there's so much circumstantial evidence against you. Come along, it's time to go.

ANDREW: [A cry] No!

DOPPLER: I'm afraid I must insist, sir! There's a police car outside.

ANDREW: [Louder] You may have a fleet of police cars out there. I'm not going!

DOPPLER: Now let's have no trouble, sir. Please don't make it difficult.

ANDREW: [Wildly] I must see a lawyer. It's my right!

[ANDREW backs away. DOPPLER makes to seize him, there is a scuffle]

DOPPLER: We can make a call from the station, sir. We wouldn't want to do anything unconstitutional. Come on, sir. Don't despair. At the most you'll only get seven years!

ANDREW: [Horrified] Seven years!

DOPPLER: Seven years to regret playing silly games that go wrong.

ANDREW: [Bitterly] It didn't go wrong. It went absolutely right. You've trapped me somehow.

DOPPLER: Yes, sir. You see, we real life detectives aren't as stupid as we are sometimes portrayed by writers like yourself. We may not have our pipes, or orchid houses, our shovel hats or deerstalkers, but we tend to be reasonably effective for all that.

ANDREW: Who the hell are you?

DOPPLER: Detective Inspector Doppler, sir, spelled as in C. Doppler,

1803–1853, whose principle it was that when the source of any wave movement is approached, the frequency appears greater than it would to an observer moving away. It is also not unconnected with Doppler meaning double in German—hence Doppleganger or double image. And of course, for those whose minds run to these things, it is virtually an anagram of the word Plodder. Inspector Plodder becomes Inspector Doppler, if you see what I mean, sir!

ANDREW: [A *shriek*] Milo!

MILO: [*Normal voice*] The same.

[MILO *peels off his disguise which apart from elaborate face and hair make-up—wig, false nose, glasses, cheek padding and moustache—also includes a great deal of body padding, and elevator shoes, which have had the effect of making him taller than* ANDREW, *where in reality he is a fraction shorter*]

ANDREW: You shit!

MILO: Just so.

ANDREW: You platinum-plated, copper-bottomed, dyed-in-the-wool, all-time knock-down drag-out, champion bastard Milo!

MILO: Thanks.

ANDREW: You weasel! You cozening coypu!

MILO: Obliged.

ANDREW: You mendacious bollock of Satan. Milo! You triple-dealing turd!

MILO: In your debt.

ANDREW: Mind you, I'm not saying it wasn't well done. It was— brilliant.

MILO: Thank you.

ANDREW: Have a drink, my dear fellow?

MILO: Let me wash first. I'm covered with make-up and spirit gum.

[ANDREW *shakily pours himself a whiskey*]

ANDREW: Just down the corridor. Cheers!

MILO: Good health.

[MILO *exits to bathroom as* ANDREW *gulps drink down*]

ANDREW: Yes, I must say, Milo, I congratulate you. It was first class. You really had me going there for a moment.

MILO: [*Quizzically*] For a moment?

ANDREW: For a long moment, I concede. Of course, I had my suspicions toward the end. Flasher's Heath indeed! That was going a bit far.

MILO: [*Off*] I was giving you one of your English sporting chances.

ANDREW: What did you think of *my* performance? The anguish of an innocent man trapped by circumstantial evidence.

MILO: [*Off*] Undignified—if it was a performance.

[MILO *returns and picks up his clothes*]

ANDREW: Of course it was, and it had to be undignified to be convincing. As I say, I had my suspicions.

MILO: Indeed? How cleverly you kept them to yourself.

[MILO *goes upstairs to the wardrobe where he dresses in his own clothes*]

ANDREW: And how well you executed it. I loved your Inspector Doppler. His relentless courtesy, his chilly rusticity, his yeoman beadiness.

MILO: [DOPPLER *voice*] I'm glad you view the trifling masquerade in that light, sir.

ANDREW: He was quite a masterpiece. Inspector Ringrose crossed with a kind of déclassé Roger Sheringham, I'd have said.

MILO: Really?

ANDREW: Oh, yes! Surely you remember "The Poisoned Chocolate Case," 1929. It was a really astounding tour de force with no less than six separate solutions.

MILO: I've never heard of it.

ANDREW: You should read it. It's a veritable textbook of the literature, not that you need any tips on plotting. I suppose you slipped in here yesterday when I was over in Salisbury.

MILO: Yes, I waited to see you leave.

ANDREW: And dumped the clothes in the wardrobe, and sprinkled a little sacrificial blood on the banisters.

MILO: Exactly. But it wasn't my blood you will be relieved to hear. It was obtained from a pig's liver.

ANDREW: Ugh! Perhaps you will do me the favor of wiping it off in a minute. I don't wish to fertilize the woodworm.

MILO: Question. Where would you find homosexual woodworms?

ANDREW: What?

MILO: In a tallboy. [ANDREW *grimaces. Then, sharply*] I'd like that drink now.

ANDREW: Yes, of course. [*He goes to drinks table and pours a brandy for* MILO] You deserve it.

MILO: [*Sits on chair under staircase*] You know I haven't congratulated you on your game yet. You brought it off with great élan.

ANDREW: Did you think so? Oh, good! Good! I must say I was rather delighted with it myself. Tell me . . . did you really think that your last moment on earth had come?

MILO: Yes.

ANDREW: You're not angry, are you?

MILO: Anger is a meaningless word in this context.

ANDREW: I've already tried to explain it to you. I wanted to get to know you—to see if you were, as I suspected, my sort of person.

MILO: A games-playing sort of person?

ANDREW: Exactly.

MILO: And am I?

ANDREW: Most certainly. There's no doubt about it.

MILO: And what exactly is a games-playing person?

ANDREW: He's the complete man—a man of reason and imagination, of potent passions and bright fancies. He's joyous and unrepenting. His weapons are the openness of a child and the cunning of a pike and with them he faces out the black terrors of life. For me personally, he is a man who dares to live his life without the crutch of domestic tension. You see, at bottom, I'm rather a solitary man. An arrangement of clouds, the secret mystery of landscape, a game of intrigue and revelation mean more to me than people—even the ones I'm supposed to be in love with. I've never met a woman to whom the claims of intellect were as absolute as they are to me. For a long time I was reticent about all this, knowing that most people would mistake my adroit heart for one of polished stone. But it doesn't worry me any longer. I'm out in the open. I've turned my whole life into one great work of happy invention.

MILO: And you think I'm like this?

ANDREW: Yes, I do.

MILO: You're wrong.

ANDREW: I'm not. Look at the way you chose to get back at me—by playing Inspector Doppler.

MILO: That was just the need for revenge. Every Italian knows about that.

ANDREW: Rubbish. You could have revenged yourself in one of many crude Mafiosi ways—cutting off the gardener's hands, for example, or staking the cleaning woman out on the gravel, or even I suppose, as a last resort, scratched loutish words on the hood of my Bentley. But no, you had to resort to a game.

MILO: I like to pay back in kind.

ANDREW: And is honor satisfied? Is it one set all?

MILO: [*Hard*] By no means. Your game was superior to mine. I merely teased you for a few minutes with the thought of prison. [*Low*] You virtually terrified me to death.

ANDREW: My dear fellow . . .

MILO: [*Slowly, thinking it out*] And that changes you profoundly. Once you've given yourself to death, actually faced the fact that the coat sleeve button, the banister, the nail on your fourth finger are the last things you're going to see ever—and then *heard* the sound of your own death—things cannot be the same again. I feel I've been tempered by madness. I stand outside and see myself for the first time without responsibility.

ANDREW: [*Nervous*] That's shock, my dear chap. It'll pass. Here, have another drink. [ANDREW *reaches for the glass.* MILO *jerks away. He is in great distress*] How cold you are. Milo, my dear fellow, I didn't realize how absolutely cold . . .

MILO: So that my only duty is to even our score. That's imperative. As you would put it "I'm three games up in the second set, having lost the first six-love." That's right, isn't it? That's about how you see it? I should hate to cheat.

ANDREW: You're being too modest, Milo. In my scoring it's one set all.

MILO: Oh, no, I can't accept that. You see, to the ends of playing the game and drawing honorably level, I *have* killed someone.

ANDREW: Killed someone?

MILO: Murdered someone. Committed murder.

ANDREW: You're not serious.

MILO: Yes.

ANDREW: What is this? Some new murder game?

MILO: Yes. But it has a difference. Both the game and the murder are real. There's absolutely no point in another pretense murder game, is there?

ANDREW: [*Soothing*] No, none. But I don't like to take advantage of you in this emotional state.

MILO: [*Shouting*] It can't wait!

ANDREW: [*Soothing*] All right. All right. Let's play your game. Who did you kill?

MILO: Your girl friend, Tẽa . . .

ANDREW: You killed Tẽa?

MILO: [*A little giggle*] She whose cobalt eyes were the secret forest pools of Finlandia. I closed them.

ANDREW: You . . .

MILO: I strangled her—right here on this rug I strangled her and . . . I had her first.

ANDREW: You raped and str . . .

MILO: No. Not rape. She wanted it.

ANDREW: You're lying. You can't take me in with a crude game like this. [*With braggadocio*] Honestly, Milo. You're in the big league now. I gave you credit for better sport than this.

MILO: You'll have all the sport you can stomach in a moment, Andrew. That I promise you.

ANDREW: Really, Milo, I think it would be better if . . .

MILO: When I was here yesterday, planning the blood and clothes for my Inspector Doppler scene, Tẽa stopped by. I strangled her. She was under that freshly dug mound of earth in the garden that so took Doppler's fancy.

ANDREW: Was? You mean she's not there now?

MILO: No. I moved her.

ANDREW: [*Derisory*] You moved her? Where to? Flasher's Heath, I suppose.

MILO: Something like that. It was too easy leaving her here . . . Too easy for the game you are going to play against the clock before the police arrive.

ANDREW: The police?

MILO: Yes. You see, about an hour ago I phoned them up and asked them to meet me here at ten o'clock tonight. They should be here in about ten minutes.

ANDREW: [*Sarcastic*] Yes, yes. I'm sure they will be. Led, no doubt, by intrepid downy Inspector Doppler.

MILO: Oh, no. It'll be a real policeman, have no fear of that. Detective Sergeant Tarrant, his name is. I told him a lot about you, Andrew. I said that I knew you to be a man obsessed with games-playing and murder considered as a fine art. Your life's great ambition, I said, of which you'd often spoken, was to commit an actual real life murder, hide the body somewhere where it couldn't be traced to you and then leave clues linking you with the crime, strewn about your house in the certain knowledge that the pedestrian and simple-minded police wouldn't recognize them for what they were.

ANDREW: Obsessed with games-playing and murder considered as a fine art! That's rather ingenious of you, Milo. But it won't work. Please, sir, Andrew Wyke can't rest until he's committed a real murder which is going to make fools out of all you coppers. Honestly! Tell that to the average desk sergeant and you'll find yourself strapped straight into the giggle jacket.

MILO: Not so in fact, I told them that if they didn't believe me, one look at your bookcase and the furnishings of your house would confirm what I said about your obsessions.

ANDREW: [*Slow*] Go on.

MILO: I also told them that two days ago your girl friend had come to my house in great distress, saying you suspected she was having affairs with other men and had threatened to kill her.

ANDREW: The police believed all that?

MILO: After some demur, yes.

ANDREW: The fuzz are watching too much T.V.

MILO: You mustn't resent imagination in public office, Andrew. Of course, I went on I had no proof that any harm had actually been done to her, but I thought I had better report the matter, particularly as I had just received an excited phone call from you, Andrew, saying you were all set to achieve your life's great ambition.

ANDREW: My dear boy, I quite appreciate you have been captivated by the spirit of games-playing and the need, as you see it, to get even, but frankly you are trying too hard to be a big boy, too soon. [*He goes to the telephone and dials*] Hullo, Joyce, this is Andrew. May I speak to Tẽa . . . she what? . . . when was this? Where . . . ? Oh, my God!

> [*He replaces the receiver and takes a drink straight from the bottle.* MILO *is very excited*]

MILO: I told you. I killed her yesterday. Now sweat for your life. You have a little over eight minutes before the law arrives. It's your giant brain against their plodding ones. Concealed in this room are two incriminating clues. And as a final expression of your contempt for the police, you hid the murder weapon itself. Do you follow me so far?

ANDREW: [*Admiringly*] You bastard!

MILO: No judgments please. Three objects. Those you don't find, be sure the police will. I should add that they're all in plain view, though I have somewhat camouflaged them to make the whole thing more fun. The first object is a crystal bracelet.

ANDREW: Not . . .

MILO: Yes, I tore it off her wrist . . . off you go. It's inscribed "From Andrew to Tẽa, a propitiatory offering to a Karelian goddess."

ANDREW: All right! All right! I know how it's inscribed.

> [*He takes off his jacket and starts his search*]

MILO: Would you like some help?

ANDREW: Yes, damn you!

MILO:
Tch! Tch! . . . "For any man with half an eye.

What stands before him may espy;
But optics sharp it needs I ween,
To see what is not to be seen."

ANDREW: [*Furious*] You said everything was in plain view.

MILO: Well, it's paradoxical old me, isn't it?

ANDREW: I'll get my own back for this . . . don't worry. That I promise you. I'll roast you for this . . . I'll make you so sorry you ever . . .

MILO: Six minutes.

ANDREW: [*Slowly to himself*] I must think . . . I must think . . . It's in plain view, yet not to be seen. H'm . . . there's a visual trick involved.

[ANDREW *searches the room*]

MILO: A propitiatory offering, eh! What was it you had to propitiate for, I ask myself.

ANDREW: None of your bloody business!

MILO: Just for being yourself, I suppose. Just for being cold, torturing Andrew Wyke. Poor Téa, I wonder if all her jewelry was inscribed with apologies for your bully boy behavior.

ANDREW: That's a cheap jibe.

MILO: Mind you, at least you gave her some. Marguerite just had the use of them.

ANDREW: I see what you're doing. You're trying to distract me . . . But you won't succeed . . . I'll solve your puzzle . . . Let me think . . . Optics sharp it needs to see what is not to be seen . . . with the naked eye? It's microscopic! You only see a fraction of it. That's it!

[ANDREW *picks up the microscope and uses it*]

MILO: You won't need the Sherlock Holmes kit, Andrew. The bracelet is full sized and in full view. Though the detective angle is not a bad one. I wonder how your man, Merry*dick*, would have gone about the search.

ANDREW: [*Furious*] Merrydew! St. John Lord Merrydew!

MILO: Perhaps he'd have clambered up on that desk to look at the plinth, hauling his great tun of port belly after him. [ANDREW *climbs up on his desk to inspect the plinth*] Or perhaps he'd have gone straight to the chimney and shoved his fat Father Christmas face right up to it. [ANDREW *runs to the chimney and climbs inside it*] "My God!" cried the noble Lord, puking on his pipe and indulging his famed taste for bad puns. "This is hardly a *sootable* place for a gentleman!"

ANDREW: [*Emerges from the chimney*] I won't listen to you. I must think . . . What are the properties of crystal? It's hard . . . It's brilliant . . . It's transparent.

MILO: You're getting warm, Andrew.

ANDREW: You look through it and you don't see it. Now the only place to conceal a transparent thing, so as to make it invisible yet keep it in plain view, is in another transparent thing like . . . [*He inspects various glass objects including* MILO'S *drink which he is holding conspicuously. Finally he crosses to the ornamental tank and lifts out the bracelet*] Suddenly it's all as clear as crystal. I don't need to destroy this, do I? She could have left this here anytime.

MILO: True, it was only planted so that the police could read the inscription. At least they'd known that your relationship with Téa hadn't always been a happy one.

ANDREW: Very subtle. What next?

MILO: The next object is much more damning. The clue is a riddle, which goes as follows:
   "Two brothers we are,
   Great burdens we bear,
   On which we are bitterly pressed.
   The truth is to say,
   We are full all the day,
   And empty when we go to rest."

ANDREW: Oh, I know that . . . don't tell me . . . full all the day, empty when we go to rest . . . it's a . . . it's a pair of shoes!

MILO: Very good. In this case, one right, high-heeled shoe. Size six. The other, I need hardly add, is on Téa's body.

ANDREW: Oh, my God! Poor Téa. [*He searches the room*]

MILO: Poor Téa, eh? Well, that's a bit better. It's the first sign of sorrow you've shown since you heard of her death.

ANDREW: It's not true! You think I don't care about Téa, don't you? But I must save myself.

MILO: You're loving it. You're in a high state of brilliance and excitement. The thought that you are playing a game for your life is practically giving you an orgasm. It's pitiable.

ANDREW: Hold your filthy tongue! What you see before you is someone using a mighty control to keep terror in check, while he tries to solve a particularly sadistic and morbid puzzle. It's a triumph of the mind over atavism! [ANDREW *searches under the stairs and in the bookshelves, and pipe racks then the sailor's foot and finally finds the shoe in a brightly decorated cornucopia attached to the stage left column*] Ah! What have we here?

MILO: Very good! Sorry it's so messy. It's only earth from Téa's first grave in your garden.

[ANDREW *burns the shoe in the stove*]

ANDREW: Now there's one thing left, isn't there? The murder weapon, that's what you said. Now you strangled her here. What with? Let's see . . . a rope . . . a belt . . . a scarf . . .

MILO: It bit into her neck very deeply, Andrew. I had to pry it loose.

ANDREW: You sadistic bloody wop!

MILO: I hope I didn't hear that correctly . . . It would be foolish to antagonize me at this stage. Because as you're certain to need a lot more help, I would hate to have to give you an oblique, Florentine sort of one, sewn with treachery and double-dealing.

ANDREW: [*Controlling himself*] All right! All right!

MILO: As Don Quixote in common with a great number of chaps remarked, "*No es oro todo que reluce.*"

ANDREW: But the other chaps, of course, didn't say it in Spanish, did they?

MILO: Well, at least you know it was Spanish, even if you can't speak it. I suppose that's what is meant by a general education in England.

ANDREW: God, you're pretty damned insufferable, Milo.

MILO: I've learned it. Let's try you on a little Latin. Every gentleman knows Latin. I'm sure you're acquainted with the Winchester College Hall Book of 1401?

ANDREW: [*Sarcastic*] Naturally. As a matter of fact I've got the paperback by my bedside.

MILO: [*Bland*] Then you will remember an entry by Alanus de Insulis—"*Non teneas nurum totum quod splendet ut aurum.*"

ANDREW: [*Sarcastic*] I'm afraid I can't have got that far yet.

MILO: Pity . . . I suppose I could put it another way. "*Que tout n'est pas or qu'on voit luire.*" The French, of course, is thirteenth century.

ANDREW: Say it again, slowly.

MILO: All-that-glitters . . .

ANDREW: All that glitters isn't gold . . . Why didn't you say that in the first place . . . [MILO *whistles a scale*] Golden notes? Golden whistle? . . . Golden cord? . . . Golden cord! You strangled her with a golden cord and put it round the bellpull. [ANDREW *runs to the bellpull, examines it, but finds nothing*] No, you didn't. [MILO *whistles "Anything Goes"*] Anything goes. In olden d . . . In olden days a . . . glimpse of stocking. It's in the spin dryer. [ANDREW *goes off down the corridor to kitchen*]

MILO: Cold, cold. It's in this room, remember.

ANDREW: [*Returning*] Where do you put stockings? On legs, golden legs . . . *He examines the golden legs of the fender, then a chair*]

MILO: [*Sings*] "In olden days a glimpse of stocking was looked on as something shocking . . ." I thought I heard something. [*He exits to hallway. A moment later, he returns*] Yes, Andrew, it's the police. They're coming up the drive.

ANDREW: [*Desperate*] Keep them out! Give me one more minute!

MILO: A glimpse of stocking, remember.

[MILO *exits to hallway*]

MILO: [*Offstage*] Good evening, Detective Sergeant Tarrant?

TARRANT: [*Offstage*] Yes, sir. This is Constable Higgs.

MILO: [*Off*] Good evening, Constable.

HIGGS: Good evening, sir.

[*The grandfather clock strikes ten*]

ANDREW: Olden days . . . A glimpse . . . Now you see it, now you don't! Of course, the clock. [*He rushes to clock and finds stocking*]

MILO: [*Off*] Nice of you to be so prompt. I apologize for keeping you waiting out there for a moment. The front door's a bit stiff.

TARRANT: [*Off*] That's all right, sir. We're used to waiting.

MILO: Won't you hang your coats up? It's a bit warm inside.

TARRANT: Thank you, sir. I expect we'll be here a little time.

[ANDREW *puts stocking into fire*]

MILO: [*Off*] Here, Constable. Let me take your helmet.

HIGGS: Thank you, sir. If it's all the same to you, I think I'll keep it with me, but I'll take my coat off.

[*Door slams offstage*]

MILO: [*Off*] Come in, gentlemen. May I introduce Mr. Andrew Wyke. Andrew, may I introduce Detective Sergeant Tarrant and Constable Higgs.

ANDREW: [*Calls*] Come in, gentlemen, come in.

[*A pause. No one enters*]

MILO: [*Off*] Or perhaps I should say, Inspector Plodder and Constable Freshface. Thank you, Sergeant. We won't be needing you after all.

TARRANT: That's all right, sir. Better to be safe than sorry, that's what I say. Good night, sir.

MILO: [*Own voice*] Good night, Sergeant. Good night, Constable. Good night, sir.

[MILO *returns from hallway.* ANDREW *sinks on the settee, shattered*]

MILO: Aren't you going to ask about Têa? She did call here yesterday looking for you when I was here setting the Doppler scene. I told her about the trick you had played on me with the gun. She wasn't a bit surprised. She knows only too well the kind of games you play—the kind of humiliation you enjoy inflicting on people. I said I wanted to play a game to get even with you, and I asked her to help me. I asked her to lend me a stocking, a shoe and a bracelet. She collaborated with enthusiasm. So did her flat-mate, Joyce. Would you like to telephone her? She'll talk to you now. Of course you don't really have much to say to her, do you? She's not really your mistress. She told me you and she hadn't slept together for over a year. She told me you were practically impotent —not at all, in fact, the selector's choice for the next Olympics.

[ANDREW *hides his head as* MILO *starts up the stairs*]

ANDREW: Where are you going?

MILO: To collect Marguerite's fur coat.

ANDREW: She's not coming back?

MILO: No. Among other things she said she was fed up with living in Hamleys.

ANDREW: Hamleys?

MILO: It's a toy shop in Regent Street.

ANDREW: Milo.

MILO: Yes?

ANDREW: Don't go. Don't waste it all on Marguerite. She doesn't appreciate you like I do. You and I are evenly matched. We know what it is to play a game and that's so rare. Two people coming together who have the courage to spend the little time of light between the eternal darkness—joking.

MILO: Do you mean live here?

ANDREW: Yes.

MILO: [Scornfully] Is it legal in private between two consenting games-players?

ANDREW: Please . . . I just want someone to play with.

MILO: No.

ANDREW: Please.

MILO: No. Most people want someone to live with. But you have no life to give anyone—only the tricks and the shadows of long ago. Take a look at yourself, Andrew, and ask yourself a few simple questions about your attachment to the English detective story. Perhaps you might come to realize that the only place you can inhabit is a dead world—a country house world where peers and colonels die in their studies; where butlers steal the port, and pert parlormaids cringe, weeping malapropisms behind green baize doors. It's a world of coldness and class hatred, and two-dimensional characters who are not expected to communicate; it's a world where only the amateurs win, and where foreigners are automatically figures of fun. To be *puzzled* is all. Forgive me for taking Marguerite to a life where people try to *understand*. To put it shortly, the detective story is the normal recreation of snobbish, outdated, life-hating, ignoble minds. I'll get that fur coat now. I presume it is Marguerite's, unless, that is, you've taken to transvestism as a substitute for non-performance.

[MILO *disappears into the bedroom.* ANDREW *sits on below, crushed and humiliated. After a minute, he rises and starts wearily across the stage. Suddenly he stops as a thought enters his mind*]

ANDREW: [*To himself*] The coat! . . . The fur coat . . . of course . . . I've got him! [*He brightens visibly—a man who realizes suddenly that he can rescue a victory out of the jaws of defeat—and crosses firmly to his desk and takes out his gun*] You see, Inspector, I was working in the morning room when I heard a noise. I seized my gun and came in here. I saw the figure of a man, apparently carrying my wife's fur coat. I shouted for him to put his hands up, but instead he ran toward the front door, trying to escape. Though I aimed low, I'm afraid I shot him dead. [INSPECTOR'S *voice*] Mustn't blame yourself, sir, could have happened to anybody!

[MILO *returns, carrying fur coat. He comes down the stairs, but does not see the gun hidden behind* ANDREW'S *back*]

ANDREW: I'm not going to let you go, you know.

MILO: No? What *are* you going to do, Andrew. Shoot me down? Play that old burglar game again?

ANDREW: Yes, that's precisely what I could do.

MILO: It wouldn't work, you know, even if you had the guts to go through with it.

ANDREW: Why not?

MILO: [*Fetches a suitcase from the hall and packs the fur coat*] Because of what happened when I left here on Friday night. I *lurched* home in the moonlight, numb and dazed, and soiled. I sat up all night in a chair—damaged—contaminated by you and this house. I remembered something my father said to me; "In this country, Milo," he said, "there's justice, but sometimes for a foreigner it is difficult." In the morning I went to the police station and told them what had happened. One of them—Sergeant Tarrant—yes, he's real—took me into a room and we had quite a long chat. But I don't think he really believed me, even though I showed him the powder burn on my head. He seemed more interested in my relationship with Marguerite, which by the way they all appeared to know about. I felt this terrible anger coming over me. I thought "they're not going to believe me because I'm a stranger from London who's screwing the wife of the local nob and has got what he deserved." So I thought of my father, and what I might have done in Italy, and I took my *own* revenge. But remember, Andrew, the police might still come.

ANDREW: [*Slowly*] Then why haven't they, then?

MILO: I don't know, perhaps they won't. But even if they don't, you can't play your burglar game now; they'd never swallow it. So you see, you've lost.

ANDREW: I don't believe one word you're saying.

MILO: [*Deliberately*] It's the truth.

ANDREW: You're lying!

MILO: Why don't you phone Sergeant Tarrant if you don't believe me.

ANDREW: And say what? Please, Sergeant, has Milo Tindle been in saying that I framed him as a burglar and then shot him? I'm not *that* half-witted.

MILO: Suit yourself.

ANDREW: I *shall* shoot you, Milo. You come here and ask my permission to steal away my wife, you pry into my manhood, you lecture me on dead worlds and ignoble minds, and you mock Merridew. Well, they're all *real* bullets this time.

MILO: I'm going home now.

[MILO *starts to leave.* ANDREW *fires.* MILO *drops in pain, fatally shot.* ANDREW *kneels and holds his head up*]

ANDREW: You're a bad liar, Milo, and in the final analysis, an uninventive games-player. Can you hear me? Then listen to this, NEVER play the same game three times running!

[*There is the sound of a car approaching and pulling to a halt. A flashing blue police car light shines through the win-*

*dow. The doorbell rings. There is a loud knocking on door.
Painfully,* MILO *lifts his head from the floor; he laughs*]

MILO: Game, set and match!

[*His laugh becomes a cough. Blood trickles from his mouth.
He grimaces in surprise at the pain and dies. The knocking
on the door is repeated more loudly.* ANDREW *staggers to his
desk and accidentally presses the button on it. This sets off
the sailor who laughs ironically. The knocking becomes more
insistent.* ANDREW *leans weakly against pillar. He shouts in
anguish as:*]

THE CURTAIN FALLS

ABSURD PERSON SINGULAR

Alan Ayckbourn

Alan Ayckbourn

During the decade of the seventies, Great Britain's leading comic dramatist, Alan Ayckbourn, was represented on four different occasions on the Broadway stage. The first of his comedies to reach there was *How the Other Half Loves*, presented in 1971 with Phil Silvers in the role originally performed in London by Robert Morley. His second, *Absurd Person Singular* (which this editor regards as his most inventive comic inspiration), opened at the Music Box Theatre on October 8, 1974, and ran for 592 performances, making it Ayckbourn's longest-running Broadway success to date. This was followed in 1975 by his trilogy, *The Norman Conquests*, and, in 1979, by the National Theatre's production of *Bedroom Farce*.

Winner of London's *Evening Standard* Award for best comedy of 1973, *Absurd Person Singular*, when it opened in New York, was evaluated by most drama critics as "the best comedy Britain has sent us in years and years." With the arrival of *Bedroom Farce*, the author was described by Walter Kerr as "an original, intelligent and hilarious British caricaturist" while Clive Barnes praised his "wit, humor, invention and class."

Alan Ayckbourn was born in London on April 12, 1939, but spent most of his childhood in Sussex. His mother was separated from his father, a musician with the London Symphony Orchestra, when he was five. Then she married a bank manager and the dramatist-to-be spent his formative years in a series of flats above local branches of Barclays bank. As he recently told an interviewer: "That's plumb center of where I set my plays now, I never go far away geographically, and, though I go up and down the social scale a bit, I always seem to return to that class."

After being educated at Haileybury, he went straight into the theatre, working as an actor and stage manager for several provincial theatres. Subsequently, he joined the Library Theatre at Scarborough as an actor and there began writing plays. All of his plays have since been performed there prior to their West End showings and, in spite of his eminence as a dramatist, he serves full-time as the theatre's Director of Productions.

Since his initial London entry, *Mr. Whatnot*, at the Arts Theatre in 1964, Mr. Ayckbourn has had more than a dozen successful West End productions. In 1975 five of his comedies were running concurrently, something of a record for a modern dramatist. Now he is an international figure, and his plays have been translated into twenty-four languages and are performed all over the world.

His first major success came with *Relatively Speaking* in 1967. Others followed in London on an almost annual basis, including: *How the Other Half Loves* (1970), *Time and Time Again* (1972), *Absurd Person Singular* (1973), *The Norman Conquests* (winner of the *Evening Standard* Award 1974), *Absent Friends* (1975), *Confusions* (1976), *Just Between Ourselves* (*Evening Standard* Award, 1977), *Bedroom Farce* (1977), and *Ten Times Table* (1978).

By and large, Mr. Ayckbourn's work is an answer to those who regard the suburbs as dull and small towns as serene. During his childhood, however, he concedes that it was far from that. "I was surrounded by relationships that weren't altogether stable, the air was often blue, and things were sometimes flying across the kitchen."

His plays raise suburban absurdities to the level of universal anxieties and his characters often come close to destroying each other, though more commonly through insensitivity than obvious malice. "We're in the twentieth century," he has reflected. "Everything and everyone conspires against us. My work is about man's inhumanity to woman and woman's inhumanity to man. It's also about the whole physical world's inhumanity to us all."

The author's twenty-first play, *Joking Apart*, opened in London in March 1979, while his twenty-second work, *Sisterly Feelings*, was testing its wings at the Library Theatre in Scarborough.

Absurd Person Singular was first produced at the Library Theatre, Scarborough, England, and subsequently by Michael Codron at the Criterion Theatre, London, opening on July 4, 1973. The cast was as follows:

JANE	*Bridget Turner*
SIDNEY	*Richard Briers*
RONALD	*Michael Aldridge*
MARION	*Sheila Hancock*
EVA	*Anna Calder-Marshall*
GEOFFREY	*David Burke*

Directed by Eric Thompson
Settings by Alan Tagg

Absurd Person Singular was first presented in New York at the Music Box Theatre on October 8, 1974, by the Theatre Guild and the John F. Kennedy Center for the Performing Arts in association with Michael Codron. The cast was as follows:

JANE	*Carole Shelley*
SIDNEY	*Larry Blyden*
RONALD	*Richard Kiley*
MARION	*Geraldine Page*
EVA	*Sandy Dennis*
GEOFFREY	*Tony Roberts*

Directed by Eric Thompson
Settings by Edward Burbridge
Costumes by Levino Verna
Lighting by Thomas Skelton

A town in England. Time—the present.

ACT ONE

Last Christmas. Sidney and Jane's kitchen.

ACT TWO

This Christmas. Geoffrey and Eva's kitchen.

ACT THREE

Next Christmas. Ronald and Marion's kitchen.

ACT ONE

SIDNEY *and* JANE HOPCROFT'S *kitchen of their small suburban house. Last Christmas.*

Although on a modest scale, it is a model kitchen. While not containing all the gadgetry, it does have an automatic washing machine, a fridge, an electric stove and a gleaming sink unit. All these are contained or surrounded by smart Formica-topped working surfaces with the usual drawers and cupboards. The room also contains a small table, also Formica-topped, and matching chairs.

When the curtain rises, JANE, *a woman in her thirties, is bustling round wiping the floor, cupboard doors, working surfaces—in fact, anything in sight—with a cloth. She sings happily as she works. She wears a pinafore and bedroom slippers, but, under this, a smart new party dress. She is unimaginatively made up and her hair is tightly permed. She wears rubber gloves to protect her hands.*

As JANE *works,* SIDNEY *enters, a small dapper man of about the same age. He has a small trimmed moustache and a cheery, unflappable manner. He wears his best, rather old-fashioned, sober suit. A dark tie, polished hair and shoes complete the picture.*

SIDNEY: Hallo, hallo. What are we up to out here, eh?

JANE: [*Without pausing in her work*] Just giving it a wipe.

SIDNEY: Dear, oh dear. Good gracious me. Does it need it? Like a battleship. Just like a battleship. They need you in the Royal Navy.

JANE: [*Giggling*] Silly . . .

SIDNEY: No—the Royal Navy.

JANE: Silly . . .

[SIDNEY *goes to the back door, turns the Yale knob, opens it and sticks his hand out*]

SIDNEY: Still raining, I see.

JANE: Shut the door, it's coming in.

SIDNEY: Cats and dogs. Dogs and cats. [*He shuts the door, wiping his wet hand on his handkerchief. Striding to the centre of the room and staring up at his digital clock*] Eighteen-twenty-three. [*Consulting his watch*] Eighteen-twenty-three. Getting on. Seven minutes—they'll be here.

JANE: Oh. [*She straightens up and looks around the kitchen for somewhere she's missed*]

SIDNEY: I've got a few games lined up.

JANE: Games?

SIDNEY: Just in case.

JANE: Oh, good.

SIDNEY: I've made a parcel for "Pass the Parcel," sorted out a bit of music for musical bumps and thought out a few forfeits.

JANE: Good.

SIDNEY: I've thought up some real devils. [*He puts his leg on the table*]

JANE: I bet. [*She knocks his leg off, and wipes*]

SIDNEY: Just in case. Just in case things need jollying up. [*Seeing* JANE *still wiping*] I don't want to disappoint you but we're not going to be out here for our drinks, you know.

JANE: Yes, I know.

SIDNEY: The way you're going . . .

JANE: They might want to look . . .

SIDNEY: I doubt it.

JANE: The ladies might.

SIDNEY: [*Chuckling knowingly*] I don't imagine the wife of a banker will particularly choose to spend her evening in our kitchen. Smart as it is.

JANE: No?

SIDNEY: I doubt if she spends very much time in her own kitchen. Let alone ours.

JANE: Still . . .

SIDNEY: Very much the lady of leisure, Mrs. Brewster-Wright. Or so I would imagine.

JANE: What about Mrs. Jackson?

SIDNEY: [*Doubtfully*] Well—again, not a woman you think of in the same breath as you would a kitchen.

JANE: All women are interested in kitchens. [*She turns to the sink*]

SIDNEY: [*Ironically*] Oh, if you're looking for a little job . . .

JANE: What's that?

SIDNEY: A small spillage. My fault.

JANE: [*Very alarmed*] Where?

SIDNEY: In there. On the sideboard.

JANE: Oh, Sidney. [*She snatches up an assortment of cloths, wet and dry*]

SIDNEY: Nothing serious.

JANE: Honestly.

[*Sidney goes to the back door, opens it, sticks a hand out*]

SIDNEY: Dear, oh dear. [*He closes the door and dries his hand on his handkerchief*]

JANE: [*Returning*] Honestly.

SIDNEY: Could you see it?

JANE: You spoil that surface if you leave it. You leave a ring. [*She returns her dish cloth to the sink, her dry cloths to the drawer and now takes out a duster and a tin of polish*] Now that room's going to smell of polish. I had the windows open all day so it wouldn't.

SIDNEY: Well then, don't polish.

JANE: I have to polish. There's a mark. [*She goes to the door and then pauses*] I know, bring the air freshener.

SIDNEY: Air freshener?

JANE: Under the sink. [*She goes out*]

SIDNEY: Ay, ay, Admiral. [*He whistles a sailor's horn-pipe, amused*] Dear, oh dear. [*He opens the cupboard under the sink, rummages and brings out an aerosol tin. He is one of those men who likes to read all small print. This he does, holding the tin at arm's length to do so. Reading*] "Shake can before use." [*He does so. Reading*] "Remove cap." [*He does so. Reading*] "Hold away from body and spray into air by depressing button." [*He holds the can away from his body, points it in the air and depresses the button. The spray hisses out over his shirt front*] Dear, oh dear. [*He puts down the tin, wipes his shirt-front with a dish cloth*]

JANE: [*Entering*] What are you doing?

SIDNEY: Just getting this to rights. Just coming to terms with your air freshener.

JANE: That's the fly spray.

SIDNEY: Ah.

JANE: Honestly. [*She takes the canister from him and puts it on top of the washing machine*]

SIDNEY: My mistake.

JANE: For someone who's good at some things you're hopeless.

SIDNEY: Beg your pardon, Admiral, beg your pardon. [*Jane puts away the duster and polish. Checking his watch with the clock*] Four and a half minutes to go.

JANE: And you've been at those nuts, haven't you?

SIDNEY: Nuts?

JANE: In there. In the bowl. On the table. Those nuts. You know the ones I mean.

SIDNEY: I may have had a little dip. Anyway, how did you know I'd been at those nuts? Eh? How did you know, old eagle-eye?

JANE: Because I know how I left them. Now come on, out of my way. Don't start that. I've got things to do.

SIDNEY: [Closing with her] What about a kiss then?

JANE: [Trying to struggle free] Sidney . . .

SIDNEY: Come on. Christmas kiss.

JANE: Sidney. No, not now. What's the matter with you? Sidney . . . [She pauses, sniffing]

SIDNEY: What's the matter now?

JANE: What's that smell?

SIDNEY: Eh?

JANE: It's on your tie. What's this smell on your tie? [They both sniff his tie] There. Can you smell?

SIDNEY: Oh, that'll be the fly spray.

JANE: Fly spray?

SIDNEY: Had a bit of a backfire.

JANE: It's killed off your after-shave.

SIDNEY: [Jovially] As long as it hasn't killed off my flies, eh. [He laughs. Suddenly cutting through this] Eighteen-twenty-eight. Two minutes.

JANE: [Nervous again] I hope everything's all right. [She moves over to SIDNEY and proceeds to brush his jacket in an effort to tidy him up]

SIDNEY: When?

JANE: For them. I want it to be right.

SIDNEY: Of course it's right.

JANE: I mean. I don't want you to be let down. Not by me. I want it to look good for you. I don't want to let you down . . .

SIDNEY: You never have yet . . .

JANE: No, but it's special tonight, isn't it? I mean, with Mr. and Mrs. Brewster-Wright and Mr. and Mrs. Jackson. It's important.

SIDNEY: Don't forget Dick and Lottie Potter. They're coming too.

JANE: Oh, well, I don't count Dick and Lottie. They're friends.

SIDNEY: I trust by the end of this evening, we shall all be friends. Just don't get nervous. That's all. Don't get nervous. [*He consults the clock and checks it with his watch*] One minute to go. [*A slight pause. The front door chimes sound*] What was that?

JANE: The front door.

SIDNEY: They're early. Lucky we're ready for them.

JANE: Yes. [*In a sudden panic*] I haven't sprayed the room.

SIDNEY: All right, all right. You can do it whilst I'm letting them in. Plenty of time.

JANE: It doesn't take a second.

> [JANE *snatches up the air freshener and follows* SIDNEY *out into the sitting-room. A silence. Jane comes hurrying back into the kitchen. She puts away the air freshener, removes her pinafore, straightens her clothing and hair in the mirror, creeps back to the kitchen door and opens it a bit. Voices are heard—*SIDNEY'S *and two others. One is a jolly hearty male voice and one a jolly hearty female voice. They are* DICK *and* LOTTIE POTTER, *whom we have the good fortune never to meet in person, but quite frequently hear whenever the door to the kitchen is open. Both have loud, braying distinctive laughs. Jane closes the door, cutting off the voices, straightens her hair and dress for the last time, grips the door handle, takes a deep breath, is about to make her entrance into the room when she sees she is still wearing her bedroom slippers*]

JANE: Oh. [*She takes off her slippers, puts them on the table and scuttles round the kitchen looking for her shoes. She cannot find them. She picks up the slippers and wipes the table with their fluffy side, where they have made a mark*] Oh. [*She hurries back to the door, opens it a fraction. Jolly chatter and laughter is heard. Jane stands for a long time, peeping through the crack in the door, trying to catch sight of her shoes. She sees them. She closes the door again. She stands lost*] Oh. Oh. Oh.

[*The door opens. Loud laughter from off.* SIDNEY *comes in laughing. He closes the door. The laughter cuts off abruptly*]

SIDNEY: [*Fiercely, in a low voice*] Come on. What are you doing?

JANE: I can't.

SIDNEY: What?

JANE: I've got no shoes.

SIDNEY: What do you mean, no shoes?

JANE: They're in there.

SIDNEY: Where?

JANE: By the fireplace. I left them so I could slip them on.

SIDNEY: Well, then, why didn't you?

JANE: I didn't have time. I forgot.

SIDNEY: Well, come and get them.

JANE: No . . .

SIDNEY: It's only Dick and Lottie Potter.

JANE: You fetch them.

SIDNEY: I can't fetch them.

JANE: Yes, you can. Pick them up and bring them in here.

SIDNEY: But I . . .

JANE: Sidney, please.

SIDNEY: Dear, oh dear. What a start. I say, what a start. [*He opens the door cautiously and listens. Silence*] They've stopped talking.

JANE: Have they?

SIDNEY: Wondering where we are, no doubt.

JANE: Well, go in. Here.

SIDNEY: What?

JANE: [*Handing him her slippers*] Take these.

SIDNEY: What do I do with these?

JANE: The hall cupboard.

SIDNEY: You're really expecting rather a lot tonight, aren't you?

JANE: I'm sorry.

SIDNEY: Yes, well it's got to stop. It's got to stop. I have to entertain out there, you know. [*He opens the door and starts laughing
heartily as he does so*]

> [SIDNEY *goes out, closing the door.* JANE *hurries about nerv-
> ously, making still more adjustments to her person and check-
> ing her appearance in the mirror. At length the door opens,
> letting in a bellow of laughter.* SIDNEY *returns, carrying* JANE's
> *shoes*]

SIDNEY: [*Behind him*] Yes, I will. I will. I'll tell her that, Dick . . .
[*He laughs until he's shut the door. His laugh cuts off abruptly.
Thrusting* JANE's *shoes at her, ungraciously*] Here.

JANE: Oh, thank goodness.

SIDNEY: Now for heaven's sake, come in.

JANE: [*Struggling into her shoes*] Yes, I'm sorry. What did Dick
say?

SIDNEY: When?

JANE: Just now? That you told him you'd tell me.

SIDNEY: I really can't remember. Now then, are you ready?

JANE: Yes, yes.

SIDNEY: It's a good job it's only Dick and Lottie out there. It
might have been the Brewster-Wrights. I'd have had a job

explaining this to them. Walking in and out like a shoe salesman. All right?

JANE: Yes.

SIDNEY: Right. [*He throws open the door, jovially*] Here she is. [*Pushing* JANE *ahead of him*] Here she is at last.

[*Hearty cries of "Ah ha" from* DICK *and* LOTTIE]

JANE: [*Going in*] Here I am.

[JANE *and* SIDNEY *exit*]

SIDNEY: [*Closing the door behind him*] At last.
[*A silence. A long one.* SIDNEY *returns to the kitchen. Conversation is heard as he opens and closes the door. He starts hunting round the kitchen opening drawers and not bothering to shut them. After a second, the door opens again, and* JANE *comes in*]

JANE: [*As she enters*] Yes, well you say that to Lottie, not to me. I don't want to know that . . . [*She closes the door*] What are you doing? Oh, Sidney, what are you doing? [*She hurries round after him, closing the drawers*]

SIDNEY: Bottle-opener. I'm trying to find the bottle-opener. I can't get the top off Lottie's bitter lemon.

JANE: It's in there.

SIDNEY: In there?

JANE: Why didn't you ask me?

SIDNEY: Where in there?

JANE: On the mantelpiece.

SIDNEY: The mantelpiece?

JANE: It looks nice on the mantelpiece.

SIDNEY: It's no use having a bottle-opener on a mantelpiece, is it? I mean, how am I . . . ?

[*The door chimes sound*]

JANE: Somebody else.

SIDNEY: All right, I'll go. I'll go. You open the bitter lemon. With gin.

JANE: Gin and bitter lemon.

SIDNEY: And shake the bottle first.

[*Sidney opens the door. Silence from the room. He goes out, closing it*]

JANE: [*To herself*] Gin and bitter lemon—shake the bottle first—gin and bitter lemon—shake the bottle first . . . [*She returns to the door and opens it very slightly. There can now be heard the chatter of five voices. She closes the door and feverishly straightens herself*]

[*The door opens a crack and* SIDNEY's *nose appears. Voices are heard behind him*]

SIDNEY: [*Hissing*] It's them.

JANE: Mr. and Mrs. Brewster-Wright?

SIDNEY: Yes. Ronald and Marion. Come in.

JANE: Ronald and Marion.

SIDNEY: Come in.

[SIDNEY *opens the door wider, grabs her arm, jerks her through the door and closes it*]

JANE: [*As she is dragged in*] Gin and bitter lemon—shake the bottle first . . .

[*Silence. Another fairly long one. The door bursts open and* JANE *comes rushing out. Murmur of voices*]

JANE: [*Over her shoulder*] Wait there! Just wait there! [*She dashes to the sink and finds a tea towel and two dish cloths*]

[RONALD, *a man in his mid-forties, enters. Impressive, without being distinguished. He is followed by an anxious* SIDNEY. RONALD, *holding one leg of his trousers away from his body. He has evidently got drenched*]

SIDNEY: Oh dear, oh dear. I'm terribly sorry.

RONALD: That's all right. Can't be helped.

JANE: Here's a cloth.

RONALD: Oh, thank you—yes, yes. [*He takes the tea towel*] I'll just use this one, if you don't mind.

SIDNEY: Well, what a start, eh? What a grand start to the evening. [*With a laugh*] Really, Jane.

JANE: I'm terribly sorry. I didn't realize it was going to splash like that.

RONALD: Well, tricky things, soda siphons. You either get a splash or a dry gurgle. Never a happy medium.

JANE: Your nice suit.

RONALD: Good God, it's only soda water. Probably do it good, eh?

JANE: I don't know about that.

RONALD: [*Returning the tea towel*] Thanks very much. Well, it's wet enough outside there. I didn't expect to get wet inside as well.

SIDNEY: No, no . . .

JANE: Terribly sorry.

RONALD: Accidents happen. Soon dry out. I'll run around for a bit.

SIDNEY: I'll tell you what. I could let you have a pair of my trousers from upstairs just while yours dry.

JANE: Oh, yes.

RONALD: No, no. That's all right. I'll stick with these. Hate to break up the suit, eh? [*He laughs*]

> [*So do* SIDNEY *and* JANE. MARION, *a well-groomed woman, a little younger than* RONALD *and decidedly better preserved, comes in*]

MARION: All right, darling?

RONALD: Yes, yes.

MARION: Oh! [*She stops short in the doorway*] Isn't this gorgeous? Isn't this enchanting.

JANE: Oh.

MARION: What a simply dishy kitchen. [To JANE] Aren't you lucky.

JANE: Well . . .

MARION: It's so beautifully arranged. Ronnie, don't you agree? Isn't this splendid.

RONALD: Ah.

MARION: Just look at these working surfaces and you must have a gorgeous view from that window, I imagine.

SIDNEY: Well . . .

MARION: It must be stunning. You must look right over the fields at the back.

SIDNEY: No—no.

JANE: No, we just look into next door's fence.

MARION: Well, which way are the fields?

JANE: I've no idea.

MARION: How extraordinary. I must be thinking of somewhere else.

SIDNEY: Mind you, we've got a good ten yards to the fence . . .

RONALD: On a clear day, eh?

SIDNEY: Beg pardon?

MARION: Oh, look, Ronnie, do come and look at these cupboards.

RONALD: Eh?

MARION: Look at these, Ronnie. [Opening and shutting the cupboard doors] They're so easy to open and shut.

JANE: Drawers—here, you see . . .

MARION: Drawers! [Opening them] Oh, lovely deep drawers. Put all sorts of things in these, can't you? And then just shut it up and forget them.

SIDNEY: Yes, yes, they're handy for that . . .

MARION: No, it's these cupboards. I'm afraid I really do envy you these. Don't you envy them, Ronnie?

RONALD: I thought we had cupboards.

MARION: Yes, darling, but they're nothing like these. Just open and shut that door. It's heaven.

RONALD: [Picking up a booklet from the counter] Cupboard's a cupboard. [He sits and reads]

JANE: [Proudly] Look. [Going to the washing machine] Sidney's Christmas present to me . . .

MARION: [Picking up the canister from the top of the washing machine] Oh, lovely. What is it? Hair spray?

SIDNEY: No, no. That's the fly spray, no. My wife meant the machine.

[He takes the spray from her and puts it down]

MARION: Machine?

JANE: Washing machine. Here . . .

MARION: Oh, that's a washing machine. Tucked under there. How thrilling. What a marvellous Christmas present.

JANE: Well, yes.

MARION: Do tell me, how did you manage to keep it a surprise from her?

SIDNEY: Well . . .

MARION: I mean, don't tell me he hid it or wrapped it up. I don't believe it.

SIDNEY: No, I just arranged for the men to deliver it and plumb it in.

JANE: They flooded the kitchen.

MARION: Super.

JANE: You see, it's the automatic. It's got—all the programmes and then spin-drying and soak.

MARION: Oh, good heavens. Ronnie, come here at once and see this.

RONALD: [Reading avidly] Just coming . . .

MARION: [Bending to read the dial] What's this? Whites—coloureds—my God, it's apartheid.

JANE: Beg pardon?

MARION: What's this? Minimum icon? What on earth is that?

JANE: No, minimum iron.

MARION: Don't tell me it does the ironing, too.

JANE: Oh, no, it . . .

MARION: Ronnie, have you seen this extraordinary machine?

RONALD: Yes. Yes . . .

MARION: It not only does your washing and your whites and your blacks and your coloureds and so on, it does your ironing.

SIDNEY: No, no . . .

JANE: No . . .

MARION: [To JANE] We shall soon be totally redundant. [She picks up the spray and fires it into the air and inhales] What a poignant smell. It's almost too good to waste on flies, isn't it. Now where . . . ? It's a little like your husband's gorgeous cologne, surely?

JANE: Oh, well . . .

[The doorbell chimes]

MARION: Oh, good gracious. What was that? Does that mean your shirts are cooked or something.

SIDNEY: No, front doorbell.

MARION: Oh, I see. How pretty.

SIDNEY: Somebody else arrived.

JANE: Yes, I'd better . . .

SIDNEY: Won't be a minute.

JANE: No, I'll go.

SIDNEY: No . . .

JANE: No, I'll go.

[JANE *hurries out, closing the door*]

MARION: I do hope your Mr. and Mrs. Potter don't feel terribly abandoned in there. They're splendidly jolly, blooming people, aren't they?

SIDNEY: Yes, Dick's a bit of a laugh.

MARION: Enormous. Now, you must tell me one thing, Mr. Hopcroft. How on earth did you squeeze that machine so perfectly under the shelf? Did you try them for size or were you terribly lucky?

SIDNEY: No, I went out and measured the machine in the shop.

MARION: Oh, I see.

SIDNEY: And then I made the shelf, you see. So it was the right height.

MARION: No, I mean how on earth did you know it was going to be right?

SIDNEY: Well, that's the way I built it.

MARION: No. You don't mean this is you?

SIDNEY: Yes, yes. Well, the shelf is.

MARION: Ronnie!

RONALD: Um?

MARION: Ronnie, darling, what are you reading?

RONALD: [*Vaguely consulting the cover of his book*] Er . . .

SIDNEY: Ah, that'll be the instruction book for the stove.

RONALD: Oh, is that what it is. I was just trying to work out what I was reading. Couldn't make head or tail.

MARION: Darling, did you hear what Mr. Hop—er . . .

SIDNEY: Hopcroft.

MARION: Sidney, isn't it? Sidney was saying . . . ?

RONALD: What?

MARION: Darling, Sidney built this shelf on his own. He went out and measured the machine, got all his screws and nails and heaven knows what and built this shelf himself.

RONALD: Good Lord!

SIDNEY: I've got some more shelves upstairs. For the bedside. And also, I've partitioned off part of the spare bedroom as a walk-in cupboard for the wife. And I'm just about to panel the landing with those knotty pine units, have you seen them?

MARION: Those curtains are really the most insistent colour I've ever seen. They must just simply cry out to be drawn in the morning.

[JANE *sticks her head round the door*]

JANE: Dear—it's Mr. and Mrs. Jackson.

SIDNEY: Oh. Geoff and Eva, is it? Right, I'll be in to say hallo.

MARION: Geoff and Eva Jackson?

SIDNEY: Yes. Do you know them?

MARION: Oh, yes. Rather. Darling, it's Geoff and Eva Jackson.

RONALD: Geoff and Eva who?

MARION: The Jacksons.

RONALD: Oh, Geoff and Eva Jackson.

MARION: That's nice, isn't it?

RONALD: Yes?

JANE: Are you coming in?

SIDNEY: Yes, yes.

MARION: Haven't seen them for ages.

JANE: They've left the dog in the car.

SIDNEY: Oh, good.

MARION: Have they a dog?

JANE: Yes.

MARION: Oh, how lovely. We must see him.

JANE: He's—very big . . .

SIDNEY: Yes, well, lead on, dear.

> [JANE *opens the door. A burst of conversation from the sit-ting-room.* JANE *goes out.* SIDNEY *holds the door open for* MARION, *sees she is not following him and, torn between his duties as a host, follows* JANE *off*]

SIDNEY: We'll be in here. [*He closes the door*]

MARION: Ronnie . . .

RONALD: [*Studying the washing machine*] Mm?

MARION: Come along, darling.

RONALD: I was just trying to work out how this thing does the iron-ing. Don't see it at all. Just rolls it into a ball.

MARION: Darling, do come on.

RONALD: I think that woman's got it wrong.

MARION: Darling . . .

RONALD: Um?

MARION: Make our excuses quite shortly, please.

RONALD: Had enough, have you?

MARION: We've left the boys . . .

RONALD: They'll be all right.

MARION: What's that man's name?

RONALD: Hopcroft, do you mean?

MARION: No, the other one.

RONALD: Oh, Potter, isn't it?

MARION: Well, I honestly don't think I can sit through many more of his jokes.

RONALD: I thought they were quite funny.

MARION: And I've never had quite such a small gin in my life. Completely drowned.

RONALD: Really? My Scotch was pretty strong.

MARION: That's only because she missed the glass with the soda water. Consider yourself lucky.

RONALD: I don't know about lucky. I shall probably have bloody rheumatism in the morning.

[SIDNEY *sticks his head round the door. Laughter and chatter behind him*]

SIDNEY: Er—Mrs. Brewster-Wright, I wonder if you'd both . . .

MARION: Oh, yes, we're just coming. We can't tear ourselves away from your divine kitchen, can we, Ronnie? [*Turning to* RONALD, *holding up the fingers of one hand and mouthing*] Five minutes.

RONALD: Righto.

[*They all go out, closing the door. Silence.* JANE *enters with an empty bowl. She hurries to the cupboard and takes out a jumbo bag of crisps and pours them into the bowl. She is turning to leave when the door opens again and* SIDNEY *hurries in, looking a little fraught*]

SIDNEY: Tonic water. We've run out.

JANE: Tonic water. Down there in the cupboard.

SIDNEY: Right.

JANE: Do you think it's going all right?

SIDNEY: Fine, fine. Now get back, get back there.

JANE: [*As she goes*] Will you ask Lottie to stop eating all these crisps? Nobody else has had any.

> [JANE *goes out closing the door behind her.* SIDNEY *searches first one cupboard, then another, but cannot find any tonic*]

SIDNEY: Oh dear, oh dear.

> [SIDNEY *hurries back to the party closing the door behind him. After a second* JANE *enters looking worried, closing the door behind her. She searches where* SIDNEY *has already searched. She finds nothing*]

JANE: Oh. [*She wanders in rather aimless circles round the kitchen*]

> [SIDNEY *enters with a glass with gin and a slice of lemon in it. He closes the door*]

SIDNEY: Is it there?

JANE: Yes, yes. Somewhere . . .

SIDNEY: Well, come along. She's waiting.

JANE: I've just—got to find it . . .

SIDNEY: Oh dear, oh dear.

JANE: I tidied them away somewhere.

SIDNEY: Well, there was no point in tidying them away, was there? We're having a party.

JANE: Well—it just looked—tidier. You go back in, I'll bring them.

SIDNEY: Now that was your responsibility. We agreed buying the beverages was your department. I hope you haven't let us down.

JANE: No. I'm sure I haven't.

SIDNEY: Well, it's very embarrassing for me in the meanwhile, isn't it? Mrs. Brewster-Wright is beginning to give me anxious looks.

JANE: Oh.

SIDNEY: Well then.

[SIDNEY *goes back in.* JANE *stands helplessly. She gives a little whimper of dismay. She is on the verge of tears. Then a sudden decision. She goes to a drawer, reaches to the back and brings out her housekeeping purse. She opens it and takes out some coins. She runs to the centre of the room and looks at the clock*]

JANE: Nineteen-twenty-two. [*Hurried calculation*] Thirteen—fourteen—fifteen—sixteen—seventeen—eighteen—nineteen . . . seven-twenty-two. [*She hurries to the back door and opens it. She holds out her hand, takes a tentative step out and then a hasty step back again. She is again in a dilemma. She closes the back door. She goes to the cupboard just inside the door and, after rummaging about, she emerges holding a pair of men's large Wellington boots in one hand and a pair of plimsolls in the other. Mentally tossing up between them, she returns the plimsolls to the cupboard. She slips off her own shoes and steps easily into the Wellingtons. She puts her own shoes neatly in the cupboard and rummages again. She pulls out a large men's gardening raincoat. She holds it up, realizes it's better than nothing and puts it on. She hurries back to the centre of the room buttoning it as she does so*] Nineteen-twenty-four. [*She returns to the back door, opens it and steps out. It is evidently pelting down. She stands in the doorway holding up the collar of the coat and ineffectually trying to protect her hairdo from the rain with the other hand. Frantically*] Oh . . . [*She dives back into the cupboard and re-emerges with an old hat. She looks at it in dismay. After a moment's struggle she puts it on and hurries back to the centre of the room*] Twenty-five.

[JANE *returns to the back door, hesitates for a second and then plunges out into the night, leaving the door only very slightly ajar. After a moment,* SIDNEY *returns still clutching the glass*]

SIDNEY: Jane? Jane! [*He looks round, puzzled*] Good gracious me. [*He peers around for her*]

[EVA *comes in. In her thirties, she makes no concessions in either manner or appearance*]

EVA: May I have a glass of water?

SIDNEY: Beg your pardon?

EVA: I have to take these. [*She holds out a couple of tablets enclosed in a sheet of tinfoil. She crosses to the back door and stands taking deep breaths of fresh air*]

SIDNEY: Oh, yes. There's a glass here somewhere, I think.

EVA: Thanks.

SIDNEY: [*Finding a tumbler*] Here we are. [*He puts it down on the washing machine*]

[EVA *stands abstractedly staring ahead of her, tearing the paper round the pills without any effort to open them. A pause.* SIDNEY *looks at her*]

SIDNEY: Er . . .

EVA: What? Oh, thanks. [*She closes the back door and picks up the glass*]

SIDNEY: Not ill, I hope?

EVA: What?

SIDNEY: The pills. Not ill?

EVA: It depends what you mean by ill, doesn't it?

SIDNEY: Ah.

EVA: If you mean do they prevent me from turning into a raving lunatic, the answer's probably yes. [*She laughs somewhat bitterly*]

SIDNEY: [*Laughing too*] Raving lunatic, yes—[*He is none too certain of this lady*]—but then I always say, it helps to be a bit mad, doesn't it? I mean, we're all a bit mad. I'm a bit mad. [*Pause*] Yes. [*Pause*] It's a mad world, as they say.

EVA: [*Surveying the pills in her hand which she has now opened*] Extraordinary to think that one's sanity can depend on these.

Frightening, isn't it? [*She puts them both in her mouth and swallows the glass of water in one gulp*] Yuck. Alarming. Do you know I've been taking pills of one sort or another since I was eight years old. What chance does your body have? My husband tells me that even if I didn't need them, I'd still have to take them. My whole mentality is geared round swallowing tablets every three hours, twenty-four hours a day. I even have to set the alarm at night. You're looking at a mess. A wreck. [*She still holds the glass and is searching round absently as she speaks, for somewhere to put it*] Don't you sometimes long to be out of your body and free? Free just to float? I know I do. [*She opens the pedal bin with her foot and tosses the empty glass into it*] Thanks. [*She puts the screwed-up tinfoil into* SIDNEY's *hand and starts for the door.* SIDNEY *gawps at her.* EVA *pauses*] My God, was that our car horn?

SIDNEY: When?

EVA: Just now.

SIDNEY: No, I don't think so.

EVA: If you do hear it, it's George.

SIDNEY: George?

EVA: Our dog.

SIDNEY: Oh, yes, of course.

EVA: We left him in the car, you see. We have to leave him in the car these days, he's just impossible. He's all right there, usually, but lately he's been getting bored and he's learnt to push the horn button with his nose. He just rests his nose on the steering-wheel, you see.

SIDNEY: That's clever.

EVA: Not all that clever. We've had the police out twice.

SIDNEY: A bit like children, dogs.

EVA: What makes you say that?

SIDNEY: Need a bit of a firm hand now and again. Smack if they're naughty.

EVA: You don't smack George, you negotiate terms.

SIDNEY: Ah. [*He retrieves the glass from the waste-bin*]

EVA: He was only this big when we bought him, now he's grown into a sort of yak. When we took him in, he—My God, was that me?

SIDNEY: What?

EVA: Did I put that glass in there?

SIDNEY: Er—yes.

EVA: My God, I knew it, I'm going mad. I am finally going mad. [*She goes to the door and opens it*] Will you please tell my husband, if he drinks any more, I'm walking home.

SIDNEY: Well, I think that might be better coming from you as his wife.

EVA: [*Laughing*] You really think he'd listen to me? He doesn't even know I'm here. As far as he's concerned, my existence ended the day he married me. I'm just an embarrassing smudge on a marriage licence.

[EVA *goes out, closing the door*]

SIDNEY: Ah. [*He puts the glass on the washing machine and finds* JANE's *discarded shoes on the floor. He picks them up, stares at them and places them on the draining-board. Puzzled, he crosses to the back door and calls out into the night*] Jane! [*He listens. No reply*]

[MARION *comes in*]

SIDNEY: Jane!!

MARION: I say . . .

SIDNEY: Rain . . . [*He holds out his hand by way of demonstration, then closes the back door*]

MARION: Oh, yes, dreadful. I say, I think you dashed away with my glass.

SIDNEY: Oh, I'm so sorry. [*Handing it to her*] Here.

MARION: Thank you. I was getting terribly apprehensive in case it had gone into your washing machine. [*She sips the drink*] Oh, that's lovely. Just that teeny bit stronger. You know what I mean. Not too much tonic . . .

SIDNEY: No, well . . .

MARION: Perfect.

SIDNEY: Actually, that's neat gin, that is.

MARION: Oh, good heavens! So it is. What are you trying to do to me? I can see we're going to have to keep an eye on you Mr.—er . . .

SIDNEY: No, no. You're safe enough with me.

MARION: Yes, I'm sure . . .

SIDNEY: The mistletoe's in there.

MARION: Well, what are we waiting for? Lead on, Mr.—er . . .

[*She ushers him in front of her*]

SIDNEY: Follow me.

[SIDNEY *goes through the door*]

MARION: [*As she turns to close it, looking at her watch*] My God.

[MARION *goes out and closes the door. A pause.* JANE *arrives at the back door still in her hat, coat and boots. She is soaking wet. She carries a carton of tonic waters. She rattles the back door knob but she has locked herself out. She knocks gently then louder, but no one hears her. She rattles the knob again, pressing her face up against the glass. We see her mouth opening and shutting but no sound. Eventually, she gives up and hurries away. After a second,* SIDNEY *returns. He has the crisp bowl which is again empty. He is about to refill it when he pauses and looks round the kitchen, puzzled and slightly annoyed. He goes to the back door and opens it*]

SIDNEY: Jane! Jane!

[SIDNEY *turns up his jacket collar and runs out, leaving the door ajar. As soon as* SIDNEY *has gone, the doorbell chimes. There is a pause, then it chimes again, several times.* RONALD *enters from the sitting-room*]

RONALD: I say, old boy, I think someone's at your front—Oh. [*He sees the empty room and the open back door. He turns and goes back into the room*] No, he seems to have gone out. I suppose we'd better . . . [*His voice cuts off as he closes the door*]

[*The doorbell chimes once more.* SIDNEY *returns, closing the back door. He finds a towel and dabs his face and hair*]

SIDNEY: Dear, oh dear. [*He shakes his head and returns to his crisps. Suddenly, the living-room door bursts open and* JANE *enters hurriedly in her strange garb, her boots squelching. She shuts the door behind her and stands against it, shaking and exhausted.* SIDNEY *turns and throws the bag of crisps into the air in his astonishment*]

JANE: Oh, my goodness.

SIDNEY: What are you doing?

JANE: Oh.

SIDNEY: [*Utterly incredulous*] What do you think you're doing?

JANE: [*Still breathless*] I went—I went out—to get the tonic. [*She puts a carton of tonic waters on the table*]

SIDNEY: Like that?

JANE: I couldn't find—I didn't want . . .

SIDNEY: You went out—and came in again, like that?

JANE: I thought I'd just slip out the back to the off-licence and slip in again. But I locked myself out. I had to come in the front.

SIDNEY: But who let you in?

JANE: [*In a whisper*] Mr. Brewster-Wright.

SIDNEY: Mr. Brewster-Wright? Mr. Brewster-Wright let you in like that? [JANE *nods*] What did he say?

JANE: I don't think he recognized me.

SIDNEY: I'm not surprised.

JANE: I couldn't look at him. I just ran straight past him and right through all of them and into here.

SIDNEY: Like that?

JANE: Yes.

SIDNEY: But what did they say?

JANE: They didn't say anything. They just stopped talking and stared and I ran through them. I couldn't very well . . .

SIDNEY: You'll have to go back in there and explain.

JANE: No, I couldn't.

SIDNEY: Of course you must.

JANE: Sidney, I don't think I can face them.

SIDNEY: You can't walk through a respectable cocktail party, the hostess, dressed like that without an apology.

JANE: [On the verge of tears again] I couldn't.

SIDNEY: [Furious] You take off all that—and you go back in there and explain.

JANE: [With a wail] I just want to go to bed.

SIDNEY: Well, you cannot go to bed. Not at nineteen-forty-seven. Now, take off that coat.

[JANE squelches to the cupboard. RONALD opens the kitchen door. He is talking over his shoulder as he comes in, carrying a glass of Scotch]

RONALD: Well, I think I'd better, I mean . . .

JANE: Oh, no!

[JANE has had no time to unbutton her coat. Rather than face RONALD, she rushes out of the back door hatless, abandoning her headgear in the middle of the kitchen table. SIDNEY, trying to stop JANE, lunges after her vainly. The door slams behind her. SIDNEY stands with his back to it]

RONALD: [*In the doorway, having caught a glimpse of violent activ-ity, but unsure what*] Ah, there you are, old chap.

SIDNEY: Oh, hallo. Hallo.

RONALD: Just popped out, did you?

SIDNEY: Yes, just popped out.

RONALD: Well—something rather odd. Someone at the door just now. Little short chap. Hat, coat, boots and bottles. Just stamped straight through. You catch a glimpse of him?

SIDNEY: Oh, him.

RONALD: Belong here, does he? I mean . . .

SIDNEY: Oh, yes.

RONALD: Ah. Well, as long as you know about him. Might have been after your silver. I mean, you never know. Not these days.

SIDNEY: No, indeed. No, he—he was from the off-licence. [*He shows* RONALD *the carton*]

RONALD: Really?

SIDNEY: Brought round our order of tonic, you see. [RONALD *stares at the hat on the table.* SIDNEY *notices and picks it up*] Silly fellow. Left his hat. [*He picks up the hat, walks to the back door, opens it and throws out the hat. He closes the door*]

RONALD: Not the night to forget your hat.

SIDNEY: No, indeed.

RONALD: [*Sitting at the table*] Mind you, frankly, he didn't look all there to me. Wild-eyed. That's what made me think . . .

SIDNEY: Quite right.

RONALD: Ought to get him to come round the back, you know. Take a tip from me. Once you let tradesmen into the habit of using your front door, you might as well move out, there and then. •

SIDNEY: Well, quite. In my own particular business, I always insist that my staff . . .

RONALD: Oh, yes, of course. I was forgetting you're a—you're in business yourself, aren't you?

SIDNEY: Well, in a small way at the moment. My wife and I. I think I explained . . .

RONALD: Yes, of course. And doing very well.

SIDNEY: Well, for a little general store, you know. Mustn't grumble.

RONALD: Good to hear someone's making the grade.

SIDNEY: These days.

RONALD: Quite. [*He picks up the booklet and looks at it*]

　　　　　[*A pause*]

SIDNEY: I know this isn't perhaps the moment, I mean it probably isn't the right moment, but none the less, I hope you've been giving a little bit of thought to our chat. The other day. If you've had a moment.

RONALD: Chat? Oh, yes—chat. At the bank? Well, yes, it's—probably not, as you say, the moment but, as I said then—and this is still off the cuff you understand—I think the bank could probably see their way to helping you out.

SIDNEY: Ah well, that's wonderful news. You see, as I envisage it, once I can get the necessary loan, that means I can put in a definite bid for the adjoining site—which hasn't incidentally come onto the market. I mean, as I said, this is all purely through personal contacts.

RONALD: Quite so, yes.

SIDNEY: I mean the site value alone—just taking it as a site—you follow me?

RONALD: Oh, yes.

SIDNEY: But it is a matter of striking while the iron's hot—before it goes off the boil . . .

RONALD: Mmm . . .

SIDNEY: I mean, in this world it's dog eat dog, isn't it? No place for sentiment. Not in business. I mean, all right, so on occasions you can scratch mine. I'll scratch yours . . .

RONALD: Beg your pardon?

SIDNEY: Tit for tat. But when the chips are down it's every man for himself and blow you Jack, I regret to say . . .

RONALD: Exactly.

[*The sitting-room door opens.* GEOFFREY *enters. Mid-thirties. Good-looking, confident, easy-going. He carries a glass of Scotch*]

GEOFFREY: Ah. Is there a chance of sanctuary here?

RONALD: Hallo.

GEOFFREY: Like Dick Potter's harem in there.

SIDNEY: Dick still at it?

GEOFFREY: Yes. Keeping the ladies amused with jokes . . .

RONALD: Is he? Oh, dear. I'd better—in a minute . . .

GEOFFREY: You'll never stop him. Is he always like that? Or does he just break out at Christmas?

SIDNEY: Oh, no. Dick's a great laugh all the year round . . .

GEOFFREY: Is he?

RONALD: You don't say?

SIDNEY: He's a very fascinating character, is Dick. I thought you'd be interested to meet him. I mean, so's she. In her way. Very colourful. They're both teachers, you know. But he's very involved with youth work of all types. He takes these expeditions off to the mountains. A party of lads. Walks in Scotland. That sort of thing. Wonderful man with youngsters . . .

RONALD: Really?

SIDNEY: Got a lot of facets.

RONALD: Got a good-looking wife . . .

SIDNEY:　Lottie? Yes, she's a fine-looking woman. Always very well turned out . . .

GEOFFREY:　Yes, she seems to have turned out quite well.

SIDNEY:　She does the same as him with girls . . .

RONALD:　I beg your pardon?

SIDNEY:　Hiking and so on. With the brownies, mainly.

RONALD:　Oh, I see.

GEOFFREY:　Oh.

　　　[*Pause*]

RONALD:　Better join the brownies, then, hadn't we? [*He laughs*]

SIDNEY:　[*At length; laughing*] Yes, I like that. Better join the brownies. [*He laughs*] You must tell that to Dick. That would tickle Dick no end.

GEOFFREY:　[*After a pause*] Nice pair of legs.

RONALD:　Yes.

SIDNEY:　Dick?

GEOFFREY:　His wife.

SIDNEY:　Lottie? Oh, yes. Mind you, I don't think I've really noticed them . . .

GEOFFREY:　Usually, when they get to about that age, they tend to go a bit flabby round here. [*He pats his thigh*] But she's very trim . . .

RONALD:　Trim, oh yes.

GEOFFREY:　Nice neat little bum . . .

SIDNEY:　Ah.

RONALD:　Has she? Hadn't seen that.

GEOFFREY:　I was watching her, getting up and stretching out for the crisps. Very nice indeed.

RONALD: Oh, well, I'll keep an eye out.

[*Pause*]

SIDNEY: That'll be the hiking . . .

GEOFFREY: What?

SIDNEY: [*Tapping his thighs; somewhat self-consciously*] This—you know. That'll be the hiking . . .

RONALD: Yes. [*After a pause*] How did you happen to see those?

GEOFFREY: What?

RONALD: Her . . . [*He slaps his thighs*] I mean when I saw her just now she had a great big woolly—thing on. Down to here.

GEOFFREY: Oh, you can get around that.

RONALD: Really?

GEOFFREY: I've been picking imaginary peanuts off the floor round her feet all evening.

[RONALD *laughs uproariously.* SIDNEY *joins in, a little out of his depth*]

RONALD: You'll have to watch this fellow, you know.

SIDNEY: Oh, yes?

RONALD: Don't leave your wife unattended if he's around.

SIDNEY: Oh, no?

RONALD: Lock her away . . .

SIDNEY: [*Getting the joke at last and laughing*] Ah-ha! Yes . . .

[JANE *suddenly appears outside the back door, peering in.* SIDNEY *waves her away with urgent gestures*]

GEOFFREY: Still raining, is it?

SIDNEY: [*Holding out his hand*] Yes. Yes.

RONALD: I'll tell you what I've been meaning to ask you . . .

GEOFFREY: What's that?

RONALD: Remember that party we were both at—during the summer—Malcolm Freebody's . . . ?

GEOFFREY: When was this?

RONALD: Eva—your wife was off sick . . .

GEOFFREY: That's nothing unusual.

RONALD: I remember it because you were making tremendous headway with some woman that Freebody was using on his public relations thing . . .

GEOFFREY: Was I?

RONALD: Blonde. Sort of blonde.

GEOFFREY: [A short thought] Binnie.

RONALD: Binnie, was it?

GEOFFREY: Binnie something. I think . . .

RONALD: Make out all right, did you?

GEOFFREY: Well—you know . . .

RONALD: Really?

GEOFFREY: You have no idea. Absolute little cracker. Married to a steward on P. and O. Hadn't seen him for eight months . . .

RONALD: [Chuckling] Good Lord . . .

SIDNEY: Ah—ha—oh—ha—ha-ha. [And other noises of sexual approval]

[The others look at him]

GEOFFREY: What have you done with yours? Buried her in the garden?

SIDNEY: [Guiltily] What? No, no. She's about. Somewhere.

GEOFFREY: Wish I could lose mine, sometimes. Her and that dog. There's hardly room for me in the flat—I mean, between the two of them, they have completely reduced that flat to rubble. I mean, I'm very fond of her, bless her, she's a lovely girl—but she just doesn't know what it's all about. She really doesn't.

RONALD: Maybe. I still think you're pretty lucky with Eva . . .

GEOFFREY: Why's that?

RONALD: Well, she must have a jolly good idea by now about your —er . . .

GEOFFREY: Yes. I should imagine she probably has . . .

RONALD: Well, there you are . . .

GEOFFREY: Oh, now, come off it. Nonsense. She chooses to live with me, she lives by my rules. I mean we've always made that perfectly clear. She lives her life to a certain extent; I live mine, do what I like within reason. It's the only way to do it . . .

SIDNEY: Good gracious.

RONALD: I wish you'd have a chat with Marion. Convince her.

GEOFFREY: Any time. Pleasure.

RONALD: Yes, well, perhaps not—on second thoughts.

GEOFFREY: No, seriously. Any man, it doesn't matter who he is— you, me, anyone—[pointing at SIDNEY]—him. They've just got to get it organized. I mean, face it, there's just too much good stuff wandering around simply crying out for it for you not . . .

[The living-room door opens. EVA appears. Behind, DICK POTTER still in full flow, laughing]

GEOFFREY: [To SIDNEY, altering his tone immediately] Anyway, I think that would be a good idea. Don't you?

EVA: [Coolly] Are you all proposing to stay out here all night?

SIDNEY: Oh, dear. We seem to have neglected the ladies.

EVA: Neglected? We thought we'd been bloody well abandoned.

GEOFFREY: Can't manage without us, you see.

EVA: We can manage perfectly well, thank you. It just seemed to us terribly rude, that's all.

GEOFFREY: Oh, good God . . .

EVA: Anyway. Your jolly friends are leaving.

SIDNEY: Oh, really. Dick and Lottie? I'd better pop out and see them off, then. Excuse me . . .

[SIDNEY *goes off to the sitting-room*]

EVA: And, darling, unless you want to see our car towed away again, horn blazing—we'd better get our coats.

GEOFFREY: He's not at it again . . .

EVA: Past his supper time . . .

GEOFFREY: Oh, honestly, Eva . . .

EVA: Don't honestly Eva me, darling. He's your dog.

GEOFFREY: What do you mean, he's my dog?

EVA: [*Sweetly*] Your house, your dog, your car, your wife—we all belong to you, darling—we all expect to be provided for. Now are you coming, please? [RONALD *smiles*] And your wife is looking slightly less than pleased, I might tell you.

[RONALD's *smile fades.* EVA *goes out*]

RONALD: Oh. [*He looks at his watch*] I suppose I'd better er . . .

GEOFFREY: Oh. Ronnie. By the way . . .

RONALD: Mmmm?

GEOFFREY: I wondered if you heard anything on the grapevine about the new building Harrison's having put up . . .

RONALD: Oh, this new shopping complex of his.

GEOFFREY: Has he got anyone yet?

RONALD: What, you mean in your line?

GEOFFREY: Yes. Has he settled on an architect? Or is it still open?

RONALD: Well, as far as I know, it's still wide open. I mean, it's still a gleam in his eye as far as I know.

GEOFFREY: Well. If you get a chance to put in a word. I know you're fairly thick with him.

RONALD: Yes, of course. I'll mention it, if the topic comes up. I mean, I'm sure you could do as good a job as anyone.

GEOFFREY: Look, I can design, standing on my head, any building that Harrison's likely to want.

RONALD: Yes, well, as I say, I'll mention it.

GEOFFREY: I'd be grateful . . .

[MARION *comes in*]

RONALD: Ah.

MARION: All right, darling, we're off . . .

RONALD: Right.

MARION: Had a nice time out here?

RONALD: Oh, yes, grand.

MARION: Good. As long as you have . . . [RONALD *goes off into the living-room*] This really is a simply loathsome little house. I mean, how can people live in them. I mean, Geoff, you're an architect, you must be able to tell me. How do people come to design these sort of monstrosities in the first place, let alone persuade people to live in them?

GEOFFREY: Well . . .

MARION: Oh, God. Now he's going to tell me he designed it.

GEOFFREY: No. I didn't do it. They're designed like this mainly because of cost and people who are desperate for somewhere to live aren't particularly choosey.

MARION: Oh, come. Nobody can be this desperate.

GEOFFREY: You'd be surprised.

MARION: Anyway, it's been lovely to see you. It's been ages. You must come up and see us . . .

[SIDNEY *and* RONALD, *now in his overcoat and carrying* MARION's *coat, return*]

RONALD: Darling . . .

MARION: Sidney, we've had a simply lovely time. Now some time you must come up and see us—and your wife, that's if you ever find her . . .

SIDNEY: Yes, yes, indeed . . .

[*They all go out, chattering, closing the door. Silence. After a pause,* SIDNEY *returns. He closes the door*]

SIDNEY: [*Rubbing his hands together*] Hah! [*He smiles. Quite pleased. He takes up his drink and sips it. He munches a crisp. There is a knock at the back door—rather tentative. It is* JANE. SIDNEY *frowns. His concentration is disturbed*] Just a minute. [*He opens the back door*]

[JANE *falls in—a sodden mass*]

SIDNEY: [*Recoiling*] My word!

JANE: I saw them leaving.

SIDNEY: Yes. All gone now. They said for me to say good-bye to you.

JANE: Oh.

SIDNEY: Where have you been?

JANE: In the garden. Where else? Where do you think?

SIDNEY: Oh—I don't know. You might have been for a stroll.

JANE: In this?

SIDNEY: Oh. Still raining, is it?

JANE: Yes. [*Pause*] Sidney, if you'd only explained to them—I could've—I mean I've been out there for ages. I'm soaking . . .

SIDNEY: Yes. Well, your behaviour made things very difficult. Explanations, that is. What could I say?

JANE: You could have explained.

SIDNEY: So could you. It was really up to you, wasn't it?

JANE: Yes, I know but—I just thought that you might have—that you would've been . . . [*She gives up*]

[JANE *starts to peel off her things*]

SIDNEY: All went off rather satisfactorily, anyway . . .

JANE: [*Emptying a Wellington boot into the sink*] Good—I'm glad . . .

SIDNEY: So am I. I mean, these people just weren't anybody. They are people in the future who can be very, very useful to us . . .

JANE: [*Emptying the other boot*] Yes . . .

SIDNEY: Now, you mustn't do that, Jane. You really mustn't. You see, you get yourself all worked up. And then what happens?

JANE: Yes.

SIDNEY: Right. Enough said. All forgotten, eh? [*Pause*] Oh dear . . .

JANE: What?

SIDNEY: We never got round to playing any of our games, did we?

JANE: No.

SIDNEY: In all the excitement. Never mind. Another year. Well. I think I'll have a look at television. Should be something. Christmas Eve. Usually is. Coming in, are you?

JANE: In a minute . . .

SIDNEY: Right then.

> [SIDNEY *goes out closing the door.* JANE *stands. She sniffs. She has finished putting away her things. Her eye lights on the dirty things scattered about. She picks up a glass or so and puts them in the sink. She picks up the damp cloth and wipes first where the glasses were standing and then slowly, in wider and wider circles, till she had turned it, once more, into a full-scale cleaning operation. As she cleans she seems to relax. Softly at first, then louder, she is heard to sing happily to herself, and—*]

THE CURTAIN FALLS

ACT TWO

GEOFFREY *and* EVA JACKSON's *kitchen in their fourth-floor flat. This Christmas.*

One door leads to the sitting-room, another into a walk-in cupboard. The room gives an immediate impression of untidiness. It is a room continually lived in, unlike the HOPCROFT's *immaculate ship's bridge. While it gives signs that the owners have a certain taste for the trendy homespun in both equipment and furnishings, some of the equipment, particularly the gas stove, has seen better days. Besides the stove, the room contains a table [natural scrubbed wood], kitchen chairs [natural scrubbed wood], a chest of drawers [natural scrubbed wood] and a fridge and sink.*

When the curtain rises EVA, *unmade-up, unkempt and baggy-eyed, sits at the table in her dressing-gown. She is writing with a stub of pencil in a notepad. Whatever it is, it is difficult to word. She and the floor around her are ringed with screwed-up pieces of paper. In front of her is an open Scotch bottle. After a minute she tears out the page she has been working on, screws that up as well, and tosses it on the floor to join the others. She starts again.*

A door slams. From the sitting-room comes the sound of a large dog barking. EVA *looks up alarmed, consults her watch, gives a moan, and quickly closes the notepad to cover up what she has been writing.* GEOFFREY's *voice is heard off.*

GEOFFREY: [*Off*] Darling? Eva—Eva! Quiet, George! [GEOFFREY *backs in from the sitting-room. George is still barking with wild glee*] George! That's enough, George! Don't be silly, boy. Sit, George. Sit, boy. At once. That's a good boy. Sit. Good George. Good . . . [*George has quietened.* GEOFFREY *goes to close the*

door. George barks with fresh vigour] George . . . ! *[Giving up]*
Oh, all right, suit yourself. *[He closes the door, turning to face*
EVA *for the first time]* Hallo, darling. *[He gives her a kiss as he*
passes. EVA *hardly seems to notice. Instead, she sits fiddling with*
one of her pieces of screwed-up paper. Her face is a tense blank]
God, I need a drink. You want a drink? *[Without waiting for an*
reply, he takes the Scotch, finds a glass and pours himself a drink]
You want one? No? *[He puts the bottle back on the table and*
drinks] Cheers. I think we're running into some sort of trouble
with the Harrison job. Helluva day. Would you believe I could
spend two months explaining to them exactly how to assemble
that central-dome. I go along this morning, they're trying to put a
bloody great pillar up the middle, straight through the fountain. I
said to them, "Listen, you promise to put it up as you're told to—
I promise it'll stay up, all right?" I now have to tell Harrison that
his super Shopperdrome that he thought was only going to cost so
much is going to finish up at twice that. He is not going to be
pleased. No, I think I'm in trouble unless I can . . . Oh well,
what the hell, it's Christmas. *[Going to the window]* You know,
I think it's going to snow. By Boxing Day, that site'll be under six
foot of slush, mark my words. That'll put us another six months
behind. *[Returning from the window]* Why didn't I pick something simple? *[Seeing the screwed-up paper]* What've you been up
to? *[He tries to take* EVA's *writing pad.* EVA *clings to the pad.*
GEOFFREY *shrugs, moves away, then turns and looks at her]* You
all right? You're still in your dressing-gown, did you know? Eva?
Are you still thinking about this morning? I phoned you at lunch,
you know. Were you out? Eva? Oh, come on, darling, we talked it
over, didn't we? We were up till four o'clock this morning talking
it over. You agreed. You did more than agree. I mean, it was your
idea. And you're right. Believe me, darling, you were right. We
can't go on. Sooner or later one of us has got to do something really positive for once in our lives—for both our sakes. And it's absolutely true that the best thing that could happen to you and me,
at this point in our lives, is for me to go and live with Sally. You
were absolutely right. You know I was thinking on the way home
—I nipped in for a quick one, that's why I'm a bit late—I was
thinking, this could actually work out terribly well. If we're adult
about it, I mean. Don't behave like lovesick kids or something.

Sally and I will probably get somewhere together—and by that time you'll probably have got yourself fixed up—we could still see each other, you know. What I'm really saying is, let's not go through all that nonsense—all that good-bye, I never want to see you again bit. Because I do want to see you again. I always will. I mean, five years. We're not going to throw away five years, are we? Eva? Eva, if you're sitting there blaming yourself for this in any way, don't. It's me, love, it's all me. It's just I'm—okay, I'm weak, as you put it. I'm unstable. It's something lacking in me, I know. I mean, other men don't have this trouble. Other men can settle down and be perfectly happy with one woman for the rest of their lives. And that's a wonderful thing. Do you think I don't envy that? [*Banging the table*] God, how I envy them that. I mean, do you really think I enjoy living out my life like some sexual Flying Dutchman? Eva, please—please try and see my side just a little, will you? Look, it's Christmas Eve. The day after Boxing Day, I promise—I'll just clear everything of mine that you don't need out of the flat. That way, you can forget I even existed, if that's what you want. But can't we try, between us to make the next couple of days . . . [*He breaks off*] Did I say it's Christmas Eve? Haven't we got some people coming round? Yes, surely we . . . What time did we ask them for? [*He looks at his watch*] Oh, my God. You didn't remember to put them off by any chance, did you? No. Well then . . . Have we got anything to drink in the house? Apart from this? [*He holds up the bottle of Scotch*] Oh well, we'll have that for a start. Now then . . . [*He finds a tray, puts it on the table and puts the Scotch bottle on the table*] What else have we got? [*He rummages in the cupboards*] Brandy. That'll do. Bottle of Coke. Aha, what's this? Tonic wine? Who's been drinking tonic wine? Is that you? Eva? Oh, for heaven's sake, Eva—you've made your point, now snap out of it, will you? We have lots of people coming round who were due five minutes ago. Now come on . . . [*He looks at her and sighs*] O.K. I get the message. O.K. There is no help or cooperation to be expected from you tonight, is that it? All systems shut down again, have they? All right. All right. It won't be the first time—don't worry. [*He returns to his hunt for bottles*] I mean, it's not as if you're particularly famous as a gracious hostess, is it? It hasn't been unheard of for you to disappear to bed in the middle of a party and be found later reading a book. [*Producing a couple more bottles—gin and sherry*] I should think our friends will be a little disappointed if you do put in an appearance. [*Finding an assortment of glasses*] When I say our friends, perhaps I should say yours. I will remind you that, so far as I can remember, all the people coming tonight come under the heading of your friends and not mine. And if I'm left to entertain them tonight because you choose to opt out, I shall probably finish up being very, very rude to them. Is that clear? Right. You have been warned. Yes, I know. You're very anxious, aren't you, that I should go and work for the up and coming Mr. Hopcroft? So is up and coming Mr. Hopcroft. But I can tell you both, here and now, I have no intention of helping to perpetrate his squalid little developments. What I lack in morals—I make up in ethics. [GEOFFREY *stamps out into the sitting-room with the tray. Off, as George starts barking again*] George—no, this is not for you. Get down. I said get down. [*There is a crash as of a bottle coming off the tray*] Oh, really—this damn dog—get out of it . . . [GEOFFREY *returns with a couple of old coffee-cups which he puts in the sink*] That room is like a very untidy cesspit. [*He finds a dish cloth*] One quick drink, that's all they're getting. Then it's happy Christmas and out they bloody well go. [GEOFFREY *goes out again. He takes with him the dish cloth.* EVA *opens her notepad and continues with her note.* GEOFFREY *returns. He still has the cloth. In the other hand he has a pile of bits of broken dog biscuit*] Half-chewed biscuit. Why does he only chew half of them, can you tell me that? [*He deposits the bits in the waste-bin. He is about to exit again, then pauses*] Eva? Eva—I am being very patient. Very patient indeed. But in a minute I really do believe I'm going to lose my temper. And we know what happens then, don't we? I will take a swing at you and then you will feel hard done and, by way of reprisal, will systematically go round and smash everything in the flat. And come tomorrow breakfast time, there will be the familiar sight of the three of us, you, me and George, trying to eat our meals off our one surviving plate. Now, Eva, *please* . . . [*The doorbell rings. George starts barking*] Oh, my God! Here's the first of them. [*Calling*] George. Now, Eva, go to bed now, please. Don't make things any more embarrassing. [*As he goes out*] George, will you be quiet.

[GEOFFREY *goes out. The door closes. Silence.* EVA *opens her notepad, finishes her note and tears it out. She pushes the clutter on the table to one side slightly. She goes to a drawer and produces a kitchen knife. She returns to the table and pins the note forcibly to it with the knife. She goes to the window.* GEOFFREY *returns. Barking and chattering are heard in the background—two voices.* EVA *stands motionless, looking out*]

GEOFFREY: [*Calling back*] He's all right. He's quite harmless. Bark's worse than his bite. [*He closes the door*] It would be the bloody Hopcrofts, wouldn't it. Didn't think they'd miss out. And that lift's broken down, would you believe it. [*Finding a bottle-opener in a drawer*] Every Christmas. Every Christmas, isn't it? Eva, come on, love, for heaven's sake. [GEOFFREY *goes out, closing the door.* EVA *opens the window. She inhales the cold fresh air. After a second, she climbs uncertainly onto the window ledge. She stands giddily, staring down and clutching onto the frame. The door opens, chatter,* GEOFFREY *returns, carrying a glass. Calling behind him*] I'll get you a clean one, I'm terribly sorry. I'm afraid the cook's on holiday. [*He laughs. The* HOPCROFTS' *laughter is heard.* GEOFFREY *closes the door*] Don't think we can have washed these glasses since the last party. This one certainly didn't pass the Jane Hopcroft Good Housekeeping Test, anyway. [*He takes a dish cloth from the sink and wipes the glass rather casually*] I sometimes think that woman must spend . . . Eva! What are you doing? [EVA, *who is now feeling sick with vertigo, moans*] Eva! Eva—that's a good girl. Down. Come down—come down—that's a good girl—down. Come on . . . [*He reaches* EVA] That's it. Easy. Come on, I've got you. Down you come. That's it. [*He eases* EVA *gently back into the room. She stands limply. He guides her inert body to a chair*] Come on, sit down here. That's it. Darling, darling, what were you trying to do? What on earth made you want to . . . ? What was the point of that, what were you trying to prove? I mean . . . [*He sees the note and the knife for the first time*] What on earth's this? [*He reads it*] Oh, no. Eva, you mustn't think of . . . I mean, what do you mean, a burden to everyone? Who said you were a burden? I never said you were a burden . . . [*During the above,* EVA *picks up the bread-knife,*

*looks at it, then at one of the kitchen drawers. She rises, unseen
by* GEOFFREY, *crosses to the drawer and, half opening it, wedges
the knife inside so the point sticks out. She measures out a run
and turns to face the knife.* GEOFFREY, *still talking, is now watching her absently.* EVA *works up speed and then takes a desperate
run at the point of the knife.* GEOFFREY, *belatedly realizing what
she's up to, rushes forward, intercepts her and re-seats her*] Eva,
now, for heaven's sake! Come on . . . [*He studies her nervously*]
Look, I'm going to phone the doctor. I'll tell him you're very
upset and overwrought. [*He backs away and nearly impales himself on the knife. He grabs it*] He can probably give you something to calm you down a bit. [*The doorbell rings*] Oh, God,
somebody else. Now, I'm going to phone the doctor. I'll just be
two minutes, all right? Now, you sit there. Don't move, just sit
there like a good girl. [*Opening the door and calling off*] Would
you mind helping yourselves? I just have to make one phone
call . . .

> [GEOFFREY *goes out. Silence.* EVA *finishes another note. A
> brief one. She tears it out and weights it down, this time with
> a tin of dog food which happens to be on the table. She gazes
> round, surveying the kitchen. She stares at the oven. She goes
> to it and opens it, looking inside thoughtfully. She reaches in-
> side and removes a casserole dish, opens the lid, wrinkles her
> nose and carries it to the draining-board. Returning to the
> oven, she removes three shelves and various other odds and
> ends that seem to have accumulated in there. It is a very
> dirty oven. She looks at her hands, now grimy, goes to the
> kitchen drawer and fetches a nearly clean tea towel. Folding
> it carefully, she lays it on the floor of the oven. She lies down
> and sticks her head inside, as if trying it for size. She is ap-
> parently dreadfully uncomfortable. She wriggles about to find
> a satisfactory position.*
>
> *The door opens quietly and* JANE *enters. The hubbub out-
> side has now died down to a gentle murmur so not much noise
> filters through.* JANE *carries rather carefully two more glasses
> she considers dirty. She closes the door. She looks round the
> kitchen but sees no one. She crosses, rather furtively, to the
> sink and rinses the glasses.* EVA *throws an oven tray onto the*

floor with a clatter. JANE, *startled, takes a step back and gives a little squeak.* EVA, *equally startled, tries to sit up in the oven and hits her head with a clang on the remaining top shelf*]

JANE: [*Covering*] Mrs. Jackson, are you all right? You shouldn't be on the cold floor in your condition, you know. You should be in bed. Surely? Here . . . [*She helps* EVA *to her feet and steers her back to the table*] Now, you sit down here. Don't you worry about that oven now. That oven can wait. You clean it later. No point in damaging your health for an oven, is there? Mind you, I know just what you feel like, though. You suddenly get that urge, don't you? You say, I must clean that oven if it kills me. I shan't sleep, I shan't eat till I've cleaned that oven. It haunts you. I know just that feeling. I'll tell you what I'll do. Never say I'm not a good neighbour—shall I have a go at it for you? How would that be? Would you mind? I mean, it's no trouble for me. I quite enjoy it, actually—and you'd do the same for me, wouldn't you? Right. That's settled. No point in wasting time, let's get down to it. Now then, what are we going to need? Bowl of water, got any oven cleaner, have you? Never mind, we'll find it—I hope you're not getting cold, you look very peaky. [*Hunting under the sink*] Now then, oven cleaner? Have we got any? Well, if we haven't, we'll just have to use our old friend Mr. Vim, won't we? [*She rummages*]

[*The door opens:* GEOFFREY *enters and goes to* EVA. *Conversation is heard in the background*]

GEOFFREY: Darling, listen, it looks as if I've got . . . [*Seeing* JANE] Oh.

JANE: Hallo, there.

GEOFFREY: Oh, hallo—anything you—want?

JANE: I'm just being a good neighbour, that's all. Have you by any chance got an apron I could borrow?

GEOFFREY: [*Rather bewildered, pointing to the chair*] Er—yes—there.

JANE: Oh, yes. [*Putting it on*] Couldn't see it for looking.

GEOFFREY: Er—what are you doing?

JANE: Getting your oven ready for tomorrow, that's what I'm doing.

GEOFFREY: For what?

JANE: For your Christmas dinner. What else do you think for what?

GEOFFREY: Yes, well, are you sure . . . ?

JANE: Don't you worry about me. [*She bustles around singing loudly, collecting cleaning things and a bowl of water*]

GEOFFREY: [*Over this, irritated*] Oh, darling—Eva, look I've phoned the doctor but he's not there. He's apparently out on a call somewhere and the fool of a woman I spoke to has got the address and no number. It'll be quicker for me to try and catch him there than sitting here waiting for him to come back. Now, I'll be about ten minutes, that's all. You'll be all right, will you?

JANE: Don't you fret. I'll keep an eye on her. [*She puts on a rubber glove*]

GEOFFREY: Thank you. [*He studies the immobile* EVA. *On a sudden inspiration, crosses to the kitchen drawer and starts taking out the knives. He scours the kitchen, gathering up the sharp implements.* JANE *watches him, puzzled. By way of explanation*] People downstairs are having a big dinner-party. Promised to lend them some stuff.

JANE: Won't they need forks?

GEOFFREY: No. No forks. They're Muslims. [*As he goes to the door*] Ten minutes.

[*The doorbell rings*]

JANE: There's somebody.

GEOFFREY: The Brewster-Wrights, probably.

JANE: Oh . . . [GEOFFREY *goes out, the dog barking as he does so, until the door is closed*] Hark at that dog of yours. Huge, isn't he?

Like a donkey—huge. Do you know what Dick's bought him? Dick Potter? He's bought George a Christmas present. One of those rubber rings. You know the ones you throw in the air. One of those. He loves it. He's been running up and down your hallway out there—Dick throwing it, him trying to catch it. But he's really wonderful with dogs, Dick. He really understands them. Do you know he nearly became a dog handler only he didn't have his proper eyesight. But he knows how to treat them. Doesn't matter what sort of dog it is . . . He knows all their ways. [*Turning to the oven*] Now then—oh, this is going to be a big one, isn't it? Dear, oh dear. Never mind. Where there's a will. [*Removing the tea towel from the oven*] You haven't been trying to clean it with this, have you? You'll never clean it with this. Good old elbow grease—that's the way. [*She sets to work, her head almost inside the oven*] Shall I tell you something—Sidney would get so angry if he heard me saying this—but I'd far sooner be down here on the floor, on my knees in the oven—than out there, talking. Isn't that terrible. But I'm never at ease, really, at parties. I don't enjoy drinking, you see. I'd just as soon be out here, having a natter with you. [*She starts to sing cheerily as she works, her voice booming round the oven*]

> [*During this,* EVA *rises, opens the cupboard, pulls out a tin box filled with first-aid things and searches through the contents. Eventually, she finds a white cylindrical cardboard pull box which is what she's looking for. She goes to the sink with it and runs herself a glass of water. She opens the box, takes out a couple of small tablets and puts the box back on the draining-board. She swallows one tablet with a great deal of difficulty and water. The same with the second. She leaves the tap running, pulls the cotton-wool out of the box—and the rest of the pills rattle down the drain.* EVA *tries desperately to save some with her finger before they can disappear, turning off the tap. This proving ineffective, she tries with a fork. The door opens. Barking and chatter are heard.* SIDNEY *enters*]

SIDNEY: Hallo, hallo. Where's everyone gone, then . . . [*Seeing* JANE] Dear, oh dear. I just can't believe it. I just can't believe my eyes. You can't be at it again. What are you doing?

JANE: She's under the weather. She needs a hand.

SIDNEY: Do you realize that's your best dress?

JANE: Oh, bother my best dress.

SIDNEY: Mr. and Mrs. Brewster-Wright have arrived, you know. Ron and Marion. I hope they don't chance to see you down there. [*Turning to* EVA *who is still fishing rather half-heartedly with the fork*] And what's the trouble over here, eh? Can I help—since it seems to be in fashion this evening? [SIDNEY *takes the fork from* EVA *and seats her in her chair*] Now. I'll give you a little tip, if you like. You'll never get a sink unblocked that way. Not by wiggling a fork about in it, like that. That's not the way to unblock a sink, now, is it? All you'll do that way is to eventually take the chrome off your fork and possibly scratch the plug hole. Not the way. Let's see now . . . [*He runs the tap for a second and watches the water running away*] Yes. It's a little on the sluggish side. Just a little. But it'll get worse. Probably a few tea-leaves, nothing more. Let's have a look, shall we? [*He opens the cupboard under the sink*] Ten to one, this is where your troubles lie. Ah-ha. It's a good old-fashioned one, isn't it? Need the wrench for that one.

JANE: He'll soon fix that for you, won't you, Sidney?

SIDNEY: Brace of shakes. Shake of braces as we used to say in the Navy. I've got the tools. Down in the car. No trouble at all. [*He turns to* EVA] Nothing serious. All it is, you see—where the pipe bends under the sink there—they call that the trap. Now then. [*He takes out a pencil*] I'll show you. Always useful to know. Paper? [*He picks up* EVA's *latest suicide note*] This is nothing vital, is it . . . ? Now then. [*He glances curiously at it, then turns it over and starts to draw his diagram on the back*] Now—here's your plug hole, do you see, here—if I can draw it—and this is your pipe coming straight down and then almost doubling back on itself like that, for a second, you see? Then it runs away here, to the drain . . .

JANE: You want to know anything, you ask Sidney . . .

SIDNEY: And this little bit here's the actual drain trap. And all you have to do is get it open and out it all comes. Easy when you know. Now I suppose I'll have to walk down four flights for my tools. [*He screws up the paper and throws it away. At the door*] Now, don't worry. Lottie's keeping them entertained at the moment and Dick's busy with George, so everybody's happy, aren't they?

> [SIDNEY *opens the door and goes out. We hear* LOTTIE's *laughter and the dog barking distantly for a moment before the door closes*]

JANE: It's at times like this you're glad of your friends, aren't you? [*She goes at the oven with fresh vigour, singing cheerily*]

> [*During the above* EVA *writes another brief note and places it in a prominent position on the table. She now rises and goes to a chair where there is a plastic washing basket filled with clean but unironed clothes. Coiled on top is a washing line. She returns to the table.* JANE, *emerging for fresh water, catches sight of her*]

JANE: Sorting out your laundry? You're a terror, aren't you? You're worse than me. [*She returns to her oven and resumes her song.* EVA *begins to pull the washing line from the basket. She finds one end and ties it in a crude noose. She tests the effectiveness of this on one wrist and, satisfied, pulls the rest of the rope from the basket. Every foot or so is a plastic clothes peg which she removes*] I think I'm beginning to win through. I think I'm down to the metal, anyway, that's something. There's about eight layers on here. [EVA *comes across a pair of knickers and two pairs of socks still pegged to the line. She removes these and replaces them in the basket*] There's something stuck on the bottom here like cement. You haven't had cement for dinner lately, have you? [*She laughs.*] EVA *now stands with her clothes line gazing at the ceiling. There are two light fittings and her eyes rest on the one immediately above the table. She crosses to the door, clicks a switch and just this one goes out*] Whooo! Where was Moses . . . ? What's happened? Bulb gone, has it? We'll get Sidney to fix that when he comes back. Keep him on the go. [*She returns to the oven again, changing her tune to something suitable like "Dancing in the Dark"*]

[EVA *climbs first onto a chair then onto the table holding her* *rope. She removes the bulb and shade in one from the socket* *and places them on the table at her feet. She is beginning to* *yawn more and more frequently and is obviously beginning to* *feel the effect of the sleeping pills. Swaying slightly, she starts* *to tie the rope round the socket. This proves a difficult opera-* *tion since she has far too much rope for the job. She finally* *manages a knot which loosely encircles it. She gives the rope* *a gentle tug—it holds. She tries again. It still remains in posi-* *tion. She gives it a third tug for luck. The rope slides down* *and pulls the socket away from the wires. The holder clatters* *onto the table and she is left clutching the rope. She stands* *swaying more pronouncedly now, a faint look of desperation* *on her face.* RONALD *enters. Behind him we hear* LOTTIE POT- TER's *laughter and, more distant, a dog barking*]

RONALD: Now then, how's our little invalid getting . . . [*Seeing* EVA] Oh, good God! [*He dashes forward and steadies* EVA] My dear girl, what on earth are you doing up there?

JANE: [*Emerging from her oven*] Oh, no. She's a real terror, you know. [*She goes to assist* RONALD *in helping* EVA *off the table and* *back onto a chair*] She can't keep still for a minute. [*Reprovingly* *to* EVA] You could have hurt yourself up there, you silly thing.

[RONALD *folds up the rope, which is looped around* EVA's *wrist, and leaves it in her hand*]

RONALD: Lucky I . . .

JANE: Yes, it was.

RONALD: I mean. What was she trying to do?

JANE: Bulb's gone.

RONALD: [*Looking up*] Yes, so it has. Well, you could have asked me to do that, you know. I'm no handyman but even I can change a bulb.

[SIDNEY *enters with a large bag of tools. Behind him we hear* LOTTIE's *laughter and a dog barking*]

SIDNEY: Here we are, back again. I've brought everything, just in case. Everything except the kitchen sink and that's already here, eh?

[*He laughs*]

RONALD: What? Oh, yes. Very good.

JANE: [*Amused*] Except the kitchen sink. Honestly.

SIDNEY: [*Noticing the light*] Hallo, hallo. More trouble? [*He puts the tool bag by the sink*]

RONALD: Nothing much. Just a bulb gone.

SIDNEY: You've lost more than a bulb, by the look of it. You've lost the whole fitting.

RONALD: Good gracious me. So we have. Look at that.

SIDNEY: Just the bare wires, you see.

RONALD: Yes. There's no thingummyjig.

JANE: Just the wires, aren't there?

SIDNEY: Don't like the look of that.

RONALD: No.

JANE: No.

SIDNEY: I mean, if that was to short across like it is . . .

RONALD: Yes.

JANE: Yes.

SIDNEY: You could finish up with a fuse, or a fire . . .

RONALD: Or worse.

JANE: Worse.

SIDNEY: I mean, you've only got to be carrying, say, for instance, a pair of aluminum steps across the room and you happen accidentally to knock against the wires, electricity would be conducted down the steps and straight into you. Natural earth, you see. Finish.

RONALD: I suppose that would go for a very tall man in, say, a tin hat, eh? [*He laughs*]

SIDNEY: True, true. Not so probable. But true.

JANE: Lucky it's not the war time.

SIDNEY: Oh, yes. In certain cases, one touch could be fatal.

RONALD: Better fix it, I suppose.

SIDNEY: I'd advise it. Going to have a go, are you?

RONALD: Well—I don't know. Looks a bit technical for me.

SIDNEY: Oh, no. Very simple. Nothing to it. Look, you've got your two wires coming down . . . Look, I'll draw it for you. [*He whips out his pencil again and, searching for a piece of paper, picks up* EVA's *suicide note. With a casual glance at it*] Nothing important this, is it? [*Without waiting for a reply, he turns it over and starts to sketch.* EVA *stares—fascinated*] You've got your two wires coming down here, you see—like that. They go through the top of the plug, here—excuse the drawing, and then they just screw into the little holes on the prongs, you see? Tighten your grubs. Screw your top to your bottom and away you go.

RONALD: Let there be light.

SIDNEY: Exactly.

    [EVA *scrawls another note*]

RONALD: Oh, well, that looks—simple enough. [*He still seems doubtful*]

SIDNEY: Right. I'll get you a screwdriver and I'll get going on the sink. [*Opening his tool bag*] Now then, let's get you fixed up. What've we got here? [*He rummages through his tools, taking out a screwdriver and a spare fitting*]

RONALD: Good gracious. What a collection.

SIDNEY: This is just the set I keep in the car.

RONALD: Really? Get a lot of trouble with it, do you?

[*During the above* EVA *climbs slowly onto her chair, steps onto the table and reaches out with both hands towards the bare wires.* JANE, *who has returned to her oven, turns in time to see her*]

JANE: Watch her!

SIDNEY: Hey-hey . . .

RONALD: Hoy . . .

[*All three of them run, grab* EVA *and pull her back in the chair*]

SIDNEY: They might have been live.

RONALD: Yes. [*A thought*] Might they?

SIDNEY: Yes.

RONALD: Well, how do we know they're not?

SIDNEY: Check the switches first.

RONALD: Yes, well, don't you think we'd better? I mean, I'm going to be the one who . . .

SIDNEY: [*Striding to the door*] Check the switches, by all means.

[SIDNEY *plays with both switches, plunging the room into darkness a couple of times*]

JANE: [*During this, still with* EVA] She's got a charmed life, honestly. The sooner that doctor gets here . . .

RONALD: He'll fix her up.

JANE: He'd better.

SIDNEY: [*Completing his check*] Yes, all safe. [*He takes off his jacket and puts it over the back of a chair*]

RONALD: Ah.

SIDNEY: Should be, anyway. Unless they've put this switch on upside down, of course.

RONALD: How do we know they haven't?

SIDNEY: Well, you'll be the first to find out, won't you? [*He roars with mirth*]

JANE: [*Equally tickled*] You'll be the first . . .

[RONALD *is less amused*]

SIDNEY: Well, let's get down to it, shall we?

RONALD: [*Gazing at the light*] Yes.

SIDNEY: Each to his own. [*He starts work under the sink*]

JANE: Each to his own. [*She returns to the oven*]

[*They prepare for their various tasks*]

JANE: This is coming up a treat.

SIDNEY: Ought to get—er—Marion out here, eh? Find her something to do.

RONALD: [*Clearing the things off the table*] No—no. I don't think she'd contribute very much. Probably better off with the Potters. Matter of fact, she's just a bit—on her pins. You know what I mean.

SIDNEY: Ah, well. Christmas.

JANE: If you can't do it at Christmas . . .

SIDNEY: Once a year, eh?

RONALD: Not in my wife's case. Festive season recurs rather more frequently. Every three or four days.

SIDNEY: [*Under the sink*] Ah-ha! You're going to be a tricky little fellow, aren't you? Nobody's opened you since you were last painted.

[SIDNEY *clatters under the sink.* JANE *scrubs cheerfully on.* RONALD *sets to work, standing on the table and on* EVA's *latest note. He tackles his own particular job extremely slowly and with many false starts. He is not particularly electrically-minded.* EVA *attempts, under the following, to rescue her note from under* RONALD's *feet. It rips. She scrawls another rapidly*]

RONALD: Must be pretty pleased with your year, I should imagine.

SIDNEY: Beg pardon?

RONALD: Had a good year. Must be pretty pleased.

SIDNEY: Oh, yes. Had a few lucky hunches. Seemed to pay off.

RONALD: I should say so.

SIDNEY: Mustn't complain, anyway.

JANE: No. Mustn't complain.

SIDNEY: As long as you're looking after our money. Eh? [*He laughs*]

RONALD: Oh, yes. Yes.

> [*They work.* SIDNEY *whistles.* RONALD *hums.* JANE *sings. Occasionally, the workers break off their respective melodies to make those sounds that people make when wrestling with inanimate objects. "Come on, you little . . . Just one more . . . get in, get in, etc." During this* EVA, *having finished her note, sees* SIDNEY'S *bag of tools. Unseen by the others, she goes to the bag and removes a lethal-looking tin of paint stripper. Also a hammer and a nail. She nails her latest note to the table with the hammer which she leaves on the table. Turning her attention to the paint stripper, she tries to get the top off. It is very stiff. She struggles vainly then goes to the room door, intending to use it as a vice.*
>
> *At this moment* MARION *enters.* EVA *is pushed behind the door, and, as it swings shut, she clings to the handle and falls across the floor. While the door is open the dog barks and raised voices are heard*]

MARION: [*Holding a gin bottle and glass*] I say—something rather ghastly's happened.

RONALD: [*Concentrating hard*] Oh, yes?

MARION: Goodness! Don't you all look busy? Darling, what are you doing up there?

> [EVA *tries to open the bottle with the walk-in cupboard door*]

RONALD: Oh, just a little light electrical work or should I say a little electrical light work? [*He laughs*]

SIDNEY: Electrical light work. [*He laughs*]

JANE: Electrical light work. [*She laughs*]

SIDNEY: I like that—yes . . .

MARION: Yes, very funny, darling. Now do come down, please, before you blow us all up. You know absolutely nothing about that sort of thing at all.

RONALD: I don't know . . .

MARION: Absolutely nothing.

RONALD: I fixed that bottle lamp with a cork in it, didn't I?

MARION: Yes, darling, and we all had to sit round admiring it while the lampshade burst into flames.

[*EVA goes to the tool bag for a screwdriver*]

RONALD: [*Irritably*] That was entirely the fault of the bloody lampshade.

MARION: I was terrified. The whole thing was an absolute death trap. I had to give it to the Scouts for jumble.

SIDNEY: What was the trouble?

MARION: It was like modern sculpture. Bare wires sticking out at extraordinary angles.

[*EVA goes and sits down in a corner*]

SIDNEY: No. I meant when you came in.

MARION: Oh, yes. What was it? Something awful. [*She remembers*] Oh, yes. I came for help, that's right. That dog . . .

JANE: George?

MARION: Is that his name—George—yes. Well, he's just bitten that Potter man in the leg.

JANE: Oh, dear.

MARION: Terribly nasty. Right through his trousers. Of course, it was entirely his fault. I mean, he was leaping about being desperately hearty with the poor animal till it had froth simply foaming from its jowls and didn't know where it was.

JANE: Oh, dear, are they . . . ?

SIDNEY: Yes, what are they . . . ?

MARION: Well, I think they were thinking of going. If they haven't gone. They seem to think he might need an anti-something.

SIDNEY: Rabies.

MARION: Probably. I'll see. [*She opens the door. Silence. Calling*] I say, hallo. Hallo there. [*There is a low growl*] Oh, dear.

RONALD: What's the matter?

MARION: It's sort of crouching in the doorway chewing a shoe and looking terribly threatening.

RONALD: Really?

MARION: I don't think it's going to let us through, you know.

RONALD: [*Picking up the tin of dog meat and moving tentatively to the sitting-room*] He's probably all right, he just needs calming down. Here, boy, boy, good boy. Hallo, boy, good boy. [*A growl.* RONALD *returns, closes the door, and goes back to his work*] No, well, best to leave them when they're like that. Just a bit excited.

SIDNEY: Mind you, once they've drawn blood, you know . . .

JANE: Old Mr. Allsop's Alsatian . . .

SIDNEY: Yes.

MARION: Yes. Well, it's lucky I brought the drink. Keep the workers going. And the invalid. How is she?

RONALD: Very groggy.

MARION: [*Peering at her*] Golly, yes. She's a dreadful color. How are you feeling?

JANE: I don't think she really knows we're here.

MARION: Hallo. Hallo, there . . . [*No response*] No, you're right. She's completely gone. Poor thing. Oh well, drink, everyone?

JANE: Not just at the moment. Nearly finished.

MARION: Jolly good. [*Nudging* SIDNEY *with her leg*] What about you?

SIDNEY: In a moment. In just a moment.

RONALD: Darling, I wouldn't drink too much more of that.

MARION: Oh, Ronnie, don't be such a misery. Honestly, he's such a misery. He's totally incapable of enjoying a party.

RONALD: No, all I'm saying is . . .

MARION: Well, Eva and I'll have one, won't we, Eva?

[MARION *pours out two glasses*]

SIDNEY: [*From under the sink*] Ah!

JANE: All right?

SIDNEY: Got it off.

JANE: Oh, well done.

MARION: What's he got off?

[EVA *finally gets the lid off the paint stripper and is about to drink it*]

SIDNEY: That was a wrestle and no mistake. But I got it off. The big question now is, can I get it on again.

MARION: Eva, dear, now you drink that. [*She puts the glass in* EVA's *hand, removing the tin of stripper*] That'll do you far more good than all the pills and patent medicines put together. [*She puts the paint stripper on the draining-board*]

RONALD: Marion, seriously, I wouldn't advise . . .

MARION: [*Hitting him on the foot with the gin bottle*] Oh, Ronnie, just shut up!

RONALD: Ah!

MARION: [*To* EVA; *confidentially*] You'd never think it but he was a really vital young man, Eva. You'd never think it to look at him, would you?

[MARION *fills* EVA'S *glass of gin so that she is forced in her inert state to drink some*]

SIDNEY: [*Emerging from his sink*] Well, time for a break. Now then, did somebody promise a drink?

MARION: [*Pushing the bottle towards him*] Help yourself.

SIDNEY: Thank you.

JANE: I think that's about as much as I can do. It's a bit better.

MARION: [*Going to the stove*] Oh, look, isn't that marvellous. Look at that splendid oven.

SIDNEY: Well done. Well done.

JANE: Bit of a difference. [*She picks up her bowl of water and carries it to the sink*]

RONALD: [*Having difficulty*] Ah . . .

SIDNEY: How's the electrical department?

RONALD: [*Muttering*] Damn fiddly thing.

SIDNEY: [*Seeing* JANE] Hey! Don't pour that down now!

JANE: Oh. Nearly forgot.

SIDNEY: You'd have been popular. [*He puts the gin bottle on the table*]

JANE: I'd have been popular.

MARION: Well, I'm just going to sit here all night and admire that oven. I think she's honestly better than our Mrs. Minns, isn't she, darling?

RONALD: Anyone's better than our Mrs. Minns.

MARION: Oh, she means well. We have our Mrs. Minns. She's a

dear old soul. She can hardly see and she only comes in for two hours a day and when she's gone we spend the rest of the time cleaning up after her. But she's got an absolute heart of gold.

RONALD: Largely paid for by us.

SIDNEY: Good health. Happy Christmas to all.

MARION: Happy New Year.

JANE: Yes.

SIDNEY: Get this lot finished, maybe there'll be time for a game . . .

JANE: Oh, yes . . .

MARION: What sort of game do you mean?

SIDNEY: You know. Some good party game. Get everyone jumping about.

MARION: What an obscene idea.

SIDNEY: Oh, they're great fun. We've had some laughs, haven't we?

JANE: Talk about laughs . . .

RONALD: Blast.

SIDNEY: What's the matter?

RONALD: Dropped the little thing. Could you see if you can see it. I've got to keep holding on to this or it'll drop off. Little thing about so big.

MARION: What little thing?

RONALD: A whajamacallit.

JANE: Small was it?

RONALD: Lord, yes. Tiny little thingy.

SIDNEY: Oh dear, oh dear.

[*They hunt,* SIDNEY *crawls on hands and knees*]

JANE: Might have rolled anywhere.

MARION: What are we looking for?

RONALD: Little whosit. Goes in here.

MARION: Darling, do be more precise. What's a whosit?

JANE: You know, one of those—one of those—isn't that silly I can't think of the word.

MARION: Well, I refuse to look till I know what we're looking for. We could be here all night. I mean, from the look of this floor it's simply littered with little whosits.

SIDNEY: [*Under the table*] Can't see it.

JANE: It's on the tip of my tongue . . . that's it, a nut. Little nut.

MARION: [*Searching by the sink*] Oh, well then, a nut. Now we know. Everyone hunt for a little nut.

[EVA *goes and sits at the table*]

SIDNEY: I didn't know we were looking for a nut.

JANE: Aren't we?

RONALD: No. A screw. That's what I'm after, a screw.

SIDNEY: A screw, yes.

JANE: Oh, a screw.

MARION: All right, everybody, stop looking for nuts. Ronnie's now decided he wants a screw. I can't see a thing, and I think it would be terribly sensible if we put the light on, wouldn't it?

RONALD: Good idea.

[MARION *goes to the light switch*]

SIDNEY: [*Realizing far too late*] No, I wouldn't turn that on . . .

[MARION *presses the switch*]

MARION: There.

[RONALD, *on the table, starts vibrating, emitting a low moan*]

SIDNEY: [*Rising*] Turn it off.

JANE: Get him away.

MARION: Darling, what on earth are you doing?

JANE: [*Reaching out to pull* RONALD *away*] Get him away.

SIDNEY: No, don't touch him, he's live. [*He goes to the switch*]

   [JANE *touches him and recoils, with a squeak*]

RONALD: [*Through gritted teeth*] Somebody turn it off.

   [SIDNEY *turns it off*]

SIDNEY: All right. Panic over.

   [RONALD *continues to vibrate*]

JANE: Turn him off, Sidney.

SIDNEY: I have.

JANE: Turn him off!

SIDNEY: He is off. [*Calming* JANE] Now, pull yourself together. Help me get him down. Get him down.

   [SIDNEY *and* JANE *guide* RONALD *down from the table and guide him to a chair.* MARION *watches them*]

MARION: Good Lord. Wasn't that extraordinary?

SIDNEY: Easy now.

JANE: Take it slowly.

   [EVA *pours herself another drink*]

MARION: Whenever he fiddles about with anything electrical it always ends in disaster. This always happens. Is he all right?

SIDNEY: He's in a state of shock.

JANE: He would be.

SIDNEY: Sit him down and keep him warm—that's the way. Pass me my jacket. Jacket. Jacket.

MARION: He looks frightfully odd.

JANE: [*Bringing* SIDNEY's *jacket*] Here.

SIDNEY: He needs more. He really needs to be wrapped up, otherwise . . .

JANE: [*Looking round*] There's nothing much here.

SIDNEY: Well, find something. In the other room. We need blankets.

JANE: Right.

[JANE *goes to the door while* MARION *looks vaguely round the kitchen*]

SIDNEY: Now easy, old chap. Just keep breathing . . .

[JANE *opens the door. There is a fierce growling. She withdraws swiftly and closes it*]

JANE: He's still there.

SIDNEY: Who?

JANE: The dog.

SIDNEY: Well, step over him. This is an emergency.

JANE: I'm not stepping over him. You step over him.

SIDNEY: Oh dear, oh dear.

MARION: [*Who has found the washing basket*] What about these bits and bobs? [*She picks up an article of clothing*]

SIDNEY: What's that?

MARION: Last week's washing, I think. [*Sniffing it*] It seems fairly clean. Might be better than nothing.

SIDNEY: Yes, well, better than nothing.

MARION: It seems dry.

JANE: Better than nothing.

[*Between them, they cover* RONALD *in an assortment of laundry, both male and female. He finishes up more or less encased in it but still quivering*]

SIDNEY: Quick as you can. Come along, quick as you can.

JANE: [*Examining a shirt*] She hasn't got this collar very clean.

SIDNEY: Jane, come along.

MARION: [*Holding up a petticoat*] Oh, that's rather pretty. I wonder where she got this.

SIDNEY: Not the time for that now. That the lot?

MARION: Yes. Only socks left. And you-know-whats.

SIDNEY: Well, it'll keep his temperature up.

MARION: Oh, my God, what does he look like? Ronnie! You know I've got a terrible temptation to phone up his chief cashier. If he could see him now . . . [*She starts to laugh*]

JANE: I don't think he's very well, you know.

MARION: Yes, I'm sorry. It's just that I've never seen anything quite so ludicrous.

SIDNEY: [*Moving a chair up beside* RONALD] Might I suggest that Marion sits down with her husband just until the doctor gets here for Mrs. Jackson . . .

JANE: Then he can look at them both.

SIDNEY: Precisely.

JANE: Lucky he was coming.

SIDNEY: Yes, well, we'd better just finish off and clear up, hadn't we?

MARION: [*Sitting beside* RONALD] Would you like a drink, darling? You look dreadful!

JANE: I'd better just go over the floor.

SIDNEY: [*Preparing to go under the sink again*] No, dear, we don't want you to go over the floor. Not now . . .

JANE: Just where we've been tramping about. If Doctor's coming. It won't take a minute.

SIDNEY: All right. Carry on, Sister. Sorry I spoke.

JANE: [*Going to the walk-in cupboard*] Now where does she keep her broom?

RONALD: [*Strained tone*] You know, I feel very peculiar.

[*JANE finds the broom and starts clearing the immediate vicinity around the table*]

MARION: Well, I hope you won't be like this all over Christmas, darling. I mean, we've got your mother over tomorrow for lunch and Edith and the twins on Boxing Day—I just couldn't face them alone, I just couldn't.

JANE: [*To EVA*] Excuse me, dear. I wonder if you could just . . . [*She winds up the rope, still looped to EVA's wrist, and puts it in EVA's hand*] Tell you what, why don't you sit up here? Just for a second. Then I won't get in the way of your feet. [*She assists EVA to sit on the edge of the table*] Upsidaisy.

SIDNEY: [*Sliding under the sink*] She all right still?

JANE: I think so. [*EVA yawns*] Just a bit tired. Neglected you in all the excitement, haven't we? Never mind. Just sit there. Doctor'll be here soon. [*She sweeps under the table*]

MARION: You know, I believe I'm beginning to feel dizzy as well. I hope I haven't caught it from her.

JANE: I hope not. What a Christmas, eh?

SIDNEY: [*From under the sink*] We'll be laughing about this.

JANE: [*Going to the sink and lifting SIDNEY's feet*] Excuse me, dear. What's that?

SIDNEY: I say, in about two weeks' time, we'll—[*JANE pours the water away in the sink*] —all be sitting down and laughing about —aaaah!

JANE: Oh, no!

SIDNEY: Put the plug in.

JANE: [*Feverishly following the plug chain*] I can't find the end.

SIDNEY: Put the plug in!

JANE: [*Putting the plug in*] I'm sorry.

SIDNEY: [*Emerging from under the sink, his top half drenched in dirty water*] Look what you've done.

JANE: I'm terribly sorry. [*She picks up a dish cloth*]

SIDNEY: Look what you have done! You silly woman! [*She tries to mop him down with the dish cloth. Beating her away*] Don't do that! Don't do that! It's too late for that. Look at this shirt. This is a new shirt.

JANE: Well, it'll wash. It'll wash. I'll wash it. It's only oven grease.

SIDNEY: I told you, didn't I? I said, whatever you do—don't pour water down there, didn't I?

JANE: I didn't think . . .

SIDNEY: Obviously.

JANE: Well, take the shirt off now and I'll . . .

SIDNEY: And I'll go home in my singlet, I suppose?

JANE: Nobody'll notice.

SIDNEY: Of course they'll notice. Otherwise, there'd be no point in wearing a shirt in the first place, would there? If nobody noticed, we'd all be walking around in our singlets.

JANE: It's dark.

SIDNEY: Don't change the subject. It would really teach you a lesson if I caught pneumonia.

JANE: [*Tearful*] Don't say that.

SIDNEY: Teach you, that would. [JANE *sniffs.* SIDNEY *strides to the door*] Dear, oh dear.

JANE: [*Following him*] Where are you going?

SIDNEY: To get my overcoat before I freeze. Where else do you think I'm going?

JANE: But, Sidney . . .

[SIDNEY *ignores her, flinging open the door and striding out, making a dignified exit. There is a burst of furious barking.* SIDNEY *reappears very swiftly and closes the door behind him*]

SIDNEY: [*To* EVA; *furiously*] That dog of yours is a liability! You ought to keep that animal under control. I can't even get to my overcoat. It's not good enough.

[EVA *slowly lies down on the kitchen table, oblivious*]

JANE: Come and sit down.

SIDNEY: Sit down? What's the point of sitting down?

JANE: Geoff should be back soon.

SIDNEY: I should hope so. This isn't what you expect at all. Not when you come round for a quiet drink and a chat. [*Almost screaming in* EVA's *ear*] This is the last time I accept hospitality in this household!

JANE: Ssh.

SIDNEY: What?

JANE: She'll hear you.

SIDNEY: I don't care who hears me. [*He sits*]

JANE: Ssh. [*She sits*]

[A *pause. The four of them are sitting.* EVA *lies.* RONALD *continues to look glassy, quivering slightly;* MARION's *drinking has caught up with her.* JANE *looks abjectly miserable.* SIDNEY *shivers in his vest*]

SIDNEY: And we're missing the television.

JANE: Ssh.

[A *silence. Then, from apparently nowhere, a sleepy voice begins to sing dreamily. It is* EVA]

EVA: [*Singing*] "On the first day of Christmas my true love sent to me, a partridge in a pear tree. On the second day of Christmas my true love sent to me, two turtle doves—

MARION: [*Joining her*]—and a partridge in a pear tree. On the third day of Christmas my true love sent to me, three French hens—

JANE: [*Joining her*]—two turtle doves and a partridge in a pear tree. On the fourth day of Christmas my true love sent to me, four calling birds—

RONALD: [*Joining them*]—three French hens, two turtle doves and a partridge in a pear tree.

ALL: On the fifth day of Christmas my true love sent to me, five gold rings, etc.

[*As the bedraggled quintet begin to open up, the singing gets bolder and more confident. Somewhere in the distance George begins to howl.* EVA, *still lying on her back, conducts them dreamily with both hands and then finally with the hammer. The door bursts open.* GEOFFREY *enters hurriedly, calling behind him*]

GEOFFREY: Through here, Doctor. Please hurry, I . . .

[GEOFFREY *is suddenly aware of the sound behind him. He turns, still breathless from his run up four flights. His mouth drops further open as he surveys the scene. The singing continues unabated, as the lights black-out and—*]

THE CURTAIN FALLS

ACT THREE

RONALD *and* MARION BREWSTER-WRIGHT's *kitchen. Next Christmas.*

They live in a big old Victorian house, and the kitchen, though modernized to some extent, still retains a lot of the flavor of the original room. A sink, an electric stove, a fridge, a dark wood sideboard, a round table and chairs form the substantial furnishings for the room. On the table is an elderly radio set. There is a door, half of opaque glass, to the hall, and a garden door.

When the curtain rises, RONALD *is sitting in an armchair near the table. He wears a scarf and a green eye-shade. Beside him is a lighted portable oil stove. At his elbow is an empty teacup. The radio is on, playing very quietly a jolly carol.* RONALD *is reading a book. He is obviously enjoying it, for every two or three seconds he chuckles to himself out loud. This continues for some seconds, until the door from the hall opens and* EVA *enters. She wears a winter coat and carries an empty teacup and a plate, which she puts down on the draining-board.*

RONALD: Oh. Hallo there.

EVA: All right?

RONALD: Oh, yes. [*He switches off the radio*]

EVA: Are you warm enough in here?

RONALD: Oh, yes. It's fine in here. Well, not too bad.

EVA: The rest of the house is freezing. I don't envy you going to bed.

RONALD: Her room's all right, though, is it?

EVA: Oh, she's got three electric fires blazing away.

RONALD: My God! That'll be the second power station I've paid for this winter.

EVA: She seems to be rather dug in up there. Almost in a state of hibernation. Doesn't she ever come out?

RONALD: Not if she can help it. Heating system went on the blink, you see—usual thing and we had a few frosty words over it and—the outcome was, she said she wasn't setting foot outside her room until I got it fixed.

EVA: [Putting on a pair of gloves] Well, how long's it been like this?

RONALD: [Vaguely] Oh, I don't know. Two or three weeks, I suppose.

EVA: Well, that's disgusting. Can't you get the men round to fix it?

RONALD: Yes, yes. I have phoned them several times. But I've been a bit unlucky up to now. They always seem to be at lunch . . .

EVA: [Taking off her coat and putting it on the back of a chair] Well, I wouldn't put up with it. I'd scream the place down till Geoffrey got it fixed. [She hunts in the cupboards]

RONALD: Yes, we've had a packet of trouble with this central heating. Always goes on the blink. Either the day before Christmas, the day before Easter or the day before Whitsun. Always seems to manage it. Don't understand the principle it works on but whatever it is, seems to be very closely tied in with the Church calendar. [He laughs] Can I help you at all?

EVA: She said she'd like a sandwich. [She puts a plate, knife, bread and a jar of peanut butter on a bread board]

RONALD: [Looking at his watch] Oh, yes. She's about due for a sandwich.

EVA: I'm looking for the butter.

RONALD: Oh, don't you bother to do that, I'll . . .

EVA: It's all right. Where do you keep your butter?

RONALD: Do you know, that's very interesting. I have absolutely no idea. A closely guarded secret kept by Mrs. Minns. I suppose we could hazard a guess. Now then, butter. Try the fridge.

EVA: Fridge?

RONALD: Keeps it soft. It's warmer in there than it is outside.

EVA: [Looking in the fridge] Right first time. [She sets about making a sandwich, taking off one glove]

RONALD: What's she want? Peanut butter?

EVA: Apparently.

RONALD: Good grief. She's got an absolute craving for that stuff lately. That and cheese footballs. All most alarming. She's not up there knitting little blue bootees, by any chance?

EVA: Not that I noticed.

RONALD: Thank God for that.

EVA: She looks a lot better than when I last saw her, anyway.

RONALD: Really? Yes, yes. Well, she got a bit overtired, I think. Principally.

EVA: Geoff'll be here in a minute to pick me up. I'll get out of your way. I just heard Marion was—I hope you didn't mind . . .

RONALD: No, very good of you to look round. Sure she appreciated it. She doesn't get many visitors. Lottie Potter looked in briefly. That set her back a couple of weeks. No, the trouble with Marion, you see, is she lives on her nerves. Far too much.

EVA: Marion does?

RONALD: Oh, yes. Very nervous, insecure sort of person basically, you know.

EVA: Really?

RONALD: That surprises you, does it? Well, I've got a pretty thorough working knowledge of her now, you know. I mean, she's calmer than she was. When I first met her she was really one of the jumpiest girls you could ever hope to meet. Still, as I say, she's much calmer since she's been with me. If I've done nothing else for her, I've acted as a sort of sedative.

EVA: You don't think that a lot of her trouble may be—drink?

RONALD: Drink? No, I don't honestly think so. She's always liked a—I mean, the doctor did say she should lay off. But that was only because it was acting as a stimulant. She hasn't touched it lately.

EVA: She has this evening.

RONALD: Really?

EVA: Yes.

RONALD: Well, you do surprise me.

EVA: She's got quite a collection up there.

RONALD: Oh, has she? Has she now?

EVA: Didn't you know?

RONALD: Well, I don't often have much cause to go into her room these days. She likes her privacy, you see. And I respect that. Not that it's not a mutual arrangement, you understand. I mean, she doesn't particularly choose to come into my room either. So it works out rather conveniently. On the whole.

EVA: Do you ever see each other at all?

RONALD: Good Lord, it's not as if we aren't in the same house. We bang into each other quite frequently. It's not always as quiet as this, believe me. In the holidays we've got the boys here. They thump about. No end of a racket. Boys, of course. Mind you, they're no trouble—they're usually out, too, most of the time— with their friends.

EVA: Pity they're not with you for Christmas.

RONALD: Oh well, it's greatly over-estimated, this Christmas business. That reminds me, would you like a drink? Seeing as it's Christmas.

EVA: No, I don't think so.

RONALD: Oh, go on. Just one. With me, for Christmas.

EVA: Well—all right, a little one.

RONALD: Right. [*He rises*] Good. I'll brave the elements then and try and make it as far as the sitting-room . . .

[*The doorbell rings*]

EVA: That's probably Geoff.

RONALD: [*Opening the door*] I'll let him in, then. [*Stopping short*] Good Lord, is that dust on the hall table or frost? Won't be a minute.

[RONALD *goes out.* EVA, *alone, looks round the room rather sadly. She leaves the sandwich and plate on the table, puts the other things back on the sideboard, returns to the table, sits and starts to eat the sandwich.* GEOFFREY *enters in his overcoat*]

GEOFFREY: Blimey. Why aren't you sitting in the garden, it's warmer.

EVA: Hullo.

GEOFFREY: Ready then?

EVA: I'm just going to have a drink with Ronnie.

GEOFFREY: Oh. And how is *she*?

EVA: Drunk.

GEOFFREY: God!

[*Pause.* EVA *munches*]

EVA: How did you get on?

GEOFFREY: Well . . .

EVA: Did you ask him?

GEOFFREY: Well . . .

EVA: You didn't. [GEOFFREY *does not reply*] You didn't damn well ask him.

GEOFFREY: It's no good. I find it impossible to ask people for money. [EVA *gives a short laugh*] I'm sorry.

EVA: He owes it you. You're not asking him a favour, you know. He owes it you.

GEOFFREY: I know.

EVA: Well then.

GEOFFREY: It doesn't matter.

EVA: Oh, my . . . Oh well, I'll have to get in touch with him then. After Christmas. I don't mind doing it.

GEOFFREY: You don't have to do that.

EVA: Well, somebody has to, darling. Don't they?

[*The door opens. A drinks trolley enters followed by* RONALD]

RONALD: Here we come. The Trans-Siberian Express. Thank you so much. We seem to be a bit depleted on the old alcohol stakes. Odd, thought I'd stocked up only recently. Probably old Mrs. Minns been knocking them off, eh? The woman must have some vices. She hasn't got much else to recommend her. Now what are we having. Eva?

EVA: Could I have just a bitter lemon.

RONALD: Good gracious, nothing stronger?

EVA: Not just now.

RONALD: Well, if that's what you want . . . Geoff, what about you?

GEOFFREY: I think I'd like the same, actually.

RONALD: What? A bitter lemon?

GEOFFREY: Just what I feel like.

RONALD: You won't last through Christmas at that rate. [*Inspecting his trolley*] Well, that seems to be the only thing I haven't brought.

EVA: Oh well, it doesn't matter. Something else.

RONALD: No, no. I'll get it, I'll get it. We've got some somewhere.

[RONALD *goes out, closing the door*]

EVA: I mean, either you want me to help you or you don't.

GEOFFREY: Yes.

EVA: I mean, if you don't just say so. I don't particularly enjoy working in that dark little office of yours. You're a terrible employer. You come in late even when I drive you to work. You take four-hour lunch breaks and then expect me to do all your damn typing at five o'clock in the evening.

GEOFFREY: That's the way I do business.

EVA: Not with me you don't.

GEOFFREY: That's what you're paid for.

EVA: That's what I'm what?

GEOFFREY: Look, if you don't like the job . . .

EVA: You asked me to help you. Now, if you didn't mean that, that's a different matter.

GEOFFREY: Well yes, I did, but . . .

EVA: All right, then. That's settled. You asked me to help you. I am bloody well going to help you.

GEOFFREY: O.K. O.K., thanks.

EVA: Not at all. [A *slight pause*] And you're not going to ask for that money?

GEOFFREY: No.

EVA: Even though we're owed it?

GEOFFREY: No.

EVA: And you won't let me ask?

GEOFFREY: No.

EVA: All right. Then we'll have to think of something else.

GEOFFREY: Exactly.

EVA: I'll phone Sidney Hopcroft after Christmas and talk to him.

GEOFFREY: Sidney Hopcroft.

EVA: He's always asking if you're interested.

GEOFFREY: If you think I'm going to get myself involved in his seedy little schemes . . .

EVA: Why not?

GEOFFREY: Have you seen the buildings he's putting up? Half his tenants are asking to be re-housed and they haven't even moved in yet.

EVA: Darling, I hate to remind you but ever since the ceiling of the Harrison building caved in and nearly killed the manager, Sidney Hopcroft is about your only hope of surviving as an architect in this city.

GEOFFREY: I can do without Sidney Hopcroft, thank you very much.

[The door opens. RONALD enters with two bottles of bitter lemon]

RONALD: Here we are. Two very bitter lemons. [He pours out two bitter lemons and a Scotch]

EVA: Thank you.

RONALD: I think I'm going to have something more than that, if you'll excuse me. Bit quieter than last Christmas, eh?

GEOFFREY: What?

RONALD: Last Christmas. Remember that? Round at your place?

GEOFFREY: Yes.

EVA: Yes.

RONALD: Good gracious me. You have to laugh now. Old Hopcroft. [He laughs] Always remember old Hopcroft. Doing very well. Did you know that? Doing frightfully well. Seems to have a flare for it.

Wouldn't think so to look at him. Always found him a bit unprepossessing. Still—the chap to keep in with. The rate he's going.

EVA: Yes.

GEOFFREY: [*Picking up* RONALD's *book*] Is this good?

RONALD: Oh, yes. Yes, quite good. Very amusing. Bit—saucy, in parts. Mrs. Minns found it under one of the boys' mattresses. Nearly finished her there and then, poor old thing. Bitter lemon—

EVA: Thanks.

RONALD: Bitter lemon.

GEOFFREY: Thank you.

RONALD: [*Raising his glass of Scotch*] Well, Happy Christmas. Good health. God bless.

EVA: Happy Christmas.

GEOFFREY: Happy Christmas.

RONALD [*After a pause*] Sorry to hear about your problems, Geoff.

GEOFFREY: How do you mean?

RONALD: I meant, the Harrison thing. Hear it fell through . . . Oh, I'm sorry, perhaps that's the wrong expression to use—bit unfortunate.

GEOFFREY: That's all right.

EVA: It wasn't actually Geoff's fault.

RONALD: No, no, I'm sure—knowing Geoff. Unthinkable. I mean, that local paper's as biased as hell. I refused to read that particular article. So did all my friends.

EVA: [*After a pause*] Just because Geoffrey was doing something totally new for a change . . .

GEOFFREY: How's the bank doing, then?

RONALD: Oh, well. We're not in the red, yet. No thanks to me, mind you. [*A bell rings*] Ah.

GEOFFREY: Is that the front door?

RONALD: No. It's the—er—bedroom bell, actually. We've never bothered to have them taken out. They always come in useful. Boys with measles and so on.

EVA: Shall I go up to her?

RONALD: No, no, I'll . . .

EVA: No, it's all right. I don't mind . . .

RONALD: Well, that's very good of you. Probably nothing important. Wants the page of her magazine turned over or something.

EVA: I hope not.

RONALD: What's the harm, I say. As long as it keeps her happy.

EVA: Yes.

[EVA *goes out, closing the door*]

RONALD: I mean, who are we to argue with a woman, eh? You can never win. Hopeless. Mind you, I'm talking to the wrong chap, aren't I?

GEOFFREY: What?

RONALD: I mean you seem to do better than most of us.

GEOFFREY: Oh, yes. [*He sits in the armchair*]

RONALD: You seem to have got things pretty well organized on the home front. [*He laughs*]

GEOFFREY: Well, it's just a matter of knowing . . .

RONALD: Ah yes, that's the point. I never really have. Not really. I mean, take my first wife. Distinguished-looking woman. Very charming. Seemed pretty happy on the whole. Then one day, she suddenly ups and offs and goes. Quite amazing. I mean, I had literally no idea she was going to. I mean, we had the flat over the bank at the time, so it wasn't as if I was even very far away and on this particular day, I came up for lunch and she'd laid on her usual splendid meal. I mean I had absolutely no complaints about that. I think my very words were something like, jolly nice that, see you this evening. And when we knocked off for tea, I came up-stairs and she'd just taken off. Well, I hunted about for a bit in case she'd got knocked down or gone shopping and lost her mem-ory or something and then she wrote, some time later, and said she'd had enough. So I was forced to call it a day. Some time later again, I took up tennis to forget her and married Marion. Of course, that's all forgotten now. All the same, sometimes in the evening I can't help sitting here and trying to work it all out. I mean, something happened. Something must have happened. I'm just not sure what. Anyway. Under the bridge, eh? All I'm saying, really, is some people seem to have the hand of it and some of us just aren't so lucky.

GEOFFREY: Hang of what?

RONALD: Well—this whole women business, really. I mean, this may sound ridiculous, but I've never to this day really known what most women think about anything. Completely closed book to me. I mean, God bless them, what would we do without them? But I've never understood them. I mean, damn it all, one minute you're having a perfectly good time and the next, you suddenly see them there like—some old sports jacket or something—lit-erally beginning to come apart at the seams. Floods of tears, smashing your pots, banging the furniture about. God knows what. Both my wives, God bless them, they've given me a great deal of pleasure over the years but, by God, they've cost me a for-tune in fixtures and fittings. All the same. Couldn't do without them, could we? I suppose. Want another one of those?

GEOFFREY: No, thanks.

[*The door opens.* EVA *enters.* GEOFFREY *rises and sits again*]

EVA: [*Coming in swiftly and closing the door*] Brrr.

RONALD: Ah.

EVA: Forgot to put my coat on. [*She puts her coat on*]

RONALD: Anything serious?

EVA: No. [*Kneeling by the stove to warm herself*] She says she wants to come down.

RONALD: Here? Is that wise?

EVA: She says she wants a Christmas drink with us since we're all here.

RONALD: Oh, well. Sort of thing she does. Calls you all the way upstairs to tell you she's coming all the way downstairs. Your drink there.

EVA: Thanks.

RONALD: And how's that mad dog of yours? Still chewing up your guests?

GEOFFREY: Er—no . . .

EVA: No, we had to—give him away.

RONALD: No, really?

EVA: Yes—he got a bit much. He was really getting so expensive to keep. And then these people we know who've got a farm—they said they'd have him.

RONALD: Oh, dear. I didn't know that. That's a shame.

EVA: Yes, it was an awful decision to make. We just felt—well . . .

GEOFFREY: You did, you mean.

EVA: Darling, we couldn't afford to keep him.

RONALD: Well, old Dick Potter will be relieved, anyway. What did he have to have? Three stitches or something, wasn't it?

EVA: Something like that.

RONALD: Doesn't seem to have done him any harm, anyway. He should be half-way up some Swiss mountain by now. Hopefully, those two lads of ours are safely roped to him.

EVA: Oh, is that where they've gone?

RONALD: Yes. Something I always meant to take them on myself. Anyway, we'll have to do without old Dick to jolly us up this year, I suppose.

GEOFFREY: That's a pity.

[*The door opens.* MARION *sweeps in. She wears a negligée. She stands dramatically and flings out her arms*]

MARION: Geoff, darling, it's sweet of you and Eva to come round and see me.

GEOFFREY: [*Rising*] Oh, that's O.K.

MARION: No, you don't know how much it means to me. It really is terribly, terribly sweet of you.

GEOFFREY: That's all right, we were . . .

MARION: And at Christmas, particularly. Bless you for remembering Christmas. [*She collapses into the armchair*]

RONALD: Look, Marion, you're going to freeze to death. For goodness' sake, put something on, woman.

MARION: I'm all right.

RONALD: Let me get you your coat. You've only just got out of bed.

MARION: Darling, I am quite all right. And I am not sitting in my kitchen in a coat. Nobody sits in a kitchen in a coat. Except tradesmen. It's unheard of. Now, offer me a drink.

RONALD: Look, dear, you know the doctor said very plainly . . .

MARION: [*Snapping fiercely*] Oh, for the love of God, Ronnie, it's Christmas. Don't be such an utter misery. [*To the others*] He's Scrooge, you know. He's Scrooge in person. Have you noticed, he's turned all the heating off. [RONALD, *dignified, goes to the trolley and pours* MARION *a drink*] Oh, it's heavenly to be up. When you've lain in bed for any length of time, on your own, no one to talk to, with just your thoughts, don't you find your whole world just begins to crowd in on you. Till it becomes almost unbearable. You just lie there thinking, oh God, it could've been so much better if only I'd had the sense to do so and so—you finish up lying there utterly filled with self-loathing.

EVA: I know the feeling.

RONALD: [*Handing* MARION *a glass*] Here you are, dear.

MARION: Heavens! I can hardly see it. Is there anything in here? No, it's all right. I'll just sit here and inhale it. [*Turning to* GEOFFREY *and* EVA] How are you anyway?

EVA: Well, as I told you we're—pretty well . . .

MARION: I don't know what it is about Christmas but—I know it's supposed to be a festive thing and we're all supposed to be enjoying ourselves—I just find myself remembering all the dreadful things—the dreadful things I've said—the dreadful things I've done and all those awful hurtful things I didn't mean—oh God, I didn't mean them. Forgive me, I didn't mean them. [*She starts to cry*]

RONALD: Look, darling, do try and jolly up just for a bit, for heaven's sake.

MARION: [*Savagely*] Jolly up? How the hell can—I—jolly—up?

EVA: Marion, dear . . .

MARION: Do you know what I saw in the hall just now? In the mirror. My face. My God, I saw my face! It was like seeing my face for the first time.

RONALD: Oh, come on. It's not a bad face, old sausage.

MARION: How could anything be so cruel? How could anything be so unutterably cruel?

RONALD: [*To* GEOFFREY] Now, you see, this is a case in point. What am I supposed to do? I mean, something I've said has obviously upset her, but you tell me—you tell me.

MARION: [*Pulling* GEOFFREY *to her*] Geoff—Geoff—Geoff—did you know, Geoff, I used to be a very beautiful woman? I was a very, very beautiful woman. People used to stare at me in the street and say, "My God, what a beautiful, beautiful woman she is." People used to come from miles and miles just to take my picture . . .

RONALD: Marion.

MARION: I mean, who'd want my photograph now? Do you want my photograph now? No, of course you don't. Nobody wants my photograph now. Can anybody think of anyone who'd want a photograph of me now? Please, someone. Someone, please want my photograph.

RONALD: [*Bellowing*] *Marion!* Nobody wants your damn picture, now shut up!

> [A *silence.* GEOFFREY *and* EVA *are stunned.* RONALD *removes his eye-shade and adjusts his scarf*]

RONALD: [*The first to recover*] Now then, what were we saying?

> [*The doorbell rings*]

EVA: [*After a pause*] Doorbell.

RONALD: Bit late for a doorbell, isn't it?

> [*They sit. The doorbell rings again*]

EVA: Shall I see who it is?

RONALD: Yes, do. Have a look through the little glass window. If you don't like the look of them, don't open the door.

EVA: Right.

> [EVA *goes into the hall*]

RONALD: Can't think who'd be ringing doorbells at this time of night.

GEOFFREY: Carol singers?

RONALD: Not at this time. Anyway, we don't get many of them. Marion always asks them in. Insists on filling them up with hot soup and chocolate biscuits as if they were all starving. Had a great row with the chap next door. She made his children as sick as pigs.

> [EVA *returns. As she does so the doorbell rings. She closes the door behind her*]

EVA: I couldn't be sure but it looks suspiciously like the Hopcrofts. Do you want them in?

RONALD: Oh, good grief, hardly.

GEOFFREY: Heaven forbid.

RONALD: If we sit quiet, they'll go away.

EVA: Well, there's the hall light.

RONALD: That doesn't mean anything. People always leave their hall lights on for burglars. I don't know why they bother. I mean, there must be very few households who actually choose to spend their evenings sitting in the hall with the rest of the house in the darkness.

GEOFFREY: If I know the Hopcrofts, they won't give up easily. They'll come round the side.

MARION: Why don't you just go in the hall and shout "Go away" through the letter-box?

RONALD: Because he happens to have a very large deposit account with my bank.

[*The doorbell rings*]

EVA: They can smell us.

RONALD: I think we'll compromise and turn off the lights in here. Just to be on the safe side. [*Going to the door*] Everybody sit down and sit tight. [*By the switch*] Ready? Here we go. [*The room plunges into darkness. Just two streams of light—one from the door and one from the window*] Now if we all keep absolutely quiet, there's no chance of them—ow! [*He cannons into* EVA *who gives a cry*] I'm terribly sorry. I do beg your pardon. Was that your . . . ?

EVA: That's all right.

GEOFFREY: Ssh.

RONALD: I wish I knew where I was.

GEOFFREY: Well, stand still. I think someone's coming round the side.

EVA: Ssh.

[MARION *starts to giggle*]

RONALD: Marion. Quiet.

MARION: I'm sorry, I've just seen the funny side . . .

GEOFFREY: **Ssh.**

> [SIDNEY *and* JANE *appear at the back door. They wear party hats, are decked with the odd streamer, have had more drinks than they are used to and have a carrier bag full of goodies. They both press their faces against the back door, straining to see in*]

MARION: It's them.

GEOFFREY: Ssh.

> [*Pause*]

RONALD: I say . . .

EVA: What?

RONALD: I've got a nasty feeling I didn't lock the back door.

> [GEOFFREY *and* EVA *hide in front of the table.* RONALD *steps up into a corner by the window. The back door opens slowly*]

SIDNEY: Hallo?

JANE: [*Unwilling to enter*] Sidney . . .

SIDNEY: Come on.

JANE: But there's nobody . . .

SIDNEY: The door was open, wasn't it? Of course there's somebody. They're probably upstairs.

JANE: But, Sidney, they might . . .

SIDNEY: Look, would you kindly not argue with me any more tonight, Jane. I haven't yet forgiven you for that business at the party. How did you manage to drop a whole plate of trifle?

JANE: I didn't clean it up, Sidney, I didn't clean it up.

SIDNEY: No. You just stood there with the mess at your feet. For all the world to see.

JANE: Well, what . . .

SIDNEY: I have told you before. If you drop something like that at a stand-up party, you move away and keep moving. Now come along.

JANE: I can't see.

SIDNEY: Then wait there and I'll find the light.

[*A pause.* SIDNEY *crosses the room.* GEOFFREY *and* EVA *creep to the sideboard. The light goes on.* SIDNEY *and* JANE *are by the separate doors. The other four are in various absurd frozen postures obviously caught in the act of trying to find a hiding-place.* JANE *gives a short squeak of alarm. A long pause*]

MARION: [*Eventually*] Boo.

SIDNEY: Good gracious!

RONALD: [*As if seeing them for the first time*] Ah, hallo there. It's you.

SIDNEY: Well, you had us fooled. They had us fooled there, didn't they?

JANE: Yes, they had us fooled.

SIDNEY: Playing a game on us, weren't you?

ALL: Yes.

EVA: Yes, we were playing a game.

SIDNEY: Completely fooled. Walked straight into that. Well, Happy Christmas, all.

ALL: [*Lamely, variously*] Happy Christmas.

SIDNEY: [*After a pause*] Well.

JANE: Well.

[*A pause*]

RONALD: Would you like a drink? Now you're here.

SIDNEY: Oh, thank you.

JANE: Thank you very much.

SIDNEY: Since we're here.

RONALD: Well. What'll it be? [*He goes to the trolley*]

SIDNEY: Sherry, please.

JANE: Yes, a sherry.

SIDNEY: Yes. We'd better stick to sherry.

RONALD: Sherry . . . [*He starts to pour*]

SIDNEY: Sorry if we surprised you.

MARION: Quite all right.

SIDNEY: We knew you were here.

RONALD: How?

SIDNEY: We saw the car.

JANE: Saw your car.

RONALD: Oh. Yes.

[*A pause.* SIDNEY *blows a party "blower"*]

EVA: Been to a party?

SIDNEY: Yes.

JANE: Yes.

GEOFFREY: You look as if you have.

SIDNEY: Yes. Up at Walter's place. Walter Harrison.

RONALD: Oh—old Harrison's.

SIDNEY: Oh, of course, you'll know him, won't you?

RONALD: Oh, yes.

GEOFFREY: Yes.

SIDNEY: [*To* GEOFFREY] Oh, yes, of course. Asking you if you know old Harrison. I should think you do know old Harrison. He certainly remembers you. In fact, he was saying this evening . . .

RONALD: Two sherries.

SIDNEY: Oh, thank you.

JANE: Thank you very much.

SIDNEY: Compliments of the season.

JANE: Of the season.

RONALD: Yes. Indeed.

[A *pause*]

SIDNEY: What a house. Beautiful.

MARION: Oh, do you like it? Thank you.

SIDNEY: No. Old Harrison's. What a place.

JANE: Lovely.

RONALD: Didn't know you knew him.

SIDNEY: Well, I won't pretend. The reason we went was half pleasure and half—well, 'nuff said. Follow me? You scratch my back, I'll scratch yours.

RONALD: Ah.

[A *pause*]

JANE: It's a nice kitchen . . .

MARION: At the Harrisons'?

JANE: No. Here.

MARION: Oh. Glad you approve.

[A *pause*]

JANE: [*Very, very quietly*] Sidney.

SIDNEY: Eh?

JANE: [*Mouthing and gesticulating towards the carrier bag*] Their presents.

SIDNEY: What's that?

JANE: [*Still mouthing and miming*] Shall we give them their presents now?

SIDNEY: Yes, yes, of course. That's why we've brought them.

JANE: We brought you a present.

SIDNEY: Just a little seasonal something.

RONALD: Oh.

MARION: Ah.

EVA: Thank you.

JANE: [*To* EVA] No, I'm afraid we didn't bring you and your husband anything. We didn't know you'd be here, you see.

SIDNEY: Sorry about that.

EVA: Oh, never mind.

GEOFFREY: Not to worry.

JANE: We could give them the hm-mm. You know that we got given this evening.

SIDNEY: The what?

JANE: You know, the hm-mm. That we got in the thing.

SIDNEY: What, that? They don't want that.

JANE: No, I meant for hm-mm, you know. Hm-mm.

SIDNEY: Well, if you want to. Now, come on. Give Ron and Marion their presents. They're dying to open them.

RONALD: Rather.

MARION: Thrilling.

JANE: [*Delving into her carrier and consulting the labels on various parcels*] Now this is for Ron. [*Reading*] "To Ron with love from Sidney and Jane."

SIDNEY: [*Handing* RONALD *the present*] That's for you.

RONALD: Thank you. [*He unwraps it*]

JANE: Now then, what's this?

SIDNEY: Is that Marion's?

JANE: No, that's from you and me to Auntie Gloria. [*Rummaging again*] Here we are. "To Marion with love from Sidney and Jane."

SIDNEY: This is for you. [*He gives* MARION *her present*]

MARION: Oh, super . . . [*To* RONALD] What've you got, darling?

RONALD: [*Gazing at his present mystified*] Oh, yes. This is very useful. Thank you very much.

MARION: What on earth is it?

RONALD: Well, it's—er—[*taking a stab at it*]—looks like a very nice set of pipe cleaners.

JANE: Oh, no.

SIDNEY: No, those aren't pipe cleaners.

RONALD: Oh, aren't they?

SIDNEY: Good gracious, no.

RONALD: Oh, no. Silly of me. Just looked terribly like them for a minute. From a certain angle.

SIDNEY: You should know those. It's a set of screwdrivers.

JANE: Set of screwdrivers.

SIDNEY: Electrical screwdrivers.

JANE: You should know those, shouldn't you?

[SIDNEY *and* JANE *laugh.* MARION *opens her present*]

MARION: [*With a joyous cry*] Oh, look! It's a lovely bottle of gin. Isn't that kind?

RONALD: Oh, my God!

SIDNEY: Bit of Christmas spirit.

MARION: Lovely. I'll think of you when I'm drinking it.

JANE: [*Still rummaging*] "To the boys with love from Sidney and Jane." [*She produces two rather ghastly woolly toys—obviously unsuitable*]

SIDNEY: That's just a little something.

JANE: For their stockings in the morning.

MARION: Oh, how nice.

RONALD: They'll love these . . .

SIDNEY: That the lot?

JANE: No, I'm just trying to find the hm-mm.

SIDNEY: Well, it'll be at the bottom somewhere, I should think.

JANE: I've got it. It's nothing very much. We just got it this eve-ning, out of a cracker actually. We were going to keep it for our budgie but we thought your George might like it. For his collar. [*She holds up a little bell on a ribbon*]

EVA: Oh.

SIDNEY: So you'll know where he is.

JANE: As if you couldn't guess.

[SIDNEY *barks genially and hands them the bell*]

SIDNEY: Woof woof!

EVA: Thank you.

SIDNEY: [*To* GEOFFREY] Woof woof. [*No response*] Woof woof.

GEOFFREY: [*Flatly*] Thanks a lot.

SIDNEY: That's your lot. No more.

RONALD: I'm terribly sorry. I'm afraid we haven't got you anything at all. Not really much of ones for present buying.

SIDNEY: Oh, we didn't expect it.

JANE: No, no.

[*A pause.* SIDNEY *puts on a nose mask.* JANE *laughs. The others look horrified.* MARION *pours herself a gin*]

SIDNEY: Well—[*He pauses*]—you know who ought to be here now?

JANE: Who?

SIDNEY: Dick Potter. He'd start it off.

JANE: With a bit of help from Lottie.

SIDNEY: True. True.

RONALD: Yes, well, for some odd reason we're all feeling a bit low this evening. Don't know why. But we were just all saying how we felt a bit down.

JANE: Oh . . .

SIDNEY: Oh dear, oh dear.

RONALD: Just one of those evenings, you know. The point is you'll have to excuse us if we're not our usual cheery selves.

MARION: I'm perfectly cheery. I don't know about anybody else.

RONALD: That is apart from my wife who is perfectly cheery.

SIDNEY: Oh, that's quite understood.

JANE: I have those sometimes, don't I?

SIDNEY: You certainly do. You can say that again. Well, that's a shame.

RONALD: Yes.

EVA: [*After a slight pause*] My husband was saying to me just now, Sidney, that he feels terribly guilty that you keep on asking him to do jobs for you and he just hasn't been able to manage them.

SIDNEY: Yes. Well, he's a busy man.

EVA: Sometimes. But he really is dying to do something for you before long.

GEOFFREY: Eh?

EVA: He's really longing to.

SIDNEY: Oh, well in that case, we'll see.

EVA: If you could keep him in mind.

SIDNEY: Yes, I'll certainly keep him in mind. Really rather depends.

GEOFFREY: Yes, it does rather.

EVA: He'd love to.

SIDNEY: [*After a pause*] Well now, what shall we do? Anyone got any ideas? We can't all sit round like this, can we? Not on Christmas Eve.

JANE: No, not on Christmas Eve.

SIDNEY: Spot of carpentry, spot of plumbing, eh? I know, what about a spot of electrical work? [*At the radio*] Well, we can have a bit of music to start off with, anyway. [*To* RONALD] This work all right, does it?

RONALD: Yes, yes, but I wouldn't . . .

SIDNEY: Get the party going, bit of music . . . [*He switches on the radio and begins to dance a little*]

JANE: Bit of music'll get it going.

SIDNEY: Hey . . .

JANE: What?

SIDNEY: You know what we ought to do now?

JANE: What?

SIDNEY: We ought to move all the chairs back and clear the floor and . . .

[*The radio warms up and the room is filled with the sound of an interminable Scottish reel which plays continually. Like most Scottish reels, without a break. This effectively drowns the rest of* SIDNEY *and* JANE's *discusion. He continues to describe with graphic gestures his idea to* JANE. JANE *claps her hands with excitement. They move the table, stove and chairs out of the way.* SIDNEY *then wheels the trolley away past* MARION's *armchair. She grabs a bottle as it goes by*]

RONALD: [*Yelling above the noise*] What the hell's going on?

SIDNEY: [*Yelling back*] You'll see. Just a minute. [*He turns the radio down a little*] Now then. We can't have this. We can't have all these glum faces, not at Christmas time.

JANE: [*Scurrying about collecting a bowl of fruit, a spoon, a tea-cosy, colander and tea towel from the dresser and draining-board*] Not at Christmas time. [*She opens the gin bottle and puts a glass near it on the trolley*]

SIDNEY: So we're going to get you all jumping about. Get you cheerful.

RONALD: No, well I don't think we really . . .

SIDNEY: No arguments, please.

RONALD: Yes, but all the same . . .

SIDNEY: Come on then, Eva, up you get.

EVA: [*Uncertainly*] Well . . .

SIDNEY: Come on. Don't you let me down.

EVA: No . . . [*She rises*]

GEOFFREY: I'm afraid we both have to . . .

EVA: No, we don't. We'll play.

GEOFFREY: What do you mean, we'll . . .

EVA: If he wants to play, we'll play, darling.

[JANE *begins to roll up the carpet*]

SIDNEY: That's grand. That's marvellous. That's two—come on—any more?

MARION: What are we all doing? Is she going to be terribly sweet and wash our floor?

JANE: No, we're playing a game.

SIDNEY: A game.

MARION: Oh, what fun . . .

RONALD: Marion, I really don't think we should . . .

MARION: Oh, don't be such a misery, Ronnie. Come on.

RONALD: Oh . . .

SIDNEY: That's telling him, that's telling him. Now then, listen very carefully, everyone. This is a version of musical chairs called Musical Dancing.

JANE: Musical Forfeits.

SIDNEY: Musical Dancing. It's called Musical Dancing.

JANE: Oh, I thought it was called Musical Forfeits.

SIDNEY: Musical Dancing. It's very simple. All you do—you start dancing round the room and when I stop the music you all have to freeze in the position you were last in . . . [GEOFFREY *sits on the high stool*] Don't let him sit down. [*To* GEOFFREY] Come on, get up.

EVA: [*Sharply*] Get up.

[GEOFFREY *gets up*]

SIDNEY: Only to make it more difficult, the last person caught moving each time gets a forfeit. At the end, the person with the least forfeits gets the prize. [*To* JANE] What's the prize going to be?

JANE: [*Producing it from the carrier*] A chocolate Father Christmas.

SIDNEY: A chocolate Father Christmas, right. Everything ready your end?

JANE: I think so.

SIDNEY: Got the list?

JANE: [*Waving a scrap of paper*] Yes.

SIDNEY: Right. You take charge of the forfeits. I'll do the music. Ready, everybody? Right. Off we go. [SIDNEY *turns up the music loud. The four stand looking faintly uneasy.* JANE *and* SIDNEY *dance about to demonstrate*] Well, come on then. Come on. I don't call that dancing. Everybody dance. Come on, dance about. Keep dancing till the music stops. [MARION *starts to dance, in what she imagines to be a classical ballet style. She is extremely shaky*] That's it. She's doing it. That's it. Look at her. Everybody do what she's doing. Lovely. [*The others begin sheepishly and reluctantly to hop about*] And—stop! [*He cuts off the music*] Right. Who was the last?

JANE: Ron.

SIDNEY: Right. It's Ron. Ron has a forfeit. What's the first one?

JANE: [*Consulting her list*] Apple under the chin.

SIDNEY: Apple under his chin, right. Put an apple under his chin.

RONALD: Eh? What are you doing?

[JANE *puts the apple under his chin*]

JANE: Here. Hold it. Go on, hold it.

RONALD: Oh, don't be so ridiculous, I can't possibly . . .

MARION: Oh, for heaven's sake, darling, do join in. We're all waiting for you. Don't be tedious.

RONALD: [*Talking with difficulty*] This is absolutely absurd, I mean how am I to be . . .

SIDNEY: [*Over this*] And off we go again. [*He turns up the music. They resume dancing.* MARION *is the only one who moves around: the others jig about on one spot.* SIDNEY *shouts encouragement*] And—stop! [*He stops the music*]

JANE: Eva!

SIDNEY: Right, Eva. What's Eva got?

JANE: [*Consulting list*] Orange between the knees.

SIDNEY: Orange between the knees, right. If you drop it you get another forfeit automatically. [JANE *gives* EVA *her orange*] And off we go again.

[*Music. From now on the forfeits come quick and fast.* JANE *reading them out,* SIDNEY *repeating them.* RONALD *gets the next (spoon in mouth). The music continues.* GEOFFREY *gets the next (tea-cosy on head). They dance on.* MARION *gets the next (ironically, swallowing a gin in one).* RONALD *opens his mouth to protest at this last forfeit of* MARION'S. *In doing so he drops his spoon]*

SIDNEY: [*Gleefully*] Another one for Ron!

JANE: Another one for Ron . . .

RONALD: What?

JANE: Pear on spoon in mouth . . .

SIDNEY: Pear on spoon in mouth . . . [*He gets up on the table and conducts*]

RONALD: Now listen I . . .

[JANE *rams the spoon handle back in* RONALD'S *mouth. She balances a pear on the other end]*

SIDNEY: And off we go . . . !

[*The permutations to this game are endless and* SIDNEY'S *list covers them all. Under his increasingly strident commands, the dancers whirl faster and faster while accumulating bizarre appendages.* JANE, *the acolyte, darts in and out of the dancers with a dedicated frenzy.* GEOFFREY *throws his tea-cosy to the floor.* JANE *picks it up and wraps a tea towel round his leg. She then pours another gin for* MARION. SIDNEY, *at the finish, has abandoned the idea of stopping the music. He screams at the dancers in mounting exhortation bordering on the hysterical]*

SIDNEY: That's it! Dance. Come on. Dance. Dance. Come on. Dance. Dance. Dance. Keep dancing. Dance . . .

[*It is on this scene that—*]

THE CURTAIN FALLS

THE EFFECT OF GAMMA RAYS ON MAN-IN-THE-MOON MARIGOLDS

Paul Zindel

Paul Zindel

The Effect of Gamma Rays on Man-in-the-Moon Marigolds was the first play of the decade to win both the Pulitzer Prize and a New York Drama Critics' Circle Award.

Yet, the play's road to ultimate success was rather circuitous. Originally presented in 1965 at the Alley Theatre in Houston, Texas, it was seen again during the summer of 1966 at the White Barn Theatre, Westport, Connecticut. During that same year, a shortened version starring Eileen Heckart was given the first of four performances on NET's New York Television Theatre. Next, it was done at the Cleveland Playhouse and, finally, on April 7, 1970, the play opened Off-Broadway at the Mercer-O'Casey Theatre. The presentation was accorded rave notices (*Variety* called it "A masterful, pace-setting drama and the most compelling work of its kind since Tennessee Williams' *The Glass Menagerie*") and in the spring of the following year it moved uptown to the New Theatre where it completed an engagement of 819 performances. Not only did *Marigolds* garner awards and acclaim for its creator, it also brought stardom to its leading lady, Sada Thompson. Later, Joanne Woodward, who appeared in the film version directed by her husband Paul Newman, was to win a 1973 Cannes Film Festival Award for her performance in the same role.

Paul Zindel was born on Staten Island, New York, on May 15, 1936. He attended several grade schools in the borough (the family moved on the average of once or twice a year) and it was during this period that he started to develop an interest in the theatre. While at Port Richmond High School, he began to write plays, including an adaptation of W. W. Jacobs' short story "The Monkey's Paw." At Wagner College, he majored in chemistry and obtained B.S. and M.S. degrees in science. He also took courses in creative writing at Wagner, where one of his teachers was Edward Albee. During his final year at college, he wrote *Dimensions of Peacocks* and it was produced Off-Off-Broadway in 1959.

After graduation, Mr. Zindel took a position as a technical writer for a chemical company. The work was not especially challenging, and when he found that he was spending more time at the movies than at the library, he resigned to become a teacher of chemistry at the Tottenville High School, Staten Island.

During ten years of teaching, Mr. Zindel continued to write plays and in 1964 he made his Off-Broadway bow with *A Dream of Swallows*. The play vanished after its opening night curtain came down; however, his next work was to more than compensate for his disappointment for it turned out to be *Marigolds*.

In 1971 the dramatist was represented on the Broadway stage with *And Miss Reardon Drinks a Little*, a vehicle that inspired exceptional performances from its three star actresses, Julie Harris, Estelle Parsons, and Nancy Marchand. In the following year, he returned with a comedy, *The Secret Affairs of Mildred Wild*, in which the heroine, performed with gusto by Maureen Stapleton, lives "a kind of Walter Mitty existence in the back of a Greenwich Village candy store cluttered with cinematic memorabilia." And in 1977, he came to Broadway once again with *Ladies at the Alamo*, a comically biting dissection of women enmeshed in a power conflict.

Mr. Zindel's other writing credits include the screenplay for the Barbra Streisand film *Up the Sandbox*, *Let Me Hear You Whisper*, a poignant drama that won wide recognition on television, *The Ladies Should Be in Bed*, a short play dealing with a group of matrons who meet for bridge and are soon drawn into more distracting matters, and a number of novels for young adults: *The Pigman*; *I Never Loved Your Mind*; *My Darling, My Hamburger*; *Pardon Me, You're Stepping On My Eyeball*; and *Confessions of a Teen Age Baboon*.

It has been written of the author—who was awarded an honorary Doctor of Humane Letters degree from Wagner College—that his plays "explore the antitheses of experience, mingling naturalism with poetic overtones, humor with anguish, and tension with tenderness."

The Effect of Gamma Rays on Man-in-the-Moon Marigolds was first presented in New York at the Mercer-O'Casey Theatre on April 7, 1970, by Orin Lehman. The cast was as follows:

TILLIE	*Pamela Payton-Wright*
BEATRICE	*Sada Thompson*
RUTH	*Amy Levitt*
NANNY	*Judith Lowry*
JANICE VICKERY	*Swoosie Kurtz*

Directed by Melvin Bernhardt
Music and Sound by James Reichert
Scenery by Fred Voelpel
Costumes by Sara Brook
Lighting by Martin Aronstein
Associate Producer: Julie Hughes

CHARACTERS:

TILLIE, *the Girl*
"In front of my eyes, one part of the world was becoming another. Atoms exploding . . . atom after atom breaking down
into something new . . . It would go on for millions of
years . . ."

BEATRICE, *the Mother*
"This long street, with all the doors of the houses shut and
everything crowded next to each other . . . And then I start
getting afraid that the vegetables are going to spoil . . . and
that nobody's going to buy anything . . ."

RUTH, *the Other Daughter*
"Well, they say I came out of my room . . . and I started
down the stairs, step by step . . . and I heard the choking
and banging on the bed . . ."

NANNY

JANICE VICKERY

ACT ONE

THE SETTING: *A room of wood which was once a vegetable store and a point of debarkation for a horse-drawn wagon to bring its wares to a small town.*

But the store is gone, and a widow of confusion has placed her touch on everything. A door to NANNY's *room leads off from this main room, and in front of the door hang faded curtains which allow ventilation in the summer. There is a hallway and a telephone. A heavy wood staircase leads to a landing with a balustrade, two doors, and a short hall.* BEATRICE *sleeps in one room;* TILLIE *and* RUTH *share the other.*

Objects which respectable people usually hide in closets are scattered about the main room: newspapers, magazines, dishes; empty bottles; clothes; suitcases; last week's sheets. Such carelessness is the type which is so perfected it must have evolved from hereditary processes; but in all fairness to the occupants, it can be pointed out that after twilight, when shadows and weak bulbs work their magic, the room becomes interesting.

On a table near the front left of the room is a small wire cage designed to hold a rabbit. Near this are several school books, notebook papers, and other weapons of high school children. A kitchen area, boasting a hot plate, has been carved near the bottom of the staircase, and the window, which was formerly the front of the vegetable store, is now mostly covered with old newspapers so that passersby cannot see in. A bit of the clear glass remains at the top—but drab, lifeless drapes line the sides of the window.

The lights go down slowly as music creeps in—a theme for lost children, the near misbegotten.

From the blackness TILLIE's VOICE *speaks against the music.*

TILLIE'S VOICE: He told me to look at my hand, for a part of it came from a star that exploded too long ago to imagine. This part of me was formed from a tongue of fire that screamed through the heavens until there was our sun. And this part of me—this tiny part of me—was on the sun when it itself exploded and whirled in a great storm until the planets came to be. [*Lights start in*] And this small part of me was then a whisper of the earth. When there was life, perhaps this part of me got lost in a fern that was crushed and covered until it was coal. And then it was a diamond millions of years later—it must have been a diamond as beautiful as the star from which it had first come.

TILLIE: [*Taking over from recorded voice*] Or perhaps this part of me became lost in a terrible beast, or became part of a huge bird that flew above the primeval swamps. And he said this thing was so small—this part of me was so small it couldn't be seen—but it was there from the beginning of the world. And he called this bit of me an atom. And when he wrote the word, I fell in love with it. Atom. *Atom*. What a beautiful word.

[*The phone rings*]

BEATRICE: [*Off*] Will you get that please? [*The phone rings again before* BEATRICE *appears in her bathrobe from the kitchen*] No help! Never any help! [*She answers the phone*] Hello? Yes, it is. Who is this? . . . I hope there hasn't been any trouble at school . . . Oh, she's always been like that. She hardly says a word around here, either. I always say some people were born to speak and others born to listen . . . You know, I've been meaning to call you to thank you for that lovely rabbit you gave Matilda. She and I just adore it and it's gotten so big . . . Well, it certainly was thoughtful. Mr. Goodman, I don't mean to change the subject but aren't you that delightful young man Tillie said hello to a couple of months back at the A & P? You were by the lobster tank and I was near the frozen foods? That delightful and handsome young man? . . . Why, I would very much indeed use the expression *handsome*. Yes, and . . . Well, I encourage her at every opportunity at home. Did she say I didn't? Both my daughters have their own desks and I put 75-watt bulbs right near them . . . Yes . . . Yes . . . I think those tests are very much overrated, anyway,

Mr. Goodman . . . Well, believe me she's nothing like that around this house . . . Now I don't want you to think I don't appreciate what you're trying to do, Mr. Goodman, but I'm afraid it's simply useless. I've tried just everything, but she isn't a pretty girl—I mean, let's be frank about it—she's going to have her problems. Are you married, Mr. Goodman? Oh, that's too bad. I don't know what's the matter with women today letting a handsome young man like you get away . . . Well, some days she just doesn't feel like going to school. You just said how bright she is, and I'm really afraid to put too much of a strain on her after what happened to her sister. You know, too much strain is the worst thing in this modern world, Mr. Goodman, and I can't afford to have another convulsive on my hands, now can I? But don't you worry about Matilda. There will be some place for her in this world. And, like I said, some were born to speak and others just to listen . . . and do call again, Mr. Goodman. It's been a true pleasure speaking with you. Goodbye. [BEATRICE *hangs up the phone and advances into the main room. The lights come up*] Matilda, that wasn't very nice of you to tell them I was forcibly detaining you from school. Why, the way that Mr. Goodman spoke, he must think I'm running a concentration camp. Do you have any idea how embarrassing it is to be accused of running a concentration camp for your own children? Well, it isn't embarrassing at all. That school of yours is forty years behind the times anyway, and believe me you learn more around here than that ugly Mr. Goodman can teach you! You know, I really feel sorry for him. I never saw a man with a more effeminate face in my life. When I saw you talking to him by the lobster tank I said to myself, "Good Lord, for a science teacher my poor girl has got herself a Hebrew hermaphrodite." Of course, he's not as bad as Miss Hanley. The idea of letting her teach girl's gym is staggering. And you have to place me in the embarrassing position of giving them a reason to call me at eight-thirty in the morning, no less.

TILLIE: I didn't say anything.

BEATRICE: What do you tell them when they want to know why you stay home once in a while?

TILLIE: I tell them I'm sick.

BEATRICE: Oh, you're sick all right, the exact nature of the illness not fully realized, but you're sick all right. Any daughter that would turn her mother in as the administrator of a concentration camp has got to be suffering from something very peculiar.

TILLIE: Can I go in today, Mother?

BEATRICE: You'll go in, all right.

TILLIE: Mr. Goodman said he was going to do an experiment—

BEATRICE: Why, he looks like the kind that would do his experimenting after sundown.

TILLIE: On radioactivity—

BEATRICE: On radioactivity? That's all that high school needs!

TILLIE: He's going to bring in the cloud chamber—

BEATRICE: Why, what an outstanding event. If you had warned me yesterday I would've gotten all dressed to kill and gone with you today. I love seeing cloud chambers being brought in.

TILLIE: You can actually see—

BEATRICE: You're giving me a headache.

TILLIE: Please?

BEATRICE: No, my dear, the fortress of knowledge is not going to be blessed with your presence today. I have a good number of exciting duties for you to take care of, not the least of which is rabbit droppings.

TILLIE: Oh, Mother, please . . . I'll do it after school.

BEATRICE: If we wait a minute longer this house is going to ferment. I found rabbit droppings in my bedroom even.

TILLIE: I could do it after Mr. Goodman's class. I'll say I'm ill and ask for a sick pass.

BEATRICE: Do you want me to chloroform that thing right this minute?

TILLIE: No!

BEATRICE: Then shut up.

[RUTH *comes to the top of the stairs. She is dressed for school, and though her clothes are simple she gives the impression of being slightly strange. Her hair isn't quite combed, her sweater doesn't quite fit, etc.*]

RUTH: Do you have Devil's Kiss down there?

BEATRICE: It's in the bathroom cabinet.

[RUTH *comes downstairs and goes to the bathroom door, located under the stairs. She flings it open and rummages in the cabinet*]

RUTH: There's so much junk in here it's driving me crazy.

BEATRICE: Maybe it's in my purse . . . If you don't hurry up you'll be late for school.

RUTH: Well, I couldn't very well go in without Devil's Kiss, now could I?

BEATRICE: Doesn't anyone go to school these days without that all over their lips?

RUTH: [*Finding the lipstick*] Nobody I know, except Tillie, that is. And if she had a little lipstick on I'll bet they wouldn't have laughed at her so much yesterday.

BEATRICE: Why were they laughing?

RUTH: The assembly. Didn't she tell you about the assembly?

BEATRICE: Ruth, you didn't tell me she was in an assembly.

RUTH: Well, I just thought of it right now. How could I tell you anything until I think of it—did you ever stop to consider that? Some crummy science assembly.

BEATRICE: [*To* TILLIE] What is she talking about?

RUTH: I thought she'd tell the whole world. Imagine, right in front of the assembly, with everybody laughing at her.

BEATRICE: Will you be quiet, Ruth? *Why were they laughing at you?*

TILLIE: I don't know.

RUTH: You don't know? My heavens, she was a sight. She had that old jumper on—the faded one with the low collar—and a raggy slip that showed all over and her hair looked like she was struck by lightning.

BEATRICE: You're exaggerating . . .

RUTH: She was cranking this model of something—

TILLIE: The atom.

RUTH: This model of the atom . . . you know, it had this crank and a long tower so that when you turned it these little colored balls went spinning around like crazy. And there was Tillie, cranking away, looking weird as a coot . . . that old jumper with the raggy slip and the lightning hair . . . cranking away while some boy with glasses was reading this stupid speech . . . and everybody burst into laughter until the teachers yelled at them. And all day long, the kids kept coming up to me saying, "Is that really your sister? How can you bear it?" And you know, Chris Burns says to me—"*She* looks like the one that went to the looney doctors." I could have kissed him there and then.

BEATRICE: [*Taking a backscratcher*] Matilda, if you can't get yourself dressed properly before going to school you're never going to go again. I don't like the idea of everybody laughing at you, because when they laugh at you they're laughing at me. And I don't want you cranking any more . . . atoms.

RUTH: [*Putting the lipstick back in* BEATRICE's *bag*] You're almost out of Devil's Kiss.

BEATRICE: If you didn't put so much on it would last longer.

RUTH: Who was that calling?

BEATRICE: Matilda turned me in to the Gestapo.

RUTH: Can I earn a cigarette this morning?

BEATRICE: Why not?

[BEATRICE *offers her the backscratcher along with a cigarette*]

RUTH: Was it Mr. Goodman?

BEATRICE: Who?

RUTH: [*Lighting the cigarette*] The call this morning. Was it Mr. Goodman?

BEATRICE: Yes.

RUTH: [*Using the backscratcher on* BEATRICE, *who squirms with ecstasy*] I figured it would be.

BEATRICE: A little higher, please.

RUTH: There?

BEATRICE: Yes, *there* . . . Why did you figure it would be Mr. Goodman?

RUTH: Well, he called me out of sewing class yesterday—I remember because my blouse wasn't all buttoned—and he wanted to know why Tillie's out of school so much.

BEATRICE: Lower. A little lower . . . And what did you tell him?

RUTH: I wish you'd go back to Kools. I liked Kools better.

TILLIE: [*Gravely concerned*] What did you tell him?

RUTH: I told him you were ill, and he wanted to know what kind, so I told him you had leprosy.

TILLIE: You didn't!

RUTH: You should have seen his face. He was so cute. And I told him you had ringworm and gangrene.

BEATRICE: What did he say?

RUTH: And I told him you had what Mother's last patient had . . . whatchamacallit?

BEATRICE: Psoriasis?

RUTH: Yeah. Something like that.

TILLIE: Tell me you didn't, Ruth!

RUTH: O.K. I didn't . . . But I really did.

BEATRICE: He knew you were joking.

RUTH: And then I told him to go look up the *history* and then he'd find out. Whenever they go look up the history then they don't bother me anymore 'cause they think I'm crazy.

BEATRICE: Ruth—

RUTH: And I told him the disease you had was fatal and that there wasn't much hope for you.

BEATRICE: What kind of *history* is it?

RUTH: Just a little folder with the story of our lives in it, that's all.

BEATRICE: How did you ever see it?

RUTH: I read the whole thing last term when Miss Hanley dragged me into the record room because I didn't want to climb the ropes in gym and I told her my skull was growing.

BEATRICE: A little *lower*, please.

RUTH: Lower! Higher! I wish you'd make up your mind. If you'd switch back to Kools it might be worth it, but ugh! these are awful. You know, I really did think my skull was growing. Either that or a tumor. So she dragged me out of gym class, and she thought I couldn't read upside down while she was sitting opposite me with the history. But I could.

BEATRICE: What does it say?

RUTH: Oh, it says you're divorced and that I went crazy . . . and my father took a heart attack at Star Lake . . . and now you're a widow—

BEATRICE: [*Referring to the backscratching*] That's it! Hold it right there! Aaah!

RUTH: And it says that I exaggerate and tell stories and that I'm afraid of death and have nightmares . . . and all that stuff.

BEATRICE: And what else does it say?

RUTH: I can't remember everything, you know. Remember this, remember that . . . remember this, that . . .

[*Go to dark. Music in*]

TILLIE'S VOICE: Today I saw it. Behind the glass a white cloud began to form. He placed a small piece of metal in the center of the chamber and we waited until I saw the first one—a trace of smoke that came from nowhere and then disappeared. And then another . . . and another, until I knew it was coming from the metal. They looked like water-sprays from a park fountain, and they went on and on for as long as I watched. And he told me the fountain of smoke would come forth for a long time, and if I had wanted to, I could have stayed there all my life and it would never have ended—that fountain, so close I could have touched it. In front of my eyes, one part of the world was becoming another. Atoms exploding, flinging off tiny bullets that caused the fountain, atom after atom breaking down into something new. And no one could stop the fountain. It would go on for millions of years —on and on, this fountain from eternity.

[*By the end of this speech, the lights are in to show* TILLIE *preparing boxes of dirt in which to plant seeds. The rabbit is in the cage near her, and* BEATRICE *is reading a newspaper on the other side of the room. She is sipping coffee from a huge coffee cup*]

BEATRICE: I thought we had everything, but leave it to you to think of the one thing we're missing . . . [*She reads from the newspaper*] Twenty-two acres in Prince's Bay. Small pond. $6,000 . . . That's cheap. I'd take a look at it if I had any money . . . What kind of seeds are they?

TILLIE: Marigolds. *They've been exposed to cobalt-60.*

BEATRICE: If there's one thing I've always wanted, it's been a living room planted with marigolds that have been exposed to cobalt-60. While you're at it, why don't you throw in a tomato patch in the bathroom?

TILLIE: Just let me keep them here for a week or so until they get started and then I'll transplant them to the backyard.

BEATRICE: [*Reading again*] Four-family house. Six and a half and six and a half over five and five. Eight garages. I could really do something with that. A nursing home . . . Don't think I'm not kicking myself that I didn't finish that real estate course. I should have finished beauty school, too . . . God, what I could do with eight garages . . . [*There is a sound from beyond the curtained door-way.* BEATRICE *gestures in that direction*] You know, I'm thinking of getting rid of *that* and making this place into something.

TILLIE: Yes.

BEATRICE: I've been thinking about a tea shop. Have you noticed there aren't many of them around anymore?

TILLIE: Yes.

BEATRICE: And this is just the type of neighborhood where a good tea shop could make a go of it. We'd have a good cheesecake. You've got to have a good cheesecake . . . [*She calculates*] Eight times ten—well, eight times eight, if they're falling down—that's sixty-four dollars a month from the garages alone . . . I swear money makes money.

[*There is a rustling at the curtains. Two thin and wrinkled hands push the curtains apart slowly and then the ancient face of* NANNY *appears. She negotiates her way through the curtains. She is utterly wrinkled and dried, perhaps a century old. Time has left her with a whisper of a smile—a smile from a soul half-departed. If one looked closely, great cataracts could be seen on each eye, and it is certain that all that can pierce her soundless prison are mere shadows from the outside world. She pervades the room with age.*

NANNY *supports herself by a four-legged tubular frame which she pushes along in front of her with a shuffling motion that reminds one of a ticking clock. Inch by inch she advances into the room.* TILLIE *and* BEATRICE *continue speaking, knowing that it will be minutes before she is close enough to know they are there*]

BEATRICE: What is cobalt-60?

TILLIE: It's something that causes . . . changes in seeds. Oh, Mother—he set the cloud chamber up just for me and he told me about radioactivity and half-life and he got the seeds for me.

BEATRICE: [*Her attention still on the newspaper*] What does half-life mean?

[NANNY *is well into the room as* TILLIE *replies*]

TILLIE: [*Reciting from memory*] The half-life of Poloniu one hundred and forty days. The half-life of Radium-2: thousand five hundred and ninety years. The half-life of _ 238 is four and one-half billion years.

BEATRICE: [*Putting away her newspaper*] Do you know you're giving me a headache? [*Then, in a loud, horribly saccharine voice, she speaks to* NANNY *as if she were addressing a deaf year-old child*] LOOK WHO'S THERE! IT'S NANNY! NANNY CAME ALL THE WAY OUT HERE BY HERSELF! I'm going to need a cigarette for this. NANNY! YOU COME SIT DOWN AND WE'LL BE RIGHT WITH HER! You know, sometimes I've got to laugh. I've got *this* on my hands and all you're worried about is planting marigolds. I'VE GOT HOTSY WATER FOR YOU, NANNY. WOULD YOU LIKE SOME HOTSY WATER AND HONEY? [NANNY *has seated herself at a table, smiling but oblivious to her environment*] I've never seen it to fail. Every time I decide to have a cup of coffee I see that face at the curtains. I wonder what she'd do . . . [*She holds pot of boiling water*] . . . if I just pour this right over her head. I'll bet she wouldn't even notice it. NANNY'S GOING TO GET JUST WHAT SHE NEEDS! [*She fills a cup for her and places a honey jar near her*] You know if someone told me when I was young that I'd end up feeding honey to a zombie, I'd tell them they were crazy. SOMETHING WRONG, NANNY? OH, DID I FORGET NANNY'S SPOON? MERCY! MERCY! I FORGOT NANNY'S SPOON. [*She gets a spoon and stands behind* NANNY] I'll give you a spoon, Nanny, I'll give you a spoon. [*She makes a motion behind* NANNY'S *back as if she's going to smack her on the head with the spoon*] Matilda! Watch me give Nanny her spoon. A SPOON FOR NANNY! [*It manages to be slightly funny and* TILLIE *yields to a laugh, along with her mother*] Fifty dollars a week. Fifty dollars. I look at you, Nanny, and I wonder if it's worth it. I think I'd be better off driving a cab. TAKE HONEY, NANNY. HONEY WITH HOTSY WATER! You should have seen her daughter bring her here last week . . . I could have used you that day . . . She came in pretending she was Miss Career Woman of the Year. She said she was in real estate and *such a busy little woman*, such a busy little woman—she just couldn't give all the love and care and affection her little momsy needed anymore . . . [*Then, with a great smile, she speaks right into* NANNY'S *uncomprehending face*] Nanny's quite a little cross to bear, now aren't you, Nanny dear? But you're a little better than Mr. Mayo was—with the tumor on his brain—or Miss Marion Minto with her cancer, or Mr. Brougham . . . what was his first name?

TILLIE: Alexander.

BEATRICE: Mr. Alexander Brougham with the worms in his legs. WHY, NANNY'S QUITE SOME LITTLE GIRL, AREN'T YOU, NANNY? A GIRL DRINKING HER HOTSY AND HONEY! . . . Cobalt-60. Ha! You take me for a fool, don't you?

TILLIE: No, Mother.

BEATRICE: Science, science, science! Don't they teach our misfits anything anymore? Anything decent and meaningful and sensitive? Do you know what I'd be now if it wasn't for this mud pool I got sucked into? I'd probably be a dancer. Miss Betty Frank, The Best Dancer of the Class of 19 . . . something. One minute I'm the best dancer in school—smart as a whip—the head of the whole crowd! And the next minute . . . One mistake. That's how it starts. Marry the wrong man and before you know it he's got you tied down with two stones around your neck for the rest of your life. When I was in that lousy high school I was one of the most respected kids you ever saw. I used to wonder why people always said, "Why, just yesterday . . . why, just yesterday . . . why, just yesterday . . ." Before I knew what happened I lost my dancing legs and got varicose legs. Beautiful varicose legs. Do you know, everything I ever thought I'd be has exploded! NANNY, YOU HURRY UP WITH THAT HONEY! Exploded! You know, I almost forgot about everything I was supposed to be . . . NANNY'S ALMOST FINISHED. ISN'T THAT WONDERFUL? She's almost finished, all right. NANNY'S DAUGHTER IS COMING TO SEE YOU SOON. WILL THAT MAKE NANNY HAPPY? The day Miss Career Woman of the Year comes to visit again I think I'll drop dead. Nobody's too busy for anything they want to do, don't you tell me. What kind of an idiot do people take me for? NANNY, YOU'RE SPILLING YOUR HOTSY! JESUS CHRIST! You know, I ought to kick you right out and open that tea shop tomorrow. Oh, it's coming. I can feel it. And the first thing I'll do is get rid of that rabbit.

TILLIE: [Hardly listening] Yes, Mother.

BEATRICE: You think I'm kidding?

TILLIE: No, I don't.

BEATRICE: You bet I'm not! [*She rummages through some drawers in a chest*] I was going to do this a month ago. [*She holds up a small bottle*] Here it is. Here's a new word for you. (*She reads*) Trichloro . . . methane. Do you know what that is, Matilda? Well, it's chloroform! [*She puts the bottle away*] I'm saving it for the Angora manure machine of yours. Speaking of manure machines, IS NANNY READY TO GO MAKE DUTY? [*She starts helping* NANNY *out of the chair and props her up with the tubular frame*] NANNY IS ALWAYS READY FOR DUTY, AREN'T YOU, NANNY? BECAUSE NANNY'S A GOODY-GOODY GIRL AND GOODY-GOODY GIRLS ALWAYS GET GOODY-GOODY THINGS. GOD LOOKS OUT FOR GOODY-GOODY GIRLS AND GIVES THEM HOTSY AND HONEY—RIGHT, NANNY? [BEATRICE *sits down in the hall and watches* NANNY *make her way toward the bathroom. There is a pause as the woman's shuffling continues. The lights go low on* TILLIE, NANNY *becomes a silhouette, and the light remains on* BEATRICE. *She starts to read the paper again, but the shuffling gets on her nerves and she flings the paper down*] Half-life! If you want to know what a half-life is, just ask me. You're looking at the original half-life! I got stuck with one daughter with half a mind; another one who's half a test tube; half a husband—a house half full of rabbit crap—and half a corpse! That's what I call a half-life, Matilda! Me and cobalt-60! Two of the biggest half-*lifes* you ever saw!

[*The set goes to dark. After a few seconds, the sound of someone dialing a phone can be heard. As the spot comes up on her, we see* BEATRICE *holding the phone and struggling to get a cigarette*]

BEATRICE: [*On the phone*] Hello—Mr. Goodman, please . . . How would I know if he's got a class? . . . Hello, Mr. Goodman? Are you Mr. Goodman? . . . Oh, I beg your pardon, Miss Torgersen . . . Yes, I'll wait . . . [*She lights her cigarette*] Couldn't you find him, Miss Torgersen? . . . Oh! Excuse me, Mr. Goodman. How are you? . . . I'll bet you'll never guess who this is—it's Mrs. Hunsdorfer—remember the frozen foods? [*She laughs*] You know, Ruth told me she's your new secretary and I certainly think that's a delight. You were paying so much attention to Matilda that I'll bet Ruth just got jealous. She does things like that, you know. I hope she works hard for you, although I can't imagine what kind of work Ruth could be doing in that great big science office. She's a terrible snoop . . . [*She takes a puff*] Your attendance? Isn't that charming. And the *cut* cards! Imagine. You trust her with . . . why, I didn't know she could type *at all* . . . imagine. Well . . . I'll . . . Of course, *too* much work isn't good for anyone, either. No wonder she's failing everything. I mean, I never knew a girl who failed everything regardless of what they were suffering from. I suppose I should say *recovering* from . . . Well, it's about the seeds you gave Matilda . . . Well, she's had them in the house for a week now and they're starting to grow. Now, she told me they had been subjected to radioactivity, and I hear such terrible things about radioactivity that I automatically associate radioactivity with sterility, and it positively horrifies me to have those seeds right here in my living room. Couldn't she just grow plain marigolds like everyone else? [*She takes a puff*] Oh . . . [*Another big puff, forming a mushroom cloud*] It does sound like an interesting project, but . . . [*The biggest puff yet*] No, I must admit that at this very moment I don't know what a *mutation* is . . . [*She laughs uncomfortably*] Mr. Goodman . . . Mr. Goodman! I don't want you to think I'm not interested, but please spare me definitions over the phone. I'll go to the library next week and pick me out some little book on science and then I'll know all about mutations . . . No, you didn't insult me, but I just want you to know that I'm not *stupid* . . . I just thought prevention was better than a tragedy, Mr. Goodman. I mean, Matilda has enough problems to worry about without *sterility* . . . Well, I was just concerned, but you've put my poor mother's heart at ease. You know, really, our schools need more exciting young men like you, I really mean that. Really. Oh, I do. Goodbye, Mr. Goodman. [*By the end of her talk on the phone, her face is left in a spotlight, and then the stage goes black. The music theme comes in, in a minor key, softly at first, but accentuated by increasingly loud pulses which transmute into thunder crashes. There is a scream heard from upstairs and we see the set in night shadows.* TILLIE *tears open her bedroom door and rushes into* BEATRICE'S *room.* RUTH *screams again*]

TILLIE: Mother! She's going to have one!

[RUTH *appears on the landing and releases another scream which breaks off into gasps. She starts down the stairs and stops halfway to scream again. There is another tremendous thunder crash as* BEATRICE *comes out of her room, puts on the hall light, and catches the hysterical girl on the stairs*]

BEATRICE: [*Shouting*] Stop it! Stop it, Ruth!

TILLIE: [*At the top of the stairs*] She's going!

BEATRICE: Ruth! Stop it!

TILLIE: She's going to go!

BEATRICE: [*Yelling at* TILLIE] Shut up and get back in your room! [RUTH *screams*] You're not going to let yourself go, do you hear me, Ruth? You're not going to go!

RUTH: He's after me!

[*She screams, lightning and thunder crash follow*]

BEATRICE: You were dreaming, do you hear me? Nobody's after you! Nobody!

TILLIE: I saw her eyes start to go back—

BEATRICE: [*To* TILLIE] Get back in your room! [*She helps* RUTH *down the rest of the stairs*] There, now, nobody's after you. Nice and easy. Breathe deeply . . . Did the big bad man come after my little girl? [*She sits* RUTH *down and then puts both hands up to her own face and pulls her features into a comic mask.* RUTH *begins to laugh at her*] That big bad bogey man? [*They both laugh heartily*] Now that wasn't so bad, was it?

RUTH: It was the dream, with Mr. Mayo again.

BEATRICE: Oh. Well, we'll just get you a little hot milk and—[*A tremendous thunder crash throws the set into shadows*] Why, the electricity's gone off. Do you remember what happened to those candles?

RUTH: What candles?

BEATRICE: The little white ones from my birthday cake last year.

RUTH: Tillie melted them down for school a long time ago.

BEATRICE: [*Searching through drawers*] She had no right doing that.

RUTH: She asked you. She used them to attach a paper straw to a milk bottle with a balloon over it, and it was supposed to tell if it was going to rain.

BEATRICE: [*Finding a flashlight*] There! It works. I don't want her wasting anything of mine unless she's positive I won't need it. You always need candles. [*She steers* RUTH *toward the couch as lightning flashes*] Why, Ruth—your skin just turned ice cold! [*She rummages through one of the boxes and grabs a blanket*] This will warm you up . . . What's the matter?

RUTH: The flashlight—

BEATRICE: What's wrong with it?

RUTH: It's the same one I used to check on Mr. Mayo with.

BEATRICE: So it is. We don't need it.

RUTH: No, let me keep it. [*Starting to laugh*] Do you want to know how they have it in the history?

BEATRICE: No, I don't.

RUTH: Well, they say I came out of my room . . . [*She flashes the light on her room*] . . . And I started down the stairs, step by step . . . and I heard the choking and banging on the bed, and . . .

BEATRICE: I'm going back to bed.

RUTH: No!

BEATRICE: Well, talk about something nice, then.

RUTH: Oh, Mama, tell me about the wagon.

BEATRICE: You change so fast I can't keep up with you.

RUTH: Mama, *please* . . . the story about the wagon.

BEATRICE: I don't know anything about telling stories. Get those great big smart teachers of yours to do that sort of stuff.

RUTH: Tell me about the horses again, and how you stole the wagon.

BEATRICE: Don't get me started on that.

RUTH: Mama, *please* . . .

BEATRICE: [*Taking out a pack of cigarettes*] Do you want a cigarette?

RUTH: [*Taking one*] Leave out the part where they shoot the horses, though.

[*They both light up*]

BEATRICE: Honey, you know the whole story—

RUTH: "Apples! Pears! Cu . . . cumbers!"

BEATRICE: No. It's "Apples! Pears! Cucum . . . bers!" [*They say it together*] "Apples! Pears! Cucum . . . bers!"

[*And they laugh*]

RUTH: How did you get the wagon out without him seeing you?

BEATRICE: That was easy. Every time he got home for the day he'd make us both some sandwiches—my mama had been dead for years—and he'd take a nap on the old sofa that used to be . . . there! [*She points to a corner of the room*] And while he was sleeping I got the horses hitched up and went riding around the block waving to everyone.

RUTH: Oh, Mama, you didn't!

BEATRICE: Of course I did. I had more nerve than a bear when I was a kid. Let me tell you it takes nerve to sit up on that wagon every day yelling "Apples! . . . [*Both together*] Pears! Cucum . . . bers!" [*They laugh again*]

RUTH: Did he find out you took the wagon?

BEATRICE: Did he find out? He came running down the street after me and started spanking me right on top of the wagon—not hard —but it was so embarrassing—and I had one of those penny marshmallow ships in the back pocket of my overalls, and it got all squished. And you better believe I never did it again . . . You would have loved him, Ruth, and gone out with him on the wagon . . . all over Stapleton yelling as loud as you wanted.

RUTH: "Apples! Pears! *Cu* . . . cumbers!"

BEATRICE: No!

RUTH: "Cu*cum* . . . bers!"

BEATRICE: My father made up for all the other men in this whole world, Ruth. If only you two could have met. He'd only be about seventy now, do you realize that? And I'll bet he'd still be selling vegetables around town. All that fun—and then I don't think I ever knew what really hit me.

RUTH: Don't tell about—

BEATRICE: Don't worry about the horses.

RUTH: What hit you?

BEATRICE: Well, it was just me and Papa . . . and your father hanging around. And then Papa got sick . . . and I drove with him up to the sanatorium. And then I came home and there were the horses—

RUTH: Mother!

BEATRICE: And I had the horses . . . taken care of. And then Papa got terribly sick and he begged me to marry so that he'd be sure I'd be taken care of. [*She laughs*] If he knew how I was taken care of he'd turn over in his grave. And *nightmares!* Do you want to know the nightmare I used to have? I never had nightmares over the fights with your father, or the divorce, or his thrombosis—he deserved it—I never had nightmares over any of that. Let me tell you about my nightmare that used to come back and back: *Well*, I'm on Papa's wagon, but it's newer and shinier, and it's being pulled by beautiful white horses, not dirty workhorses—these are like circus horses with long manes and tinsel—and the wagon is blue, shiny blue. And it's full—filled with yellow apples and grapes and green squash. You're going to laugh when you hear this. I'm wearing a lovely gown with jewels all over it, and my hair is piled up on top of my head with a long feather in it, and the bells are ringing. Huge bells swinging on a gold braid strung across the back of the wagon, and they're going DONG, DONG . . . DONG, DONG. And I'm yelling "APPLES! PEARS! CUCUM . . . BERS!"

RUTH: That doesn't sound like a nightmare to me.

BEATRICE: And then I turn down our street and all the noise stops. This long street, with all the doors of the houses shut and everything crowded next to each other, and there's not a soul around. And then I start getting afraid that the vegetables are going to spoil . . . and that nobody's boing to buy anything, and I feel as though I shouldn't be on the wagon, and I keep trying to call out. But there isn't a sound. Not a single sound. Then I turn my head and look at the house across the street. I see an upstairs window, and a pair of hands pull the curtains slowly apart. I see the face of my father and my heart stands still . . . Ruth . . . take the light out of my eyes.

[A long pause]

RUTH: Is Nanny going to die here?

BEATRICE: No.

RUTH: How can you be sure?

BEATRICE: I can tell.

RUTH: Are you crying?

BEATRICE: What's left for me, Ruth?

RUTH: What, Mama?

BEATRICE: What's left for me?

[The stage goes slowly to dark as the drizzling rain becomes louder and then disappears.
When the lights come up again NANNY is seated at the

kitchen table with a bottle of beer and a glass in front of her.
TILLIE *comes in the front door with a box of large marigold plants and sets them down where they'll be inconspicuous. She gets the rabbit out of its cage, sits down near* NANNY *and gives her a little wave.* BEATRICE *suddenly appears at the top of the stairs and drops a stack of newspapers with a loud thud. She goes back into her room and lets fly another armful of junk]*

TILLIE: What are you doing?

BEATRICE: A little housecleaning, and you're going to help. You can start by getting rid of that rabbit or I'll suffocate the bastard. *[She takes a drink from a glass of whiskey]* You don't think I will, do you? You wait and see. Where's Ruth? She's probably running around the schoolyard in her brassiere.

[She comes downstairs]

TILLIE: Mother, they want me to do something at school.

BEATRICE: NANNY! DID YOU HEAR THAT? THEY WANT HER TO DO SOMETHING AT SCHOOL! ISN'T THAT MOMENTOUS, NANNY? Well I want you to do something around here. Like get rid of that bunny. I'm being generous! I'll let you give it away. Far away. Give it to Mr. Goodman. I'd chloroform the thing myself, but that crazy sister of yours would throw convulsions for fifty years . . . and I hate a house that vibrates. And get rid of those sterile marigolds. They stink! HI, NANNY—HOW ARE YOU, HONEY? HOW WOULD YOU LIKE TO GO ON A LONG TRIP? You see, everybody, I spent today taking stock of my life and I've come up with zero. I added up all the separate departments and the total reads zero . . . zero zero zero zero zero zero zero zero zero zero zero zero zero zero zero zero zero zero . . . And do you know how you pronounce that, with all your grammatical schoolin' and foolin'? You pronounce it o,o,o,o,O,O,O,O,O,O! o,o,o,o,O,O,O,O,O,O,O,O! Right Nanny? RIGHT, NANNY? So, by the end of the week, you get rid of that cottontail compost heap and we'll get you a job down at the five-and-ten-cent store. And if you don't do so well with the public, we'll fix you up with some kind of machine. Wouldn't that be nice?

[RUTH *enters at a gallop, throwing her books down and babbling a mile a minute*]

RUTH: [*Enthusiastically*] Can you believe it? I didn't, until Chris Burns came up and told me about it in Geography, and then Mr. Goodman told me himself during the eighth period in the office when I was eavesdropping. Aren't you so happy you could bust? Tillie? I'm so proud I can't believe it, Mama. Everybody was talking about it and nobody . . . well, it was the first time they all came up screaming about her and I said, "Yes, she's my sister!" I said it, "She's my sister! My sister! My *sister!*" Give me a cigarette.

BEATRICE: Get your hands off my personal property.

RUTH: I'll scratch your back later.

BEATRICE: I don't want you to touch me!

RUTH: Did he call yet? My God, I can't believe it, I just can't!

BEATRICE: Did who call yet?

RUTH: I'm not supposed to tell you, as Mr. Goodman's private secretary, but you're going to get a call from school.

BEATRICE: [*To* TILLIE] What is she talking about?

TILLIE: I was in the Science Fair at school.

RUTH: Didn't she tell you yet? Oh, Tillie, how could you? She's fantastic, Mama! She's a finalist in the Science Fair. There were only five of them out of hundreds and hundreds. She won with all those plants over there. They're freaks! Isn't that a scream? Dr. Berg picked her himself. The principal! And I heard Mr. Goodman say she was going to be another Madam Pasteur and he never saw a girl do anything like that before and . . . so I told everybody, "Yes, she's my sister!" Tillie, "You're my sister!" I said. And Mr. Goodman called the Advance and they're coming to take your picture. Oh, Mama, isn't it crazy? And nobody laughed at her, Mama. She beat out practically everybody and nobody laughed at her. "She's my sister," I said. "She's my sister!" [*The telephone rings*] That must be him! Mama, answer it—I'm afraid.

[*Ring*] Answer it before he hangs up! [*Ring*] Mama! He's gonna hang up! [RUTH *grabs the phone*] Hello? . . . Yes . . . [*Aside to* BEATRICE] It's him! . . . Just a minute, please . . . [*Covering the mouthpiece*] He wants to talk to you.

BEATRICE: Who?

RUTH: The *principal!*

BEATRICE: Hang up.

RUTH: I told him you were here! Mama!

[BEATRICE *gets up and shuffles slowly to the phone*]

BEATRICE: [*Finally, into the phone*] Yes? . . . I know who you are, Dr. Berg . . . I see . . . Couldn't you get someone else? There's an awfully lot of work that has to be done around here, because she's not as careful with her home duties as she is with man-in-the-moon marigolds . . . Me? What would you want with me up on the stage? . . . The other mothers can do as they please . . . I would have thought you had enough in your *history* without . . . I'll think about it . . . Goodbye, Dr. Berg . . . [*Pause, then screaming*] I SAID I'D THINK ABOUT IT!

[*She hangs up the phone, turns her face slowly to* RUTH, *then to* TILLIE, *who has her face hidden in shame in the rabbit's fur*]

RUTH: What did he say?

BEATRICE: [*Flinging her glass on the floor*] How could you do this to me? HOW COULD YOU LET THAT MAN CALL OUR HOME! I have no clothes, do you hear me? I'd look just like you up on the stage, ugly little you! DO YOU WANT THEM TO LAUGH AT US? LAUGH AT THE TWO OF US?

RUTH: [*Disbelievingly*] Mother . . . aren't you proud of her? Mother . . . it's an *honor.*

[TILLIE *breaks into tears and moves away from* BEATRICE. *It seems as though she is crushed, but then she halts and turns to face her mother*]

TILLIE: [*Through tears*] But . . . nobody laughed at me.

[BEATRICE's *face begins to soften as she glimpses what she's done to* TILLIE]

BEATRICE: Oh, my God . . .

[TILLIE *starts toward her.* BEATRICE *opens her arms to receive her as music starts in an lights fade. A chord of finality punctuates the end of Act One*]

ACT TWO

About two weeks later.

The room looks somewhat cheery and there is excitement in the air. It is early evening and preparations are being made for TILLIE *to take her project to the final judging of the Science Fair.*

TILLIE *has been dressed by her mother in clothes which are clean but too girlish for her awkwardness. Her hair has been curled, she sports a large bow, and her dress is a starched flair.*

RUTH *has dressed herself up as well. She has put on too much makeup, and her lipstick has been extended beyond the natural line of her lips. She almost appears to be sinister.*

A large three-panel screen stands on one of the tables. THE EFFECT OF GAMMA RAYS ON MAN-IN-THE-MOON MARIGOLDS *is printed in large letters running across the top of the three panels. Below this on each panel there is a subtopic:* THE PAST; THE PRESENT; THE FUTURE. *Additional charts and data appear below the titles.*

RUTH: The only competition you have to worry about is Janice Vickery. They say she caught it near Princess Bay Boulevard and it was still alive when she took the skin off it.

TILLIE: [*Taking some plants from* RUTH] Let me do that, please, Ruth.

RUTH: I'm sorry I touched them, really.

TILLIE: Why don't you feed Peter?

RUTH: Because I don't feel like feeding him . . . Now I feel like feeding him. [*She gets some lettuce from a bag*] I heard that it screamed for three minutes after she put it in because the water wasn't boiling yet. How much talent does it take to boil the skin off a cat and then stick the bones together again? That's what I want to know. Ugh. I had a dream about that, too. I figure she did it in less than a day and she ends up as one of the top five winners . . . and you spend months growing atomic flowers.

TILLIE: Don't you think you should finish getting ready?

RUTH: Finish? This is it!

TILLIE: Are you going to wear that sweater?

RUTH: Look, don't worry about me. I'm not getting up on any stage, and if I did I wouldn't be caught dead with a horrible bow like that.

TILLIE: Mother put it—

RUTH: They're going to laugh you off the stage again like when you cranked that atom in assembly . . . I didn't mean that . . . The one they're going to laugh at is Mama.

TILLIE: What?

RUTH: I said the one they're going to laugh at is Mama . . . Oh, let me take that bow off.

TILLIE: It's all right.

RUTH: Look, just sit still. I don't want everybody making fun of you.

TILLIE: What made you say that about Mama?

RUTH: Oh, I heard them talking in the Science Office yesterday. Mr. Goodman and Miss Hanley. She's getting $12.63 to chaperon the thing tonight.

TILLIE: What were they saying?

RUTH: Miss Hanley was telling Mr. Goodman about Mama . . . when she found out you were one of the five winners. And he wanted to know if there was something wrong with Mama because she sounded crazy over the phone. And Miss Hanley said she *was* crazy and she always has been crazy and she can't wait to see what she looks like after all these years. Miss Hanley said her nickname used to be *Betty the Loon.*

TILLIE: [*As* RUTH *combs her hair*] Ruth, you're hurting me.

RUTH: She was just like you and everybody thought she was a big weirdo. There! You look much better! [*She goes back to the rabbit*] Peter, if anybody stuck you in a pot of boiling water I'd kill them, do you know that? . . . [*Then to* TILLIE] What do they call boiling the skin off a cat? I call it murder, that's what I call it. They say it was hit by a car and Janice just scooped it up and before you could say *bingo* it was screaming in a pot of boiling water . . . Do you know what they're all waiting to see? Mama's feathers! That's what Miss Hanley said. She said Mama blabs as though she was the Queen of England and just as proper as can be, and that her idea of getting dressed up is to put on all the feathers in the world and go as a bird. Always trying to get somewhere, like a great big bird.

TILLIE: Don't tell Mama, please. It doesn't matter.

RUTH: I was up there watching her getting dressed and sure enough, she's got the feathers out.

TILLIE: You didn't tell her what Miss Hanley said?

RUTH: Are you kidding? I just told her I didn't like the feathers and I didn't think she should wear any. But I'll bet she doesn't listen to me.

TILLIE: It doesn't matter.

RUTH: It doesn't matter? Do you think I want to be laughed right out of the school tonight, with Chris Burns there, and all? Laughed right out of the school, with your electric hair and her feathers on that stage, and Miss Hanley splitting her sides?

TILLIE: Promise me you won't say anything.

RUTH: On one condition.

TILLIE: What?

RUTH: Give Peter to me.

TILLIE: [*Ignoring her*] The taxi will be here any minute and I won't have all this stuff ready. Did you see my speech?

RUTH: I mean it. Give Peter to me.

TILLIE: He belongs to all of us.

RUTH: For me. All for me. What do you care? He doesn't mean anything to you anymore, now that you've got all those crazy plants.

TILLIE: Will you stop?

RUTH: If you don't give him to me I'm going to tell Mama that everybody's waiting to laugh at her.

TILLIE: Where are those typewritten cards?

RUTH: I MEAN IT! Give him to me!

TILLIE: Does he mean that much to you?

RUTH: Yes!

TILLIE: All right.

RUTH: [*After a burst of private laughter*] Betty the Loon . . . [*She laughs again*] That's what they used to call her, you know. Betty the Loon!

TILLIE: I don't think that's very nice.

RUTH: First they had Betty the Loon, and now they've got Tillie the Loon . . . [*To rabbit*] You don't have to worry about me turning you in for any old plants . . . How much does a taxi cost from here to the school?

TILLIE: Not much.

RUTH: I wish she'd give me the money it costs for a taxi—and for all that cardboard and paint and flowerpots and stuff. The only time she ever made a fuss over me was when she drove me nuts.

TILLIE: Tell her to hurry, please.

RUTH: By the way, I went over to see Janice Vickery's pot, that she did you know what in, and I started telling her and her mother about the worms in Mr. Alexander Brougham's legs, and I got thrown out because it was too near dinner time. That Mrs. Vickery kills me. She can't stand worms in somebody else's legs but she lets her daughter cook a cat.

TILLIE: [*Calling upstairs*] Mother! The taxi will be here any minute.

[BEATRICE *comes to the top of the stairs. Her costume is strange, but not that strange, by any means. She is even a little attractive tonight, and though her words say she is greatly annoyed with having to attend the night's function, her tone and direction show she is very, very proud*]

BEATRICE: You're lucky I'm coming, without all this rushing me.

TILLIE: Mama, you look beautiful.

BEATRICE: Don't put it on too thick. I said I'd go and I guess there's no way to get out of it. Do you mind telling me how I'm supposed to get up on the stage? Do they call my name or what? And where are you going to be? If you ask me, they should've sent all the parents a mimeographed sheet of instructions. If this is supposed to be such a great event, why don't they do it right?

TILLIE: You just sit on the stage with the other parents before it begins.

BEATRICE: How long is this thing going to last? And remember, I don't care even if you do win the whole damn thing, I'm not making any speech. I can hold my own anywhere, but I hated that school when I went there and I hate it now . . . and the only thing I'd have to say is, what a pack of stupid teachers and vicious children they have. Imagine someone tearing the skin off a cat.

RUTH: She didn't tear it. She boiled it off.

BEATRICE: You just told me upstairs that girl tore the skin off with an orange knife and . . . do you know, sometimes you exasperate me? [*To* TILLIE] If you've got all the plants in this box, I can manage the folding thing. Do you know I've got a headache from doing those titles? And you probably don't even like them.

TILLIE: I like them very much.

BEATRICE: Look, if you don't want me to go tonight, I don't have to. You're about as enthusiastic as a dummy about this whole thing.

TILLIE: I'm sorry.

BEATRICE: And I refuse to let you get nervous. Put that bow back in your hair.

RUTH: I took it out.

BEATRICE: What did you do that for?

RUTH: [*Taking the rabbit in her arms*] Because it made her look crazy.

BEATRICE: How would you know what's crazy or not? If that sweater of yours was any tighter it'd cut off the circulation in your chest. [*Fussing over* TILLIE] The bow looks very nice in your hair. There's nothing wrong with looking proper, Matilda, and if you don't have enough money to look expensive and perfect, people like you for *trying* to look nice. You know, one day maybe you will be pretty. You'll have some nice features, when that hair revives and you do some tricks with makeup. I hope you didn't crowd the plants too close together. Did you find your speech?

TILLIE: Yes, Mother.

BEATRICE: You know, Matilda, I was wondering about something. Do you think you're really going to win? I mean, not that you won't be the best, but there's so much politics in school. Don't laugh, but if there's anyone who's an expert on that, it's me, and someday I'm going to write a book and blast that school to pieces. If you're just a little bit different in this world, they try to kill you off.

RUTH: [*Putting on her coat*] Tillie gave Peter to me.

BEATRICE: Oh? Then you inherited the rabbit droppings I found upstairs. What are you doing with your coat on?

RUTH: I'm going out to wait for the taxi.

BEATRICE: Oh, no you're not. You start right in on the rabbit droppings. Or you won't get another cigarette even if you scratch my
back with an orange knife.

RUTH: I'm going down to the school with you.

BEATRICE: Oh, no you're not! You're going to keep company with
that corpse in there. If she wakes up and starts gagging just slip
her a shot of whiskey. [*The taxi horn blows outside*] Quick! Grab
the plants, Matilda—I'll get the big thing.

RUTH: I want to go! I promised Chris Burns I'd meet him.

BEATRICE: Can't you understand English?

RUTH: I've got to go!

BEATRICE: Shut up!

RUTH: [*Almost berserk*] I don't care. I'M GOING ANYWAY!

BEATRICE: [*Shoving* RUTH *hard*] WHAT DID YOU SAY?

TILLIE: Mother!

[*After a pause, the horn blows again*]

BEATRICE: Hurry up with that box, Matilda, and tell him to stop
blowing the horn. HURRY UP! [TILLIE *reluctantly exits with the box
of plants*] I don't know where you ever got the idea you were
going tonight. Did you think nobody was going to hold down the
fort? . . . Now you know how I felt all those years you and everybody else was running out whenever they felt like it—because
there was always me to watch over the fifty-dollar-a-week corpse. If
there's one thing I demand it's respect. I don't ask for anything
from you but respect.

RUTH: [*Pathetically*] Why are you ashamed of me?

BEATRICE: I've been seen with a lot worse than you. I don't even
know why I'm going tonight, do you know that? Do you think I
give one goddam about the whole thing? . . . [*She starts to fold
the large three-panel screen with the titles:* THE PAST, THE PRES-

ENT, *and* THE FUTURE] Do you want to know why I'm going?
Do you really want to know why this once somebody else has to
stick with that dried prune for a few minutes? Because this is the
first time in my life I've ever felt just a little bit proud over something. Isn't that silly? Somewhere in the back of this turtle-sized
brain of mine I feel just a little *proud!* Jesus Christ! And you
begrudge me even that, you little bastard.

[*The taxi horn blows impatiently*]

RUTH: [*In a hard voice*] Hurry up. They're waiting for you . . .
They're *all* waiting for you.

BEATRICE: [*Carrying the folded screen so that* THE PAST *is face out
in bold black letters*] I hope the paint is dry . . . Who's waiting
for me?

RUTH: Everybody . . . including Miss Hanley. She's been telling all
the teachers . . . about you . . . and they're all waiting.

BEATRICE: You're such a little liar, Ruth, do you know that? When
you can't have what you want, you try to ruin it for everybody
else.

[*She starts to the door*]

RUTH: Goodnight, *Betty the Loon.*

[BEATRICE *stops as if she's been stabbed. The taxi horn blows
several times as* BEATRICE *puts down the folding screen*]

BEATRICE: [*Helplessly*] Take this thing.

RUTH: What for?

BEATRICE: Go with Matilda.

RUTH: I don't want to go now.

BEATRICE: [*Blasting*] GET OUT OF HERE!

RUTH: [*After a long pause*] Now Tillie's going to blame it on me
that you're not going—and take the rabbit back. [*The taxi beeps
again, as* RUTH *puts her coat on*] I can't help it what people call

you. [*She picks up the screen*] I'll tell Tillie you'll be down later, all right? . . . Don't answer me. What do I care! [RUTH *exits*]

[BEATRICE *breaks into tears that shudder her body, and the lights go down slowly on her pathetic form. Music in. Suddenly a bolt of light strikes an area in the right stage—* JANICE VICKERY *is standing in the spotlight holding the skeleton of a cat mounted on a small platform. Her face and voice are smug*]

JANICE: *The Past:* I got the cat from the A.S.P.C.A. immediately after it had been killed by a high-altitude pressure system. That explains why some of the rib bones are missing, because that method sucks the air out of the animal's lungs and ruptures all cavities. They say it prevents cruelty to animals but I think it's horrible. [*She laughs*] Then I boiled the cat in a sodium hydroxide solution until most of the skin pulled right off, but I had to scrape some of the grizzle off the joints with a knife. You have no idea how difficult it is to get right down to the bones. [*A little gong sounds*] I have to go on to *The Present,* now—but I did want to tell you how long it took me to put the thing together. I mean, as it is now, it's extremely useful for students of anatomy, even with the missing rib bones, and it can be used to show basic anatomical aspects of many, many animals that are in the same family as felines. I suppose that's about the only present uses I can think for it, but it is nice to remember as an accomplishment, and it looks good on college applications to show you did something else in school besides dating. [*She laughs, and a second gong sounds*] *The Future:* The only future plans I have for Tabby—my little brother asked the A.S.P.C.A. what its name was when he went to pick it up and they said it was called Tabby, but I think they were kidding him—[*She laughs again*] I mean as far as future plans, I'm going to donate it to the science department, of course, and next year, if there's another Science Fair perhaps I'll do the same thing with a dog. [*A third gong sounds*] Thank you very much for your attention, and I hope I win!

[JANICE *and her spotlight disappear as suddenly as they had arrived, and music returns as the lights come up slowly on* BEATRICE.

She has obviously been drinking and is going through a phone book. Finding her number, she goes to the phone and dials]

BEATRICE: *[Into the phone]* I want to talk to the principal, please . . . Well, you'll have to get him down off the stage . . . It's none of your goddam business who I am! . . . Oh, I see . . . Yes. I have a message for him and Mr. Goodman, and you, too . . . And this is for Miss Hanley, too . . . Tell them Mrs. Hunsdorfer called to thank them for making her wish she was dead . . . Would you give them that message, please? . . . Thank you very much.

[She hangs up the phone, pauses, then surveys the room. Her attention fixes on the store window covered with newspapers. The phone rings several times but she ignores it. She goes to the window and proceeds to rip the paper from it. That finished, she turns and surveys the room again. She goes to the kitchen table and rearranges its position. She spies a card table with school supplies and hurls them on the floor. Next, she goes to a bureau and rummages through drawers, finding tablecloths and napkins. She throws cloths on two or three tables and is heading toward the kitchen table when the phone rings again. The ringing triggers off something else she wants to do. She empties a cup filled with scraps of paper and finds a telephone number. She lifts the receiver off the ringing phone and hangs up immediately. She lifts the receiver again, checks to make sure there's a dial tone, and then dials the number on the scrap of paper]

BEATRICE: *[Into the phone]* Hello. This is Mrs. Hunsdorfer . . . I'm sorry if I frightened you, I wouldn't want you to think Nanny had deceased or anything like that—I can imagine how terrible you'd feel if anything like that ever happened . . . Terrible tragedy that would be, Miss Career Woman of the Year . . . Yes, I'll tell you why I am calling. I want her out of here by tomorrow. I told you when you rolled her in here I was going to try her out for a while and if I didn't like her she was to get the hell out. Well, I don't like her, so get her the hell out . . . It's like this. I don't like the way she cheats at solitaire. Is that a good enough reason? . . .

Fine. And if she's not out of here by noon I'll send her collect in an ambulance, you son of a bitch!

[*She slams down the phone and bursts into laughter. The laughter subsides somewhat as she pours herself another drink. She takes the drink to a chair and as she sits down her foot accidentally hits the rabbit cage. She gives the cage a little kick and then an idea strikes. She gets up and finds a large blue towel which she flings over her shoulder. She gets the bottle of chloroform and approaches the cage. Having reached a decision she picks up the cage and takes it upstairs. Music in and lights fade.*

From the darkness a beam of light falls on TILLIE *in the same way* JANICE VICKERY *had been presented*]

TILLIE: [*Deathly afraid, and referring to her cards*] The Past: The seeds were exposed to various degrees . . . of gamma rays from radiation sources in Oak Ridge . . . Mr. Goodman helped me pay for the seeds . . . Their growth was plotted against . . . time. [*She loses her voice for a moment and then the first gong sounds*] The Present: The seeds which received little radiation have grown to plants which are normal in appearance. The seeds which received moderate radiation gave rise to mutations such as double blooms, giant stems, and variegated leaves. The seeds closest to the gamma source were killed or yielded dwarf plants. [*The second gong rings*] The Future: After radiation is better understood, a day will come when the power from exploding atoms will change the whole world we know. [*With inspiration*] Some of the mutations will be good ones—wonderful things beyond our dreams—and I believe, I believe this with all my heart, THE DAY WILL COME WHEN MANKIND WILL THANK GOD FOR THE STRANGE AND BEAUTIFUL ENERGY FROM THE ATOM.

[*Part of her last speech is reverberated electronically. Deep pulses of music are added as the light focuses on* TILLIE'*s face. Suddenly there is silence, except for* RUTH *picking up* TILLIE'*s last words.*

The lights come up on the main set, and the room is empty.

RUTH *bursts in the front door. She is carrying the three-panel*

*card and a shopping bag of plants, both of which she drops
on the floor]*

RUTH: MAMA! MAMA! She won! Mama! Where are you? She won!

[She runs back to the front door and yells to TILLIE] Hurry up!
Hurry! Oh, my God, I can't believe it! *[Then yelling upstairs]*
Mama! Come on down! Hurry! [TILLIE *comes in the front door,
carrying the rest of her plants, and the large trophy.* RUTH *takes
the trophy]* Give me that! *[She starts upstairs]* Mama! Wait till
you see this!

> [BEATRICE *appears at the top of the stairs. She has been drink-
> ing a great deal, and clings fast to a bunch of old cheap cur-
> tains and other material]*

RUTH: Mama! She won . . . [BEATRICE *continues mechanically on
down the stairs]* Didn't you hear me? Tillie won the whole
thing! . . . Mama? What's the matter with you? What did you
rip the paper off the windows for?

> [BEATRICE *commences tacking up one of the curtains]*

TILLIE: Mama? Are you going to open a . . . shop?

RUTH: What's the matter? Can't you even answer?

BEATRICE: *[To* TILLIE] Hand me some of those tacks.

RUTH: *[Screaming]* I SAID SHE WON! ARE YOU DEAF?

BEATRICE: Ruth, if you don't shut up I'm going to have you put
away.

RUTH: They ought to put *you* away, BETTY THE LOON!

> *[There is a long pause]*

BEATRICE: The rabbit is in your room. I want you to bury it in the
morning.

RUTH: If you did anything . . . I'LL KILL YOU!

> *[She runs upstairs]*

TILLIE: Mother, you didn't kill it, did you?

BEATRICE: Nanny goes tomorrow. First thing tomorrow.

[*There is a cry from upstairs*]

TILLIE: Ruth? Are you all right?

BEATRICE: I don't know what it's going to be. Maybe a tea shop. Maybe not. [RUTH *appears in the doorway of her room. She is holding the dead rabbit on the blue towel. As she reaches the top of the stairs, she begins to moan deeply*] After school you're going to have regular hours. You'll work in the kitchen, you'll learn how to cook, and you're going to earn your keep, just like in any other business.

[TILLIE *starts slowly up the stairs toward* RUTH]

TILLIE: [*With great fear*] Mama . . . I think she's *going to go.*

[RUTH *commences to tremble.* TILLIE *speaks softly to her*] Don't go . . . don't go . . . [RUTH'S *eyes roll in her head, and the trembling of her body becomes pronounced throbbing. She drops the rabbit with the towel covering it*] Help me! Mama! Help me!

BEATRICE: Snap out of it, do you hear me? RUTH, DON'T LET YOUR-SELF GO! [*To* TILLIE] Help me get her downstairs!

[*By the time the trio reaches the bottom of the stairs,* RUTH *is consumed by a violent convulsion.* BEATRICE *holds her down and pushes* TILLIE *out of the way*]

BEATRICE: [*Screaming*] Get the wooden spoon!

[TILLIE *responds as* BEATRICE *gets* RUTH *onto a sofa. The convulsion runs its course of a full minute, then finally subsides.* TILLIE *gets a blanket and covers* RUTH]

TILLIE: Shall I call the doctor? [*There is a long pause*] Shall I call the doctor?

BEATRICE: No. She'll be all right.

TILLIE: I think we should call him.

BEATRICE: I DIDN'T ASK YOU WHAT YOU THOUGHT! . . . We're going to need every penny to get this place open.

[BEATRICE *spreads a tablecloth on one of the tables and places a pile of old cloth napkins on it. She sits down and lights a cigarette*]

TILLIE: [*Picking up the rabbit on the stairs*] I'd better bury him in the backyard.

[*She starts out*]

BEATRICE: Don't bury the towel.

[TILLIE *stops, sobs audibly, then gets control*]

TILLIE: I'll do it in the morning.

[*She gently lays the rabbit near the door. She tucks* RUTH *in on the couch and sits a few minutes by her sleeping sister.*
Music starts in softly as BEATRICE *continues folding napkins with her back to the others.*
There is the sound of someone at the curtained doorway, and NANNY *commences negotiating herself into the room. Slowly she advances with the tubular frame—unaware, desiccated, in some other land*]

BEATRICE: [*Weakly*] Matilda?

TILLIE: Yes, Mama?

BEATRICE: I hate the world. Do you know that, Matilda?

TILLIE: Yes, Mama.

BEATRICE: I hate the world.

[*The lights have started down, the music makes its presence known, and a spot clings to* TILLIE. *She moves to the staircase and the rest of the set goes to black during the following speech. As she starts up the stairs her recorded voice takes over as in the opening of the play*]

TILLIE's VOICE: *The Conclusion:* My experiment has shown some of the strange effects radiation can produce . . . and how dangerous it can be if not handled correctly. Mr. Goodman said I should tell in this conclusion what my future plans are and how this experiment has helped me make them. For one thing, the effect of gamma rays on man-in-the-moon marigolds has made me curious about the sun and the stars, for the universe itself must be like a world of great atoms—and I want to know more about it. But most important, I suppose, my experiment has made me feel important—every atom in me, in everybody, has come from the sun —from places beyond our dreams. The atoms of our hands, the atoms of our hearts . . . [*All sound out.* TILLIE *speaks the rest live —hopeful, glowing*] Atom. *Atom.* What a beautiful word.

THE END